Charles Mohnike

SAMS
Teach Yourself

ColdFusion

in 21 Days

SAMS

A Division of Macmillan USA
201 West 103rd St., Indianapolis, Indiana, 46290 USA

Sams Teach Yourself ColdFusion in 21 Days

Copyright © 2000 by Sams Publishing

International Standard Book Number: 0-672-31796-6

Library of Congress Catalog Card Number: 99-65392

Printed in the United States of America

First Printing: August 2000

03   02   01   00   4   3   2   1

Trademarks

Warning and Disclaimer

ASSOCIATE PUBLISHER
Bradley Jones

ACQUISITIONS EDITOR
Sharon Cox

DEVELOPMENT EDITOR
Steve Rowe

MANAGING EDITOR
Charlotte Clapp

PROJECT EDITOR
Paul Schneider

COPY EDITORS
Michael Henry
Mary Ellen Stephenson

INDEXER
Rebecca Salerno

PROOFREADERS
Kathy Bidwell
Juli Cook

TECHNICAL EDITOR
Gregory Snortland

TEAM COORDINATOR
Meggo Barthlow

MEDIA DEVELOPER
J. G. Moore

INTERIOR DESIGNER
Gary Adair

COVER DESIGNER
Aren Howell

PRODUCTION
Jeannette McKay

Contents at a Glance

Contents

About the Author

CHARLES MOHNIKE is an experienced ColdFusion developer and consultant, who has been building dynamically generated, award-winning sites for businesses since 1994. With a background in print publishing, Charles heads a northern California consulting firm specializing in ColdFusion site planning and deployment. He writes on Web topics for publications such as *Wired, Microsoft Bookshelf, Smart TV*, and *Videomaker*. Charles also contributes freelance articles on computers, politics, and vintage music genres to daily and weekly newspapers around the country.

About the Technical Editor

GREG SNORTLAND is the manager of Web development for CaregiverZone, a startup eldercare portal providing resources for a wide variety of issues, including an e-commerce site. The site is being developed using ColdFusion Enterprise and Spectra software. Greg and his team of programmers spend every waking moment working to make CaregiverZone.com the premier site for family caregivers, elder care professionals, and seniors. Prior to rejoining the rat race in the bay area of California, Greg was president and owner of Unlimited Data Systems, an award-winning Web integration company headquartered in Great Falls, Montana. While enjoying Big Sky country, Greg built the compliance database for Intel Corporation's Y2K inventory tracking and Year 2000 rollover tracking systems. In addition, he has done work for clients small and large across the country. Greg has been an Allaire Alliance Partner for more than two years. When he can tear himself away from the computer (which he does often), Greg enjoys the outdoors with his wife, Ann, and children Abby and Hadley. His favorite activity is to enjoy a day of boating on Seeley Lake in western Montana.

Dedication

For Heavy Metal Mandi

Acknowledgments

Thanks to Steve Rowe and Sharon Cox at Macmillan, and to all those who aided in the thought processes necessary to produce this book: Don Van Vliet, Charlie Parker, Hank Williams I and III (not II), John Coltrane, Tom Waits, Elvises Costello and Presley, Count Basie, Dick Dale, Lux Interior, Howlin' Wolf, and Perez Prado.

Helping-hand thanks to Kristin Windbigler at Wired Digital, Bill Newlin at Moon Travel Handbooks, and—naturally—Mom and Dad.

Tell Us What You Think!

As the reader of this book, *you* are our most important critic and commentator. We value your opinion and want to know what we're doing right, what we could do better, what areas you'd like to see us publish in, and any other words of wisdom you're willing to pass our way.

As an Associate Publisher for Sams, I welcome your comments. You can fax, email, or write me directly to let me know what you did or didn't like about this book—as well as what we can do to make our books stronger.

Please note that I cannot help you with technical problems related to the topic of this book, and that due to the high volume of mail I receive, I might not be able to reply to every message.

When you write, please be sure to include this book's title and author as well as your name and phone or fax number. I will carefully review your comments and share them with the author and editors who worked on the book.

Fax: 317-581-4770

Email: adv_prog@mcp.com

Mail: Brad Jones, Associate Publisher
        Sams Publishing
        201 West 103rd Street
        Indianapolis, IN 46290 USA

Introduction

Who Should Read This Book?

As the author of this book, naturally, I'm going to say "everyone" should read it because the goal here is for you to actually place dollars on the counter and take this volume home to savor the many pearls of wisdom within. But I'd be misleading you if I didn't mention the following:

- You'll need to have some basic knowledge of building Web pages using HTML code and a text editor.
- You'll need to know how to transfer files to a server via an FTP program or other means.
- You'll definitely need a computer.

This tutorial will be particularly useful if you belong to one of the following groups.

Non-Programming Web Developers

Say you've built a few sites using standard HTML, and you now know your way around an <A HREF> tag better than you do the functions on your cell phone. You're naturally feeling a little sure of yourself, but one day you get a call from a client or boss, who has met with "the committee" and produced a huge laundry list of features to include on the company Web site. The committee wants Web-based email, a login function, a guest-book, user-customizable pages, and the ability to add new content daily. Oh yeah, and, of course, they want it *yesterday*.

You have several options at this point. You can quit this computer thing altogether and go back to your part-time job at the Jiffy Mart. You can phone up a programmer buddy and offer to trade him your prized Spock ears for a few hours' consulting time. Or, you can sit down and actually try to build the thing within the insane time frame the committee requires. Assuming that you're not experienced in C or Perl programming, you'd first have to scour the Web for prewritten programs that will perform all the fancy functions the company wants. Then you'd have to install, configure and customize each of these programs to your liking, and, if you've ever tried to troubleshoot someone else's freeware programs, you know that this is no easy task.

But there's a better method, one that will save you plenty of teeth gnashing and just might get you in before the company deadline. You could instead opt to install ColdFusion on the company's Web server and purchase a copy of this book (thank you) to help you create all of those special functions without having to learn a lick of C code or install a single Perl module. In just 21 days, you'll be the talk of the town and the envy of your peers.

Web Programmers

If you *do* have programming knowledge, you'll find that ColdFusion works just fine alongside the existing Web tools you've built, and that it can help you add new functions to your sites in a fraction of the coding time you're used to. And with all of that programming experience already whizzing around in your head, you can zip through the sections in this book that deal with familiar concepts such as variables and if-then statements.

The Teeming Millions

Even if you're not in the business of Web design, you may have a pet project that's been barking to get on the Web. Maybe you've collected lots of data on Hummel figurines or your city's exciting zoning ordinances and just can't wait to share them with the world. ColdFusion is a great way to build a feature-rich site with lots of information—without having to dedicate all of your spare hours to learning a programming language just for your pet project.

Overview

The first seven lessons in this book introduce you to ColdFusion and explain how it is used to build Web applications that will help you quickly accomplish a variety of tasks not possible with standard HTML code. You'll learn how to install ColdFusion server, how to use the SQL language to select and serve database records on the Web, and how to use forms to change the contents of your Web databases. By the end of Week 1, you'll have enough knowledge to begin building simple but functional ColdFusion-driven sites that make it look as if you've really worked your tail off when, in reality, you spent merely a few hours constructing a few *template* pages.

Week 2 introduces ColdFusion Studio, the optional development application that helps you build template pages. You'll also learn about tools like variables and functions, both of which allow you to create Web sites that *do things* other than just sit there and look nice. You'll learn how to control the flow of your application with if-then statements, and how to use ColdFusion to send and receive mail via the Web.

Finally, Week 3's lessons will show you how to make the most of your programming hours with ColdFusion. You'll learn about timesaving devices such as advanced variable types, advanced SQL procedures, and ColdFusion's Verity search engine. You'll find out how to combat the Web's inherent statelessness with client and session variables. In the final chapters, you'll learn how ColdFusion is used to construct e-commerce applications, and how to troubleshoot template pages that just won't behave.

Conventions Used in This Book

This book uses the following typeface conventions:

- Menu names are separated from menu options by a comma. For example, File, Open means "select the Open option from the File menu."
- New terms are set off by the icon **NEW TERM** and appear in *italic*.
- In some listings, we've included both the input and output. For these, all code that you type in (input) appears in **boldface monospace**. Output appears in standard monospace. The combination icon **INPUT/ OUTPUT** indicates that both input and output appear in the code.

  The input icon **INPUT** and output icon **OUTPUT** also identify the nature of the code.
- Many code-related terms within the text also appear in `monospace`.
- Placeholders in code appear in *`italic monospace`*.
- When a line of code is too long to fit on one line of this book, it is broken at a convenient place and continued to the next line. A code continuation character (➡) precedes the continuation of a line of code. (You should type a line of code that has this character as one long line without breaking it.)
- Paragraphs that begin with the analysis icon **ANALYSIS** explain the preceding code example.
- The syntax icon identifies syntax statements.

SYNTAX

Special design features enhance the text material:

- Notes
- Tips
- Cautions

Note

Notes explain interesting or important points that can help you understand SQL concepts and techniques.

Tip

Tips are little pieces of information that will help you in real-world situations. Tips often offer shortcuts to make a task easier or faster.

Caution

Cautions provide information about detrimental performance issues or dangerous errors. Pay careful attention to Cautions.

WEEK 1

At a Glance

Week 1 is your introduction to ColdFusion, seven lessons that will help you better understand what ColdFusion is, what it can and can't do, and how Web developers most often use it. If you're still deciding whether you might benefit from ColdFusion's magic, a look through this week's lessons should be enough to clinch the decision. If you're already sold on the product and are ready to start developing, this week will give you the foundation you need to begin building the template pages that make up a ColdFusion application.

Because ColdFusion works closely with both your Web server and your databases, using it successfully requires knowledge of more than just the program itself. This week will introduce you to all the concepts you need to know, including the following:

- Day 1, "Introducing ColdFusion," presents ColdFusion, provides some history, and gives examples of how ColdFusion is most often used in Web development.

- Day 2, "Anatomy of a ColdFusion Application," provides an overview of a basic ColdFusion application, introduces you to the way ColdFusion works with your Web server and your databases, and shows you what goes on behind the scenes.

- Day 3, "Setting Up ColdFusion and Defining a Datasource," walks you through the process of setting up ColdFusion Server and introduces you to the concept of the datasource.

- Day 4, "Building a Database and Organizing Data," presents a tutorial on databases, showing you how they work and how to design a database that will work efficiently with ColdFusion.

1

2

3

4

5

6

7

- Day 5, "Finding the Data You Need: An Introduction to Queries and SQL," examines Structured Query Language, or SQL, the language ColdFusion uses to communicate with your database.

- Day 6, "Creating Your First Web Application," gives a step-by-step example of how to create a complete ColdFusion application, from defining a datasource to building the template pages your users will see on the Web.

- Day 7, "Changing the Contents of a Database with ColdFusion," takes your application-building skills a step further by illustrating how ColdFusion can be used to alter the contents of a database.

DAY 1

Introducing ColdFusion

Let's begin with a basic fact that will put your upcoming 21-day journey into perspective, and maybe even make it less wearing on your psyche: *ColdFusion is all about saving time.*

Like other Web development and application-server tools, it was developed by people like you and me who grew tired of living in their computer chairs, folks who wanted to get their projects finished and get out to see the world.

The 21 days you now begin to invest will pay off later in the form of time—time spent doing things other than hard-coding HTML documents and formatting boring text passages. How you spend that free time is entirely up to you, and way beyond the scope of this book.

In Day 1, you'll

- Get your first look at Allaire's ColdFusion
- Learn how it can make you the talk of your computing buddies, and find out whether it's the right tool for your project
- Cover the basic theory behind creating *dynamic* pages
- Look briefly at the client/server relationship that makes all this high-tech wizardry possible

What Is ColdFusion?

A couple computer types, brothers Jeremy and J.J. Allaire, created ColdFusion in 1995. Jeremy, the business-minded one, had a print publication he needed to regularly post to the Web, so he approached the coding brother, J.J, and asked him to help build a simple application that would speed the task. When the project was complete, both realized they had a hot property on their hands and Allaire Corporation was born. Today, ColdFusion is in its fourth major release and both brothers wear fine suits and drive fancy cars.

The official description of ColdFusion calls it a *Web application server,* but depending on how you choose to use it, it can also be considered a page-development tool, a database server, or your ticket to the high life. At the heart of the program is a *database-to-Web gateway.* It allows you to take an existing database file and serve it up via the Web, record-by-record, without having to create new HTML files for each record.

Exploring a Sample ColdFusion Application

To clarify this concept, let's use an example. Using a common database program, Microsoft Access, I've been maintaining a database of Elizabeth Taylor's husbands, as illustrated in Figure 1.1.

FIGURE 1.1

A sample database table in Microsoft Access containing data on the men in Liz Taylor's life.

ID	name	occupation	hair	eyes	worth
1	Nicky Hilton	hotel magnate	pompadour	green	loaded
2	Michael Wilding	actor	pompadour	brown	not hurting
3	Michael Todd	film producer	pompadour	brown	loaded
4	Eddie Fisher	singer	Beaver Cleaver-style	brown	not hurting
5	Richard Burton	actor	yes	brown	not hurting
6	John Warner	senator	grey	green	loaded
7	Larry Fortensky	trucker/construction	mullet	brown	none

NEW TERM   A *field* is an element in a database that categorizes information by type. If I create a database containing names, occupations, eye color, hair color, and net worth, I'd define each of these types as a field.

Now assume that I've decided it's vital that the world has this information readily available. The traditional way to get this stuff on the Web would be to sit down, fire up the text editor, and start coding HTML documents, seven in all—or eight if you count the fact that she married Richard Burton twice.

But, hey, I know that creating seven or eight Web pages with the same type of information on each is a waste of my time. Instead I'll use ColdFusion to create the pages *dynamically.*

New Term Generating a page *dynamically* means to create it on-the-fly, or at the moment it is requested by the user's browser. The opposite of a dynamic page is a *static* page, or a plain old HTML document that physically resides on a server.

I upload the database to my ColdFusion–compatible Web service provider, set it up as a *datasource* (don't worry—I'll get to this in Day 3, "Setting Up ColdFusion and Defining a Datasource"), and then create a single *template* file to serve up the information.

New Term A ColdFusion *template* file is a Web page that contains text and code directing ColdFusion to perform an action or actions. Templates use the file extension .CFM.

When someone accesses my template file from the Web and requests the record for the little-known Larry Fortensky, it looks like Figure 1.2.

FIGURE 1.2

ColdFusion output for the database record containing "Larry Fortensky".

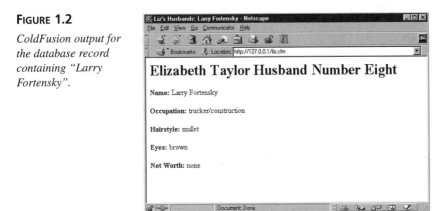

Looks a lot like a regular Web page, right? That's an important point to catch— ColdFusion is transparent to the end user, save for the file extension .CFM instead of the standard .HTML. Because it's a *back-end* application, the average surfer won't even know you're using it. He'll think you spent hours building pages just for his benefit, and that's not necessarily a bad thing.

New Term A *back-end* application is one that runs behind the scenes and is transparent to the Web surfer. Various back-end apps are used to serve Web content, to gather data on site visitors, and to control advanced features such as chat rooms, message boards, and so on.

Why Should I Use ColdFusion?

Hopefully at this point light bulbs are popping over your head and bells are ringing in your ears with reasons to use this great tool on your own projects. Just in case there aren't, in the next few sections I'll cover a few reasons why ColdFusion is a tool you will want to add to your repertoire of development applications.

Database-Driven Sites

ColdFusion gives you the ability to control some of or all of your entire Web site's content from a database. The beauty of this may not strike you just yet, but consider a situation where you might be working with others who aren't as HTML-savvy as yourself. Without ColdFusion, a change in content means that someone has to come in and code a new HTML page, and that someone will probably be you, regardless of the importance of whatever you were doing when your pager went off. With ColdFusion, Web content can be changed or updated by anyone who knows his way around an input form and an enter key. This means that anyone in the company—even those without database experience—can update their Web projects without you having to drive down to the office and possibly miss the bonus round on "The Price Is Right."

In addition, database-driven sites give you the ability to present lots and lots of material on the Web, and you only need to design a single template file. Take my Liz database, for example. It's pretty small now, but someday if that database should stretch into hundreds or thousands of husbands, my initial template page would easily handle all of them. I'd have one killer Web site that looked as if I'd spent hours designing pages.

Database-driven sites also present interesting opportunities to keep tabs on your visitors. If your site required users to register with a login name and password, for example, you could then use the database behind the scenes to track their interests by logging the pages they visit. The concepts behind this are covered further in Day 7, "Changing the Contents of a Database with ColdFusion."

Ready for Business

Many businesses love databases, and these businesses may come to love ColdFusion. It's not hard to see why. Many businesses maintain a database of their products or services, and for an existing database, ColdFusion makes it a short hop to a full-featured Web site. Show me a business with a large product catalog and I'll show you, the Web developer, a quick way to deliver a full-featured Web site that will have your client dancing in the streets.

Real-Time Web Presentation

Many businesses can use ColdFusion directly with their active databases. This means that the moment someone in the warehouse records a product as shipped, the pages on the Web site immediately reflect the change in inventory. In most cases, businesses can continue to use the same database, spreadsheet, or word processing software they've always used in the same way they've always used it. Just imagine the reception when you march into a business and tell its owners that you can put their entire operation online in real-time—without their forking over a cent to retrain employees.

Interfacing With Intranets

Due to the nature of their product or service, some businesses don't really require an extensive Web presence, but this doesn't mean that you, the ColdFusion developer, need to pass them by. Lots of businesses use ColdFusion as an *intranet* tool.

NEW TERM   An *intranet* is an internal network that is usually not available to Web users. Intranets are used within businesses for employee tasks such as information sharing, maintaining the company database, or vital communications such as "Hey, Jim in accounting, how was the big bash last night?"

Many businesses have found that using Web-like interfaces to control their intranets helps new employees assimilate quickly and easily. Many have at least experimented with a Web browser, so by presenting intranet data in the form of Web pages, businesses can avoid having to acquaint new hires with several applications.

ColdFusion is ideal for building these Web-based interfaces, and its database functions are just as valuable on intranets as they are on the Web outside.

Business Security

Site security is generally a pretty big concern for businesses, whether it's keeping the advertising staff from rewriting editorial copy or keeping outsiders from rifling through the company secrets. ColdFusion has several security measures built in to the program, meaning that even inexperienced CF designers don't need to worry much about leaving their sites open to hackers and ne'er-do-wells.

E-Commerce

ColdFusion is e-commerce ready, with lots of built-in tools and tricks that make it easy to build sites offering secure online transactions. I'll cover this in depth in Day 20, "Using ColdFusion for E-Commerce Applications," but for now just let the concept sink in. We have a tool here that allows you to quickly serve up a huge database of products or services, plus the ability to easily make them available for sale online. Bells ringing yet?

Data Collection

It's not just about business, either. ColdFusion is also used by government bureaucrats to get their reams of data on the Web. It is used by community organizations that maintain lists of other community organizations, and by common folk like you and me who just want to share our database of Boxcar Willie's bootleg recordings with the world at large.

Neither is ColdFusion just about outputting documents to the Web. It features a handy tool called CFINSERT, which I'll cover in Day 7. This feature alone opens up whole new worlds of uses because it allows you to collect user input from the Web, via a standard HTML *form* or other methods, and automatically input it into a database on your server.

NEW TERM A *form* is a Web page designed to take input from the user. When you type a keyword into the text box on a search engine and hit "submit," you're using a form.

Let's say that you're with one of the community organizations mentioned previously, and you want to assemble a database of support groups for average Joes who confess an addiction to watching "COPS." Using ColdFusion, you'd post an input form on the Web with fields for "name of group," "meeting place," "time," and so on, as shown in Figure 1.3.

FIGURE 1.3

A Web input page designed with ColdFusion behind the scenes.

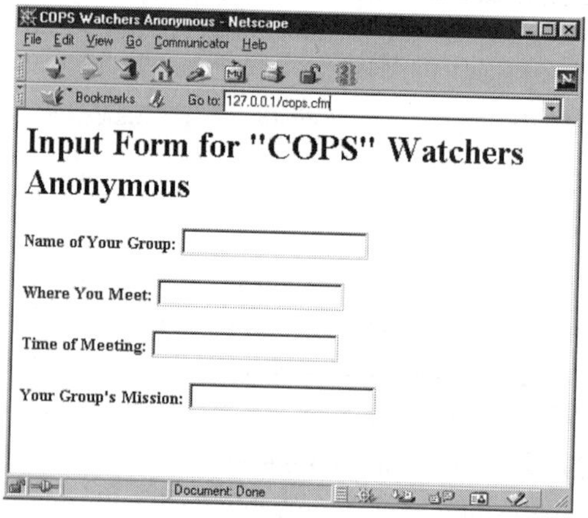

Each time a user fills out and submits the form, you have a new record in your database. And then it's up to you what to do with the data. You could serve it up on the Web as mentioned previously, or you could create a snail-mail list to send out form letters to all those "COPS" Watchers Anonymous groups around the globe.

1

In the same way, ColdFusion can be a huge asset to those who've embarked on a personal quest to share their interests with the world at large. For example, I'm quite the fan of '50s mambo music, but due to financial constraints (and time spent writing this book) I don't have the time on my hands to code Web pages for each of the hundreds of mambo LPs I own. If not for time-saving programs like ColdFusion, the world might never get to share my extensive knowledge of the mambo and would be all the poorer for it.

Better Than CGI

For the uninitiated, CGI scripts are tools Web developers use for handling stuff like input data from forms, email, and site-specific searches. These scripts are essentially small programs written in languages like Perl and C that run on the Web server and vastly extend the capabilities of an HTML page by allowing the server to actually *do* stuff other than just blindly serve up Web pages.

OUTPUT *CGI* stands for *Common Gateway Interface*, a set of commands understood by all standard Web server packages.

ColdFusion does pretty much everything a CGI script will, so you needn't quiver when I mention Perl and C.

If you're already familiar with common CGI tasks, you'll find ColdFusion extends the capabilities of these and other functions. It offers sophisticated mail and search handling (I'll cover these in Days 13, "Using ColdFusion to Handle Email," and 17, "Finding Text with Verity") without your having to work with scripting. It also handles stuff like environment variables with elegance and can evaluate complex if-then decisions with only a few lines of code.

NEW TERM *Environment variables* are variables used in CGI scripts to do things like determine the current time, date, page hits, and so on.

If you know about programming languages, you'll be glad to know that ColdFusion works seamlessly with your existing CGI scripts and you won't have to replace all those scripts you slaved on last year.

ColdFusion is a little less risky than CGI when it comes to security as well. If you've ever written a CGI application, you've probably dealt with subroutines that handle malicious input from outside users. Even a simple CGI mail handling script can leave potential security holes, and without special precautions Jodie Foster may someday receive threatening mail traceable to your client's server. ColdFusion builds security measures into the server, so there's less worry.

Custom Applications

Advanced ColdFusion programmers have also used the tool to build a variety of common Web applications such as chat rooms, message boards, and shopping cart systems. These apps often have advantages over their standard CGI incarnations because they allow use of a database behind the scenes. Chatters can have their email logged to a database field, shopping carts can keep tabs on who's buying what, and so on.

Many of those super-swift coders have made their pre-coded ColdFusion apps publicly available, either free or for insane sums. An average ColdFusion user can pop a pre-written app onto her Web site without having to reinvent the wheel and thus make it appear to customers and clients that she's really on the ball.

Tip

> Allaire lists hundreds of pre-coded ColdFusion applications on its Web site, www.allaire.com. A quick browse through these makes a good starting point for new CF users. You'll learn how other coders use ColdFusion and gain a better understanding of what's possible with the program.

However, don't take this to mean that you can simply go out and spend a few bucks for a pre-written ColdFusion app and skip the rest of this book. You'll need a good grasp of ColdFusion theory to tailor the application to your site's needs.

Dynamic Page Generation

ColdFusion's true finesse lies in its capability to produce *dynamic* Web pages. As defined earlier in today's lesson, the term "dynamic" is not used here as a measure of greatness (that's up to your content), but describes the way a page gets from your server to the user's screen. The opposite of a dynamic page is a *static* page, or a plain old HTML document that lives on the Web server and gets served up when someone enters a URL into his browser. Dynamic pages, by contrast, are created on-the-fly by the server. They may only partially exist on the server until a user requests them; then they're assembled and sent to the browser.

Take the previous example of Liz's husbands. The template file I created to display each database record is not a complete HTML page. It may contain elements of HTML such as headers and footers, but the actual data on Larry Fortensky, his mullet, and his truck-driving career is missing. Larry's data is added to the page only at the moment the user's browser makes a request to the Web server. On the user's end, a dynamically generated page looks identical to a static one.

Dynamically generated pages have other attributes as well. They may contain code that makes decisions on-the-fly, such as deciding whether a user is surfing with Netscape Communicator or Internet Explorer, and then delivering a page optimized for that specific browser.

Let's look at a simple example of dynamic page generation in action. My Liz Web site will have a constant *header* and *footer* throughout, as shown in Figure 1.4.

FIGURE 1.4

One page from my sample Web site, showing the use of a header above and a footer below.

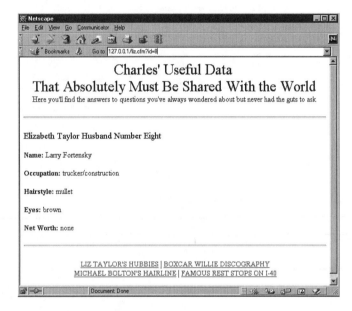

NEW TERM *Header* and *footer* are terms used by Web designers that mean "stuff that appears at the top of the page" (such as a navigation bar or icons) and "stuff that appears at the bottom of the page" (such as site credits, disclaimers, and so on), respectively.

The same header and footer appear with different body text in Figure 1.5.

Note that both pages have the same text up top, as well as the same links at the base of the page. Only the body text changes from page to page.

If you are new to this whole Web design thing, you might approach this the hard way by manually typing in the code for each header and footer as you design each individual page. If you've been around the Web scene for a while, you might be a little wiser and save some time. You'd create a template page with a header and footer, and then paste in the body text for each page, saving the page as a new file each time.

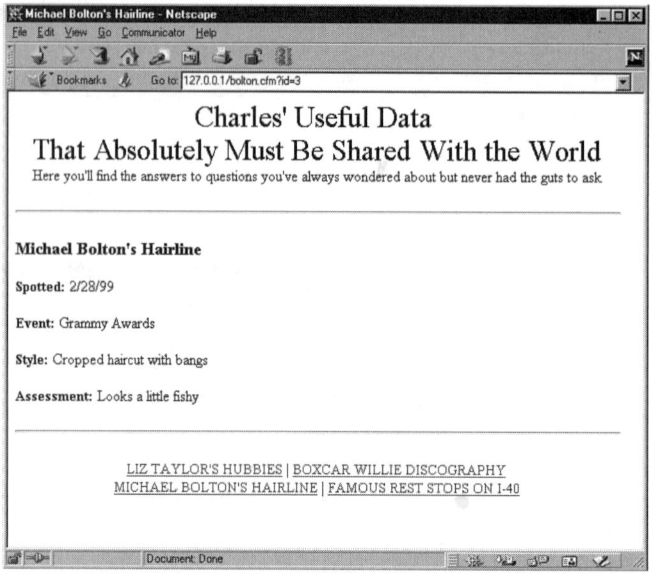

FIGURE 1.5

Another page from my site, with the same header and footer information from the one in Figure 1.4.

But you're even smarter than that. Instead of duplicating the header and footer information on every page in the site, you can generate pages dynamically and let ColdFusion do the work. Using a standard text editor like Windows Notepad, I'll create two simple files—first, one called `header.html`.

```
<CENTER>

<FONT SIZE="+2">Charles' Useful Data That Absolutely Must Be Shared With the
➥World</FONT>
<BR>

Here you'll find the answers to questions you've always wondered about but never
➥had the guts to ask

</CENTER>

<HR>
```

In Listing 1.2, I'll create `footer.html` with the code necessary to create links.

```
<HR>

<CENTER>

<A HREF="somelink.html">LIZ TAYLOR'S HUBBIES</A> |
<A HREF="somelink.html">BOXCAR WILLIE DISCOGRAPHY</A>

<BR>
```

```
<A HREF="somelink.html">MICHAEL BOLTON'S HAIRLINE</A> |
<A HREF="somelink.html">FAMOUS REST STOPS ON I-40</A>
```

Finally, I can use the magic of dynamically generated pages to automatically insert my header and footer into each page on the site at the moment the page is requested by a user. I do it with a handy ColdFusion tag called `<CFINCLUDE>`. As you'll learn in tomorrow's lesson, ColdFusion tags work much the same way as HTML tags, but they vastly extend the capabilities of regular old HTML.

Now I could add text like Listing 1.3 to each of the pages I create for my site.

```
<HTML>

<BODY>

<CFINCLUDE template="header.html">

Some body text goes here

<CFINCLUDE template="footer.html">

</BODY>

</HTML>
```

When a user requests that page, ColdFusion quickly finds the files titled `header.html` and `footer.html` and sticks them into the page. The user sees only the dynamic output, as in Figure 1.4.

One of many advantages to doing things this way is that if I'd like to change a link or a graphic later in the game, I only change it once in the relevant header or footer file—and it's immediately updated throughout my site.

Dynamic pages can also be written to perform computations on variables, such as totaling an order and applying sales tax. In short, they bring Web pages alive, and once you begin using them you'll probably lie awake nights dreaming up new uses for dynamic pages.

Understanding Clients and Servers

To really understand ColdFusion and how it serves up your pages, it's important to grasp the basic concepts behind Web service. Let's start with the *server*, which is any computer connected to the Internet. PC, Mac, Silicon Graphics—the make isn't important as long as it can connect to the Net and has software running that allows it to serve up Web pages.

TCP—TRANSMISSION CONTROL PROTOCOL
IP — INTERNET PROTOCOL

The server is—in a perfect world—always on and connected, just waiting, hoping, pleading for a client machine to send it a request. The *client* is the user's computer, the home or office machine on which the user does his Web surfing. The client makes its requests in the form of Uniform Resource Locators (URLs) that specify which server they want to connect to, and what file they want to retrieve or execute. Without getting too technical on the theories of packets and TCP/IP networking, lets just say that once the client requests a URL, magic fairies carry it to the designated server. A list of what servers ColdFusion will run on is covered more in depth in Day 3.

When the server receives a request from a client, it performs whatever function the client has requested. Most often, the client has requested an HTML page or an image file, so the server's task is simple—send the requested file back to the client. Pull out your highlighter now, because here comes the key concept: Sometimes the client's request, though still a URL, asks that the server perform an action, and then return the results of that action to the user's browser. This is the basis of the CGI scripts mentioned previously, and it is the key element that makes the wonder of dynamically generated pages possible.

When a client requests a ColdFusion template or the name of a CGI script, the server performs an action—depending on the request, it might search a database, run a computation on figures, or run a short program. It then returns the *output,* or results of the action, to the client in the form of an HTML document. The client doesn't care what goes on behind the scenes; it's only concerned with the HTML output.

How ColdFusion Works Within the Client/Server Relationship

In the client/server relationship, ColdFusion resides on the server computer, running in conjunction with Web server software. It waits for a client to send a request URL that has the .CFM extension designating a ColdFusion template file, such as

```
http://www.blahblah.com/stuff.cfm
```

and then goes to work. It momentarily seizes control on the Web server, does whatever is requested of it in the template file, and then gives the results back to the Web server to hand over to the magic fairies for delivery to the client.

Tag Processing

Open up any ColdFusion template in a text editor and you'll find a lot of familiar HTML markup, including code such as <BODY>, <TITLE>, and text formatting tags such as <I> (italic) and <B> (bold). You'll also find some not-so-familiar tags such as <CFQUERY>,

`<CFOUTPUT>`, and the aforementioned `<CFINCLUDE>`. These are *ColdFusion Markup Language* (CFML). They're similar to HTML tags except that they're recognized only by ColdFusion and require that ColdFusion Application Server is running concurrently with your Web server before they'll do anything other than place errors neatly up and down your page.

> **Tip**
>
> Most ColdFusion tags use opening and closing brackets just like HTML tags. For example, to designate a bold passage with HTML tags, you'd use a `<B>` before the relevant text and a `</B>` to stop the bolding. ColdFusion uses the same characters to denote a beginning and ending tag, such as `<CFQUERY>` and `</CFQUERY>`.

When a ColdFusion server processes a template or `.CFM` file, it first looks for CFML tags. These may tell ColdFusion to search a database, to output some information, or to include a file (as in the earlier example).

You'll find a complete listing of ColdFusion 4.5 tags in Appendix B of this book, and I'll discuss most of them in depth in lessons to come.

Database Connectivity

Once a ColdFusion server examines the tags on a page, it begins executing the commands specified within the CFML tags.

One of the most common requests is a database search. To search efficiently, ColdFusion needs to have the database ready for access when requests come in. If each time the program received a request it had to open the database file, search the records, and then close the file, it would be hopelessly inefficient and unable to deal with multiple requests pouring in simultaneously.

ColdFusion works this out by requiring you to set up your database as an Open Database Connectivity (ODBC) source. An ODBC source sets up a data pipeline in and out of the database, making it readily accessible to ColdFusion.

Once a database is connected to ColdFusion via ODBC, developers can use a special set of commands, called *structured query language*, or SQL, to communicate with the database. SQL commands can be used to search a database, change the information within, or even to create new databases.

You'll look at SQL, datasources (DSNs), and ODBC in Days 3 through 5. For today, just marvel at the acronyms and sleep tight knowing you've covered the basic concepts.

Summary

Two guys, who wanted to save time on their Web coding, so they could do other stuff, created ColdFusion. By mastering the software and using it in your own Web projects, you too can save many hours of coding and remain free to venture into the daylight.

At the heart of the program is a database-to-Web gateway, a means of sharing database information with Web users. ColdFusion can take databases containing thousands of records and serve them up as individual Web pages via a single template file. It also handles input, allowing Web users to contribute to a database.

ColdFusion server is an ideal tool for business and organizations because it allows the creation of very large sites with a minimum design time. It features built-in security and commerce tools for those wanting to serve data selectively, or those who offer products or services for sale online.

Q&A

Q **Where can I get more information on ColdFusion before shelling out the dollars for it?**

A Allaire's Web site at `http://www.allaire.com/` has extensive information on Web software compatible with ColdFusion, and a 30-day demo available for download. You might also try reading the rest of this book.

Q **Does ColdFusion work with all database types?**

A Yes, pretty much. But knowing that there will be someone out there running some arcane office suite, I'd recommend checking the Web site for a current list of supported file formats. I'll cover databases in depth in Day 4, "Building a Database and Organizing Data," and Day 5, "Finding the Data You Need: An Introduction to Queries and SQL."

Q **What about scalability? I have a huge product database and a Web site that gets thousands of hits per day.**

A Scalability is one of ColdFusion's biggest selling points. Right out of the box, it can handle everything from the simplest fan site to a huge database on a busy server. As you'll learn in Day 3, it also includes options to tailor its own performance to the capabilities of your server.

Workshop

The workshop provides quiz and exercise questions to test your understanding of today's material. Answers to quiz questions can be found in Appendix A at the back of the text.

Quiz

1. What is ColdFusion's primary function? Name two good uses for the program.
2. How does ColdFusion work with CGI scripts?
3. What is dynamic page generation?
4. How does a ColdFusion-driven Web page get from a server to a client?
5. Who was Elizabeth Taylor's most recent husband?

Exercises

1. Check out Allaire's Web site and browse the Frequently Asked Questions (FAQ) section on ColdFusion 4.
2. Also on Allaire's site, check out some of the links to other ColdFusion-driven pages. Note some of the ways others use ColdFusion in their design and compare them to your own design needs.

Day 2

Anatomy of a ColdFusion Application

Day 1, "Introducing ColdFusion," provided your first look at a ColdFusion application. You might recall that a database archiving Liz Taylor's various marriages was created, and then a ColdFusion template file was designed to display that data on the Web. This type of application uses one of the most popular ColdFusion functions—searching a database for information and presenting it in a Web page. In Day 2, you'll look at the three main components of this type of ColdFusion application and learn about the function of each. This day covers

- The database file
- The ColdFusion datasource
- The template
- Query and output elements
- The relationship between queries and output

Connecting Your Database to the Web

Although ColdFusion boasts many functions that work independently of databases, it's most often used by developers who want to integrate their database with the Web. For the majority of ColdFusion applications, your database will be the key element. It contains the actual text of all that useful stuff you or your client wants to serve up on the Web—names, dates, prices, whatever—all indexed in a format that's easy for computers to access, but ugly to the eyes of most humans. Actually, there are humans existing on our planet who love gazing at databases, but with your prayers and financial support, science will someday find a cure.

ColdFusion's primary function is to take that ugly glob of data and turn it into a page or series of pages that the average surfers can access by simply poking around your Web site with a mouse. If you're lucky, they might even *read* your valuable data. Again, all this magic happens behind the scenes, so home users see only standard HTML pages and never need to know you're working with a database instead of creating each page by hand. Don't go telling them either, because you'll spoil the dream for the rest of us who work our tails off trying to make it look as if we'd worked our tails off.

I'll cover databases in exhausting depth in Day 4, but today, here's just a quick intro for neophytes. A database is a file created in programs like Microsoft Access, Oracle, FoxPro, FileMaker Pro, and so on. Each of these applications has its unique features, but essentially they all perform the same business. They assemble your reams of valuable input data into a single file in which each individual chunk of data (a name, a price, an address) relates to other chunks of data and is organized for easy access.

Database organization makes things easier for both the user and other programs that will be used to access the information. For example, if you needed to find an address corresponding with a certain name, it's a pretty easy task to pop open a database, find the table containing names and addresses, look for the name you want, and note the related address. As you'll learn in this and later sections, ColdFusion and other programs that work with databases use a similar method, for instance the SQL language, when they search for stuff.

Before we move on, let's quickly define a few terms for those who haven't yet experienced the pleasure of working with databases. Veteran database handlers will find these definitions expanded in Day 4, "Building a Database and Organizing Data."

Understanding Tables

The main elements in any database file are *tables*, or collections of data grouped by relevance. Let's look at a sample in Figure 2.1.

Figure 2.1

A sample Microsoft Access database table.

ID	title	year	rating
1	King Creole	1958	watchable
2	Blue Hawaii	1951	watchable
3	Kid Galahad	1962	aaaahhh!
4	Harum Scarum	1965	aaaahhh!
5	Roustabout	1964	he's going to hell for this
6	Speedway	1968	pretty good, actually
7	Charro	1969	watchable
8	Clambake	1967	pretty good, actually
9	Flaming Star	1960	watchable
10	Kissin' Cousins	1964	he's going to hell for this

Here I've created a sample database using Microsoft Access. Within that database file, I've created a table containing a catalog of several bad Elvis movies, ranking each by its individual level of badness. In that same database file, I can also create other tables that might contain information about Elvis' worst songs, his outfits, or whatever. For the moment, I'll concentrate on the movie table and examine some of the elements within.

The Fields

The movie table contains three columnar *fields,* or categories of information I've collected: title, year, and rating.

I've chosen names for these fields based on the type of information I want to store in my table. Not surprisingly, these names are called *field names* in database jargon. In Figure 2.1, the field names appear in bold text and run horizontally across the top of the figure.

After I have defined field names, I'm free to type in the actual data, or relevant information for each field. As I enter the data for each film, I'm automatically creating rows in the database.

The Rows

The subset of data for each of these fine Elvis flicks represents a *row,* or *record,* in the table. Take a look at Figure 2.1 again. The information for the film *Speedway,* including its title, year, and rating, represents a row.

To understand the relationship of data in a record or row, visualize an object you probably never thought you'd see mentioned in a computer tutorial—a 3" × 5" index card. Say I have a plastic box full of index cards; that box is equivalent to my table. On each card, I've printed the information for each movie. This is equivalent to a record.

Just as with a box of index cards, I can choose to sort my Elvis entries by a variety of topics (fields) and sorting methods. I can arrange them alphabetically by movie title, numerically in the order that I created each record, or chronologically by the date the movie was released. Via the magic of computer processing, however, sorting a database file is a bit easier than shuffling around a bunch of index cards.

> **Tip**
>
> Your database software will have its own methods for sorting records in a table. By sorting the order in which records are viewed, you can arrange a series of names alphabetically, organize dates chronologically, and so on. Check your software's "help" documentation for details.

Databases can contain just a few rows, like mine, or in the case of a store with thousands of products, they can go on seemingly forever. As you'll see in later chapters, ColdFusion doesn't much care how many rows your table contains.

The Key

Note that each row is numbered on the left side of the screen, under the heading "ID". Microsoft Access automatically supplied this number, called a *key,* as I entered each new row of information. A key is a identifier (most often a number) that refers to a specific row in a table. No two rows may share the same key. This unique number will make for easy reference to individual rows later. We'll discuss keys in depth in Day 4.

Cross-Referencing Data

Each data chunk in my table has two reference points. It has a related row and a related field. If I want to look up the year *Speedway* was released, I can use programs such as ColdFusion to search my table for the row containing *Speedway* and then look for the data in the year field of that row.

This is a simple example of a *data relationship*.

NEW TERM *Data relationships* are methods for grouping data by common traits, such as grouping a name with a related address, or grouping an address with other addresses.

These data relationships, much like human relationships, will become more complex further down the road.

Data relationships represent the advantage of using databases over *flat* files, or plain text documents, that will simply dump all your data in a list indicating no relationships between the data chunks.

Retrieving data from databases is far more efficient than doing so from simple text because databases provide their own cataloging system. Every data entry is cross-referenced by record and field—much like a library catalogs its books. It's less time-consuming to ask a library worker to go to aisle five, shelf six, and bring back *The Mouse and the Motorcycle* than it is to say, "It starts with like 'M' or something, and it's about a rat with half a Ping-Pong ball on its head. It's in this building somewhere, just keep looking around until you find it."

Because the library stores its books on shelves and aisles instead of in one massive stack, it's a pretty easy task for the worker to find the specific book I want. Also, the library has taken the time to order the books by subject, title, or author, which makes the selection process even more efficient. Understand this, and you've grasped the basic concept behind using databases.

The Datasource and ODBC

After we've created a database and populated it with vital information, we're only a few steps away from serving up that data on the Web. The next task is to "link" your database with ColdFusion. This link is called a *datasource,* or *DSN*.

Note

> Manuals for older releases of ColdFusion were peppered with references to "DSNs," but you'll find newer versions prefer the term "datasource." Why the change? Who knows, but it might have something to do with the fact that "DSN" is a lot like the acronym "DNS," which refers to an Internet *domain name server*, a whole different animal we don't need to mess with here.

The term *datasource* is, for the purposes, interchangeable with another three-dollar acronym you'll hear bantered about at computer geek parties—*ODBC*, or *Open Database Connectivity*. A datasource or ODBC source is essentially a database, but when I refer to it as a datasource, I mean that I've readied it for ColdFusion access by defining it in ColdFusion Administrator (see Day 3). When we did, we "told" ColdFusion, and the system, a few important things about the database:

- That it does, in fact, exist.
- Where it exists on the server's hard drive (the *file path*).
- What kind of database file it is (Microsoft Access, Oracle, FileMaker Pro, and so on).
- And, most important, that we want ColdFusion to create a data pipeline in and out of the database so it's ready for quick access.

An open pipeline is a crucial concept; it lets ColdFusion quickly rummage around in a database looking for information, without having to open the file, search it, and then close the file each time. In terms of the miniscule database of Elvis' flop films, this might not sound like such a Herculean task, but in the real world, with databases holding hundreds or thousands of records, searching files can turn into pretty heavy-duty work for a server's processor.

Selecting a database as a datasource also lets you send commands to the database file, telling it things like what records you want to retrieve or what information you want to add or change. These commands are sent in a concise but whoppingly powerful language called *SQL*, *structured query language*, which I'll introduce in Day 4.

NEW TERM   *Structured query language* (SQL) is a universal set of commands that programs such as ColdFusion use to "communicate" with a database. Commands can include searching for and retrieving data; inputting data; creating and deleting table fields; and much more.

The datasource also enables instant access to the database. If you need to add a new record or change existing information, just pop the thing open and do your work. No program shutdown, updating, or reloading is necessary to have your changes reflected instantly on your Web site. The sample database of Elvis' films probably won't change much, but if we were archiving a list of Liz Taylor's husbands as detailed in Day 1, you can see where up-to-the-minute updates would be a bonus feature.

Datasources are defined in the ColdFusion Administrator, the configuration utility we'll explore in Day 3, "Setting Up ColdFusion and Defining a Datasource." Defining a data-source is pretty easy—just use your Web browser to navigate a standard dialog window, tell ColdFusion where your database resides on your hard drive, give the datasource a suitable name, and you're set.

From that point on, when you refer to the database in a ColdFusion document, just call it by the datasource name, in this case `elvis`. It's much easier than having to type in the full *file path* to the database file each time you reference it, such as

`c:\my documents\bad stuff\elvis site\database\elvis.mdb`

UNIX users are familiar with file paths, but Windows users who navigate "folders" might not be.

NEW TERM   A *file path* is the text that points to a file on your hard drive. For example, if a file called `DOCUMENT.ZIP` is in the `STUFF` folder on your `C` drive, its file path will be `c:\STUFF\DOCUMENT.ZIP`.

I've briefly introduced the database and how to put it into use as a datasource. These concepts show how ColdFusion secretly works behind the scenes, but let's take a look at the element closest to the end user. I'll now move on to the ColdFusion template, the third vital piece that completes the puzzle.

Exploring the ColdFusion Template

A ColdFusion *template* determines the layout and content of what the user actually sees in the browser when she accesses your expertly coded ColdFusion site. Templates use the file extension .CFM, rather than .HTML. When a user's browser requests a .CFM file, the server knows to turn the handling over to ColdFusion.

Templates are constructed in the same way as HTML pages—that is, either they can be hand-coded in text editors such as Notepad, Vi, or EMACS, or they can be created with *graphic user interfaces* (GUIs) such as Allaire's companion product, ColdFusion Studio. (We'll get to Studio in Week III, "Maximizing and Customizing ColdFusion Applications.") In fact, you can even use templates to create other templates, but I'm getting all lathered and jumping the gun here.

To introduce you to the template, let's use my database of Elvis movies as the sample datasource.

Suppose that I wanted to create a template that will retrieve the information for *Speedway*, that fine film in which Elvis stars as a frustrated racecar driver who also just happens to be a rock and roll singer.

Other than the different file extension and a few lines of code, my template file will look a lot like a standard HTML document. In fact, if you open this or any ColdFusion template in a text editor, you'll see something like Figure 2.2.

Note the special tags beginning with CF. These are ColdFusion Markup Language, which was briefly discussed in Day 1. CFML tags are processed exclusively by ColdFusion, and when you use them you tell ColdFusion that you want it to do something. In this case, you have two CFML tag sections, the *query* section and the *output* section.

2

FIGURE 2.2

A sample ColdFusion template containing a query section, an output section, and standard HTML markup tags.

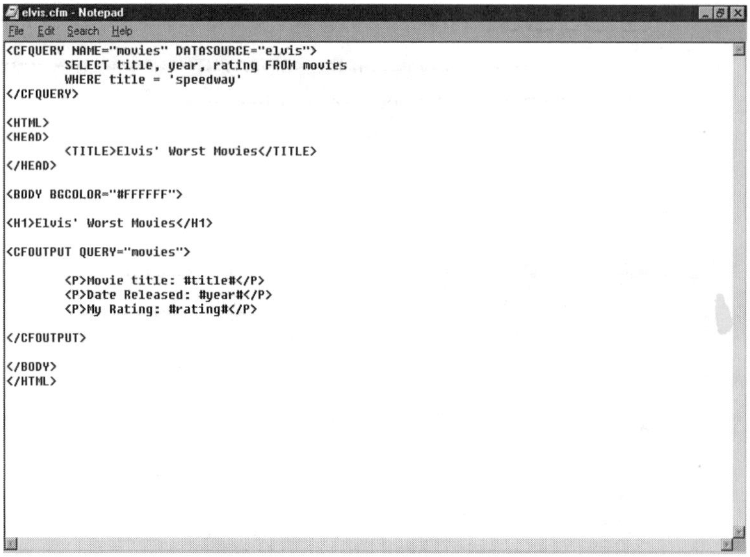

```
elvis.cfm - Notepad
File  Edit  Search  Help
<CFQUERY NAME="movies" DATASOURCE="elvis">
        SELECT title, year, rating FROM movies
        WHERE title = 'speedway'
</CFQUERY>

<HTML>
<HEAD>
        <TITLE>Elvis' Worst Movies</TITLE>
</HEAD>

<BODY BGCOLOR="#FFFFFF">

<H1>Elvis' Worst Movies</H1>

<CFOUTPUT QUERY="movies">

        <P>Movie title: #title#</P>
        <P>Date Released: #year#</P>
        <P>My Rating: #rating#</P>

</CFOUTPUT>

</BODY>
</HTML>
```

The Query

The first section, enclosed in the <CFQUERY> tags, defines a *query*, a set of instructions we want to send to the database. In Figure 2.2, the query is performing a simple search of records, looking for the one in which title is 'Speedway'. If the actual instructions rattle your brain, don't worry. You'll find more information on SQL than you ever wanted to know in Day 5, "Finding the Data You Need: An Introduction to Queries and SQL."

Basic queries like this example tell ColdFusion three things: which datasource you want to use, which table or tables you want to work with, and what function you want to perform on that table's data—a search, a modification, a new entry, and so on.

HTML Markup

The second section in Figure 2.2 begins with the <HTML> tag, and will look awfully familiar to anyone who's labored over a hand-coded Web page. The usual HTML tags define the page title, header, and so on. The only deviation from standard HTML markup is in the <CFOUTPUT> section, which opens and closes with the <CFOUTPUT> and </CFOUTPUT> tags, respectively.

The Output

The output section lies between the `<CFOUTPUT>` tags. It, too, looks strikingly similar to HTML markup, but contains *variables* like these:

```
#title#
#year#
#rating#
```

NEW TERM A *variable* is a symbol or a name that stands for a value. ColdFusion output variables stand for values returned by a ColdFusion query.

Note the *hash marks* around each word—these tell ColdFusion that something's up, and that the text between the marks is not your average HTML code, but is instead a reference to a variable. When ColdFusion sees hash marks that lie within `<CFOUTPUT>` tags, it treats the text within the marks as a variable.

NEW TERM *Programmers* and Web developers call the number sign (#)a *hash mark*, to signify that it no longer retains its value as a number sign, but has become a placeholder or marker designating something else. In ColdFusion, hash marks designate variables.

In Figure 2.2, ColdFusion processes the query specified in the `<CFOUTPUT>` tag and returns the value of each variable.

To understand this, let's look at the query section again, in Listing 2.1.

INPUT   **LISTING 2.1** A Sample ColdFusion Query Section

```
1: <CFQUERY NAME="movies" DATASOURCE="elvis">
2: SELECT title, year, rating FROM movies WHERE title = 'Speedway'
3: </CFQUERY>
```

Using SQL terms such as `SELECT`, `FROM`, and `WHERE`, you've asked ColdFusion to search the `"movies"` table for records where `title` is `'Speedway'` and then to remember the data contained in the fields called `title`, `year`, and `rating`. These field names correspond exactly to the variables referenced in the `<CFOUTPUT>` section. If a user's browser requested this template, ColdFusion would run the specified query, and then plug in the returned values wherever the corresponding variable appears. The result would look like Figure 2.3.

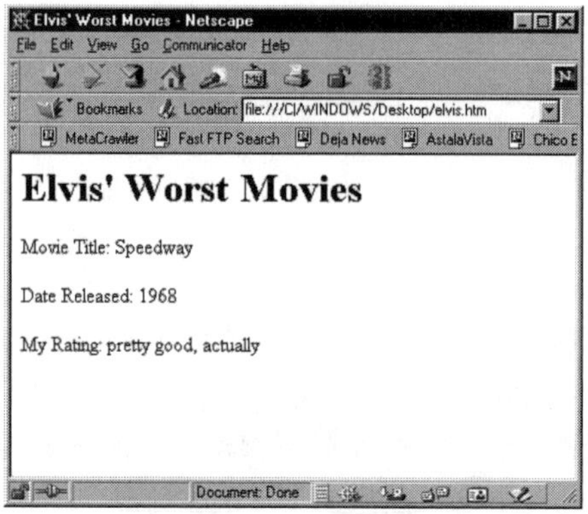

FIGURE 2.3

Sample output from the template illustrated in Figure 2.2.

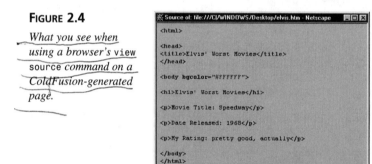

If the user were savvy enough to use the *view source* command in her browser, she'd see only the text in Figure 2.4.

FIGURE 2.4

What you see when using a browser's view source *command on a ColdFusion-generated page.*

```
<html>

<head>
<title>Elvis' Worst Movies</title>
</head>

<body bgcolor="#FFFFFF">

<h1>Elvis' Worst Movies</h1>

<p>Movie Title: Speedway</p>

<p>Date Released: 1968</p>

<p>My Rating: pretty good, actually</p>

</body>
</html>
```

NEW TERM   A browser's *view source* command lets the user see the actual text and HTML code that make up a Web page. In Netscape Navigator, choose the View menu and select Page Source. In Internet Explorer, choose View and then Source.

No query, no variables, just pristine, unrevealing HTML code. That's because ColdFusion generates the page *dynamically* at the moment the user's browser requests the page and sends just the HTML text. Let the user pay no attention to that designer behind the curtain.

Exploring the Relationship Between Query and Output

To better understand the relationship between ColdFusion query and output sections, let's see what happens when we make some changes to the query.

In the template file illustrated in Figure 2.2, the query was very specific. Using SQL commands, it asked ColdFusion to retrieve the data from only a single record—the one in which `title` was `'Speedway'`. To further understand ColdFusion output, look at an example where the query isn't so picky, in Figure 2.5.

2

FIGURE 2.5

A new sample template file, identical to Figure 2.2 except for the query section.

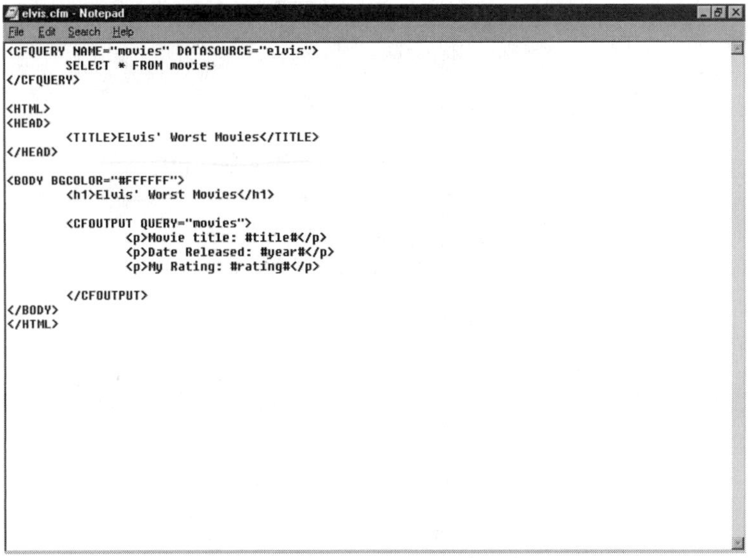

```
elvis.cfm - Notepad
File  Edit  Search  Help
<CFQUERY NAME="movies" DATASOURCE="elvis">
        SELECT * FROM movies
</CFQUERY>

<HTML>
<HEAD>
        <TITLE>Elvis' Worst Movies</TITLE>
</HEAD>

<BODY BGCOLOR="#FFFFFF">
        <h1>Elvis' Worst Movies</h1>

        <CFOUTPUT QUERY="movies">
                <p>Movie title: #title#</p>
                <p>Date Released: #year#</p>
                <p>My Rating: #rating#</p>

        </CFOUTPUT>
</BODY>
</HTML>
```

Note that the new query section uses a *wildcard* character, the asterisk.

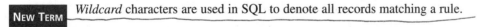

NEW TERM *Wildcard* characters are used in SQL to denote all records matching a rule.

The asterisk is a special SQL command that means "everything." In Figure 2.5, you've changed the query from "get the record where `title` is `'Speedway'`" to "get everything"—all the records in the table. Note that the output section hasn't changed, nor has the HTML code.

The output from Figure 2.5 would look like this:

```
Title: King Creole
Year Released: 1958
My Rating: watchable

Title: Blue Hawaii
Year Released: 1951
My Rating: watchable

Title: Kid Galahad
Year Released: 1962
My Rating: aaaahhh!

Title: Harum Scarum
Year Released: 1965
My Rating: aaaahhh!

Title: Roustabout
Year Released: 1964
My Rating: he's going to hell for this

Title: Speedway
Year Released: 1968
My Rating: pretty good, actually

Title: Charro
Year Released: 1969
My Rating: watchable

Title: Clambake
Year Released: 1967
My Rating: pretty good, actually

Title: Flaming Star
Year Released: 1960
My Rating: he's going to hell for this watchable

Title: Kissin' Cousins
Year Released:1964
My Rating: he's going to hell for this
```

Instead of displaying just one film, the output now shows the data for all films in the table, running vertically down the page. But referring back to Figure 2.2, you see only one <CFOUTPUT> section, with only one set of variables. How did all those other movies get there?

They appear because ColdFusion, by default, repeats the output section for every record returned by a query. Any text or variables appearing within the <CFOUTPUT> and </CFOUTPUT> tags will repeat until every record is exhausted. If the query returns one record, you get one output section, and so on. I'll discuss ways to use this feature, and how to limit it, in later chapters.

Using URL Variables to Select Output

By now I hope you're beginning to understand the basic relationship between a ColdFusion query and the output it generates as a page in your browser. If so, then you might be starting to wonder about all these time-saving features I raved about in Day 1. For example, if I want to design a site in which every Elvis film is listed on its own page, wouldn't I have to create a separate ColdFusion template for each film? Each template's query would have to refer to a specific film, right?

Of course, the answer is no, and the reason behind it is one of the key elements that make ColdFusion worthy of a book this size.

You can use a single template file to generate hundreds of Web pages because ColdFusion accepts variables in the query sections. Instead of a query that says "get the record where `title` equals `'Speedway'`," you can instead say "get the record where `title` equals a variable" and then supply the variable later. Each time you change the variable, you get an output page showing a different record.

I realize that we're moving into some pretty heady concepts here for only the second chapter, but bear with me. It's important that you grasp the idea behind this variable stuff, but not so important that you fret over the details—yet.

Let's look at the contents of a new template page in Listing 2.2.

INPUT   **LISTING 2.2** A Complete ColdFusion Template, with Query and Output Sections

```
<CFQUERY NAME="get_movies" DATASOURCE="elvis">

SELECT * FROM movies WHERE ID = '#code#'

</CFQUERY>

<HTML>

<TITLE>Elvis Movies</TITLE>

<CFOUTPUT QUERY="get_movies">

<B>Title:</B> #title# <P>

<B>Year Released:</B> #year# <P>

<B>My Rating:</B> #rating# <P>

</CFOUTPUT>

</HTML>
```

2

Note that the query now contains a variable, the word `code`, which is enclosed in hash marks. In this query we've asked ColdFusion to search the `"movies"` table for records in which the ID field is the same as the variable `#code#`. Let's look at the `"movies"` table again, in Figure 2.6.

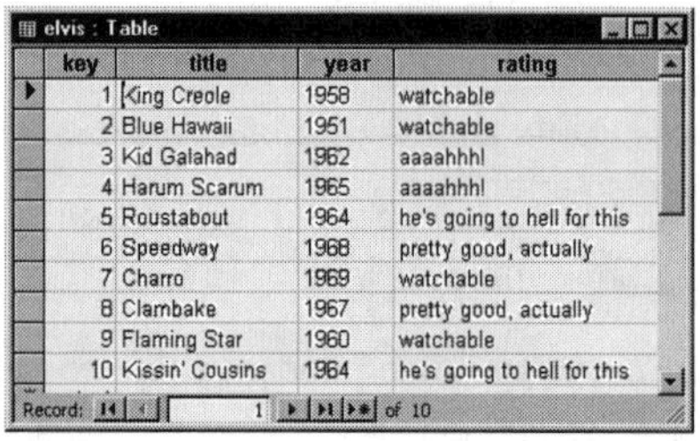

key	title	year	rating
1	King Creole	1958	watchable
2	Blue Hawaii	1951	watchable
3	Kid Galahad	1962	aaaahhhl
4	Harum Scarum	1965	aaaahhhl
5	Roustabout	1964	he's going to hell for this
6	Speedway	1968	pretty good, actually
7	Charro	1969	watchable
8	Clambake	1967	pretty good, actually
9	Flaming Star	1960	watchable
10	Kissin' Cousins	1964	he's going to hell for this

FIGURE 2.6

The `"movies"` table—note the ID field.

You might recall in the discussion of databases earlier in this section that the ID field is a key field. My database software automatically generated the key field as I entered the row for each Elvis film. Every row in my table has a unique number in the ID field, making it ideal for selecting a certain record.

In the query shown in Listing 2.2, I've asked ColdFusion to get the records where the ID field equals the variable `#code#`. But what's "code"? It's not a field in the database, so how does ColdFusion know what to plug in for the variable?

We'll tell it what to plug in. One of ColdFusion's handiest functions is the capability to pass variables to a template file via the page URL. We can use any variables we'd like as long as they appear somewhere in the template file. Look at Figure 2.7.

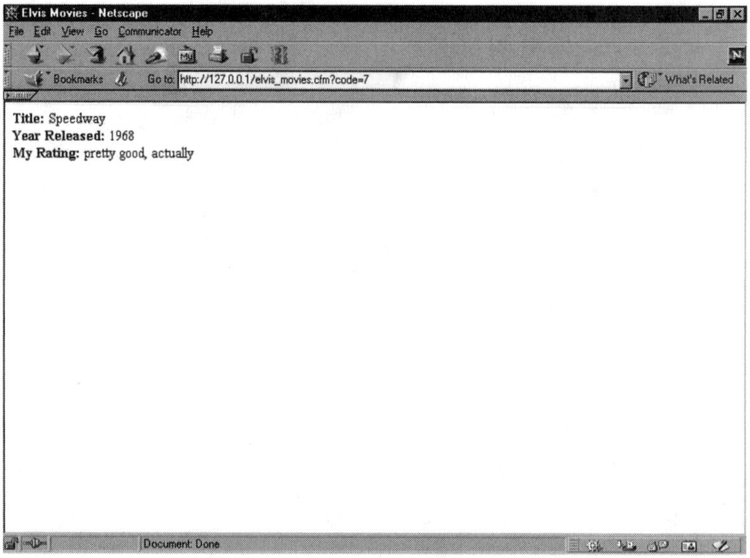

FIGURE 2.7

The output from Listing 2.2, as it appears in a browser.

Here I've entered a special URL into my browser. I've called up my template file, `elvis_movies.cfm`, and appended a variable to it using the question mark (?) symbol. In this case I've defined a simple variable called `code` and set it equal to the number 7.

 Note   ColdFusion, like many CGI programs, uses the question mark symbol to denote variables in the URL. For this reason, it's important to avoid question marks in variable names and field names. ColdFusion might misinterpret them and return an error.

The template page in Listing 2.2 would then produce a Web page like Figure 2.7.

If I use the same template page, but change the value of `code` in the URL to 2, I'd get the output for a different Elvis movie. Behind the scenes, ColdFusion plugs in the `code` value that I supplied in the browser URL for the variable `#code#` in the template's query section. So when my URL looks like this:

```
http://www.myserver.com/movies.cfm?code=3
```

ColdFusion interprets the query section in the `movies.cfm` template as shown in Listing 2.3.

INPUT

LISTING 2.3 A Sample Query Section Using an ID Number to Select a Specific Record

```
<CFQUERY DATASOURCE="elvis">

SELECT title, year, rating FROM movies WHERE ID = 3

</CFQUERY>
```

By changing the URL I use to access the template page, I can generate output for any movie in my database. If my database had hundreds or even thousands of records, I could view formatted output for any one of them with this single template. Now we're talking saving time, right?

Again, don't worry too much if the mechanics of URL variables aren't crystal clear yet. The important concept here is that a template page's query section determines the output to the user, and that using variables in a query lets you view lots of records from a single template. I'll revisit URL variables in depth during the coming days.

Summary

Most ColdFusion applications you'll build have a database at their heart. If you're new to databases, think of them as mini-libraries that organize and relate data by common traits. If you know someone's name, databases make it easy to find the corresponding address, and so on.

When you use a database as the backbone of a ColdFusion application, define it as a datasource with CF's Administrator software. Doing so tells the program where the database is on the system, and opens up an ODBC pipeline that connects ColdFusion directly to the database.

When the database is active as a datasource, you can build template files that will output items from the database as Web pages. Each template file has three elements—a query section, an output section, and standard HTML markup tags. When a user views these templates in a Web browser, he sees the output in HTML format.

The query section of a template tells ColdFusion what datasource you want to work with, which table to work with, and what you want to do. One of the most common query tasks is a search in which you tell ColdFusion to retrieve database records matching a condition. By changing the conditions (as variables) in a query, you can manipulate the output the user sees in his browser.

Q&A

Q What other programs use ODBC? What are the advantages of these programs?

A ColdFusion is only one example of an ODBC-compatible application. Others include word processors, spreadsheet programs, address books, and mail programs. The advantages these programs have over their non-ODBC counterparts is that, as with ColdFusion, you can use them to generate documents from a database. For example, consider a mail program: With ODBC, you can link your mailer to a database and create an instant form mail to every name and address listed in a table.

Q Where are ColdFusion template files stored on my Web server?

A Older versions of CF required you to define a directory to hold your template files, but from version 3.0 on, you could place them anywhere in your Web directory structure—just as with standard HTML pages. As long as your templates use the `.cfm` file extension, ColdFusion will recognize them.

Q Can multiple queries be used in a single ColdFusion template file?

A Yes, and in later sessions, I'll discuss specific advantages to doing this. In fact, queries can even be used to generate search parameters for other queries in the same template.

Q What happens when I place text and HTML markup outside a ColdFusion output section?

A It displays normally, just as it would in a standard HTML file. ColdFusion essentially ignores anything not appearing in a `<CF>` and simply returns it to the user's browser verbatim.

Q What happens if a ColdFusion query doesn't match with any records in a table?

A The template page displays normally, but the text within the `<CFOUTPUT>` tags doesn't appear. This has both advantages and disadvantages that I'll cover in later sections.

Workshop

Just to see whether you were dozing through today's discussion, here are a few quiz questions and exercises. Answers to quiz questions can be found in Appendix A at the back of the text.

Quiz

1. What are the three components of a ColdFusion application?
2. What does a user see at home when using his browser's `view source` function on a ColdFusion template?
3. What are the three sections in a ColdFusion template?
4. What does SQL stand for, and what is it?

Exercises

1. Open a database file and identify the following elements: a table, a field, and a record.
2. Open a database table and picture ways a record might be served up as a Web page.
3. Open one of the sample template files included on the ColdFusion installation CD-ROM and identify the query and output sections.

DAY 3

Setting Up ColdFusion and Defining a Datasource

Now that you've examined the basic components of a ColdFusion application, it's time to either install the software or to get set up with a remote ColdFusion provider so you can start working miracles with your own templates. If you're not already the proud owner of ColdFusion Server, you have a few decisions to make at this point. This section will help you decide whether you need to shell out the dollars for your own copy, or whether you'd be better served—pardon the bad pun—by hosting your CF documents on someone else's server. I'll also cover

- Issues to consider when choosing a remote provider
- Web servers compatible with ColdFusion Server
- The three varieties of ColdFusion Server
- Installing ColdFusion Server
- Verifying ColdFusion Server installation

- Understanding ColdFusion Administator
- Defining a ColdFusion datasource
- Starting and stopping ColdFusion service

If you're one of the few, the proud, who host their own Web servers, you might skip the following sections and move to "Exploring ColdFusion Server Varieties," which looks at the two types of ColdFusion Servers and helps you decide which one you'll need.

If you're among us folk who can't afford our own T-1 Net connection, read on. I'll look at some important issues in choosing an outside Web provider and help you decide whether you need to run your own copy of ColdFusion for testing purposes.

Deciding What to Buy or Not to Buy

If you've made your decision to host your ColdFusion site with a remote provider, you face a dilemma. Because ColdFusion only works in conjunction with a Web server, you can't simply preview CF templates in your browser as you can with standard HTML pages. You'd really like the ability to try out templates on your computer before uploading them to your provider's server, but for all its benefits ColdFusion Server is a pretty pricey purchase if you're just using it to test templates.

Allaire provides a solution with a special development package for Windows users, called ColdFusion Studio. It sells for a fraction of the price of the fully blown ColdFusion Server applications, and it comes with a special single-user server. This mini-ColdFusion server runs just fine alongside the freebie Microsoft Personal Web Server that comes bundled with several Microsoft products, such as FrontPage and Windows 98. It provides a fully featured and relatively inexpensive way to test CF templates on your local computer before uploading them to a remote Web host.

The package also includes an expanded copy of Allaire's HomeSite, a semi-graphic interface for building Web pages. It provides graphic shortcuts for HTML and ColdFusion tags and includes timesaving features such as tag checking and query-building aids. I'll take a closer look at ColdFusion Studio and the HomeSite editor in the third and final week of this tutorial.

Tip

ColdFusion Studio is often called a *semi-graphic* interface because it enables developers to work with HTML and CFM files as text pages, but includes graphic shortcuts that aid in the coding process. By contrast, programs like Adobe PageMill and Microsoft FrontPage are considered *graphic* interfaces because the developer most often sees a page as it will appear in a browser, rather than working directly on the HTML text.

Questions to Ask a Potential ColdFusion Provider

If you've settled on hosting your ColdFusion site with an outside Web provider rather than on your own server, it's important to compare prices and features.

> **Tip**
>
> To find providers offering ColdFusion as an option, start with a search in your favorite Web index. Use terms like "ColdFusion" (obviously), "service," "provider," "hosting," and "Windows NT" or "Solaris." Several good provider indices provide price and feature breakdowns of several major Web hosts.

It's vital that you take the time to seek out a provider who really *knows* the software. ColdFusion is a very hot property in today's Web-service market, and plenty of fly-by-night hosting services want in on the action. For every knowledgeable provider who knows the ins and outs of ColdFusion service, there are at least as many who installed the software yesterday and don't have the faintest idea how it works. When you start asking pointed questions like those that follow, it won't take long to find out which providers know their DSNs from their DNSs.

ColdFusion Version

For obvious reasons, it's important to know what software version your potential provider is running *before* you start creating templates. Although most templates written for version 4.0 are compatible with 3.0, there are a few nifty features in the later version that won't seem so nifty when they don't work and you have to edit them out of all your pages.

Because the ColdFusion boom developed fairly recently, you'll find a majority of providers working with versions 3.x or 4.x. Beware those who use anything older, because the first and second versions of the software are vastly different from recent releases. With ColdFusion versions 1 and 2, templates use a different file extension (.dbm instead of .cfm) and must reside in a single, predetermined directory. I've migrated older ColdFusion sites to newer servers, and, trust me, it's a task best left to the sort of people who enjoy repetitive, menial tasks like arranging their sock drawers by color and style.

> **Tip**
>
> If you're migrating an extensive ColdFusion site that was built in an earlier version of the software, your CF server's administrator might be able to help out with a few tricks such as enabling the .dbm file extension for templates.

Email or phone potential providers and ask them what version(s) they support. If they don't know, take that as your first hint to keep looking elsewhere.

Number of Datasources Supported

So far, I've discussed ColdFusion applications only on a conceptual level, and all my examples have used only a single datasource. I should mention here that there are certain advantages to having more than one datasource, particularly if you're dealing with very large databases.

For example, a huge online department store will gain much by keeping a separate product database for each department and setting up each as a separate datasource. Why? Picture yourself inside a *physical* department store and you'll understand. If I sent you inside to find a pair of red cotton Underoos with a Spiderman logo—waist 34, please— but didn't tell you in which department to look, you could be in there all day. If I narrowed the search by first pointing you to Menswear, you'd be back in a flash, and I'd soon be at home sipping iced tea in my new underpants.

Now extend this delightful metaphor to ColdFusion. If the online department store lists thousands of products in a single datasource, the software might be in your database plundering around all day looking for the specific product requested by a query. Well, maybe not *all day,* because computers are pretty quick at that kind of stuff, but you get the point. You can cut down on the time it takes for ColdFusion to return pages to your users by keeping your databases small, and by using multiple datasources when necessary.

As an example, take a look at two ways to configure a store's data in Figure 3.1 and Figure 3.2.

FIGURE 3.1

A sample data structure for a store, with all departments sharing one data-source.

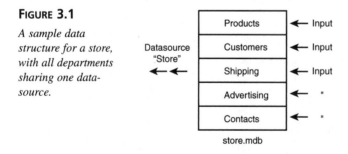

In Figure 3.1, I've illustrated the layout of a ColdFusion site that lumps everything into one datasource. All of the store's operations, including customer databases, shipping information, and products are handled with a single datasource. Each time ColdFusion searches for a record, it must begin by navigating that massive collection of data.

FIGURE 3.2

A second sample structure, this time using a separate datasource for each department.

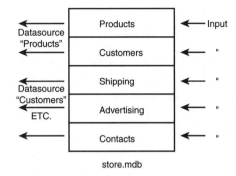

store.mdb

By contrast, Figure 3.2 shows a site organized with several databases, each set up as an individual datasource. When ColdFusion searches for data on a product, it only needs to search the datasource that contains information on products, and not those that contain shipping information, customer names, etc.

It's important to have some idea of how many datasources your site will require. Small to medium-sized sites will do fine with just one, and coincidentally that's the number the vast majority of Web hosts allow. If you anticipate your site someday needing more than one datasource, some sweet-talk or additional host-shopping might be required.

If your potential provider doesn't know how many it allows, or the host seems confused by the term "datasource," draw a sad face next to its name and continue down your list of potentials.

Updating Datasources

Updating of datasources is an important factor that's often overlooked when shopping for ColdFusion Web hosts. Ignore it and you might find yourself pecking away at the keyboard during all those hours you had hoped to save by building your site with ColdFusion.

When you host a remote ColdFusion site, times will come when you'll need to *update* your datasource. This might occur because you've manually added data to your database, or because you've added new tables or fields. Either way, you want to have the database on your Web provider's machine synchronized with the one on your local system.

With most providers, it's as simple as uploading your modified database and overwriting the older file that resides on the provider's server. Your database-driven pages will be unavailable while the file is in transit, but it's fairly easy to compensate for this by scheduling your uploads during "off peak" hours in the middle of the night, when all but the true geeks are asleep. When the upload finishes, your Web site will automatically reflect the new database entries, and all's well.

I say *most* providers offer this feature, because a surprising number haven't yet caught on to the simple wisdom of this method, and still others can't offer it because they run older versions of ColdFusion or have super-strict security requirements. With providers such as these, the update process is not so simple. Each time you need to update your data, you'll upload your database and then have to email or phone your provider's tech support department to ask it to update the datasource manually.

If your database doesn't change often, the latter method probably won't bother you much. However, if you've built a ColdFusion site for a client whose sales department wants to add five new products on a Friday afternoon for a special promotion, you might spend your weekend testing the *true* limits of "round-the-clock tech support." Similarly, if you have to call and update your datasource two or three times a day, you might earn a spot on your techperson's "Cubicle Wall of Shame," right next to the pic of Bill Gates with the inked-in devil horns.

Ask potential providers what they require you do to update an existing datasource. Ask them to be very specific and don't settle for vague answers like, "Well, you just upload it and then we do some stuff here…"

Where to Put Your Database

Many providers require that your database be uploaded to a certain directory or folder on their server before they'll initialize it as a datasource. Ask potential hosts where this directory resides, and whether it is directly accessible by you, the developer.

For security reasons, some providers won't let you upload your database right into the directory where ColdFusion expects it to reside. This means that, after uploading, you must email a techie and wait for him to make the changes for you. This puts you in a position similar to the one in the last section—every time you make a manual change to your database, you rely on your provider's tech support folks to do additional work behind the scenes.

Again, if your database doesn't change often, a couple emails back and forth won't slow you down much. On the other hand, if you're constantly updating data or adding new tables, you might want to seek out a provider that offers direct database uploading.

Exploring ColdFusion Server Varieties

Allaire's ColdFusion Server comes in three varieties. The first is the *Professional Edition*, which is the standard package that will perform all the tasks covered in this

CORBA—COMMON OBJECT REQUEST BROKER ~~ARHIC~~ ARCHITECTURE

book. The *Enterprise Edition* adds increased security and system failsafe measures for those who plan to run very sophisticated e-commerce applications and require interface with tools like CORBA. The third and newest variety is ColdFusion Express, Allaire's free application offering a limited feature set of the full versions.

> **Note**
>
> The coding examples later in this book are designed for use with ColdFusion Professional Edition or Enterprise Edition. The examples covered in Week 1 will also work with ColdFusion Express, but the advanced chapters use features not offered by Express.

If you're not sure which version you need, stick with the *Professional* edition, which works just fine for the majority of sites—even those hosting e-commerce functions.

Professional Edition Compatibility

ColdFusion Server *Professional Edition* is compatible with systems running Windows NT Server version 4.0 or greater, with Windows 95 and 98 systems, and with Red Hat Linux 6.0 or 6.1. ColdFusion 4.x works with Web server packages that support any of these common Web server *Application Programmers' Interfaces* (APIs):

Netscape Server API

Internet Server API

WebSite Server API

Apache 1.3.2 or higher

Common Gateway Interface, or CGI (limited functionality)

Enterprise Edition Compatibility

ColdFusion Server *Enterprise Edition* is compatible with Windows NT 4.0 or greater; Red Hat Linux 6.0 or 6.1; HP-UX 11; and SPARC Solaris 2.5.1, 2.6, and 2.7. On NT machines, ColdFusion 4.x is compatible with all the Web server packages listed previously; on Solaris systems, it supports the following:

Apache API 1.3.2 or higher

Common Gateway Interface (CGI)

API — APPLICATION PROGRAMMING INTERFACE

Installing ColdFusion Server on Windows Platforms

Compared to what I'll get into later, installing ColdFusion Server is a breeze. When you pop in the CD-ROM, the setup proceeds pretty much along the lines of every Windows program you've ever used before.

Before installing, make sure the files and directories on your server are generally "cleaned up"—that is, you don't have old stuff hanging around from previously installed apps you've since deleted.

> **Note** Depending on your operating system, ColdFusion Server Professional Edition needs 50–100MB of space available on your hard drive; Enterprise Edition requires 120–200MB.

Make sure that you have Web server software installed and running *before* you begin ColdFusion installation. If you're not sure whether you're running a Web server, open a browser on your system and enter this URL:

```
http://127.0.0.1/
```

If you see your site's home page, or other text provided by your Web server, you know things are running correctly. If you don't, consult your Web server's documentation for help.

Because you're evidently maintaining your own Web server, I'll assume you've reached Big Kid status and I won't offend you here by detailing installation basics such as click on the "setup" icon, enter your name and serial number, and so on. Beyond that, the installation app will offer some options. I recommend choosing the default install directory unless you have a *really good* reason not to. You'll then be asked which ColdFusion components you want to install. If disk space isn't an issue, go ahead and let the installer default to add all of them. If you find a component you don't use, you can always delete it later.

The installer will next present a list of compatible server APIs and ask you to choose the one that matches your brand of Web server software. If you're running a server that is only partially supported by ColdFusion, it's a good idea to check the documentation at this point and read over the features offered by different compatibility modes.

Caution   Windows users installing ColdFusion for use with Apache Web servers will need to make a couple manual modifications to the server. Check the ColdFusion help file for details.

Next you'll be asked to choose an administrator password, which you'll need later to access the ColdFusion Administrator.

ColdFusion will, by default, install its documentation as HTML and CFM pages. This might seem a little strange if you're used to reading application docs in Microsoft Word or other text formats, but when you start browsing the pages you'll understand the method behind the apparent madness. By coding some of the pages in `.CFM` template files, Allaire is able to actively demonstrate sample output for each of ColdFusion's tags.

After the setup files decompress, the installer will ask you to reboot your server so ColdFusion can make the necessary link with your system ODBC.

Tip   Depending on your system platform, ColdFusion "runs" in a variety of ways. On Windows NT, it becomes a system service, accessible from the Services Control Panel. On Solaris systems, it runs as a process, and is initiated by a script. On Windows 9x systems, the program runs as an ordinary executable and is accessible from the system tray.

Installing ColdFusion Server on UNIX-Based Platforms

ColdFusion is distributed as a "package" file, a familiar concept to UNIX or Solaris administrators. As with all package files, ColdFusion is installed and managed with `pkgadd`, `pkgrm`, and `pkginfo` utilities. To begin the installation, log in to your system as root and mount the installation CD. Type the following to begin:

```
pkgadd -d /cdrom/cdrom0
```

A list of relevant package files appears, from which you can select the ColdFusion file. From here, it's a fairly standard program installation. ColdFusion will ask for a serial number, a default install directory, and the make of your Web server. You'll also be asked for a username under which you want ColdFusion server to run.

Users running UNIX-based systems with certain Apache- or Netscape-based Web servers might need to manually configure their software to work with ColdFusion. Check the files in `/opt/coldfusion/webserver/apache/README` or `/opt/coldfusion/webserver/NSAPI/README` for details.

After the install program finishes copying files, a shell script will restart your Web server and begin ColdFusion service for the first time.

Verifying Server Setup

After completing the initial setup phase, it's important to test ColdFusion Server. Open a browser on your system and enter this URL:

`http://127.0.0.1/CFIDE/Administrator/index.cfm`

If all went well, you'll see the ColdFusion Administrator login page, as shown in Figure 3.3.

FIGURE 3.3

The entry page in ColdFusion Adminstrator.

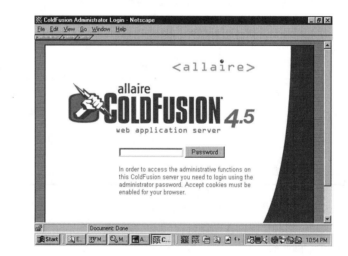

If you don't see the administration page, or your Web server software returns a 404 error (page not found), check the following:

- Did you use the default installation paths when installing the software? If you specified a directory or folder other than the default, the Administrator page will be at a location other than `http://127.0.0.1/CFIDE/Administrator/index.cfm`.

- Did the installation fully complete? In some cases, other programs on your computer—such as anti-virus software—might cause the installation to hang. Disable the offending program and start the ColdFusion installation again.

- Is your Web server running? ColdFusion absolutely requires that your Web server software be enabled.

That's about it. It's a deceptively simple setup—even easier than installing your average Web browser. Don't get over-confident on me though. You still have 19 days to go, and you'll be tackling more complex issues ahead!

Understanding the ColdFusion Administrator

Starting with ColdFusion 3.0, Allaire recognized that system administrators don't always have the luxury of sitting right at the keyboard of the server they're administering. For this reason, Allaire developed a very nifty Web interface for its program's configuration utility, the ColdFusion Administrator. You can now fire up the Administrator interface by clicking a desktop icon, right-clicking a taskbar icon (on Windows 9x platforms), or by remotely accessing a special URL in any Web browser. Assuming you used the default directories when you installed ColdFusion server, the URL to access Administrator is

```
http://your.hostname/CFIDE/Administrator/index.cfm
```

It's a good idea to bookmark the ColdFusion Administrator page in your browser at this point. I'll be referring to it often in coming chapters as I define datasources, discuss setting up access to your server's mail system, and explore template debugging.

Whichever method you choose to start the Administrator, the result will be the same. Your system's default Web browser will bring up the ColdFusion Administrator login screen. Enter the password you specified in the install process and you'll see a set of page frames like Figure 3.4 offering access to ColdFusion options.

Server Options

This section provides options to tune ColdFusion's performance. You probably won't need to make any adjustments to the default settings initially, but if your site becomes heavily trafficked, these server options can help avoid performance problems.

Included in Server Options are

- Version information
- Ways to define and configure special ColdFusion variables
- Password and security setup
- Directory mapping

FIGURE 3.4

The main configura-tion page in ColdFusion Adminstrator.

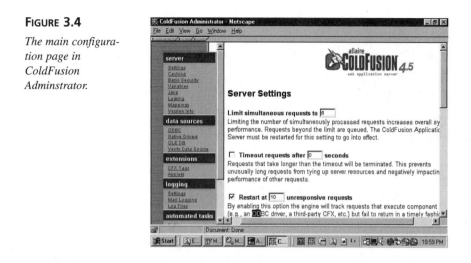

NEW TERM   *Directory mapping* defines the location of key directories on your Web server, such as the root or home directory.

Datasource Options and Setup

Before ColdFusion can communicate with a database, the database file must be config-ured as a datasource in ColdFusion Administrator.

To begin defining a datasource, move your database to a spot on your hard drive where you can keep it for a while. It's no problem if you need to move it later, but it would require re-defining the datasource information.

> **Tip**
>
> ColdFusion provides a default directory for databases, but it's only a sug-gested storage spot and you're not required to keep your databases there. Some developers like to keep all their databases in one directory. I work on several clients' sites and like to keep my databases in the respective client folder. In this way, I ensure that, when I make a backup copy of a client's pages, I also include the database.

After the database is stored somewhere, launch ColdFusion Administrator with its special URL:

```
http://your.hostname/CFIDE/Administrator/index.cfm
```

After logging in, click on the "ODBC" link under "Datasources" and see something like Figure 3.5.

FIGURE 3.5

The ODBC configura-
tion page in
ColdFusion
Administrator.

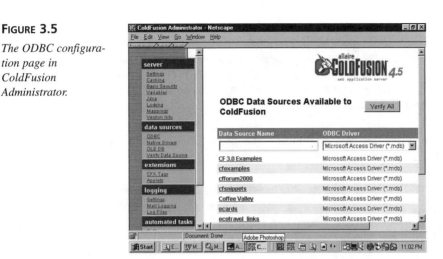

ColdFusion has provided an input form that requests several parameters; options are described in the following sections.

Datasource Name

Type the name of your datasource in the Data Source Name field. You can call your data-source anything you like, but it's always helpful to keep it similar to the file name of your database. For example, I've set up a datasource called "elvis" for my database titled `elvis.mdb`. As I'll discuss in Day 4, "Building a Database and Organizing Data," I like to use all lowercase letters when naming files and substitute the underscore character (_) for spaces.

> **Caution**
>
> Don't use the words "cookie" or "registry" when naming a datasource. These words are used by ColdFusion to perform other functions.

ODBC Driver

The ODBC Driver pull-down box enables you to select the driver that goes with the make of software in which you created a database. For my file, it's pretty straightforward—I just chose Microsoft Access. Depending on whether you've installed other ODBC applications in the past, and on what platform you run ColdFusion, this box will contain a variety of supported formats.

3

> If you don't see your database software listed in the ODBC box, it's usually because your system doesn't have an ODBC driver installed for your file format. Check your manufacturer's Web site for updates, or check the distribution site for your system software for supported ODBC drivers.

To define an entirely new datasource, click the Add button for an expanded dialog and see something like Figure 3.6.

FIGURE 3.6

The expanded dialog for defining a new ColdFusion datasource.

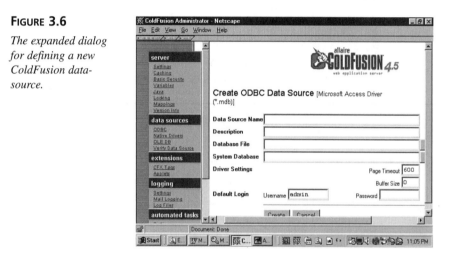

Description

Entering a description of your datasource in the expanded dialog box is optional, but if you plan to set up several, a brief description of the database contents can help you figure what's what further down the road.

Database File

In the Database File field, either type in the full path to the database file (such as `c:\my documents\Web\databases\elvis.mdb`) or use the "browse" button to find the file using a standard navigation window.

For most applications, that's all you need to enter to get things rolling. In some situations you might also want to define the following:

- Login Timeout: The number of seconds ColdFusion will wait when trying to log in to a datasource

- Limit Connections: The number of requests a datasource will handle at one time
- ColdFusion Login: The username and password required to access a database
- Maintain Database Connections: Determines whether ColdFusion connects directly to a database on every request, or whether it caches database information to aid server performance
- Restrict SQL Operations: A security measure that will enable only certain SQL commands to be executed on a database file

Finally, click Create and the datasource is set.

Verifying a Datasource

It's always a good idea to verify your datasources in ColdFusion Administrator immediately after defining them. By doing so, you'll ensure that the program can, in fact, find and access your database file, and you'll have eliminated a bad datasource setup as a potential cause for any errors that might appear later in the template-building process.

To do this, return to the main Administrator page and select Verify Data Source under the Data Sources link. The page looks like Figure 3.7.

FIGURE 3.7

Verifying a datasource setup in ColdFusion Administrator.

In the list, you can see the name of the datasource just defined, "elvis." If you don't see the name there, you know that something's wrong; return to the datasource setup to check all the entries.

If the new datasource appears in the list, select it and click Verify. If ColdFusion can connect to the database, it gives you the thumbs-up; if it can't, it generates an error message.

> **Tip**
>
> Some of the most common reasons for bad datasources include
>
> - Misspelled file names.
> - The database file has been moved or renamed since it was initially set up.
> - The database is password protected and ColdFusion wasn't supplied with the username and password necessary for access.
> - The database file type isn't compatible with the ODBC driver selected in the setup dialog.
> - The database file is corrupt or otherwise unreadable.

After a datasource has been defined and successfully verified, it's ready for use with ColdFusion. In a few days you'll begin to build templates that will draw information from datasources, but today let's remain on the subject of databases and explore a few key topics.

Logging Options

This section allows you to define an administrator email address that will be alerted when a ColdFusion process generates an error. It's also the place to set the location of ColdFusion's general *log file* and the mail log that tracks actions when messages are sent using ColdFusion's mail functions.

New Term *Log files* are text documents used to track the actions made by an application. Both ColdFusion and your Web server software use log files to track events like Web page hits, report errors, or note when users log in or out of password-protected areas of your site.

Automated Tasks

In the Automated Tasks section, you'll find a setup dialog for defining and scheduling automated tasks such as log cycling and link testing. Tasks can be configured to run for any duration and interval.

Extensions Options

This section of Administrator is the place to register Java applets, CFX tags, and custom tags written in C++. I'll discuss extensions in Week III, "Maximizing and Customizing ColdFusion Applications."

Other Options

There are several other Administrator options that might not make sense to you yet, but will become important as I get into ColdFusion's more advanced functions. These include

- Setting up a default mail server for mail handling
- Debugging options for testing your templates
- The Verity options page for building and maintaining search indices

Starting and Stopping ColdFusion Service

When you install ColdFusion Server, the program assumes that you're going to want it running all the time and it automatically configures your system accordingly. When you reboot your system after the program installation, ColdFusion will begin to run, and won't stop unless you manually turn off its services.

In most cases, there's never really much reason to turn ColdFusion off, but there are a few instances when you might need to. You might need to upgrade your Web server or ColdFusion software at some point, and this will require shutting down the program.

To do this, click the Stop-Start icon in ColdFusion's program group. After logging in with the administrator password, you'll see a dialog like Figure 3.8 in your browser.

FIGURE 3.8

ColdFusion's Stop-Start utility.

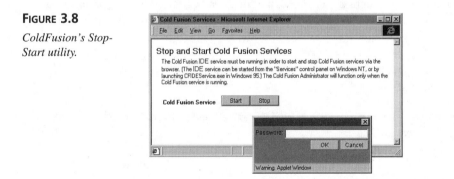

> **Tip**
>
> If you've stopped the program to perform software upgrades or make other system changes, these changes might require you to reboot your system. If you want to keep ColdFusion from restarting after the boot, you'll also need to disable it so that it doesn't automatically resume service. This process differs depending on your system platform. Check your ColdFusion documentation for details specific to your operating system.

Summary

Depending on you or your client's needs, you might choose either to run ColdFusion on your own server or to go with one of the many Web providers now offering ColdFusion support as an optional feature. With either method, you have a few decisions to make at this point.

If you host your site with someone else, you'll probably still want to be able to test your ColdFusion applications on your local system before uploading them. Allaire's special ColdFusion Studio package is ideal for this function because it provides a single-user version of ColdFusion server.

It's important to spend some research time before choosing a Web provider to run ColdFusion. Find out from potential hosts what version of the software they support, how many datasources they allow, and what is required to update a datasource. Compare these with you or your client's needs.

If you plan to run ColdFusion on your own system, you'll need to choose between the Professional Edition and the Enterprise Edition, depending on your site's requirements and your system software. With either edition, the software installation is a very straight-forward process. Use the default settings and you'll do just fine. After the software is installed, all changes to ColdFusion operation are handled through the Administrator, which is accessed locally or remotely by a special Web page.

For ColdFusion to recognize a database, the file must be defined in CF Administrator as a datasource. Datasource setup supplies a name for the connection, tells ColdFusion where the database file resides, and specifies which ODBC driver to use, depending on the make of database software that created the file. After you define a datasource, Administrator offers a "verify" function that will quickly tell whether ColdFusion is able to access the database.

In tomorrow's discussion I'll look at the key element behind every ColdFusion application—the database.

Q&A

Q Will ColdFusion someday offer direct support for my server software, *Server X, Y, or Z?*

A With each consecutive ColdFusion release, Allaire has increased the number of directly supported Web server APIs. The company's Web site is your best source of up-to-date news on future developments. If your brand isn't supported, it probably wouldn't hurt to use Allaire's contact addresses to do a little lobbying for your preferred server.

Q **Why is the ColdFusion *Enterprise Edition* so much more expensive than the *Professional Edition*? Is it really that much better?**

A The Enterprise Edition offers some high-end features like CORBA support to the basic ColdFusion package. The actual uses of these features go beyond the scope of this book, but it's safe to say that most users will do just fine with the less-expensive Professional Edition. It's easy to upgrade later if you discover you need Enterprise's added attractions.

Q **Can I really configure my ColdFusion server from any computer, anywhere?**

A Yes. Beginning in version 3.0, the new ColdFusion Administrator interface enables you to make configuration changes from any Web-connected machine. With the Web interface, you can run admin tasks like cycling logs, adding and removing datasources, and starting and stopping ColdFusion service.

Workshop

Just to see whether you were dozing through today's discussion, here are a few quiz questions and exercises. Answers to quiz questions can be found in Appendix A at the back of the text.

Quiz

1. Name at least three questions you should ask a potential ColdFusion Web provider.
2. What is ColdFusion Studio, and how is it different from ColdFusion Server?
3. What are the two varieties of ColdFusion Server? How do they differ?
4. Which Web servers require special attention when installing ColdFusion Server?
5. Name two ways to start the ColdFusion Administrator.
6. Describe the process of setting up a database as a ColdFusion datasource.
7. Name a reason you might need to stop ColdFusion service and describe how to do it.

Exercises

1. If you don't already own a copy, download the demonstration edition of ColdFusion Server from Allaire's Web site and install it on your local computer.
2. If you plan to host your site remotely, make a list of potential Web providers and contact them with the questions I discussed. Keep notes on their replies and compare them to hosting prices.
3. Set up a sample datasource using a database existing on your system. Verify it using the verification utility in ColdFusion Administrator.

DAY 4

Building a Database and Organizing Data

Now that we've covered database concepts, it's time to start thinking about real-life stuff such as what kind of information you're actually going to share with the world. When you design a database for use with ColdFusion or any other Web application, it's important to plan ahead and work to keep your file size to a minimum. Smaller, well-organized databases make for faster search times, happier users, and fewer hassles when you have to make changes or updates. For the same reasons, it's important to spend a few moments in thoughtful reflection before setting up ColdFusion datasources.

In this section I'll look at the following:

- Database software supported by ColdFusion
- ColdFusion as a database-to-Web gateway
- Creating a data map
- Introducing data relationships
- Designing a sample database

- Creating data relationships
- Table and database security issues
- Populating a database

Database Software Supported by ColdFusion

ColdFusion supports a pretty wide variety of database packages. Even if you don't own one of the applications listed, your preferred database software can probably export data to one of several common file formats, including dBASE and plain text.

ColdFusion works with the following database file types on Windows platforms:

- Microsoft SQL Sever
- Microsoft Access
- Microsoft FoxPro
- Oracle
- Borland Paradox
- Borland dBASE
- Microsoft Excel
- Clipper

On SPARC Solaris systems it supports these:

- DB2
- dBASE
- FoxPro
- Informix
- OpenIngres
- Oracle
- Sybase SQL Server
- Sybase System 10 and 11

ColdFusion as a Database-to-Web Gateway

In Net jargon, ColdFusion is often called a database-to-Web gateway. Such gateways allow developers to "link" a database to a Web site and display one, some, or all of the database records as standard HTML pages, as described in Day 1, "Introducing ColdFusion," and Day 2, "Anatomy of a ColdFusion Application."

ColdFusion is by no means the only application of this kind. Several programs perform similar functions, but few can match the power and simplicity of ColdFusion. In addition, ColdFusion goes beyond simple database tasks by adding tools that allow developers to create complete Web-based applications.

The program works by intercepting Web requests from a user's browser, taking over when a Web server receives a request for a `.cfm` file instead of the standard `.html` documents Web servers usually work with.

Figure 4.1 illustrates how ColdFusion integrates with an existing Web server.

FIGURE 4.1

The flow of data from a browser request to output.

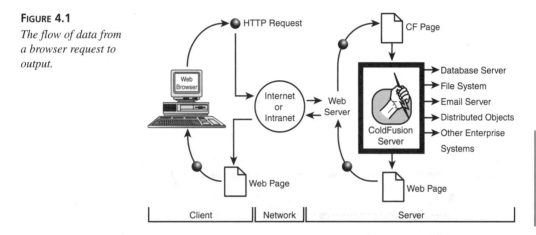

When ColdFusion intercepts a request, it has a broad range of computing power at its demand. It can perform many of the functions common to CGI, or *Common Gateway Interface,* applications, as well as its own unique handling of database searches. As a "gateway" program, ColdFusion provides an active link between your Web server and a database, but the actual linking process is handled by your system's *object database connectivity source,* or ODBC.

ODBC

I've already discussed ODBC briefly in Day 2 but let's take things a step further. ODBC is an application programming interface (API) that gives programmers the ability to write applications (such as ColdFusion) that can "talk" directly to databases. Think of it as a mediator between your application and your database. When we run ODBC-compatible software such as word processors, spreadsheets, ColdFusion, and so on, this mediation function enables our application to communicate with our database using standardized commands. Without it, every database-friendly application would have to know the languages of every database package on the market.

When we install ODBC on our system, it installs a set of *drivers* that are compatible with a variety of common database apps.

NEW TERM A *driver* is software that enables your system software to communicate with hardware or other software. Your operating system communicates with your video card, your sound card, and your printer by way of drivers.

Other programs that communicate with our database now do so by way of the driver, which essentially translates program commands into a language the database can understand. By default, most ODBC-compatible programs support most common database formats right out of the box, ColdFusion included.

ODBC drivers are specific to the make of software used to create the database. Some drivers, such as those for Microsoft products, Oracle, and Sybase, extend the capabilities of communicating with a database by adding special features. These include functions such as special SQL commands and text formatting. Check your database software to see what features it supports.

Creating a Data Map

Regardless of the complexity of your data, it's always a good idea to create a *schema* before you begin assembling a database on the computer.

NEW TERM A *schema* is a visual representation of a database, a plan showing the names of all tables and fields.

For a sample schema, you'll create a real-life paper-and-pencil map showing each table, illustrating how they relate to each other, and defining how each one receives input. Sit down at the largest table in your home or office and obtain the biggest piece of paper you can find. Some companies have special schema forms just for this purpose, whereas the rest of us make do with the deli paper off the sliced ham.

Working with a pencil might seem foreign after your many hours spent at the keyboard, but it's like riding a bike—it'll come back to you. Start by making a list of each of the categories your data will require, including a short sentence to describe each one.

For this example, we're going to have to leave the Elvis database for a moment because the King no longer serves our immediate needs. Let's say instead that you're launching a mail order Web business that will manufacture and sell pasta shaped like the profiles of famous TV cops. I'm thinking Jack Lord rigatoni, T.J. Hooker fettuccini, and maybe little ravioli in the likenesses of Ponch and John from *CHiPs*. Database categories will look like Table 4.1.

TABLE 4.1   Database Categories for TV Cop Pasta, Inc.

Database Category	What It Holds
Product	Lists products, prices, and descriptions
Customer	Lists previous Web customers and those who've "opted in" to our email list
Orders	Lists current and past orders
Suppliers	Where we get our raw pasta
Wholesalers	Distributors carrying our products

> **Tip**
>
> When dividing your data into categories, think about how you (or others) might access your database on an average workday. For example, if you're designing a site for a company with a shipping department, a sales department, and a design department, consider each department separately. Shipping might deal primarily with the Products data, sales with the Customer data, and so on.

Now it's time to get artsy. For each data category, draw a large box, as shown in Figure 4.2.

4

FIGURE 4.2

A sample database schema, with each data category listed in a box.

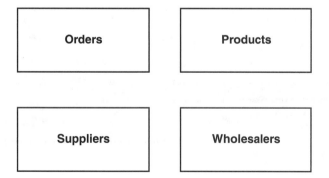

Circles work fine instead of boxes, but use more-fanciful shapes like hearts and stars if you're dealing with a conservative client. Each box represents a table in the soon-to-be-constructed database; flesh these out by adding the names of the fields each table should contain. You're still in the planning phase, so don't worry too much about getting everything dead accurate. You can always make modifications later—that's the purpose of a schema, after all.

Next, you need to illustrate how each of the tables will receive its input. For example, Products, Suppliers and Wholesalers table data can be keyed in by your company's staff (hire the neighbor kid to do this), whereas Customers data will come from the Web, and the Orders records will be generated by the sales department (the neighbor kid with a cordless headset).

Draw big arrow outlines to indicate input, so that the map now looks like Figure 4.3.

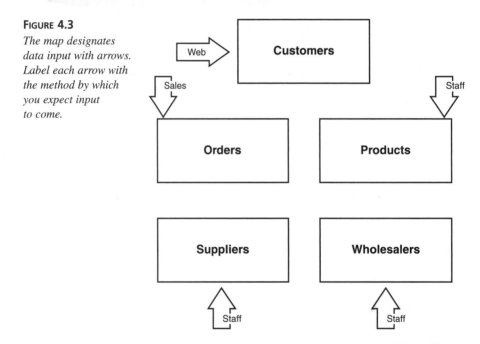

FIGURE 4.3

The map designates data input with arrows. Label each arrow with the method by which you expect input to come.

By virtue of the map, you can already see areas where you'll be duplicating data, and that's exactly what you're trying to avoid in this exercise. Names and addresses in the Orders table will duplicate listings in the Customer table. You don't want to pay the neighbor kid to enter these twice, so you need to *link* some data from one table to another.

Introducing Data Relationships

Herein lies the beauty of relational databases. Instead of keying in customer information for each of my orders and then duplicating the effort when I add new customers to the Customers table, I can *link* the data across tables.

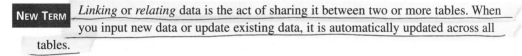

NEW TERM *Linking* or *relating* data is the act of sharing it between two or more tables. When you input new data or update existing data, it is automatically updated across all tables.

Figure 4.4 illustrates the relationships on the map.

FIGURE 4.4

The lines on the map show where data will be linked between tables.

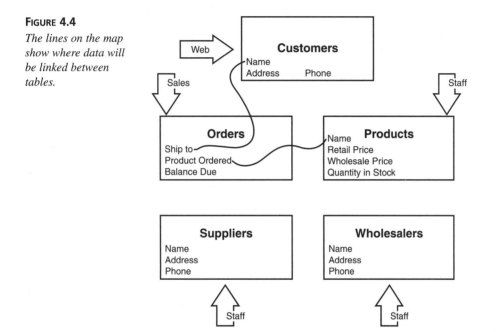

Already you've saved at least a couple of working hours, and have bought yourself time for a couple rounds of mini golf at the Pitch N' Putt. When we move onto coding templates, you'll see that ColdFusion doesn't care a bit whether a cell contains actual data, or a link to data somewhere else in the database. It sees the contents of a cell only as text, regardless of origin.

Search the map for other places where you can link data and save input time. The Orders table in Figure 4.5 has a Product Ordered field that can easily be drawn from the Products table.

The data map is starting to look like the wiring schematic on a '73 Plymouth Fury, but you now have a complete visual representation of your database for reference. As you move into the actual design phase, you'll know what each of the tables will be named, what fields they'll contain, where they'll get their input, and which tables will share linked data.

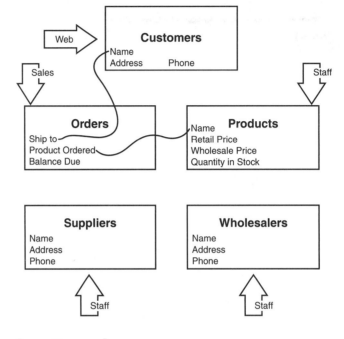

Figure 4.5

The Product Ordered field can draw information from the Products table.

Designing the Database

Now let's move to a more familiar spot—the computer chair—and begin designing the database. It's tough to get too specific here because your actual mileage will vary depending on the brand of database software you use. Each software manufacturer has its own methods for creating tables and defining fields, but most are surprisingly similar. For this example, I'll use the common package Microsoft Access. If you use a different package and run into trouble, consult your application's documentation.

First you'll use your database package to create a new file. To create the database file, open Microsoft Access and select *File|New Database*. Access offers several templates to start from; keep it simple and select the default, *blank database*. Access then prompts for a filename—use `tv_cop_pasta_inc.mdb`. The `.mdb` extension is specific to Microsoft Access software—other manufacturers use other extensions.

Tip

When designing a database, it's important to develop a convention for naming files, tables, and fields. I use lowercase letters throughout, and use the underscore character (_) to denote a space. Lowercase names mean that I'll never have to wonder whether I capitalized a letter when I refer to my database in a ColdFusion template. The use of underscores isn't always necessary—newer versions of ColdFusion do recognize spaces—but by using it I'm ensuring that my database will be portable to any Windows- or UNIX-based server.

Using the data map as guide, your next step is to create the tables. In Microsoft Access, select the New button in the Table dialog box. As you make each table, the program will offer several ways to *view* the new table.

NEW TERM A table *view* is the way you choose to look at your data. Microsoft Access offers two views: *datasheet view* and *design view*.

Access' datasheet view creates a new table with a grid pattern, showing fields listed horizontally across the top of the screen, and rows running down. If you've worked in a spreadsheet application, this view might elicit a familiar groan. *Design view* doesn't display the actual data; it just lists fields, making it easy to define new table fields. We'll look at the design view in a moment.

Because you're only creating tables and not yet inputting data, just select the default *datasheet view*, which produces a blank grid.

> **Tip**
>
> Note that when you create a new table, Access (like most database apps) also lists an option for *importing* data. If you had an existing table or text file created in another application, this feature would enable you to incorporate the existing information into the database you're building.

4

For the moment, you're on fire creating tables and don't want to mess with the contents. Click the Close button for each new table, and Access will ask whether you want to define a *primary key* for the table. For now answer "yes," (I'll explain why in a moment). Nest Access prompts you for a name for the table, which is what you've been trying to input all along. Like a good coder, you'll again use the lowercase and underscore naming conventions for your table.

Repeat the process for each of these table names:

- Products
- Customers
- Orders
- Suppliers
- Wholesalers

Some database programs allow space for a short description of each table you create. It never hurts to use this feature in case someone else needs to work with your database later. A good description might keep your pager from going off someday.

Defining Fields

Next open each table and begin setting up fields, again drawing upon your handy map. There are a couple ways to do this. The easiest is simply to double-click each field title (field1, field2, and so on) and rename it as you choose. Again, I recommend using all lowercase letters and replacing spaces with the underscore character.

This method works fine if you only have a few fields to set up, but if you have, say, 10 or 20, it's pretty inefficient. Unless you have a monitor the size of a garage door, you can't view all the defined fields without scrolling horizontally across the database.

Horizontal scrolling is a real pain and will make you crazy faster than a noisy neighbor who owns just one CD. Particularly in database apps, navigating horizontally means that you can never see a whole line of information on screen at one time. Avoid it wherever possible.

To cut down on the back-and-forth, use the previously discussed Access feature called *design view.* Other packages will have similar functions. The design view is a handy tool in defining field names because it displays several at once. In this view, you can see whether you've already entered a field name, and what type of data it will contain. Figure 4.6 illustrates a design view of one of the sample tables.

Note in Figure 4.6 that each entry contains a field name, a data type, and space for an optional description. In this view, you can easily define a bunch of fields quickly.

After you've entered the fields, use Access' pull-down View menu to switch back to datasheet view; you'll see the table in the conventional grid format, as in Figure 4.7.

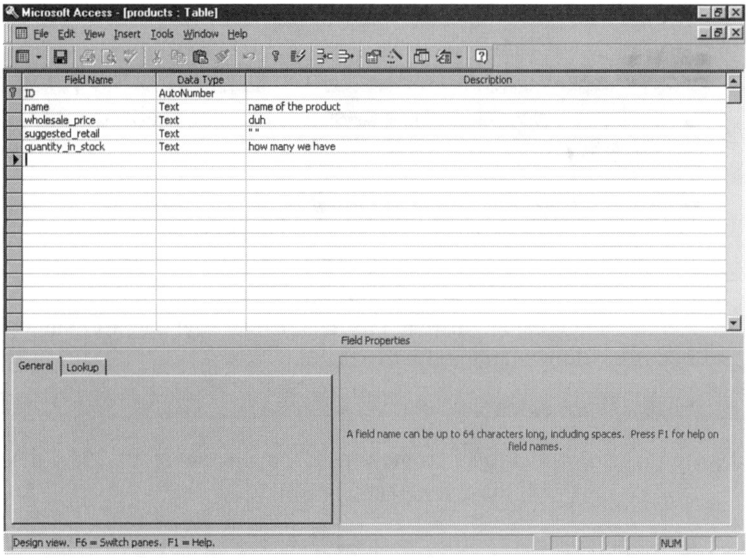

FIGURE 4.6

FIGURE 4.6

A sample table in design view with fields defined.

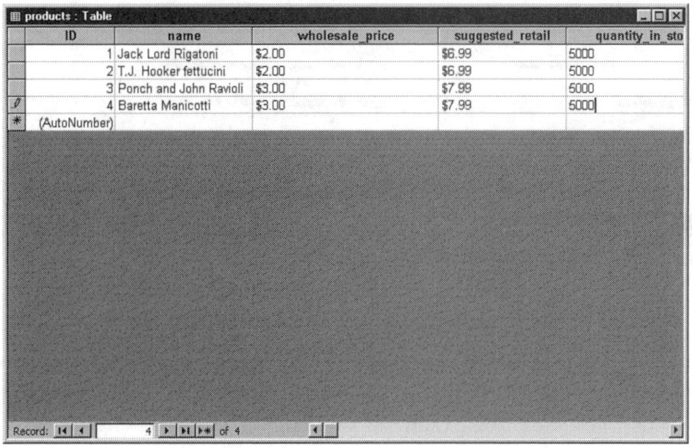

FIGURE 4.7

The table from Figure 4.6, shown in datasheet view.

Data Types

Back to the design view for a moment. Each field you've defined has an associated *data type*. A data type lets you tell your database program what kind of information that a field will contain. For example, Access' "Yes/No" data type will place a simple checkbox in the field. The currency data type will automatically supply a dollar sign and decimal when you input a number. The text data type (*char* for users of MSQL Server) lets you to type in any old text string.

Other database applications vary in the data types used, but most support these basics.

Assigning the proper database types to fields is essential to good database design—it helps speed up searches, it preserves the integrity of your data, and it can help you validate whether the right type of data (a date, a number, a dollar figure, etc.) is being added to a field.

However, certain data types present a problem for new ColdFusion users. Say that in Microsoft Access I create a table and set one of the fields to a date data type. I might then type in a date that a product was ordered, such as "January 1, 2000." When I later create a template to display this data, I'll see the date formatted the way Microsoft Access stores it internally, like this:

```
2000-01-01 00:00:00
```

or if I set a field to a currency data type and entered "$25," I'd see something like this when my ColdFusion template is displayed

```
25.0000
```

which is the way my database software stores a dollar value.

In both cases, my database application is giving me more information than I probably want to display to a Web user—the date data type adds on hours, minutes, and seconds, while the currency data type extends my dollar figure to four decimal places.

In Day 14,"Using ColdFusion Functions to Manipulate Data," you'll learn how to use this extra information to your advantage and control the way it is displayed to users. Until then, it's best to stick with text and memo data types for your fields as you work the examples in Weeks 1 and 2.

Back to the table design—as you enter each field, Access defaults to the text data type. This enables the field to accept up to 255 characters of text or numbers; if you need more room, use the memo data type, which supports up to 65,000 characters. Both of these data types store text exactly as it is entered.

For now, leave out the fields designated as containing *linked* data on my map. You first need to make some decisions on how to link them—that is, which tables will contain the actual data, and which will merely link to another table. For this, it's time to discuss keys and how to define relationships.

The Importance of Keys

To illustrate use of a database *key* field, look at the Orders table in Figure 4.8. Just like in a cooking show, I've pulled it from the oven already brimming with pasta orders to be shipped all over the globe.

FIGURE 4.8
The Orders table with fields defined and data entered.

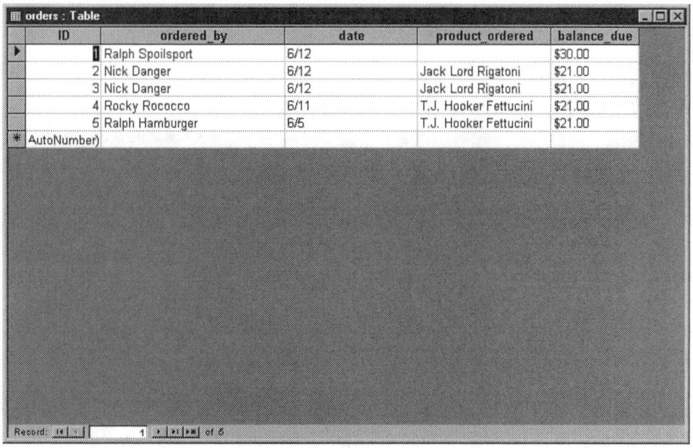
orders : Table

ID	ordered_by	date	product_ordered	balance_due
1	Ralph Spoilsport	6/12		$30.00
2	Nick Danger	6/12	Jack Lord Rigatoni	$21.00
3	Nick Danger	6/12	Jack Lord Rigatoni	$21.00
4	Rocky Rococco	6/11	T.J. Hooker Fettucini	$21.00
5	Ralph Hamburger	6/5	T.J. Hooker Fettucini	$21.00
(AutoNumber)				

Record: 1 of 5

Look at the second and third rows. They're both orders from the same guy, Nick Danger, and he ordered exactly the same thing twice on the same day—he must be quite the *Hawaii Five-O* fan. When I access this table with a ColdFusion template, how will the program know these are two separate orders, rather than a single order I duplicated accidentally?

It will know because when I created my table I allowed the database software to define a *primary key*, which is the number you see in the left column of the illustration. In Figure 4.8, it appears in the ID field, which Microsoft Access supplies automatically as a user inputs a row of data. Access calls this field ID by default.

NEW TERM A *primary key* is a value in a field that uniquely identifies a record.

Even if all the other fields contain the same data as another record, You'll always have the key to let you know that you're looking at a unique set of data.

The Customers table also has its own primary key, as shown in Figure 4.9.

For ColdFusion developers, key fields also present a very efficient way to designate records. If your ColdFusion template queries ask the program to search for the record where the product is Jack Lord Rigatoni, ColdFusion has to wade through several cells of text until it finds an exact match for those letters. If instead you told it to fetch the record with the ID "10" (its primary key), ColdFusion would know exactly where to go, and would return the requested data in a fraction of the time.

4

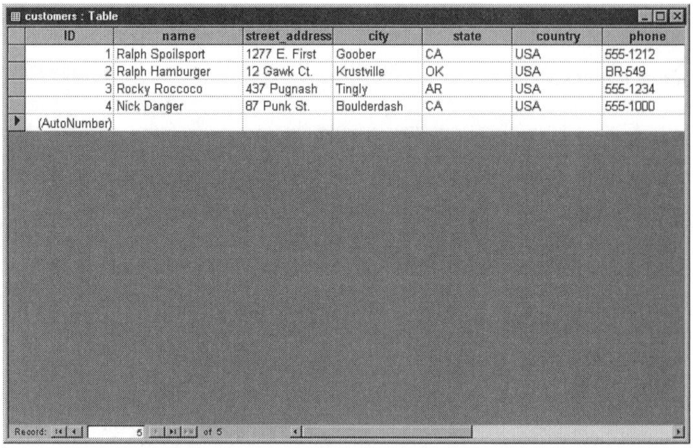

FIGURE **4.9**

The Customers table uses its own primary key, also titled ID by Access default.

Creating Data Relationships

Now we'll revisit the all-important data relationship. On your map you've already illustrated potential *relationships*, or fields that might be shared across tables. It's now time to put these relationships into a table.

The subject of data relationships is a pretty broad one—to cover it completely here would easily raise the page count of this book to biblical proportions. Different database applications have widely varying methods for creating relationships, and, in fact, some consultants have built entire careers around mastering the methods of just one application. For this 21-day tutorial, I'll detail a fairly simple relationship—the *list box*—and hope that the concept gets your mental gears spinning and causes you to seek out other ways to share table data.

One goal of sharing or relating data is to cut down on the time you actually spend typing stuff into your database. For example, after you've entered a new product in the Products table, it would be a real timesaver to be able to make that product name available in other tables, such as Orders.

To illustrate I've created a sample list box for the Product Ordered field in the Orders table. It looks like Figure 4.10.

Each time a new product name is entered in the Products table, it will also appear as a choice in the list box in the Orders table.

To define this type of relationship in Microsoft Access, use the design view to change the attributes of the Products Ordered field. Leave the data type set to the default "text" because the field will ultimately contain a product name. Then designate the list box in the Field Properties window at the bottom left of the design view, as shown in Figure 4.11.

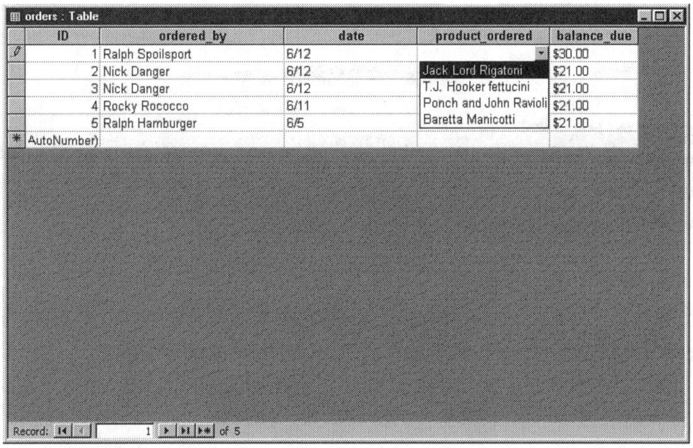

FIGURE 4.10

This list box in the Orders table gets its information from data in the Products table.

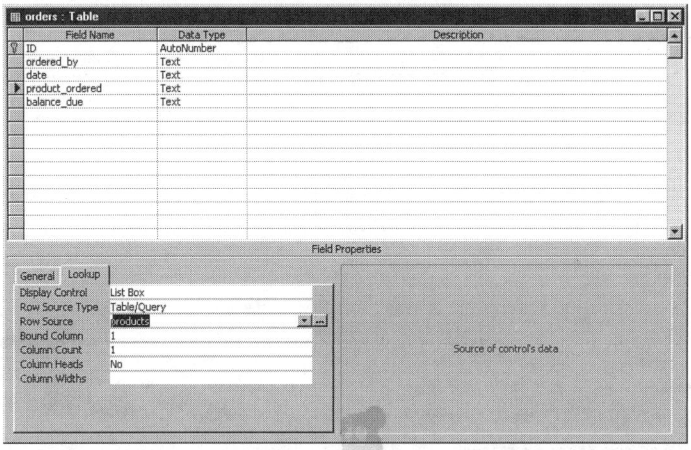

FIGURE 4.11

The Lookup tab in Field Properties allows me to assign a list box to the Product Ordered field.

Under the Lookup tab, set the Display Control to "list box", the Row Source Type to "query" (because your list will come from another table), and the Row Source to "products".

> **Note**
>
> Microsoft Access uses list boxes as one way to create data relationships—your software may use other methods. For details, check your program's help file for a section on "defining relationships."

So far so good. You've told Access that you want the Ordered by field to be a list box, and it should get its data from the Products table. But how does it know which field in Products to show in the list? To specify the Products field, you'll have to create a simple

SQL (structured query language) query within Access. I'll cover SQL in blathering detail in Day 5, "Finding the Data You Need: An Introduction to Queries and SQL," but for now you'll use an easy visual interface that comes with Access: the Query Builder.

Start the query builder by clicking the button labeled … next to the Row Source selection box. In writer's jargon, we call those three periods an ellipse. In Access, as in writing, the ellipse implies "something more," and that's what we're hoping to get at. The button opens the Query Builder as seen in Figure 4.12.

FIGURE 4.12

Microsoft Access'
Query Builder.

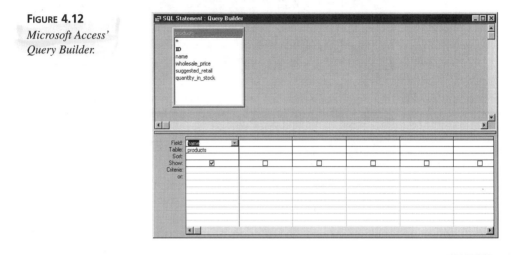

Look at Figure 4.11 again. Because I selected the Products table in the Row Source box before clicking the Query Builder, I can now see that table and its fields at the top of the screen. In the first square below that, I've dragged and dropped the Name field from the Products table into the Field box. This builds a quick query that says "go to the Products table and bring me back all the values in the field called Name."

> **Tip**
>
> Microsoft Access' Query Builder is one of many applications used to visually create SQL statements. Other database programs offer similar built-in interfaces, and there are also several good external programs that build queries.

Save this query by closing it, and then saving the new table design. When you switch back to datasheet view and access the Orders table again, you'll see a list box like the one back in Figure 4.10.

You've saved another healthy chunk of time by doing this, and you've likely eliminated potential shipping errors as well. If the neighbor kid had to type in the product name each time a customer placed an order, sooner or later he'd make a typo, someone wouldn't get their Baretta Manicotti, and you'd be out a customer.

Table and Database Security

While we're on the subject of databases, let's be forthright, responsible developers and briefly consider security issues.

You'll find security covered throughout this book, particularly in the sections on e-commerce. What follows is only an introduction to protecting your database on the Web. After all, I know that by Day 8, "Understanding ColdFusion Studio," when you start building templates, you'll be anxious to put your database right on the Web and start serving up pages. Before you do, there are a few things to consider.

In the sample store, two tables will be accessible on the Web, Products and Customers. Looking at the data map, you see that Customers won't be taking any input from the Web—it will only output to the ColdFusion templates. Still, you know that your competitors over at Famous Corporate CEO's Pasta are pretty sneaky folks; you'd like some assurance they can't somehow hack in and replace your product descriptions with their own cheeky humor. You'll want to set up security that will allow only you (or the neighbor kid) to input data into this table.

The second table, Customers presents a more difficult situation. You need to make it accessible to Web users so that they can key their vitals into a ColdFusion form and thus subscribe to your Cop Pasta newsletter. But you'd also like to protect the table so the Famous Corporate CEO's Pasta people can't steal your mailing list and send their worthless propaganda to all your customers.

Both situations can be neatly handled by assigning *permissions* to the tables.

Table Permissions

Most database packages include some provision for defining permissions on individual tables. In general, you create a "user" or "users" in your database software, give each user a password, and then assign *user permissions* to each table. In the Cop Pasta database, you should create usernames and passwords for the neighbor kid and yourself, and then restrict "write" or input access to just the two of you. The next time you open the database, you'll be asked for your username and password before you can make any modifications. *Read* permissions, or the ability to access the database for viewing, remains unchanged because you want all Web users to see your product data.

Security on the second table, Customers, gets a little stickier. Only the neighbor kid and you should be able to view the table, but Web users should have "write" access so they can submit their information via your Web form. Some database packages will give tables "write" access by default, whereas others might require you to set up a catch-all user—often named "browser" or "guest"—to designate someone accessing your database from the Web. Depending on your Web server's security setup, this generic user might also need to be added in ColdFusion Administrator's datasource properties before your database will allow any input from the Web. Check with your system administrator and your database documentation to find out how write permissions are assigned to Web users.

Table permissions can usually also be assigned to *groups*, or predetermined sets of users. This would greatly simplify matters if the store staff suddenly grew from just you and the neighbor kid to a full staff of salespeople, shipping clerks, and a public-relations team. You could create a username for each employee, arranging them in groups corresponding to the needs of each department. You could give the sales staff access to the Orders table, keep the shipping clerks out of the Products descriptions, and deny the P.R. people access to everything.

> **Tip**
>
> In Microsoft Access, setting security is a two-step process. First, choose *Tools| Security|User and Group Accounts*. This opens a dialog box that allows you add or remove users, and to create or change user passwords. Once you've defined the users who will access your database, choose *Tools|Security|User and Group Permissions*. There you'll find a second dialog box allowing you to assign user permissions to each table in your database.

Writing Data into a Database

The easiest method of entering data is to open the table, put your cursor into the proper cell, and just start typing. This is a great method if all your data consists of only a word or two, but if you need to enter long sentences or lists you're going to be doing a lot of horizontal scrolling to see your text. Horizontal scrolling is a royal pain in the butt, so there must be a better way.

There are four primary methods for getting data into a database. The first, typing information directly into the cells, is the most basic, but let's look at some others.

The Input Form

The input *form* is a handy feature offered by most modern database packages. Input forms let you view your database one record at a time. After you create a form, it's neatly packaged in your database along with your data for later use. Let's look at one I created for inputting data into my Orders table in Figure 4.13.

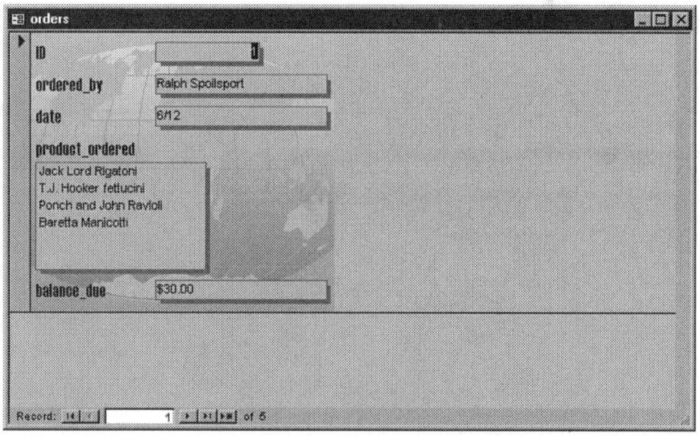

FIGURE 4.13

*A sample input form
used to enter data in
the Orders table.*

This is a simple form I created with one hand tied behind my back, using Access' Form
Wizard (Microsoft supplied the fancy background). It's a vast improvement over typing
my data directly into the table cells because it enables me to see all my fields on a single
screen and gives me more elbowroom for editing text. To access other records or to enter
a new one, I just navigate the arrow keys at the bottom of the display.

Importing Data

The fastest method to get stuff into a database is to draw data from an existing source, or
import it. Depending on your brand of database software, you might be able to import
data from databases created in other software packages, spreadsheets, text files, HTML
pages, or word-processing documents. This is a useful feature if someone hands you, say,
a floppy disk containing a text list of international cheese varieties—just import it into
your database and you're an instant cheese authority.

Your database software has specific import methods and supported file formats. I have
neither the space nor the endurance necessary to cover all of them here, so check your
manufacturer's documentation for the particulars.

Tip

If your database software doesn't allow the importing of data from a certain
file type, it might be because you didn't install the proper data translator
when you initially set up your software. Run your database program's installation again, using the Custom Install setting, and look for a list of supported
data translators.

Input forms and data importing are fine input methods for anyone who has direct access
to my database and also owns a copy of my preferred database software. But what if I
want any user to have the ability to input data from the Web?

Web Input

ColdFusion handles data input with the <CFINSERT> tag. Using <CFINSERT>, you can design a special form template that looks and behaves a lot like the mail and search forms you've seen all over the Web. When a user accesses your input template, they'll see a form, as shown in Figure 4.14.

FIGURE 4.14

A ColdFusion-driven input form designed to be accessible from the Web.

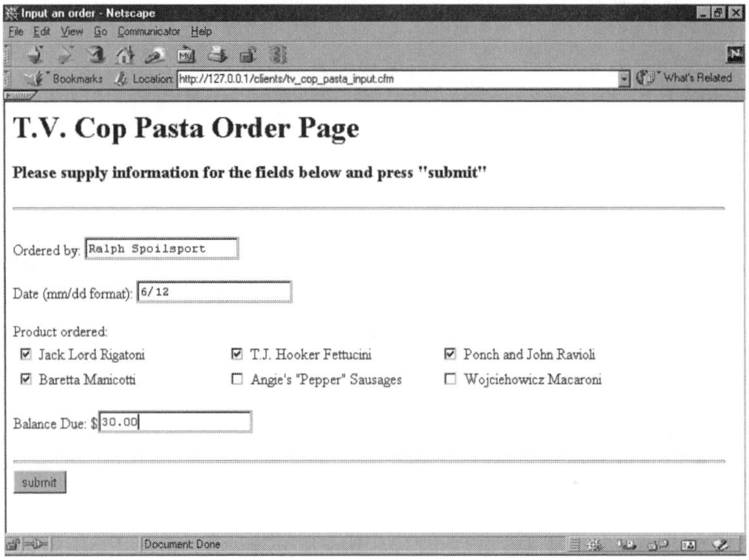

Each input box corresponds to a field in Cop Pasta tables. When the user submits this form, it will send their input data to your datasource, which will make it instantly appear in your database and in any relevant Web templates.

> **Caution**
>
> Depending on the moral fiber of your users, accepting Web input can get a little risky. Even the most virtuous sometimes succumb to the temptation to enter four-letter expletives and dirty limericks into Web input forms. It's a good idea to set up an approval mechanism so that you can preview your users' wisdom before sharing it with the world at large. We'll talk about specific methods in Day 7, "Changing the Contents of a Database with ColdFusion."

Summary

ColdFusion works with most common database formats, and, for those not directly supported, it can instead work with exported data in the form of text files. When working with databases, ColdFusion functions as a gateway program, using a system's ODBC capabilities to create an open pipeline in and out of a database.

Good database design is crucial in optimizing the performance of ColdFusion applications, and a well-planned database will save coding time in building templates. It's important to create a visual representation of a database before you actually sit down at the computer to identify tables, fields, input, and data relationships.

Sharing data across tables saves input time and helps keep things organized. It's also important to define table keys, which will keep ColdFusion's search time to a minimum and give you an easy way to refer to unique records when you create templates later. Because you'll probably be using your new database to test your templates in future days, it's also crucial that you understand basic database security issues to protect your data.

There are a variety of methods for populating a database. Data can be input by database forms, data importing, and Web forms. Well-designed sites will likely use a combination of these methods.

In Day 5, we'll take a closer look at structured query language (SQL), the first step to building ColdFusion templates.

Q&A

Q If my database software isn't supported by ColdFusion, can I still use it?

A Yes, if you have the ability to *export* database files in one of the many formats ColdFusion recognizes. Most modern database packages support exporting to at least a few other file formats. At the very least, you can always export your data to a tab-delimited text file. It's a much less efficient method than using an actual database file, but it will work.

Q Are there other database-to-Web gateway applications?

A Yes, other popular development applications include PHP, Microsoft's Active Server Pages, Microsoft SQL Server, and mini-SQL. These represent a pretty wide range of price and features.

Q Are there other programs that use ODBC? Can I use these with databases I've created for use with ColdFusion?

A Yes, and yes. ODBC-compatible programs are great ways to read and write information to databases. As an example, let's say that I'm designing the layout of an article in a magazine. Using an ODBC design application, I can pull the content of my article from a database. The content might have been entered in the database by another ODBC application such as a word processor used by the article's author.

Q Does it help to look at other people's data maps when I'm designing my own?

A Yes. Observing the ways experienced database designers structure their files is a great way to gain insight for your own design. Many database models exist on the Web. Try performing a search in a comprehensive engine such as AltaVista or HotBot. Use keywords such as "database," "structure," "model," and "schema."

Q I see now that relating and sharing data across tables is my ticket to the big time. Where can I find more information?

A Your database software's help file is the best place to begin. Programs like Microsoft Access offer a detailed look at data relationships and use real-world examples to illustrate. Their stuffy examples won't be as exciting as TV Cop Pasta, but you'll gain ideas on how to use relationships in your tables.

Q I'm confused by the Access Query Builder. Should I be worried?

A No. Stick around for tomorrow's introduction to SQL, and all will be revealed.

Workshop

Just to see if you were dozing through today's discussion, here are a few quiz questions and exercises. Answers to quiz questions can be found in Appendix A at the back of the text.

Quiz

1. What is an ODBC driver?

2. How is ColdFusion considered a "gateway" application?

3. What is a *schema*?

4. Why is it important to create a visual representation of a database before creating the actual file?

5. On a 1973 Plymouth Fury, what color is the wire that switches between high and low headlight beams?

6. Why did I use lowercase letters and underscores in naming my database and tables?

7. What is a *primary key*?

8. Briefly describe the process of setting permissions on a table.

9. Name three ways to get information into a database.

Exercises

1. Dream up a goofy, fictitious business and create a data map for it. If you have a real business, you can leave the goofy and fictitious parts out.

2. Design a small database for your "business" and enter some sample data.

3. If you use a database application that supports list boxes (such as Microsoft Access), create a list box in one of your tables. It should draw information from another table in your database.

4. Create a user in your database software. Set permissions on one of your tables to enable write permission from that user. Set another table to enable read-only access.

5. Input some sample data into a database and explore input methods offered by your software.

6. Check your word processing software's documentation to see whether it's ODBC compatible. If so, explore methods for reading and writing database information from word processing documents.

4

DAY 5

Finding the Data You Need: An Introduction to Queries and SQL

In Day 2, "Anatomy of a ColdFusion Application," I introduced you to your first ColdFusion template page and illustrated the way it uses a query to select data to present on the Web. I designed a few simple queries, and gave examples of the output they might generate. In today's session, we'll take a closer look at the query and how it uses *structured query language* (SQL) to select records from a database. We'll cover

- Examining the ColdFusion query
- Basics of the SELECT statement
- Qualifying a SELECT statement with conditions
- Sorting and evaluating data
- Using SQL to change a database

Examining the ColdFusion Query

To briefly recap the principle behind queries, let's take a closer look at a query from Day 2. This one works with my database of Elvis trivia, specifically examining the table `"movies"`.

Here's the code for that query section, as it will appear in a ColdFusion template:

```
<CFQUERY NAME="movies" DATASOURCE="elvis">
SELECT title, year, rating FROM movies WHERE title = 'Speedway'
</CFQUERY>
```

If I used that query section in a template page along with a simple <CFOUTPUT> section to present the results, the user would see something like Figure 5.1 in his browser.

The SQL statement in this query directed ColdFusion to go to my database, look for the `"movies"` table, then select the `title`, `year`, and `rating` fields from all records where the `title` field contains the word `'Speedway'`.

When we begin an SQL command with SELECT, we're using what's called a *SELECT statement*. These are used most often to look for something in a database. Other statements include UPDATE, which would enable us to change the contents of a record or records, and INSERT, which adds a new record to the table we specify. Let's examine each of these in more depth.

Note

One of the nice things about SQL is that it doesn't stray too far from plain English. Re-read the SQL statement in the coded example and you'll see that it's pretty close to one I used to describe it in the previous paragraph. Part of the reason for this is that applications like ColdFusion examine a database in pretty much the same way humans do. If we wanted to find a chunk of information ourselves, we'd open the database file, find the table we need, and then scan the records looking for the word or phrase we want.

Exploring the Basics of the SELECT Statement

SELECT statements give SQL its seemingly magical powers. They do this by giving ColdFusion the capability to find a specific record or set of records based on criteria you choose.

Let's start with a sample table. In Table 5.1, I've reproduced the contents of the songs table from my database of Elvis trivia.

TABLE 5.1 songs

ID	Title	Released	Rating
1	Baby, Let's Play House	1954	yeee-haw!
2	Good Rockin' Tonight	1954	yeee-haw!
3	Money Honey	1956	yeee-haw!
4	Teddy Bear	1957	OK, I guess
5	A Big Hunk O'Love	1959	OK, I guess
6	Bossa Nova Baby	1963	uh-oh
7	Devil In Disguise	1963	yeee-haw!
8	Do The Clam	1965	uh-oh
9	Don't Cry Daddy	1969	the end is near

Pretty basic stuff—three fields, plus the ID, or *key* field, that my database program supplied automatically. Recall that the key field is a unique identifier for each row in my table.

Let's start with a query that will return all the fields for all the records in the table. Check out Listing 5.1.

5

LISTING 5.1   A Sample Query That Retrieves the Contents of Four Fields
from the songs Table

```
<CFQUERY NAME="get_songs" DATASOURCE="elvis">
SELECT ID, title, released, rating FROM songs
</CFQUERY>
```

I've asked ColdFusion to get the contents of all four fields from every record in my table.
I didn't use a WHERE parameter, so ColdFusion isn't comparing any text with my table
entries—it's just fetching the whole thing.

Notice also that I've asked ColdFusion to return the data for all four fields in my table,
ID, title, released, and rating. Instead of listing each of these, I might instead use the
wildcard character, or asterisk, to denote all fields, as in Listing 5.2.

LISTING 5.2   A Query That Retrieves the Contents of All Fields in the songs Table

```
<CFQUERY NAME="get_songs" DATASOURCE="elvis">
SELECT * FROM songs
</CFQUERY>
```

This will return the same output as Listing 5.2, and will save a little typing time, particularly if I have lots of fields to select.

> **Caution**   The wildcard character, or asterisk, can be a time-saver if you really want to
> retrieve data for all fields in a database, but don't overuse it. If you only
> need the data from a few fields, list them separately and avoid the wildcard.
> This cuts down on ColdFusion's search time and will keep your site running
> quickly.

Further down my template page, I'll use a <CFOUTPUT> section like Listing 5.3 to display
the results of my query.

LISTING 5.3   An Output Section to Display the Results of a Query

```
<CFOUTPUT QUERY="get_songs">
Title: #title# <BR>
Date Released: #released# <BR>
My Rating: #rating# <BR>
<P>
</CFOUTPUT>
```

In this output section, I've specified the query I want to associate with this output ("get songs"), and then I've placed some text headings followed by variables. Each line ends with a <BR>, the standard HTML code for a carriage return.

Even though I selected it in my query, I didn't use the ID field in my <CFOUTPUT> section. I figured the average Web user doesn't really care how I number entries in my database, so I just left it out. ColdFusion didn't complain with an error message because it will only output the data I ask it to.

Note that the text that appears within my <CFOUTPUT> tags will repeat for every record in the database, giving Listing 5.3 an output like the following:

OUTPUT

```
Title: Baby, Let's Play House
Release Date: 1954
My Rating: yeee-haw!

Title: Good Rockin' Tonight
Release Date: 1954
My Rating: yeee-haw!

Title: Money Honey
Release Date: 1956
My Rating: yeee-haw!

Title: Teddy Bear
Release Date: 1957
My Rating: OK, I guess

Title: A Big Hunk O'Love
Release Date: 1959
My Rating: OK, I guess

Title: Bossa Nova Baby
Release Date: 1963
My Rating: uh-oh

Title: Devil In Disguise
Release Date: 1963
Rating: yeee-haw!

Title: Do The Clam
Release Date: 1965
My Rating: uh-oh

Title: Don't Cry Daddy
Release Date: 1969
My Rating: the end is near
```

5

> **Tip**
>
> A line of whitespace separates the records from one another because I used the HTML paragraph marker (<P>) at the end of my <CFOUTPUT> section. In Day 6, "Creating Your First Web Application," and beyond, we'll talk about other ways to dress up output.

The query in Listing 5.3 is useful if I just wanted the Web user to see the entire contents of my database, but usually we need to be more specific. Let's say that I wanted to show only the records from 1954, which incidentally was Elvis' best year. I'd rewrite my query as in Listing 5.4.

LISTING 5.4 A Query Section That Selects Data for a Specific Year of Release

```
<CFQUERY NAME="get_songs" DATASOURCE="elvis">
SELECT title, released, rating FROM songs WHERE released = '1954'
</CFQUERY>
```

In Listing 5.4 I've added a WHERE clause to my SELECT statement to pare things down a bit. I'm now looking for only the records in which year is 1954.

> **Note**
>
> When you use a text string for comparison in a WHERE clause, you must always use single quotes (') to denote the beginning and end of the text string. The single quotes tell ColdFusion to read the contents as text, rather than as an operator in your query. Numeric strings, such as 1954, don't require quotes.

Using the same <CFOUTPUT> section shown in Listing 5.3, my new query will produce the following output.

OUTPUT
```
Title: Baby, Let's Play House
Release Date: 1954
My Rating: yeee-haw!

Title: Good Rockin' Tonight
Release Date: 1954
My Rating: yeee-haw!
```

Only two records displayed this time, both of them 1954 releases, and the WHERE clause made it all possible. Let's move on to some other examples of refining the WHERE clause.

Qualifying a SELECT Statement with Conditions

By adding one or more conditions to my WHERE clause, I can get very specific as to which records I want my query to retrieve. Each condition functions like a true-false statement: If the query examines a record in which the conditional statement is true, the record is returned as output. If the statement is false, the query ignores the record and moves on.

SQL uses two types of operators to build conditional statements, *relational operators* and *logical operators*.

Relational Operators

Thus far, all my queries have used the equals operator (=), which determines whether the contents of a field are equal to the text I supply. The equal sign works just fine for comparing text strings such as "Baby, Let's Play House," but if we're dealing with numbers, we have some other tricks at our disposal.

Table 5.2 illustrates the six relational operators available in SQL commands.

TABLE 5.2 Relational Operators

Operator	Definition
=	Equal to
<>	Not equal to
<	Less than
>	Greater than
<=	Less than or equal to
>=	Greater than or equal to

If I wanted to write a query to display all the songs in my table that were released in the year 1959 or later, I'd use the greater than or equal to operator (>=) in my WHERE clause, as in Listing 5.5.

LISTING 5.5 A Sample Query Using Greater Than or Equal To

```
<CFQUERY NAME="get_songs" DATASOURCE="elvis">
SELECT ID, title, released, rating FROM songs WHERE released >= '1959'
</CFQUERY>
```

This will produce five entries, including all the songs in which `year` is `1959` and those in which the year is a number higher than 1959, as follows:

OUTPUT

```
Title: A Big Hunk O'Love
Release Date: 1959
My Rating: OK, I guess

Title: Bossa Nova Baby
Release Date: 1963
My Rating: uh-oh

Title: Devil In Disguise
Release Date: 1963
Rating: yeee-haw!

Title: Do The Clam
Release Date: 1965
My Rating: uh-oh

Title: Don't Cry Daddy
Release Date: 1969
My Rating: the end is near
```

Tip

> Relational operators are particularly valuable when your query deals with dates or dollar figures. These operators allow your query to look for values greater than, less than, or equal to a value you specify. Sample uses include:
>
> - A table of customers might be queried to find those who spent more than $500 in the last year
> - A `"products"` table might be queried to find items that have sold in quantities of more than 1,000 units
> - A table containing news headlines might be queried to display items entered only in the last week
> - A `"what's new"` page might query a table to retrieve only the latest additions to a Web site

Logical Operators

If I need to specify more than one condition in a WHERE clause, I can use logical operators to set up a flow among the conditions. To do this, I might use *Boolean terms* to create true-false statements that will determine whether a particular record is returned by my query.

NEW TERM   *Boolean terms* are words like "and" and "or" that qualify search conditions. They're used extensively in SQL, but also in programming languages, flow charts, and even Web searches.

Let's say I want to query my songs table to show only the songs that were released in 1965 and, of those, only the ones that received my "yeee-haw!" rating. By using the AND operator in my WHERE clause, I can join two conditions and select a record only if it satisfies *both* conditions.

I'd use a query like Listing 5.6.

LISTING 5.6   A Query Section Using the Boolean Operator AND

```
<CFQUERY NAME="get_songs" DATASOURCE="elvis">
SELECT title, released, rating FROM songs
➥WHERE released = '1965' AND rating = 'yeee-haw!'
</CFQUERY>
```

I've included the AND operator, giving my WHERE clause two conditions to satisfy. Using the same <CFOUTPUT> section as the previous examples, this template will return only one record, the one for "Devil In Disguise." I'm pretty selective with my "yeee-haw!"s.

If I wanted to display all songs recorded in the years 1956 and 1957, I can use the Boolean OR operator to join two conditions, returning a record if its data satisfies *either* condition. My query is shown in Listing 5.7.

LISTING 5.7   A Query Section Using the Boolean Operator OR

```
<CFQUERY NAME="get_songs" DATASOURCE="elvis">
SELECT title, released, rating FROM songs WHERE released = '1956' OR released =
➥'1957'
</CFQUERY>
```

5

Listing 5.7 will produce the following output:

OUTPUT
```
Title: Money Honey
Release Date: 1956
My Rating: yeee-haw!

Title: Teddy Bear
Release Date: 1957
My Rating: OK, I guess
```

Logical operators can also be used in conjunction with any of the six relational operators. Let's say that I wanted to find all songs released in 1959 or later that received a "yeee-haw!". My query will look like Listing 5.8.

LISTING 5.8   A Query Section Using Both Relational and Boolean Operators

```
<CFQUERY NAME="get_songs" DATASOURCE="elvis">
SELECT title, released, rating FROM songs
➥ WHERE released >= '1959' AND rating = 'yeee-haw!'
</CFQUERY>
```

Logical operators can also be chained together to form *compound conditions*.

NEW TERM   A *compound condition* is a WHERE clause that contains more than one logical operator. As in algebra, compound conditions are evaluated from left to right.

To illustrate a common compound condition, lets say that I want to display all songs released 1959 or later *and* songs that received either a "yeee-haw!" or "OK, I guess" rating. Listing 5.9 shows my query.

LISTING 5.9   A Query Section Using a Compound Condition

```
<CFQUERY NAME="get_songs" DATASOURCE="elvis">
SELECT title, released, rating FROM songs
➥WHERE released >= '1959' OR rating = 'yeee-haw!'
➥OR rating = 'OK, I guess'
</CFQUERY>
```

Using the <CFOUTPUT> section from previous examples, the query in Listing 5.9 will output all records that satisfy any one of the three conditions.

OUTPUT
```
Title: Baby, Let's Play House
Release Date: 1954
My Rating: yeee-haw!

Title: Good Rockin' Tonight
Release Date: 1954
My Rating: yeee-haw!

Title: Money Honey
Release Date: 1956
My Rating: yeee-haw!

Title: Teddy Bear
Release Date: 1957
My Rating: OK, I guess

Title: A Big Hunk O'Love
Release Date: 1959
My Rating: OK, I guess
```

```
Title: Bossa Nova Baby
Release Date: 1963
My Rating: uh-oh

Title: Devil In Disguise
Release Date: 1963
Rating: yeee-haw!

Title: Do The Clam
Release Date: 1965
My Rating: uh-oh

Title: Don't Cry Daddy
Release Date: 1969
My Rating: the end is near
```

Both the AND and OR operators can be used in a single query, but as you'll see, it gets a little tricky for ColdFusion to know which condition should be processed first. To designate which condition I want processed before it is evaluated against another, SQL uses a trick from high school algebra textbooks, as shown in Listing 5.10.

LISTING 5.10   A Query Section Using Parentheses to Specify Processing Order

```
<CFQUERY NAME="get_songs" DATASOURCE="elvis">
SELECT title, released, rating FROM songs
➥WHERE released >= '1959'
➥AND (rating = 'yeee-haw!' OR rating = 'OK, I guess')
</CFQUERY>
```

Note the parentheses in Listing 5.10. This query appears similar to the one in Listing 5.9, but the use of the AND operator and the parentheses will produce a very different output.

The parentheses tell ColdFusion that I want the contents to be evaluated *first*, and then the results compared to any other conditions. In the case of Listing 5.10, the query will first examine a record to see whether the rating equaled either "yeee-haw!" or "OK, I guess." If either condition proved true, it would *only then* check the released field for a value of 1959 or greater.

The query in Listing 5.10 will produce the following output:

OUTPUT
```
Title: A Big Hunk O'Love
Release Date: 1959
My Rating: OK, I guess

Title: Devil In Disguise
Release Date: 1963
Rating: yeee-haw!
```

The query retrieves just two songs, the only tunes released in 1959 or later, AND rated either "OK, I guess" OR "yeee-haw!"

OUTPUT
```
Title: A Big Hunk O'Love
Release Date: 1959
My Rating: OK, I guess

Title: Devil In Disguise
Release Date: 1963
Rating: yeee-haw!
```

> **Tip**
>
> Compound conditions are one of SQL's most powerful functions. By using them in your queries, you can bring even the largest databases down to size. Sample uses include
>
> - A "products" table might be queried to show items priced more than $100 that have sold in quantities of 1,000 or more units in the last six months
> - A table of customers might be queried to show those residing in a certain ZIP code area who have purchased more than $500 in products in the last year
> - An "organizations" table might be queried to find only non-profit groups with an annual budget more than $100,000, that cater to the disabled

Using the IN and BETWEEN Operators

The IN and BETWEEN operators don't add any new functions to SQL; instead they're shortcuts designed to simplify your queries. Let's say that we want to select songs that received a rating of "OK, I guess," "uh-oh," or "the end is near," denoting the downfall of Elvis' music career. A query using logical operators will look like Listing 5.11.

LISTING 5.11 A Sample Query Using Two OR Operators

```
<CFQUERY NAME="get_songs" DATASOURCE="elvis">
SELECT title, released, rating FROM songs
➥WHERE rating = 'OK, I guess' OR rating = 'uh-oh' OR rating = 'the end is near'
</CFQUERY>
```

OUTPUT
```
Title: Teddy Bear
Release Date: 1957
My Rating: OK, I guess

Title: A Big Hunk O'Love
```

```
Release Date: 1959
My Rating: OK, I guess

Title: Bossa Nova Baby
Release Date: 1963
My Rating: uh-oh

Title: Do The Clam
Release Date: 1965
My Rating: uh-oh

Title: Don't Cry Daddy
Release Date: 1969
My Rating: the end is near
```

The OR list is starting to get a little unwieldy. Enter the IN command, which performs the same selection with a simplified query by replacing multiple OR operators. An example is shown in Listing 5.12.

LISTING 5.12   A Query Section Using IN to Replace Multiple OR Operators

```
<CFQUERY NAME="get_songs" DATASOURCE="elvis">
SELECT title, released, rating FROM songs
➥WHERE rating IN ('OK, I guess', 'uh-oh', 'the end is near')
</CFQUERY>
```

The query in Listing 5.12 replaces the equals operator with IN, following it with a comma-delimited list of terms. The parentheses mark the beginning and end of the list. The output from Listing 5.12 is identical to that of Listing 5.11.

Note that the comma in my rating "OK, I guess" doesn't confuse the IN operator because it's enclosed in single quotes.

Similarly, the BETWEEN operator provides a shortcut for the less than (<) and greater than (>) operators. To show all songs released between 1954 and 1965, I can use the conventional method as pictured in Listing 5.13.

LISTING 5.13   A Query Section Using Multiple Relational Operators

```
<CFQUERY NAME="get_songs" DATASOURCE="elvis">
SELECT title, released, rating FROM songs
➥WHERE released >= '1954' AND released <= '1965'
</CFQUERY>
```

But the BETWEEN operator will clean this up nicely, as in Listing 5.14.

5

LISTING 5.14 A Query Replacing Multiple Relational Operators with BETWEEN

```
<CFQUERY NAME="get_songs" DATASOURCE="elvis">
SELECT title, released, rating FROM songs
➥WHERE released BETWEEN '1954' AND '1965'
</CFOUTPUT>
```

Listings 5.13 and 5.14 will return the same output, displaying all songs released between 1954 and 1965.

OUTPUT

```
Title: Baby, Let's Play House
Release Date: 1954
My Rating: yeee-haw!

Title: Good Rockin' Tonight
Release Date: 1954
My Rating: yeee-haw!

Title: Money Honey
Release Date: 1956
My Rating: yeee-haw!

Title: Teddy Bear
Release Date: 1957
My Rating: OK, I guess

Title: A Big Hunk O'Love
Release Date: 1959
My Rating: OK, I guess

Title: Bossa Nova Baby
Release Date: 1963
My Rating: uh-oh

Title: Devil In Disguise
Release Date: 1963
Rating: yeee-haw!

Title: Do The Clam
Release Date: 1965
My Rating: uh-oh
```

Using LIKE

Earlier in this chapter, I illustrated the use of a wildcard character, the asterisk, to tell ColdFusion I want to retrieve the data for *all* fields in a table. The WHERE clause has its own wildcard operator, LIKE, which signals that I'm not sure of the exact text I'm searching for and need to match just a few numbers or letters in a field.

Say I wanted to list all songs that were released in 1960 or later. I could write this query the hard way, using the OR operator to search for records where released is 1960 OR 1961 OR 1962, and so on. But as you might suspect, SQL provides an easier method. I've illustrated it in Listing 5.15.

LISTING 5.15   A Query Using the LIKE Operator

```
<CFQUERY NAME="get_songs" DATASOURCE="elvis">
SELECT title, released, rating FROM songs WHERE released LIKE '196%'
</CFQUERY>
```

Listing 5.15 uses the LIKE operator in conjunction with another of SQL's wildcard characters, the percent sign (%). This symbol denotes any possible character or characters that might appear in that position, including spaces, letters, numbers, and even punctuation marks.

LIKE and the percent sign always appear together in SQL commands. The percent can appear either before, after, or within a text string. As an example, let's say that I wanted to display an alphabetic list of song titles, and for the current page I want to list all titles starting with the letter "D." My query will appear as in Listing 5.16.

LISTING 5.16   A Query Using the LIKE Operator to Find Titles Beginning with "D"

```
<CFQUERY NAME="get_songs" DATASOURCE="elvis">
SELECT title, released, rating FROM songs WHERE title LIKE 'D%'
</CFOUTPUT>
```

Listing 5.16 will produce output for three songs, "Devil In Disguise," "Don't Cry Daddy," and "Do The Clam."

By using LIKE with a percent sign both before and after my text string, I can query the database for song titles that include the word "Baby," as in Listing 5.17.

LISTING 5.17   A Query Using the LIKE Operator to Find a Word Within a Title

```
<CFQUERY NAME="get_songs" DATASOURCE="elvis">
SELECT title, released, rating FROM songs WHERE title LIKE '%Baby%'
</CFOUTPUT>
```

When combining Listing 5.16 with a <CFOUTPUT> section, I'd see just two songs—both with "Baby" in the title.

5

Title: Baby, Let's Play House
Release Date: 1954
My Rating: yeee-haw!

Title: Bossa Nova Baby
Release Date: 1963
My Rating: uh-oh

> **Tip**
>
> The LIKE command and the percent sign are great tools for querying large databases, and for queries in which you need to find a keyword. Sample uses include
>
> - By using LIKE to query several fields, a "product" table can be searched by keyword, and will return results if the keyword appeared in the product name, product description, or product class.
> - A table of names, addresses, and phone numbers might be queried to produce customers residing in a certain area code or ZIP code area.

Sorting and Evaluating Query Results

If I've built a successful query that returns just the records I want, sometimes I'm content to just let them display in any old order, as in the examples listed so far. But I may also want to build an application that will sort data alphabetically or numerically based on the contents of a certain field. SQL provides a tool for this in ORDER BY.

Ordering Output with ORDER BY

By default, ColdFusion queries return records in the order they find them. In all the query examples from my database of songs, the output results have appeared in the order they're shown in the table in Table 5.1. For my small Elvis database, this hasn't been a problem, but let's look at another example in which I might want to change the output order.

Table 5.3 shows a subsection of the "orders" table from my business TV Cop Pasta, Inc. To keep things simple, I've only illustrated a few of the fields.

TABLE 5.3   orders

purchased_by	product_ordered	amount
Beaumont, Hugh	Jack Lord Rigatoni	$30.00
Eden, Barbara	T.J. Hooker Fettuccini	$10.00
York, Dick	Jack Lord Rigatoni	$30.00

purchased_by	product_ordered	amount
Mathers, Jerry	Ponch & John Ravioli	$20.00
Eden, Barbara	Baretta Manicotti	$50.00
Eden, Barbara	Jack Lord Rigatoni	$30.00
Denver, Bob	T.J. Hooker Fettuccini	$10.00

There are few things to notice in Table 5.3. First, the entries don't appear in any particular order. They were keyed in at the time the sale was made, so they aren't arranged alphabetically, or by order amount.

Second, note that one customer, a "Barbara Eden" placed three different orders, for three different dollar amounts.

If I wanted to search Table 5.3 for all of Barbara's orders and list them by dollar value, I'd use a query like Listing 5.18.

LISTING 5.18   A Query That Sorts Results with ORDER BY

```
<CFQUERY NAME="get_orders" DATASOURCE="tv_cop_pasta">
SELECT purchased_by, product_ordered, amount FROM orders
➥WHERE purchased_by = 'Eden, Barbara" ORDER BY amount
</CFQUERY>
```

In Listing 5.18, I've constructed a pretty basic query, but I've tacked on the ORDER BY command at the end. This tells SQL to sort my query results based on the amount field. In this case, the field contains numeric data, so ColdFusion will default to sorting it numerically from lowest value to highest value.

Using a standard <CFOUTPUT> section, the query in Listing 5.18 will look like this:

```
Eden, Barbara
T.J. Hooker Fettuccini
$10.00

Eden, Barbara
Jack Lord Rigatoni
$30.00

Eden, Barbara
Baretta Manicotti
$50.00
```

The ORDER BY amount clause caused the records to be sorted from lowest dollar value to highest.

5

Similarly, if I wanted to sort output by the purchased_by field, which contains alphabetic data, ColdFusion will output my query results ordered from A to Z.

The ORDER BY command will accept more than one sort field. Say that I want to output all the orders in my table, and that I want to sort them alphabetically by customer, but when a customer has made more than one transaction, I want to arrange his or her entries by dollar value.

The query in Listing 5.19 handles this nicely.

LISTING 5.19   A Query Using ORDER BY to Sort by Two Fields

```
<CFQUERY NAME="get_orders" DATASOURCE="tv_cop_pasta">
SELECT * FROM orders ORDER BY purchased_by, amount
</CFQUERY>
```

I used a comma to delimit the ORDER BY fields, and I placed purchased_by before amount to produce output like this:

OUTPUT
```
Beaumont, Hugh
Jack Lord Rigatoni
$30.00

Denver, Bob
T.J. Hooker Fettuccini
$10.00

Eden, Barbara
T.J. Hooker Fettuccini
$10.00

Eden, Barbara
Jack Lord Rigatoni
$30.00

Eden, Barbara
Baretta Manicotti
$50.00

Mathers, Jerry
Ponch & John Ravioli
$20.00

York, Dick
Jack Lord Rigatoni
$30.00
```

My orders are now sorted alphabetically by customer name, and where a customer has placed more than one order, those entries are sorted numerically.

> **Tip**
>
> By default, the ORDER BY command assumes that you want to sort character data from A to Z, and numeric data from lowest to highest. If you require the opposite, use the DESC (descending) parameter (such as ORDER BY *name* DESC) to output query results in reverse order.

Checking For Duplicates with DISTINCT

Sticking with my "orders" data in Table 5.3, let's assume I want to generate a simple list of all customers who've placed an order with my company. This sounds like a pretty straightforward query, but if I just ask ColdFusion to get all the purchased_by fields and sort them alphabetically, my output will look like this:

OUTPUT
```
Beaumont, Hugh
Denver, Bob
Eden, Barbara
Eden, Barbara
Eden, Barbara
Mathers, Jerry
York, Dick
```

Even though I'm a big fan of Barbara Eden, I might not want her name to appear three times in my list. To avoid this, I'll use a query like Listing 5.20.

LISTING 5.20   A Query Section Using DISTINCT to Limit a Selection

```
<CFQUERY NAME="get_customer_list" DATASOURCE="tv_cop_pasta">
SELECT DISTINCT purchased_by FROM orders ORDER BY purchased_by
</CFQUERY>
```

SQL's DISTINCT command tells ColdFusion to only select a record if the specified field contains a new value. In Listing 5.20, I've followed the DISTINCT command with the purchased_by field, so ColdFusion will return only one record with the name "Eden, Barbara" in that field.

Summary

SQL, or *structured query language* is a set of commands ColdFusion uses to communicate with a database. The most common use of SQL is to search a database table for records that match a set of conditions. A ColdFusion template defines the terms of these searches in the <CFQUERY> section, then arranges the resulting output in the <CFOUTPUT> section.

SQL uses conditions such as WHERE X = Y in a template's <CFQUERY> section to tell ColdFusion which records to select. By refining this WHERE clause with relational operators such as greater than or less than, or with logical operators such as OR and AND, you can restrict queries to return a very specific subset of your tables.

Additional terms such as IN and BETWEEN provide shortcuts for what will otherwise be lengthy queries. Terms such as ORDER BY and DISTINCT enable further control of output by changing the way records returned by a query appear in the user's browser.

Q&A

Q Does my database software fully support all SQL commands?

A In most cases, yes. ColdFusion uses the ANSI, or standard, set of SQL commands to maintain compatibility with most databases. In fact, your database software might even support special commands unique to that application. To use these extra commands, you'll need to make sure that you're using the correct ODBC driver for your database brand. Check your database app's documentation for details.

Q Do SQL commands such as WHERE and SELECT have to be in all capital letters?

A No, but it's not a bad idea to use this convention. When you're examining a query, the uppercase letters make it easy to distinguish between SQL commands and table fields, which use lowercase names.

Q Is there a limit on the length of SQL query statements?

A Longer query statements require more processing time from ColdFusion, but there's no limit on length. The queries illustrated in this chapter are very short; more sophisticated ColdFusion apps will use queries that might cover 20 or more lines of code.

Workshop

Just to see whether you were dozing through today's discussion, here are a few quiz questions and exercises. Answers to quiz questions can be found in Appendix A at the back of the text.

Quiz

1. What ColdFusion tags denote the beginning and end of a query section?

2. In a basic SQL SELECT statement, what follows the word "FROM"?

3. What are the two types of operators used in a WHERE clause?

4. Why are single quotes necessary when using a text string in a query?

5. What is the character that always appears in conjunction with the LIKE operator?

6. Which SQL command orders output alphabetically or numerically? How is it used?

Exercises

1. Construct a sample database table with at least five fields. Set it up as a ColdFusion datasource and design a basic template that will query and output all records.

2. Using the same template file, refine the <CFQUERY> section to return only records where a field is equal to a value you specify. Use ORDER BY to sort the results alphabetically.

3. Refine your <CFQUERY> by using LIKE and the percent sign to search for a wild-card text string within a field, such as 'A%'.

4. Construct a sample query that will search a hypothetical "orders" table for orders made between two calendar dates.

5

WEEK 1

DAY **6**

Creating Your First Web Application

If you're working your way through this book sequentially, so far you've been very patient as I prattled on about intangibles such as the theories behind ColdFusion, how it queries a database, and so on. At this point, you're probably a little antsy to start building your own Web application. I promise not to let you down—this chapter draws on concepts we've already discussed and I walk you through each step of building a Web application. We'll cover

- A sample real-world application
- Preparing a client's database
- Constructing the application
- Previewing your work
- Troubleshooting basic problems

Defining a Sample Application

There you are, dozing peacefully on your design firm's break room couch when a call comes in from Gargantuan Electronics, Inc. Gargantuan's representative tells you that her company sells a variety of computer hardware. And, in the process of providing tech support for its products, Gargantuan has built a database listing the weirdest support calls it has received. Upon hearing the word *weird*, you set your soda aside and listen carefully.

She tells you that at the end of each nine-to-five shift, Gargantuan's phone support people get together and decide on the strangest call of the day. They've been recording this information in a database for the last two weeks, and now they want to share it with all Gargantuan employees via their corporate Intranet. You begin to see imaginary dollar signs, but you remain calm.

She says the company managers have thought this through and decided that they want to keep the site very simple. They envision a home page that chronologically lists each of the funny calls along with a short description. When a Gargantuan employee clicks one of the items, he or she should be taken to a page showing the full details of the call.

The managers discussed the idea of building the site with standard HTML pages, but quickly realized that this would require coding a new page every day and that the home page would have to be modified daily to link to each day's entry. They figure this is a lot of trouble to go through just to let their employees read about goofy callers, so they're looking to you for a solution.

She tells you that her company's sales department has ColdFusion installed on the Intranet server (you begin a silent dance), but that the goofy caller page is an endeavor of the tech department and no one in that department knows the first thing about CF. Can you help her?

Yes, you say with great authority. You agree on a price and ask her to send you the current database of calls as an email attachment. You tell her that although your company is very, very busy, you're willing to begin right away.

After thanking her and hanging up, you move to your computer, close the solitaire game you had in progress, and start work.

Examining the Database

First, you pop open the database she has sent. It's a fairly standard Microsoft Access file called `calls.dbm`. It looks like Figure 6.1.

FIGURE 6.1

Gargantuan Electronics' database of weird tech support calls.

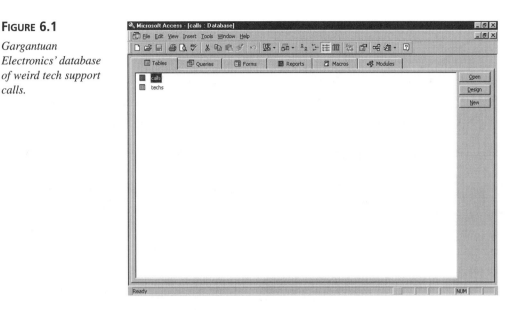

 Note

You'll find a copy of this database along with other sample files used in this book on the Sams Publishing Web site at http://www.samspublishing.com. The database is available as a Microsoft Access file or as a generic, tab-delimited text file for use with software packages other than Access.

There are just two tables—one containing the details of the calls and one listing the names of the techs who work in the department. You click the "calls" table to view the contents, shown in Figure 6.2.

FIGURE 6.2

The "calls" table in calls.mdb.

6

ID	date_of_call	tech_who_took_call	callers_first_name	short_description	long_description
1	10/4/99	Billy	Ed	Customer couldn't find	Customer called intitially
2	10/5/99	Dougie	Tad	Customer dials own I	Customer thought trouble
3	10/6/99	Jackie	Biff	Customer couldn't fit	Customer called requestir
4	10/7/99	Barbie	Eda	Customer can't find C	Customer tried to load a C
5	10/8/99	Jenny	Bud	Customer requesting	Customer purchased our
6	10/11/99	Bobby	Kay	Customer needed he	Customer experienced cc
7	10/12/99	Joey	?	Customer left messa	Customer called after hou
8	10/13/99	Buffy	Cap	Customer used a har	Customer had problems c
9	10/14/99	Jenny	Dot	Customer gets "no d	Customer called to report
10	10/15/99	Bobby	Art	Customer tries to fix	Customer had trouble witl
(AutoNumber)					

Nothing out of the ordinary here, just a small table showing the date of the call, the tech person who took the call, and the caller's first name. The short_description field provides a one-sentence summary of each call, whereas long_description contains a complete account of the weirdness.

You notice that when you place your mouse over the tech_who_took_call field, you see a drop-down box, as shown in Figure 6.3.

FIGURE 6.3

The drop-down box listing tech persons who work in the department.

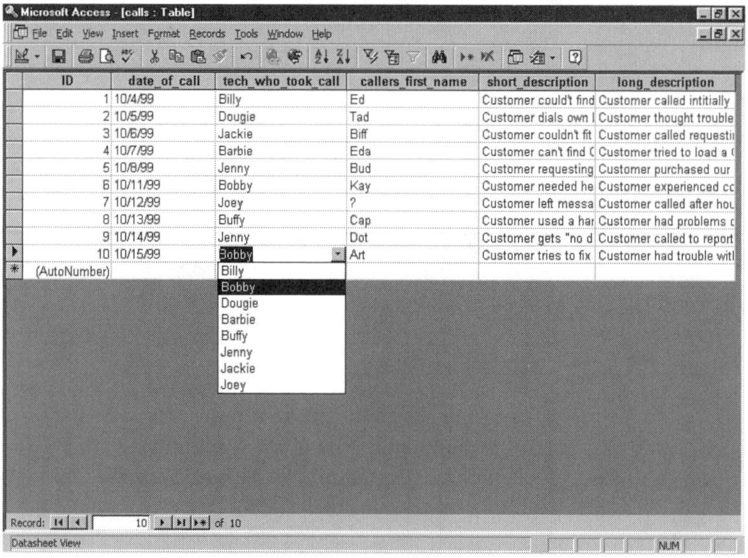

This drop-down box gets its information from the other table in the database, "techs". By adding or removing a name in the "techs" table, Gargantuan employees can change the list of names that appear in the drop-down box.

Tip

Drop-down boxes are a good way to limit the information a database user may input into a field. In Microsoft Access, drop-down boxes are created with a simple query. For an example of this, flip back to the database discussion in Day 4, "Building a Database and Organizing Data."

Everything looks fine—the client didn't use any spaces or odd characters when the tables and fields were named, so you don't have to make any modifications to the database.

Creating and Sharing Folders

In your Webserver directory structure, you now create a directory called gargantuan that will house all of this client's files. You must put the database file in a permanent spot before defining it as a datasource, so you create a subfolder of gargantuan called odbc and place the file inside it.

> **Tip**
>
> As with any Web site, it's always a good idea to arrange ColdFusion files in the same way they will appear on your client's server. During the development phase, if you place the client's database in a folder called odbc and pictures in a folder called images, the remote server should mirror this structure exactly.

When you create a new folder or directory to hold your Web files, both your Webserver software and ColdFusion require that you share it.

NEW TERM   *Sharing* a folder or directory means setting its security level so that its contents are available on the Web or a local Intranet.

The process of sharing a folder or directory is unique to your Webserver and/or operating system—check your software's help file for details. For Windows 95/98 users running Microsoft Personal Webserver, it's usually a matter of right-clicking over the folder name in Explorer and choosing "Properties, Sharing," as shown in Figure 6.4.

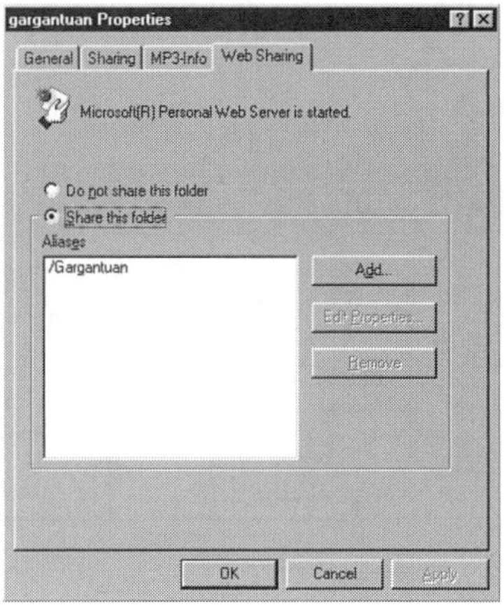

FIGURE 6.4

Sharing a Web folder on Windows platforms.

6

UNIX-based operating systems use the CHMOD command to assign permissions to directories.

Folders that will contain CFM files must also have *script* or *execute* permissions enabled. This tells your Webserver that you want to allow users to run or execute programs or scripts from that directory. Again, check your Webserver's help file for details.

> **Caution**   Depending on your brand of Webserver, you might need to share all new folders you create. For example, if you create folders titled images and odbc within the folder titled gargantuan, your Webserver might not automatically assign those folders the same security level as their parent folder.

Setting Up the Datasource

The file calls.mdb now resides in a shared folder and is ready to be set up as a datasource. Next, log in to ColdFusion Administrator using the special URL:

http://127.0.0.1/cfide/Administrator/index.cfm

After you supply your password, you will see the main Administrator page in your browser. Click ODBC to set up a new datasource, and you will see something like Figure 6.5.

FIGURE 6.5

Defining a new datasource in ColdFusion Administrator.

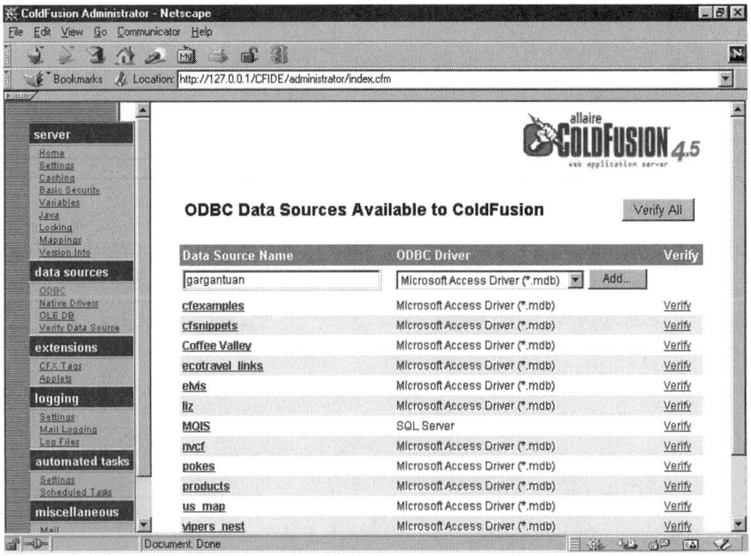

You'll call the datasource gargantuan and select the Microsoft Access driver to signify that the database is an Access file. Clicking the Add button takes you to a screen like Figure 6.6.

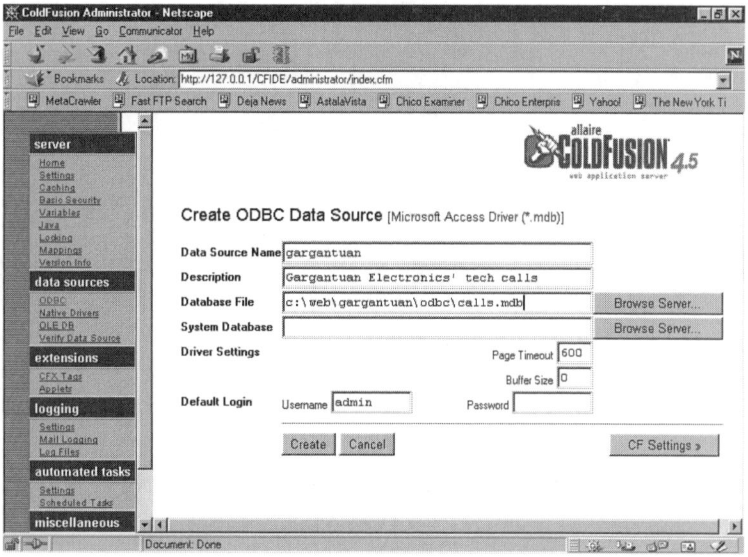

FIGURE 6.6

Supplying datasource details in ColdFusion Administrator.

For the expanded dialog screen in Figure 6.6, supply a description of the datasource contents, use the Browse button to locate the file on your hard drive, and click Create to complete the ODBC connection process.

ColdFusion automatically attempts to verify the datasource. That is, ColdFusion makes a connection to the file to see whether it can access the data within. If all goes well, you'll next see a screen listing your new datasource with the word Verified in the Status column, as shown in Figure 6.7.

If you see the word Failed next to the datasource details, something has gone wrong. You'll find a list of common datasource problems in Day 3, "Setting Up ColdFusion and Defining a Datasource."

Otherwise, you're set to fly.

6

FIGURE 6.7

The gargantuan *data-source, listed as veri-fied and ready for action.*

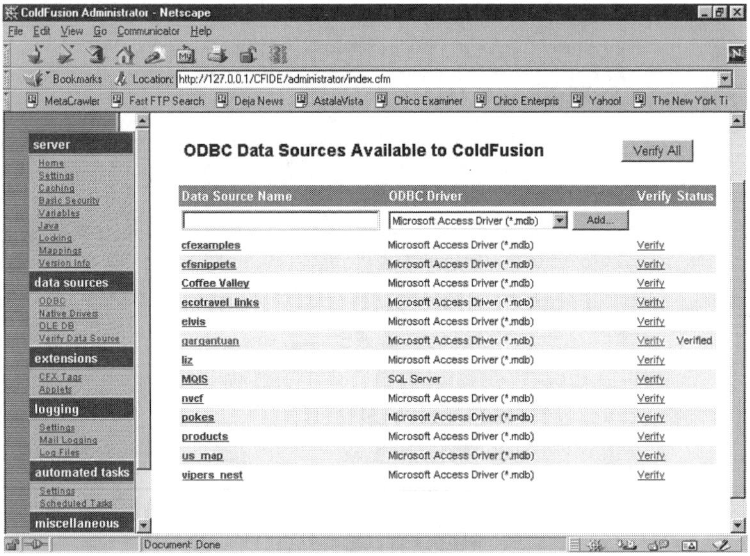

Constructing Your First Templates

You've been mulling over your client's vision of the site, and have decided that the whole thing can be constructed with two ColdFusion template pages—how's that for economy? The first page, the home or index page, will query the database for all records and list the calls as a series of links running down the page. When a user clicks one of these links, he or she is taken to your second template, a details page that shows a longer description of the selected call. In Web jargon, this is called a drill-down application.

NEW TERM A *drill-down* application is one that presents a list of items on one page and uses another page to show a more detailed view of a selected item.

Let's start with the index page. Open your favorite text editor and create a new file called `index.cfm` in the `gargantuan` folder.

Tip

After a CFM or template file is created, Windows users might have some trouble later opening the file for editing. If you simply double-click the file, Windows tries to send it to its "associated" program, ColdFusion, rather than your text editor. A better solution is to add a text editor (such as Notepad) to the Windows Send To menu by creating a shortcut to the editor in the folder `C:\WINDOWS\SENDTO`. After you've done this, you can right-click a template file in Explorer and choose Send To | Notepad.

> **Note**
>
> Allaire makes an excellent semi-graphic interface for building pages, ColdFusion Studio. We'll discuss it in detail in future sections, but for this first coding experiment we'll stick to creating pages in a standard text editor. The lesson is twofold: first, that ColdFusion templates are nothing more than text files containing CF code; second, that you don't necessarily have to have a copy of ColdFusion Studio handy to create or modify template files.

After creating the file, use ColdFusion comment tags to block out the various sections your template will contain.

NEW TERM   ColdFusion's *comment tags* are similar to those used in HTML. Any text or code appearing between the "begin comment" symbol <! - - - and the "end comment" symbol - - -> will not be parsed by ColdFusion Server. This makes the tags ideal for tasks such as announcing query and output sections, placing comments to aid other developers, and troubleshooting problems by commenting out sections of code.

My blocked-out template file looks like Figure 6.8.

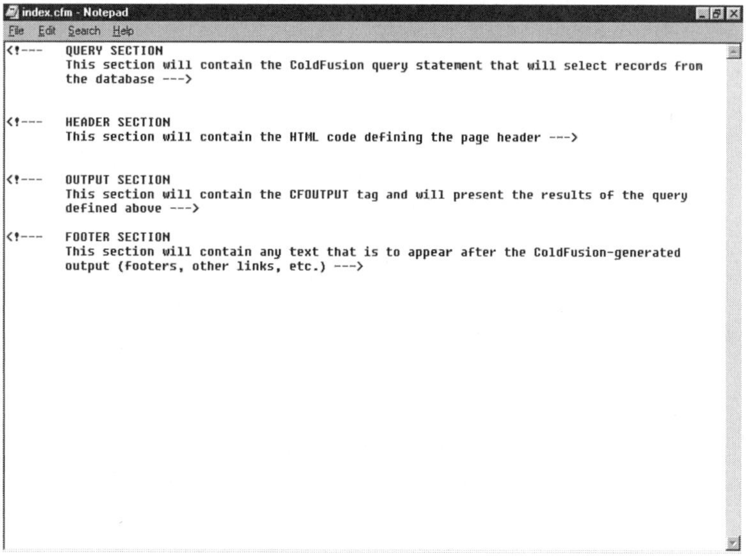

FIGURE 6.8

A new template file with comment tags to identify areas that will contain code.

Next, you'll start filling in the code for each of these four identified sections, starting with the query.

The Query

Your client wants her site's home page to list all the calls in the database. That sounds like a pretty straightforward query. However, you won't need the field long_description because it will appear only on the details page.

You need a query that selects all records from the table "calls", and gathers just the data in the fields date_of_call, tech_who_took_call, callers_first_name, and short_description. You should also select the autonumber field ID for reasons I'll explain in a moment. You might use a query like the one in Listing 6.1.

LISTING 6.1   A Query Section Selecting All Records from the "calls" Table

```
 1: <!--- BEGIN QUERY SECTION --->
 2:
 3: <CFQUERY name="get_calls" datasource="gargantuan">
 4:     SELECT ID,
 5:   date_of_call,
 6:   tech_who_took_call,
 7:   callers_first_name,
 8:   short_description
 9:     FROM calls
10: </CFQUERY>
11:
12: <!--- END QUERY SECTION --->
```

Note a couple things about this query. First, carriage returns are used after each field name instead of listing them all in a row. ColdFusion doesn't care whether you do this or not—it reads the query the same either way. It's just a coding trick to keep things organized and aid in any troubleshooting that might come later.

Second, note that the query doesn't include a WHERE clause. This is because we want to select all records in the database and don't need any qualifiers.

Also notice that we've modified the original commented sections to identify the beginning and end of the query section. This might sound like overkill on a short template page like this one, but it's a good habit to develop and it will save you lots of hair-pulling when you graduate to more sophisticated coding.

The Header

This section is just standard HTML code of the type you've probably used before. You must define a title for the page, set up a header defining the page content, and supply a sentence or two introducing the list of calls that will appear below this section.

My header section is shown in Listing 6.2.

LISTING 6.2   A Header Section Defining Gargantuan's Calls Page

```
 1: <!--- BEGIN HEADER SECTION --->
 2:
 3: <HTML>
 4:
 5: <TITLE>Gargantuan's Greatest Hits</TITLE>
 6:
 7: <BODY BGCOLOR="#FFFFFF">
 8:
 9: <H1>Gargantuan's Greatest Hits</H1>
10:
11: This page compiles the weirdest tech-support calls of each business day,
as selected by Gargantuan Electronics' tech support staff. These are
actual calls, and not figments of our staff's warped imagination.<P>
12:
13: <H3>Select a call to view complete details</H3>
14:
15: <!--- END HEADER SECTION --->
```

In Listing 6.2, we've used the HTML tag `BGCOLOR` in the body section to set the page background color to white. Not a very adventurous color, but we're keeping the design elements simple until we get the ColdFusion stuff working properly.

The header section ends with the text `Select a call to view complete details`, which introduces the `<CFOUTPUT>` that appears later.

The Output Section

You might assume that your client would like the listing of calls to appear something like this:

```
Date of Call: (date of call appears here)
Caller Name: (caller name appears here)
Call Taken By: (techperson's name appears here)

(The short description of the call appears here)
```

To create output that looks like this, you use an output section like Listing 6.3.

6

LISTING 6.3 An Output Section Displaying the Results of the Query in LISTING 6.1

```
 1: <!--- BEGIN OUTPUT SECTION --->
 2:
 3: <CFOUTPUT query="get_calls">
 4:
 5: <BLOCKQUOTE>
 6:
 7: <HR>
 8:
 9: <B>Date of Call:</B> #date_of_call#<BR>
10: <B>Caller Name:</B> #callers_first_name#<BR>
11: <B>Call Taken By:</B> #tech_who_took_call#
12:
13: <P>
14:
15: #short_description#
16:
17: </BLOCKQUOTE>
18:
19: </CFOUTPUT>
20:
21: <!--- END OUTPUT SECTION --->
```

Note the all-important <CFOUTPUT> tag. Within it, we've specified a query, get_calls, which is the same name we used in the query section. In this case, we have only one query, but note that template pages may contain several. For this reason, <CFOUTPUT> requires the QUERY parameter to associate output with the results of a particular query.

My output section adds a few HTML tags to dress up the output a bit. We've used bold tags (<B>) to set off the descriptive titles, carriage return tags (<BR>) after each item, and a paragraph marker (<P>) to add a little whitespace before the short call description. We've also placed a horizontal line (<HR>) before the entry, which helps divide the records as they run down the page.

Go ahead and format your template's output any way you like. Just remember one vital rule of ColdFusion output: Anything you place within the <CFOUTPUT> and </CFOUTPUT> tags repeats for every record returned by a query. For example, if we used the <BLOCKQUOTE> tag to indent our text but forgot to also supply the closing </BLOCKQUOTE> within the output section, our output would stagger itself down the page, like a staircase descending to the right.

So far so good, but you're missing one key element. Each record returned must somehow link to the details page for that particular record. Assume that you'll call the details page details.cfm and that you'll use the first line of each call record, the Date of Call line, as the text link. That line would be amended to look like Listing 6.4.

LISTING 6.4   Creating the Date of Call Line

```
<A HREF="details.cfm?call_number=#ID#">
<B>Date of Call:</B> #date_of_call#</A><BR>
```

We used the `<A HREF>` tag to make the whole Date of Call line linkable to the soon-to-be-developed page `details.cfm`. We also defined a new variable, `call_number`, to be equal to the number that appears in a record's ID field.

When a user clicks this link, her browser takes her to the Details template, and it passes the variable `call_number` to that template for parsing. We'll come back to this in a moment.

The Footer Section

For the footer, you assume that Gargantuan wants just the basic copyright information. If it wants to place links to other pages in the organization, it's easy to supply those later. My footer looks like Listing 6.5.

LISTING 6.5   Developing the Footer Section

```
 1: <!--- BEGIN FOOTER SECTION --->
 2:
 3: <P>
 4:
 5: <FONT SIZE="-1">
 6:
 7: <BLOCKQUOTE>
 8:
 9: This page and its contents are Copyright 1999
by Gargantuan Electronics. All rights reserved.
10:
11: </BLOCKQUOTE>
12:
13: </FONT>
14:
15: </BODY></HTML>
16:
17: <!--- END FOOTER SECTION --->
```

6

This section is just plain old HTML code. It starts with a paragraph mark to put a little space between the footer and the calls that appear above it, and then sets the font size down a bit so the text isn't too obtrusive. The final tags identify the end of the page with `</BODY>` and `</HTML>`. They're not entirely necessary, but we're being responsible coders who cover all the angles.

Our complete template file now looks like Figure 6.9

FIGURE 6.9

The complete index template, viewed in Windows Notepad.

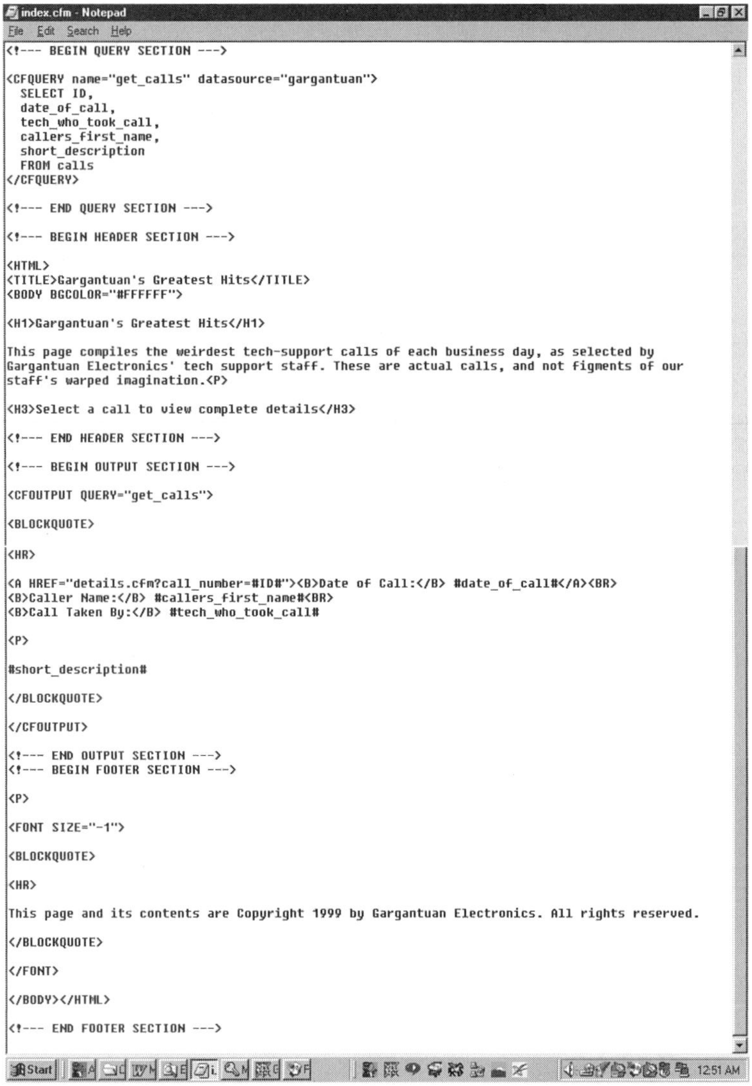


```
<!--- BEGIN QUERY SECTION --->

<CFQUERY name="get_calls" datasource="gargantuan">
  SELECT ID,
  date_of_call,
  tech_who_took_call,
  callers_first_name,
  short_description
  FROM calls
</CFQUERY>

<!--- END QUERY SECTION --->

<!--- BEGIN HEADER SECTION --->

<HTML>
<TITLE>Gargantuan's Greatest Hits</TITLE>
<BODY BGCOLOR="#FFFFFF">

<H1>Gargantuan's Greatest Hits</H1>

This page compiles the weirdest tech-support calls of each business day, as selected by
Gargantuan Electronics' tech support staff. These are actual calls, and not figments of our
staff's warped imagination.<P>

<H3>Select a call to view complete details</H3>

<!--- END HEADER SECTION --->

<!--- BEGIN OUTPUT SECTION --->

<CFOUTPUT QUERY="get_calls">

<BLOCKQUOTE>

<HR>

<A HREF="details.cfm?call_number=#ID#"><B>Date of Call:</B> #date_of_call#</A><BR>
<B>Caller Name:</B> #callers_first_name#<BR>
<B>Call Taken By:</B> #tech_who_took_call#

<P>

#short_description#

</BLOCKQUOTE>

</CFOUTPUT>

<!--- END OUTPUT SECTION --->
<!--- BEGIN FOOTER SECTION --->

<P>

<FONT SIZE="-1">

<BLOCKQUOTE>

<HR>

This page and its contents are Copyright 1999 by Gargantuan Electronics. All rights reserved.

</BLOCKQUOTE>

</FONT>

</BODY></HTML>

<!--- END FOOTER SECTION --->
```

Viewing the Index Template

Now you're ready to check out your handiwork. Fire up your preferred browser and point it to the index file via your Webserver. If you used the default folder locations I suggested earlier, the URL is

```
http://127.0.0.1/gargantuan/index.cfm
```

If all goes well, you'll see the first half of the page, as shown in Figure 6.10.

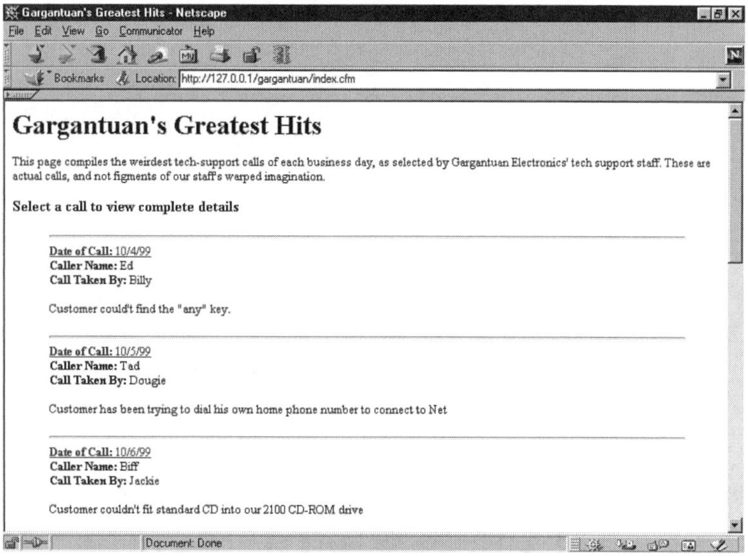

FIGURE 6.10

The output from the template in Figure 6.9, viewed in a browser.

Caution If you try to preview a template file and your browser asks a seemingly odd question such as, "Which program do you wish to use with this file type?", it usually means that you've tried to view a CFM file directly from your hard drive. In order for ColdFusion to parse your templates, you must access them through your Webserver, using its IP address, domain name, or the default 127.0.0.1 in the URL. When your mind is tied up with variables, queries, and output, it's easy to forget.

Basic Troubleshooting

If you *don't* see a page like Figure 6.10, it's time to do some poking around and find out what went wrong. First, read the error message in your browser to determine whether your Webserver or ColdFusion is generating the error.

Common Webserver errors include

- `404 Not Found`—If you get this error, double-check the location of the `gargantuan` folder and the file `index.cfm`.
- `Permission Denied`—Make sure you've enabled execute or script permissions on the folder `gargantuan` as described earlier in this chapter.
- `Host Not Found` or `Timed Out`—Make sure your Webserver is up and running properly.

Common ColdFusion errors include

- `Data Source Not Found`—You have incorrectly identified the datasource in your query section.

- `Error Resolving Parameter #some_variable#`—You've either used a variable that doesn't correspond to the field names in the database, or you haven't correctly identified the query name in the `<CFOUTPUT query="get_calls">` tag.

- `ColdFusion Service Not Running`—This should be fairly self-explanatory.

- Erratic output—If you see lines or characters that seem to repeat more often than you hoped, double-check your template file's `<CFOUTPUT>` section. Any text or code appearing between it and the `</CFOUTPUT>` closing tag repeats for each record returned by your query.

- `Wrong Number of Parameters`—This ColdFusion error is usually the result of a misspelled field name in your query. It can also occur if you forget to place a comma between two field names.

Creating the Second Template Page

At this point, you've successfully designed your first ColdFusion template and you might be tempted to hit the town and whoop it up with your computing buddies. If you do, keep it short because the more you retain from the previous sections, the easier it will be to create the second, or detail, page.

The detail page is the second part of the drill-down application. When a user clicks a link on your index page, he will see this second page showing the details of just one phone call. This page will contain all the fields shown on the index page, except that it will substitute the `long_description` field for the `short_description` field to give readers the full rundown on the tech-support call.

To begin, open your text editor and create a new file in the folder `gargantuan`. Name this file `details.cfm`.

The Query

Once again, start with the query section. You might recall that on the index page we supplied a link to the details page for each record. Each record was uniquely identified by its ID field, which we assigned to the variable `call_number`.

To see how this works, open your `index.cfm` file via your Webserver URL and place your mouse over one of the links. You'll see something like this in the bottom panel of your browser:

`http://127.0.0.1/gargantuan/details.cfm?call_number=1`

This is because ColdFusion plugged in the value of the ID field when it generated the page, creating the full URL you see here. This special URL tells ColdFusion to fetch the page `details.cfm` and pass to it the variable that appears after the question mark symbol.

When ColdFusion does this, you're able to use this variable as a dynamic parameter in your query. My query looks like Listing 6.6.

LISTING 6.6 A Query Section Selecting Data for One Distinct Call in the `"calls"` table

```
 1: <!--- BEGIN QUERY SECTION --->
 2:
 3: <CFQUERY name="get_details" datasource="gargantuan">
 4: SELECT date_of_call,
 5:    tech_who_took_call,
 6:    callers_first_name,
 7:              long_description
 8:      FROM calls
 9:      WHERE ID = #call_number#
10: </CFQUERY>
11:
12: <!--- END QUERY SECTION --->
```

This single query and template will serve you for all the records in your database because it creates a dynamic SQL statement that plugs in the value of `call_number` and compares it to the ID field in the table. Each number matches only one record in the table, so your details page shows only a single record at a time. The query gets the value of `call_number` from the link on the index page.

Note that we haven't included the `ID` field in the list of fields to select, because we won't need it anymore. There's no reason to output it to the page because the average user doesn't really care how Gargantuan has numbered the calls in the database. We're using `ID` only behind the scenes, as a means of selecting a particular record.

The Header and Output Sections

Our details page uses a header much like the one on the index page, but we're also going to be a little tricky. Check out Listing 6.7.

6

Listing 6.7 An Output Section Displaying Data for a Single Call

```
 1: <!--- BEGIN HEADER SECTION --->
 2:
 3: <HTML>
 4:
 5: <!--- BEGIN CFOUTPUT SECTION --->
 6:
 7: <CFOUTPUT query="get_details">
 8:
 9: <TITLE>Gargantuan Tech Call Dated #date_of_call#</TITLE>
10:
11: <BODY BGCOLOR="##FFFFFF">
12:
13: <H1>Gargantuan Tech Call Dated #date_of_call#</H1>
14:
15: <!--- END HEADER SECTION --->
16:
17: <B>Date of Call:</B> #date_of_call#<BR>
18: <B>Caller Name:</B> #callers_first_name#<BR>
19: <B>Call Taken By:</B> #tech_who_took_call#
20:
21: <P>
22:
23: #long_description#
24:
25: </CFOUTPUT>
26:
27: <!--- END CFOUTPUT SECTION --->
```

For this page, we're combining the header and output sections by placing the <CFOUTPUT> tag *before* the <TITLE> tag. We want the page title to be generated dynamically from the query results.

Caution

> When you use a number sign within <CFOUTPUT> tags to designate anything other than a variable, you have to tell ColdFusion that the sign should be interpreted as plain text. In Listing 6.7, we need to use a number sign in the <BODY BGCOLOR> tag to identify the hex code for the color white. We do this by using two number sign characters in sequence. That tells ColdFusion that the number sign is not being used as part of a variable name.

The Footer

Here we'll use just the standard copyright information, and we'll add a link back to the index page. It looks like Listing 6.8.

LISTING 6.8 Linking Back to Another Web Page

```
1: <!--- BEGIN FOOTER SECTION --->
2:
3: <P>
4:
5: <A HREF="index.cfm">Return to Call Listings</A>
6:
7: <HR>
8:
9: <FONT SIZE="-1">
10:
11: <BLOCKQUOTE>
12:
13: This page and its contents are Copyright 1999
by Gargantuan Electronics. All rights reserved.
14:
15: </BLOCKQUOTE>
16:
17: </FONT>
18:
19: </BODY></HTML>
20:
21: <!--- END FOOTER SECTION --->
```

Viewing all these sections together in a text editor, you'll see something like Figure 6.11.

Viewing the Details Template

You're now ready to view your first full application in a browser. Sure, it's comprised of only two pages, but with those two short template files, your client could effectively present hundreds of records to a Web user. You're now a bona fide solution provider. Others merely talk about solutions, but you *provide*, baby.

Caution

Before checking out your new template, be aware of the fact that the page details.cfm *absolutely requires* that the variable call_number is defined. That means you can't simply point your browser to the file and pop it open—you must access it via one of the links on the index page or by manually typing text such as **?call_number=3** after the filename in your browser's URL window.

6

Call up the index page with the URL you used previously:

`http://127.0.0.1/gargantuan/index.cfm`

FIGURE **6.11**

*The complete code for
the detail page, dis-
played in Windows
Notepad.*

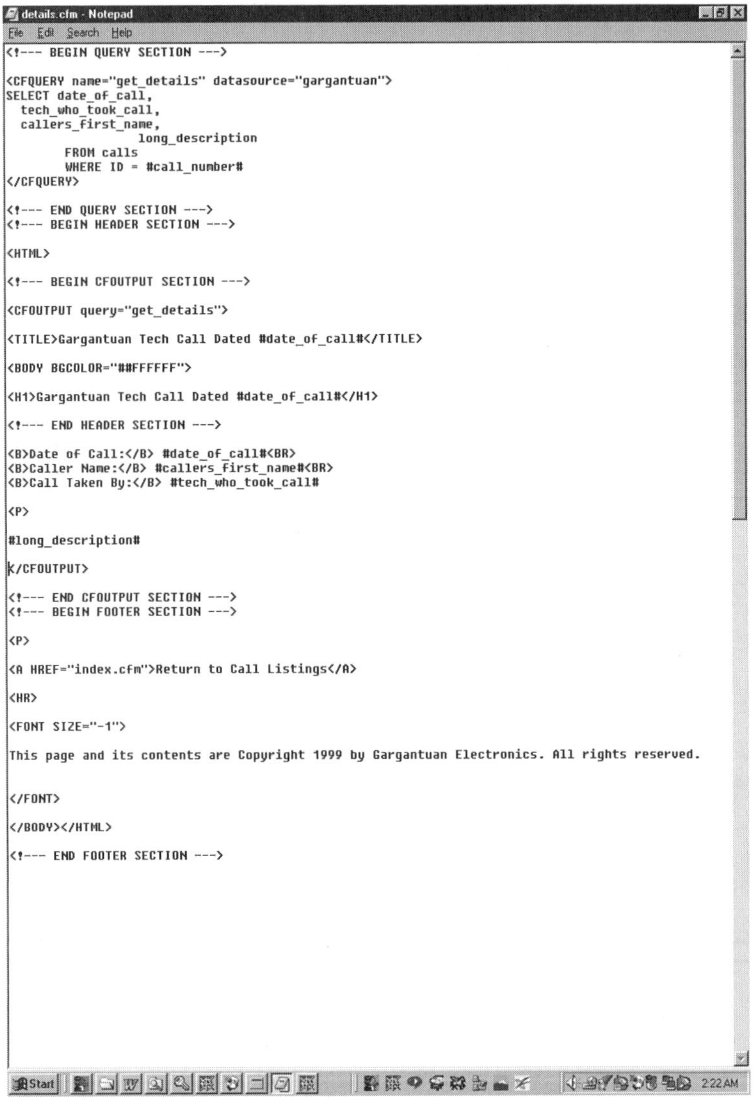

```
details.cfm - Notepad
File  Edit  Search  Help
<!--- BEGIN QUERY SECTION --->

<CFQUERY name="get_details" datasource="gargantuan">
SELECT date_of_call,
  tech_who_took_call,
  callers_first_name,
                 long_description
       FROM calls
       WHERE ID = #call_number#
</CFQUERY>

<!--- END QUERY SECTION --->
<!--- BEGIN HEADER SECTION --->

<HTML>

<!--- BEGIN CFOUTPUT SECTION --->

<CFOUTPUT query="get_details">

<TITLE>Gargantuan Tech Call Dated #date_of_call#</TITLE>

<BODY BGCOLOR="##FFFFFF">

<H1>Gargantuan Tech Call Dated #date_of_call#</H1>

<!--- END HEADER SECTION --->

<B>Date of Call:</B> #date_of_call#<BR>
<B>Caller Name:</B> #callers_first_name#<BR>
<B>Call Taken By:</B> #tech_who_took_call#

<P>

#long_description#

</CFOUTPUT>

<!--- END CFOUTPUT SECTION --->
<!--- BEGIN FOOTER SECTION --->

<P>

<A HREF="index.cfm">Return to Call Listings</A>

<HR>

<FONT SIZE="-1">

This page and its contents are Copyright 1999 by Gargantuan Electronics. All rights reserved.

</FONT>

</BODY></HTML>

<!--- END FOOTER SECTION --->
```

Click through to one of the links. If the gods are smiling on you today, you'll see
something like Figure 6.12.

To better understand the use of the `call_number` variable, manually enter a new URL,
such as

`http://127.0.0.1/gargantuan/details.cfm?call_number=10`

You'll see something like Figure 6.13.

FIGURE 6.12

Output from the details page when call_number *is* 4.

FIGURE 6.12

Output from the details page when call_number *is* 4.

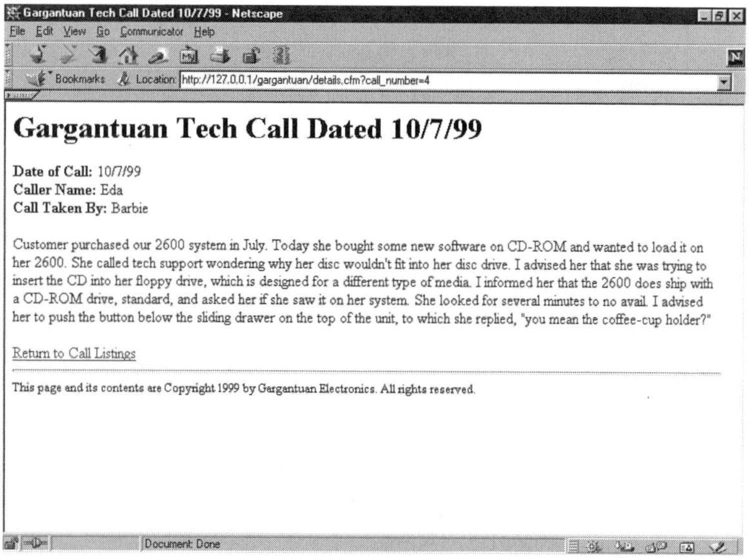

FIGURE 6.13

Output from the details page when call_number *is* 10.

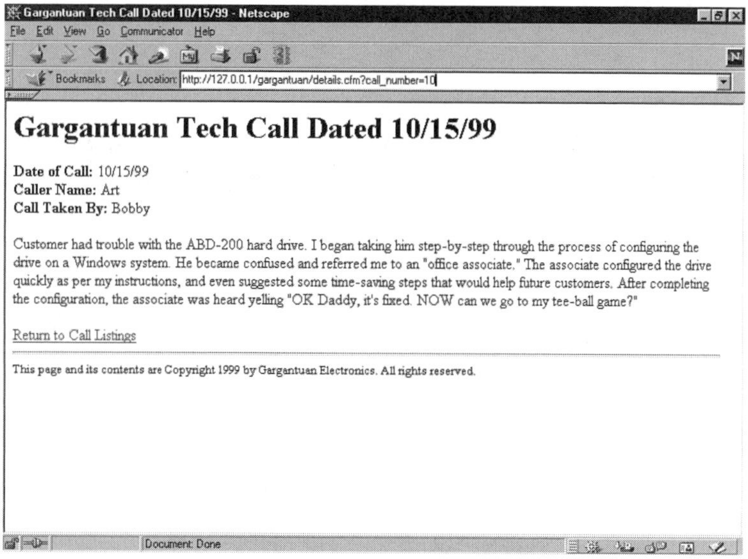

Go ape! You've built your first ColdFusion application, and it seems to be working. All that remains is loading the two template files to your client's Intranet server via FTP, and then walking the client through the process of setting up their own copy of the database as a ColdFusion datasource.

You'll sleep soundly tonight knowing that you've provided a genuine solution, and most important, that you will soon have a hefty check coming from the satisfied folks at Gargantuan Electronics.

Summary

For your first Web application, a hypothetical client asked you to build a site around an existing database. You first examined the database to familiarize yourself with its structure, and to ensure that field and table names were ColdFusion compatible.

In building the application, you first defined and verified the client's database as a datasource. You then created a folder on your Webserver to house the template files, sharing it and enabling executable access.

From your client's description, you envisioned the site as a single-level drill-down application. You created two templates to handle the data: the first templates briefly lists all records in the database and the second provides a more detailed look at a single record. You then previewed the templates in your browser, and used a few basic troubleshooting techniques to track down errors.

Q&A

Q What if the sample client's database had contained thousands of records. Would I have approached the application differently?

A Essentially no, but the client might not want to wait while the index page loads data on 1,000 calls. In later chapters, we'll discuss methods for limiting the number of records that appear on the page.

Q What if the client had asked for a fancier site, say with graphics and backgrounds?

A You would use the development process described in today's lesson first, and then go on to add the fancy stuff. In general, it's best to design the ColdFusion portion of a site first. Get it working on ugly bare-bones pages, and then move on to the graphic elements.

Q What if the client's database *had* contained field names that used spaces or nonalphabetic characters?

A You would first have to consult with the client. If the database stands alone on the client's Intranet, they probably won't object to changing it a bit. However, there might be cases in which a client database is an integral part of their Intranet, linked to other databases, forms, and so on. In cases like those, you're not able to change field names arbitrarily and should use one of the workarounds I will describe in subsequent chapters.

Workshop

Answers to quiz and exercise questions can be found in Appendix A at the back of the text

Quiz

1. What is a *drill-down* application?
2. When you create a new folder to host ColdFusion template files, what two things do you need to do it?
3. What symbols open and close a ColdFusion comment?
4. In a URL passed to ColdFusion, what does the question mark (?) stand for?
5. When should you use two hash marks (#) together?

Exercises

1. Return to the index and detail pages you built in this chapter and experiment with different ways of formatting the ColdFusion output. Try moving the fields around, making them bold, and so on.
2. Modify your template pages to produce some of the ColdFusion errors described in the section "Basic Troubleshooting." By understanding what creates these errors, you are better prepared to handle them when they occur in other projects.
3. Make your pages presentable by adding graphics and backgrounds. Use at least one graphic in the <CFOUTPUT> section.

6

DAY 7

Changing the Contents of a Database with ColdFusion

In Day 6, "Creating Your First Web Application," you built your first ColdFusion templates to create a two-page drill-down application. Your templates used basic queries to draw information from a client's database and present the data to users as an HTML page. In today's lesson we'll look at the other side of ColdFusion—input. You'll learn how standard Web forms can be used to get information into a ColdFusion database. We'll also cover

- The <CFINSERT> and <CFUPDATE> tags
- An introduction to Web forms
- Creating forms to insert or update data
- Troubleshooting insert and update operations

Defining a Sample Application

After successfully completing your first Web application for Gargantuan Electronics as described in Day 6, you return from your Mexican vacation to find your answering machine full of messages from the Gargantuan rep. She loves the application you created, but it has now become so popular with the Gargantuan's tech department that all the employees want the ability to personally log their strange calls, rather than leaving it to the "database guy."

When you phone her back, the rep tells you the problem is that not all the tech-support employees are familiar with using database software. She wants you to build a Web interface that will enable any techperson to input the details of a call, right from his Web browser.

However, having seen other paperwork submitted by tech-support personnel, she knows that certain members of the department can't spell or punctuate their way out of a wet grocery sack. For this reason she also requests that you create a special administrator page that will enable her to edit the text in existing entries.

After she hangs up, you remove your sombrero and huraches, hang your new velveteen Elvis tapestry near your desk, and set to work.

Introducing <CFINSERT> and <CFUPDATE>

You'll need to understand two new ColdFusion tags to create the new pages, <CFINSERT> and <CFUPDATE>. Both are used when you want to change the information in a database. Both work like SQL queries in reverse—instead of selecting information from a database table, these tags change or add values to the fields you specify.

Use <CFINSERT> when you need to add a new record to an existing table. It doesn't require any qualifying statements to do its work. It simply takes the variables you've defined, matches them with field names in your table, and inputs the lot as a new record.

<CFUPDATE> is used to update an existing record in the table. It requires some sort of match to work—that is, you first need to inform the tag which record you want to update. Usually this is done by matching the value of a field, such as telling <CFUPDATE> to find the record where the ID field is 7, and then to change the data in that record to your specifications.

Both of these tags usually get data they need from Web forms.

Understanding Web Forms

> **Tip**
>
> If you're venturing into the world of ColdFusion you probably already have some experience with HTML forms. If not, this section will introduce the basic concepts behind forms. You'll find complete coverage of forms in any good HTML reference in print or on the Web.

Forms are increasingly common on the Web, particularly among businesses that want to gather information from their customers. If you've ever typed your email address or credit-card number on a Web page, you've used a form. A form page is simply an HTML document designed to gather information. On its own, it does nothing out of the ordinary—the real magic happens when you click the "submit" button.

HTML forms are always used in conjunction with at least one other page or program called the "action." The action is almost always a program or script of some kind, but as we'll see in the next section, it can also be a ColdFusion page.

Let's look at a simple form in Figure 7.1.

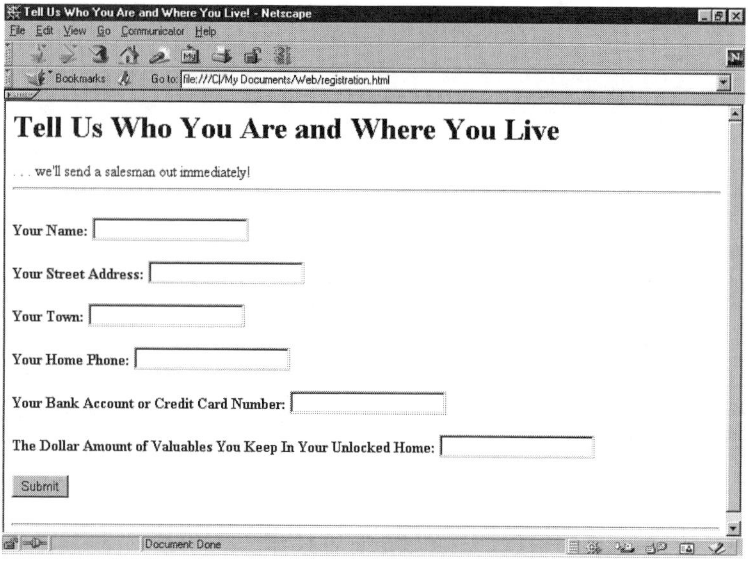

FIGURE 7.1

A sample user input form.

A form like this one doesn't require ColdFusion. It's coded in standard HTML—pretty basic HTML, in fact. The source appears in Listing 7.1.

LISTING 7.1   A User Form Created in HTML

```
 1: <HTML>
 2:
 3: <HEAD>
 4: <TITLE>Tell Us Who You Are and Where You Live!</TITLE> 5: </HEAD>
 6:
 7: <BODY>
 8:
 9: <H1>Tell Us Who You Are and Where You Live</H1>
10:
11: . . . we'll send a salesman out immediately!
12:
13: <HR>
14:
15: <FORM ACTION="send_out_the_dogs.exe " METHOD="post">
16:
17:     <B>Your Name: <INPUT TYPE="text" NAME="name">
18:     <P>
19:     Your Street Address: <INPUT TYPE="text" NAME="address">
20:     <P>
21:     Your Town: <INPUT TYPE="text" NAME="town">
22:     <P>
23:     Your Home Phone: <INPUT type ="text" NAME="phone">
24:     <P>
25:     Your Bank Account or Credit Card Number: <INPUT TYPE="text" NAME="bank">
26:     <P>

27: The Dollar Amount of Valuables You Keep In Your Unlocked Home:
➥<INPUT TYPE="text" NAME="valuables">
28:     <P></B>
29:     <INPUT TYPE="submit" VALUE="Submit">
30:
31: </FORM>
32: </BODY>
33. </HTML>
```

The <FORM> tag in line 15 opens the form section by defining an action that will happen when a user hits the Submit button. In this case, it's a CGI script titled send_out_the_ dogs.exe that might perform a variety of operations on the data passed to it by the form. It might add the data to a Web page, or it might place the data into an email message and send it to a designated address.

Also included in the <FORM> tag is a method, whose values are GET or POST. The first is used when the data you collect doesn't require any external processing; the second, when you want to pass form data on to another page or program.

Within the `<FORM>` and `</FORM>` tags on lines 15 and 31 are listed the variables this form will submit to the CGI script for processing. The variables appear in the `<INPUT>` tags, and they are assigned names by the `name` parameter.

Tip

> The form source in Listing 7.1 uses `INPUT TYPE="text"` for all the input sections. This tells your browser to draw a text box to receive input. Other "types" include drop-down select boxes, checkboxes, and radio buttons. These will be covered in Days 6 and 11.

For example, if I were to fill out this form and hit "submit," the information passed to the CGI script would include these variables:

NAME="Charles "Mohnike"

address="yeah, right"

town="Disneyworld, USA"

phone="nope"

bank="First Acme"

valuables="none"

Note that each of these variables corresponds to a `name` in the `<INPUT>` tags on lines 17-25, and that each variable now contains whatever text the user happened to type into the relevant input box.

You usually don't see this variable information "posting," or passing to the action program when you click the submit button. The variables and the data they contain are typically passed in the form of a URL, but its passing occurs behind the scenes.

This method of passing data via a URL makes forms ideal for ColdFusion work. As you learned in Day 6, ColdFusion is very adept at taking variables from the URL and using them as input. You'll exploit this capability in the input pages you're about to build. Instead of using a CGI script as the action of a form, you'll use a ColdFusion template designed to process the incoming data.

Tip

> ColdFusion has extended the capabilities of forms with a special tag, `<CFFORM>`. When using this tag in place of the standard HTML `<FORM>`, you can access an expanded range of form features such as sliders to select values or input validation, and a grid control to display tabular data. `<CFFORM>` is covered in Day 11, "Enhancing Input Pages with Basic `<CFFORM>` TAGS."

7

Creating an Input Form to Insert Data

Returning to the Gargantuan Electronics project, you determine that an input interface will require two elements, a Web form to collect the data, and an insert page to perform the action of putting the information into the `calls.mdb` database.

You begin to mentally sketch out the design of the input form based on the fields in the client's `"calls"` table. The contents are shown in Figure 7.2.

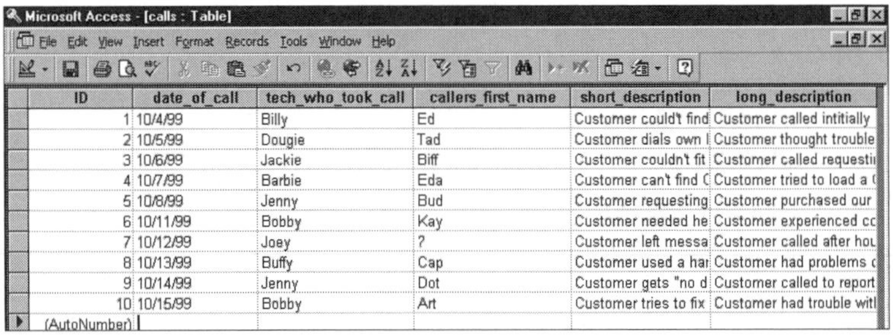

ID	date_of_call	tech_who_took_call	callers_first_name	short_description	long_description
1	10/4/99	Billy	Ed	Customer could't find	Customer called intitially
2	10/5/99	Dougie	Tad	Customer dials own l	Customer thought trouble
3	10/6/99	Jackie	Biff	Customer couldn't fit	Customer called requesti
4	10/7/99	Barbie	Eda	Customer can't find C	Customer tried to load a
5	10/8/99	Jenny	Bud	Customer requesting	Customer purchased our
6	10/11/99	Bobby	Kay	Customer needed he	Customer experienced cc
7	10/12/99	Joey	?	Customer left messa	Customer called after hou
8	10/13/99	Buffy	Cap	Customer used a hai	Customer had problems c
9	10/14/99	Jenny	Dot	Customer gets "no d	Customer called to report
10	10/15/99	Bobby	Art	Customer tries to fix	Customer had trouble witl
(AutoNumber)					

FIGURE 7.2
The `"calls"` table from Gargantuan Electronics database.

You envision that the fields `date_of_call`, `callers_first_name`, `short_description`, and `long_description` will be input manually by the tech taking the call, but you also have a trick or two up your sleeve. Because the list of tech employees is stored in a second table called `"techs"`, why not make that field a drop-down box listing all tech persons currently working in the department? In this way, when a tech records a call, she doesn't have to manually type in a name each time.

You begin by creating a new template page in the folder `gargantuan`. You name the page `input.cfm` and proceed to block out comment sections to identify the various components. Normally you wouldn't need a query section for this type of page, but our trick with the drop-down list will require one. The blocked-out page looks like Figure 7.3.

Tip

If your form uses ColdFusion elements, it must be named with the `.cfm` extension. If it doesn't, create it as an `.html` document instead. Standard form elements don't require ColdFusion, and will load faster as HTML documents.

FIGURE 7.3

The new file input.cfm, *commented to show major elements to be coded.*

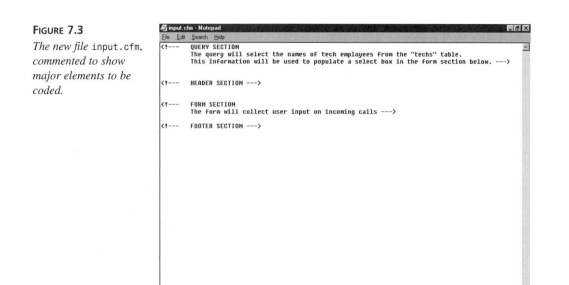

The Query

For the query section just concern yourself with selecting the names of the techpersons. We'll discuss what to do with those names later.

My query looks like Listing 7.2.

LISTING 7.2 The Query Section

```
1: <!--- BEGIN QUERY SECTION --->
2:
3: <CFQUERY NAME="get_techs" DATASOURCE="gargantuan">
4:     SELECT * from techs
5: </CFQUERY>
6:
7: <!--- END QUERY SECTION --->
```

The above is just a basic query with no qualifiers. Because there's only one field in the "techs" table, I didn't even identify fields to select. By default the query will get all fields—in this case, it retrieves just the field tech.

7

The Header

As with the templates described in Day 6, you needn't worry about prettying headers up too much. Let's stick to a basic header that defines the page and sets the background color to white. Mine looks like Listing 7.3.

LISTING 7.3 Creating a Header Section

```
 1: <!--- BEGIN HEADER SECTION --->
 2:
 3: <HTML>
 4:
 5: <HEAD><TITLE>Tech Call Input Form</TITLE></HEAD>
 6:
 7: <BODY BGCOLOR="#FFFFFF">
 8:
 9: <H1>Tech Call Input Form</H1>
10:
11: This is the page for tech-support employees to log their weirdest
➥ support calls of the day. Please complete all fields before submitting. <P>
12:
13: <!--- END HEADER SECTION --->
```

Here I defined the page headers and included a short message reminding employees to provide information for all the fields. Note that in the <BODY> tag, I wasn't required to use double hash marks for the BGCOLOR parameter because the <BODY> tag doesn't occur between <CFOUTPUT> markers.

The Form

Here we get to the good stuff. You need to define a form and an associated action, as well as textboxes that will become variables when a user fills them in. We'll agree to call the to-be-created "action" page insert.cfm. We'll also use text input types for all the fields except tech_who_took_call, which will require special consideration because we want it to reflect values returned by the query.

The first part of my form section looks like Listing 7.4.

LISTING 7.4 The Form Section

```
 1: <!--- BEGIN FORM SECTION --->
 2:
 3: <FORM action="insert.cfm" method="post">
 4:
 5:     <B>
```

```
 6: Date of Call: <INPUT TYPE="text" NAME="date_of_call"><P>
 7:
 8: Caller's First Name: <INPUT TYPE="text" NAME="callers_first_name"><P>
 9:
10:     Describe Call in a Single Sentence:<BR>
11: <TEXTAREA COLS="50" rows="2" NAME="short_description"></TEXTAREA><P>
12:
13:     Describe Call At Length:<BR>
14: <TEXTAREA COLS="50" rows="4" NAME="long_description"></TEXTAREA><P>
```

This first part of the form is pretty standard form fare. I've defined a form with the action insert.cfm and used the POST parameter to specify that the form will pass collected data along to that page.

I've also defined simple text input areas for the shorter fields. The two longer fields, short_description and long_description will require a little more space for the user to type, so I used the <TEXTAREA> tag and set column and row parameters to define the size of the text box.

 Caution | Unlike the other INPUT types, <TEXTAREA> requires the closing tag </TEXTAREA>.

The important thing to note here is that the input fields in Listing 7.4 are named *exactly* like the names of the fields in the "calls" table. This is important because later when we send these variables to the insert page, each variable name will look for a corresponding field in which to insert its assigned value.

Now on to the rest of the form section. Without ColdFusion, you would use code like Listing 7.5 to create a select box within a form.

LISTING 7.5   Creating the Select Box

```
 1: <SELECT NAME="tech_who_took_call">
 2:     <OPTION>Billy</OPTION>
 3:     <OPTION>Dougie</OPTION>
 4: <OPTION>Jackie</OPTION>
 5: <OPTION>Barbie</OPTION>
 6: <OPTION>Jenny</OPTION>
 7: <OPTION>Bobby</OPTION>
 8: <OPTION>Joey</OPTION>
 9: <OPTION>Buffy</OPTION>

11: </SELECT>
```

7

This would produce a select box like Figure 7.4.

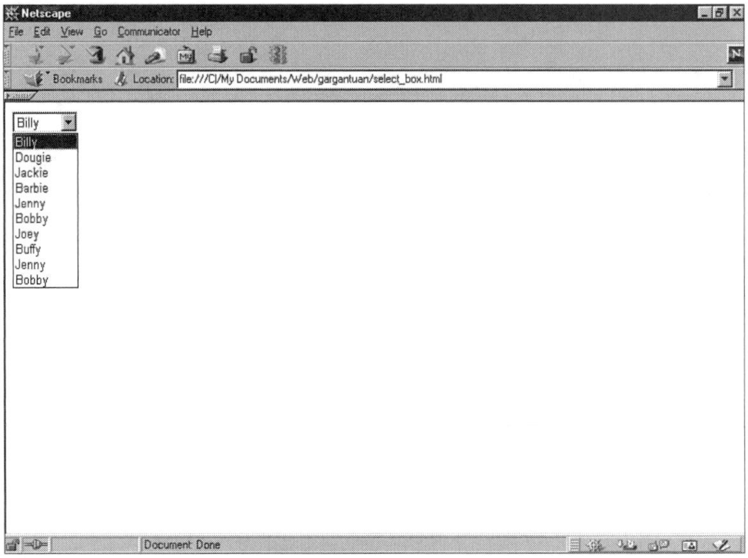

FIGURE 7.4

A form select box
populated with
Gargantuan tech-
support employees.

Using the manual-coding method in Figure 7.6, someone would have to edit the input form's code each time an employee was added or deleted. Instead, I'll use a <CFOUTPUT> snippet in conjunction with the earlier query to generate the names. This would make the second half of my form section look like Listing 7.6.

LISTING 7.6   Using <CFOUTPUT> to Populate a SELECT Box

```
 1: Your Name: <SELECT NAME="tech_who_took_call">
 2:
 3:     <CFOUTPUT query="get_techs">
 4:
 5:         <OPTION>#tech_name#</OPTION>
 6:
 7:     </CFOUTPUT>
 8:
 9:     </SELECT><P>
10:
11:     <INPUT TYPE="submit">
12:
13: </FORM>
14:
15: <!--- END FORM SECTION --->
```

The code in Listing 7.6 defines a <SELECT> box in line 1 and then begins a <CFOUTPUT> section in line 3 to provide option values. Because they're enclosed in the output tags, the <OPTION> tag in line 5 will replicate itself around each name returned by the query.

When this template is viewed in a browser, ColdFusion will plug in the values from the query, and the browser will see it just as if you'd built the SELECT box manually, as in Listing 7.5.

I added a simple footer, and now my completed template page looks like Figure 7.5.

FIGURE 7.5

The complete template page input.cfm.

```
input.cfm - Notepad
File  Edit  Search  Help
<!--- BEGIN QUERY SECTION --->

<CFQUERY name="get_techs" datasource="gargantuan">
        SELECT * from techs
</CFQUERY>

<!--- END QUERY SECTION --->
<!--- BEGIN HEADER SECTION --->

<HTML>

<BODY BGCOLOR="#FFFFFF">

<TITLE>Tech Call Input Form</TITLE>

<H1>Tech Call Input Form</H1>

This is the page for tech-support employees to log their weirdest support calls of the day.
Please complete all fields before submitting. <P>

<!--- END HEADER SECTION --->
<!--- BEGIN FORM SECTION --->

<FORM action="insert.cfm" method="post">

        <B>
        Date of Call: <INPUT type="text" name="date_of_call"><P>

        Caller's First Name: <INPUT type="text" name="callers_first_name"><P>

        Describe Call in a Single Sentence:<BR>
        <TEXTAREA cols="50" rows="2" name="short_description"></TEXTAREA><P>

        Describe Call At Length:<BR>
        <TEXTAREA cols="50" rows="4" name="long_description"></TEXTAREA><P>

        Your Name: <SELECT name="tech_who_took_call">

        <CFOUTPUT query="get_techs">

                <OPTION>#tech_name#</OPTION>

        </CFOUTPUT>

        </SELECT><P>

        <INPUT TYPE="submit">

</FORM>

<!--- END FORM SECTION --->
<!--- BEGIN FOOTER SECTION--->

<P>

<HR>

<A HREF="index.cfm">Return to List of Calls</A>

</BODY>
</HTML>
```

7

Testing the Template

When you preview the template in Figure 7.5 via your Web browser, you will see something like Figure 7.6.

FIGURE 7.6

The form page created by the template in Figure 7.5.

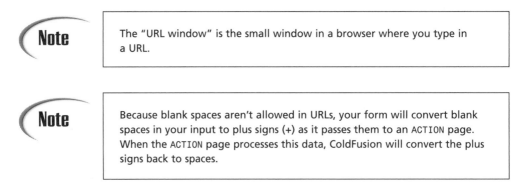

Obviously, clicking the Submit Query button will get you nowhere, because you haven't yet designed the ACTION page insert.cfm. But go ahead and enter a few values into the text boxes and submit the form anyway. You'll get an error, but if you check your browser's URL window you'll find a behind-the-scenes look at how your input is passed via a URL.

 Note The "URL window" is the small window in a browser where you type in a URL.

 Note Because blank spaces aren't allowed in URLs, your form will convert blank spaces in your input to plus signs (+) as it passes them to an ACTION page. When the ACTION page processes this data, ColdFusion will convert the plus signs back to spaces.

Creating the Insert Page

Now that you've developed a working form to collect data, it's time to design the insert page that will process the data and add it to the database. This action is transparent to the user—by default his browser will never know it has happened. For this reason, it's always a good idea to send a confirmation message back to the user so that he knows the information has successfully been added.

Fortunately, ColdFusion can handle both operations with a single template. The page you design in this section will add all submitted form data to the "calls" table in the form of a new record, and it will send confirmation to the user.

You begin by creating the ACTION page insert.cfm within the folder gargantuan. Because there's no query on this page, your blocked out sections will include an insert section, a header section, and a body section (to show the confirmation message).

The Insert

To perform this insert action, you'll need to use the <CFINSERT> tag along with two parameters: the name of the datasource and the name of the table in which to insert data. The insert section looks like Listing 7.7.

LISTING 7.7   The Insert Section

```
1: <!--- BEGIN INSERT SECTION --->
2:
3: <CFINSERT DATASOURCE="gargantuan" TABLENAME="calls">
4:
5: <!--- END INSERT SECTION --->
```

This insert action retrieves all the variables posted by the form page and inserts them as a new record in the "calls" table. If any one of the posted variable names didn't match up exactly with a field name in the "calls" table, ColdFusion would return an error.

Another parameter often used with the <CFINSERT> tag is formfields, followed by a comma-delimited list of the posted variables (fields) you want to insert. In this case, you need to insert all of them, which ColdFusion does by default if no fields are specified.

The Body and Footer

The body and footer sections are just plain HTML text. The body will give a confirmation such as "thanks for submitting your data" and the footer will provide a link back to the list of calls on index.cfm. With this link, the user can immediately view the results of her input. I've added a reminder for the user to reload the index.cfm page so that the call she's just submitted will appear on the page.

7

The complete insert template looks like Figure 7.7.

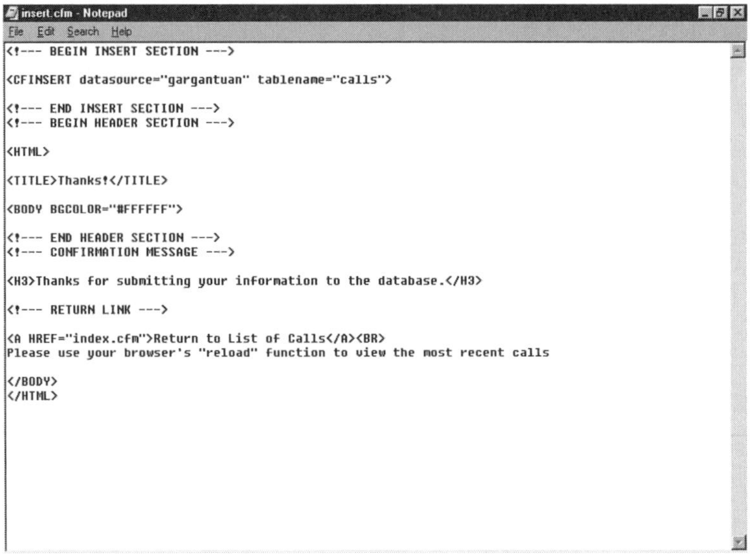

```
<!--- BEGIN INSERT SECTION --->

<CFINSERT datasource="gargantuan" tablename="calls">

<!--- END INSERT SECTION --->
<!--- BEGIN HEADER SECTION --->

<HTML>

<TITLE>Thanks!</TITLE>

<BODY BGCOLOR="#FFFFFF">

<!--- END HEADER SECTION --->
<!--- CONFIRMATION MESSAGE --->

<H3>Thanks for submitting your information to the database.</H3>

<!--- RETURN LINK --->

<A HREF="index.cfm">Return to List of Calls</A><BR>
Please use your browser's "reload" function to view the most recent calls

</BODY>
</HTML>
```

FIGURE 7.7
The complete `insert.cfm` *template.*

Now it's time to load up the page `input.cfm` in a browser, type in some sample text, and see what happens on submission. I like to use text like `test entry` just so my submissions don't get confused with actual tech-department entries. I can easily delete it later.

If all goes well, you will see the confirmation message, as shown in Figure 7.8.

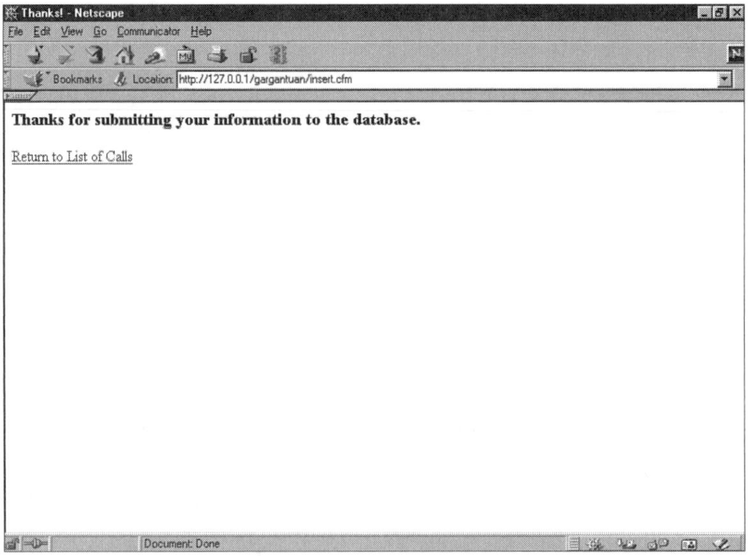

FIGURE 7.8
The `insert.cfm` *page displays a confirmation that posted information has been added to the database.*

So far so good. Now for the real test: You'll use the link back to the list of calls on `index.cfm`, hit reload, and see whether the `test entry` record appears there. Scrolling down to the bottom of the calls list, you'll see a screen like Figure 7.9.

If you didn't see the confirmation message or your test entry listed on `index.cfm`, check out the troubleshooting section near the end of today's discussion.

Creating the Edit Interface

With the input page completed, you'll now move on to the second part of Gargantuan's Web interface. The rep has asked that you create an administration interface that will enable her to edit entries in the database. She'd like the ability to pull up a specific call entry and then make spelling and punctuation corrections as needed.

You envision the editing interface in three parts: the first, a list from which you can select a call to be edited; the second, a form in which to edit the text; and the third, an `ACTION` page to add edited text to the database.

The first template sounds simple enough. You'll just need to query the database for all records, which will appear in a list, as they do in `index.cfm`. In fact, you can even re-use the code from that page.

You'll begin by opening `index.cfm` and saving it to a new file, `admin_list.cfm`, also in the folder `gargantuan`. You'll need to make a few modifications to make the code work as an administration page. My modified page appears in Figure 7.10.

7

Tip

Re-using code is a great way to make the most of ColdFusion's timesaving functions. As you begin to develop more templates, you'll find yourself coding certain types of queries and output sections frequently. When you begin developing a new template, you might be able to cut-and-paste snippets from previous applications to cut down on design time. You'll probably have to change a few variable names to match your current project, but you'll save yourself from re-inventing the wheel.

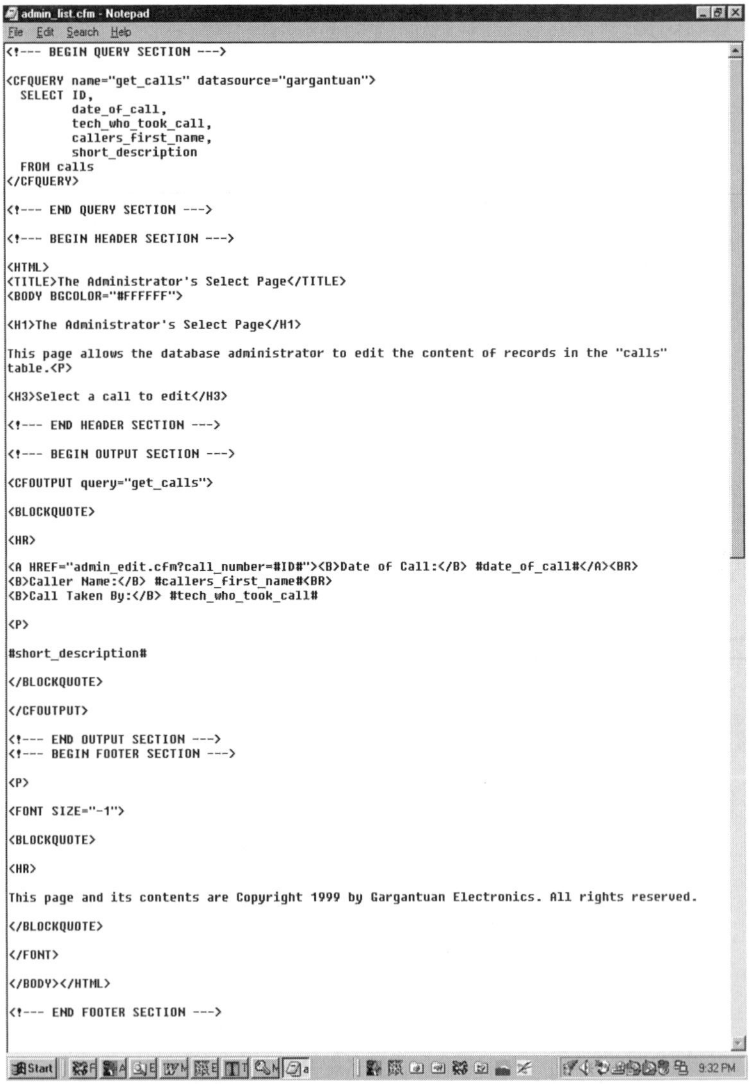

FIGURE 7.10

By modifying the code in index.cfm *and saving it to a new file, I create the new template* admin_list.cfm.

```
admin_list.cfm - Notepad
File  Edit  Search  Help

<!--- BEGIN QUERY SECTION --->

<CFQUERY name="get_calls" datasource="gargantuan">
  SELECT ID,
         date_of_call,
         tech_who_took_call,
         callers_first_name,
         short_description
  FROM calls
</CFQUERY>

<!--- END QUERY SECTION --->

<!--- BEGIN HEADER SECTION --->

<HTML>
<TITLE>The Administrator's Select Page</TITLE>
<BODY BGCOLOR="#FFFFFF">

<H1>The Administrator's Select Page</H1>

This page allows the database administrator to edit the content of records in the "calls"
table.<P>

<H3>Select a call to edit</H3>

<!--- END HEADER SECTION --->

<!--- BEGIN OUTPUT SECTION --->

<CFOUTPUT query="get_calls">

<BLOCKQUOTE>

<HR>

<A HREF="admin_edit.cfm?call_number=#ID#"><B>Date of Call:</B> #date_of_call#</A><BR>
<B>Caller Name:</B> #callers_first_name#<BR>
<B>Call Taken By:</B> #tech_who_took_call#

<P>

#short_description#

</BLOCKQUOTE>

</CFOUTPUT>

<!--- END OUTPUT SECTION --->
<!--- BEGIN FOOTER SECTION --->

<P>

<FONT SIZE="-1">

<BLOCKQUOTE>

<HR>

This page and its contents are Copyright 1999 by Gargantuan Electronics. All rights reserved.

</BLOCKQUOTE>

</FONT>

</BODY></HTML>

<!--- END FOOTER SECTION --->
```

Start 9:32 PM

I've only made a couple changes to the code. First, I've modified the page title, header, and description to let the administrator know she's reached the correct page.

Second, and most importantly, I've changed the name of the page that links to the detailed description. In the index template I linked each outputted call to details.cfm, a page designed to merely display details. In this case, I've pointed the link to the to-be-created file admin_edit.cfm. This page will also display all details of the call, but it will do so in a form interface to enable the administrator to make changes.

Viewing the new template in your browser, you'll see a page that looks similar to index.cfm, except for the headers, description, and link information. Mine appears in Figure 7.11.

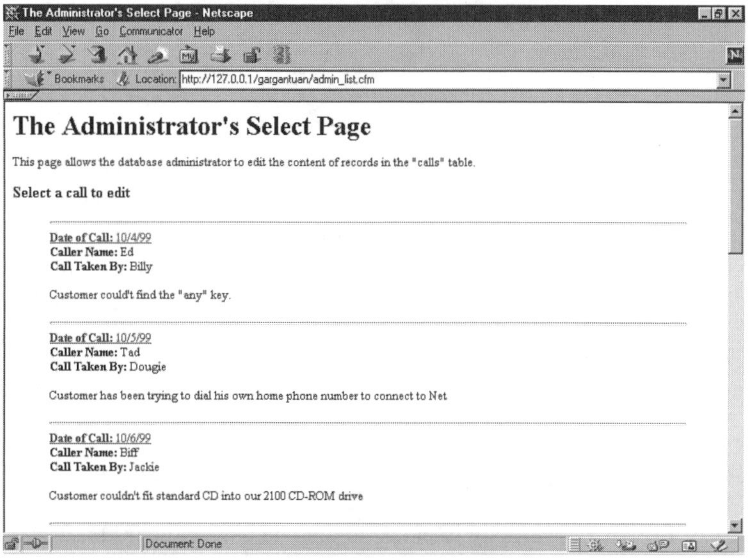

FIGURE 7.11

The completed admin_list.cfm page. Note the link location that appears in the bottom bar of the browser when I hold the mouse over it.

Creating a Form to Edit Existing Data

Constructing the edit form will draw on two principles you've learned in the last two days. First, it will query the "calls" table, looking for contents in the ID field that match the numeric variable passed to it from admin_edit.cfm. Second, it will create a standard Web form, inserting the values from the specified record into the entry boxes for editing.

To better understand this, let's work backwards and take a look at a completed version of the page we want to create. It appears in Figure 7.12.

7

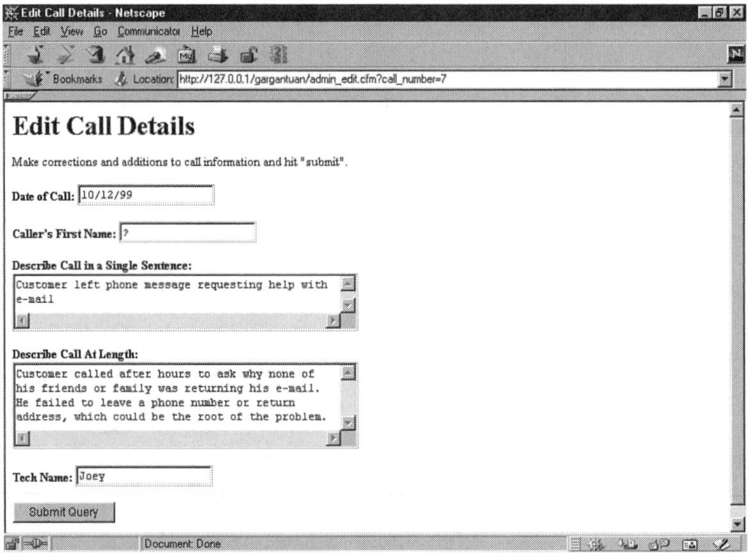

FIGURE **7.12**

The completed page admin_edit.cfm.

Figure 7.12 shows what you'll see when you click on a call's link on the page admin_list .cfm. By matching the call_number variable in the URL with the ID field in the table, this template pulls up the information for the specified record. It then inserts that text into form boxes ready for editing. The administrator sees the text originally entered by the techperson. From here she can make any necessary changes, and then submit the changed information back to the database.

Now let's examine the form source.

The Query

The query is exactly identical to the one used in details.cfm. That is, it pulls the call_number variable from the linking URL and matches that number with the ID field in the table "calls". I cut-and-pasted my query from the details file, as in Listing 7.8.

LISTING 7.8   The Query Section

```
1: <!--- BEGIN QUERY SECTION --->
2:
3: <CFQUERY NAME="get_details" DATASOURCE="gargantuan">
4: SELECT * FROM calls
5:    WHERE ID = #call_number#
6: </CFQUERY>
7:
8: <!--- END QUERY SECTION --->
```

The only modification made to the query was to add the asterisk (*) on line 4 rather than listing the fields we wanted the query to select. For this page, you'll need the data from all the fields.

The Header and Form Sections

You'll want to provide a simple header to let the administrator know that she's reached the edit page—no problem there. The form section is a little trickier. For this template, you'll need to introduce the <CFOUTPUT> tag before the <FORM> tag, because the goal is to populate the form with information from the selected record. To get the data into the form's text boxes, you'll use a parameter in your <INPUT> tags called value.

The value parameter defines a default text string that will appear in a form's text box. It's often used to create forms in which default text is already filled in, such as defaulting to "United States" for an address form or defaulting to "1" for a quantity ordered. If the user wants to change the text, he is free to type his own value over it; otherwise, it is submitted to the form's ACTION as-is.

Caution

> The sample form also uses the <TEXTAREA> tag as an input device where larger text boxes are required. This tag doesn't use a value parameter. Instead, the default text is inserted between the <TEXTAREA> and </TEXTAREA> tags.

In the interest of saving time, I cut-and-pasted my form section from the input.cfm file and added a few modifications. The form section appears in Listing 7.9.

LISTING 7.9   Using <CFOUTPUT> to Populate <FORM> Entries

```
 1: <!--- BEGIN CFOUTPUT AND FORM SECTION --->
 2:
 3: <CFOUTPUT query="get_details">
 4:
 5:     <FORM action="update.cfm" method="post">
 6:
 7:         <INPUT TYPE="hidden" NAME="ID" VALUE="#ID#">
 8:
 9:         <B>
10: Date of Call: <INPUT TYPE="text" NAME="date_of_call"
➥VALUE="#date_of_call#"><P>
11:
12: Caller's First Name: <INPUT TYPE="text" NAME="callers_first_name"
➥VALUE="#callers_first_name#"><P>
13:
```

7

continues

LISTING **7.9**   continued

```
14:          Describe Call in a Single Sentence:<BR>
15: <TEXTAREA COLS="50" rows="2"
    ➥NAME="short_description">#short_description#</TEXTAREA><P>
16:
17:          Describe Call At Length:<BR>
18: <TEXTAREA COLS="50" rows="4"
    ➥NAME="long_description">#long_description#</TEXTAREA><P>
19:
20: Tech Name: <INPUT TYPE="text"
    ➥NAME="tech_who_took_call" VALUE="#tech_who_took_call#">
21:
22:          <P>
23:
24:          <INPUT TYPE="submit">
25:
26:      </FORM>
27:
28: </CFOUTPUT>
29:
30: <!--- END CFOUTPUT AND FORM SECTION --->
```

Note the differences between this form section and the one in input.cfm. First, the entire form section appears within <CFOUTPUT> tags because I need to dynamically generate the text that will appear in the input boxes. Second, I've changed the form's ACTION to the to-be-created "update.cfm". This page will work much like the insert page you created earlier today, but it will be designed to update an existing record rather than create a new one.

Also notice that I've added value parameters to each of the <INPUT> tags, and that I've used ColdFusion output variables to define each. For the larger input boxes that use the <TEXTAREA> tags, I've enclosed the CF variable between them.

One more thing: I added a new input field at the top of the form. I defined the record's ID field as a variable, but I used the type "hidden" to specify that this data doesn't need to appear as part of the form. It will, however, be added to the variables posted to the ACTION page—this is crucial, as you'll see in the next section.

> **Caution**
>
> "Hidden" input fields provide a way to post data to an ACTION page behind the scenes. These fields are "hidden" only in the sense that they aren't visible in the form seen by the user. If the users were to use a browser's "view source" function, they *would* see your hidden field embedded in the code. For this reason, avoid using private information (such as email addresses you don't want made public) in hidden fields.

My complete template appears in Figure 7.13.

FIGURE 7.13

The complete template page admin_edit.cfm.

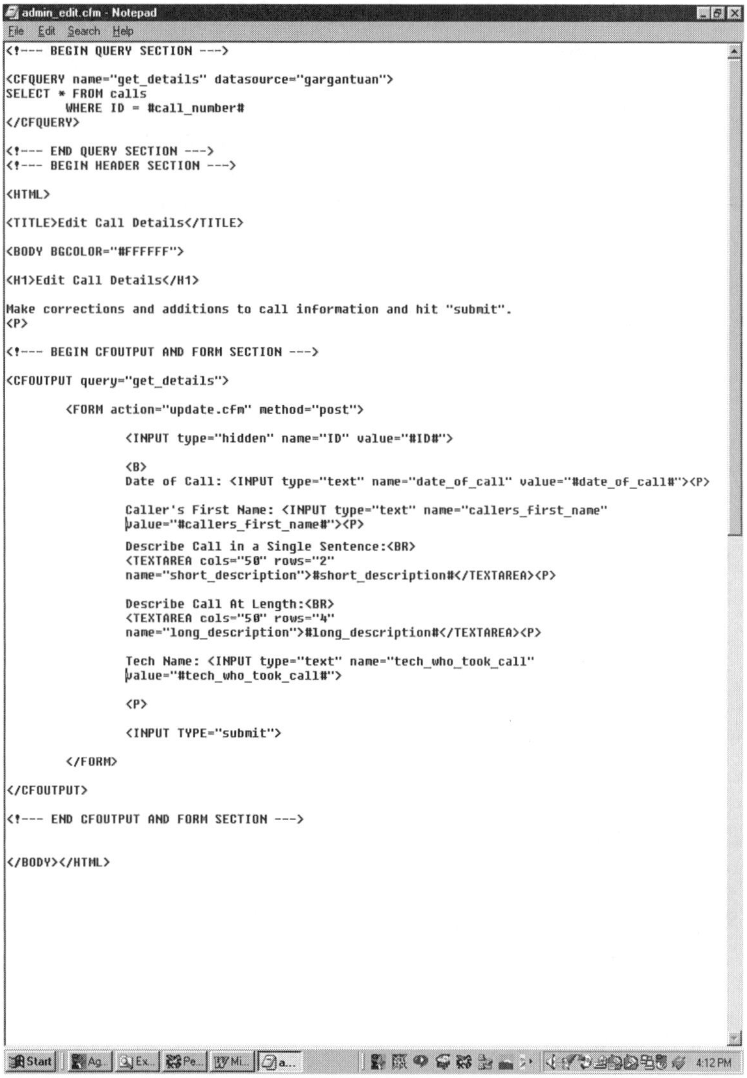

```
admin_edit.cfm - Notepad
File  Edit  Search  Help
<!--- BEGIN QUERY SECTION --->

<CFQUERY name="get_details" datasource="gargantuan">
SELECT * FROM calls
        WHERE ID = #call_number#
</CFQUERY>

<!--- END QUERY SECTION --->
<!--- BEGIN HEADER SECTION --->

<HTML>

<TITLE>Edit Call Details</TITLE>

<BODY BGCOLOR="#FFFFFF">

<H1>Edit Call Details</H1>

Make corrections and additions to call information and hit "submit".
<P>

<!--- BEGIN CFOUTPUT AND FORM SECTION --->

<CFOUTPUT query="get_details">

        <FORM action="update.cfm" method="post">

                <INPUT type="hidden" name="ID" value="#ID#">

                <B>
                Date of Call: <INPUT type="text" name="date_of_call" value="#date_of_call#"><P>

                Caller's First Name: <INPUT type="text" name="callers_first_name"
                value="#callers_first_name#"><P>

                Describe Call in a Single Sentence:<BR>
                <TEXTAREA cols="50" rows="2"
                name="short_description">#short_description#</TEXTAREA><P>

                Describe Call At Length:<BR>
                <TEXTAREA cols="50" rows="4"
                name="long_description">#long_description#</TEXTAREA><P>

                Tech Name: <INPUT type="text" name="tech_who_took_call"
                value="#tech_who_took_call#">

                <P>

                <INPUT TYPE="submit">

        </FORM>

</CFOUTPUT>

<!--- END CFOUTPUT AND FORM SECTION --->

</BODY></HTML>
```

Creating the Update Page

After the administrator makes changes to call details via the form admin_edit.cfm, she'll hit the "submit" button, which will post the edited data to the ACTION page we'll now create, update.cfm.

To create this page, you'll use ColdFusion's <CFUPDATE> tag. <CFUPDATE> *requires* that one of the fields you post to it be the table's primary key, in this case, the ID field. It searches the table for the record matching the specified ID and updates the other fields using the text you supply.

In every other sense, <CFUPDATE> is identical to <CFINSERT>, so we'll cut-and-paste the code from the page cfinsert.cfm. It appears, slightly modified, in Figure 7.14.

FIGURE 7.14

The ACTION *page* update.cfm.

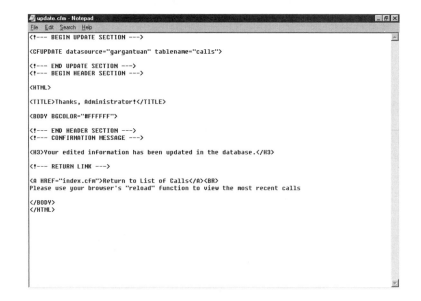

Other than a few changes to the text and changing <CFINSERT> to <CFUPDATE>, this page is just like insert.cfm. The key to making it work actually happened on the form in admin_edit.cfm, where we were careful to include the ID field as hidden input so ColdFusion would know which record to update.

To test your new templates, load admin_list.cfm via your Web server, select a call, and make a change or two to the text. When you submit the form, you will see something like Figure 7.15.

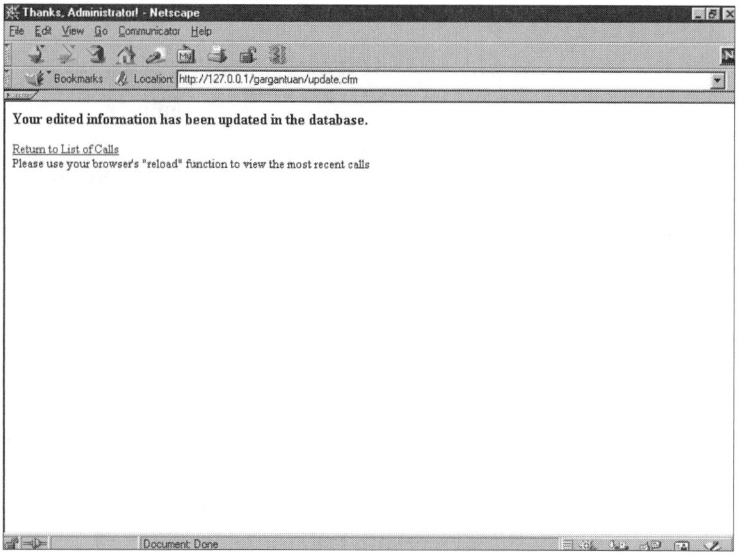

FIGURE 7.15

The confirmation message on update.cfm, *showing that edited text has been updated.*

Troubleshooting Insert and Update Operations

If you don't see the confirmation message for either the insert or update page, check the following:

- Does your datasource point to a database or table that is password protected? If so, you'll need to specify the username and password in the datasource setup to enable ColdFusion to "write" data to your table.

- Do all the field names posted by your form exactly match those in your table? If you've added any form fields for other purposes, ColdFusion might be trying to insert or update those, and won't do so because it can't find a matching field in the table. If this is the problem, specify which forms you want to be updated or inserted by using the `formfields` parameter in your `<CFINSERT>` or `<CFUPDATE>` tag.

- If your database seems to be truncating the text you entered from an input form, check the data type for that field. For example, in Microsoft Access, the text data type allows up to only 256 characters. Longer text strings will require you to change the field's data type to memo.

7

Summary

ColdFusion's interaction with databases goes far beyond simple output. ColdFusion tags like <CFINSERT> and <CFUPDATE> give you the ability to create Web-based forms that can change the contents of your database. In doing so, you can allow yourself, your clients, or your users to make instant changes to stuff that appears on your Web sites.

Most often, these types of changes are made through Web forms built with standard HTML tags like <FORM>. Your forms collect user input and pass it along to ACTION pages—pages that employ ColdFusion to make the necessary changes to your database. You use the <CFINSERT> tag in your ACTION pages when you want to add a new record to a database, or the <CFUPDATE> tag when you want to alter the contents of an existing record.

Q&A

Q What if my site already uses forms that link to CGI scripts? Do I have to replace the scripts with ColdFusion templates?

A Nope. ColdFusion will work just fine with existing CGI scripts, including mail handlers, banner rotators, and so on.

Q How can a ColdFusion page be the ACTION of a form? Don't ACTIONs have to be programs?

A ACTION pages generally have to "do" something, but they don't have to be freestanding programs. In the case of ColdFusion, the template page acts like a script, working in conjunction with the CF server to make things happen.

Q Is there any limit to the length of variables a form will accept? If I type my life story into a <TEXTAREA> input box, will ColdFusion still handle it?

A Variable length is determined by the data types you've set in your database tables. ColdFusion will happily pass your life story to the ODBC datasource, but your data type will need to be set to memo (or your database's equivalent) to handle such a big chunk of text.

Workshop

Just to see if you were dozing through today's lesson, here are a few quiz questions and exercises. Answers to quiz questions can be found in Appendix A at the back of the text.

Quiz

1. What is the primary function of a form page?
2. In the preceding examples, how does data input into a form page get to the action program or page?

3. What's the primary difference between the <CFINSERT> and <CFUPDATE> tags?

4. Do input forms have to be coded as ColdFusion templates (.cfm files)?

5. What is a "hidden" form field used for?

6. Why does the <CFUPDATE> tag have to be supplied with a primary key, or ID field?

Exercises

1. Modify the confirmation page insert.cfm so that it also shows users the data they've just submitted to the database.

2. Design a Web form that will enable the Gargantuan administrator to add employee names to the Techs table.

3. Create a new file called snippets.cfm. Inside it, paste bits of queries or output you think might be useful on other projects. Describe each with "commented" text.

Week 1

In Review

Now that you've finished your first week with ColdFusion, you should know what the program is and some general facts about what it can do. If you're really on the ball, you might have started to envision ways in which ColdFusion applies to your specific projects.

Day 1, "Introducing ColdFusion," introduced you to ColdFusion and presented a short sample application to show one of ColdFusion's most common uses. You learned a bit about the relationship between a client and a server, and how ColdFusion exploits that relationship to work its magic. You now understand how ColdFusion works on the Web, and how it can save developers coding hours by automating common tasks.

Day 2, "Anatomy of a ColdFusion Application," provided an outline of a simple ColdFusion application, showing you how a database is used to serve information on the Web via ODBC. You also learned about templates, the building blocks of all ColdFusion applications. You now understand how a ColdFusion template page communicates with a database, and how it presents output to the user.

Day 3, "Setting Up ColdFusion and Defining a Datasource," gave you hands-on experience with ColdFusion as you learned how to set it up on a server. If you plan to use ColdFusion on a remote Web host rather than your own server, you gained some valuable tips for provider shopping. You also learned a little more about datasources and set up your first DSN by using ColdFusion Administrator. At this point, you either have a working copy of ColdFusion installed on your server, or you have a ColdFusion-ready account with a remote provider.

Day 4, "Building a Database and Organizing Data," provided an introduction to databases and how they work. You learned why it's important to create a map or *schema* before designing a database, and you learned how to create new databases in applications such as Microsoft Access. You now have a better understanding of database technology, and you know how to design a database that is optimized for the ColdFusion applications you'll build later.

Day 5, "Finding the Data You Need: An Introduction to Queries and SQL," gave you an inside view of SQL, or *Structured Query Language*. You learned how SQL is used within ColdFusion to search a database for certain records, and you learned about tools such as SELECT, LIKE, BETWEEN, and IN that help you extract just the data you need. You know now how to use SQL in ColdFusion queries.

Day 6, "Creating Your First Web Application," walked you through the creation of your first ColdFusion Web application. You learned how to build a template that pulls data from a database and displays it to users on a Web page. You now have a feel for the way ColdFusion works with dynamic data.

Day 7, "Changing the Contents of a Database with ColdFusion," introduced you to the <CFUPDATE> and <CFINSERT> tags. You learned how both are used in conjunction with HTML form pages to enable you and your users to change the contents of your database. You can now design a complete Web application that will both accept and serve data via the Web.

WEEK 2

At a Glance

Week 2 takes you beyond the basics by introducing several timesaving tools that can help you get the most out of ColdFusion. These seven lessons will help you better understand how ColdFusion's various features are commonly used in Web applications to automate otherwise tedious tasks. You'll also learn how to build more complex applications that give your users more interactivity with the data you present in your sites. You'll cover the following:

- Day 8, "Understanding ColdFusion Studio," introduces you to Allaire's powerful (but optional) visual development interface, ColdFusion Studio.

- Day 9, "Enhancing Your Applications with Variables and If-Then Statements," shows you how to use variables in your ColdFusion applications, and how to create if-then constructs to control how your applications execute.

- Day 10, "Enhancing Output with Tables and Groups," gives you examples of how to use tables and data grouping to display ColdFusion pages that are well-organized and easy to navigate.

- Day 11, "Enhancing Input Pages with Basic <CFFORM> Tags," discusses ColdFusion's enhanced form capabilities and explains how to use them to collect user input.

- Day 12, "Using Advanced <CFFORM> Techniques to Validate and Display Data," takes the form discussion in Day 11 one step further, showing you how to create pages that will validate user input and give your users access to your site's data, no matter how complex it is.

8

9

10

11

12

13

14

- Day 13, "Using ColdFusion to Handle Email," covers ColdFusion's email functions and how they can be used to integrate mail with your Web pages.
- Day 14, "Using ColdFusion Functions to Manipulate Data," introduces the concept of the ColdFusion *function*, a special programmer's tool that gives you control over the way variables are displayed and processed by your pages.

WEEK 2

DAY 8

Understanding ColdFusion Studio

So far, you've created all your ColdFusion templates using a plain old text editor. Text editors are like the survivalist tools of ColdFusion coding—for what they lack in fancy features, they're always available, they use an interface with which you're already familiar, and they take up a miniscule amount of space on your hard drive. But now that you've grasped the basics of CF coding, it's time to introduce you to a powerful tool that will help you quickly build templates and troubleshoot your code—ColdFusion Studio.

Today, we'll cover

- What is ColdFusion Studio?
- How to install Studio
- The components of the Studio interface
- Configuring Studio
- Studio's help and reference functions

Introducing ColdFusion Studio

Studio is Allaire's companion product to ColdFusion Server. Studio was built around the software company's popular HomeSite HTML editor, and contains all the time-saving functions of that program along with some features unique to building ColdFusion applications.

If you're comfortable coding your CF applications in a standard text editor, you can skip this section. However, every serious ColdFusion developer should at least browse Studio's feature set to learn what the app can do. If you don't have access to a copy of Studio, visit Allaire's Web site at http://www.allaire.com/ to download an evaluation copy.

Studio is such a complex application that it deserves a complete text of its own; in fact, several good guides are available in print and online. New users don't have to worry, though: The Studio interface is designed to get you coding without digesting a manual's worth of instructions.

Today's discussion provides a basic overview of the program, including just enough to get you started. As you begin using the program, you'll naturally find yourself seeking ways to automate this or that process. By browsing Studio's extensive help reference (detailed later today), you'll gradually learn more about the program's more sophisticated functions.

Installing Studio

ColdFusion Studio is strictly a Windows application, compatible only with Windows 95/98 and Windows NT platforms. It requires at least 32MB of RAM, and approximately 17MB of disk space for the full installation. To begin the install, either double-click the evaluation program or insert the distribution CD-ROM.

Note

If you're running ColdFusion *Server* on a platform other than Windows, don't worry. You can still use Studio on a separate Windows machine to connect to and modify your non-Windows datasources.

From there, you are taken through a pretty standard Windows software installation. When possible, choose the default folders for storing program files. It's also a good idea to install all documentation, an option illustrated in Figure 8.1.

FIGURE 8.1

The options menu that appears during a ColdFusion Studio installation.

Following the install, you'll find a program group and startup icon in your Windows Start|Program Files menu.

Studio Components

Open Studio, and let's look at some of the basic components. The initial screen is pictured in Figure 8.2.

editing tools

main toolbar   tag tools

edit window

FIGURE 8.2

The primary components of ColdFusion Studio.

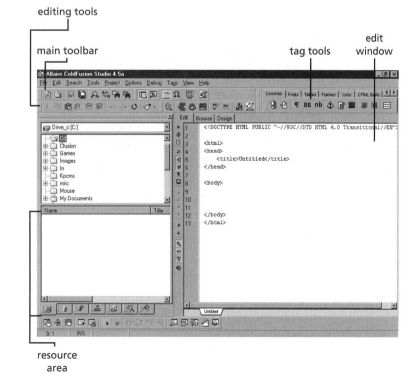

resource area

Editing Components

The most prominent window on the right of the screen is the edit window. This is where your coding happens, and the tools immediately surrounding the window are all designed to aid in the coding process. At the bottom of the edit window, notice the tab (which is labeled "untitled" if you've just opened Studio). If you have several documents open at a time, each is labeled with a tab and an "x" next to the filename if the file has been modified but not yet saved.

Immediately to the left of the edit window is a vertical row of icons that toggle various edit functions such as word wrapping, line numbering, indents, and Studio's various tag-writing aids. The icons in the second horizontal toolbar are also used for editing. Most of these functions are familiar to Windows users: cut, paste, copy, undo, redo, and so on.

> **Tip**
>
> If the meaning of an icon isn't readily apparent to you, use Studio's tooltips feature by holding your mouse pointer over a button or tab. You'll see a short description of that tool's function.

The tabs just above the main edit window contain some of Studio's most useful functions. Each tab contains a row or rows of icons that will insert their related code into your edit windows. The functions behind each tab are described in Table 8.1.

TABLE 8.1   Studio's Edit Tabs

Tab Name	Functions Within
Common	Contains buttons to add basic HTML features such as paragraph markers, line breaks, horizontal lines, alignment, and image sources
Fonts	Includes font-related tags such as style, headers, bold, italic, and size
Tables	Contains Studio's Table Wizard function, as well as manual table tags such as row, data, and size
Frames	Includes the Frame Wizard and tools to set frame type, size, and behavior
Lists	Includes icons for the various HTML list types: ordered list, unordered list, and definition list
CFML Basic	Contains launch icons for building queries, generating output, inserts, updates, includes, and comment tags
CFML Advanced	Includes the not-as-common, advanced ColdFusion functions such as cookies, CFMail, CFPOP, and so on
CFForm	Contains launch icons for building custom forms using CFForm's advanced features

Tip

The edit tabs described in Table 8.1 are those Studio displays by default. To use other tabs that might be useful to your application, right-click over the tabs area to see a complete list.

To use any of the code icons in the edit tabs, either place the cursor in the edit window where you want the code to appear, or highlight a string of existing text and choose a code to associate with it. For example, I typed the words `This Is a Page Header`, selected the text, and then navigated to the Fonts tab to select the H1 icon. Studio automatically generated the necessary header tags around my selected text, as shown in Figure 8.3.

FIGURE 8.3

Studio's edit tabs provide icons that automatically enter HTML or CFML codes into your documents.

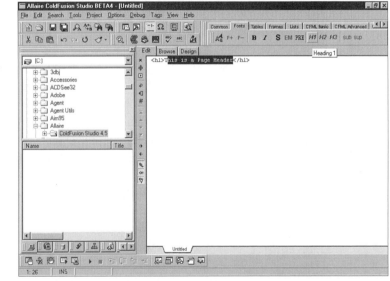

You'll learn more about Studio's editing functions later today.

Resource Components

The two smaller windows to the left of the edit window are called the *resource area*. The uppermost resource window displays a folder navigator that may be set to display either the contents of your hard drive or the datasources you've set up on a local or remote server. As you browse folders or datasources in the upper window, the contents of your selection appear in the lower window.

> **Tip**
>
> To gain screen space in the editing window, the resource area may be toggled on and off by clicking the Resource Tab button on the top toolbar, or by pressing F9.

At the bottom edge of the lower window are *resource tabs*, which select what is displayed in the resource area. Tabs are illustrated with icons, but by holding your mouse over each one you'll see a text description of the tab. A description of each tab's function is shown in Table 8.2.

TABLE 8.2   Studio's Resource Tabs

Tab Name	Purpose
Local Files	When this tab is selected, the resource windows display the contents of your hard drive or your local network. Use this view for opening existing files or projects.
Remote Files	Displays files existing on remote servers. By right-clicking in the upper window, you can add and remove servers you want to display.
Database	Allows access to ColdFusion datasources on either local or remote servers.
Projects	Studio enables you to arrange groups of files or folders into projects for easy access and editing. Those projects are accessed here.
Site View	Presents a graphic representation of hyperlinks, starting with the current document.
Snippets	Provides an interface to organize, store, and retrieve short bits of HTML or CFML code for reuse.
Help	Studio's comprehensive reference section, containing help on both Studio and ColdFusion Server, as well as a complete guide to CFML and HTML tags.
Tag Inspector	Provides a drill-down view of the current page's tags and their attributes.

Accessing Remote Servers

One of Studio's best features lies in the capability to work on remote ColdFusion applications. For example, if you were to sign on a client that needs modifications to a CF app already existing on the client's server, the traditional method requires downloading both the client's database and all the necessary ColdFusion files. You have to define the client's database as a datasource on your local machine, make the necessary modifications to the templates, and then reload everything back to the client's server.

That process is not necessarily required with Studio. The remote access feature enables you to connect to datasources and files anywhere on local or remote networks and, in most cases, to make changes directly to the active files as you edit them in Studio.

Defining a Local or Remote Server

When you begin working with a project in Studio, the first step is to connect with the project's associated server. Depending on the way you use ColdFusion, that server might be either part of your local network or another machine somewhere on the Net. Either way, the process is similar.

Start by selecting the Remote Files tab at the base of the resource area. In the uppermost resource window, you'll see a list of defined servers. To add a new server, right-click in the window and choose one of the following types of servers.

Add RDS Server

RDS, or *Remote Development Services*, are used to connect to remote servers running ColdFusion. When the link is active, you have access to all datasources defined on that server, as well as the entire file system of templates and HTML documents.

The dialog to add an RDS server appears in Figure 8.4.

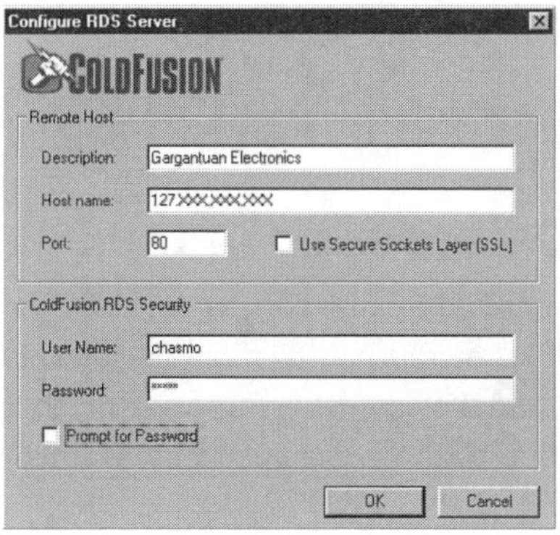

FIGURE 8.4
To add an RDS server, you'll need to supply a hostname, username, and password.

> **Caution**
>
> Some server configurations don't support connections via RDS. For example, if you maintain a site with a Web host that services many users with a single copy of ColdFusion, RDS won't work. In cases like those, you can still access template files remotely via FTP, but you have to maintain a copy of your database on a local machine for testing.

If you're defining a local server, use the special 127.0.0.1 IP address (which uniquely identifies the computer you're working on), and supply the password you use to log in to ColdFusion Administrator. Unless your server uses a custom port number, the default "80" will work fine.

Add FTP Server

If a remote server doesn't support RDS or is not running ColdFusion Server, you can still use the FTP standard to work on remote files. This method doesn't support viewing remote datasources, but it enables you to modify documents right on the server.

To add an FTP server, you need to provide the same kind of information you would supply to an external FTP program. The dialog looks like Figure 8.5.

FIGURE 8.5

Connecting to a remote server via FTP.

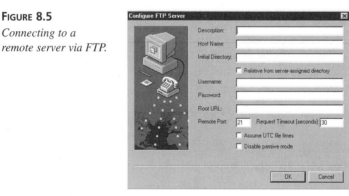

Viewing Files or Datasources in the Resources Area

After you've successfully connected to a remote server, you have access to template files just as if they were on your local hard drive. To view the contents of remote folders, select the Remote Files tab and expand the contents of a server by clicking on the plus sign (+) next to the server name. In Figure 8.6, I've connected to Gargantuan Electronics' server.

Clicking a file in the lower-left window loads it in Studio's editor, just as if the file resided on your local hard drive. When you edit the page and choose File|Save, Studio connects to the remote server and overwrites the old file with your more recent, edited version.

To view the contents of a datasource, choose the Database tab at the base of the resource area. You'll see a list of available servers in the uppermost window. You should see your local server listed, as well as any remote machines you have defined.

In the pane just below the server window, you'll see a list of datasources currently active on the server you selected.

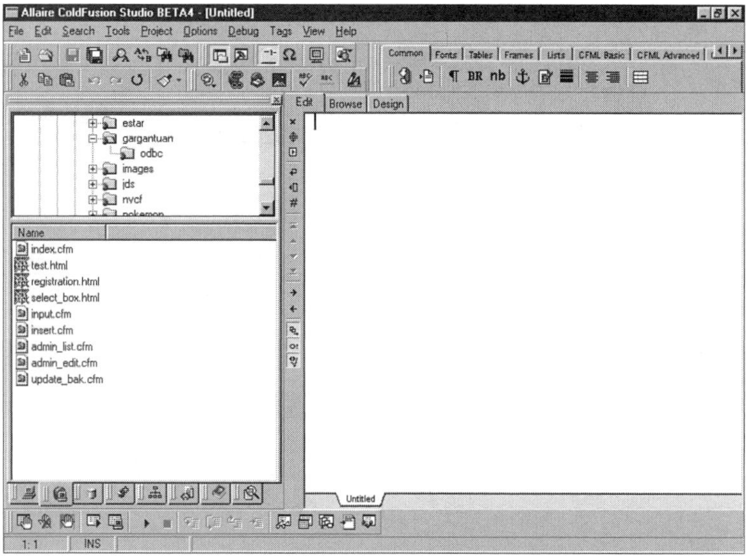

FIGURE 8.6

Viewing the files on a remote server. The folder structure is shown in the top resources window; files are displayed below.

8

Tip

Viewing the contents of a datasource can come in handy when you're creating template files and need to recall the exact name of a field in your database. By using Studio's Database resource, you can open your datasource and get a list of all tables and fields within.

Expand a datasource by clicking the plus sign (+) next to it, and you'll see a list of tables in the datasource; expand a table, and you'll find a list of fields, along with a description of their datatypes. Figure 8.7 shows an expanded view of the gargantuan datasource used in Days 6, "Creating Your First Web Application," and 7, "Changing the Contents of a Database with ColdFusion."

Tip

Studio enables you to drag and drop table and field names from the resource area and to make them appear as text in the edit window. This is a great feature if you're dealing with long names and need to get the spelling just right.

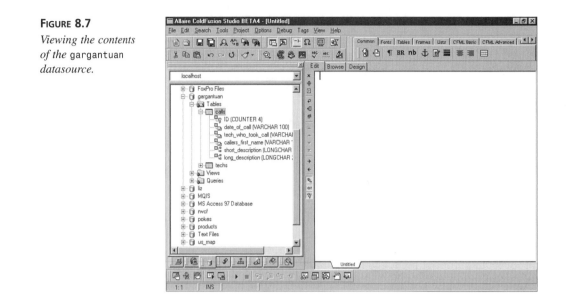

FIGURE 8.7

Viewing the contents of the gargantuan *datasource.*

Working with the Editor

To load an existing file into Studio's edit area, choose either the Local Files or Remote Files resource tab and navigate to the file you want to open. To create a new file, simply start typing in the blank template Studio provides by default.

When you load or create an html or .cfm document, Studio automatically color-codes the text within that document. Each tag type has an associated color, whereas text appears in black. This makes it easy to identify opening and closing tags, and it's an excellent tool for catching coding errors. Figure 8.8 shows a sample template with color-coding.

Studio's developers took great pains to streamline the editing interface for easy access. For this reason, some of the editor's most powerful features lie hidden behind the right mouse button. The right button is context sensitive, meaning that you get a different dialog depending on where you click.

For example, when I place the mouse cursor inside a form input tag and right-click, I get a dialog like Figure 8.9.

FIGURE 8.8

Studio color-codes documents to help developers distinguish tags from text.

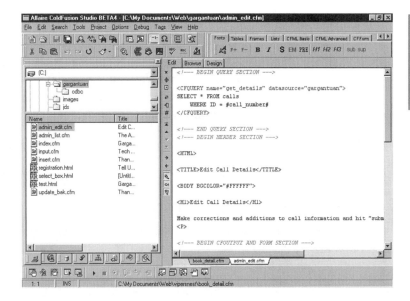

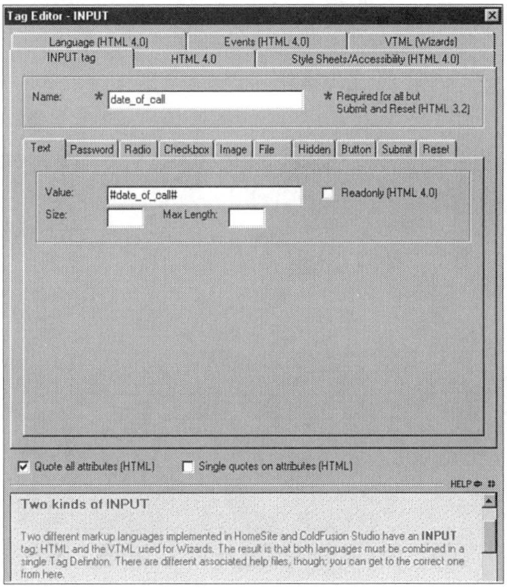

FIGURE 8.9

Right-clicking over an input tag brings up an expanded dialog of input options.

Studio's editor has three viewing modes, which are selected by the three tabs immediately above the main edit window. These viewing modes are explained in detail in the following sections.

Edit View

Edit view displays a page as source, showing the complete text as well as HTML and CFML tags. Many designers prefer this view because it allows the greatest degree of control over page formatting and ColdFusion query and output. When in Edit view, choosing any of the tag icons in the edit tab bar either inserts a tagset at the cursor or, if text is selected, brackets the text with the appropriate tag.

Browse View

After opening or creating a document, you can use the Browse view to preview the code that will appear in a browser window. By default, only HTML code can be previewed this way because CFML tags must be processed via the Web server.

However, the latest versions of Studio offer a great feature called *development mapping* in which you can tell Studio the related URL of your Web server and, thus, preview even .cfm pages with the browse function.

To define your server's location, click the Development Mappings icon on Studio's lowermost toolbar. Studio requires two things to define a mapping: the location of the folder in which your template files are stored and the URL to access that folder as it would appear in a browser. In Figure 8.10, I've defined a mapping for the gargantuan project developed in Days 6 and 7.

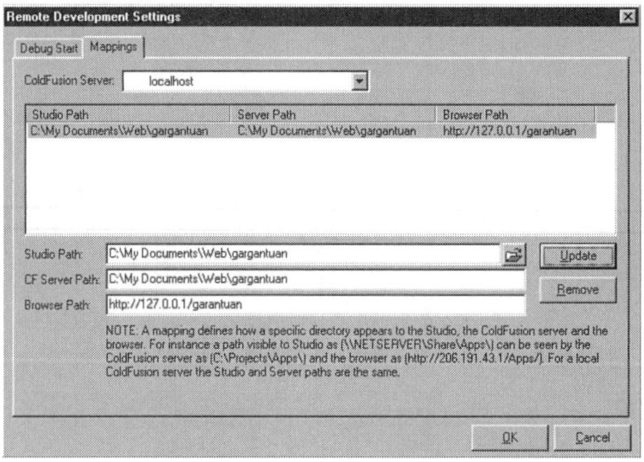

FIGURE 8.10

Defining a development mapping enables you to preview ColdFusion templates in Studio's browse view mode.

Design View

Another new function in Studio, Design view presents your page in a graphic interface that will be familiar to those who've developed sites with tools such as Microsoft FrontPage and Adobe PageMill.

Caution | Design view requires that you've installed Microsoft Internet Explorer version 4.01 or later.

8

Tip | Design view is a great way to block out the look of a page by inserting graphics and text in their approximate locations. After you've placed the basic elements, you can switch to the more sophisticated Edit view to fine-tune your code.

Studio's Helping Hand

As part of its sophisticated editing functions, Studio provides several shortcuts that help even veteran developers save time. The edit interface includes several wizards and tag functions that guide you through setting tag parameters and inserting the generated code into your document.

Tag Tools

Studio provides three features that help you set tag parameters. All three are toggled on and off by their respective buttons on the vertical bar immediately to the left of the edit window.

Tag Insight

In a new document, manually type a <BODY> tag. But before adding the final bracket (>), pause for a moment. That pause activates Studio's Tag Insight feature, which presents a drop-down box of valid parameters for the tag, as shown in Figure 8.11.

When you choose one of these parameters, Studio automatically adds the relevant text (such as bgcolor in the <BODY> example) and then, if applicable, provides another drop-down box with values for that parameter.

Tag Completion

When you click a tag icon in the edit tabs or manually type a tag into the edit window, ColdFusion automatically follows it with its related closing tag. When it does, your cursor remains between the opening and closing tags, allowing you to type text within.

In Figure 8.12, note the position of the cursor. I typed the <STRONG> tag, and Studio completed it by adding the related </STRONG> tag.

Figure 8.11

Studio's Tag Insight function provides a list of valid parameters associated with a selected tag.

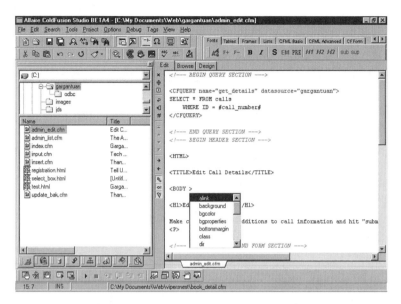

Figure 8.12

Studio's Tag Completion function provides the associated closing tag for each opening tag you type.

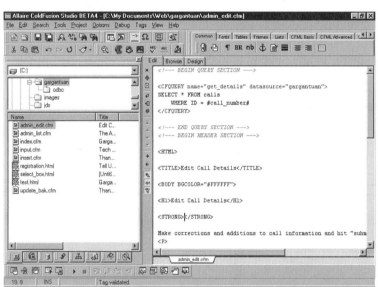

Tag Validation

Studio's Tag Validation feature "watches" your tags as you type them in, and reports any possible problems in the status bar at the bottom of the screen. For example, if I mistype the <STRONG> tag as <STORNG>, Studio catches this error, triggers a system alert sound, and reports the error in red, as shown at the bottom of Figure 8.13.

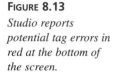

FIGURE 8.13

Studio reports potential tag errors in red at the bottom of the screen.

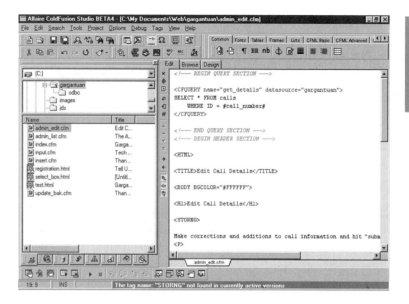

The Table Wizard

The Table Wizard provides a graphic interface to help you visualize the layout of an HTML table. From your specifications, the wizard generates the necessary HTML code and inserts it into your document.

To access the Table Wizard, choose the Tables tab above the edit window and select the related icon. You'll see a dialog box similar to Figure 8.14.

FIGURE 8.14

Studio's Table Wizard enables you to define HTML tables in a graphic interface.

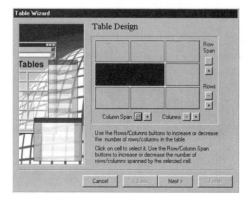

By selecting rows or cells and using the + (plus sign) and - (minus sign) buttons, you can easily create complex tables in which rows span multiple columns, and vice versa. After defining a basic layout, click the Next button and you will see a properties dialog like Figure 8.15.

FIGURE 8.15

Setting table properties in Studio's Table Wizard.

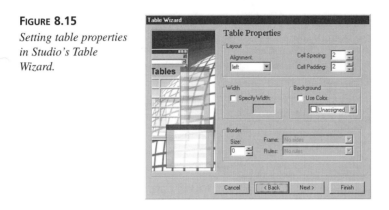

This dialog enables you to edit table parameters such as width, alignment, and background color. Clicking Next again produces a third dialog box that defines the properties of individual cells. Finally, the Finish button inserts the HTML code for our defined table into the document, as shown in Figure 8.16.

FIGURE 8.16

Using parameters we supplied in the Table Wizard, Studio creates the necessary code automatically.

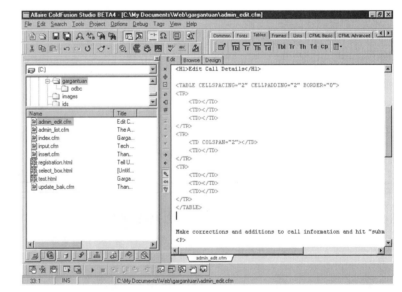

The Frame Wizard

The Frame Wizard interface is similar to the one used by the Table Wizard. It displays a graphic representation of a browser screen and enables you to define the number and properties of frames that appear within. Using your specified parameters, Studio generates the code for a frameset page and the related pages that make up the frame content.

To access the Frame Wizard, select the Frames edit tab above the main edit window and choose the Frame Wizard icon. You'll see a dialog similar to the one in Figure 8.17.

FIGURE 8.17

Building a frameset with Studio's Frame Wizard.

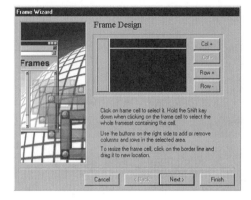

After you've blocked out the look of a frame page, clicking the Next button produces a properties dialog like the one shown in Figure 8.18. In this dialog, you can give each frame a name and define parameters such as margins, scrolling, and so on. Use the "source URL" field to define the name of the entire frameset, such as my_frames_page .html.

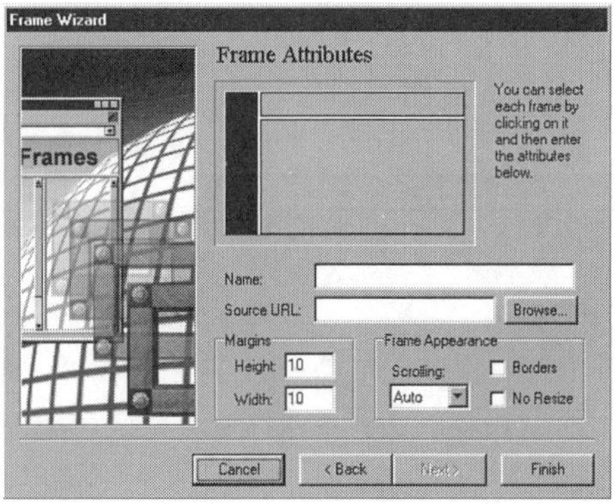

FIGURE 8.18

Defining frame properties with Studio's Frame Wizard.

Finally, clicking the Finish button inserts the appropriate code to generate the frameset.

The SQL Builder

Studio's SQL builder enables you to create complex queries by navigating a drag-and-drop interface. When you create a new query, Studio connects to the relevant datasource and shows the fieldnames and content for the table you select. By dragging and dropping fieldnames into the SQL builder, you can see exactly which fields and what type of data the query will produce.

To create a new query, select the CFML Basic tab above the edit window and choose the CFQUERY icon. Studio presents a dialog window in which you can name the query, specify the datasource, and manually edit other query parameters, if necessary. The dialog appears in Figure 8.19.

FIGURE 8.19

Creating a new query in Studio.

After defining query basics, you can either supply a manual SQL statement by simply typing it into the box provided, or you can choose the icon next to the box to launch the visual SQL builder.

When you launch the builder, Studio enables you to navigate to a datasource and select a table to use with your SQL statement, as shown in Figure 8.20.

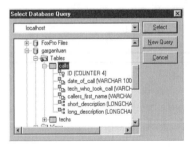

After selecting the table you want to query, click the New Query button and Studio launches its drag-and-drop SQL interface. If you've used SQL builders in programs such as Microsoft Access, this interface will be familiar to you. The main builder screen is shown in Figure 8.21.

FIGURE 8.21

The SQL builder automatically creates a text SQL statement as you navigate its graphic interface.

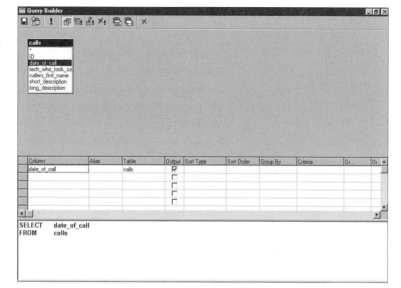

In Figure 8.21, the uppermost window displays the names of the fields in the selected table. By dragging each of these names into the Column box, you can specify which fields your query should select. The boxes to the right of Column are used to define further selection criteria (such as WHERE statements) or to order or sort records returned by the query.

As you drag and drop fieldnames and change criteria, the related SQL statement appears as text at the bottom of the screen. When your query is complete, click the Close button and supply a name. Studio inserts the generated text into your current document.

Configuring Studio for Your Work

Depending on how you use ColdFusion, some of the advanced features might either help or hinder your coding. For example, the Tag Completion function is excellent for creating a new Web page, but it might add unnecessary closing tags if you're editing an existing document. Tag Completion and other automatic functions are toggled on and off via the vertical toolbar left of the editor.

Other configuration options are available by choosing Options|Settings. Setting categories are described in Table 8.3.

TABLE 8.3   Studio's Configuration Settings

Setting Category	Function
General	Enables you to set the position and style of resource tabs; controls program warnings, long filename usage, and splash screens
HTML	Sets preferences for tags, including lowercase or uppercase tag text, hex code for colors, and whether to provide the closing </P> tag on paragraphs
Startup	Defines which windows are opened by default when Studio is launched
Locations	If you didn't use the default directories when installing Studio, you can point it to the help libraries here; also defines the location of saved code snippets and the default template file
File Settings	Defines recognized file extensions for text and graphics
Editor	Configures settings for tag-help functions, color-coding, and default templates
Browse	Defines the default internal browser and server mappings
Design	Sets attributes for Design view function
Validation	Sets the tag validator function to compare your tags with established standards such as HTML 2, 3, or 4, as well as Netscape and Internet Explorer extensions
Spelling	Enables you to use either MS Word's spelling module (if present) or an external spellcheck program
Dreamweaver	Enables integration with Macromedia Dreamweaver
Codesweeper	Setting for Studio's Codesweeper function
Projects	Defines file types to be included in Studio projects
Tag Definitions Library	Some markup languages use identical tags; this tab enables you to set the order in which Studio searches languages to obtain tag definitions

> **Tip**
>
> To quickly access Studio's configuration utility from the keyboard, press F8.

Studio's Help and Reference Functions

As previously mentioned, today's discussion provides only a basic overview of ColdFusion Studio. Fortunately, the application provides a very comprehensive, searchable help reference that details not only the Studio interface, but also ColdFusion Server, the CFML tagset, and HTML functions.

8

To access the reference section, choose the Help icon in the resource tabs near the bottom left of the screen. Studio presents an expandable help index in the left window.

To search the index for a keyword or words, click the Search icon (illustrated with a pair of binoculars) in the upper part of the resource window. Studio provides a search box where you can enter keywords to help you find a suitable help topic.

Tip

> When searching for a common term such as *form* or *input*, use the search dialog's checkboxes to narrow the categories searched.

Summary

ColdFusion Studio is Allaire's companion product to CF Server. It provides a semi-graphic interface for creating template files, as well as several automatic features to aid in the coding process. If you don't already have access to a copy of Studio, you can visit Allaire's Web site to obtain an evaluation copy.

One of the application's biggest values lies in its capability to work with remote files and datasources. Remote and local servers must be defined in Studio's resources area prior to accessing their contents.

Studio also provides a very powerful editor based on Allaire's HomeSite HTML editor. In it, all HTML and CFML tags are color-coded for easy viewing, and any tag can be inserted into a document at the push of a button. The editor provides a multiple document interface that makes it easy to open and edit an entire project's worth of files.

Q&A

Q Is the Studio evaluation copy limited in any way?

A Only in duration. The evaluation copy expires after 30 days.

Q I already own Allaire's HomeSite editor. Is it compatible with ColdFusion?

A Yes, but it doesn't include the ColdFusion-specific functions present in Studio.

Q I use Netscape or browser *X* to preview my files. Can I configure Studio to launch it by default?

A Yes. Choose Options|Settings|Browse and supply the path to your browser.

Workshop

Answers to the quiz and exercise questions can be found in Appendix A at the back of the text.

Quiz

1. Where are Studio's resource tabs located by default?
2. Before accessing remote files or datasources, what must you do first?
3. How do you access Studio's Tag Insight function?
4. How do you launch the Table Wizard or Frame Wizard?
5. What does the SQL builder do?
6. How do you toggle the resource area on and off?
7. What must you first do to preview ColdFusion templates in the editor's Browse view?

Exercises

1. If you don't already have access to a copy of Studio, download the evaluation version from Allaire's Web site.
2. Define your local server in the resources area, or connect to a remote server and verify your connection by browsing the remote datasource and template files.
3. Create one of the sample template files from Day 7 using Studio. Use the SQL builder to create the necessary query.
4. Define a project using the Projects tab in the resource area. If you have more than one CF project on your system, define each of them.
5. Browse Studio's help references. Try a search for a keyword that interests you.

DAY **9**

Enhancing Your Applications with Variables and If-Then Statements

In Days 6 and 7, you created a dynamic Web application capable of both input and output. In doing so, you made extensive use of variables—you used query variables to create output and form variables to pass data from one template to another. Today's lesson will introduce you to two powerful tags that use variables to control when and how data is processed.

This chapter covers

- Using the `<CFIF>` tag with variables
- Creating basic password protection with `<CFIF>`
- Creating and defining ColdFusion variables
- Using variables to create a simple counting mechanism

Defining a Sample Application

Gargantuan Electronics is on the phone again, and their rep can't say enough about the great work you did for them in Days 6 and 7. Gargantuan's tech support department now has a working ColdFusion application that lets employees log the weirdest tech support calls they receive each day. They can now input information from a simple Web form, and the rep says that her employees have taken to this method like cats to a wiggly string.

She says there's one small problem though, and she needs you to provide a solution. You inform her that "Solution" was, in fact, your middle name until you had it legally changed last year to avoid an unfair advantage over your competitors.

The problem is that the easy-access method you created has unwittingly led to the inevitable inter-office pranks. Some techs have been logging phony calls into the database and attributing the bogus records to other employees. She says that a recent entry showed that "Joey" received a call from the "U.S. Surgeon General," asking whether second-hand cigarette smoke would harm his Gargantuan CD-ROM drive. Joey swears he had nothing to do with the entry.

She'd like you to design a simple password-protection method for her application's input page. Each tech will be assigned a password that will be required before the database accepts any entries to the database. She says she doesn't need 128-bit PGP encryption or any extreme security measures, just a simple method to keep her techs on the up-and-up.

She also mentions that she's hosting a contest for the Gargantuan tech department in which participating employees who log the greatest number of goofy tech calls over a period will receive some sort of prize, like maybe an industrial-sized bottle of aspirin. She'd like you to create a method of counting each employee's future submissions to the database, and to give employees the option to participate or not.

You assure her that you've built hundreds of password-protected applications, and that this one will be a breeze. After hanging up, you frantically search this book's index for the word "password" and set to work.

Introducing the `<CFIF>` Tag

To add password protection to Gargantuan's application, you'll use a powerful ColdFusion tag called `<CFIF>`. `<CFIF>` is used in conjunction with variables to set up a *conditional* statement in a template. Essentially, it tells ColdFusion, "If *this* is true, then do *that*," leaving it up to you, the developer, to define just what "this" and "that" are.

NEW TERM *Conditional* statements are used to control ColdFusion processes by stating that before action A can take place, condition B must be satisfied.

First, let's look at a simple if-then construct using <CFIF>. I've designed a basic form that asks a question. The user answers my question by clicking either the True or False link, as shown in Figure 9.1.

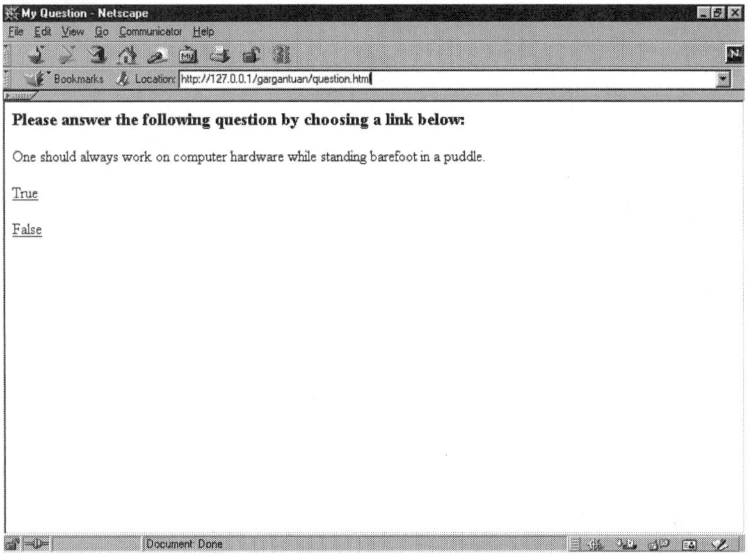

FIGURE 9.1

My sample question page.

Just a simple question—in fact, I didn't even use a ColdFusion template to create it, just standard HTML. The code is shown in Listing 9.1.

LISTING 9.1 question.html

```
 1: <HTML>
 2:
 3: <TITLE>My Question</TITLE>
 4:
 5: <H3>Please answer the following question by choosing a link below:</H3>
 6:
 7: One should always work on computer hardware while
    ➥standing barefoot in a puddle.<P>
 8:
 9: <A HREF="answer.cfm?reply=true">True</A><P>
10: <A HREF="answer.cfm?reply=false">False</A><P>
11:
12: </HTML>
```

Note that the `true` and `false` links in lines 9 and 10 both point to the same template page, `answer.cfm`. In the links, I've also defined the variable `reply` and set it to `True` for the `true` link, and `False` for the `false` link.

The idea is that, instead of creating two pages, one to handle each possible answer, I'll use a single ColdFusion template, and create an if-then construct to handle either reply. The code for my answer page appears in Listing 9.2.

LISTING 9.2   `answer.cfm`

```
 1: <HTML>
 2:
 3: <CFOUTPUT>
 4:
 5: <TITLE>Your answer was: #reply#</TITLE>
 6:
 7: </CFOUTPUT>
 8:
 9: <CFIF reply IS 'true'>
10:
11:      Ummmmm....no. You really should go back and
         ➥read those operator manuals again.
12:
13: </CFIF>
14:
15: <CFIF reply is 'false'>
16:
17:      You are correct. You have successfully completed your
         ➥electronics-licensing test and should receive your
         ➥license in 4-6 weeks.
18:
19: </CFIF>
20:
21: </HTML>
```

This template page does three things. First, it uses a `<CFOUTPUT>` tag on line 3, before the `<TITLE>` bar, so that I can display the value of the variable posted by the question page. Second, it uses `<CFIF>` on line 9 with a qualifying statement that determines whether the variable `reply` matches the text `'true'`. If so, the template displays the text between that first `<CFIF>` tag on line 9 and the next `</CFIF>` on line 13.

If the statement doesn't match, it ignores the first text and moves on to the second `<CFIF>` tag on line 15. If the variable reply matches `'false'`, the template displays the text enclosed in the `<CFIF>` tags at lines 15 and 19.

Note also that I didn't use hash marks around the `reply` variable in the IF statements on lines 9 and 15. `<CFIF>` will automatically recognize "reply" as a variable and act accordingly. Also notice that I used single quotes around the variable values to denote that it is text to be interpreted literally.

Note When you use <CFIF>, ColdFusion automatically assumes that you're going to follow it with a variable match or other conditional statement.

The results of this template appear in Figures 9.2 and 9.3.

FIGURE 9.2

The template page answer.cfm when reply is 'false'.

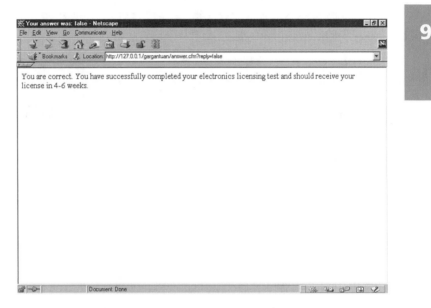

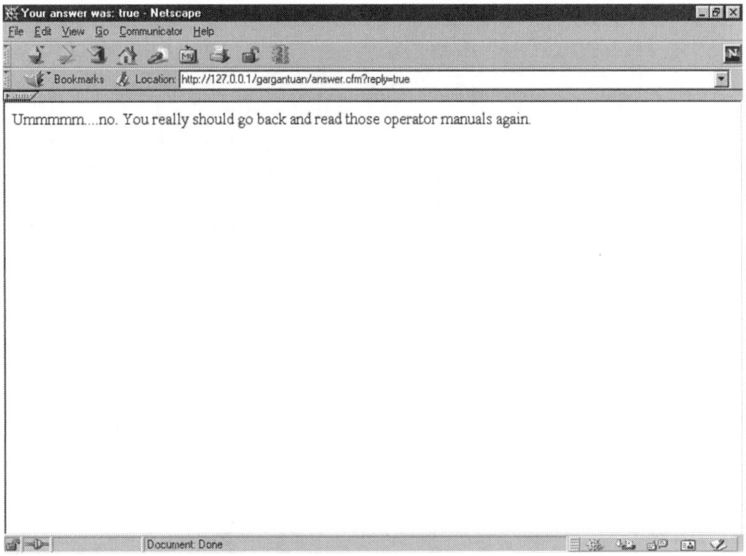

FIGURE 9.3

The template page answer.cfm when reply is 'true'.

The <CFELSE> Tag

The <CFIF> tag is often used in conjunction with a second tag, <CFELSE>. Just like it sounds, <CFELSE> is used to say, "If something else, then…" Recall that <CFIF> says, "If *this* is true, do *that*" and by following it with <CFELSE>, you tell ColdFusion, "If it wasn't true, do *this* instead."

To illustrate the use of <CFELSE>, I've modified my question page to include a third answer "I Don't Know" as shown in Figure 9.4.

FIGURE 9.4

My question page, new and improved with three possible answers.

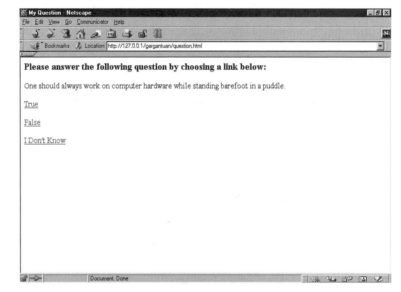

To create the third choice, I added the following text to the original question page:

```
<A HREF="answer.cfm?reply=dont_know">I Don't Know</A><P>
```

It's just another link, this time with the variable `reply` set to `dont_know`. Note that I omitted the apostrophe because ColdFusion might interpret it as a single quote mark when it is passed to the answer page. I also replaced the space with the underscore character.

> **Tip**
>
> ColdFusion has a few tools that will handle characters such as apostrophes when they appear in variables—some of these are discussed later in this chapter. However, as a time-saving measure, it's easiest to avoid these characters whenever possible.

With my new question page, I have three possible outcomes for my answer page to process, True, False, or I Don't Know. I can create three separate `<CFIF>` statements, but there's an easier way.

The gist of my question is "True or False: One should always work on computer hardware while standing barefoot in a puddle?" Obviously, False is the answer we're looking for, but if someone clicks either True or I Don't Know, there's a serious and equal cause for alarm. I can use the same response for either a True or I Don't Know answer—essentially that the user is a danger to him or herself and others and should seek help.

I'll use `<CFELSE>` to say in essence, "If the answer is anything but false, do this." Listing 9.3 shows how this appears in my template `answer.cfm`.

LISTING 9.3   The Modified Output Section of `answer.cfm`

```
 1: <HTML>
 2:
 3: <CFOUTPUT>
 4:
 5: <TITLE>Your answer was: #reply#</TITLE>
 6:
 7: </CFOUTPUT>
 8:
 9: <CFIF reply is 'false'>
10:
11:     You are correct. You have successfully completed
        ➥your electronics licensing test and should
        ➥receive your license in 4-6 weeks.
12:
13: <CFELSE>
14:
15:     Please step away from your computer immediately.
        ➥Your answer suggests that you need adult supervision
        ➥while working with electronics.
16:
17: </CFIF>
18:
19: </HTML>
```

Note   `<CFELSE>` is *part of* a `<CFIF>` construct, that is, it always appears within `<CFIF>` and `</CFIF>` tags and never alone.

The code in Listing 9.3 matches the value of the `reply` variable with the word `'false'`. If the match proves true, it returns the text that appears before the `<CFELSE>` tag. If the answer is anything other than the word `'false'`, the template outputs the second text string instead. In this way, I've handled three possible answers with just one `<CFIF>` statement.

Creating an Application with `<CFIF>`

Now let's return to Gargantuan's project. Gargantuan wants its tech employees to supply a password with each entry they input, and you can probably already see where `<CFIF>` is going to come in handy.

You envision that the best place to insert the password protection is in the input template you built in Day 7, "Changing the Contents of a Database with ColdFusion." In this way, when the employee wants to add the details of a goofy tech-support call, she must also supply a password associated with her username. When the form is posted, ColdFusion will evaluate the password to see whether it matches the one supplied to the employee. If the match is successful, the database will be updated with the call description the user supplied. If not, ColdFusion will return an error message.

First you'll need to add some passwords to the database. Recall from Day 6, "Creating Your First Web Application," that the names of all employees are listed in the `"techs"` table of Gargantuan's database.

> **Tip**
>
> If you maintain a duplicate copy of a database on your local server, always be careful not to overwrite the client's existing database with an older version.

Open the table and add the new field `password`, as I've done in Figure 9.5.

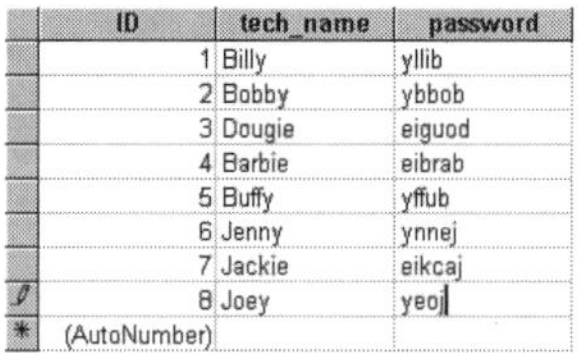

FIGURE 9.5

The modified `"techs"` table in the database `calls.mdb`.

ID	tech_name	password
1	Billy	yllib
2	Bobby	ybbob
3	Dougie	eiguod
4	Barbie	eibrab
5	Buffy	yffub
6	Jenny	ynnej
7	Jackie	eikcaj
8	Joey	yeoj
(AutoNumber)		

Just for testing purposes, I've supplied each employee name with a password. I just spelled their names backwards—hardly the height of security, but the Gargantuan rep can always change these later.

The Password-Check Page

To create the password page, start by opening the input form you created in Day 7 and making a few additions to create the password entry field. My modified page reads like Listing 9.4.

> **Tip**
>
> If you read the introduction to ColdFusion Studio in Day 8, "Understanding ColdFusion Studio," use Studio to complete the exercises in this chapter. If you don't have access to a copy of Studio, you can still use a standard text editor.

9

LISTING 9.4   A Modified `tech_calls.cfm`

```
 1: <!--- BEGIN QUERY SECTION --->
 2:
 3: <CFQUERY name="get_techs" datasource="gargantuan">
 4:     SELECT * from techs
 5: </CFQUERY>
 6:
 7: <!--- END QUERY SECTION --->
 8: <!--- BEGIN HEADER SECTION --->
 9:
10: <HTML>
11:
12: <BODY BGCOLOR="#FFFFFF">
13:
14: <TITLE>Tech Call Input Form</TITLE>
15:
16: <H1>Tech Call Input Form</H1>
17:
18: This is the page for tech-support employees to log their weirdest support
    ➥calls of the day. Please complete all fields before submitting. <P>
19:
20: <!--- END HEADER SECTION --->
21: <!--- BEGIN FORM SECTION --->
22:
23: <FORM action="insert.cfm" method="post">
24:
25:     <B>
26:     Date of Call: <INPUT type="text" name="date_of_call"><P>
27:
28:     Caller's First Name: <INPUT type="text" name="callers_first_name"><P>
29:
30:     Describe Call in a Single Sentence:<BR>
31:     <TEXTAREA cols="50" rows="2" name="short_description"></TEXTAREA><P>
32:
33:     Describe Call At Length:<BR>
34:     <TEXTAREA cols="50" rows="4" name="long_description"></TEXTAREA><P>
```

continues

LISTING 9.4   continued

```
35:
36:     Your Name: <SELECT name="tech_who_took_call">
37:
38:         <CFOUTPUT query="get_techs">
39:
40:             <OPTION>#tech_name#</OPTION>
41:
42:         </CFOUTPUT>
43:
44:     </SELECT><P>
45:
46:     Your Password: <INPUT type="password" name="password"><P>
47:
48:     <INPUT TYPE="submit">
49:
50: </FORM>
51:
52: <!--- END FORM SECTION --->
53: <!--- BEGIN FOOTER SECTION--->
54:
55: <P>
56:
57: <HR>
58:
59: <A HREF="index.cfm">Return to List of Calls</A>
60:
61: </BODY>
62: </HTML>
```

For the "password" form box in Listing 9.4, I used the input type `"password"` instead of `"text"`.

Note   When a user types in a password box, he sees only asterisks, regardless of the characters he enters. This feature helps guard against wily shoulder surfers.

When viewed in a browser, the input form now looks like Figure 9.6.

When this form is submitted by a user, it will pass an additional field, `password` on to the action page `insert.cfm`.

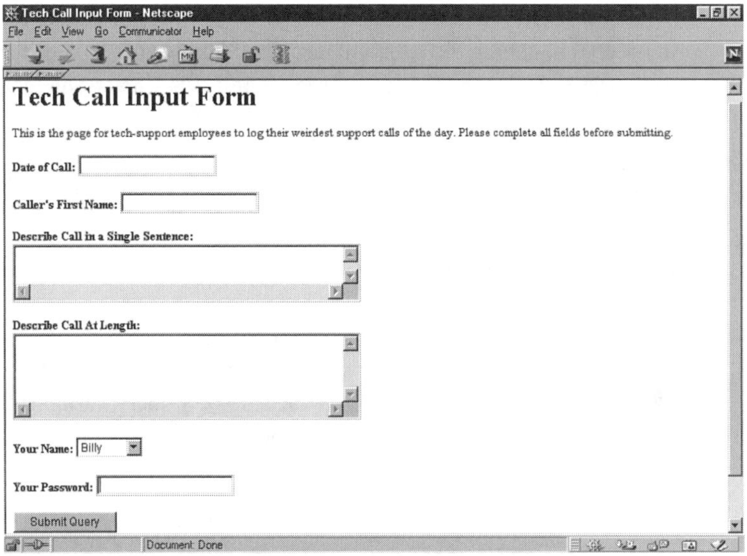

FIGURE 9.6

The modified input page now prompts for a password.

The Insert Page

You'll need to add a couple of new functions to the insert page. You'll first have to query the "techs" table to get the password that matches the user's name, and then compare that with the text the user typed into the form. If the match is true, then you can continue with the update process. If not, you need to provide a grave error message.

The Query

Start by opening insert.cfm in the gargantuan folder. You'll first need a query that will take the name passed in the variable #tech_who_took_call# and find the related password for that employee. My query looks like Listing 9.5.

LISTING 9.5 The Query Section for insert.cfm

```
1: <!--- BEGIN QUERY SECTION --->
2:
3: <CFQUERY name="get_pass" datasource="gargantuan">
4:     SELECT password FROM techs
5: WHERE tech_name = '#tech_who_took_call#'
6: </CFQUERY>
7:
8: <!--- END QUERY SECTION --->
```

This query will select only one piece of data—the contents of the password field in the record matching the user's name. That data is now stored in the query variable #password# and is available for processing further down the template page.

But wait—there's one problem. The input form has also passed a variable named #password# from the information supplied by the user. Now you have *two* variables with the same name working in this template—how do you distinguish between them?

Using Variable Scopes

You distinguish between the two variables by *scoping* the variable.

NEW TERM A variable *scope* is a prefix attached to the variable name that identifies the type of variable, such as a form variable or a query variable. To scope a variable, you supply a prefix before the variable name followed by a period, such as form.username or some_query.address.

For example, one of your password variables was derived from the new query titled "get_pass" so the scoped variable name will be get_pass.password. Similarly, variables that are sent to a template from a form use the "form" scope, so the passed variable can also be referred to as form.password.

Note Scopes are useful for the coder (and ColdFusion) to keep track of variables, particularly on templates where you may need to compare two variables with the same name such as form.password and get_pass.password. As you'll learn in later lessons, variable scopes can also be used to define special variables such as application, session, and client variables.

The <CFIF> Statement

I used variable scopes to identify the two password variables in my <CFIF> statement. The complete code for insert.cfm appears in Listing 9.6.

LISTING 9.6 insert.cfm

```
1: <!--- BEGIN QUERY SECTION --->
2:
3: <CFQUERY name="get_pass" datasource="gargantuan">
4:    SELECT password FROM techs
5: WHERE tech_name = '#tech_who_took_call#'
6: </CFQUERY>
```

```
 7:
 8: <!--- END QUERY SECTION --->
 9: <!--- BEGIN PASSWORD CHECK ---!>
10:
11: <CFIF form.password IS NOT get_pass.password>
12:
13:     Error: You have entered an incorrect password for the tech name you
        ➥provided. If you think you've received this message in error, please
        ➥contact the Administrator.
14:
15: <CFELSE>
16:
17:     <CFINSERT datasource="gargantuan" tablename="calls"
18:     formfields="date_of_call,
19:     tech_who_took_call,
20:     callers_first_name,
21:     short_description,
22:     long_description">
23:
24:     <H3>Thanks for submitting your information to the database.</H3>
25:
26: </CFIF>
27:
28: <!--- END PASSWORD CHECK --->
29:
30: <A HREF="index.cfm">Return to List of Calls</A><BR>
31:
32: </BODY>
33: </HTML>
34:
```

The <CFIF> statement on lines 11-26 compares the password data submitted by the user with the password returned by the query. If the two don't match, the user sees the Error message on line 13; in all other cases (<CFELSE>), the new record is inserted into the table "calls" (lines 17-22) and the user sees a confirmation.

Also note that I've added a list of form fields to the <CFINSERT> tag. This was necessary because this template is now working with some new variables, form.password and get_pass.password, that I don't want to submit to the "calls" table with the other call details. Recall that, by default, <CFINSERT> will attempt to send all variables to the database for insertion, and in this case I will have received a ColdFusion error because there isn't a password field in the "calls" table.

In a browser, the modified insert.cfm page looks like Figure 9.7.

FIGURE 9.7

Gargantuan's insertion page, modified to perform a password-check.

```
insert.cfm - Notepad
File  Edit  Search  Help
<!--- BEGIN QUERY SECTION --->

<CFQUERY name="get_pass" datasource="gargantuan">
       SELECT password FROM techs
       WHERE tech_name = '#tech_who_took_call#'
</CFQUERY>

<!--- END QUERY SECTION --->
<!--- BEGIN PASSWORD CHECK --->

<CFIF FORM.password IS NOT get_pass.password>

        Error: You have entered an incorrect password for the tech name you provided. If you
        think you've received this message in error, please contact the Administrator.
<CFELSE>

        <CFINSERT datasource="gargantuan" tablename="calls"
               formfields="date_of_call,
               tech_who_took_call,
               callers_first_name,
               short_description,
               long_description">

        <H3>Thanks for submitting your information to the database.</H3>
</CFIF>

<!--- END PASSWORD CHECK --->
<!--- RETURN LINK --->

<P>
<A HREF="index.cfm">Return to List of Calls</A><BR>
Please use your browser's "reload" function to view the most recent calls

</BODY>
</HTML>
```

When a user inputs call data in the form pictured in Figure 9.6, he'll see a confirmation like Figure 9.8 if he has supplied his correct password. If the password doesn't match, he'll see the error pictured in Figure 9.9.

FIGURE 9.8

A correct password entry produces this confirmation message and inserts user data into the "calls" table.

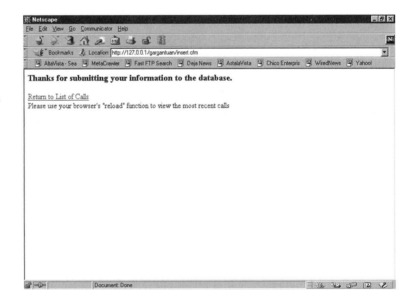

Netscape
File Edit View Go Communicator Help
Bookmarks Location: http://127.0.0.1/gargantuan/insert.cfm
AltaVista - Sea   MetaCrawler   Fast FTP Search   Deja News   AstalaVista   Chico Enterpris   WiredNews   Yahoo!

Thanks for submitting your information to the database.

Return to List of Calls
Please use your browser's "reload" function to view the most recent calls

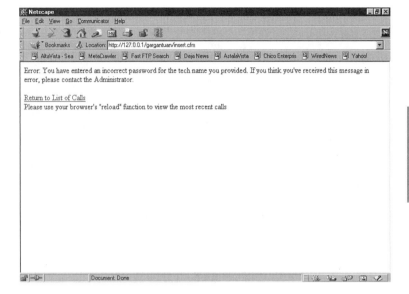

FIGURE 9.9

Supplying an incorrect password displays this error message and halts the insertion process.

9

Defining Variables with `<CFSET>`

The second portion of Gargantuan's requested changes is the submission counter in which employees can choose to have their logged calls count toward a prize. When an employee submits new call information to the database, the confirmation message he receives should allow him to add the submitted call to his overall count. At the end of a predetermined period, Gargantuan will reward the employee with the most calls counted.

ColdFusion offers several ways to "count" things, but for the purpose of this illustration, we'll look at just one—the `<CFSET>` tag. `<CFSET>` gives the developer the ability to create new variables that aren't defined by queries or form data. Using `<CFSET>` you can create any variable you'd like, assign any value necessary, and use it anywhere in your template file.

For example, to create a simple text variable to display my name, I'd use a `<CFSET>` tag like the following:

```
<CFSET developer = 'Charles Mohnike'>
```

Within that template, I can cause my name to appear anywhere within `<CFOUTPUT>` tags by referring to the variable `developer`. I didn't use hash marks when I created the variable, but I do have to use them when I refer to it later in a document.

Unlike some programming and scripting languages, ColdFusion uses "type-less" variables, meaning that you don't need to tell the program whether a variable value is numeric, text, yes/no, or time-date.

Admittedly, turning a two-word name into a one-word variable probably isn't going to save you much time, but read on for other ways to use <CFSET>.

Variables created with <CFSET> are not always designed to be displayed to the user. They can be, but, more often, <CFSET> is used behind the scenes to control some factor in page output or database modifications.

Creating the Counting Mechanism

To enhance Gargantuan's application by including a counter, use <CFSET> to create a counting mechanism. Through a query, find the previous number of submissions an employee has contributed, and then use <CFSET> to create a new variable whose value adds the number 1 to the previous count. The new variable will reflect the employee's current count.

First, you'll need to create a field in Gargantuan's database that will hold the employee's current count figure. Because tech department employees are all listed in the table "techs", this is a good place to do it. In Figure 9.10, I've added the new field submissions to the "techs" table and given each an initial value of 0.

FIGURE 9.10

The "techs" table in Gargantuan's database, modified to include a submissions count.

ID	tech_name	password	submissions
1	Billy	yllib	0
2	Bobby	ybbob	0
3	Dougie	eiguod	0
4	Barbie	eibrab	0
5	Buffy	yffub	0
6	Jenny	ynnej	0
7	Jackie	eikcaj	0
8	Joey	yeoj	0
(AutoNumber)			

Next you'll need to add some text to the existing template insert.cfm. When a user gets a confirmation message that her submission has been entered in the database, she will also see a button or link that enables her to "count" that call and thus participate in the contest. When a user clicks the button, her username and new count value will be sent to an action page that will update the database using the <CFUPDATE> tag.

I thought a button might be a nice way to do this, so I added a short form to insert.cfm, as illustrated in Listing 9.7.

LISTING 9.7 Confirming Password Data and Entering Call Details

```
 1: <!--- BEGIN QUERY SECTION --->
 2:
 3: <CFQUERY name="get_user_info" datasource="gargantuan">
 4:     SELECT * FROM techs
 5:     WHERE tech_name = '#tech_who_took_call#'
 6: </CFQUERY>
 7:
 8: <!--- END QUERY SECTION --->
 9: <!--- BEGIN PASSWORD CHECK --->
10:
11: <CFIF FORM.password IS NOT get_user_info.password>
12:
13:     Error: You have entered an incorrect password for the tech name you
       ➥ provided. If you think you've received this message in error, please
       ➥ contact the Administrator.
14: <CFELSE>
15:
16:     <CFINSERT datasource="gargantuan" tablename="calls"
17:         formfields="date_of_call,
18:         tech_who_took_call,
19:         callers_first_name,
20:         short_description,
21:         long_description">
22:
23:     <H3>Thanks for submitting your information to the database.</H3>
24:
25:     To participate in Gargantuan's tech-calls contest, click the button
       ➥below to receive credit for the call you just logged.
26:
27:     <CFSET submissions = get_user_info.submissions + 1>
28:
29:     <FORM action="count.cfm" method="post">
30:
31:         <CFOUTPUT>
32:
33:         <INPUT type="hidden" name="ID" value="#get_user_info.ID#">
34:
35:         <INPUT type="hidden" name="tech_name" value="#get_user_info.tech
           ➥name#">
36:
37:         <INPUT type="hidden" name="submissions" value="#submissions#">
38:
39:         </CFOUTPUT>
40:
```

continues

LISTING 9.7   continued

```
41:           <INPUT type="submit" value="yes, add this call to my total!">
42:
43:      </FORM>
44:
45: </CFIF>
46:
47: <!--- END PASSWORD CHECK --->
48: <!--- RETURN LINK --->
49:
50: <P>
51: <A HREF="index.cfm">Return to List of Calls</A><BR>
52: Please use your browser's "reload" function to view the most recent calls
53:
54: </BODY>
55: </HTML>
```

First, notice that I've slightly modified the query section on lines 3-6 to select all (*) fields from the techs database. My previous query selected only the tech's password, but now I'll need to get the values for ID and submissions as well. Recall that the ID field is the primary key for this table, and that <CFUPDATE> will require me to specify the primary key in the action page.

Because I changed the name of the query from get_pass to the more inclusive get_user_info, I've also changed the variable scope in the <CFIF> statement on line 11 from get_pass.password to get_user_info.password.

Note that I've added the <CFSET> and form sections within the <CFELSE> and final </CFIF> tag on lines 14-45. I want the text to display only if the user successfully submitted a call to the database.

The <CFSET> tag on line 27 creates the variable submissions. The variable name is important, because it will need to match with a field name in the "techs" table when I perform an update on the action page. The value of submissions is set to the employee's previous submissions value, plus one.

Finally, I used a <CFOUTPUT> section on lines 31-39 to create hidden values the form will post to the action page. I didn't specify a query name with <CFOUTPUT>, because that would make all variable values default to the output returned by the query. This would give me the *old* value for submissions, when I instead want to post the modified, plus-one value.

As an alternative, I used a generic <CFOUTPUT> tag and within it used variable scopes to identify exactly which variable values should be posted by the form. ID and tech_name are scoped to use values returned by the query get_user_info, whereas submissions has no scope and thus uses the value defined by the <CFSET> tag at line 27.

The source in Listing 9.7 returns a page like Figure 9.11 when a user successfully submits data.

FIGURE 9.11

The result of a successful submission.

Next you'll need to create the *count.cfm* template to serve as an action for the form. Because the actual "counting" happened in the previous page, *count.cfm* is used only to update the posted values to the *"techs"* table. The update confirmation page looks like Listing 9.8.

LISTING 9.8   Updating the Datasource with <CFUPDATE>

```
 1: <!---BEGIN UPDATE SECTION--->
 2:
 3: <CFUPDATE datasource="gargantuan" tablename="techs">
 4:
 5: <!---END UPDATE SECTION--->
 6:
 7: <HTML>
 8:
 9: <HEAD>
10:
11: <CFOUTPUT>
12:
13: <TITLE>Thanks, #tech_name#</TITLE>
14:
15: </HEAD>
16:
17: <BODY>
18:
19: <H3>Thanks for participating, #tech_name#</H3>
```

continues

LISTING 9.8   continued

```
20:
21: Your current call total is #submissions#. Good luck!
22:
23: </CFOUTPUT>
24:
25: </BODY>
26: </HTML>
```

Because `count.cfm` requires so few elements, I elected to add a few bonus features to mine. I used the values in `tech_name` and `submissions` to notify the user of his current count. In a browser, this confirmation looks like Figure 9.12.

FIGURE 9.12

Gargantuan tech employees receive a confirmation and current count when they participate in the contest.

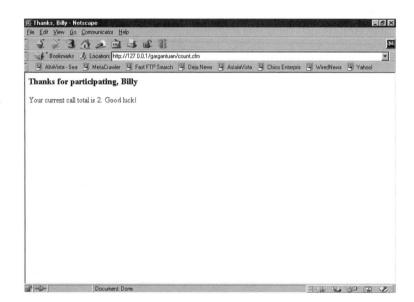

Finally, I'll upload the new files I've created to Gargantuan's server, and its enhanced application is complete.

Summary

Using ColdFusion variables to control or enhance input and output is one of the keys to creating more sophisticated applications. CF templates work with several types of variables; some are defined by query results, some by user input, and still others can be defined arbitrarily by the developer. Any of these variable types can be used in conditional statements to produce enhanced output.

A powerful tool, ColdFusion's <CFIF> tag family enables the developer to state a condition or conditions that must occur before an action is taken. An example is a password-protected application in which a user's supplied password must match with one stored in a database before further surfing or input is permitted.

Developer-defined variables are established with the <CFSET> tag. While these variables can be used to define commonly used phrases to be output, most often they're used behind the scenes as a tool to give developers more control over their applications. An example is the counting mechanism described in this chapter, in which <CFSET> is used to add the number 1 to an existing value each time a user accesses a certain page.

9

Q&A

Q What are some other uses of the <CFIF> tag?

A In addition to the uses described in this chapter, <CFIF> is also a common way to create single templates that handle a variety of activities. For example, a site might offer three types of text searches: by keyword, by data type, or by alphabetic list. By using <CFIF> and defining a "search type" parameter, a developer can handle all three search types with a single template.

Q Should I use <CFIF> to password-protect areas of my site?

A Not if security is a big concern. The sample application used in this chapter was designed to illustrate the use of <CFIF>, not to provide an impenetrable defense. In Week 3, "Maximizing and Customizing ColdFusion Applications," I'll cover ColdFusion's security functions in greater detail.

Q Can I "nest" <CFIF> statements by placing one within another?

A Yes, and by doing so you'll be harnessing some of CF's most useful powers. When using nested <CFIF> statements, it's very important to use indents in your source code because the conditional flow can quickly become hard to read without them.

Q Can I use computations other than addition with <CFSET>?

A Yes. <CFSET> canbe used in conjunction with any mathematical computation, as well as text-string functions such as masking and de-shouting (making letters lowercase). You'll find descriptions of various text-massaging functions in future chapters of this book.

Workshop

Answers to quiz and exercise questions can be found in Appendix A at the back of the text.

Quiz

1. Name three ways variables can be defined in ColdFusion applications.
2. Do `<CFIF>` statements have to be enclosed in `<CFOUTPUT>` tags?
3. Describe, in plain language, the flow of a `<CFIF>`-`<CFELSE>` statement.
4. What is the distinguishing feature of the form input type password?
5. Why are ColdFusion variables called "typeless"?
6. What is a variable scope?
7. True or False: Hash marks are always used when defining a variable with `<CFSET>`.

Exercises

1. Using `<CFIF>`, create a two-template application that asks a question and returns a response depending on the user's answer.
2. Use `<CFIF>` to create a simple form validation page in which a user must complete all fields before the form will be processed.
3. Design a database table containing a list of people and their ages. Using this as a datasource, create a page using `<CFSET>` that will display the difference between two people's ages.

WEEK 2

DAY 10

Enhancing Output with Tables and Groups

So far, the `<CFOUTPUT>` sections we've discussed have been designed simply to churn out the results of `<CFQUERY>` statements. We've used only basic paragraph or line-return tags to determine how the output displays in the user's browser. This design method works fine if a client's only aim is to display the contents of a database without any fancy formatting, but in the real world, your clients are likely to want more. They might want page data displayed in tables, grouped by type, or indexed for easy navigation. Today's discussion shows you how to make use of ColdFusion, SQL, and HTML features to enhance the look and readability of your output sections. We'll cover

- ColdFusion's `<CFTABLE>` tag
- Displaying ColdFusion output in standard HTML tables
- Using `<CFOUTPUT>`'s GROUP parameter to organize output
- Using SQL's DISTINCT parameter to create a page index

Understanding <CFTABLE>

ColdFusion provides a quick-and-dirty way to display query results with its <CFTABLE>
tag. <CFTABLE> offers only a limited set of display features as compared to HTML tables,
but it's by far the easiest and fastest way to display output data in tabular format. You
simply specify the variables you want displayed and supply a few parameters. <CFTABLE>
automatically does the rest, creating the necessary table code at the time the data is output dynamically in the user's browser.

> **Note**
>
> <CFTABLE> works with a pretty limited feature set. If your application
> requires tables that use custom cell colors, multiple-column spanning, or
> other advanced features, you need to work with HTML's more advanced
> <TABLE> tag. Both tags are detailed today.

Let's look at an example that might benefit from tabular output. Assume that I maintain a
database table for all of the 8-track tapes I carry around in my 1970s Cadillac (which is
equipped with an 8-track player, naturally). Using the ColdFusion techniques we've covered so far, it is pretty easy to create a template with a query and output section that displays a page like the one shown in Figure 10.1.

FIGURE 10.1

*My query's output dis-
played as linear text.*

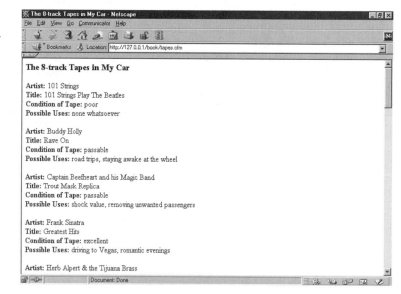

This page layout serves my purpose, but that's about it. It gets the data on the page, but it's not very attractive, nor is it a good use of the user's screen. I have a page that scrolls down for several screens, but I'm wasting lots of white space to the right of my text.

One way to correct this and make my query results more readable is with the <CFTABLE> tag.

Creating Output Tables with <CFTABLE>

<CFTABLE> is unique among the CFML tags we've covered thus far in that it works as a replacement to the <CFOUTPUT> tag, rather than within it.

<CFTABLE> has two modes—one mode that displays data as plain text, organized in tabular fashion, and another mode that actually creates HTML 3.0 tables on-the-fly as it displays data. The first mode is used when you want to ensure compatibility with all browsers; the second is used when you need a little more control over table features.

10

<CFTABLE> in Text Mode

By default, <CFTABLE> creates output tables in text mode using HTML's <PRE> tag to insert white space between columns. I'll use my previous 8-track database to illustrate. My template page is illustrated in Listing 10.1.

INPUT   **LISTING 10.1**   tapes_pre_table.cfm

```
 1: <!---BEGIN QUERY SECTION--->
 2:
 3: <CFQUERY NAME="tapes" DATASOURCE="music">
 4: SELECT * FROM 8tracks ORDER BY artist
 5: </CFQUERY>
 6:
 7: <!---END QUERY SECTION--->
 8:
 9: <HTML>
10: <HEAD>
11:     <TITLE>The 8-track Tapes in My Car</TITLE>
12: </HEAD>
13:
14: <BODY>
15: <H3>The 8-track Tapes in My Car</H3>
16:
17: <!---BEGIN OUTPUT SECTION--->
18:
19: <CFTABLE QUERY="tapes" COLHEADERS>
20:     <CFCOL header="Artist" width="16" text="#artist#">
21:     <CFCOL header="Title" width="30" text="#title#">
22:     <CFCOL header="Condition" width="10" text="#condition#">
```

continues

LISTING 10.1 continued

```
23:    <CFCOL header="Uses" width="50" text="#uses#">
24: </CFTABLE>
25:
26: <!---END OUTPUT SECTION--->
27:
28: </body>
29: </html>
```

I used a basic query that returns all values in all fields in my database table "8tracks".
To display the results, I used <CFTABLE> in place of <CFOUTPUT> on line 19 and specified
the query "tapes" from which to grab output. I also supplied the optional parameter
COLHEADERS on line 19, which tells ColdFusion that I plan to use a header name for
each of my columns.

Within the <CFTABLE> and closing </CFTABLE> tags on lines 19 and 24, I defined four
<CFCOL>s, or columns, to display. Each includes parameters to define the text of the
header, the width (in characters) of the column, and the query variable that should be
displayed in the column.

Because I didn't supply the HTMLTABLE parameter in the <CFTABLE> tag, ColdFusion will,
by default, generate my table in text mode. When <CFTABLE> creates the display, it won't
use table tags such as <TR> and <TD>. Instead, it will use the HTML tag <PRE> and insert
blank spaces to make the text display in columnar format. The Browser view and View
Source text are displayed in Figures 10.2 and 10.3, respectively.

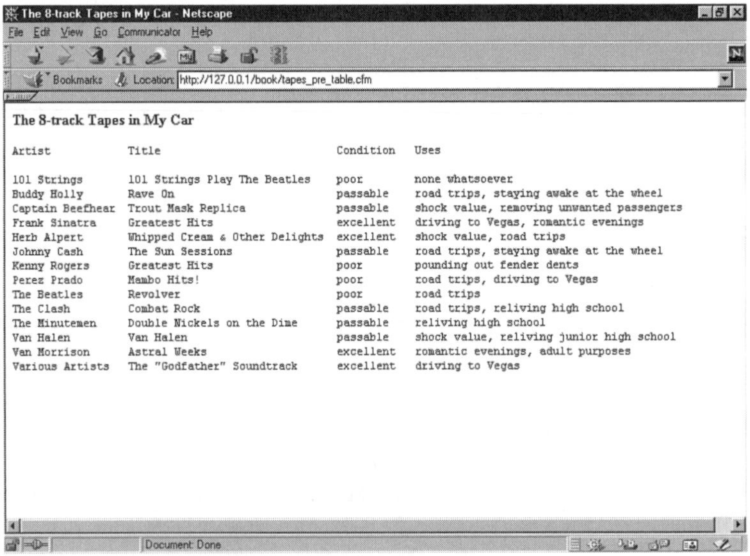

FIGURE 10.2

*By default, <CFTABLE>
creates table data as
plain text.*

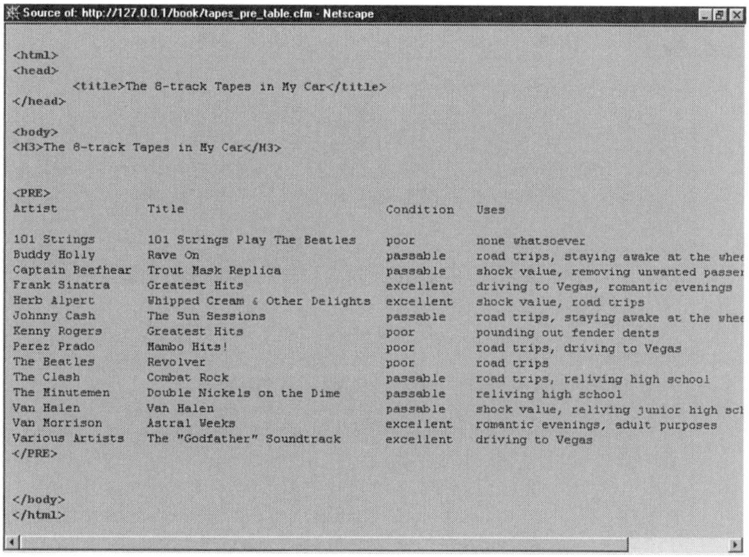

```
Source of: http://127.0.0.1/book/tapes_pre_table.cfm - Netscape

<html>
<head>
        <title>The 8-track Tapes in My Car</title>
</head>

<body>
<H3>The 8-track Tapes in My Car</H3>


<PRE>
Artist            Title                          Condition   Uses

101 Strings       101 Strings Play The Beatles   poor        none whatsoever
Buddy Holly       Rave On                        passable    road trips, staying awake at the whe
Captain Beefhear  Trout Mask Replica             passable    shock value, removing unwanted passe
Frank Sinatra     Greatest Hits                  excellent   driving to Vegas, romantic evenings
Herb Alpert       Whipped Cream & Other Delights excellent   shock value, road trips
Johnny Cash       The Sun Sessions               passable    road trips, staying awake at the whe
Kenny Rogers      Greatest Hits                  poor        pounding out fender dents
Perez Prado       Mambo Hits!                    poor        road trips, driving to Vegas
The Beatles       Revolver                       poor        road trips
The Clash         Combat Rock                    passable    road trips, reliving high school
The Minutemen     Double Nickels on the Dime     passable    reliving high school
Van Halen         Van Halen                      passable    shock value, reliving junior high sc
Van Morrison      Astral Weeks                   excellent   romantic evenings, adult purposes
Various Artists   The "Godfather" Soundtrack     excellent   driving to Vegas
</PRE>


</body>
</html>
```

FIGURE 10.3

The source of a default <CFTABLE> *shows the use of HTML's* <PRE> *tag.*

10

Because this method doesn't require HTML tables, it is compatible with pretty much any browser you're likely to run across.

Tip

> Text-mode <CFTABLE>s are great for dealing with columns of figures, or short text strings such as the ones used in this example. However, the plain-text display isn't particularly eye-catching, and because the <PRE> tag doesn't allow text wrapping, you can see how longer text would cause the table to run off the right side of the screen. To gain more control over tables, use <CFTABLE> along with the HTMLTABLE parameter.

<CFTABLE> in HTMLTABLE Mode

As <CFTABLE>'s second display option, HTMLTABLE enables you to create HTML 3.0–compatible tables to display your output. However, it still doesn't boast the full set of features available in standard HTML tables—we'll cover those in the next section.

To create a <CFTABLE> using HTML 3.0 tags, I've used the template illustrated in Listing 10.2.

```
 1: <!---BEGIN QUERY SECTION--->
 2: <CFQUERY NAME="tapes" DATASOURCE="music">
 3: SELECT * from 8tracks ORDER BY artist
 4: </CFQUERY>
 5: <!---END QUERY SECTION--->
 6: <HTML>
 7: <HEAD>
 8:     <TITLE>The 8-track Tapes in My Car</TITLE>
 9: </HEAD>
10:
11: <BODY>
12: <H3>The 8-track Tapes in My Car</H3>
13:
14: <CFTABLE QUERY="tapes" COLHEADERS HTMLTABLE BORDER="1">
15:     <CFCOL header="<B>Artist</B>" text="#artist#">
16:     <CFCOL header="<B>Title</B>" text="#title#">
17:     <CFCOL header="<B>Condition</B>" text="#condition#">
18:     <CFCOL header="<B>Uses</B>" text="#uses#">
19: </CFTABLE>
20:
21: </BODY>
22: </HTML>
```

This template uses exactly the same query as Listing 10.1, with some modifications to the <CFTABLE> section on line 14. When the HTMLTABLE parameter is added, it opens up a few new options not available in the <PRE> table we created in the last section. Specifically, we can now specify a border width (I used "1"), and we no longer have to specify column widths for each field because HTML 3.0 tables do this automatically in the user's browser. Note also on lines 15–18 that the HTML I've inserted (bold text) is enclosed in quotes so that ColdFusion recognizes it as my column headers.

I've also bolded each column header with the <B> tag just to fancy up the display.

> **Tip**
>
> Using <CFTABLE>'s HTMLTABLE parameter also enables a few other customizable features. See the tag definitions in Appendix B of this book for a complete list of available parameters in <CFTABLE>.

Figures 10.4 and 10.5 show browser and source output for this template in Listing 10.2.

FIGURE 10.4

Using <CFTABLE>'s HTMLTABLE parameter causes ColdFusion to create HTML 3.0 tables.

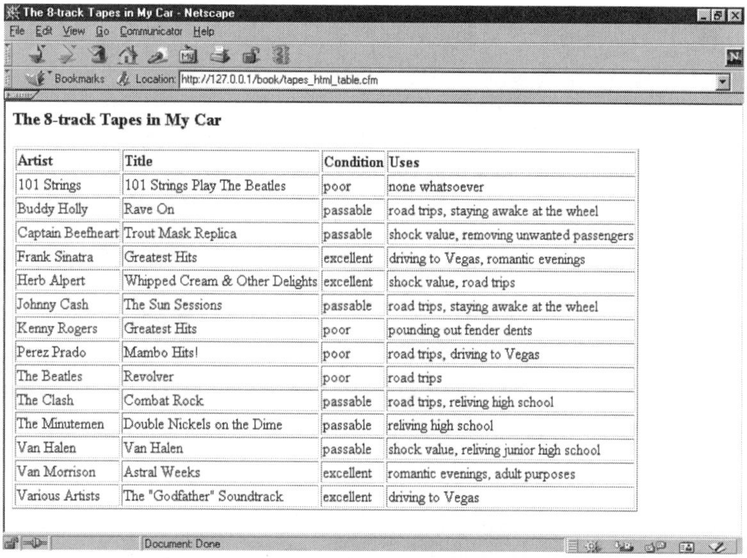

FIGURE 10.5

The View Source look at Figure 10.4, showing the use of <TR> and <TD> tags to create rows and columns.

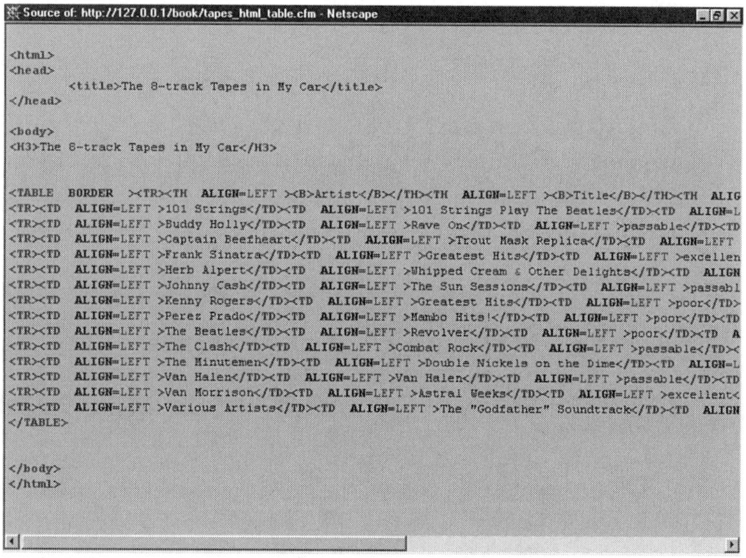

The HTMLTABLE parameter helps to create a much nicer-looking display, but it still leaves <CFTABLE> fairly limited if you need to work with more sophisticated table features such as colored backgrounds, and so on. To use these, you need to create output display tables manually, using a combination of <CFOUTPUT> and HTML's <TABLE> tags.

Creating Output Tables with HTML's <TABLE> Tag

Using HTML's standard table tags to organize your query output can make for some very sleek page designs, but it can also be one of the most frustrating tasks you'll ever complete with ColdFusion. HTML tables can be taxing enough on their own—one missed </TD> tag can keep your table from displaying at all. Add a repeating <CFOUTPUT> section, and you have a potentially nail-biting experience.

For those reasons, it's a good idea to use extensive comments and indentations in your code to help organize table rows and columns. If you take the time to organize table code carefully so that it illustrates the flow of your table, you'll save many troubleshooting hours later.

> **Tip**
>
> ColdFusion Studio users can take advantage of their program's table-creation aids to make the process even easier. Studio's Table Wizard helps in designing the table structure, whereas the editor automatically color-codes and indents table text to keep your code easy to read.

To illustrate, assume that I want to create a table displaying my 8-track collection that requires a few features not available in the limited <CFTABLE> method. I want to add a title row that spans all my columns, and I want to use a custom background and font color to offset the title from the rest of my data. I'm shooting for something like Figure 10.6.

FIGURE 10.6

To create this table, you'll need to use both <CFOUTPUT> and HTML's <TABLE> tags.

The 8-track Tapes in My Car			
Artist	**Title**	**Condition**	**Use**
101 Strings	101 Strings Play The Beatles	poor	none whatsoever
Buddy Holly	Rave On	passable	road trips, staying awake at the wheel
Captain Beefheart	Trout Mask Replica	passable	shock value, removing unwanted passengers
Frank Sinatra	Greatest Hits	excellent	driving to Vegas, romantic evenings
Herb Alpert	Whipped Cream & Other Delights	excellent	shock value, road trips
Johnny Cash	The Sun Sessions	passable	road trips, staying awake at the wheel
Kenny Rogers	Greatest Hits	poor	pounding out fender dents
Perez Prado	Mambo Hits!	poor	road trips, driving to Vegas
The Beatles	Revolver	poor	road trips
The Clash	Combat Rock	passable	road trips, reliving high school
The Minutemen	Double Nickels on the Dime	passable	reliving high school
Van Halen	Van Halen	passable	shock value, reliving junior high school
Van Morrison	Astral Weeks	excellent	romantic evenings, adult purposes
Various Artists	The "Godfather" Soundtrack	excellent	driving to Vegas

Because <CFTABLE> doesn't provide for custom background colors or rows that span multiple columns, we'll create a manual HTML table and use <CFOUTPUT> to fill in the data. The template looks like Listing 10.3.

INPUT **LISTING 10.3** `tapes_manual_table.cfm`

```
 1: <!---BEGIN QUERY SECTION--->
 2:
 3: <CFQUERY name="tapes" datasource="music">
 4: SELECT * from 8tracks ORDER by artist
 5: </CFQUERY>
 6:
 7: <!---END QUERY SECTION--->
 8:
 9: <HTML>
10: <HEAD>
11:     <TITLE>The 8-track Tapes in My Car</TITLE>
12: </HEAD>
13:
14: <BODY>
15:
16: <!---DEFINE TABLE--->
17:
18: <TABLE align="center" border="2" cellpadding="4">
19:
20: <!---FIRST TABLE ROW
21:     This row spans all four columns that will appear below--->
22:
23: <TR>
24:     <TD colspan="4" align="center" bgcolor="#000000"><FONT COLOR=
        ➥"#FFFFFF"><B>The 8-track Tapes in My Car</B></FONT></TD>
25: </TR>
26:
27: <!---SECOND TABLE ROW
28:     Creates the four columns and fills each with a header--->
29:
30: <TR>
31:      <TD align="center"><B>Artist</B></TD>
32:     <TD align="center"><B>Title</B></TD>
33:     <TD align="center"><B>Condition</B></TD>
34:     <TD align="center"><B>Use</B></TD>
35: </TR>
36:
37: <!---THIRD TABLE ROW AND BEYOND
38:     This section uses CFOUTPUT to generate the rest of the table--->
39:
40: <CFOUTPUT query="tapes">
41:
```

continues

LISTING 10.3 continued

```
42: <TR>
43:      <TD>#artist#</TD>
44:      <TD>#title#</TD>
45:      <TD>#condition#</TD>
46:      <TD>#uses#</TD>
47: </TR>
48:
49: </CFOUTPUT>
50:
51: <!---CLOSE TABLE AFTER CLOSING CFOUTPUT--->
52:
53: </TABLE>
54:
55: </BODY>
56: </HTML>
```

First, notice that I inserted comments for each table element, and indented <TD>, or table data, sections to set them off from the <TR>, or table row, sections.

The query used in Figure 10.9 is identical to previous examples. On line 4, it selects all fields in all records of the "8tracks" database table. The tough stuff doesn't begin until we reach the <TABLE> tag on line 18.

When we define the table, we haven't yet specified a <CFOUTPUT> section. That is because we want the first two rows of my table (the title and the headers) to appear only once. If we enclosed those rows in <CFOUTPUT> tags, they would repeat for every record returned by my query.

The table uses a border width of "2" and a cellpadding parameter of "4" , which adds a little space around each text element that appears within. We also used align="center", which centers the table in the user's browser.

The first table row on line 23 contains the text that will become the table's title. It spans all four columns using the COLSPAN parameter, and uses a black background (hex code #000000) via the BGCOLOR parameter. Over this background, we used a white font (hex code #FFFFFF) to make the title stand out.

The second table row on line 30 sets up the four columns that will serve as headers and provides bold text for each. We used the align="center" parameter within each <TD>, or table data tag, to show that the headers should lie in the center of their respective columns.

For the third row that begins on line 42, we first begin with the <CFOUTPUT> tag on line 40. From this point until the closing </CFOUTPUT> tag appears on line 49, every text string, tag, and variable will repeat for each record returned by the query, so we must be careful.

> **Tip**
>
> When creating tables manually with <CFOUTPUT>, most errors are the result of table tags that should or shouldn't be enclosed in the <CFOUTPUT> section of your page. If you preview such a page and your table doesn't display properly (or at all), go back and carefully review the elements that appear within and without your <CFOUTPUT> section(s).

Each record should lie in its own row, so use the <TR> tag to create a row, followed by four <TD> tags to create the four columns. Each <TD> contains one of the variables returned by the query, and we must be careful to make sure these appear in the same order as the headers above. We close each <TD> tag after the variable, close the <TR> tag after identifying all four rows, and finally close the <CFOUTPUT> tag and the table itself on lines 49 and 53.

This example creates a fairly simple table, but you can see how things can become pretty complex as tables become more sophisticated and as more than one <CFOUTPUT> section is used within a table tag. The exercises at the end of today's discussion will help you create other types of tables that will put your ColdFusion skills to the test.

Grouping Data to Organize Output

Let's leave tables behind for a moment and look at another ColdFusion output trick that will help make your pages more readable. Look back at Figure 10.1, which illustrates the contents of the "8tracks" table in linear format. Notice that the records aren't displayed in any particular order—in fact, by default, they appear in the same order in which they were entered into the database.

You might recall that in Day 5, "Finding the Data You Need: An Introduction to Queries and SQL," I illustrated how the ORDER BY parameter could be used in an SQL query to change the display order of records. For example, if I had used the phrase ORDER BY condition in the query that created Figure 10.1, the records would have been arranged alphabetically by condition so that all the tapes in excellent condition would have been appeared first, and so on.

This certainly gets the job done, but for better page organization, it might be helpful to display certain records together as a group. Check out Figure 10.7.

FIGURE 10.7

My "8tracks" *table, ordered and grouped by the* condition *field.*

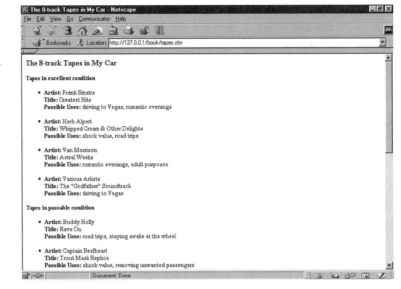

This page shows the benefits of grouping output data.

NEW TERM   *Grouping* data means to arrange it by a common trait. In the example in Figure 10.7, records have been grouped by the contents of the condition field.

By arranging the results of your query in groups, you can make your pages more readable and easier to navigate. A page like the one in Figure 10.7 makes it easy for me to browse my collection of 8-tracks and see which tapes are in playable condition, and which ones I might as well leave at home on the next road trip.

Tip

By choosing different fields from which to group your data, you can create custom views to appeal to different user audiences. For example, a table containing product orders might be grouped by customer to show all the orders placed by various customers, by product to show which products are most popular, or by address to show which locales are ordering which products.

Creating Output Using the GROUP Parameter

To create pages like Figure 10.7, you use an ORDER BY clause in your <CFQUERY> in conjunction with the GROUP parameter in your <CFOUTPUT> statement. Recall that ORDER BY causes the results of your query to be returned in a certain order, arranging records alphabetically or numerically by the field you specify.

Note ColdFusion's GROUP output parameter only works properly if you've supplied an ORDER BY statement in your SQL query. In order for <CFOUTPUT> to accurately group a set of records, it must receive the records pre-ordered by the "grouped" field.

The GROUP parameter then takes over in a template's <CFOUTPUT> section to arrange ordered records into definable groups. To illustrate, look at the code that produced Figure 10.7, shown in Listing 10.4.

INPUT   **LISTING 10.4**   tapes.cfm

```
 1: <!---BEGIN QUERY SECTION--->
 2:
 3: <CFQUERY name="tapes" datasource="music">
 4: SELECT * from 8tracks ORDER by condition, artist
 5: </CFQUERY>
 6:
 7: <!---END QUERY SECTION--->
 8:
 9: <HTML>
10: <HEAD>
11:     <TITLE>The 8-track Tapes in My Car</TITLE>
12: </HEAD>
13:
14: <BODY>
15: <H3>The 8-track Tapes in My Car</H3>
16:
17: <!---BEGIN GROUPED OUTPUT--->
18:
19: <CFOUTPUT query="tapes" group="condition">
20:     <B>Tapes in #condition# condition</B>
21:     <UL>
22:
23: <!---OUTPUT RECORDS FOR CURRENT GROUP--->
24:
25:     <CFOUTPUT>
26:     <LI>    <B>Artist:</B> #artist#<BR>
27:             <B>Title:</B> #title#<BR>
28:             <B>Possible Uses:</B> #uses#<P>
29:     </CFOUTPUT>
30:     </UL>
31:
32: <!---END CURRENT GROUP--->
33:
34: </CFOUTPUT>
```

10

continues

LISTING **10.4**   continued

```
35:
36: <!---END GROUPED OUTPUT--->
37:
38: </BODY>
39: </HTML>
```

First, look at the query section on lines 3-5. It uses a simple SELECT statement that gets the contents of all records in the "8tracks" table. The SQL statement uses the ORDER BY clause to specify that the results should be returned to ColdFusion arranged alphabetically by the contents of the field condition, and arranged secondarily by the contents of the field artist. If we used this query without any further modifications, our page would simply display a list of tapes with the ones in excellent condition displayed first, and the excellent tapes ordered alphabetically by artist, and so on.

Second, notice that two <CFOUTPUT> sections are used on lines 19 and 25 to display the query data, one nested inside the other.

| NEW TERM | *Nesting* occurs when you place one set of <CFOUTPUT> tags (the "child") within an existing <CFOUTPUT> section (the "parent"). |

The first, or parent, tagset on line 19 identifies the query from which to retrieve the data and uses the GROUP parameter to specify which field is used for the group. Think of each group's contents as a subset of all the records returned by the query.

Immediately following this tag, the text Tapes in #condition# condition is used to serve as a group. ColdFusion will fill in the #condition# variable as it processes each group. The <UL> or unordered list tag on line 21 is used to create a bulleted list of items.

Nested within this output section is the second set of <CFOUTPUT> tags, beginning on line 25. This time, we didn't specify a query name because ColdFusion assumes by default that we want to use data returned by the query referenced in the parent tag.

Within each group, we used the <LI>, or list item, tag to show that each record in the current group should be an object of its group's <UL>, or unordered list. This causes each record to display as bulleted, indented text below its related group header. Note that unordered lists and list items aren't required to group output—we just used them here to better clarify our page's organization.

Next, we close the inner, or child, <CFOUTPUT> tags on line 29. We then close the <UL> tag with </UL> on line 30 to specify that this is the end of one group's list. Finally, we end the parent <CFOUTPUT> section with </CFOUTPUT> on line 34.

> **Tip**
>
> If your grouped pages look like stair steps, with each line indented further than the preceding line, it's likely that you haven't closed a `<UL>` tag before closing the `<CFOUTPUT>` parent.

Making Long Pages Accessible with Index Links

My `"8tracks"` table has only three `condition` types: `"poor"`, `"passable"`, and `"excellent"`. This makes it an ideal candidate for a simple grouped page, but what if my database housed hundreds of records and had 10 or more `condition` types? A grouped page would certainly help organize things, but a user would still have to do quite a bit of scrolling to get to the group he or she wants to see.

To increase accessibility on lengthy pages, I can use a trick that has been available to HTML developers since the very early days of the Web: page indices or anchors. Page anchors allow the developer to place a list of topics at the top of a document, and to make each topic name a link to text further down the page.

Look at an example in Figure 10.8.

FIGURE 10.8

The first screen of a long page, with index links that navigate to text sections below.

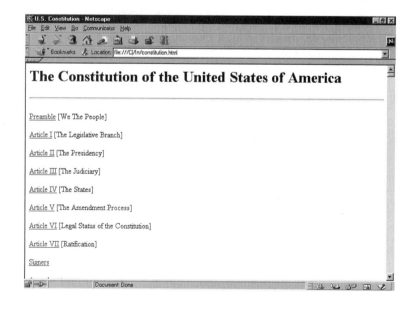

The entire Constitution has already loaded as a single page in the browser, but it's a very long document that would require a lot of scrolling to see it all. The index links enable the user to immediately navigate to the part of the page he wants to see. Clicking any of these links causes the user's browser to move down the page to the relevant topic.

The HTML tag that makes this happen is <A NAME>. To set up a page index, you first anchor your page's subsections with the <A NAME> tag like this:

```
<A NAME="topic3"><H3>Article III</H3></A>
```

At the top of your page, you use the following link:

```
<A HREF="#topic3">Article III</A>
```

You can see how index links might come in handy with a grouped page such as the one described in the last section. Let's see how ColdFusion templates might build their own index links.

Using SQL's DISTINCT to Create Dynamic Index Links

To add index links dynamically, we can use the DISTINCT command in our template's SQL statement. Recall from Listing 5.20 in Day 5 that DISTINCT tells ColdFusion to get only one item of each type. For example, this query

```
SELECT DISTINCT condition FROM 8tracks
```

returns the following from our table:

    poor

    passable

    excellent

There are just three items, even though there are 14 records in the table. In effect, we're using DISTINCT to list the various classifications of the field condition.

If you use a DISTINCT query in conjunction with a grouped page, you can dynamically create links to groups. I've built a template for this in Listing 10.5.

INPUT   **LISTING 10.5**   Dynamically Creating Links to Groups

```
1:  <!---BEGIN QUERY SECTION--->
2:
3:  <CFQUERY name="tapes" datasource="music">
4:  SELECT * from 8tracks ORDER by condition, artist
```

```
 5: </CFQUERY>
 6:
 7: <CFQUERY name="get_conditions" datasource="music">
 8: SELECT DISTINCT condition FROM 8tracks
 9: </CFQUERY>
10:
11: <!---END QUERY SECTION--->
12:
13: <HTML>
14: <HEAD>
15:     <TITLE>The 8-track Tapes in My Car</TITLE>
16: </HEAD>
17:
18: <BODY>
19: <H3>The 8-track Tapes in My Car</H3>
20:
21: Click on a link below to view tapes in that condition<P>
22:
23: <BLOCKQUOTE>
24:
25: <CFOUTPUT query="get_conditions">
26:
27:     <A HREF="###condition#">Tapes in #condition# condition</A><BR>
28:
29: </CFOUTPUT>
30:
31: </BLOCKQUOTE>
32:
33: <HR>
34:
35: <!---BEGIN GROUPED OUTPUT--->
36:
37: <CFOUTPUT query="tapes" group="condition">
38:     <A NAME="#condition#">
39:     <B>Tapes in #condition# condition</B>
40:     </A>
41:     <UL>
42:
43: <!---OUTPUT RECORDS FOR CURRENT GROUP--->
44:
45:     <CFOUTPUT>
46:     <LI>    <B>Artist:</B> #artist#<BR>
47:             <B>Title:</B> #title#<BR>
48:             <B>Possible Uses:</B> #uses#<P>
49:     </CFOUTPUT>
50:     </UL>
51:
52: <!---END CURRENT GROUP--->
53:
54: </CFOUTPUT>
```

continues

LISTING **10.5**   continued

```
55:
56: <!---END GROUPED OUTPUT--->
57:
58: </BODY>
59: </HTML>
```

We started with the grouping template from Listing 10.4 and added some new features. Notice the additional query, titled get_conditions. We used DISTINCT to get one of each condition. There's also a new <CFOUTPUT> section associated with the query.

Let's first look at the second <CFOUTPUT> section in which I've used the <A NAME> tag to anchor the groups. We used <A NAME="#condition#"> so that ColdFusion will dynamically plug in the name of each condition type as it groups the data. This in itself causes nothing new to appear in the user's browser—it just sets up anchor points.

Now look back at the first <CFOUTPUT> section. Here we used the results of the get_conditions query to dynamically create index links. Each of these will link to a group header.

Caution Because index links use the hash mark (#) to refer to <A NAME> sections further down a page, you must "escape" the symbol with an additional hash mark when it is used within <CFOUTPUT> tags. This lets ColdFusion discern between a literal hash mark and one that identifies a variable.

In the first output section, the three hash marks together can be a little confusing, but let's break them down. The first two provide the single hash mark necessary for the index link. For example, if I were to hand-code these links, they'd look like this:

```
<A HREF="#poor">Tapes in poor condition</A>
<A HREF="#passable">Tapes in passable condition</A>
<A HREF="#excellent">Tapes in excellent condition</A>
```

I have to use two hash marks to get one in this case because I'm working within a <CFOUTPUT> tag. The third hash mark is the beginning identifier for the variable #condition#. This variable is also used in the text that identifies the link:

```
<B>Tapes in #condition# condition</B>
```

To the user, this page looks like Figure 10.9.

Figure 10.9

A dynamically grouped and indexed page.

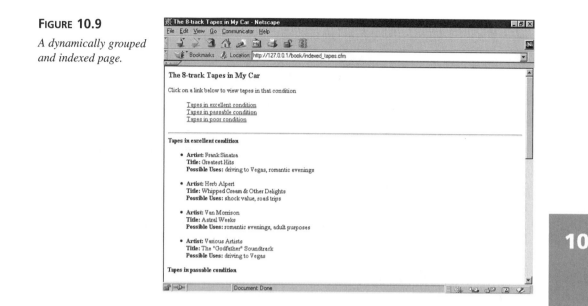

When a user clicks Tapes in excellent condition at the top of the page, his or her browser immediately moves to that group. For a small database like this, the page isn't really that hard to navigate manually, but you can see how larger databases will benefit from grouping and indexing.

Summary

Building readable, easy-to-navigate pages is a big part of successful Web design, and it's just as important when creating ColdFusion templates. CF has several features that enable you to format query output to your liking, including tabulated data and organizational tools such as grouping and sorting.

<CFTABLE> provides a quick way to turn queried data into a table. It's designed to replace the <CFOUTPUT> tag in your templates, and requires only a few parameters to display a basic table. It has a limited feature set, however, so if you need advanced table properties, it's best to work with standard HTML tables and populate the cells with <CFOUTPUT>.

Grouping data is another output tool designed to make your application easier to navigate. By using the GROUP parameter in <CFOUTPUT> sections, you can organize your data by a common field. Longer pages particularly benefit from grouping, and may also be indexed using the SQL command DISTINCT.

Q&A

Q Why don't my bold headers show up in a `<CFTABLE>`?

A By default, `<CFTABLE>` creates your table with the `<PRE>` tag, which doesn't recognized bolded text. To use bold headers, add the `HTMLTABLE` parameter to `<CFTABLE>` to build your table in HTML 3.0.

Q Can I use graphics in a `<CFTABLE>`?

A Yes, if you add the `HTMLTABLE` parameter. The easiest way to add graphics is to create a field in your database that lists the link path to the graphic. When you run a query, ColdFusion will return the link as one of your variables, which can then be added to a `<CFTABLE>`.

Q I used HTML tables with `<CFOUTPUT>` and now my table doesn't display at all. What should I do?

A Go through your table code line-by-line and pay careful attention to what appears within and without the `<CFOUTPUT>` tag. Errors often come from unclosed `<TD>` or `<TR>` tags, or even an unclosed `<TABLE>`.

Q I used the `GROUP` parameter in a `<CFOUTPUT>` section. ColdFusion created groups, but there are several groups of the same type and only one record per group.

A This happens when you don't use the `ORDER BY` clause in your template's query. ColdFusion will group records with a common field, but only if it receives them ordered by that field.

Workshop

Just to see if you were dozing through today's discussion, here are a few quiz questions and exercises. Answers to quiz and exercise questions can be found in Appendix A, "Quiz Answers," at the back of the text.

Quiz

1. What are the two modes of `<CFTABLE>`?
2. If your table requires header fields, what parameter must you include in `<CFTABLE>`?
3. If your table requires rows that span multiple columns, which tool should you use to build it?
4. What is *nesting*?

5. How many <CFOUTPUT> tags are necessary to build a grouped page?

6. What's the function of the HTML tag <A NAME>?

7. I have a database field that contains the following values: yes, yes, yes, no, maybe, yes, no, no. How many records would a query return if I used the DISTINCT tag on this field?

Exercises

1. Create a page that uses <CFTABLE> to display the contents of a database. First, use the default <PRE> mode to display data, and then use HTMLTABLE.

2. Create a table using HTML <TABLE> tags and ColdFusion output. Use a title row that spans all columns, and end the table with a similar footer row. Use BGCOLOR to make one of your data columns display over a colored background.

3. Create a page that groups data into tables. Each group should have a header, followed by a table populated with data from that group.

4. Using SQL's DISTINCT, create index links to each of the grouped tables in the last exercise.

10

DAY **11**

Enhancing Input Pages with Basic <CFFORM> Tags

ColdFusion's <CFFORM> tag serves as a replacement for HTML's <FORM> tag, offering an enhanced set of features that can improve the look and functionality of your input pages. Today's lesson will cover <CFFORM> and several of its associated tags including sections on

- Understanding how <CFFORM> works
- Using <CFFORM> in your templates
- Using the <CFINPUT> tag to accept and validate user input
- Using the <CFTEXTINPUT> tag to customize input boxes
- Using <CFSELECT> tag to populate selections from a query
- Using the <CFSLIDER> tag for number selection

Understanding <CFFORM>

In Day 7, "Changing the Contents of a Database with ColdFusion," you learned how ColdFusion works with standard HTML forms to insert and update data stored in a database. The examples in that chapter showed how to create a Web input form using the HTML <FORM> tag, and how to designate a ColdFusion template as the action page of that form. When a user filled out the form and pressed the "submit" button, the collected data was sent to the designated ColdFusion template in the form of a URL.

ColdFusion's <CFFORM> serves as a more feature-rich replacement for HTML's <FORM> tag. <CFFORM> works with similar elements like <FORM>, it also requires a defined ACTION page, and also submits collected data via a URL. But it goes beyond the capability of standard HTML forms by giving you new ways to display data and validate the user's entries.

Today's lesson will cover the basic input and selection tags available within <CFFORM>.

> **Note**
>
> Unlike HTML forms, the <CFFORM> tag only works when it appears in a template, or .cfm file. The standard <FORM> tag can be used in either .cfm or .html files.

> **Tip**
>
> If you've already built action pages to handle input from standard HTML forms, you can still use them as the action of <CFFORM> pages without changing a thing. The advanced features of the tag only affect the user-input side of things—they don't change the way that data is processed by an action page.

<CFFORM> creates enhanced form tools with JavaScript, but you needn't worry if you're not a programmer. In your template pages you'll simply use the various <CFFORM> tags as you would for a standard form, and then ColdFusion generates the necessary JavaScript at the time the user's browser requests the form page.

For example, one of <CFFORM>'s features is the sliding selection bar, implemented by the <CFSLIDER> tag within the form. The form section in your template file will look like Listing 11.1.

INPUT **LISTING 11.1** Creating a Sample Form Section with <CFFORM>

```
 1: <CFFORM action="some_page.cfm" method="post">
 2:    Choose a number between 1 and 100 by sliding the bar below:
 3:    <P>
 4:    <CFSLIDER    NAME="pick_a_number"
 5:                 LABEL="Your Number: %value%"
 6:                 RANGE="1,100"
 7:                 WIDTH="200"
 8:                 REFRESHLABEL="yes">
 9:    <P>
10:    <INPUT TYPE="submit">
11: </CFFORM>
```

When a user views the page created in Listing 11.1 in a browser, he sees something like Figure 11.1.

FIGURE 11.1

When a user moves the slider in a <CFSLIDER> tag, the input value changes within a pre-determined range of numeric values.

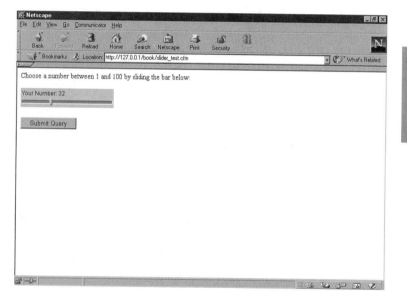

11

If users were crafty enough to use their browser's view source command on the slider page, they'd see what was happening behind the scenes, as in Listing 11.2.

LISTING 11.2 The Source Code That Appears in a User's Browser When Using <CFSLIDER>

```
 1: <script LANGUAGE=JAVASCRIPT>
 2: <!--
 3: function _CF_getSlider(sliderInstance)
 4:    {
 5:          return sliderInstance.cf_getSlider();
 6:    }
 7: function  _CF_checkCFForm_1(_CF_this)
 8:    {
 9:    _CF_this.__CFSLIDER__CFForm_1__pick_a_number.value = _
       ➥CF_getSlider(document.pick_a_number );
10:    return true;
11:    }
12: //-->
13: </script>
14: <FORM NAME="CFForm_1" ACTION="some_page.cfm" METHOD=POST onSubmit="return
    ➥_CF_checkCFForm_1(this)">
15:        Choose a number between 1 and 100 by sliding the bar below:
16:        <P>
17:        <APPLET NAME="pick_a_number" CODE="allaire.controls.CFSliderApplet"
           ➥ CODEBASE="/CFIDE/classes/" HEIGHT=40 WIDTH=200> <param NAME=
           ➥"ApplicationClass" VALUE="allaire.controls.cfslider">
18: <param NAME="sliderparm" VALUE="40%02200%021%02100%02%03%021%02Y
    ➥our+Number%3A+">
19: <B>Browser must support Java to <Br>view Cold Fusion Java Applets!</B><Br>
20: </APPLET>
21:        <P>
22:        <INPUT TYPE="submit">
23: <INPUT TYPE="HIDDEN" NAME="__CFSLIDER__CFForm_1__pick_a_number"> </FORM>
```

Don't be scared by the JavaScript in Listing 11.2. You won't need to be at all familiar with JavaScript to use <CFFORM>, and that's the point—you simply use <CFFORM> elements to create a page. ColdFusion creates the JavaScript behind the scenes, and the user sees an expertly formatted form page, thinking you've really outdone yourself.

Note For browsers that don't support JavaScript or have it disabled, <CFFORM> will display a generic error message letting the user know they're missing out on some features. If you want to customize this message, use the NotSUPPORTED parameter, as covered in the next section.

Now let's look at the parameters used with <CFFORM> and code some sample pages using the tag and its related tools.

Using <CFFORM>

Just like HTML's <FORM>, ColdFusion's tag requires an "action" parameter to define the form's action page, and a "method" parameter to determine how the collected data is sent. To define a form section anywhere in a ColdFusion template page, I use text like this:

```
<CFFORM action="some_page.cfm" method="post">

</CFFORM>
```

Note   <CFFORM> accepts all the same parameters as HTML <FORM>, including TARGET for use with frame sets, and ENCTYPE for determining the way the form is encoded. In addition, <CFFORM> also accepts two Java-specific parameters, ENABLECAB and ONSUBMIT. These aren't necessary for normal form processing, but can come in handy for Java programmers who want to add custom features to form pages.

After a <CFFORM> section is defined in a template page, I can use a variety of input and display elements. I can use standard HTML form elements like INPUT and TEXTAREA interchangeably or in conjunction with ColdFusion's more advanced tools.

We'll look at all these enhanced tags in more detail, but first realize that, because all <CFFORM>'s companion tags are driven by JavaScript behind the scenes, they have some common parameters that enable you to customize the way they look and work. Table 11.1 lists these common parameters. If any of these parameters don't make sense to you at this point, don't worry. You'll begin to understand how they work as we examine each of <CFFORM>'s enhanced tags.

11

TABLE 11.1   Common Parameters Used with All <CFFORM> Tags

Parameter	Function
NAME (required)	All <CFFORM> tags require a name.
NotSUPPORTED	The message to display if the user's browser doesn't support Java, or has it turned off. If you don't specify a message, ColdFusion displays a generic one by default.
ONVALIDATE	The name of a JavaScript function to validate user input. If you don't specify one, ColdFusion uses its own validation methods when the VALIDATE parameter is used in a <CFFORM> tag.

continues

TABLE 11.1   continued

Parameter	Function
ONERROR	A Javascript function to run if validation fails. Again, ColdFusion does this by default, so you only need to use this parameter if you have a custom-built function.
ALIGN	Means the same as HTML's standard alignment functions, but applies only to the <CFFORM> element that specifies it.
BOLD	Bolds the text for any <CFFORM> element.
ITALIC	Italicized text for any <CFFORM> element.
FONT	You can specify any font name supported by JavaScript to customize the appearance of your <CFFORM> elements.
FONTSIZE	The size of the font specified previously.
HEIGHT	The height, in pixels, of the <CFFORM> element.
HSPACE	Horizontal spacing of the <CFFORM> element.
VSPACE	Vertical spacing of the <CFFORM> element.
WIDTH	The width, in pixels, of the <CFFORM> element.

The <CFINPUT> Tag

<CFINPUT> is a cousin to the standard HTML form tag <INPUT>. Depending on the parameters used with it, the tag can be used to collect user input in the form of a text box, radio buttons, a check box, or a password box.

One of the primary advantages to using <CFINPUT> instead of its HTML counterpart is that it can also validate user input—that is, it can examine the text a user types in and see if it matches a certain format, such as a five-digit ZIP code or a nine-digit Social Security number. If the match fails, the user is advised to check her entry and resubmit.

Say that a client has asked me to design a simple online poll to determine how its users feel about crime. The envisioned page will look something like Figure 11.2.

This form contains two questions. For the first question, I used a standard radio button selector. When one button is selected, the others are automatically deselected to ensure that the user can only choose one answer for the question. Radio buttons are easily handled by standard HTML form codes, so I'm free to use either the <INPUT> or <CFINPUT> tags to create this question. The first part of my form was created from the code in Listing 11.3.

FIGURE 11.2

This form built with the <CFFORM> tag looks like a standard HTML form, but includes a "validate" feature to examine user input.

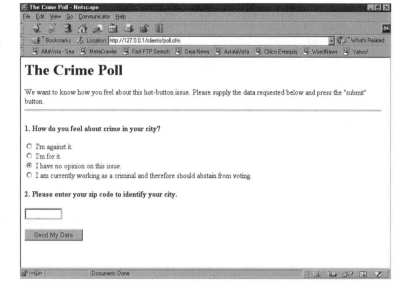

 LISTING 11.3 Creating Radio Buttons

```
1: <HEAD>
2:     <TITLE>The Crime Poll</TITLE>
3: </HEAD>
4: <BODY>
5: <H1>The Crime Poll</H1>
6: We want to know how you feel about this hot-button issue. Please supply
    ➥the data requested below and press the "submit" button.
7: <HR>
8: <!--- BEGIN CFFORM SECTION --->
9: <CFFORM ACTION="submit_data.cfm" METHOD="post">
10: <!--- BEGIN FIRST QUESTION --->
11:     <B>1. How do you feel about crime in your city?</B><P>
12:     <CFINPUT TYPE="radio" NAME="feelings" VALUE="against">
13:     I'm against it.<BR>
14:     <CFINPUT TYPE="radio" NAME="feelings" VALUE="for">
15:     I'm for it.<BR>
16:     <CFINPUT TYPE="radio" NAME="feelings" VALUE="no opinion">
17:     I have no opinion on this issue.<BR>
18:     <CFINPUT TYPE="radio" NAME="feelings" VALUE="criminal">
19:     I am currently working as a criminal and therefore should abstain from
        ➥voting.
20:     <P>
```

I've set up four possible answers to the question and assigned variables to each of them with the VALUE parameter. The variable passed to the action page will be either "for" (line 14), "against" (line 12), "no opinion" (line 16), or "criminal" (line 18).

The second question on the form enables me to make use of <CFINPUT>'s validation function. The client wants to see how users in different cities respond to the question, so he has asked me to collect a postal ZIP code with each submission. To verify that the user actually enters a five-digit ZIP, I used the text in Listing 11.4 to create the second question and then close the form.

LISTING 11.4   The Second Half of an Input Form, Using VALIDATE to Check
INPUT   for a Valid ZIP Code Entry

```
 1: <!--- BEGIN SECOND QUESTION --->
 2:
 3:    <B>2. Please enter your zip code to identify your city.</B><P>
 4:
 5: <CFINPUT TYPE="text" NAME="zip" SIZE="5" VALIDATE="zipcode" MESSAGE
    ➥"The text you entered in the ZIPCODE field is not a valid five-digit zip.
    ➥Please try again.">
 6:    <P>
 7:
 8: <INPUT TYPE="submit" VALUE="Send My Data">
 9:
10: </CFFORM>
11:
12: </BODY>
13: </HTML>
```

The second form question uses a couple of new parameters with the <CFINPUT> tag on line 5: VALIDATE and MESSAGE. VALIDATE tells ColdFusion that I want to compare the text typed in by the user with one of a variety of formats to see whether they got the right idea.

For this particular question, I've used ZIP code validation, which makes sure that the user has entered five digits. If the user typed in too few or too many characters, or used letters, their browser would return an error when they used the "submit" button, as shown in Figure 11.3.

Note

Depending on the user's browser and how it handles JavaScript, the error message can appear in different ways. Figure 11.3 shows an error message as a pop-up window in Netscape 4.6. Other browsers and versions might return a Web page with the error message rather than a separate window.

FIGURE 11.3

An error message generated by <CFINPUT>'s VALIDATE parameter.

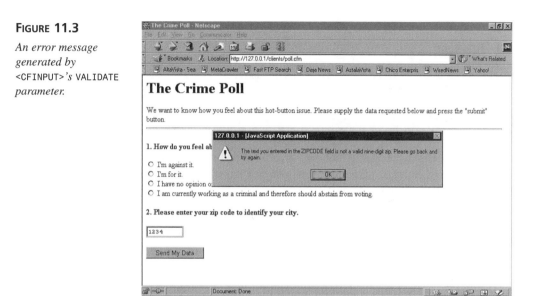

There are several validation types available for use with the VALIDATE parameter. They're designed to check for most of the common data types collected by forms, as shown in Table 11.2.

TABLE 11.2 Accepted Types Used with <CFINPUT>'s VALIDATE Parameter

Validation Type	Function
date	Verifies U.S. date entry in mm/dd/yyyy format.
eurodate	Verifies valid European date entry in dd/mm/yyyy format.
time	Verifies a time entry in hh:mm:ss format.
float	Verifies a floating point entry.
integer	Verifies an integer entry.
telephone	Verifies a telephone entry in the format ###-###-####. The hyphen (-) can also be replaced with a blank space.
creditcard	Strips blanks and dashes from the number input and checks it against the mod10 algorithm.
social_security_	Verifies a nine-digit number in the number format ###-##-####. The hyphen(-) can also be replaced with a blank space.

Look back at the code in Listing 11.4. Along with the new VALIDATE parameter, I've also used the parameter MESSAGE. The supplied text is what the user will see as an error if she don't input text that satisfies the VALIDATE type.

> **Caution**
>
> Because the MESSAGE parameter uses quote marks (") for demarcation, avoid using quotes in your error message itself. For example, instead of please use your browser's "back" button, try please use your browser's BACK button.

Note also in Listing 11.4 that I've used a SIZE parameter of "5" to really hammer it home to the user that I'm looking for a ZIP code here. By setting the SIZE to a certain number of characters, I can control both how the box looks on the page, and how many characters can be typed into it.

If a user selected an answer for question one and supplied five digits for the ZIP code in question two (line 5), my form would then send the results to an action page, in this case submit_data.cfm as defined in Listing 11.3, line 9. The action page would probably use a <CFINSERT> tag to input the collected data to a datasource, but I'll leave the possibilities to your imagination and the requirements of your own applications.

The <CFTEXTINPUT> Tag

This tag is the hot-rodded relative to both HTML's <INPUT TYPE="text"> and ColdFusion's <CFINPUT TYPE="text">. Like the other tags, it uses JavaScript to work its magic behind the scenes, but <CFTEXTINPUT> takes things a step further by creating the *entire input box* as a JavaScript function.

What does this mean to you, the developer? It means more control over the way your text input boxes look on the page. With <CFTEXTINPUT> you can customize the font, text color, and box color of your text input elements. Let's look at an example in Figure 11.4.

The first box in Figure 11.4 comes from a standard HTML <FORM> tag:

```
<INPUT TYPE="text" NAME="HTML">
```

The second uses the <CFINPUT> tag:

```
<CFINPUT TYPE="text" NAME="CFINPUT">
```

The third uses the enhanced features of <CFTEXTINPUT>:

```
<CFTEXTINPUT NAME="CFTEXTINPUT" FONT="Arial" BGCOLOR="Blue" TEXTCOLOR="White"
➥REQUIRED="No" BOLD="No" ITALIC="No">
```

FIGURE 11.4

Three types of input boxes, each generated by different code.

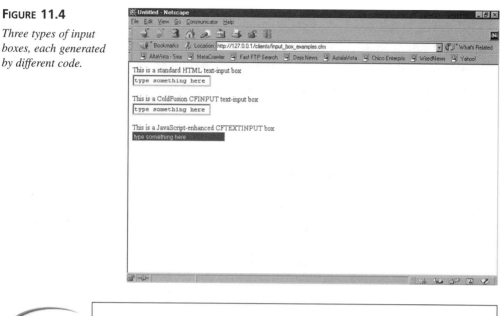

> **Note**
>
> The appearance of text boxes is a little more elegant with <CFTEXTINPUT> because the whole thing is generated by JavaScript, rather than relying on standard HTML boxes.

11

In addition to its aesthetic enhancements, <CFTEXTINPUT> also supports input validation for the various data types detailed in the last section on <CFINPUT>. Table 11.3 shows a complete list of parameters accepted by <CFTEXTINPUT>.

TABLE 11.3 Parameters for <CFTEXTINPUT>

Parameter	Function
NAME (required)	A name for the input box.
REQUIRED	Setting this to "yes" requires the user to supply some text before submitting the form.
RANGE	If you're asking the user for numeric data, this will set upper and lower limits for an acceptable range of numbers.
VALIDATE	Determines a data type the user must enter. Valid data types are covered in the previous section on <CFINPUT>.
MESSAGE	The text that will appear if validation fails.
BGCOLOR	Sets the background color of the text box.
TEXTCOLOR	Sets the color of the text a user types in.
MAXLENGTH	The maximum number of characters the user can type.

The <CFSELECT> Tag

<CFSELECT> is arguably the most valuable tag available in <CFFORM> because it has the greatest potential to save you time and hair-pulling. To see why, let's look at an example.

Remember my database of 8-track tapes back in Day 10? I built a database table that stored the names of all the tapes currently riding around in my car. Let's say I want to let Web users vote for their favorite tape via a form. I'll use a pull-down SELECT box that will list all the tapes, as shown in Figure 11.5.

FIGURE 11.5

This form uses a standard SELECT box to enable users to choose a value.

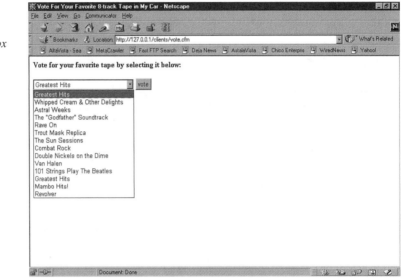

To create this form, I did things the old way for purposes of illustration. I used a <CFQUERY> to get all the tapes from the database, and then used the returned data to populate my SELECT box. I used only standard <FORM> tags, not the ColdFusion versions. The code looks like Listing 11.5.

INPUT   **LISTING 11.5**   vote.cfm

```
1: <!--- GET ALL DATA FOR THE TAPES --->
2:
3: <CFQUERY name="tapes" datasource="music">
4: SELECT * from 8tracks
5: </CFQUERY>
6:
7: <HTML>
8: <HEAD>
```

```
 9:     <TITLE>Vote For Your Favorite 8-track Tape in My Car</TITLE>
10: </HEAD>
11:
12: <BODY>
13: <B>Vote for your favorite tape by selecting it below:</B>
14:
15: <!--- BEGIN THE VOTING FORM --->
16:
17: <FORM ACTION="send_vote.cfm" METHOD="post">
18:
19:     <SELECT NAME="tape">
20:
21: <!--- USE DATA FROM THE QUERY TO POPULATE THE SELECT OPTIONS --->
22:
23:         <CFOUTPUT query="tapes">
24:             <OPTION VALUE="#ID#">#title#</OPTION>
25:         </CFOUTPUT>
26:
27: <!--- NOW CLOSE THE SELECT STATEMENT --->
28:
29:     </SELECT>
30:     <INPUT TYPE="submit" VALUE="vote">
31:
32: </FORM>
33:
34: </BODY>
35: </HTML>
```

11

Because I placed the <OPTION> tag (line 24) within the <CFOUTPUT> section (lines 23-25), each record returned by my query will become an option in the SELECT box.

Notice in the browser display in Figure 11.5 that the names of the tapes appear in no particular order—in fact, they're listed in the order in which I typed them into the database. So when the user comes to my form page, the tape they'll see listed in the select box is the one that occurs first in the database, in this case, the Sinatra album "Greatest Hits."

Of course, when they click the "down" arrow as I did in Figure 11.5, they'll see the whole list. But I'm thinking maybe I can sway the voting a little by setting *my own* favorite tape as the default selection value. I'm kinda partial to the mambo sounds of Perez Prado, so I'll make the tape "Mambo Hits!" be the default selected value and hope that other users see the wisdom in this selection.

Now this gets a little tricky because I'm populating my SELECT box with ColdFusion query output. I need to add SELECTED="yes" to just the "Mambo Hits!" entry. To do this *without* <CFSELECT>'s enhanced features, I'd have to do some pretty crafty coding, as shown in Listing 11.6.

LISTING 11.6   Using SELECTED=yes to Choose a Default Item

```
 1: <!--- BEGIN VOTING FORM --->
 2:
 3: <FORM ACTION="send_vote.cfm" METHOD="post">
 4:
 5:     <SELECT NAME="tape">
 6:
 7: <!---POPULATE SELECT BOX WITH QUERY OUTPUT--->
 8:
 9:         <CFOUTPUT query="tapes">
10:             <OPTION VALUE="#ID#"
11:
12: <!--- ADD "SELECTED=yes" TO THE "MAMBO HITS!" OPTION --->
13:
14:             <CFIF title IS 'Mambo Hits!'>
15:                 SELECTED="yes"
16:             </CFIF>
17:
18: <!--- CONCLUDE OPTION STATEMENT --->
19:
20: #title#</OPTION>
21:
22:         </CFOUTPUT>
23:
24: <!--- CONCLUDE SELECT STATEMENT --->
25:
26:     </SELECT>
27:
28:     <INPUT TYPE="submit" VALUE="vote">
29:
30: </FORM>
```

This method examines each row of query output, looking for the title "Mambo Hits!" When it finds it, the <CFIF> statement adds the text SELECTED="yes" to just that one OPTION statement.

This is a pretty simple form with just one SELECT box, but you can see how your code could get really confusing if you had several of these on a page. That's where <CFSELECT> comes in. It offers a much more compact way to populate SELECT boxes with query data, and even provides for fancy stuff like selecting a certain record.

To use <CFSELECT> to create the voting page, I first change the HTML <FORM> tag to <CFFORM>. I'll use the same query as before, but now my form section will look like Listing 11.7.

LISTING 11.7   Using <CFSELECT> to Select a Default Item

```
1: <CFFORM ACTION="send_vote.cfm" METHOD="post">
2:
3:     <CFSELECT NAME="tape" QUERY="tapes" VALUE="ID" DISPLAY="title"
        ➥SELECTED="6">
4:     </CFSELECT>
5:     <INPUT TYPE="submit" VALUE="vote">
6:
7: </CFFORM>
```

<CFSELECT> provides a much easier way to populate the SELECT box. It uses the NAME and VALUE parameters just like a regular <SELECT>, but also includes some other features, as listed in Table 11.4.

TABLE 11.4   Parameters for <CFSELECT>

Parameter	Function
NAME (required)	The variable name that will be assigned to the selected data
SIZE	The size of the SELECT box in rows
REQUIRED	If set to "yes," a value must be selected for the form to process
MESSAGE	The text that appears if REQUIRED is set to "yes" and nothing is selected on submit
ONERROR	The name of a JavaScript function to run if validation fails
MULTIPLE	Allows the user to select more than one value in the SELECT box
QUERY	The name of the query that will populate the box
SELECTED	The value(s) of one or more entries in VALUE that will appear as selected by default
VALUE	The query field that will be passed to the action page as a variable
DISPLAY	The query field that will display in the SELECT box

Look back at the code in Listing 11.7. In my <CFSELECT> statement on line 3, I specified a NAME and VALUE for my SELECT box, and then used the SELECTED parameter to supply a certain VALUE that should be selected. Recall that the ID field is the primary key in my database and is unique for each record, so it makes a good selector. Looking at my database, I saw the "Mambo Hits!" tape has an ID of 6, so I used that for the SELECTED value.

11

Note

SELECTED must be a value that appears in the VALUE parameter. In the previous example, I used the ID field as the value, so I had to supply a valid ID number as the SELECTED record.

The `<CFSLIDER>` Tag

`<CFSLIDER>` isn't a big time-saving device like `<CFSELECT>`, but it's kind of a neat way to enable users to choose a numeric value in a form.

To illustrate, let's say I want to create a form that will let users rate each of my tapes on a scale from 1 to 10. It will look like Figure 11.6.

FIGURE 11.6

`<CFSLIDER>` *lets users select a number by sliding a JavaScript bar across a range of values.*

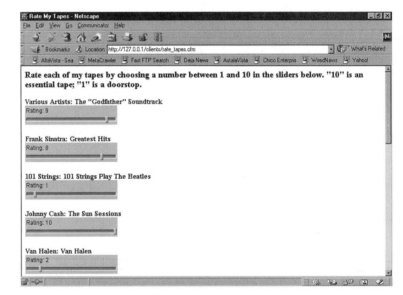

Tip

`<CFSLIDER>` absolutely requires a Java-enabled browser to run. If you think your users might not be Java-ready, use a standard SELECT box instead.

To create this page, I used a basic query to get all the tapes in my database, and then created a `<CFFORM>` to display the results and collect a rating for each. The code is shown in Listing 11.8.

LISTING 11.8   rate_tapes.cfm

```
 1: <CFQUERY NAME="tapes" DATASOURCE="music">
    ➥SELECT * from 8tracks
    ➥</CFQUERY>
 2: <HTML>
 3: <TITLE>Rate My Tapes</TITLE>
 4: <CFFORM action="some_page.cfm" method="post">
 5:     <H3>Rate each of my tapes by choosing a number between 1 and 10
        ➥in the sliders below. "10" is an essential tape; "1" is a
        ➥doorstop.</H3>
 6: <CFOUTPUT query="tapes">
 7:         <B>#artist#: #title#</B><BR>
 8: <CFSLIDER    NAME="#ID#"
    ➥LABEL="Rating: %value%"
    ➥RANGE="1,10"
    ➥WIDTH="200"
    ➥REFRESHLABEL="yes">
 9:         <P>
10:     </CFOUTPUT>
11:     <INPUT TYPE="submit">
12: </CFFORM>
13: </HTML>
```

11

In the <CFSLIDER> tag, I again used the ID field as the name because unique numbers make good selectors. When a user clicks the "submit" button on this form, it will pass a series of ID numbers with rating values for each.

<CFSLIDER> accepts the parameters shown in Table 11.5.

TABLE 11.5   Parameters Used with <CFSLIDER>

Parameter	Function
LABEL	A label that appears above the slider. If you'd like the current value of the slider to be shown in the label, use the variable %value% and also set REFRESHLABEL to "yes."
REFRESHLABEL	If set to "yes," the label will update as the user moves the slider.
IMG	An image file to use in the slider groove.
IMGSTYLE	Determines how the IMG file is displayed. Can be "tiled," "centered," or "scaled."
RANGE	The upper and lower values for the slider, separated by a comma. For example, RANGE="1,10" will enable users to choose a number between 1 and 10.
SCALE	Specifies the increments between values. For example, if RANGE was set to show numbers between 1 and 500, SCALE=100 would show only the numbers 100, 200, 300, and so on.

continues

TABLE 11.5 continued

Parameter	Function
VALUE	Determines the default slider setting.
ONVALIDATE	The name of a JavaScript function used to validate input.
MESSAGE	Text that will appear if validation fails.
ONERROR	A JavaScript function to run if validation fails.
GROOVECOLOR	Instead of an IMG file, you can also illustrate the slider with a valid HEX color.
BGCOLOR	The background color of the slider label.
TEXTCOLOR	The text color of the slider label.

Summary

ColdFusion's <CFFORM> tag provides a variety of ways to customize and enhance the way users can input data on your site. Though it offers more features than HTML's standard <FORM> tag, it passes collected data in exactly the same way. For this reason, ColdFusion-enhanced forms can be used with existing action pages and CGI scripts.

ColdFusion-enhanced forms use JavaScript to create the custom features in the user's browser; you, the developer, don't need to know a thing about Java to use the tools. You simply use the required <CFFORM> tags in your templates, and ColdFusion does the rest behind the scenes.

Included in <CFFORM>'s enhanced tagset are <CFINPUT> and <CFTEXTINPUT> for creating text boxes that will automatically validate user entries to make sure the user is supplying valid phone numbers, ZIP codes, Social Security numbers, or other formats you specify. <CFFORM> also enables you to customize the way these selection devices are displayed, including colored fonts, backgrounds, and bold and italic entries.

Particularly useful to ColdFusion developers is the <CFSELECT> tag, which greatly simplifies the process of populating a SELECT box with query results. <CFSLIDER> lets you create a JavaScript-driven selector for numeric values.

Q&A

Q **I'm migrating an HTML-only site to ColdFusion. Should I go through my pages and upgrade all my <FORM> tags to <CFFORM> and put them on template pages?**

A If it ain't broke, don't fix it. The advantage to keeping your existing HTML forms is that they don't require Java and are consequently faster-loading and foolproof for all users. However, if you find a form that might benefit from the enhanced features of <CFFORM>, go for it.

Q **What if my site is targeted to a user base that doesn't use Java-compatible browsers?**

A You can supply alternative HTML-only forms to non-Java users by customizing the error message in the NotSUPPORTED parameter of <CFFORM> sections.

Q **If I'm an experienced JavaScript programmer, can I customize the behavior of <CFFORM> tags?**

A Yes. <CFFORM> tags enable you to specify JavaScript functions that run when certain actions occur, such as a successful or failed validation.

Workshop

Answers to quiz questions can be found in Appendix A at the back of the text.

Quiz

1. What happens when a user with a non-Java browser tries to view a ColdFusion-enhanced form page?

2. Name the main feature supported by <CFINPUT> that is not supported by the standard HTML <INPUT> form tag.

3. What's the difference between <CFINPUT> and <CFTEXTINPUT>?

4. What's the main benefit of using <CFSELECT> instead of a standard form <SELECT>?

5. What is the parameter used with a query-driven <CFSELECT> to specify which option should be selected by default?

6. If you want to create a <CFSLIDER> that will show the values 5, 10, 15, 20, and so on up to 100, what are the two parameters to use with the tag?

Exercises

1. Create a form that requires users to input a valid Social Security number. Customize the error message so that it reads "You Loser!" if they don't.

2. Create a form that will collect user input in text boxes. Use <CFTEXTINPUT> to customize the color, font, and size of the boxes.

3. Create a form that enables users to select more than one value from a SELECT box. Use <CFSELECT> and a query to create selections, and specify a selection to appear as the default.

4. Create a slider that enables users to choose a decade between 1900 and the present using <CFSLIDER>.

DAY **12**

Using Advanced Form Techniques to Manage Input

In previous lessons, you've learned much about Web forms and how they're used to handle input from users. In today's discussion, you'll learn about some advanced design techniques that will enable you to get more from your forms. You'll find out how to handle custom insertion, update, and delete actions, as well as how to consolidate your forms and make them easy to manage if your site's databases change structure. This lesson also introduces two <CFFORM> tags not covered in yesterday's lesson, both of which provide new ways to display complex data and accept user input.

Today's lesson covers

- Using SQL to update, insert, and delete records
- Creating multifunction form pages
- Displaying and selecting data with <CFTREE>
- Displaying, selecting, and updating data with <CFGRID> and <CFGRIDUPDATE>

Understanding SQL Updates, Inserts, and Deletes

Way back in Day 5, "Finding the Data You Need: An Introduction to Queries and SQL," you learned how to use the <CFUPDATE> and <CFINSERT> tags to edit and add records in a database. For simple sites, these tools work fine—they enable you to take user data from a form and perform some action on your database. But as your knowledge of ColdFusion grows and your applications become more sophisticated, you might find that you need more flexibility in working with your database. Take a look at Figure 12.1 for a basic example.

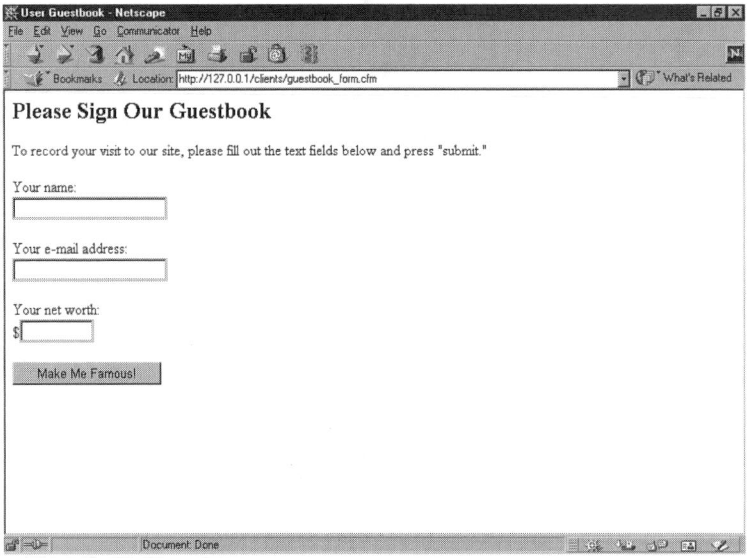

FIGURE 12.1

A basic input form that collects data from the user.

To input this data into a table, you'd use an action page like Listing 12.1.

LISTING 12.1 guestbook_submit.cfm

```
1: <CFINSERT    DATASOURCE="gargantuan"
2:              TABLENAME="visitors"
3:              FORMFIELDS="name,email,net_worth">
4:
5: <HTML>
6: <HEAD>
7:    <TITLE>Thanks For Submitting Your Entry</TITLE>
8: </HEAD>
9:
```

```
10: <BODY>
11: <H2>Thanks For Submitting Your Entry</H2>
12:
13: <B>The text you entered reads as follows:</B><P>
14:
15: <CFOUTPUT>
16:     <B>Your name:</B> <I>#form.name#</I><P>
17:     <B>Your e-mail address:</B> <I>#form.email#</I><P>
18:     <B>Your net worth:</B> <I>#net_worth#</I>
19:
20: </CFOUTPUT>
21:
22: </BODY>
23: </HTML>
```

ANALYSIS   Note the <CFINSERT> tag in line 1 of Listing 12.1—that's the part that inserts the user data.

> **Note**
>
> For a review of <CFINSERT> and <CFUPDATE>, see Day 7, "Changing the Contents of a Database with ColdFusion."

<CFINSERT> is a great tool if you want to work just with form data, but what if you have other information that you'd like to insert—information that doesn't come from the form? To illustrate, let's say that you want to input the current time and date at the moment the user's information is added to the database. You could use a special ColdFusion function called Now() on your ACTION page to generate the current time and date, but because that value isn't being passed by the form, <CFINSERT> won't "see" it. The <CFINSERT> tag only enables you to list form fields to insert, so clearly that won't work.

> **Note**
>
> ColdFusion *functions* are covered in detail in Day 14, "Using ColdFusion Functions to Manipulate Data." For now, just know that #Now()# creates a variable that holds the current time and date reported by your Web server.

In situations like these in which you need to input data that doesn't come directly from a form, you can use alternative methods to add or edit your database contents. These methods are the SQL commands UPDATE, INSERT, and DELETE. All are used in the context of a standard SQL query in place of the now-familiar SELECT command. The next sections examine all three commands in detail, but first consider a few situations in which you'd want to use these SQL methods instead of their simpler ColdFusion equivalents:

12

- When you need to insert data that isn't passed from a form
- When you need to insert data into more than one table
- When your insert or update action is generally too complex to be handled with <CFINSERT> or <CFUPDATE>
- When you need to delete a record or records from a table

Using SQL's INSERT Command

To see how to insert data with SQL, start with the following example. The ACTION page in Listing 12.1 contained an insert function like this:

```
<CFINSERT     DATASOURCE="gargantuan"
              TABLENAME="visitors"
              FORMFIELDS="name,email,net_worth">
```

But, now you'd like to insert the current date/time into the database, and the forms hasn't passed that information. You might replace the previous statement with an SQL query like this:

```
<CFQUERY DATASOURCE="gargantuan">
        INSERT INTO visitors(name,email,net_worth,date)
        VALUES('#name#',
               '#email#',
               '#net_worth#',
               #Now()#)
</CFQUERY>
```

An SQL insert like this is much more flexible than <CFINSERT> because it gives you more control over what—and where—data is inserted.

Take a closer look at the statement. It begins with a standard <CFQUERY> tag, although no NAME is used because this query won't be outputting any data. It specifies the name of a table to INSERT INTO and follows with a comma-delimited list of field names in parentheses. The order of these is important, because it must correspond exactly to the order of the data listed in VALUES.

The final value of INSERT, #Now()#, will place the current date and time reported by the Web server into the visitors table at the moment the user inputs the form. This special function isn't surrounded by single-quotes because it isn't a text string—it's actually something called a *date/time object,* but you'll learn more about that in Day 14.

Assuming a user inputs typical data into the form, my Microsoft Access database now contains a record like Figure 12.2. Note that the ID field is automatically supplied by Access as each new record enters the table.

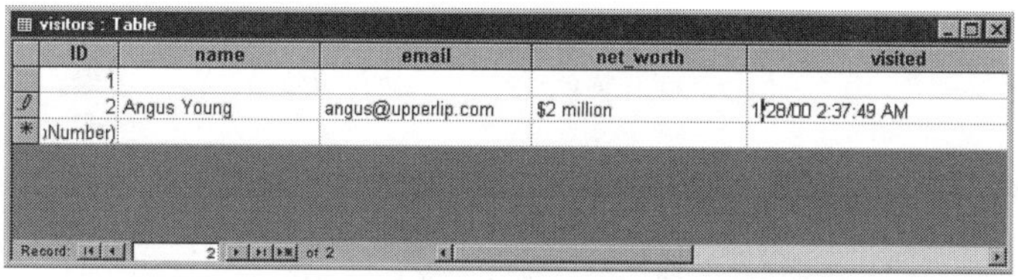

FIGURE 12.2

FIGURE 12.2

A record inserted with SQL's INSERT command, containing the date and time of the insertion.

> **Note**
>
> Depending on your database software and the data type in your table, date/time objects such as Now() may require special formatting before your database will accept them in an INSERT action. If you have trouble with the INSERT described above, try using text data types for the examples in this chapter. When you learn more about date/time objects in Day 14, you can then use ColdFusion functions to put Now() into a date format accepted by your database.

Using SQL's UPDATE Command

The UPDATE command is similar to INSERT, but it takes a different set of parameters. To illustrate how it is used, suppose that you want to create a page that will enable users to edit erroneous information submitted in the previous example. You'd use a form that would select the user's existing record from the database and display it as VALUEs in a form, like Figure 12.3.

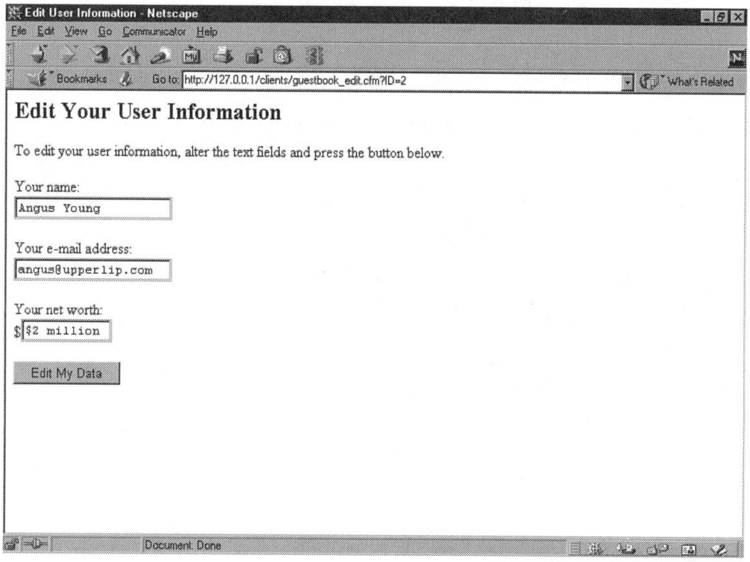

FIGURE 12.3

A form that lets users edit previously submitted data.

12

The code that produced this form is shown in Listing 12.2. The page requires an ID field to be supplied in the URL (or possibly from a previous form) to grab the user's record.

LISTING 12.2 guestbook_edit.cfm

```
 1: <CFQUERY NAME="get_user" DATASOURCE="gargantuan">
 2: SELECT * FROM visitors WHERE ID = #ID#
 3: </CFQUERY>
 4:
 5: <HTML>
 6: <HEAD>
 7:    <TITLE>Edit User Information</TITLE>
 8: </HEAD>
 9:
10: <BODY>
11: <H2>Edit Your User Information</H2>
12:
13: To edit your user information, alter the text fields and press
    ➥the button below.
14:
15: <CFOUTPUT QUERY="get_user">
16: <FORM ACTION="guestbook_edit_submit.cfm" METHOD="post">
17: Your name:<BR>
18: <INPUT TYPE="text" NAME="name" VALUE="#name#"><P>
19:
20: Your e-mail address:<BR>
21: <INPUT TYPE="text" NAME="email" VALUE="#email#"><P>
22:
23: Your net worth:<BR>
24: $<INPUT TYPE="text" NAME="net_worth" VALUE="#net_worth#" SIZE="11"><P>
25:
26: <INPUT TYPE="hidden" NAME="ID" VALUE="#ID#">
27:
28: <INPUT TYPE="submit" VALUE="Edit My Data">
29:
30: </FORM>
31: </CFOUTPUT>
32: </BODY>
33: </HTML>
```

Note

Notice that Listing 12.2 includes a "hidden" field on line 26 containing the ID number associated with the record. This is important, because it will be required on the ACTION page to perform an update with either <CFUPDATE> or SQL's UPDATE command.

The form enables the users to work with their existing data—correct spelling errors, increase their net worth, whatever—and then resubmit the new information to the database where it will overwrite their previous records.

To accomplish this last task, you might use a <CFUPDATE> tag like this on the ACTION page:

```
<CFUPDATE    DATASOURCE="gargantuan"
             TABLENAME="visitors"
             FORMFIELDS="name,email,net_worth">
```

Note

<CFUPDATE> is covered in detail in Day 7's lesson.

As long as you're sure to pass ID (the table's primary key) as a hidden field, <CFUPDATE> will take the user's edited data from the form and overwrite the record. But let's say that you want to get a little tricky and overwrite the existing date field with the new date at the time the user submits his edited data. Like <CFINSERT> in the last section, <CFUPDATE> doesn't have any provision for updating data not sent by the form. You'll have to improvise with SQL's UPDATE command, as illustrated in Listing 12.3, which contains the ACTION page for the form.

LISTING 12.3   guestbook_edit_submit.cfm

```
 1: <CFQUERY DATASOURCE="gargantuan">
 2:          UPDATE visitors
 3:          SET name='#name#',
 4:              email='#email#',
 5:              net_worth='#net_worth#',
 6:              visited=#Now()#
 7:          WHERE ID=#ID#
 8:
 9: </CFQUERY>
10:
11:
12: <HTML>
13: <HEAD>
14:     <TITLE>Thanks For Submitting Your Entry</TITLE>
15: </HEAD>
16:
17: <BODY>
18: <H2>Thanks For Submitting Your Entry</H2>
```

12

continues

LISTING 12.3 continued

```
19:
20: <B>The text you entered reads as follows:</B><P>
21:
22: <CFOUTPUT>
23:     <B>Your name:</B> <I>#form.name#</I><P>
24:     <B>Your e-mail address:</B> <I>#form.email#</I><P>
25:     <B>Your net worth:</B> <I>#net_worth#</I>
26:
27: </CFOUTPUT>
28:
29: </BODY>
30: </HTML>
```

ANALYSIS Listing 12.3 contains a query that uses SQL's UPDATE rather than <CFUPDATE>. It specifies a table to UPDATE, and then lists field names and the variable values that will overwrite the old data. Note that, as in the last section, the #Now()# function isn't surrounded by single quotes because it is not a simple text string. The UPDATE query ends with the required line

```
WHERE ID=#ID#
```

This tells ColdFusion exactly which record you want to replace—without it, the update would fail, and you'd see an error message.

Using SQL's DELETE Command

Unlike INSERT and UPDATE, SQL's DELETE command has no corresponding ColdFusion tag. This means that, when you want to delete data from your tables with ColdFusion, you *always* have to use the DELETE command in the context of an SQL query.

> **Caution**
>
> When you remove a database record or records with DELETE, it's gone forever. There are no second chances or "wish-I-woulda's." Because of this, it's important to exercise extreme caution in creating pages that enable users to delete information.

Take a look at a sample delete form in Figure 12.4.

FIGURE 12.4

A form designed to delete a user record from the database.

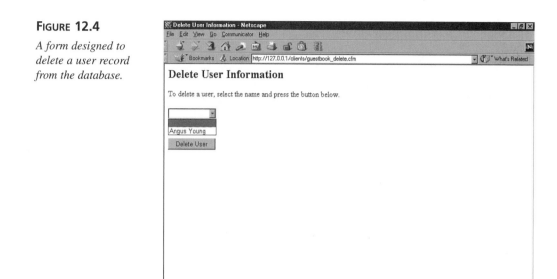

The code that produced Figure 12.4 is shown in Listing 12.4.

LISTING 12.4 guestbook_delete.cfm

```
 1: <CFQUERY NAME="get_users" DATASOURCE="gargantuan">
 2: SELECT * FROM visitors
 3: </CFQUERY>
 4:
 5: <HTML>
 6: <HEAD>
 7:     <TITLE>Delete User Information</TITLE>
 8: </HEAD>
 9:
10: <BODY>
11: <H2>Delete User Information</H2>
12:
13: To delete a user, select the name and press the button below.
14:
15:
16: <FORM ACTION="guestbook_delete_action.cfm" METHOD="post">
17:
18: <SELECT NAME="ID">
19:
20: <CFOUTPUT QUERY="get_users">
21:
22: <OPTION VALUE="#ID#">#name#</OPTION>
```

continues

12

LISTING 12.4   continued

```
23:
24: </CFOUTPUT>
25:
26: </SELECT>
27:
28: <BR><BR><BR>
29:
30: <INPUT TYPE="submit" VALUE="Delete User">
31:
32: </FORM>
33: </BODY>
34: </HTML>
```

ANALYSIS   It's a pretty straightforward form page, but there are a few things to note. First, the query section on lines 1-3 gets the data for all users from the visitors table. These are output as OPTION values in the form's SELECT box on lines 18-26. Note that, although the SELECT box will display the user's name, the variable that will be passed is actually #ID#. Again, this is important because you need to send a unique value to the ACTION page where the actual deletion will occur. The ID number is perfect for this because it ensures that you won't delete the wrong record.

Listing 12.4 passes just one variable to the ACTION page guestbook_delete_action.cfm, the record's ID. This page is shown in Listing 12.5.

LISTING 12.5   guestbook_delete_action.cfm

```
 1: <CFQUERY DATASOURCE="gargantuan">
 2:         DELETE FROM visitors
 3:         WHERE ID=#form.ID#
 4:
 5: </CFQUERY>
 6:
 7:
 8: <HTML>
 9: <HEAD>
10:     <TITLE>Entry Deleted</TITLE>
11: </HEAD>
12:
13: <BODY>
14: <H2>Thanks For Submitting Your Entry</H2>
15:
16: <B>The record for user ID <CFOUTPUT>#form.ID#</CFOUTPUT> has been
    ➥deleted.</B>
17:
18: <P>
19:
20: </BODY>
21: </HTML>
```

SQL's DELETE command is *very* simple to use, and therein lies one of its great dangers. It requires only one parameter to work—in this case, the #ID# passed by the previous form. You simply specify a table name to delete from and, *flash*, the record is gone.

> **Tip**
>
> When building pages that use DELETE, don't forget that it's best to use a test table or datasource to try out your handiwork. Use an active datasource, and you risk zapping crucial data.

Combining Multiple Form Actions

In the previous examples, you created three sets of form and ACTION pages that performed three different functions. In an actual Web application, you might consolidate two or more of these actions on a single page—both to make your site easier for users to navigate, and to save yourself coding time if you need to alter field names or form functions later. Take a look at Figure 12.5 for an example.

FIGURE 12.5

A multifunction administration form with two possible actions.

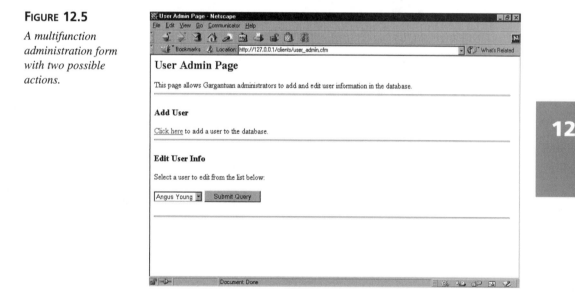

This page enables two different actions, an insert and an update. Both link to the same ACTION page, but only the edit function will pass a variable. Take a look at Listing 12.6 to see what's going on behind the scenes.

Listing 12.6 user_admin.cfm

```
 1: <CFQUERY NAME="get_users" DATASOURCE="gargantuan">
 2: SELECT * FROM visitors
 3: </CFQUERY>
 4:
 5: <HTML>
 6:
 7: <TITLE>User Admin Page</TITLE>
 8: <BODY>
 9: <H2>User Admin Page</H2>
10:
11: This page allows Gargantuan administrators to add and edit user
    ➥information in the database.
12:
13: <HR>
14: <H3>Add User</H3>
15: <A HREF="user_edit.cfm">Click here</A> to add a user to the database.
16:
17: <HR>
18:
19: <H3>Edit User Info</H3>
20: Select a user to edit from the list below:<BR>
21:
22: <FORM ACTION="user_edit.cfm" METHOD="post">
23:
24:     <SELECT NAME="ID">
25:
26:     <CFOUTPUT QUERY="get_users">
27:         <OPTION VALUE="#ID#">#name#</OPTION>
28:     </CFOUTPUT>
29:
30:     </SELECT>
31:
32:     <INPUT TYPE="submit">
33:
34: </FORM>
35: <HR>
36:
37: </HTML>
```

Analysis   The <CFQUERY> in line 1 retrieves all users from the table for display in the drop-down "edit" list, just like the form in the previous section on SQL's UPDATE command. The "add" function doesn't require anything special—it's just a simple link to the page user_edit.cfm.

The ACTION page is where the fancy footwork comes into play. Note that if a user chooses the "add" option, they're taken to user_edit.cfm, and no variable is passed. If they choose a name from the "edit" list, they're taken to the same page, but the variable #ID#

is passed from the form. You can use the presence of the #ID# variable to let the ACTION page know what's going on. Take a look at Listing 12.7 to see how one page can accommodate either type of action.

LISTING 12.7   user_edit.cfm

```
 1: <CFIF IsDefined("ID")>
 2:
 3:     <CFSET to_do = "edit">
 4:
 5: <CFELSE>
 6:
 7:     <CFSET to_do = "add">
 8:
 9: </CFIF>
10:
11: <CFIF to_do IS "edit">
12:
13:     <CFQUERY NAME="get_user" DATASOURCE="gargantuan">
14:         SELECT * FROM visitors WHERE ID=#form.ID#
15:     </CFQUERY>
16:
17: </CFIF>
18:
19: <HTML>
20:
21: <HEAD>
22:     <TITLE>User Admin Page</TITLE>
23:
24: </HEAD>
25: <BODY>
26: <H2>Add or Edit User Info Below:</H2>
27:
28: <FORM ACTION="user_update.cfm" METHOD="post">
29:
30: Name: <INPUT TYPE="text" NAME="name"
31:
32: <CFIF to_do IS "edit">
33:     VALUE="<CFOUTPUT>#get_user.name#</CFOUTPUT>"
34: </CFIF>
35:
36: >
37:
38: <P>
39:
40: E-mail: <INPUT TYPE="text" NAME="email"
41:
42: <CFIF to_do IS "edit">
43:     VALUE="<CFOUTPUT>#get_user.email#</CFOUTPUT>"
```

continues

LISTING 12.7   continued

```
44: </CFIF>
45:
46: >
47:
48: <P>
49:
50: Net Worth: <INPUT TYPE="text" NAME="net_worth"
51:
52: <CFIF to_do IS "edit">
53:     VALUE="<CFOUTPUT>#get_user.net_worth#</CFOUTPUT>"
54: </CFIF>
55:
56: >
57:
58: <P>
59:
60: <CFIF to_do IS "edit">
61:     <INPUT TYPE="hidden" NAME="ID" VALUE="<CFOUTPUT>#get_user.
        ➥ID#</CFOUTPUT>">
62: </CFIF>
63:
64: <INPUT TYPE="submit">
65:
66: </FORM>
67:
68: </HTML>
```

ANALYSIS   As you can see, things get a little complex here, but the time you save will be well worth it if you need to change your form or your database later. Take a look at the code. The first item on the page uses a special function called `#IsDefined()#` to check for the existence of an `#ID#` variable. Again, you'll learn much more about functions in a future chapter—for now just know that `#IsDefined()#` checks whatever variable name lies between its parentheses.

If the variable `#ID#` has been passed from the previous form, this ACTION page creates a variable called to_do using `<CFSET>` and defines it as "edit" on line 3. If no variable is passed (say, if the user is adding a *new* record), to_do is set to "add" on line 7.

If to_do is "edit", the page uses a `<CFQUERY>` on lines 13-15 to get the data for the selected user. If to_do is defined as "add", it doesn't run the query.

In the form section starting on line 28, the to_do variable is used again to see whether a new record is being added or an existing record is being edited. If to_do is "edit", a VALUE parameter is added to each form field so that the user information is displayed on the page. If to_do is "add", no VALUE is specified and the input boxes will be empty, ready for new information to be added.

Finally, just before closing the form, a hidden field containing the record's ID is added at line 61 if to_do is "edit". Recall that update actions require an ID or primary key specifier to work, so you'll need to pass that to the next page if you're performing an update. If the record is new, no ID needs to be passed.

Clear so far? If not, you might want to read through this section again. It takes a little time to understand how these multifunction pages work, but it'll all pay off eventually.

The result of Listing 12.7 is that the Web user will see one of two pages. If he chose "add user" on the previous form, he'll see empty form boxes. If he chose "edit user", he'll see the same form boxes with the user's data in them, ready for editing.

Now consider the final ACTION page, user_update.cfm. Again this page will need to perform one of two actions. If the record is new, it will do an insert and place the user data into the table. If the record is an existing one that has been edited, the ACTION page will need to perform an update instead.

This final page uses the same #IsDefined()# check to see whether an ID variable has been passed. Check out Listing 12.8.

LISTING 12.8 user_update.cfm

```
 1: <CFIF IsDefined("ID")>
 2:
 3:     <CFSET to_do = "edit">
 4:
 5: <CFELSE>
 6:
 7:     <CFSET to_do = "add">
 8:
 9: </CFIF>
10:
11: <CFIF to_do IS "edit">
12:
13:     <CFUPDATE DATASOURCE="gargantuan" TABLENAME="visitors" FORMFIELDS=
        ➥"name,email,net_worth">
14:
15: </CFIF>
16:
17: <CFIF to_do IS "add">
18:
19:     <CFINSERT DATASOURCE="gargantuan" TABLENAME="visitors" FORMFIELDS=
        ➥"name,email,net_worth">
20:
21: </CFIF>
22:
23: <HTML>
```

continues

LISTING 12.8   continued

```
24:
25: <HEAD>
26:    <TITLE>User Information Updated</TITLE>
27: </HEAD>
28:
29: The information for user <CFOUTPUT>#form.name#</CFOUTPUT> has been updated.
30:
31: </HTML>
```

ANALYSIS   This page does a quick check to see if an #ID# variable has been passed. If so, it assumes that you want to perform an update and acts accordingly. If not, it inserts a new record. Note that the page uses <CFUPDATE> and <CFINSERT> to perform these actions because nothing fancy is being input—just fields passed by the form.

You've now created a multifunction form that can perform two possible actions with one set of pages.

 Tip   Though space doesn't permit discussion here, you can probably see how you might add a third action (a delete) with some further trickery.

Understanding <CFTREE> and <CFTREEITEM>

Recall from yesterday's lesson that, by using <CFFORM> in place of a standard HTML <FORM>, you open up a new arsenal of selection and input methods. Your final instruction today will cover two of the most feature-rich <CFFORM> tags, <CFGRID> and <CFTREE>. I've held off on introducing them until now because you need to be familiar with the concepts in the previous sections to really get the most from these powerful tags.

Using <CFTREE>

<CFTREE> provides a pretty neat way to display form data, particularly data you want to sort by one or more categories. To understand this, first take a look at a sample tree in Figure 12.6.

For this form, I've used a query that selects all tapes in my table of 8-track tapes and sorts the results by the "condition" field. When I use <CFTREE> within a <CFFORM> to display the results, the user sees a special navigation window in his browser. Each category of "condition" is displayed as a folder. These folders work much like hard-drive browsing programs such as the Explorer in Windows. When I click on a folder, it "expands," and I see something like Figure 12.7.

FIGURE 12.6

A sample <CFTREE> describing 8-track tapes in my database.

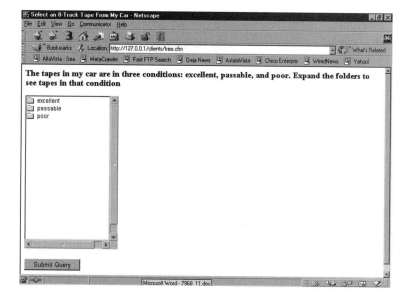

FIGURE 12.7

The <CFTREE> from Figure 12.6, with folders expanded to show contents.

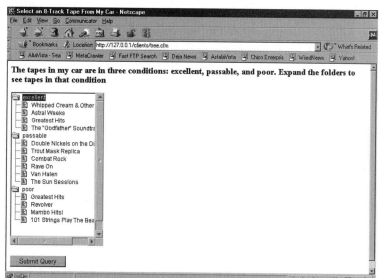

12

My database doesn't take full advantage of <CFTREE> because it only contains two levels of information. But you can see that if you were building a site for a business client who had departments and subdepartments and wanted to generate a categorized employee list, this would be your tool.

Tip

Although <CFTREE> is designed as a form element to collect user input, it's also a nice way to simply display information on a site. For example, it makes an excellent tool for displaying categorized lists of URLs, such as a bookmark list or a site map.

In structure, <CFTREE> works a lot like the <SELECT> tag. That is, you first define a tree, and then use the companion tag <CFTREEITEM> to populate the tree, just as you'd use the <OPTION> tag within a <SELECT> statement. Take a look at the code that generated my tree in Listing 12.8.

LISTING 12.8 my_tapes.cfm

```
 1: <CFQUERY NAME="tapes" DATASOURCE="music">
 2:     SELECT * FROM 8tracks ORDER BY condition
 3: </CFQUERY>
 4:
 5: <HTML>
 6:
 7: <HEAD>
 8:
 9:     <TITLE>Select an 8-Track Tape From My Car</TITLE>
10:
11: </HEAD>
12:
13: <BODY>
14:
15: <H3>The tapes in my car are in three conditions: excellent, passable,
    ➥and poor. Expand the folders to see tapes in that condition</H3>
16:
17: <CFFORM ACTION="some_page.cfm" METHOD="post">
18:
19: <!--- BEGIN TREE --->
20:
21: <CFTREE NAME="tapes">
22:
23: <!--- DEFINE TREE ELEMENTS --->
24:
25:         <CFTREEITEM VALUE="condition,title" IMG="folder,document" QUERY=
            ➥"tapes" EXPAND="no">
26:
27: <!--- CLOSE TREE --->
28:
29:     </CFTREE>
30:
31:     <P>
```

```
32:
33:    <INPUT TYPE="submit">
34:
35: </CFFORM>
36:
37: </BODY>
38:
39: </HTML>
```

ANALYSIS Not much code there, but that's one of the beauties of <CFTREE>. First, note that my query sorts results by the "condition" field using the ORDER BY parameter. This is because I want the <CFTREE> tag to receive data in groups, with all the "poor" condition tapes together, and so on.

To define my <CFTREE>, I just give it a name, which will consequently be the variable name sent to the ACTION page when the user submits data. Optional parameters are listed in Table 12.1.

TABLE 12.1 Parameters Used with <CFTREE>

Parameter	Function
REQUIRED	"Yes" requires that the user make a selection.
BORDER	Places a border around the tree, as by default.
HSCROLL	"Yes" specifies that your tree will have a horizontal scrollbar.
VSCROLL	"Yes" specifies that your tree will have a vertical scrollbar.
HIGHLIGHTREF	If a tree item is a URL, it will be highlighted by default. Use "no" with this parameter to disable the feature.

When a user selects a tape from my list and submits the form, <CFTREE> passes the selected variable as *TAPES.PATH=selected_item*, using the name I gave my tree and (optionally) the folder-by-folder path to the selected item. There are also <CFTREE> parameters to control the way these paths are sent, as shown in Table 12.2.

TABLE 12.2 Parameters Used with <CFTREE> to Control the Way Data Is Passed

Parameter	Function
COMPLETEPATH	Defaults to "no". Determines whether the entire path to a selected item is passed as a variable. For example, if a user selected the tape "Revolver," the passed variable would be tapes. path=revolver if COMPLETEPATH was set to "no" or unspecified, and tapes.path=poor\revolver if COMPLETEPATH was set to "yes".
DELIMITER	The character used to separate elements in the path variable. The default character is \.

12

Using <CFTREEITEM>

After I defined a <CFTREE> structure, I used the companion tag <CFTREEITEM> to add the contents. In my example, the contents came from a query, so I only used one line for <CFTREEITEM> and let ColdFusion do the rest. I used the QUERY parameter to specify the query from which I want to draw data and set the EXPAND parameter to "no" to specify that I want the category folders to appear unexpanded when the user first loads the form.

In addition, I set a very important parameter, VALUE, to determine the structure of the table. I used VALUE="condition,title" to show the two query fields to display in the tree, and selected them in the order in which they should be sorted. Corresponding to these two items, I also used <CFTREE>'s IMG parameter to show that I want to illustrate the "condition"s with a folder icon, and the "title"s with a document icon.

A complete list of <CFTREE> parameters is shown in Table 12.3.

TABLE 12.3   Parameters Used with <CFTREEITEM>

Parameter	Function
VALUE (required)	This parameter serves two functions: First, it determines the value that will be passed to the form's ACTION page; second, it determines which values to display in the tree. Values are separated by commas.
DISPLAY	The label for a tree item. The default is the value supplied in VALUE. To set DISPLAY names other than those in VALUE, use a comma-separated list that corresponds to the items listed in VALUE.
PARENT	The "parent" category under which a tree item should be classified. It is generally only used if you're building tree contents manually rather than with a query.
IMG	The image to display next to the tree item, with a default of the folder icon. Other values include fixed, floppy, document, and element. Use a comma-separated list to associate images with items listed in the VALUE parameter. You can also use external images by supplying the pathname to the image.
IMGOPEN	Specifies a separate image to display if the tree item is expanded. Also accepts external images.
HREF	A URL to associate with a tree item. Uses a comma-separated list in the same order as the elements in VALUE.
TARGET	The target for URLs created with HREF previously, for use with frame pages. Uses a comma-separated list in the same order as elements in VALUE.
QUERYASROOT	Defines the specified QUERY as the root of your tree.
EXPAND	Although the <CFTREE> tag has its own EXPAND parameter, you can also specify individual tree items to appear expanded with this parameter. The default is "yes".

Note

<CFTREEITEM> contents usually come from a query, but they can also be hand-coded by using the PARENT parameter to determine tree structure.

Tip

<CFTREE> is often used in conjunction with the file-management tag <CFFILE>, which is covered in Day 18 "Working with Files and Directories." When used together, they enable you to quickly design graphic interfaces that let users view and manage files existing on your server.

Understanding <CFGRID>

Like <CFTREE>, <CFGRID> is a form tag that goes well beyond what you'd probably expect from a form. Although it can be used to collect user data just like a text input box, its main strength lies in the fact that it can display complex tabular data in a spreadsheet format. Take a look at Figure 12.8 to get a feel for this tag.

FIGURE 12.8

A <CFGRID> displaying a database table.

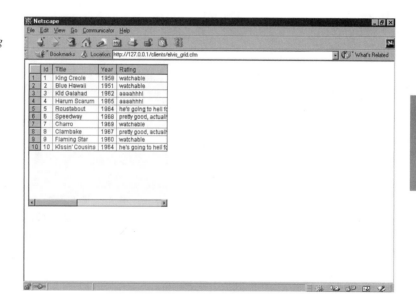

12

<CFGRID> uses JavaScript behind the scenes to display your table data in much the same way that it appears in a database application. It might not be such a useful tool for displaying a database of Elvis flicks, but consider situations in which you might need to display a company's Web site statistics or marketing data. Designing traditional tables to format these could be a nightmare, but <CFGRID> handles it easily. Check out the code in Listing 12.9 that produced Figure 12.8.

LISTING 12.9 elvis_grid.cfm

```
 1: <CFQUERY NAME="get_movies" DATASOURCE="elvis">
 2:     SELECT * FROM movies
 3: </CFQUERY>
 4:
 5: <CFFORM NAME="grid" ACTION="grid_action.cfm" METHOD="post">
 6:
 7:     <CFGRID NAME="movies" QUERY="get_movies">
 8:     </CFGRID>
 9:
10: </CFFORM>
```

ANALYSIS Listing 12.9 contains just a few lines, but, once again, that's the point of these advanced tags. To display a basic view of a database table, you just create a <CFFORM> and use <CFGRID> with the name of a valid query.

The grids it displays are infinitely customizable, of course. The many parameters for <CFGRID> are listed in Table 12.4.

TABLE 12.4 Parameters Used with <CFGRID>

Parameter	Function
APPENDKEY	Selecting yes or no sets whether the value CFGRIDKEY should be set to whatever text a cell contains.
BGCOLOR	Defines background color; accepts any standard JavaScript color name or hex value.
COLHEADER	Yes causes column headers to display (default); no will produces a table sans headers.
COLHEADERALIGN	Determines whether column headers are aligned left, right, or center.
COLHEADERBOLD	Yes creates bolded column headers; no is default.
COLHEADERFONT	Defines a font face for column headers.
COLHEADERFONTSIZE	Defines a font size for column headers.
COLHEADERITALIC	Yes creates italicized column headers; default is no.
GRIDDATAALIGN	Determines alignment of text within cells—left, right, or center.
HIGHLIGHTREF	Determines whether URLs are underlined; defaults to yes.
HREF	The URL to be retrieved when a cell is selected.
MAXROWS	The maximum number of rows to display in the grid.

QUERY	The name of the query to display.
ROWHEADER	Same as COLHEADER, but for row text.
ROWHEADERALIGN	Same as COLHEADERALIGN, but for row text.
ROWHEADERBOLD	Same as COLHEADERBOLD, but for row text.
ROWHEADERFONT	Same as COLHEADERFONT, but for row text.
ROWHEADERFONTSIZE	Same as COLHEADERFONTSIZE, but for row text.
ROWHEADERITALIC	Same as COLHEADERITALIC, but for row text.
ROWHEADERWIDTH	Specifies a pixel width of the row header.
SELECTCOLOR	The background color displayed when cells are selected.
SELECTMODE	Determines what happens when a user clicks over the grid. SINGLE selects a cell, ROW selects a row, COLUMN selects a column, and EDIT enables users to edit cell data. Default is BROWSE, where no selections are permitted.
TARGET	The target window for URLs, which is used in framed sites.

Tip

Like <CFTREE>, <CFGRID> also enables you to build graphic displays manually, rather than from the results of a query. This is done much like an HTML table, using the tags <CFGRIDROW> and <CFGRIDCOLUMN>. Check your ColdFusion documentation for more on these tags.

<CFGRID> is a good tool for simply displaying data, but, because it belongs to the <CFFORM> family, it also has valuable functions for selecting data and sending it to an ACTION page. <CFGRID> can be used for something as simple as the selection of a name or number to pass along to an action, or it can be used with its companion tag <CFGRIDUPDATE> to perform more complex actions.

Using <CFGRIDUPDATE>

To illustrate the use of <CFGRIDUPDATE>, I've added the parameter SELECTMODE="edit" to my grid of Elvis films. When users view the grid, they can now edit the text that appears in the cells, as shown in Figure 12.9.

12

FIGURE 12.9

Using <CFGRIDUPDATE> to let users update table data.

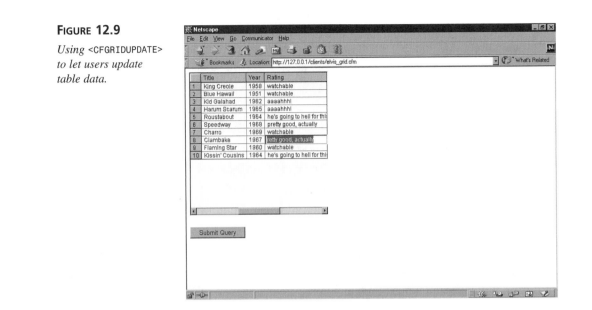

The code is shown in Listing 12.10. It's still pretty basic stuff.

LISTING 12.10   elvis_grid_edit.cfm

```
1: <CFQUERY NAME="get_movies" DATASOURCE="elvis">
2:     SELECT * FROM movies
3: </CFQUERY>
4:
5: <CFFORM NAME="grid" ACTION="grid_action.cfm" METHOD="post">
6:
7:     <CFGRID NAME="movies" QUERY="get_movies" SELECTMODE="edit">
8:     </CFGRID>
9:
10:     <P>
11:
12:     <INPUT TYPE="submit">
13:
14: </CFFORM>
```

Finally, on the ACTION page for this form, I use <CFGRIDUPDATE>, as illustrated in Listing 12.11.

LISTING 12.11   grid_action.cfm

```
1: <CFGRIDUPDATE GRID="movies"
2:               DATASOURCE="elvis"
3:               TABLENAME="movies">
```

```
4:
5:  <HTML>
6:
7:  <H2>Your edits have been added to the database</H2>
8:
9:  </HTML>
```

 ANALYSIS Listing 12.11 has just a few lines of code, but I've now created an interface enabling users to easily edit information in my table, all without using a single `<TABLE>` tag. `<CFGRIDUPDATE>` requires the name of a grid used on the form page (line 1), a datasource name (line 2), and a table to update (line 3).

> **Tip**
>
> `<CFGRID>` and `<CFGRIDUPDATE>` provide an easy way to build quick-and-dirty edit or input forms for tables that contain lots of fields and would otherwise require lots of coding to produce a standard form.

Summary

Forms are your users' link to the inner workings of your sites. By mastering their advanced incarnations, you can build truly interactive sites. In Day 7, you first learned how to change the contents of a database by using forms in conjunction with `<CFUPDATE>` and `<CFINSERT>` tags in your ACTION pages. Today's lesson introduced you to three SQL commands that pick up where ColdFusion's basic tags leave off: UPDATE, INSERT, and DELETE.

The first two of these are used in place of their ColdFusion equivalents when data to be added comes from sources other than a form. The third, DELETE, is unique to SQL and has no corresponding tag in CFML. DELETE is used to delete records from a database table, and should always be used with extreme caution.

By using multifunction form pages, you can create Web interfaces that enable users to add, edit, or delete data from a single start page. You use tools such as `<CFIF>` to determine which of these should occur on your form's ACTION page, and you save yourself plenty of coding time in the process.

Finally, today's lesson covered two advanced tags used with `<CFFORM>`, ColdFusion's enhanced version of the HTML `<FORM>` tag. The first, `<CFTREE>`, creates a graphic interface for selecting items that occur in a branching structure—directories and files, for example. The second, `<CFGRID>`, is an extremely powerful tag that can both display complex data tables and enable your users to edit content directly from `<CFGRID>`'s JavaScript interface.

12

Q&A

Q Why doesn't ColdFusion have a `<CFDELETE>` tag?

A That would be too easy and too dangerous. By requiring developers to use the SQL `DELETE` command rather than a simple tag, ColdFusion ensures that you really know what you're doing before you put your data at risk.

Q Why doesn't `<CFINSERT>` require that a primary key be specified, as `<CFUPDATE>` does?

A `<CFINSERT>` inputs data in much the same way as your database software does when you manually type in a new record. If you use the "autonumber" function in your database (most do this by default), a primary key will be provided for the new record.

Q How can I ensure that `DELETE` actions aren't misused?

A You can password-protect pages that use the command, or you can restrict the pages to be viewed only by computers at certain IP addresses. You'll learn more about this in Day 16, "Using ColdFusion Client and Session Management."

Q How can a form page be used as its own `ACTION` page?

A By using `<CFIF>` to determine whether data is being input or passed along, you can create one page to do all your dirty work. This has two advantages: It consolidates your code, and it lets the user immediately perform another action without having to click back to a form page.

Q I'm confused about how multifunction form pages work. What am I missing?

A It might be helpful to revisit Day 9, "Enhancing Your Applications with Variables and If-Then Statements." This lesson will help you understand how variables may be used to control actions such as `INSERT`s and `UPDATE`s.

Q Why can't my users see my forms that use `<CFGRID>` and `<CFTREE>`?

A Like all enhanced `<CFFORM>` tags, they require that the user's browser be JavaScript compatible. Most browsers are these days, but, if you have a significant user base running older browsers, you'll need to provide alternative forms.

Workshop

Answers to quiz questions can be found in Appendix A.

Quiz

1. Name the three situations in which you should use SQL updates instead of the ColdFusion equivalents.

2. How do you recover a record that has been accidentally removed with the DELETE command?

3. What ColdFusion tag makes multifunction form pages possible?

4. What are the primary differences between a form page designed to add a new record and one designed to edit an existing record?

5. Name some uses for the <CFGRID> tag.

Exercises

1. Create three sets of input forms and ACTION pages that use the SQL commands INSERT, UPDATE, and DELETE.

2. Create a multifunction form page that enables users to add, edit, or delete a database record. Use <CFIF> on your ACTION page(s) to determine which action should occur.

3. Choose one of your database tables that contains five or more fields and design pages using <CFTREE> and <CFGRID> to display table contents. Create an ACTION page for your <CFGRID> to enable users to edit data in the grid.

12

DAY **13**

Using ColdFusion to Handle Email

ColdFusion's developers thought of nearly everything in the development of their application. Though you still can't use CF to clean your refrigerator, you *can* use it to send, receive and process email by way of two powerful tags named <CFMAIL> and <CFPOP>. In today's lesson we'll look at those two tags in detail and discuss ways to use ColdFusion email services with your Web applications. We'll cover

- Understanding the <CFMAIL> tag
- Using queries to create mail
- Customizing your message with HTML tags
- Sending email attachments with <CFMAIL>
- Viewing incoming mail with <CFPOP>
- Deleting read mail with <CFPOP>

Understanding the <CFMAIL> Tag

Think of the <CFMAIL> tag as ColdFusion's database-to-mail or Web-to-mail gateway. By using it in your pages, you can use all the data-collection and processing features of ColdFusion to manage mail that gets sent to one or more users. The tag can serve as simple a use as a mail processor for a form (mimicking CGI programs like mailto.exe), or as complex a use as a complete autoresponder and mailing-list manager.

<CFMAIL> is most often used within action pages, getting its required data from a form. To actually send mail, it works with either your network's existing mail (or *SMTP*) server or with a remote mail server to which your system has access.

NEW TERM *SMTP* stands for Simple Mail Transfer Protocol. It's the Internet standard for sending mail from one host to another. An *SMTP server* is a machine running mail software that adheres to the SMTP protocol.

Let's look at a simple <CFMAIL> application to illustrate its capabilities. Say I've signed on a client named "Buddy," who wants to provide a user feedback form on the Web. As the developer, I could use such a form in conjunction with one of many common CGI scripts like mailto.exe, sendmail.exe, and so on, or I could link the form to a ColdFusion template that contains only a few lines of code, as shown in Listing 13.1.

INPUT **LISTING 13.1** feedback.cfm

```
 1: <CFMAIL    TO="buddy@client.com"
 2:            FROM="server@buddy.com"
 3:            SUBJECT="feedback from user #user#">
 4:
 5: #user# has sent you feedback from the client.com Web site.
 6:
 7: Comments:
 8:
 9: #feedback#
10:
11: The user's e-mail address is:
12:
13: #email#
14:
15: </CFMAIL>
16:
17: <HTML>
18:
19: Thanks for your mail. You should receive a response within 3-5 working
➥months.
20:
21: </HTML>
```

I didn't show the form code here for the sake of saving space, but suffice to say that it will provide input boxes for a user's name (line 5), email address (line 13), and comments (#feedback# on line 9). When the user submits the form, these variables are passed to the action page in Figure 13.1, where they're intercepted by the <CFMAIL> tag and sent to my pal "buddy@client.com" as an email. Buddy then gets a message like Figure 13.1.

FIGURE 13.1

When a user sends mail from a Web form, the recipient sees something like this.

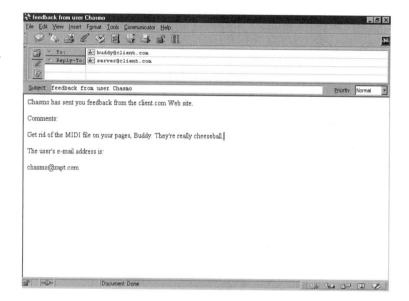

The mail is sent behind the scenes, so the template that contains this tag might also include a brief confirmation message in the HTML section to let the user know that all's well.

Note that the <CFMAIL> tag and its accompanying parameters define where the mail is sent, who it's from, and the subject. From there, everything before the closing </CFMAIL> tag will appear in the body of the email sent to Buddy.

Sure, this simple little app is nothing to scream about, because there are scores of freeware CGI programs that will do the same thing. But read on—you'll learn how <CFMAIL> can use ColdFusion's dynamic functions and database support to do stuff that will make your coder's heart beat like a kettle drum.

Using <CFMAIL>

The first <CFMAIL> tag you configure will be the toughest. It might take a little fiddling to get some of the parameters working with your system's mail server, but, when you know the drill, you'll be using it like a pro.

Note

Due to the proliferation of spamming, many system administrators now keep their SMTP servers under extremely tight security. This means that the mail server will be very picky about the address you designate as FROM in your <CFMAIL> tags. It will likely have to be a user and domain that is authorized to send mail from your server.

<CFMAIL> accepts the parameters shown in Table 13.1.

TABLE 13.1 Parameters Used with <CFMAIL>

Parameter	Function
TO (required)	The recipient of the message. This can be either a static address or a specific variable containing an address, or a query variable that will send mail for every row returned by the query.
FROM (required)	The sender of the message, either a static address or one provided by a variable.
SUBJECT (required)	The subject of the email. May be static, dynamic, or both if you want a subject that reads email from #user#, for example.
SERVER (required)	The name or IP address of an SMTP server that will accept outgoing mail from your ColdFusion server. The default is the server name that is defined in ColdFusion administrator.
CC	Other addresses that will receive a carbon copy (CC) of the mail.
BCC	Other addresses that will receive a blind carbon copy (BCC) of the mail. Addresses that are copied blindly aren't visible to the primary recipient.
TYPE	If you don't supply a value for this parameter, your email will be sent as plain text. If you specify TYPE="HTML", the recipient's mail reader software will treat your mail like an HTML page and parse tags to produce boldface and italic fonts, HTML headers, and so on.
MAXROWS	Specifies the maximum number of email messages you want to send.
MIMEATTACH	Provides the path to a file on your system, and it will be sent with your email as a MIME attachment.
QUERY	The name of the CFQUERY from which you want to draw data for your mail. Use this parameter to send more than one email or to send the results of a query within a message.
GROUP	If you use the ORDER BY command in your query, you can group messages by the contents of a particular field and send mail to only that group by specifying it with the GROUP parameter.

Parameter	Function
GROUPCASESENSITIVE	If your GROUPed field contains case-sensitive data such as "MARKET-ING" and "marketing," you can use "yes" or "no" with this parameter to determine whether these will be considered as one group. The default is "yes."
STARTROW	Specifies the row in the query to start from.
PORT	By default, this is set to port 25, the standard listening port for SMTP servers. If your server isn't standard, you can set a port with this parameter.
TIMEOUT	If you're working with a particularly slow or remote server, you can specify a number (in seconds) that ColdFusion will wait before timing out and reporting a connection failure.
MAILERID	Specifies a mailer ID to be passed in the X-Mailer SMTP header. This particular header identifies the software that sent the mail; the default is "Allaire ColdFusion Application Server."

Don't worry if some of these parameters don't make sense yet. In the following sections, we'll design some sample mail apps that will help you understand how the parameters are used.

Defining a Default Mail Server in ColdFusion Administrator

As outlined in Table 13.1, <CFMAIL> requires that you define a valid SMTP server to process outgoing mail. If you don't specify one, ColdFusion will attempt to use the default server defined in ColdFusion Administrator.

To add or change the default server, log in to Administrator and choose the Mail link under Miscellaneous. You'll see a dialog like Figure 13.2.

13

> **Note**
> If you're hosting your site with a remote Web provider, you probably won't have access to ColdFusion Administrator. In these cases, check with your provider to see if they've defined an SMTP server.

Supply the name or IP address of your system's mail server, set the port if your server doesn't use the default port 25, and choose a connection time or use the default 60 seconds. Click Apply to complete the setup.

FIGURE **13.2**

*ColdFusion
Administrator's mail
server definition
screen.*

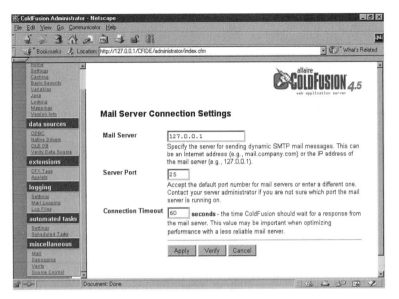

Using Queries to Autorespond
and Create Content

There's really a lot of ground to cover with `<CFMAIL>`, so stick with me as I introduce you to two concepts at once. Say I have a client who sells a tech item, a monitor-viewing aid that's selling like hotcakes. It's called the SuperView 2000, and it consists of a 8"×8" block of wood designed to be placed under a user's monitor to bring it up to eye level.

Some of her users have had trouble installing and configuring the SuperView 2000, so she wants to set up a system of product-support FAQs users can request via the Web site. Users will go to a form page, enter their email address, choose one of four *FAQ* documents, and in a few moments receive mail containing the selected FAQ page.

NEW TERM   *FAQ* is Internet shorthand for a list of "Frequently Asked Questions." These lists are generally assembled by users experienced in a certain topic, with the aim of answering common questions asked by new users. These expert users post their FAQs to the Web or to a newsgroup, after which they can tell new users to simply "Read the FAQ!" in answer to common questions. Businesses also use FAQs to help support their products.

You'll learn two new concepts with this example—using `<CFMAIL>` to autorespond to specified address, and using a standard `<CFOUTPUT>` query to generate the text to be sent.

First, I'll set up a basic form, using either HTML's <FORM> tag or ColdFusion's <CFFORM>—nothing too tricky is happening in this particular form, so it really doesn't matter which one I choose. My completed form looks like Figure 13.3.

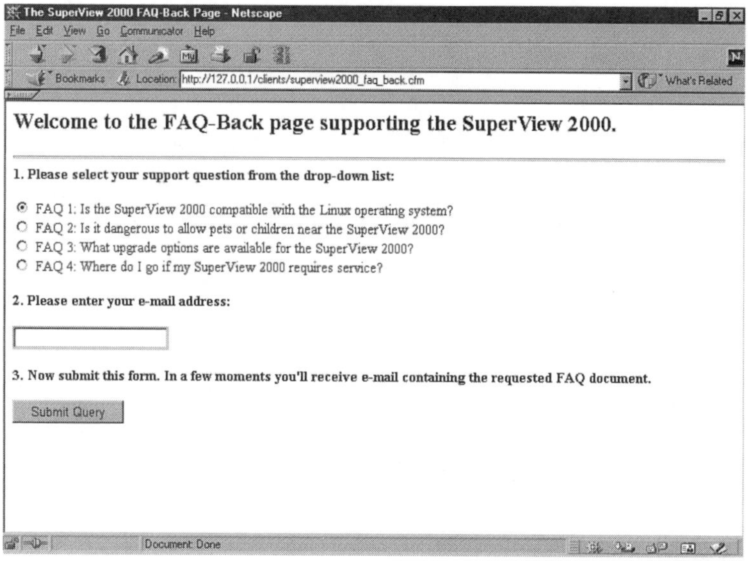

FIGURE 13.3

A sample input form for a FAQ-back system driven by <CFMAIL>.

This form will send two variables to its action page. The first, question, will contain the number of the FAQ selected by the user. The second, email, will contain the email address supplied by the user.

Next I'll design a quick-and-dirty database table containing two fields. The first, FAQ_NUMBER will contain a label (FAQ1, FAQ2, and so on), so I'll use the text data type. The second, text, will contain the actual text of the related FAQ that will be sent to users. It's likely to be a longer block of text, so I'll use the memo data type. Because I have only four FAQs, my table will contain only four records.

After I ask the client to populate the database table with the text of their FAQs, I set about designing an action page that will receive the results of my form, as shown in Listing 13.2.

13

INPUT　**LISTING 13.2**　action.cfm

```
1: <!--- RUN QUERY TO GET FAQ TEXT FROM DATABASE --->
2:
3: <CFQUERY NAME="get_faq" DATASOURCE="clients">
➥SELECT FAQ_number,text FROM superview_faqs WHERE FAQ_number =
➥'#FAQ_number#'
```

continues

LISTING 13.2   continued

```
 4: </CFQUERY>
 5: <!--- SEND FAQ TO USER VIA CFMAIL --->
 6: <CFMAIL TO="#email#" QUERY="get_faq"
 7:          FROM="support@superview2000.com"
 8:          SERVER="smtp.superview2000.com"
 9:            SUBJECT="Your requested FAQ on the SuperView 2000">
10:       #text#
11: </CFMAIL>
12: <!--- REPORT SUCCESS TO USER BY WEB --->
13: <HTML>
14: <HEAD>
15:     <TITLE>Mail Has Been Sent</TITLE>
16: </HEAD>
17:
18: <BODY>
19: <!--- USE CFOUTPUT TO ADD USER'S E-MAIL ADDRESS TO CONFIRMATION MESSAGE --->
20: <CFOUTPUT>
21:     The document you requested has been mailed to #email#. Please check
         ➥your mail in a few moments.
22:     <P>
23:     Enjoy your SuperView 2000!
24: </CFOUTPUT>
25:
26: </BODY>
27: </HTML>
```

The query on line 3 should be old hat by now—it just takes the variable information from the form and searches the database for the corresponding FAQ text. Next, I configured `<CFMAIL>` on line 6 to point to SuperView's mailserver and supplied a valid SuperView address in the FROM parameter. For the TO address, I used the variable #email#, which will be supplied dynamically by the user input in the form page.

Between the opening and closing `<CFMAIL>` tags, I included the variable #text#, which will reproduce the contents of that field from the FAQ table. Finally, I supplied some basic HTML to display a confirmation message back to the user. I also fancied things up a little with a `<CFOUTPUT>` tag so I could again use the #email# variable in the confirmation message.

Tip

<CFMAIL> works entirely behind the scenes and displays nothing in a user's browser even when mail is sent successfully. For this reason, it's a good idea to include some sort of confirmation message in all templates that use <CFMAIL>. You'll find an example in Listing 13.2.

The mail sent to the user will look something like Figure 13.4.

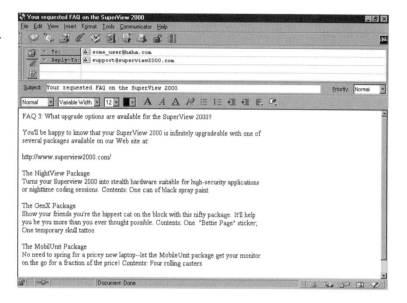

Customizing Your Message with HTML Tags

A message like that shown in Figure 13.4 is fine if my client is happy with sending out just plain text. But you know how those business-types are, always wanting to get their logos in wherever possible.

To dress up a text message, I can use `<CFMAIL>`'s capability to send a message as an HTML document. I do this by adding the TYPE parameter to the `<CFMAIL>` tag in my action page, as in Listing 13.3.

INPUT   **LISTING 13.3**   action.cfm

```
1: <CFMAIL QUERY="get_faq"   TO="#email#"
   ➥FROM="support@superview2000.com"
   ➥SERVER="smtp.superview2000.com"
   ➥SUBJECT="Your requested FAQ on the SuperView 2000"
   ➥TYPE="HTML">
2: #text#
3: </CFMAIL>
```

By using TYPE="HTML" at the end of line 1, I'm now free to enhance the text of my message with any valid HTML tags I'd like. I can use image links to pictures on SuperView's server, clickable URLs pointing to their Web pages, bold text, and so on.

13

I created some HTML text like Listing 13.4 in a text editor, and then cut-and-pasted it into the "text" field in the client's database.

INPUT   **LISTING 13.4**   A Sample FAQ Built with HTML Code

```
 1: <HTML>
 2:
 3: <CENTER>
 4: <IMG SRC="http://www.superview2000.com/images/logo.gif">
 5: </CENTER>
 6: <P>
 7: <BLOCKQUOTE>
 8: <FONT FACE="Arial">
 9:
10: <H4>FAQ 3: What upgrade options are available for the SuperView 2000?</H4>
11:
12: You'll be happy to know that your SuperView2000 is infinitely
    ➥upgradeable with one of several packages available on our Web site at:
13: <P>
14:
15: <A HREF="http://www.superview2000.com/">http://www.superview2000.com/</A>
16: <P>
17:
18: <FONT FACE="Arial" COLOR="#400000">
19: <B>The NightView Package</B><BR>
20: </FONT>
21:
22: <FONT FACE="Arial">
23: Turns your Superview 2000 into stealth hardware suitable for high-
    ➥security applications or nighttime coding sessions. Contents:
    ➥One can of black spray paint.
24: <P>
25:
26: <FONT FACE="Arial" COLOR="#400000">
27: <B>The GenX Package</B><BR>
28: </FONT>
29:
30: <FONT FACE="Arial">
31: Show your friends you're the hippest cat on the block with this nifty
    ➥package. It'll help you be you more than you ever thought possible.
    ➥Contents: One "Bettie Page" sticker; One temporary skull tattoo
32: </FONT>
33:
34: </BLOCKQUOTE>
35:
36: </HTML>
```

Note

For the end user to view a message as HTML, his mail software must support the HTML type. Most mail readers do, but keep in mind that if they don't, the reader will see all your fancy formatting as plain text—including the HTML tags.

In my client SuperView's case, the text to be sent as mail is stored in a database, so I'd add my HTML formatting to the text stored there. In a case where the text *isn't* generated dynamically, I could simply type it into the action page between the <CFMAIL> tags and supply the necessary formatting along with the text.

My HTML-enhanced page for SuperView would show up in a user's mailbox looking something like Figure 13.5.

FIGURE 13.5

An HTML-enhanced mail message generated by <CFMAIL>. *The image link points to a file residing on the SuperView server.*

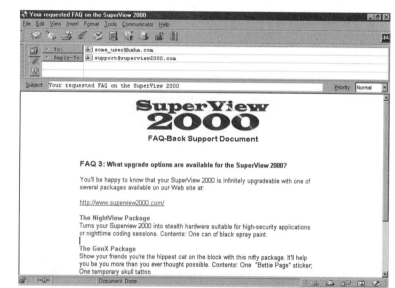

Sending Attachments

For some applications, even HTML won't do. You or your client might want to include attached files with messages generated by <CFMAIL>. For this you'd use the MIMEATTACH parameter in the action page's <CFMAIL> tag, and specify either a pathname to t a query variable that contains a valid pathname.

For example, if SuperView requested that its standard product catalog be inclu every FAQ-back document, I'd use a <CFMAIL> tag, as shown in Listing 13.5.

INPUT **LISTING 13.5**   A <CFMAIL> Section Creating an Autoresponder

```
1: <CFMAIL      TO="#email#"
   ➥FROM="support@superview2000.com"
   ➥SERVER="smtp.superview2000.com"
   ➥SUBJECT="Your requested FAQ on the SuperView 2000"
   ➥MIMEATTACH="c:/files/catalog.pdf">
2: #text#
3: </CFMAIL>
```

This example assumes that SuperView wants to send the Adobe Acrobat (PDF) file called `catalog.pdf`, and that the file resides in the `files` folder on its server.

I could also supply the pathname dynamically by including a field in my database table that would specify a different file to accompany each FAQ the user requests. For example, I might create a new field in SuperView's database called `file` and within it supply the full pathname to a file that will be sent with each type of FAQ.

I would then alter my query on the action page to also SELECT the contents of the `file` field, and use the resulting variable #file# in the MIMEATTACH parameter of my mail tag.

Using Queries to Send Mail to a List

Because ColdFusion is very adept at pulling multiple values from a database, let's look at how to use that function with <CFMAIL>. Let's say that, over the few months SuperView has been in business, the company has been collecting users' email addresses via a Web form and storing them in the database table "users".

Now the client has asked me to create an administration page for internal use that will enable SuperView employees to send mail to all registered users. The form she wants to use looks something like Figure 13.6.

This form will pass only one variable to its action page—the variable "text," which will contain whatever the administrator types into the text box. The code for the form is shown in Listing 13.6.

FIGURE 13.6

A sample form designed to send email to multiple users via <CFMAIL>.

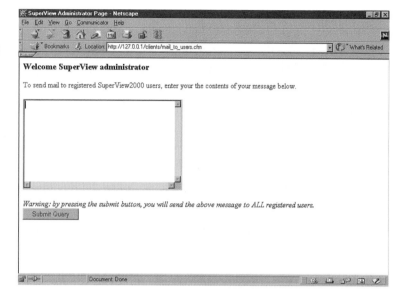

INPUT   **LISTING 13.6**   form.html

```
 1: <html>
 2: <head>
 3:     <title>Send Text</title>
 4: </head>
 5:
 6: <body>
 7:
 8:     <h3>Welcome SuperView Administrator</H3>
 9:
10:     <CFFORM ACTION="email.cfm" METHOD="POST">
11:         To send mail to SuperView users, enter the contents of your
            ➥message below.<P>
12:
13:         <TEXTAREA NAME="text" COLS="50" ROWS="12"></TEXTAREA><P>
14:
15:         <I>Warning, by pressing the submit button, you will be sending mail
            ➥ to ALL registered users.</I><P>
16:         <INPUT TYPE="Submit">
17:
18:     </CFFORM>
19:
20: </body>
21: </html>
```

13

ColdFusion will do the rest by way of the action page's <CFMAIL> tag and a query. It'll supply the addresses from a database table, generate the necessary messages, and send them one by one to each registered user in the table. For this action page, I used a template like that created in Listing 13.7. It assumes names and addresses are stored in a table called "users".

INPUT   LISTING 13.7   email.cfm

```
 1: <!--- GET ALL USERS FROM DATABASE --->
 2: <CFQUERY NAME="get_users" DATASOURCE="superview">
 3:     SELECT * FROM users
 4:     </CFQUERY>
 5: <!--- SEND MAIL TO EACH ADDRESS RETRIEVED BY QUERY --->
 6: <CFMAIL    TO="#email#"
 7: FROM="support@superview200.com"
 8:         SUBJECT="mail from our support department"
 9:         QUERY="get users">
10:
11: <!--- INSERT CONTENTS OF "TEXT" VARIABLE FROM FORM PAGE --->
12:         #text#
13: </CFMAIL>
14:
15: <!--- SEND A CONFIRMATION TO THE USER THAT MAIL HAS BEEN SENT --->
16: <HTML>
17: <HEAD>
18:     <TITLE>Mail Sent</TITLE>
19: </HEAD>
20: <BODY>
21: <H3>The text you supplied has been mailed to all registered users in the
22: ➥SuperView 2000 database.</H3>
23: <!--- USE CFOUTPUT TO LIST ALL THE NAMES AND EMAIL ADDRESSES --->
24: <CFOUTPUT QUERY="get_users">
25: #name# #email#<BR>
26: </CFOUTPUT>
27: </BODY>
28: </HTML>
```

Caution

As with any tool capable of sending multiple emails, there is a potential of spam abuse with <CFMAIL>. It's a good idea to keep unwanted users out by password-protecting pages or sections designed to be used internally. It's also good policy to counsel your client on the dangers of sending unsolicited mail, and to create only <CFMAIL> applications that will send to users who've either "opted-in" to a mailing list or specifically requested return mail.

Getting Incoming Mail with <CFPOP>

The powerful companion tag to <CFMAIL> is <CFPOP>, which works on the receiving end to enable users to view and manage *incoming* email from a ColdFusion template page. <CFPOP> works its magic by acting like a mail client using the *POP3* mail protocol, and can be customized to take advantage of many features available to POP3 users.

NEW TERM *POP3* stands for *Post Office Protocol*, a common Internet standard used to retrieve email. POP3-compatible mail servers store users' mail until it is requested by a POP3-compatible mail client such as Microsoft Outlook, Eudora, or Netscape Mail. When you download new messages from your Internet Service Provider (ISP), you're probably using POP3.

One of the advantages of POP3 over other mail protocols is its capability to fetch only mail *headers*—without retrieving the body of the message itself. Using this method, POP3 client programs can allow users to peruse their mailboxes and delete unwanted messages before having to download the actual body text. <CFPOP> includes provisions for this feature as well.

NEW TERM An email's *header* is the part of the message that defines who the mail is from, to whom it's addressed, its subject, when and how it was sent, and other control data. The other component of an email is the *body*, which is the actual text of the message.

When you use the <CFPOP> tag, you supply parameters one of two ways:

- dynamically, say from a form page or a query variable
- statically, by actually supplying the parameters in the template

You give parameters specifying the name of a POP3 mailserver, a username, and a password. When a user loads a template page containing the <CFPOP> tag, ColdFusion will retrieve all messages waiting for that user or, alternatively, only the headers.

<CFPOP> "remembers" retrieved mail information in the same way <CFQUERY> stores the results of a database query. By using special variables like #FROM# #SUBJECT# and #BODY# in conjunction with <CFPOP>, you can display the contents of a user's mail as output in a template.

13

Let's look at a sample use of <CFPOP> in Listing 13.8. Assume that the user is an employee at SuperView 2000's vast headquarters. All SuperView workers use the mailserver "pop.superview2000.com" to retrieve their incoming mail.

INPUT   **LISTING 13.8**   Fetching Mail Headers from a POP3 Mail Server

```
1: <!--- GET MAIL HEADERS FROM POP SERVER --->
2:
3: <CFPOP     NAME="get_mail"
4: SERVER="pop.superview2000.com"
5:         USERNAME="jethro"
6:         PASSWORD="1ellie_mae1"
7:         ACTION="GETHEADERONLY">
```

Think of <CFPOP> as a query run on the contents of your mailbox. Like a standard query, it requires a defined name. You'll use that name later in <CFOUTPUT> sections to specify that you want to use the results of <CFPOP> in your page. In addition, the tag requires the name of a POP3-compatible server and a username and password associated with an account on that mail server.

Notice the ACTION parameter in Listing 13.8—I used GETHEADERONLY to specify that this query will only gather information from the headers of waiting messages, rather than spend the extra time downloading the whole message. <CFPOP> supports two other actions, GETALL and DELETE. The first is used to collect the entire contents (header *and* body) of waiting messages. The second is used to remove a message from the server, generally after a user has viewed or downloaded mail with one of the other actions.

To display the mail headers collected by the <CFPOP> tag in Listing 13.8, I'd use a <CFOUTPUT> section like Listing 13.9.

INPUT   **LISTING 13.9**   Displaying Headers Retrieved by <CFPOP>

```
1: <!--- DISPLAY HEADERS RETRIEVED BY CFPOP --->
2:
3: <CFOUPUT QUERY="get_mail">
4:
5: <B>From:</B> #from#<BR>
6: <B>Subject:</B> #subject#<P>
7:
8: </CFOUTPUT>
```

To display the results of a <CFPOP> mail retrieval, I use the same techniques I would with a standard <CFQUERY>. I reference the name, and then use variables that will plug in the necessary output when the user views the page.

Unlike <CFQUERY>, the output variable names used by <CFPOP> aren't definable. To reference them, I have to use variable names supplied by ColdFusion. Table 13.2 shows a complete list of variables returned by <CFPOP>.

TABLE 13.2   Variable Names Returned by <CFPOP>

Variable Name	Contents
DATE	Contains the time and date the message was mailed.
FROM	The name of the person who sent the message.
TO	The email address to which the message was sent.
ATTACHMENTS	If any files were attached to the message, they will be listed here in tab-delimited format.
CC	The addresses of others who might have been carbon copied by the sender.
REPLYTO	The email address to which replies will be sent.
SUBJECT	The subject of the message.
MESSAGENUMBER	A number assigned to each message as it is retrieved. This variable is useful for control purposes, such as coding an action to delete message "5."
BODY	Assigned only if the GETALL action is used in the <CFPOP> tag, BODY contains the actual text of the message.

To display the contents of any of these variables in a <CFOUTPUT> section, I just reference the variable the same way I would a query variable, using hash marks like this: #subject# or #from#.

Deleting Mail with <CFPOP>

Using the techniques described in this chapter, I can design a complete email client using nothing but ColdFusion. I'd use <CFPOP> in my template pages to get and display users' messages, and <CFMAIL> to send outgoing mail. But so far I've only covered reading and sending mail—what if I want to remove it from the server after the user has read it?

I'd use the third <CFPOP> action, DELETE. This action always works in conjunction with the parameter MESSAGENUMBER to define a specific message to be deleted.

Caution

When you use <CFPOP>'s DELETE parameter to remove a message from a mail server, the message is pretty much unrecoverable. If the mail server's sysadmin takes a liking to you, he might opt to restore the message from a backup (if one is available), but that's not likely. Use the DELETE action with care.

13

Assume that I've already designed a simple mail client for the employees of SuperView 2000. To create a template that will allow me to delete messages, I'd probably start with a form page that would collect the user's account name and password, then pass this data to a template using <CFPOP> to obtain and display the user's current messages.

For more functionality, I might present the user's mail as elements in a form. By using check boxes or SELECT boxes and using the #messagenumber# returned by <CFPOP> to set their values, I can also allow users to delete unwanted messages. If it has been awhile since you've designed a form, check out Day 11 for some samples.

Check out the sample form pictured in Figure 13.7.

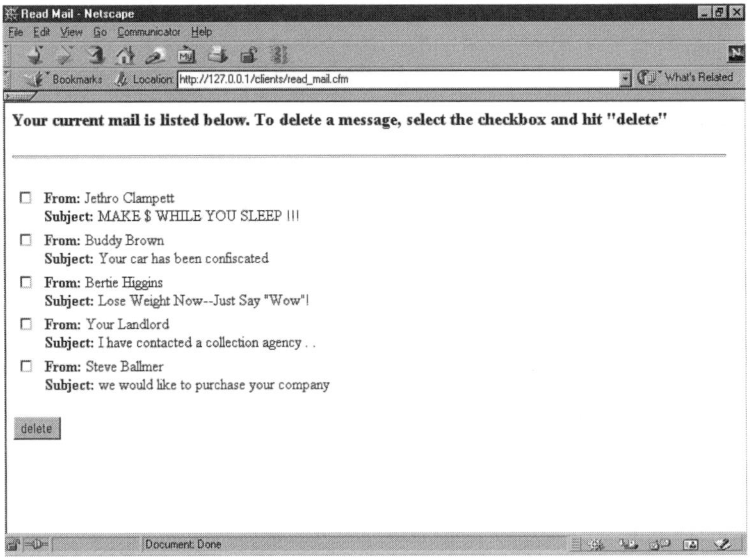

FIGURE 13.7

A basic form displaying user email. By checking a box, the user can delete a message from the mail server.

In the code for this form, I defined each message's checkbox with the number returned by the standard <CFPOP> variable #messagenumber#, like this:

```
<INPUT TYPE="checkbox" name="messagenumber" value="#messagenumber#">
```

When the user selects a message to delete and submits the form, the passed variable will be messagenumber=1 or messagenumber=2, and so on. The form's action page would then use <CFPOP> and the DELETE action to remove that particular message, as illustrated in Listing 13.10.

INPUT **LISTING 13.10**   delete_mail.cfm

```
1: <!--- DELETE MESSAGE SELECTED IN FORM PAGE --->
2:
3: <CFPOP     NAME="delete_mail"
4: SERVER="pop.superview2000.com"
5:         USERNAME="jethro"
6:         PASSWORD="ellie_mae1"
7:         ACTION="DELETE"
8: MESSAGENUMBER="#messagenumber#">
9: <HTML>
10: <H2>Delete Successful</H2>
11:
12: Your message has been deleted.
13: </HTML>
```

An action page like this uses <CFPOP> on line 3 to access the specified mail server on line 4 and delete the message checked by the user (#messagenumber#). Again, ColdFusion doesn't display a confirmation by default, so it's up to you let the user know his or her selected message has been nuked, as I've done on lines 9 through 13.

Summary

Like many readily available CGI scripts, ColdFusion lets you process and send mail at the server level. But unlike those basic scripts, it also enables you to use mail features in conjunction with database selection and input, making it a very powerful mail tool that doesn't require nearly as much coding know-how as a custom CGI script.

To handle incoming mail, developers use a special tag called <CFMAIL>. It works by sending mail to a SMTP server, defined either in the tag itself or in ColdFusion Administrator. <CFMAIL> accepts parameters that enable you to specify who the mail is from and to whom it's going, and gives you the ability to send plain text, HTML-enhanced message bodies, or MIME-encoded attachments. You can supply any of <CFMAIL>'s parameters dynamically, making it a great tool to automate mailing lists or provide instant feedback from the Web.

The tag <CFPOP> is <CFMAIL>'s companion, offering the capability to receive mail from POP3 servers anywhere on the Net. <CFPOP> includes an option to retrieve only the headers of messages, which enables readers to peruse and delete mail before downloading the actual message bodies. Used together, <CFPOP> and <CFMAIL> can create an entire Web-driven mail client.

13

Q&A

Q **I host my ColdFusion site with a remote Web provider. What SMTP server should I specify in my `<CFMAIL>` tags?**

A If your Web provider has done its homework, it will have already defined a mailserver in ColdFusion Administrator. If so, you don't need to supply a name in `<CFMAIL>`—but do be sure that your FROM address is one that will be accepted by that server.

Q **When I access a template that uses `<CFMAIL>`, I get an error relating to the mail server. What's the problem?**

A First, make sure that the machine on which ColdFusion runs has rights to send mail on the SMTP server specified. If you haven't defined a server, check the default setup in ColdFusion administrator (or have your provider check it) to be sure that one is defined.

Q **Rather than type the contents of my messages into a database, can I keep text files on my server and then have `<CFMAIL>` retrieve them by filename?**

A Yes. Use a tag called `<CFINCLUDE>`, which performs a server-side include of the file you specify. For example, this line between your opening and closing `<CFMAIL>` tags:

```
<CFINCLUDE TEMPLATE="mytext.txt">
```

would plug the contents of `mytext.txt` into your message body. You can also supply the name of the included template dynamically with a variable.

Workshop

Here are a few quiz questions and exercises. Answers to quiz and exercise questions can be found in Appendix A at the back of the text.

Quiz

1. What is the primary function of the `<CFMAIL>` tag?
2. What does `<CFMAIL>` display when it successfully sends a message?
3. How do you use the results of a `<CFQUERY>` with a `<CFMAIL>` tag?
4. What parameter must be set to use HTML code in message bodies?
5. Name the three ACTION types used with `<CFPOP>`.
6. How does `<CFPOP>` return the results of a mail check?

Exercises

1. Create a database table containing names and email addresses of friends and family. Use <CFMAIL> to create a template that will send the same message to all of them. Tell them how you're destined for the high life as a ColdFusion developer.

2. Create a form page and an action page that will enable users to supply an email address, type in some text, and have that text returned to them as an email.

3. Create a template using <CFPOP> that will display the messages currently waiting on your mail server. Design a second page using <CFPOP>'s DELETE action that will enable you to remove unwanted messages.

13

DAY 14

Using ColdFusion Functions to Manipulate Data

As you move into building advanced templates, there will be times when you'll wish you could do more with the contents of your variables than just display them on the page as-is. To enable you to do this, ColdFusion borrows a concept found in several programming languages—the *function*. Functions are tools that offer greater control in the way your variables are used and displayed. Functions can be used to compare variables, to trim extra characters from them, to convert them to uppercase or lowercase, and even to see whether the variables exist at all. Today's lesson will look at three types of ColdFusion functions and describe those most commonly used. In today's lesson, you'll learn to

- Understand ColdFusion functions
- Understand Display and formatting functions
- Understand String functions
- Understand Date/Time functions

Understanding Functions

To understand how functions work, it's helpful to think of them as real-time manipulators of data. I say *real-time* because the manipulation occurs at the moment a user views a template page including your expertly coded function.

Functions use the format *SomeFunction(SomeVariable)*, where the variable you want to manipulate is placed between the parentheses. When you use functions within <CFOUTPUT> tags, you enclose the entire function string in hash marks (rather than enclosing the variable), like this:

```
#SomeFunction(SomeVariable)#
```

ColdFusion reads the entire hash-delimited string, performs whatever manipulations the function requires, and returns the results as output.

> **Note**
>
> When functions are used as part of a ColdFusion tag, such as
>
> ```
> <CFIF SomeFunction(SomeVariable)>
> ```
>
> hash marks aren't required. In general, functions follow the same rule as ColdFusion variables.

To illustrate how this works in a real ColdFusion template, let's use one of the most common functions, DollarFormat(). Assume that I've set up an input form that collects user data and adds it to a guestbook. My form looks like Figure 14.1.

FIGURE 14.1

The user who filled out this form doesn't use a decimal point or commas in the net worth field.

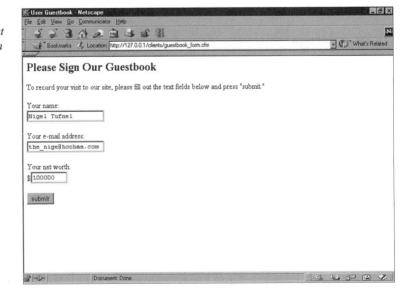

When users supply a figure for the net worth box, sometimes they use commas (100,000), sometimes a decimal point (100000.00), and sometimes they don't use either. Because my guestbook displays their figures only as text, this usually is not a problem.

But what if I later want to display user entries in a tabular format, and have all the dollar figures line up nicely on the page? If I just use the net worth numbers as submitted, I see something like Figure 14.2.

FIGURE 14.2

Without formatting, the Net Worth column shows numbers exactly as the users typed them in.

This display gets the job done, but it would be much more effective if each net worth entry shared a common format, such as using commas to set off thousands, and a decimal point. To accomplish this, I can use a <CFOUTPUT> section such as the one in Listing 14.1.

LISTING 14.1   guestbook_table.cfm

```
 1: <HTML>
 2: <HEAD>
 3:       <TITLE>Users Who've Signed My Guestbook</TITLE>
 4: </HEAD>
 5:
 6: <BODY>
 7:
 8:       <H1>Users Who've Signed My Guestbook</H1>
 9:
10: <!---CREATE TABLE--->
11:
12: <TABLE BORDER="1">
13:
14: <!---USE QUERY OUTPUT TO POPULATE TABLE ROWS--->
15:
16: <CFOUTPUT QUERY="guestbook">
17: <TR>
18: <TD>#name#</TD>
19: <TD>#email#</TD>
20:
```

14

continues

LISTING 14.1 continued

```
21: <!---USE DOLLARFORMAT TO FORMAT NET_WORTH FIGURE
22: RIGHT-ALIGN COLUMN TO LINE UP NUMBERS--->
23:
24: <TD ALIGN="right">#DollarFormat(net_worth)#</TD>
25:
26: </TR>
27:
28: <!---CLOSE CFOUTPUT AT END OF TABLE ROW--->
29:
30: </CFOUTPUT>
31:
32: <!---CLOSE TABLE--->
33:
34: </TABLE>
35: </HTML>
```

Take a close look at the variable that creates the Net Worth table cell in Listing 14.1. I've used the regular query variable net_worth inside the function DollarFormat(). Note that the variable's hash marks surround the whole function, rather than surrounding just the variable name.

Caution

If the user *does* supply a dollar sign ($) with his input, DollarFormat() causes ColdFusion to return an error. That is why my form page places a dollar sign to the left of the input box: to indicate the user should type in only a number.

When I use a function like DollarFormat(), ColdFusion changes the way the variable is displayed to the user—but it doesn't make any lasting changes to the actual variable content. If I were to take a look at my guestbook table after viewing this page, I'd still see the user's original input without commas or the decimal point.

Tip

Although ColdFusion functions don't make permanent changes to the contents of variables, you can use them in conjunction with tags such as <CFUPDATE> if you want to alter permanently the data in your tables.

Using the <CFOUTPUT> section illustrated in Listing 14.1, I now have a page that looks like the one shown in Figure 14.3.

FIGURE 14.3

The function
`DollarFormat()`
causes variables to
display with dollar
signs, commas, and
decimal points.

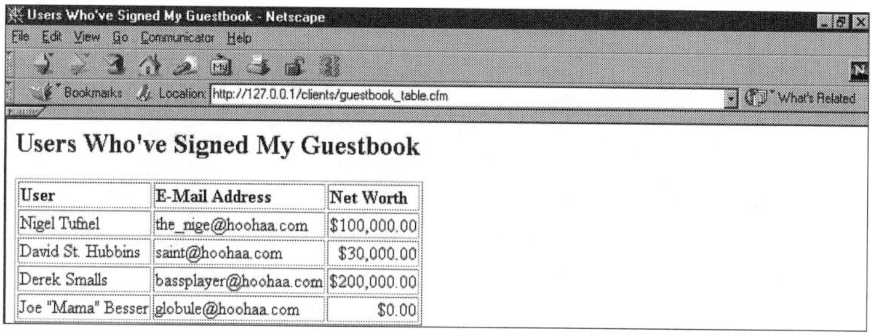

Because I also used the HTML tag `<TD ALIGN="right">` for the Net Worth column, I now have a nicely formatted list of dollar values.

Note

`DollarFormat()` is what ColdFusion's documentation calls a *display and formatting* function. Like other functions in that category, `DollarFormat()` is used primarily to change the way a variable is displayed. However, display and formatting functions can also be used behind the scenes to get variables into a certain format; for instance, if you wanted to create a sum total for all net worth figures.

General Function Rules

No matter what purpose they serve, all ColdFusion's functions share a few common traits.

Function Input

All ColdFusion functions accept either a string or a variable as input. That means you can either supply a specific value you want to format (rare) or use a valid variable name to format (common).

For example, this code

```
<CFOUTPUT>
#DollarFormat(123456)#
</CFOUTPUT>
```

produces the same output as the following code:

```
<CFSET number="123456">

<CFOUTPUT>
#DollarFormat(number)#
</CFOUTPUT>
```

14

However, it's more likely that I would use a variable such as #number# from the results of a <CFQUERY> instead of manually defining it with <CFSET>.

Case-Insensitive Function Names

Function names can be specified in any combination of uppercase and lowercase letters and still be recognized by ColdFusion. The program's documentation uses capital letters (such as DateFormat()) to denote words in function names, and it's not a bad idea to follow company convention in your templates.

Delimiting Functions

When functions are used as part of a CFML tag, they don't require the hash-mark delimiter. For example

```
<CFSET price="DollarFormat(20000)">
```

sets price to a value of $20,000.00.

When functions are used outside a tag, they must be placed within <CFOUTPUT> tags and delimited with hash marks so that ColdFusion knows to treat them as functions rather than as literal text.

Nesting Functions

Like many ColdFusion tools, functions may be nested. For example, to trim extra leading spaces from a variable *and* cause it to display in all capital letters, nest the UCase() and LTrim() functions like this

```
#UCase(LTrim(my.variable))#
```

Tip   The order in which functions are nested is important. The innermost function executes first, followed by the outer function(s).

The sections following will introduce you to some of the ColdFusion functions most commonly used by developers. For a full listing of available functions, along with usage examples, check the help documentation that comes with ColdFusion Server and ColdFusion Studio.

Note   Some functions are specifically designed to work in conjunction with certain ColdFusion tools (such as list, structure, and array functions for data manipulation or authentication functions for security purposes). These functions are covered in later lessons along with the tools they support.

> **Tip**
>
> You won't need to be familiar with all the following functions to continue to the lesson in Day 15. But take a few moments to skim through the following sections to familiarize yourself with the types of functions available and to understand some of the tasks that functions can handle.

Display and Formatting Functions

Display and formatting functions are some of the most commonly used functions in the bunch. Like `DollarFormat()` (discussed earlier today), display and formatting functions convert the contents of a variable to specified format.

Display and formatting functions are often used to standardize a user's form input so that it matches the format of other data in a database or display. They can also help you deal with a client's database in which dollar values or dates are listed a certain way that is different than the variable with which you want to match them.

DateFormat()

Usage: `DateFormat(date, mask)`

`DateFormat()` enables you to specify the way a variable containing a date is displayed. It accepts two parameters: a *date* (or a variable containing a date) and an optional *mask*.

NEW TERM   A *mask* is a series of characters that gives you precise control over how data is displayed. Many ColdFusion functions can accept mask parameters that use placeholder characters to determine display format, such as `DD/MM/YY` for a date.

If you don't specify a mask, ColdFusion formats the date like `03-Mar-99`. Masks are assembled from the characters in Table 14.1.

TABLE 14.1   Mask Characters Used with `DateFormat()`

Mask Character	Output
D	Day as a number. If the day is only one digit, no leading `0` is used.
DD	Day as a number. If the day is only one digit, a leading `0` is supplied.
DDD	Day as a three-letter abbreviation, such as `Sun`, `Sat`, and so on.
DDDD	Day as a full word: `Sunday`, and so on.
M	Month as a number, with no leading `0` for single-digit months.
MM	Month as a number, with `0` supplied for single-digit months.

continues

14

TABLE 14.1 continued

Mask Character	Output
MMM	Month as a three-letter abbreviation.
MMMM	The full name of the month.
Y	The last two digits of the year, with no leading 0 for numbers less than 10.
YY	The last two digits of the year, with a 0 supplied for numbers less than 10.
YYYY	All four digits of the year.

For example, this code

```
#DateFormat("Dec. 8, 2000", "D MMMM YYYY")#
```

produces the text 8 December 2000 and this code

```
#DateFormat("Dec. 8, 2000", "MM/DD/YY")#
```

produces the text 12/08/00.

> **Tip**
>
> DateFormat() is most useful when it is used to format ColdFusion date/time objects. These are special data units that will be covered in the next section.

DecimalFormat()

Usage: DecimalFormat(*number*)

DecimalFormat() causes values or variables to be displayed with commas to denote thousands and a decimal point followed by two digits.

For example, this code

```
#DecimalFormat(123456)#
```

produces the text 123,456.00.

This function is particularly useful for formatting numbers for tabular display.

DollarFormat()

Usage: DollarFormat(*number*)

DollarFormat(), as illustrated earlier in today's lesson, causes a value to be displayed with a dollar sign, a comma for thousands, and a decimal point.

For example, this code

```
#DollarFormat(123456)#
```

produces the text $123,456.00.

> **Tip**
>
> If you're working with currency values other than U.S. dollars, you'll be happy to learn that ColdFusion also supports a variety of international functions. They can be used to manipulate and display currencies, numbers, dates, times, and numbers in the proper format native to your users. Check your ColdFusion documentation for a complete list of supported locales and details on the functions available.

NumberFormat()

Usage: NumberFormat(*number*, "*mask*")

Like DateFormat(), the NumberFormat() function allows precise control over the way your text is displayed via use of a mask. If no mask is supplied, the number displays as all digits. Mask characters are listed in Table 14.2.

TABLE 14.2 Mask Characters Used with NumberFormat()

Mask Character	Output
9	Holds the place for a digit
.	Orients the decimal point
0	Pads the number with 0s
( )	Shows parentheses around numbers less than 0
+	Displays a plus sign before positive numbers and a minus sign before negative numbers
-	Displays a minus sign before negative numbers and a space before positive numbers
,	Separates thousands with a comma
C	Centers the number within the width of the mask
L	Left-justifies the number within the mask width
$	Places a dollar sign before the number
^	Specifies the exact location for positioning a number within the mask length

14

For example, this code

```
#NumberFormat(1234.56787, "9999")#
```

produces the number 1235, rounding the number up because no decimal point position was supplied in the mask.

```
#NumberFormat(1234.56787, "$9999.99")#
```

instead rounds the number to two decimal places and adds a dollar sign to show $1234.57. To display a comma in that same figure, you'd use a mask like this:

```
#NumberFormat(1234.56787, "$9,999.99")#
```

which would return the value $1,234.57.

ParagraphFormat()

Usage: ParagraphFormat(text)

ParagraphFormat() is useful for displaying text that has embedded carriage returns. For example, text that comes from email messages often contains hard returns after a certain number of characters. If you insert that sort of text into an input form's <TEXTAREA>, you'll see some strange wraps. ParagraphFormat() formats this type of text for proper HTML display.

For an example of how this works, take a look at Listing 14.2.

LISTING 14.2   paragraph_format.cfm

```
 1: <!---SET A STRING THAT INCLUDES HARD CARRIAGE RETURNS--->
 2:
 3: <CFSET text="
 4: Today we both went
 5: to the store and got new G.I. Joe dolls and
 6: I lost mine and got mad and tried to
 7: steal
 8: Buddy's, but he hit me in the head and took
 9: all
10: of my lunch
11: money.">
12:
13: <!--DISPLAY THE STRING WITH AND WITHOUT ParagraphFormat()--->
14:
15: <HTML>
16:
17: <H4>Without ParagraphFomat ()</H4>
18: <FORM ACTION="action.cfm" METHOD="post">
19: <CFOUTPUT>
```

```
20: <TEXTAREA NAME="text" COLS="50" ROWS="10" WRAP="virtual">#text#</TEXTAREA>
21: </CFOUTPUT>
22: </FORM>
23:
24: <H4> Using ParargraphFormat()</H4>
25: <FORM ACTION="action.cfm" METHOD="post">
26: <CFOUTPUT>
27: <TEXTAREA NAME="text" COLS="50" ROWS="10" WRAP="virtual">#ParagraphFormat
     ➡(text)#</TEXTAREA>
28: </CFOUTPUT>
29: </FORM>
30:
31: </HTML>
```

Listing 14.2 contains two <FORM> sections. The first displays the variable #text# as-is, the second uses ParagraphFormat(). The two methods look like Figure 14.4 when viewed in a browser.

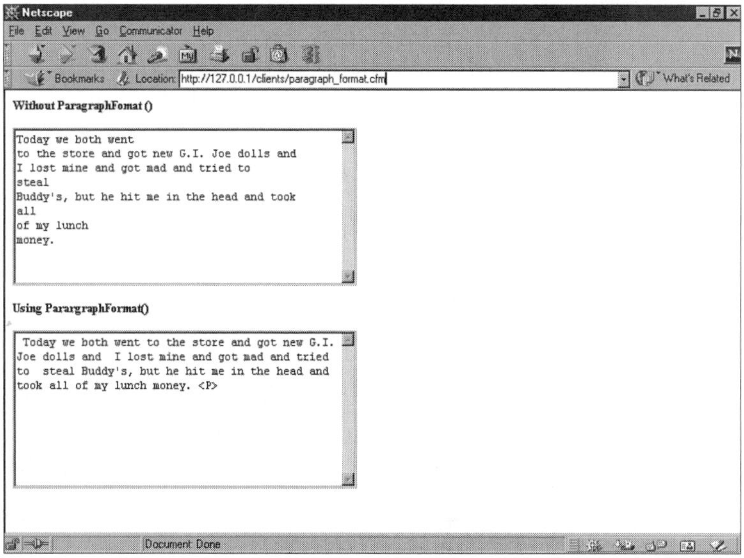

FIGURE 14.4

Using
ParagraphFormat()
*to eliminate hard
carriage returns*

TimeFormat()

Usage: TimeFormat(*date, mask*)

Like DateFormat(), the TimeFormat() function displays time-related text or variables according to the optional mask you specify. Mask characters are listed in Table 14.3.

14

TABLE 14.3 Mask Characters Used with `TimeFormat()`

Mask Character	Output
h	A lowercase h shows hours in a 12-hour format with no leading 0s for single digits
hh	Shows hours in a 12-hour format; adds leading 0s for single digits
H	An uppercase H shows hours in a 24-hour format with no leading 0s for single digits
HH	Shows hours in a 24-hour format; adds leading 0s for single digits
m	Shows minutes without leading 0s for single digits
mm	Shows minutes; adds leading 0s for single digits
s	Shows seconds without leading 0s for single digits
ss	Shows seconds; adds leading 0s for single digits
t	Shows a.m. or p.m. as one character, A or T
tt	Shows AM or PM

For example, this code

```
#TimeFormat("13:20:08", "h:m tt")#
```

produces the text 1:20 PM.

```
#TimeFormat("13:20:08", "HH:mm tt")#
```

produces the text 13:20 PM.

> **Tip**
>
> `TimeFormat()` is most useful when it is used to format ColdFusion date/time objects. These are special data units that will be covered in the next section.

YesNoFormat()

Usage: `YesNoFormat(value)`

`YesNoFormat()` changes true and false values to the text Yes and No. It's a useful tool when dealing with databases that record yes/no values as 0 or 1 (such as checkboxes). With this function, you can cause the contents of such tables to display in a more user-friendly format.

For example, the code

```
#YesNoFormat(0)#
```

produces the text No, whereas using a 1 in place of 0 produces Yes. YesNoFormat() may also be used in conjunction with other ColdFusion tools that produce output such as TRUE or FALSE and will output Yes or No, respectively.

Using String Functions

String functions are used to manipulate text or numeric strings. They can be used to replace characters in a string, to compare the value of two strings, to find text within a string, and many other operations. ColdFusion offers more than 30 such functions; I'll detail only the most commonly used functions here.

Find() and FindNoCase()

Usage: Find(search_string, target_string)

These two functions search for text within a string. Find() performs a case-sensitive search for the specified text, whereas FindNoCase() ignores case. The first parameter specifies the text to look for, the second the string in which to search.

If the search doesn't find any matching text, both Find() and FindNoCase() return a 0. If they do find matching text, they return the number at which the first matching character occurs in the specified string.

For example:

```
#Find("donald", "Gary Eddie Harry")#
```

returns a 0 because the first string is not found within the second, whereas

```
#Find("donald", "Gary Eddie Harry Donald")#
```

still returns a 0 because "donald" (with a lowercase "d") isn't found in the string. But using FindNoCase():

```
#FindNoCase("donald", "Gary Eddie Harry Donald")#
```

returns the number 18 because the case-insensitive text "Donald" occurs at position 18 in the text string.

14

GetToken()

Usage: GetToken(*string, index, delimiters*)

GetToken() is an extremely useful function for extracting a certain word or number from a string. The *delimiters* parameter is optional.

Assume that a string variable called #claim# contains the sentence "I have played Twister many times". By default, the GetToken() function uses spaces as delimiters to determine what exactly makes up a token. As such, the previous sentence contains six tokens (one for each word), so if I wanted to get the value of the fourth word in the sentence, I would use code like this

```
#GetToken(claim, 4)#
```

Because I didn't specify a delimiter, the function assumes that I want to use spaces to determine tokens. It looks for the fourth token, which is the word Twister.

Insert()

Usage: Insert(*source_string, target_string, position*)

The function Insert() provides a good way to put text into a string. It takes three parameters: The first parameter denotes a string that contains the text you want to insert, the second contains the string in which to insert the text, and the third contains a number designating the character position at which to perform the insertion.

For example, to add the area code 555 to a phone number, use code like this

```
#Insert("(555) ", "555-1212", 0)#
```

In an actual application, I would probably use variables for the first and second parameters, but you see what I'm after here. This would return the text (555) 555-1212.

LCase() and UCase()

Usage: LCase(*string*) and UCase(*string*)

Despite the relative sophistication of other ColdFusion functions, LCase() and UCase() are probably the functions used most often by developers. LCase() and UCase() convert text or a variable to all lowercase or uppercase characters, respectively.

> **Tip**
>
> The LCase() and UCase() functions are often used to format form input from users who have gone crazy with the Shift key, and to create uppercase section headers.

For example, the following code:

```
#LCase("wOw, aIn't ThAt keW1, hAcKeR dOOdz")#
```

produces the text `wow, ain't that kewl, hacker doodz`.

Similarly, the UCase() function might be used on a string to convert it to uppercase.

```
#UCase("contents of my glove box")#
```

produces `CONTENTS OF MY GLOVE BOX`, which might make a nice header for a listing of items.

Len()

Usage: Len(*string*)

Len() might not seem like the most exciting of ColdFusion's functions, but it's a deceptively handy tool for many purposes. It calculates the character length of a string or binary object and returns a number. Used alone, the function might validate user input to be sure that it has a certain number of characters, but it is also used with other string functions to gain control over individual characters in a string.

For example, if my form requires a user to supply a 12-digit product number, I could check the length of the user's input like this

```
#Len(FORM.product_number)#
```

Then, with other tools such as <CFIF>, I could evaluate the number returned by Len() to make sure it is equal to 12. For example, code like this would return an error message if the user has supplied text that isn't exactly 12 characters long:

```
<CFSET length = Len(URL.product_number)>
<CFIF length IS 12>
```

14

```
Thanks for supplying a valid product number.
<CFELSE>
You have not entered a valid 12-digit product number. Please try again.
</CFIF>
```

LTrim() and RTrim()

Usage: LTrim(*string*) or RTrim(*string*)

This pair of functions is extremely valuable for cleaning up text strings that contain unwanted characters. For example, you've probably received a form letter at one time or another that looked like this:

Dear   **Charles**;

I am writing to you personally,   **Charles**, to tell you how much I value your opinion on **excessive ATM fees**   and to let you know that I will be presenting your thoughts to my Senate colleagues at the very next congressional session. It is because of citizens like you,   **Charles**, and your outspoken views on   **excessive ATM fees**   that we are able to maintain this wonderful democracy in which we live.

Thanks again   **Charles** for taking the trouble to write, and hope to see you and your lovely wife   **no entry supplied**   at the voting booth next November.

Your Senator,

J. Hutchins Hornswoggle

Form letters like this one occur when either the user or an unknowing computer inserts extra characters before or after a string. LTrim() can guard against this sort of thing.

```
Dear #LTrim(user_name)#;
```

produces the text Dear Charles, automatically stripping any preceding spaces that appear in the variable. Similarly, RTrim() does the same for trailing spaces.

RepeatString()

Usage: RepeatString(*string, count*)

RepeatString() takes just two parameters: a string you want to display, and the number of times you want to display it. For example, to create a line of asterisks 40 characters long, you use the function this way:

```
#RepeatString("*", 40)#
```

Replace()

Usage: Replace(*string, replace_what, replace_with*) or ReplaceNoCase(*string, replace_what, replace_with*)

These two functions search a string for occurrences of a substring you specify (the *replace_what* parameter) and replace it with a second substring (the *replace_with* parameter).

Confusing? Imagine that I have a text string called my_statement. It reads: Molly will always be the girl of my dreams, come what may. Some time has passed since I originally wrote the statement, and now I need to make a few changes.

#Replace(my_statement, "Molly", "Daphne")#

This would produce the text Daphne will always be the girl of my dreams, come what may.

Note

By default, Replace() works only on the first occurrence of a substring. If your text includes more than one occurrence of a substring (such as "Molly") and you want to change them all, use the optional ALL parameter as a scope:

#Replace(my_statement, "Molly", "Daphne", "ALL")#

Replace() performs a case-sensitive search when it examines your string. If you need a case-insensitive search, use the companion function ReplaceNoCase().

Tip

For even more control over searches and replacements, check the ColdFusion documentation on the REReplace() and REReplaceNoCase() functions. These work in the same way as Replace(), but rather than performing simple text matches, they allow the use of regular expressions. Regular expressions are used in many programming languages to perform sophisticated text searches and replacements, such as finding text that appears between two HTML tags, finding the first word in a phrase, and so on.

Date and Time Functions

14

To understand how ColdFusion functions work with dates, it's important to first understand the difference between dates and times that are treated as plain text, and more complex date/time objects.

So far in this book, dates and times have been treated simply as text. When a user types a date into a form, for example, I've thus far stored the entry exactly as the user types it. The date is stored in my database table as plain text, the same as any other text string. When I need to display the date later, I can use a formatting function such as DateFormat() to change the way it appears in my pages, but that's about it.

To gain more control over dates and times, I can instead use date/time objects. *Date/time objects* are special internal variables ColdFusion uses to hold a specific date and time down to one-second accuracy. Date/time objects are usually not displayed as-is because they often contain more information than the average Web page requires (such as seconds). Instead, I can use ColdFusion's arsenal of date and time functions to display a date/time object in a way that's meaningful to people surfing my site.

Defining Date/Time Objects

To create a new date/time object, ColdFusion offers three different functions: CreateDate(), CreateDateTime(), and CreateTime(). Each of these accepts the parameters you might expect, such as

CreateDate(*year*, *month*, *day*)

CreateDateTime(*year*, *month*, *day*, *hour*, *minute*, *second*)

CreateTime(*hour*, *minute*, *second*)

> **Note**
>
> When you create any of these objects, ColdFusion automatically sets any undefined parameters to the value 0.

For example, to create a date/time object that marks the day my first bicycle was stolen, I would use the CreateDate() function along with a <CFSET> tag to define the date/time object as a variable:

<CFSET fateful_day=#CreateDate(1974, 5, 28)#>

In this case, I'm supplying CreateDate() with literal values, but I could have also used variables that came from a query or from user input.

Working with Date/Time Objects

After I have an object defined, I can perform some pretty fancy operations on it. In fact, there are 25 ColdFusion functions that work specifically with date/time objects. I'll give a few general examples in this section and leave it to ColdFusion's documentation to address the finer points.

Assume that after defining a date/time object for my traumatic bike incident, I want to display that object as a day of the week, such as in a sentence like, "I remember it well—the horrible, life-changing incident occurred on a _____."

To do this, I would use a couple of functions. The first, DayOfWeek() examines my date/time object and returns the day of the week as a number from 1 to 7. Because I want to display the name of the day, not a number, I can use a second function—DayOfWeekAsString()—to convert that number to a name that will be output on my page. I do this by nesting the two functions:

```
I remember it well—the horrible, life-changing incident occurred on a
➥#DayOfWeekAsString(DayOfWeek(fateful_day))#.
```

DayOfWeek() examines my date/time object fateful_day and returns a number, whereas the parent function DayOfWeekAsString() turns that number into the corresponding text. The output is, "I remember it well—the horrible, life-changing incident occurred on a Tuesday."

To take things a step further, let's say that I want to calculate the number of years between my horrible loss and today's date. I want to use the resulting value in a sentence like "I guess I should be over it by now, after all it has been _____ years since my bike was stolen."

To do this, I'll use the function DateDiff(), which compares two date/time objects and returns the difference. I can also specify how I want the difference displayed: either in days, years, months, or weeks. I need a current date to compare it to, so I'll use the function Now().

Note

Now() is a special date/time object that generates the current time. It is set to the moment the page is displayed—that is, if a user views a page today and then again two weeks from now, he or she will see two different values displayed for Now().

```
I guess I should be over it by now, after all it has been
➥#DateDiff("YYYY", fateful_day, Now())# years since my bike was stolen.
```

When a user views the page containing this code, he or she will see the number of years between the date of the incident (May 28, 1974) and the date on which the page is viewed (Now()). Viewing the page in the year 2000, I see the number 25.

The function DateDiff(), like many of the date and time functions, takes a specifier as one of its parameters. In the previous line of code, the specifier was YYYY, which told the

14

function that I want to display the results of my comparison in number of years. Table 14.4 lists the specifiers used with date/time objects.

TABLE 14.4 Specifiers Used with Date/Time Objects

Specifier	What It Displays
D	Day
H	Hour
M	Month
N	Minute
Q	Quarter
S	Second
W	Day of week
WW	Week
Y	Day of year
YYYY	Year

The previous examples provide only a brief introduction to ColdFusion's date and time functions. There are others that work specifically with hours, minutes, and seconds that might be useful in your applications. Check the documentation that comes with ColdFusion Server and ColdFusion Studio for a complete list of date and time functions.

Tip

As it can with currency values, ColdFusion can also display date and time objects in a variety of international formats. Check ColdFusion's documentation on international functions for a complete list of tools that enable you to convert and display international dates and times.

Summary

ColdFusion functions are tools that help take your applications to the next level of sophistication. Although they're only a word long, they work in real-time, like miniature programs. As you begin to develop more advanced templates, you'll encounter coding situations for which there seems to be no solution—chances are it will be one of ColdFusion's many functions that comes to the rescue.

ColdFusion offers scores of functions, and the list grows with each new release of the software. Today's lesson introduced you to the concept of functions and detailed only those functions commonly used in building applications. You'll find an extensive section listing all functions and their use in your ColdFusion Server and ColdFusion Studio documentation.

Functions take the form *#SomeFunction(some_variable)#*. They don't make permanent changes to your data unless you use them with tags such as <CFUPDATE> and <CFINSERT>, and they execute only at the moment a page is loaded by a user. Different functions may be nested within each other to perform more than one operation at a time.

Display and formatting functions such as DecimalFormat() and DollarFormat() enable you to change the way variables are displayed. They take an existing query or form variable and display it according to parameters you define, such as rounding to two decimal places or showing only whole dollar figures. String functions such as Replace() and LCase() are also valuable tools for tasks such as replacing words in a string and converting an uppercase string to lowercase. There are also functions that work specifically with dates and times, both to control the way they're displayed and to perform comparisons between them.

Q&A

Q Do I need to be familiar with every ColdFusion function before moving on to other lessons?

A Not at all. As mentioned in today's lesson, most developers discover ColdFusion functions one at a time, when they reach a coding impasse and think, "There must be some tool to fix that."

Q Are all functions supported by all versions of ColdFusion Server?

A No. Functions are version-specific. Check the documentation that ships with your version of ColdFusion to find a list of supported items.

Q How many functions can be nested within one another?

A In theory, you can nest as many functions as you like, as long as the inner functions produce output recognized by the outer functions. In practice, however, each function requires a bit of processing power, so to keep your pages loading quickly it's not a good idea to nest more than three or four at a time. Too many nested functions also make for templates that are hard to debug.

14

Workshop

Just to see whether you were dozing through today's discussion, here are a few quiz questions and exercises. Answers to quiz questions can be found in Appendix A at the back of the text.

Quiz

1. When do ColdFusion functions require hash-mark delimiters?
2. Are function names case-sensitive?
3. Name two functions that might be used to trim leading or trailing spaces from a text string.
4. Briefly describe a date/time object.
5. In the jargon of functions, what is a token?
6. What is a mask?

Exercises

1. Create a table in which at least one field contains dollar values. Add some values that contain commas for thousands, some that contain decimal points and trailing zeros, some that are whole numbers, and so on. Using ColdFusion functions, create a template that will query your table and display the results neatly aligned, each with dollar signs, commas, and two decimal places.

2. Create a table that contains the birth dates of friends and relatives. Using date and time functions, create a template that shows how many days separate two of the dates. Also list the number of weeks, years, and months that separate the dates. (If you plan to display your handiwork to others, it's best not to use older people in your comparisons.)

3. Using <CFOUTPUT>'s GROUP parameter, create a template that displays records in groups, such as all employees in Production followed by all employees in Marketing. Use UCase() to create uppercase headers to identify each group.

WEEK 2

In Review

Now that you've finished your second week with ColdFusion, you should be able to build basic Web applications with ease. You learned about some of ColdFusion's more advanced tools for working with templates and data, and gained some insight as to how those tools are used in real-world Web sites.

Day 8, "Understanding ColdFusion Studio," introduced you to ColdFusion Studio, Allaire's development application for ColdFusion. You examined the basic components of Studio and learned how it can aid in remote development. You also tried out the program's powerful editing and tag functions, so you now have a good grasp of what Studio does and can use it in developing the examples in future lessons.

Day 9, "Enhancing Your Applications with Variables and If-Then Statements," showed you how variables and if-then statements can make ColdFusion behave like a programming language. You learned how to use <CFIF> to generate a basic password-protection function, and how to use it to create templates that perform more than one action. At this point, you understand ColdFusion's method of controlling program flow.

Day 10, "Enhancing Output with Tables and Groups," covered the aesthetic end of development by showing how you can use tables and groups to create output that's easy to read and navigate. You learned about ColdFusion's special <CFTABLE> tag and how it is used to quickly format results from a query. You also learned about the GROUP parameter and how it can be used to arrange output by similar characteristics. Now you can make your pages readable and logical in construction.

Day 11, "Enhancing Input Pages with Basic <CFFORM> Tags," focused on ColdFusion's powerful replacement for HTML forms, the <CFFORM> tag. You learned how the tag automatically builds form-input devices in JavaScript to create some pretty useful tools. You can now create form pages that go far beyond the limitations of standard HTML.

Day 12, "Using Advanced Techniques to Select and Display Data," showed you some advanced techniques for dealing with user input. You learned how SQL can be used to put data into tables, and how it can replace ColdFusion's more basic input methods when your data gets complex. You learned a few tips for saving on coding time such as creating multifunction forms that can handle several actions. You also learned about <CFTREE> and <CFGRID>, two powerful input tags available in <CFFORM>. You should now have no problem getting any data, no matter how complex, into your database quickly and easily.

Day 13, "Using ColdFusion to Handle Email," focused on ColdFusion's email functions, teaching you how to build template pages that can both send and receive email. You also learned how to create tools such as autoresponders and list managers in ColdFusion. With the tools covered in this lesson, you can build a complete email client with a ColdFusion Web interface.

Day 14, "Using ColdFusion Functions to Manipulate Data," covered the unsung heroes of ColdFusion development, the functions. You learned how functions are used to manipulate the contents of variables—that they can control what is displayed and how. At this point, you should have a feel for how functions work and should be familiar with their syntax.

WEEK 3

At a Glance

Week 3 shows you how ColdFusion applications can be customized to the specific needs of your data. Although the two previous weeks have looked at ColdFusion applications as a collection of template pages, this week's lessons will help you begin to look at ColdFusion applications as a whole. In doing so, you'll learn how you can take advantage of application-wide features such as sharing data from page to page. You'll also learn several tricks that will help in real-world development environments, and how to troubleshoot your applications when errors occur. This week covers the following:

- Day 15, "Using Lists, Structures, and Arrays to Package Data," takes you beyond simple variables by introducing data storage units such as lists, structures, and arrays.

- Day 16, "ColdFusion Client and Session Management," introduces ColdFusion's unique client and session management tools, and shows you how to build applications in which each page works as part of a whole.

- Day 17, "Finding Text with Verity," covers the search tool Verity, and provides step-by-step instructions to quickly build search engines for even the most complex sites.

- Day 18, "Working with Files and Directories," illustrates how ColdFusion can interact with files and directories on your server, and how you can create applications that enable your users to add, remove, and modify such files.

- Day 19, "Using Advanced SQL Techniques," examines advanced SQL techniques that will give you more power over how your queries select data and help you work with databases that don't comply with ColdFusion requirements.

- Day 20, "Using ColdFusion for E-Commerce Applications," looks at e-commerce and introduces you to concepts that will help you build successful commerce sites with ColdFusion.

- Day 21, "Using ColdFusion's Debugging Tools to Troubleshoot Your Code," wraps up your journey by looking at the various types of error messages that a ColdFusion application can generate and showing you what to do when they occur.

DAY 15

Using Lists, Structures, and Arrays to Package Data

You're now beginning your third week of developing with ColdFusion, and the concept of variables probably seems like old hat. You've learned how to generate both form variables and query variables, and have learned how to pass them from one template to another. In today's lesson you'll learn how to assemble a bunch of variable values into packages called lists, arrays, and structures. By using these unique data packages, you can save loads of coding time and handle tricky situations you never thought possible. We'll cover

- Defining and assigning values to lists, arrays, and structures
- Reading data from a package
- The uses and advantages of lists, arrays, and structures
- Using data packages in your applications

Understanding ColdFusion Lists

Until now, you've dealt only with variables that hold a single value, be it a word, a text string, or a number. ColdFusion lists are variables that can hold more than one value, by storing values in a comma-delimited list, such as:

```
names="Bobby,Peter,Greg,Cindy,Marsha,Jan"
```

Instead of using five separate variables like

```
name1="Bobby"
name2="Peter"
```

and so on, I can assemble individual values into a list and then get at the contents later either by looping through values one by one, or by referring to the specific *offset* of one list item or another.

NEW TERM A variable's *offset* value is the order number in which it appears in a list. In a list like Bobby,Peter,Greg,Cindy,Marsha,Jan, the name "Bobby" has an offset value of "1," "Peter" is "2," and so on.

When I have values in a list like #names#, I can use a nifty tag called <CFLOOP> to cause ColdFusion to process each value in the list. Essentially, <CFLOOP> says to perform some action for each value in a list; if my list has six values, <CFLOOP> will perform six actions.

Suppose I need to search a database for one of these names. I might use a lengthy query like Listing 15.1.

LISTING 15.1 Finding One of Several Names with OR

```
 1: <CFQUERY NAME="find_siblings" DATASOURCE="family">
 2:
 3: SELECT * FROM siblings
 4:     WHERE name = 'Bobby' OR
 5:     name = 'Peter' OR
 6:     name = 'Greg' OR
 7:     name = 'Cindy' OR
 8:     name = 'Marsha' OR
 9:     name = 'Jan'
10:
11: </CFQUERY>
```

That's a pretty long query, and I'm only dealing with six names here. For a shorter chunk of code, I can package all the values into a list and then use a shorter query like Listing 15.2.

LISTING 15.2   Using a List to Build a Query

```
 1: <CFQUERY NAME="find_siblings" DATASOURCE="family">
 2:
 3: SELECT * FROM siblings WHERE 0=1
 4:
 5: <CFLOOP INDEX="name" LIST="#names#">
 6:
 7:     OR name = '#name#'
 8:
 9: </CFLOOP>
10:
11: </CFQUERY>
```

In Listing 15.2, I begin my query with a SELECT statement in line 3, but then I stop short at the WHERE clause, in the place I'd usually type in the name of a field and a value for which to search. Instead of a standard WHERE clause, I use the "dummy" statement 0=1, which won't match anything. You'll learn why in a moment.

Starting on line 5, I use <CFLOOP> along with my list #names# to tell ColdFusion that I want to perform a search for each name in the list. <CFLOOP> will pull each value from my list and make it part of the query, stopping only after it reaches the last value. I've placed an OR before the name statement, so the SELECT statement built by the <CFLOOP> will be interpreted by ColdFusion as this:

```
SELECT * FROM siblings WHERE 0=1 OR name = 'Bobby' OR name = 'Peter'
➥OR name = 'Greg' OR name = 'Cindy' OR name = 'Marsha' OR name = 'Jan'
```

Note that for each item in my list variable, <CFLOOP> adds OR name = 'some_name' to the query. This is why I supplied the dummy statement 0=1—otherwise my WHERE clause would begin with an OR and I'd get an SQL syntax error. Since the dummy statement is untrue, ColdFusion will simply pass it by and move on to the rest of the WHERE checks.

Got that? Don't worry if you're fuzzy on the details—I'll offer more specific descriptions in the next sections.

Creating ColdFusion Lists

There are several ways to package values into a list. You can hard-code them, or actually type in the names of the variables you want to package. You can also use a query to fill a list with values, or you can use data passed from a form page. Each of these methods has its associated tags and techniques.

- When you want to define a new list, such as the siblings list in the previous section, use <CFSET>.
- When you want to add a value to an existing list, use <CFSET> with the ListAppend() function.
- When you want to create a list from the results of a query, use the ValueList() function.

The following sections examine each of these methods in detail. Note that in these examples, you'll learn only how lists are packaged. We'll talk about how to read data from your lists in the section covering <CFLOOP>.

Populating a List with <CFSET>

Let's start with the most basic way to get data into a list, the <CFSET> tag.

<CFSET> is arguably ColdFusion's easiest tag to understand because it does only one thing—it assigns a value to a variable. Say that I had a long phrase that I didn't want to have to type out each time I wanted to display it in my page. I'd use <CFSET> to assign that text string to a variable name, like this:

```
<CFSET phrase="My name is Charles Mohnike and I was sent here from another
➡planet to help Earthlings learn about ColdFusion software distributed
➡by Allaire. Someday I will return to my home planet and report on my success
➡to my immediate superiors, who each have two heads and breathe through
➡their eyelids.">
```

When I want to display that text later, I can just use the variable #phrase# within a <CFOUTPUT> tag and save myself from having to type it out each time.

In the same way, I can use <CFSET> to create a list by simply separating the values with commas.

```
<CFSET names="Bobby,Peter,Greg,Cindy,Marsha,Jan">
```

Note

ColdFusion doesn't really care if my variable is a list or a simple text string, so I don't need to do anything special to alert it that I'm creating a list. If I reference the variable #names# without using any of the tools associated with lists, ColdFusion will just return the whole string of names, commas included.

Populating a List with `<CFSET>` and the `ListAppend` Function

ColdFusion's `ListAppend` function offers another way to package data into a list. It is typically used either when you want to add a value to an existing list, or when you want to use the results of a query to populate a list.

From our discussion of ColdFusion's functions in Day 14, "Using ColdFusion Functions to Manipulate Data," recall that functions manipulate variables. In this case, we're adding a value, and `ListAppend` works like this:

```
<CFSET names=ListAppend(names, "Mike")>
<CFSET names=ListAppend(names, "Carol")>
```

Note

> `ListAppend` is designed to add values to an existing variable. If you try to add values to a variable that doesn't already exist, `ListAppend` will return an error. You must first define an empty variable with `<CFSET>`, such as `<CFSET names="">`.

Each variable I add with `ListAppend` will be placed at the end of my list. After adding the values `Mike` and `Carol`, the value of the list `#names#` is now:

```
Bobby,Peter,Greg,Cindy,Marsha,Jan,Mike,Carol
```

Populating a List with a Query

By itself, the `ListAppend` function doesn't have many advantages over typing values into a list with the `<CFSET>` tag. But when I use it in conjunction with a query, the tag begins to show its power.

Suppose I'm working on a project in which it would be useful to have a list of all of Liz Taylor's husbands. I can use a standard query to get their names from the database table used as an example in Day 1, "Introducing ColdFusion," and then use `<CFOUTPUT>` and `ListAppend` to package those names into a list, as shown in Listing 15.3.

LISTING 15.3 Populating a List with Query Results

```
1: <!--- GET ALL HUSBANDS' NAMES FROM THE husbands TABLE --->
2:
3: <CFQUERY NAME="get_husbands" DATASOURCE="liz">
4:
5: SELECT name FROM husbands
```

continues

LISTING 15.3 continued

```
 6:
 7: </CFQUERY>
 8:
 9: <!--- DEFINE AN EMPTY VARIABLE TO HOLD THE LIST --->
10:
11: <CFSET liz_taylor_husbands="">
12:
13: <!--- USE CFOUTPUT TO LOOP THROUGH EACH NAME --->
14:
15: <CFOUTPUT QUERY="get_husbands">
16:
17: <!--- USE LISTAPPEND TO ADD EACH NAME TO liz_taylor_husbands --->
18:
19: <CFSET liz_taylor_husbands=ListAppend(liz_taylor_husbands, "#name#")>
20:
21: </CFOUTPUT>
```

As the <CFOUTPUT> section on lines 15 though 21 cycles through each record returned from the query, ListAppend steps in on line 21 and adds the value of the query variable #name# to the list variable #liz_taylor_husbands#.

As usual, ColdFusion also provides a shorthand method to perform this same task—another function called ValueList. ValueList works specifically with variables returned by a query. Instead of processing each record individually, the way <CFOUTPUT> does, ValueList gets all returned values for a query variable and assembles them into a comma-delimited list. Not coincidentally, this list is in the exact format I need to create a data list. Check out Listing 15.4.

LISTING 15.4 Using ValueList() to Build a List from Query Results

```
 1: <!--- GET ALL HUSBANDS' NAMES FROM THE husbands TABLE --->
 2:
 3: <CFQUERY NAME="get_husbands" DATASOURCE="liz">
 4:
 5: SELECT name FROM husbands
 6:
 7: </CFQUERY>
 8:
 9: <!--- CREATE A LIST OF HUSBANDS FROM QUERY RESULTS--->
10:
11: <CFSET liz_taylor_husbands=ValueList(get_husbands.name)>
```

In Listing 15.4, I economized on code; no `<CFOUTPUT>` tag was necessary, and I didn't need to predefine a variable to hold the list because I was not appending anything. I just created a new variable with `<CFSET>` and set it equal to the text generated by `ValueList`. The function itself took the results of the query `get_husbands`, specifically examined the `name` field, and automatically created a comma-generated list.

If I then used a `<CFOUTPUT>` tag to display the contents of `#liz_taylor_husbands#`, I'd see that it holds something like this:

```
Nicky Hilton,Michael Wilding,Michael Todd,Eddie Fisher,Richard Burton,
➥John Warner,Larry Fortensky
```

Populating a List with Data Passed by a Form

Form pages—both standard HTML forms and souped-up `<CFFORM>`'s—use commas to separate values if the form collects more than one value for a given variable name.

To illustrate, check out this basic form page I've created to let users vote for their favorites among Liz's husbands (see Figure 15.1).

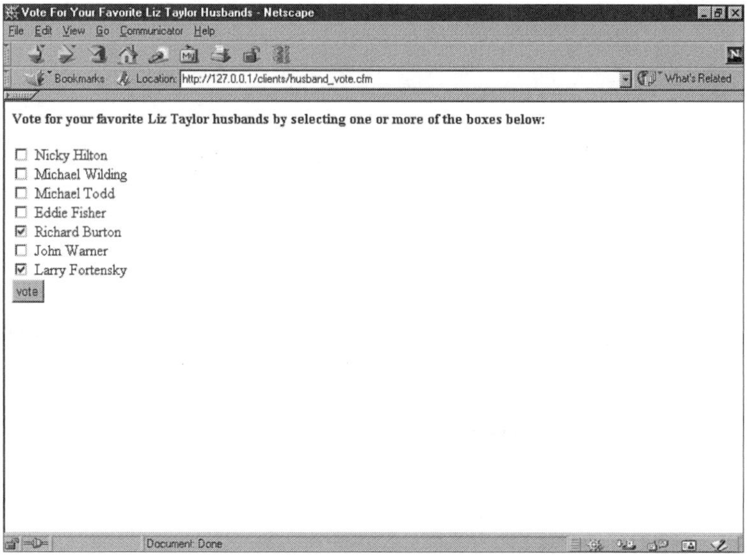

FIGURE 15.1

This input form lets the user select more than one value.

The form uses check boxes to enable users to select more than one value. Listing 15.5 shows its code.

LISTING 15.5   husband_vote.cfm

```
 1: <!--- GET HUSBAND NAMES --->
 2:
 3: <CFQUERY name="get_husbands" datasource="liz">
 4: SELECT name from husbands
 5: </CFQUERY>
 6:
 7: <HTML>
 8: <HEAD>
 9:     <TITLE>Vote For Your Favorite Liz Taylor Husbands</TITLE>
10: </HEAD>
11:
12: <BODY>
13: <B>Vote for your favorite Liz Taylor husbands by selecting one or more of
    ➥ the boxes below:</B>
14:
15: <!--- BEGIN THE VOTING FORM --->
16:
17: <FORM ACTION="send_husband_vote.cfm" METHOD="post">
18:
19:        <CFOUTPUT query="get_husbands">
20:            <INPUT TYPE="checkbox" NAME="husband" VALUE="#name#"> #name#<BR>
21:        </CFOUTPUT>
22:
23:    <INPUT TYPE="submit" VALUE="vote">
24:
25: </FORM>
26:
27:
28: </BODY>
29: </HTML>
```

Because the NAME of each check box is husband, when a user selects more than one box, there will be one or more potential values for the passed variable #husband#. Recall that when this occurs, forms pass multiple values by separating them by commas. This makes them ideal for packaging into a list.

> **Tip**
>
> Check boxes are a good way to pass multiple values for a single variable, but they're not the only method. You can also use multiple text-input boxes that share the same NAME attribute, or <CFFORM>'s <CFSELECT> tag with the parameter MULTIPLE="yes". The latter will create a select box in which the user can highlight more than one value.

On my action page for the form in Figure 15.1, I can package the values into a list with a simple <CFSET> tag, as shown in Listing 15.6.

LISTING 15.6   send_husband_vote.cfm

```
 1: <!---PACKAGE PASSED VALUES INTO husbands--->
 2:
 3: <CFSET husbands="#form.husband#">
 4:
 5: <!---SHOW A CONFIRMATION MESSAGE --->
 6:
 7: <html>
 8: <head>
 9:    <title>Thanks for Voting</title>
10: </head>
11:
12: <body>
13: <B>Thanks for your vote. The husbands you selected are:</B><P>
14:
15: <!---DISPLAY CONTENTS OF husbands--->
16:
17: <CFOUTPUT>
18: #husbands#
19: </CFOUTPUT>
20:
21: </body>
22: </html>
```

I've now illustrated three ways to get data into a list, but you might be wondering why go to all the trouble? Is a comma-delimited text string really all that valuable? Read on to learn how to use these lists you've so expertly packaged.

Reading List Values with <CFLOOP>

By using the tag <CFLOOP>, all the extra time I spent packaging data into lists really starts to pay off. I covered the tag briefly in the introduction to data lists, but this section takes things a step further.

Let's say that in my off hours I've assembled a massive database that contains the details of every episode of the 1970's TV show *The Munsters*. I now have 70 records in my table, with each one listing the episode's title and plot synopsis.

I've decided it's vital that Web users be able to access this information, so I want to create a search page that lets them search my table by keywords. I'll start with the input form shown in Figure 15.2.

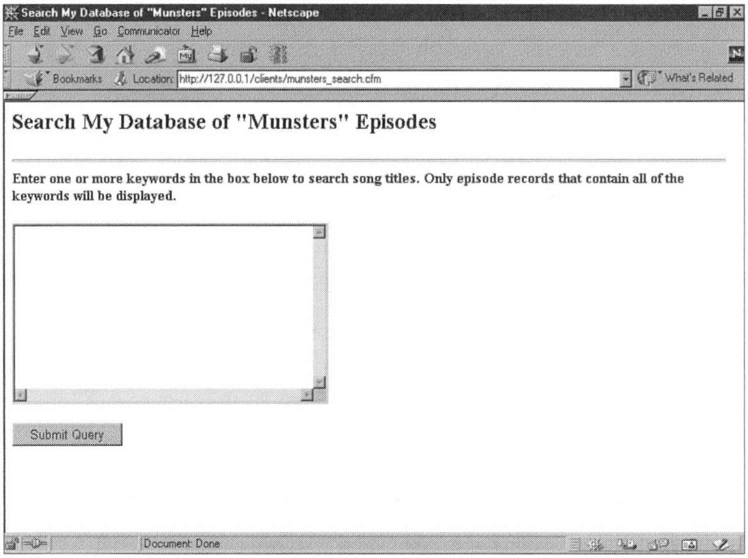

FIGURE 15.2

*This form collects one
or more keywords and
passes them to an
action page.*

I won't display the code for this search page because it's pretty basic stuff. I just created a standard HTML form with a <TEXTAREA> input box to collect the user's keywords. When the user submits the form, the passed variable keywords might look like this:

```
keywords=Eddie Grandpa school
```

Because the variable reflects exactly what the user has typed in, it doesn't use commas to separate the keywords. That's okay, though—we'll handle this on the action page.

> **Note**
>
> Data lists use commas as the *default* delimiter, but you can use other characters, such as spaces. Specify the desired delimiter in <CFLOOP> statements.

When my action page processes this search, I want it to examine my table's synopsis field, checking for the occurrence of all keywords submitted by the user. I've created an action page like Listing 15.7.

LISTING 15.7   munsters_search_action.cfm

```
1: <!---QUERY DATABASE--->
2:
3: <CFQUERY NAME="get_episodes" DATASOURCE="tv">
4:
5:     SELECT title,synopsis from shows
```

```
 6:     WHERE series = 'Munsters'
 7:
 8:     <!---LOOP THROUGH SUBMITTED KEYWORDS--->
 9:
10:     <CFLOOP INDEX="search_word" LIST="#keywords#" DELIMITERS=" ">
11:         AND synopsis LIKE '%#search_word#%'
12:     </CFLOOP>
13:
14: </CFQUERY>
15:
16: <!---SHOW RESULTS--->
17:
18: <HTML>
19: <HEAD>
20:     <TITLE>Your Search Results</TITLE>
21: </HEAD>
22:
23: <BODY>
24: <H2>Here are the results of your search:</H2>
25: <HR>
26: <CFOUTPUT QUERY="get_episodes">
27:     <B>Episode Title: </B>#title#<BR>
28:     <B>Plot Synopsis: </B>#synopsis#<P>
29: </CFOUTPUT>
30:
31: </BODY>
32: </HTML>
```

Take a close look at the SQL statement on lines 5-12. It performs an initial check to be sure that the series field contains 'Munsters' (as opposed to 'I Dream of Jeannie', or the other shows I've archived) and then uses AND (line 11) to specify other conditions.

These conditions are generated dynamically by <CFLOOP> on lines 10–14. The tag takes the variable passed by the search form and treats it as a list. Because I've specified the delimiting character as " " (a blank space), <CFLOOP> will treat each word as an item in my list and create an AND clause for each word listed. If I were to look at the actual SQL statement used behind the scenes, I'd see something like this:

```
SELECT title,synopsis from shows
        WHERE series = 'Munsters'
AND synopsis LIKE '%Eddie%'
AND synopsis LIKE '%Grandpa%'
AND synopsis LIKE '%school%'
```

This statement sets up a compound condition in which all the keywords must appear in the field "synopsis" before SQL will select that record. The output of the search page looks like Figure 15.3 in the user's browser.

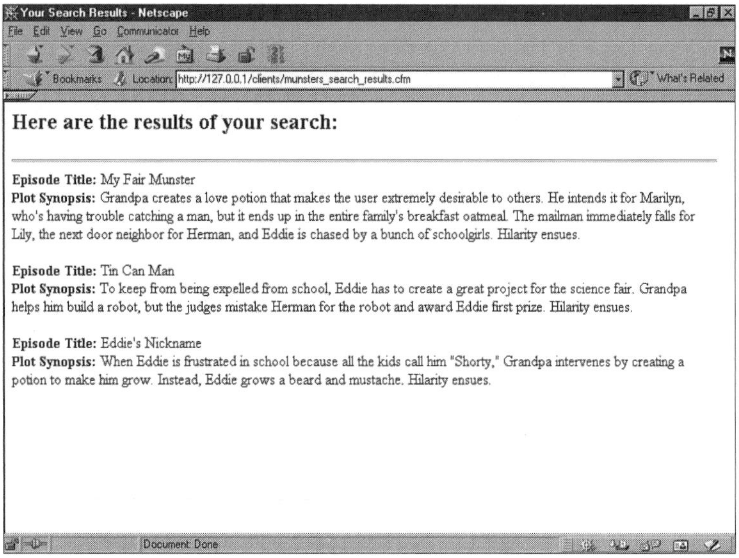

FIGURE 15.3

The results of my search, using <CFLOOP> with a data list to check for multiple keywords.

> **Tip**
>
> Lists are most often used in conjunction with tags like <CFLOOP> that cause something to occur for each item in the list. If you need to display or work with a single value in a list, use the function ListGetAt() along with an offset value. For example, #ListGetAt(siblings, 2)# would return "Peter," the second element in the list siblings.

> **Note**
>
> ColdFusion provides several functions to help you manipulate and access data lists. You've already learned about two of the most essential, ListAppend and ValueList, but there are several others you might find useful. You can use functions to find text in a list, count the number of items in a list, or return the text that appears at a specific list position. Check ColdFusion's documentation for a complete rundown of list functions.

Understanding ColdFusion Structures

Like lists, ColdFusion structures are special variables that can hold more than one chunk of data at a time. *Unlike* lists, structures have the capability to package *pairs of related data*.

When I package or read variable data from a list, I use functions to reference each list item by its offset number, say to add a new list item at position 10, or to retrieve the value of list item 7. Structures handle this differently. Instead of using a number to find a certain chunk of data, they use *keys*. Keys are user-definable, just like variables.

NEW TERM   A *structure key* is an identifer within a structure variable that refers to a specific element in the structure. For example, the key "name" might refer to the value "Jeff".

When I create a new structure, I populate it by specifying key names, along with the text associated with each key. For example, if I wanted to store a name and address and maintain unique variables for each element, I might use a basic method like this:

```
<CFSET first_name="Buddy">
<CFSET last_name="Bradley">
<CFSET street_address="12 Suburban Ct.">
<CFSET city="Seattle">
<CFSET state="WA">
```

It's a simple method, but I now have five unique variables to handle. If I want to pass this information to a query or page, I have to worry about passing each element.

Structures can package this information into a single variable, like this:

```
<CFSET user=StructNew()>
<CFSET user.first_name="Buddy">
<CFSET user.last_name="Bradley">
<CFSET user.street_address="12 Suburban Ct.">
<CFSET user.city="Seattle">
<CFSET user.state="WA">
```

The first line defines a new structure called "user"; the following lines define keys in the structure "user" (first_name, last_name, and so on) and assign a value to each. The resulting structure is called #user#.

> **Note**
>
> There is one drawback to using structures and arrays to package your data. Because they're complex data formats, they can't simply be passed from template to template in the URL as lists can. Instead, structures and arrays are often stored as *application* or *session variables* and require a little extra code to make them work. You'll find a full account of application and session variables in Day 16, "ColdFusion Client and Session Management."

Structures are often more valuable than lists because they allow you to refer to stored values by a key name rather than an offset number, such as with a list. This feature also makes your code easier to follow. For example, a structure reference like #user.address# is pretty self-explanatory, while a list reference like #ListGetAt(user, 3)# is less so.

Viewing the Contents of a Structure

The easiest way to view the contents of a structure is to specify its name and the key that contains the data you want to display, as follows:

```
<CFOUTPUT>
Name: #user.first_name# #user.last_name#<BR>
Address: #user.street_address#<BR>
City: #user.city#<BR>
State: #user.state#<BR>
</CFOUTPUT>
```

A more dynamic way to output structure content is to use the <CFLOOP> tag with a special parameter called COLLECTION.

The COLLECTION parameter tells <CFLOOP> that it's dealing with a data structure more complex than simple text. In fact, you might think of a structure as a small database. To display the contents of the structure #user#, I'd use a <CFLOOP> tag like this:

```
<CFLOOP COLLECTION=#user# ITEM="key">
<CFOUTPUT>
        #key#: #StructFind(user,key)#<BR>
</CFOUTPUT>
</CFLOOP>
```

Note that there's a second element at work here, the function StructFind. I first use <CFLOOP> to loop through my structure #user# and return each key value I assigned earlier. Using the database analogy again, a key can be compared to a field name.

<CFLOOP> displays the value of each key, and then uses the StructFind function to find and display the related value for that key. This repeats for every item in my structure. The output looks like this:

```
CITY: Seattle
FIRST_NAME: Buddy
LAST_NAME: Bradley
STATE: WA
STREET_ADDRESS: 12 Suburban Ct.
```

Understanding ColdFusion Arrays

Like lists and structures, ColdFusion arrays are special variables that can hold more than one chunk of data at a time. But whereas lists can store only individual bits of data and structures can hold only sets of data, arrays expand on the capabilities of both by letting you store data in *multiple dimensions*, as in a spreadsheet grid or a database table.

NEW TERM   An array's *multi-dimensionality* refers to its capability to relate one, two, or three bits of data to another. ColdFusion supports arrays of up to three dimensions.

To understand the concept, picture arrays as temporary, transportable database tables. Arrays have the capability to store columns and rows of information, preserving the relationships between them. A two-dimensional array, for example, can contain as much data as a database table with two fields—and the whole thing will be packaged into a single variable, or *array name*.

Table 15.1 illustrates the way an array holds data. Keep in mind that arrays are abstract constructs—you'll never actually see them laid out like Table 15.1, but it's helpful to visualize them this way.

TABLE 15.1 An Abstract View of a Two-Dimensional Array

Big Guy	Company
Bill Gates	Microsoft
Lee Iacocca	Chrysler
Steve Forbes	Forbes, Inc.
Hugh Hefner	Playboy Enterprises
Bernie Jefferson	Craaaazy Bernie's Shoe Repair and Taco Stand

Just like a database, an array has rows and columns. The first column in Table 15.1 lists powerful business magnates; the second column shows the business with which they're associated. To reference a certain bit of data, I can ask ColdFusion for the value of column 1, row 4, and it will return the text "Hugh Hefner."

The reasons for using arrays are a lot like those for using structures. In an array, you can temporarily store user-submitted data that you don't need committed to a database. Arrays also provide a good way to send complex data structures from one template to another by way of session or application variables, which we'll cover in Day 16.

Defining and Populating Arrays

To create an array like the one in Table 15.1, I'd start with a <CFSET> tag and the ArrayNew function, like this:

```
<CFSET business_magnates=ArrayNew(2)>
```

The 2 means that I want to create a two-dimensional array that will store two columns of data. Next I'll populate the first row by specifying each column by number:

```
<CFSET business_magnates[1][1]="Bill Gates">
<CFSET business_magnates[1][2]="Microsoft">
```

The first bracketed number refers to the row number, the second to the column. This method works fine if I plan to manually type in all the values in my array. But if I plan to populate my array dynamically, maybe with the results of a query, I'll need a better method. Not surprisingly, ColdFusion provides one, as shown here:

```
<CFSET business_magnates[ArrayLen(business_magnates)+1][1]="Lee Iacocca">
```

The preceding example uses the ColdFusion function ArrayLen to determine the number of records in the array *before I place the current record into it*. If I had already placed Bill Gates' entry into the array, the ArrayLen function would return a value of 1 or one record. The +1 in the first <CFSET> statement says that I want to place the current data in the next available row.

To add the name of a business associated with "Lee Iacocca", I'd use a tag like this:

```
<CFSET business_magnates[ArrayLen(business_magnates)][2]="Chrysler">
```

Note that I didn't need the +1 here because I automatically created a new row when I placed the text "Lee Iacocca" into it. This second <CFSET> statement says to get the number of the last row, and insert the text "Chrysler" into column 2 of that row.

To use this technique to populate an array from the results of a query, I'd use code like Listing 15.8.

LISTING 15.8 Populating an Array With Query Results

```
 1: <!---SELECT TITLE, YEAR FROM ALL RECORDS--->
 2:
 3: <CFQUERY name="get_movies" datasource="elvis">
 4: SELECT title, year from movies
 5: </CFQUERY>
 6: <!---CREATE A NEW ARRAY--->
 7: <CFSET movies=ArrayNew(2)>
 8: <!---USE CFOUTPUT TO POPULATE THE ARRAY--->
 9: <CFOUTPUT query="get_movies">
10:     <!---USE "+1" TO ADD DATA TO THE NEXT AVAILABLE ROW--->
11:     <CFSET movies[ArrayLen(movies)+1][1]="#title#">
12:     <CFSET movies[ArrayLen(movies)][2]="#year#">
13: </CFOUTPUT>
```

Listing 15.8 uses my database of Elvis movies as its datasource. The query selects the title and year from all records. I then create a new array, and populate it with the results of the query. Each time <CFOUTPUT> loops to a new record, the value of ArrayLen(movies) increases by one and the data is inserted in the next available row.

Tip

There are several ways to dynamically populate an array without using <CFSET>. Other common methods include the function ArraySet for one-dimensional arrays, and the <CFLOOP> tag for two- and three-dimensional arrays. Check ColdFusion's help documentation on these two tools for further explanation.

Reading Data from an Array

Just as with structures, there are lots of ways to reference specific data packaged in an array. The most basic method is to refer to a specific row and column number, like this:

```
<CFOUTPUT>
#movies[2][2]#
</CFOUTPUT>
```

This would cause ColdFusion to output the text "1957," which appears in the second column of the second row of my database table, and also in my array #movies#.

If I want to display all the data stored in an array, I can also use the <CFLOOP> tag, as illustrated in Listing 15.9.

LISTING 15.9 Populating and Displaying an Array

```
 1: <!---GET TITLE, YEAR FOR ALL MOVIES--->
 2:
 3: <CFQUERY name="get_movies" datasource="elvis">
 4: SELECT title, year from movies
 5: </CFQUERY>
 6: <!---CREATE A NEW ARRAY CALLED "MOVIES"--->
 7: <CFSET movies=ArrayNew(2)>
 8: <!---POPULATE THE ARRAY WITH QUERY RESULTS--->
 9: <CFOUTPUT query="get_movies">
10:     <CFSET movies[ArrayLen(movies)+1][1]="#title#">
11:     <CFSET movies[ArrayLen(movies)][2]="#year#">
12: </CFOUTPUT>
13: <!---BEGIN A CFLOOP TO DISPLAY EACH ELEMENT IN THE ARRAY--->
14: <CFLOOP INDEX="Counter" FROM=1 TO="#get_movies.RecordCount#">
15:     <CFOUTPUT>
16:         Movie: #movies[Counter][1]#<BR>
17:         Year Released: #movies[Counter][2]#<P>
18:     </CFOUTPUT>
19: </CFLOOP>
```

In a very roundabout way, the code in Listing 15.9 accomplishes something that can be done with a simple <CFQUERY> and a <CFOUTPUT> section, but it's still an excellent method to introduce the concepts behind displaying arrays. The query gets all movie listings from my database table; then I use <CFOUTPUT> to fill a two-dimensional array with movie titles and their associated years of release.

Look carefully at the <CFLOOP> tag that starts displaying the array. Note that I've used an INDEX called "Counter" and have defined a range for the counter from 1 to #get_movies.RecordCount#.

The reserved ColdFusion variable RecordCount returns the number of records selected by a query. The prefix get_movies specifies that I want to find the number of records returned by the "get_movies" query, and use it as the upper limit on my <CFLOOP> count. In this way, <CFLOOP> does its stuff only as many times as the number of records returned. Ten records in the query means that <CFLOOP> will display array values only ten times.

The output from Listing 15.9 looks like Figure 15.4 in my browser.

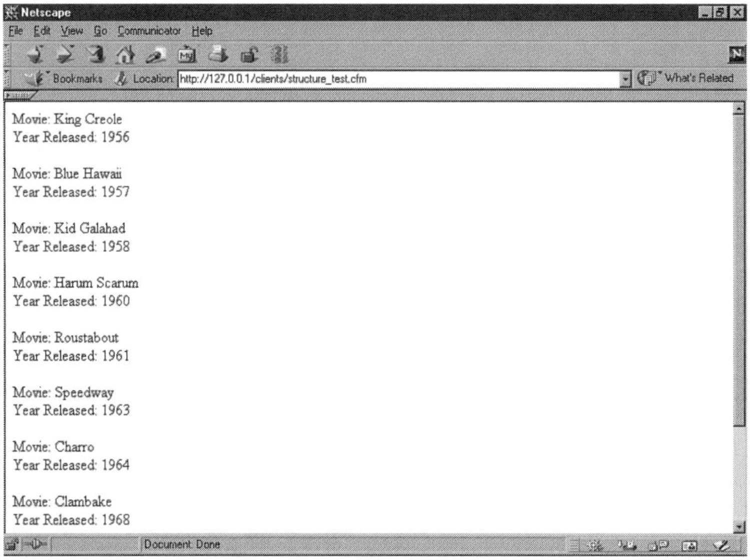

FIGURE 15.4

Output drawn from arrays can be format- ted and arranged like any <CFOUTPUT>.

Since arrays work like portable database tables, they are extremely valuable for storing related data such as shopping carts that might contain data on several products a user has selected for purchase (you'll learn more about shopping carts and arrays in Day 20, "Using ColdFusion for E-Commerce Applications").

Note that today's lesson has only scratched the surface of arrays and structures. Both are complex data structures that have a variety of uses and techniques. Use today's principles as a starting point in your own applications, and then check ColdFusion's help documentation for details on other uses of arrays and structures.

Summary

Until this chapter, the variables I've used and discussed have been simple variables capable of holding only one bit of data at a time. Day 15 introduced you to the concept of "packaging" your data, or using special variable constructs called lists, structures, and arrays to store more than one bit of data in a single variable. The contents of all three variable types can be displayed with the <CFLOOP> tag.

Lists are comma-delimited values that can be passed from template to template by way of URLs, just like standard variables. Lists can be created with the <CFSET> tag, by the results of a query, or by a form that returns multiple values for a single variable. Once defined, lists are valuable tools for tasks such as performing searches with multiple keywords or populating table fields with keyword lists.

Structures take the concept of data packaging a step further by enabling developers to store related sets of data. Structures use *keys* to create relationships, for example, the key first_name might identify the text "Buddy."

Arrays offer even more flexibility because they're multi-dimensional and, in ColdFusion, are capable of storing up to three related levels of data. In the abstract, arrays function much like database tables, with rows and columns that identify each specific cell. Because of their complexity, arrays, like structures, can't be passed to other templates with a URL, but they can be temporarily stored in a ColdFusion server's RAM for later access, as I'll cover in Day 16.

Q&A

Q I've designed an input form that assembles user selections into a list. I want to use the list to create a dynamic query, but my SQL statement requires that each list item appear in single quotes. What to do?

A When you use the list variable in your query, surround it with the function QuotedValueList, like this:

```
#QuotedValueList(form.variable)#
```

This will cause ColdFusion to insert single quotes around each item in your list.

Q How do I guard against errors if my query calls on an empty list, for example, if a user hits "submit" without typing anything into a search box?

A There are several solutions. The simplest is to use the `<CFPARAM>` tag on your `results` page to define a default value for your list. You might also use a `<CFIF>` statement that will only perform the query if the list has values in it. You can also design your form with the `<CFFORM>` tagset and use the `REQUIRED` parameter on all input boxes.

Q I've used lists, structures, and arrays in other programming languages. Are the ColdFusion versions similar?

A In concept, yes, although the ColdFusion versions have certain limitations versus those used in languages such as Perl and C.

Q Are there limits on the amount of data that can be stored in a list, structure, or array?

A In theory, no, but massive variables of any type can put a strain on your server in their extremes.

Workshop

Answers to quiz and exercise questions can be found in Appendix A at the back of the text.

Quiz

1. What is the default delimiter character for a list?
2. Name three ways to get data into a list.
3. What is a structure *key*?
4. Which of the three variable types covered in this chapter can be passed via a URL?
5. When assigning data to arrays, what do the two bracketed numbers after the array name stand for?
6. What does the function `ArrayLen` do, and where would you use it?

Exercises

1. Create a Web form that lets users input a comma-delimited list of keywords. Use their input to search a database and return the results.
2. Use the results of a query to populate a structure. On the same page, create a `<CFOUTPUT>` section that draws information from your structure.
3. Use a query to create an array that mimics a two-dimensional table in your database.

DAY **16**

Using ColdFusion Client and Session Management

In the examples leading up to today's lesson, you've created several types of templates that perform tasks like retrieving, displaying, or storing data. So far, you've looked at each type of template as a unique entity unto itself, but realize that in a real-life scenario, you or your clients' sites are likely to require several types of templates that perform a variety of tasks.

Together, these various templates are called a ColdFusion *application.* In to-day's lesson, you'll learn how to deal with your site as a complete application—rather than as individual templates. This enables you to implement a variety of features, including sharing data from one template to another, maintaining a user's preferences throughout a site, or tracking the comings and goings of visitors. In today's lesson, you'll learn about

- ColdFusion's Web application framework
- The `Application.cfm` file
- Application, client, and session variables
- Client-state management
- Using cookies with ColdFusion

Understanding ColdFusion's Web Application Framework

To understand how several ColdFusion templates can work as a whole, think about visiting an online store that sells videotapes. It's likely you'd first be asked to log in or register. During the process, the site might present a form that would ask you some very personal questions, such as what your hobbies are, your favorite color, and so on.

As you browse the site, you see content tailored to the answers you provided to the questions on the login form. If you specified your favorite color as ochre, you'd now see a yellow background and navigation bar; if you listed "fish" as one of your interests, you'd now be shown lots of Jacques Cousteau videos, and so on. If you select a video to purchase and then continue to browse, the site "remembers" your selection by placing it in some kind of shopping cart, where it remains as you continue to browse.

Say that some pressing concern tears you away from your computer that night, and you forget all about the video site. If you happen to return to it a week or a month later you'd still see your favorite yellow background, with your selected videos still waiting in your shopping cart.

ColdFusion enables you to easily build a site like this through the use of its unique Web application framework. By working with your various templates as a single application, you can define a default set of preferences throughout your pages, pass data from one page to another without using lengthy URLs, and even store user data from one viewing session to another.

> **Note**
>
> Today's lesson is designed only as an introduction to ColdFusion's Web application framework and client-state management techniques. After finishing this chapter you'll have enough information to get started, but keep in mind that there are many more tasks that can be accomplished than there is room to list here.

Using `Application.cfm`

The key to all of this high-tech magic is a special template file called `Application.cfm` that resides in a folder along with your application's templates and subfolders. `Application.cfm` is a lot like the `.ini` files used by many Windows applications, or the `.conf` files familiar to users of UNIX-based operating systems. It defines a set of parameters to be used throughout your application, including

- The name of your application
- Default variable values
- Custom error pages
- Data sources
- Default style settings
- Security settings

16

By creating an `Application.cfm` file to accompany your various template files, you can specify a set of values to be used by every template that resides in that folder, or folders below it in the directory tree. For example, if you've built 10 template pages that use a common datasource for queries, you can define that datasource in `Application.cfm` rather than in the individual templates. If the name of your datasource changes later (say, if you move your site to another server), you only have to change the datasource name once in `Application.cfm`, rather than 10 times in your templates.

In the same way, you can use `Application.cfm` to define font styles to be used throughout your pages. When you do, changing the look of your site is as simple as editing a single file.

Every time you or a user requests a template page on your site, ColdFusion looks for an `Application.cfm` file. If it doesn't find one in the same folder as the template, it continues searching in parent folders until it *does* find one. When Coldfusion finds an `Application.cfm` page, it inserts the contents of the file into the requested template page, just as a `<CFINCLUDE>` might add a header or a footer. You don't see this happening, but still it happens.

Note

UNIX-based operating systems use case-sensitive filenames, so for compatibility ColdFusion uses the specific case-sensitive name `Application.cfm`, with the capital "A". This gives the file a unique name that's not likely to conflict with other template pages.

Since ColdFusion uses the first `Application.cfm` file it finds, it's possible to use more than one in an application. For example, you might have a folder titled "search forms" with an `Application.cfm` file in that folder, and another titled "products" with its own `Application.cfm`. But until you become more comfortable using application files, it's best to stick with one—otherwise it can be difficult to track which file your templates are using.

Setting Values In `Application.cfm`

Take a look at a sample `Application.cfm` file in Listing 16.1.

LISTING 16.1   Application.cfm

```
 1: <!--- CREATE A NAME FOR THE APPLICATION --->
 2: <CFAPPLICATION NAME="elvis">
 3:
 4: <!--- DEFINE A DEFAULT DATASOURCE --->
 5: <CFSET ODBC_Datasource = "elvis">
 6:
 7: <!--- DEFINE A DEFAULT BACKGROUND COLOR --->
 8: <CFSET BG_Color = "FFFFFF">
 9:
10: <!--- DEFINE A DEFAULT FONT --->
11: <CFSET Font_Face = "Helvetica">
```

ANALYSIS   The first entry in Listing 16.1 is the `<CFAPPLICATION>` tag. This defines a name for your application, and ensures that any client, session, or application variables you use within it are unique to the application. You'll learn more about such variables later in today's lesson.

A page like Listing 16.1 uses `<CFSET>` to define default variables that you could use in place of static values in your application's template pages. If you wanted to change a value later, you'd only do it once—in `Application.cfm`.

If `Application.cfm`'s sole purpose were to set application variables, it would still be a pretty handy tool. But it does much more, including setting *application* and *session* variables, as well as defining *client states*. The following sections explain what these mean.

Understanding Statelessness

When a user views one of your template files, it's likely there are several variables at work. If the page includes a query, there are query variables being passed between `<CFQUERY>` and `<CFOUTPUT>` to produce results, or the page might be processing variables passed by a previous form. But when the user moves on to another page, the variables and their values vanish into the ether. There's no physical record of them ever having existed. If the user returns to your site the next day, he or she has to start all over again.

This is what technical types call the Internet's *statelessness*. Variable values are relative to the page on which they're displayed, and the HTTP protocol that drives the Web doesn't provide any way to save these values, or to preserve the state of a page when a user leaves it.

To overcome statelessness, Web developers and software engineers have come up with a variety of ways to preserve user settings and maintain the state of variables. They've traditionally used one of three methods:

- Tracking user IP addresses
- Passing data in URLs
- Using cookies to store data

Tracking User IP Addresses

Recall from Day 1, "Introducing ColdFusion," that an IP address is a unique number assigned to every machine that connects directly to the Net. In theory, this would be a good way to keep track of a user's actions—but, in practice, it doesn't work. Most modem users are assigned IP addresses dynamically by their Web providers, so that each time the users dial up, they're at a new address.

Also, many business networks use only a single connection to the Internet, letting their employees surf the Web behind a firewall or proxy server. Imagine a user's surprise if she has been browsing the "vegetarian cuisine" portions of your site, but you mistake her IP address and serve up a recipe for Buffalo Bob's BBQ Spareribs.

Passing Data in URLs

You've already worked with two examples of this method—form ACTION pages and ColdFusion templates. Both will accept variable(s) as input and return a page based on variable values. This method also has a limited capability to save the state of a user. For example, a user could bookmark a ColdFusion template with a URL such as

```
http://your_server/elvis_movie.cfm?code=7
```

If the user calls up the page a day or a week later, she can see the movie with the appropriate code number (assuming you haven't restructured your site).

One problem with URL data is that, as a user moves from page to page within your site, you have to pass every single variable collected to each page she visits. You'd end up with extremely long URLs that would gradually become more time-consuming for servers to parse. There's also a security risk involved, because others can easily track URL data.

Using Cookies to Store Data

Cookies offer improvements over either of the other two methods. They can be reasonably secure, they can save variables as a user browses, and they can maintain a user's state between browsing sessions.

NEW TERM A *cookie* is a small text file that a Web application sends to a user's machine. As a user browses, information such as preferences and other variables are stored in the cookie and can be recalled either during the user's current session, or if he returns to the site later.

The main problems with cookies are that older browsers do not support them, and some users might have turned off the cookie feature.

Understanding ColdFusion's Client-State Management

ColdFusion provides its own weapon against statelessness, called *client-state management*.

When a user visits an application page that employs client-state management, ColdFusion will automatically generate two special variables to identify the user, CFID and CFTOKEN. Think of these as labels on a "drawer" of information specifically for a particular user. When a user has an assigned CFID and CFTOKEN, any template page in the application can either add information to the user's drawer by referencing those two variables, or read information already in the drawer, also by referring to CFID and CFTOKEN.

Note By default, ColdFusion saves a user's "drawer" in the system registry, but it can also be configured to save the data in an SQL database or in a cookie on the user's machine. Sites that save lots of information might want to use one of these alternative storage methods. Check your ColdFusion documentation for details on <CFAPPLICATION>'s CLIENTSTORAGE variable.

ColdFusion passes the CFID and CFTOKEN data to the user's machine as a cookie, where it is saved either until the user deletes it or reaches a "time out" date (see the section "Understanding Cookies" later in this day). Note that only the CFID and CFTOKEN values are sent to the user—the user's drawer remains stored on the server unless your configuration says otherwise.

When the user has been associated with a specific CFID and CFTOKEN, your template pages can read from and write data to their drawers using the CLIENT scope on variables:

```
<CFSET CLIENT.favorite_color = "blue">
```

or

```
<CFOUTPUT>
Your Age: #CLIENT.age#
</CFOUTPUT>
```

Any data added to the user's drawer remains there for future sessions. When your users return to your site, their preferences and state will be maintained.

Using Client-State Management

Say that you've been approached by a guy named Crazy Eddie, who runs a wholesale business selling everything from surplus Barbie doll heads to railroad spikes. He's very adamant about giving his customers the full "Crazy Eddie experience," so he's asked you to create a site that will greet each customer by name on every page they visit. He'd also like to allow his users to choose their favorite color as the background for their pages.

To use client-state management, for this task, you first have to create a new folder in which to store your application's files. Within that folder, you create an Application.cfm file to define parameters for the application.

You plan to use ColdFusion's client-state management to handle Eddie's odd requests, so you first enable the feature by adding the CLIENTMANAGEMENT parameter to your <CFAPPLICATION> tag in the Application.cfm page accompanying your templates:

```
<CFAPPLICATION NAME="crazy_eddie"
               CLIENTMANAGEMENT="yes">
```

Now you can start creating templates. The login page for new users might look something like Listing 16.2.

LISTING 16.2   Crazy Eddie's Login Page

```
 1: <HTML>
 2: <HEAD>
 3:    <TITLE>Crazy Eddie's Bargain Junction</TITLE>
 4: </HEAD>
 5:
 6: <BODY>
 7: <H1>Crazy Eddie's Bargain Junction</H1>
 8:
 9: Welcome to Crazy Eddie's, your home for quality products at crazy prices.
    ➡Eddie's so nuts he's sellin' stuff for less than he paid for it,
    ➡and now YOU can cash in on his craziness!<P>
10: <HR>
11: To start your browsin' experience, tell Eddie yer name and yer
    ➡favorite color:
12: <FORM ACTION="howdy.cfm" METHOD="post">
13: <INPUT TYPE="text" NAME="name"><P>
```

continues

LISTING 16.2 continued

```
14: <SELECT NAME="color">
15:     <OPTION VALUE="BB0000">Red</OPTION>
16:     <OPTION VALUE="00BB00">Green</OPTION>
17:     <OPTION VALUE="0000BB">Blue</OPTION>
18: </SELECT>
19: <INPUT TYPE="submit">
20: </FORM>
21:
22:
23: </BODY>
24: </HTML>
```

ANALYSIS Nothing new here—just a simple form to collect the user's name and favorite color. Note that the SELECT box on lines 14-18 uses hexadecimal color values as VALUEs. That's because these will be used in the <BODY> tags on future pages to create the necessary background hue.

The form looks like Figure 16.1 in your browser.

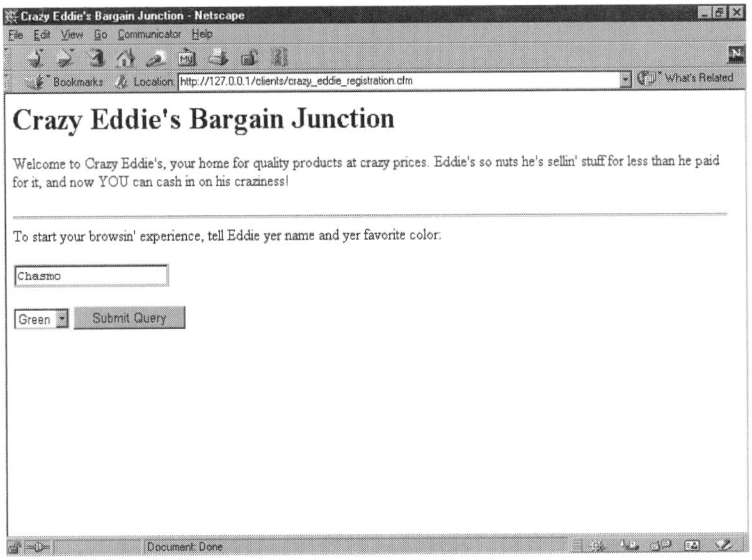

FIGURE 16.1

Crazy Eddie's login form.

Next you need to create an ACTION page that will perform two tasks.

Recall that because you enabled client-session management in the Application.cfm file, Eddie's users will automatically be assigned a CFID and CFTOKEN when they view the form in Figure 16.1.

Your `ACTION` page's first task is to use the `<CFSET>` tag to add the user's name and color selection to his drawer. You do this by defining variables using the special `CLIENT` scope, like this:

```
<CFSET CLIENT.name = "#name#">
<CFSET CLIENT.color = "#color#">
```

This inserts the form values into the "drawer" associated with a specific user's `CFID` and `CFTOKEN` values. Note that you can use any variable names you'd like as long as they use the `CLIENT` scope and don't conflict with the reserved variable names used by `CLIENT`. (You'll learn about those in a moment.)

Next you'll use a `<CFOUTPUT>` tag to insert the user's name and color preference into the page. The whole `ACTION` page looks like Listing 16.3.

LISTING 16.3 howdy.cfm

```
 1: <CFSET CLIENT.name = "#name#">
 2: <CFSET CLIENT.color = "#color#">
 3:
 4: <HTML>
 5: <HEAD>
 6: <CFOUTPUT>
 7:    <TITLE>Howdy #CLIENT.name#!</TITLE>
 8: </HEAD>
 9:
10: <BODY BGCOLOR="#CLIENT.color#">
11: <H1>Howdy #CLIENT.name#!</H1>
12: </CFOUTPUT>
13: Thanks fer registerin'. Hope ya like the new look!<P>
14:
15: Browse the Bargains:
16:
17: <UL>
18: <LI><A HREF="dog_sweaters.cfm">Check out our new dog sweaters!</A>
19: <LI><A HREF="hubcaps.cfm">Browse our collection of hub caps!</A>
20: <LI><A HREF="lumber.cfm">Look at our prices on quality lumber!</A>
21: </UL>
22:
23:
24: </BODY>
25: </HTML>
```

When the user has registered, he can browse anywhere on Eddie's site and still see his name and preferred background color as long you use the variables #CLIENT.name# and #CLIENT.color# for these values.

16

If the user leaves the site today and returns next week, he'll still see his personalized pages. It's just what Eddie wanted.

> **Note**
>
> If you're concerned that your users' browsers might not support cookies, you can still use client-state management. You do so by passing the CFID and CFTOKEN values along with each link on your site, using a special URL-compatible variable:
>
>   http://your_server/crazy_eddie/dog_sweaters. cfm?#CLIENT.URLtoken#
>
> User-associated variables still go into a "drawer" on the server, but because there's no cookie to identify the user, your links have to "remind" each template which user is visiting.

Reserved Client Variables

CLIENT has a small set of reserved variables that can come in pretty handy for quite a few tasks. Besides the previously mentioned CFID and CFTOKEN, these are

- CLIENT.LastVisit   Records the date and time a user last visited your application pages.
- CLIENT.HitCount   Stores the number of times the user has visited your site.
- CLIENT.TimeCreated   The date and time the client first visited your site and was assigned a CFID.
- CLIENT.URLToken   A special variable that appends the CFID and CFTOKEN values into a single variable for passing with a URL. This method is used as an alternative to storing CFID and CFTOKEN in a cookie.

To see an example of these reserved variables in action, take a look at Listing 16.4.

LISTING 16.4   status.cfm

```
1: <HTML>
2: <HEAD>
3: <CFOUTPUT>
4:     <TITLE>Howdy #CLIENT.name#!</TITLE>
5: </HEAD>
6:
7: <BODY BGCOLOR="#CLIENT.color#">
8: <H1>Howdy #CLIENT.name#!</H1>
9: You've been visitin' Crazy Eddie since #DateFormat(CLIENT.TimeCreated,
➥"MMMM D, YYYY")#<P>
```

```
10: You've been here #CLIENT.HitCount# times and your last visit was
    ➥#DateFormat(CLIENT.LastVisit, "MMMM D, YYYY")#.<P>
11:
12: </CFOUTPUT>
13: We're a-watchin' you!
14:
15: </BODY>
16: </HTML>
```

This page uses the DateFormat() function to put the values returned by the CLIENT variables into a readable format. In a browser, it looks like Figure 16.2.

FIGURE 16.2

Using client variables to display user statistics.

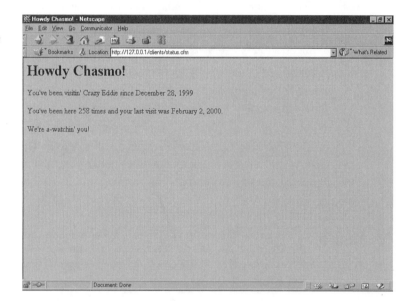

Checking and Listing Client Variables

As a user browses your application, various variables will be added to the user's drawer. For example, a user might register, adding a name and a color to his drawer; then select a product or two; and then perhaps request to hear Crazy Eddie's custom MIDI file as he browses.

As you create pages on a site like this one, remember that your pages don't already "know" which variables are in the user's drawer. For example, if you use a variable such as #CLIENT.zipcode# on an order page, and your user hasn't yet visited the "Enter your address" page, the user will see an error because that particular variable hasn't been defined.

There are a couple of ColdFusion tools to help you work with variables that might or might not exist:

- IsDefined()   This function checks for the existence of a variable and returns TRUE or FALSE. It is most often used with a `<CFIF>` statement, like this:

```
<CFIF IsDefined("CLIENT.Name")>
    Thanks, #CLIENT.Name#, for logging in today.
<CFELSE>
    You haven't logged in yet. Please proceed to the login page.
</CFIF>
```

  Note that no hash marks are used around the variable name, since we're asking if the variable name—not the actual value of the variable—is defined.

- `<CFPARAM>`   This tag specifies a default value for a variable, if one hasn't already been defined. For example,

```
<CFPARAM NAME="CLIENT.Name" DEFAULT="Mud">
```

  would set the user's name to "Mud" if she hadn't already logged in. If a value did appear in `#CLIENT.Name#`, `<CFPARAM>` wouldn't do anything.

- GetClientVariablesList()   This function will generate a comma-delimited list of all the variable names that appear in a user's drawer. That's not a very useful feature by itself, but, when used with a tag like `<CFLOOP>` to extract individual values, it becomes pretty handy.

> **Note**
>
> Client variables exist until they're either redefined or deleted. To delete a client variable, use the function DeleteClientVariable(). This function returns a "YES" if it succeeds, or "NO" if it doesn't find the specified variable.

Understanding Variable Scopes

In the last section, you learned about client variables, one of the three special variable types available to you when you use an Application.cfm file. Recall that a client variable is only valid for a particular client—if a new client visits your site, a new set of client variables comes into play. Also remember that client variables use the prefix client. before the actual variable name. This is called a *scope*, a term you were introduced to back in Day 9, "Enhancing Your Applications with Variables and If-Then Statements."

When using Application.cfm files and thus employing ColdFusion's client and session management, the scope of your variables becomes very important. There are four variable scopes available, each with its own uses. Look at Table 16.1 for a list and descriptions.

TABLE 16.1   Variable Scopes in Client and Session Management

Scope	Description	How To Enable
client scope	Client variables are used when you need values that are specific to one client, such as user preferences. They remain active every time a client visits your site.	Set CLIENTMANAGEMENT=yes in Application.cfm.
session scope	Session variables are similar to client variables, but they last only as long as the user continues a browsing session. When a user leaves your site, session variables no longer retain their values. They may be set to expire after a certain time.	Set SESSIONMANAGEMENT=yes in Application.cfm.
application scope	Application variables retain their value throughout your application, for every user on every visit. They are reset only when ColdFusion server is restarted. They may also be set to expire after a certain time.	Application variables are automatically enabled when you use an Application.cfm file. They may also be defined in ColdFusion Administrator.
cookie scope	Cookie variables retain their value as long as the cookie remains on the client's machine, or until the cookie "expires."	To use cookie variables, you must first set a cookie with the <CFCOOKIE> tag.

16

Notice that application, session, and cookie variables may be set to "time out" or expire at a certain time. As an example of how this might be used, consider a situation where a user browses a store site, adding products to a shopping cart. If the user leaves the site before checking out, you may want to retain those products as session or cookie variables for a few days so that if he returns to the site the products still "live" in his shopping cart. But if the user visits your site months or weeks after the first session, you may want him to start with an empty cart since he's probably not interested in the selected products anymore.

Note

Depending on the variable scope, timeout values may be set in Application.cfm, ColdFusion Administrator, or in the <CFCOOKIE> tag. If you need custom timeout values, check your ColdFusion documentation for details.

The following sections cover session, application, and cookie variables in more detail.

Using Session Variables

Now that you've learned the basics of client variables, *session* variables will be a breeze.

As their name implies, session variables stick around only as long as a user's session lasts. When the user leaves your application pages, the session variables vanish into the ether. However, they're still extremely valuable tools for storing data that doesn't necessarily need to be permanently saved as client data.

Suppose that Crazy Eddie has added several "featured products of the week" to his site. He wants to offer different products to different customers, based on information they supplied during registration. For example, someone who said his hobby was "cars" would see Eddie's custom chain steering wheel as the featured product this week. Someone who specified "pets" might see Eddie's rhinestone dog muzzle.

Eddie wants the featured product to appear on every page the user browses, and he also wants the ability to change the range of products each week to feature new stuff.

Obviously this is a job for a database. Featured products could be listed in a table, with a field for "interests" that would match those supplied by users during registration. But, what about the fact that the selected product needs to appear on every page? You might use a client variable to store the name of the user's product, but then in a week, Eddie would rotate the products, and you'd have to redefine the variable.

Session variables offer a good way to handle a situation like this. Because they're only valid for a user's session, they won't save any permanent information to the user's drawer. When the user returns a week from now, he will see a different product related to his interests. Session variables are also application-wide, meaning that, like client variables, they can be defined once and then used throughout the site—for as long as the user's session lasts.

To create a feature like this, you first have to "tell" ColdFusion that you'll be using session variables. You do this in your application's `Application.cfm` file:

```
<CFAPPLICATION NAME="crazy_eddie"
               CLIENTMANAGEMENT="yes"
               SESSIONMANAGEMENT="yes">
```

> **Note**
>
> Like application variables, session variables are enabled and disabled under ColdFusion Administrator's "variables" link.

Next, on the login page, you would add a query that would find the product to feature to the user that week. Assuming that the user's hobby was previously saved as `#CLIENT.hobby#`, you'd use a query like this:

```
<CFQUERY NAME="get_featured_product" DATASOURCE="crazy_eddie" MAXROWS="1">
SELECT product, description, price FROM featured WHERE related_hobby =
➥'#CLIENT.hobby#'
</CFQUERY>
```

This query would find the product that matched the hobby specified by the user in his first registration session way back when. The MAXROWS=1 parameter tells the query to only select one item, just in case Crazy Eddie hasn't maintained his database properly.

You'd next use the <CFSET> tag to assign the query results to session variables:

```
<CFSET SESSION.product = get_featured_product.product>
<CFSET SESSION.description = get_featured_product.description>
<CFSET SESSION.price = get_featured_product.price>
```

Now, for as long as the user continues to surf the site, you can use the variables #SESSION.product#, #SESSION.description#, and #SESSION.price# to display the featured product on any page in your application. When the user returns next week, the session variables will have expired, and Eddie will have rotated the products in the database.

Note

> Session variables and application variables can be manually set to expire, or "time out," after a certain period. This can be done with the APPLICATION-TIMEOUT and SESSIONTIMEOUT parameters in Application.cfm, or under the "variables" link in ColdFusion Administrator.

Understanding Application Variables

The practice of using application variables is very similar to the other scopes, but remember that application variables persist throughout your application and retain their values for every user session. They expire only when ColdFusion Server is restarted, or if you have defined a custom timeout value in Application.cfm or ColdFusion Administrator.

Note

> Application variables can be enabled and disabled under ColdFusion Administrator's "variables" link. Some Web hosting services might not support application variables—check with your host's administrator to find out.

To illustrate, say that you want to maintain some kind of running count that persists as users visit your site. You've designed a form that allows users to vote "yes" or "no" on a question, and you want to keep a running total of user responses without logging their information to a database. The ACTION page for your form might contain the following snippet of code:

16

```
<CFPARAM NAME="application.yes_votes" DEFAULT="0">
<CFPARAM NAME="application.no_votes" DEFAULT="0">
<CFIF form.vote IS 'yes'>
    <CFSET application.yes_votes=application.yes_votes + 1>
<CFELSE>
    <CFSET application.no_votes=application.no_votes + 1>
</CFIF>
```

This would keep a running count of "yes" and "no" votes that could be displayed with
<CFOUTPUT> or used for other computations. The tally would continue for each voting
user, and would continue to build until ColdFusion Server is restarted or the application
variable times out (if you've used a custom timeout setting).

Understanding Cookies

There might be times when you don't need the advanced features of client-state management, but you still have some user-specific data you'd like to preserve, for example, a
quick check to see if a user has "logged in." Or, you might find yourself in a situation
wherein a Web hosting service doesn't support client-state.

In either case, ColdFusion enables you to use cookies independently of its client-state
management feature. It does this with a tag called <CFCOOKIE>, and using it is very similar to the methods described in the previous sections.

Setting Cookies

To set a cookie, you specify a name, a value and an expiration date within the tag:

```
<CFCOOKIE NAME="some_variable"
          VALUE="some_value"
          EXPIRES="7">
```

The cookie will be passed to the user's browser, where it will remain until its expiration
date. EXPIRES can be set to a specific number of days, to a date using MM/DD/YY format, or to never.

Reading Cookies

When the cookie is in place, you can read the data it contains by specifying the name of
the variable:

```
<CFIF cookie.logged_in is 'yes'>
    Howdy Friend!
<CFELSE>
    You are not logged into the system. Please return beneath the rock from
whence you came.
</CFIF>
```

> **Note**
>
> In practice, references to cookies are almost always used with the `IsDefined()` function to see if the cookie exists. Even if you're sure that you placed a cookie on the user's machine, the user might have deleted it. Code like this will do the trick:
>
> ```
> <CFIF IsDefined("cookie.logged_in")>
>   some action
> </CFIF>
> ```

16

To see how this works in practice, recall the "Crazy Eddie" example in Listing 16.1. The form collects a user name and background color preference, then passes those along to an ACTION page. In Listing 16.2, you used client variables to store this information so that it would be preserved each time the user visits Eddie's site.

To do the same thing with cookies, you'd use an ACTION page like Listing 16.5. Note that to test this page with the form in Listing 16.1, you need to change the form's ACTION to cookie_howdy.cfm.

LISTING 16.5   cookie_howdy.cfm

```
 1: <CFSET CLIENT.name = "#name#">
 2: <CFSET CLIENT.color = "#color#">
 3:
 4: <HTML>
 5: <HEAD>
 6: <CFOUTPUT>
 7:     <TITLE>Howdy #CLIENT.name#!</TITLE>
 8: </HEAD>
 9:
10: <BODY BGCOLOR="#CLIENT.color#">
11: <H1>Howdy #CLIENT.name#!</H1>
12: </CFOUTPUT>
13: Thanks fer registerin'. Hope ya like the new look!<P>
14:
15: Browse the Bargains:
16:
17: <UL>
18: <LI><A HREF="dog_sweaters.cfm">Check out our new dog sweaters!</A>
19: <LI><A HREF="hubcaps.cfm">Browse our collection of hub caps!</A>
20: <LI><A HREF="lumber.cfm">Look at our prices on quality lumber!</A>
21: </UL>
22:
23:
24: </BODY>
25: </HTML>
```

Removing Cookies

For obvious security reasons, browsers don't allow you to "get" things from users' machines. So, when you want to delete a cookie, you can't just simply go in and snatch it back.

To remove an unwanted cookie, reset it and use an expiration setting of now:

```
<CFCOOKIE NAME="some_variable"
          VALUE="some_value"
          EXPIRES="now">
```

Secure Cookies

ColdFusion also supports sending cookies using the Secure Socket Layer (SSL) supported by many browsers. To send a cookie this way, add the SECURE parameter to your <CFCOOKIE> tag:

```
<CFCOOKIE NAME="some_variable"
          VALUE="some_value"
          EXPIRES="7"
          SECURE>
```

Summary

ColdFusion's Web Application Framework requires you to begin thinking of your templates as a whole. In doing so, you can design a site that shares common data between templates, uses default parameters, and saves user states between sessions. The keys to ColdFusion applications are configuration files called Application.cfm that reside in the upper-most folder of each of your application trees. In these files, you can set common variables for your applications and enable features such as client and session management.

Client-state management is ColdFusion's method for dealing with the statelessness of the Web. It gives you the ability to save user data between sessions and to read and write *client variables* that are specific to individual users. *Session variables* work in similar ways, although they only remain defined for as long as a user continues to browse your site.

Client-state management makes use of the cookie, a feature of most modern browsers that enables Web applications to transparently send bits of data to a user's machine for storage. ColdFusion also supports the setting of cookies independently from its client-state features.

Q&A

Q Because ColdFusion's client-state management uses cookies, how is it any better than other cookie-driven Web tools?

A There are several Web tools that support cookies, but in most cases these tools store *all* of a user's collected data in the cookie. ColdFusion stores the user data on the server and uses the cookie only for identification. This has benefits both in security and in speed.

16

Q Because my users never actually look at my `Application.cfm` page, how do my other templates get information from it?

A A good way to think of `Application.cfm` is as an "included" file on each of your templates. Any variable definitions or parameters that appear in `Application.cfm` are implicitly added to the beginning of each of your templates as users view them.

Q My client runs a clustered server setup. Won't this cause problems if user data is saved to an individual system's registry?

A Yes, and the solution is to use a central database to store user information. This is done with either the `CLIENTSTORAGE` parameter in `Application.cfm` or the "variables" link in ColdFusion Administrator.

Q How secure are cookies sent using the `SECURE` parameter?

A As secure as Web pages that use this feature. SSL has become a fairly well-respected method for sending secure data.

Workshop

Answers to quiz questions can be found in Appendix A at the back of the text.

Quiz

1. Describe the Web's statelessness.
2. Where should `Application.cfm` reside on your server?
3. How long does an application variable persist?
4. In client-state management, when would you use the `#CLIENT.URLToken#` variable?
5. In client-state management, what data is saved on the user's machine?
6. How do you delete a cookie set with `<CFCOOKIE>`?

Exercises

1. Create a two-page application consisting of a form and an ACTION page. Create an Application.cfm file to set default parameters for the page including background color, font face, and datasource name.

2. Using the application from the previous exercise, enable client-state management and modify your ACTION page so that it adds the form input to client variables. Create a third page that reads these variables, using code such as #CLIENT.some_variable#. Use at least one of the reserved client variables in your display.

3. Using the same application, use session variables to create a text display that appears for as long as the user browses in the current session. When the user leaves the session and returns later, she should see a new text message.

Finding Text with Verity

In 1997, Allaire made a move that probably induced blubbering tears of joy in veteran ColdFusion programmers who managed large sites. It partnered up with a company called Verity to provide an extremely advanced search technology as part of the standard ColdFusion package. Verity's innovative search tools offer you the ability to design full-text search engines for your own ColdFusion sites—engines that mimic the sophistication of popular Web search engines like HotBot and AltaVista. And the best news is that it can all be done without having to troubleshoot a single SQL statement. In today's lesson, you'll learn to

- Understand Verity
- Create and manage Verity collections
- Search Verity collections
- Integrate databases into Verity collections

Understanding Verity

In the lessons you've read so far, you've learned quite a bit about SQL statements and how they're used to sniff out chunks of data hiding in the nether regions of your database files. But in the real world of Web development, the average Web site hosts a lot more than just databases. Your average corporate site might contain static HTML documents and text files, or maybe even some word-processor documents or spreadsheets the company has made available for download. SQL will handle the database stuff, but what about the rest?

Verity's search tools provide a solution by allowing you to index and search a variety of file types, files that might be scattered all over your server or network or those of your client. Verity technology can dramatically increase the user-friendliness of your sites by providing a single, all-inclusive search page that will hunt down a phrase, whether it appears in a Word document on the marketing V.P.'s desktop or in a long-neglected spreadsheet on the accounting department's server.

With a little massaging, Verity will also search the contents of your ColdFusion datasources in much the same way that SQL does. In some applications, it even offers significant improvements over standard SQL searches because Verity automatically emulates the advanced features of powerful Web search engines.

To illustrate, assume you're using a Web search like HotBot to find pages on Magic Eightballs, those fortune-telling orbs that people couldn't get enough of in the late '70s. In a Web search, typing the words

```
magic eightball
```

would probably return hundreds of pages that contain those two words, whether or not they appear next to each other. (You'd probably get a lot of pool-related page, for example.) You could narrow your search a bit by enclosing the phrase in quotes:

```
"magic eightball"
```

which would tell the search engine that you only want pages where those two words appear together. Because "Magic Eightball" is a trade name, you might also capitalize the phrase:

```
"Magic Eightball"
```

which would perform a case-sensitive search for the exact phrase.

Now consider a situation where you want to add these same features to a search page that looks at documents on your own site. It could be done using very lengthy and complex SQL statement with lots of parentheses and whatnot, but do you want to be the person to create it? Not likely.

With Verity, such features are built in to the engine. To use Verity, you begin by creating a *collection*.

NEW TERM A Verity *collection* is a subset of files that reside on a local or remote network. It contains the names of files and directories to be searched.

When Verity has the names and locations of your files, you can tell the software to create an *index* of the data contained in the collection's files.

NEW TERM A Verity *index* is a map of your searchable files, containing data that describes the files and their contents.

After an index has been created, Verity searches will examine the index rather than the files themselves. This obviously saves quite a bit of processing time, and not coincidentally it's the same method used by the larger Web search engines.

Finally, after a collection has been defined and an index created, you can build standard ColdFusion templates to perform searches on the assembled data. In doing so, you use a special set of CFML tags that ColdFusion uses to "talk" to the Verity engine.

17

Note

If you host your ColdFusion site on a third-party commercial server, you might not have access to Verity search features. Check with your host's system administrator to find out whether it's supported.

To get a feel for how this all works, start by checking out the Verity tool that ColdFusion uses to search product documentation. Open up ColdFusion Administrator, log in, and look for the Product Documentation link on the main administration page. Click there, and you'll see something like Figure 17.1.

FIGURE 17.1
The Product Documentation overview page in ColdFusion Server 4.5.

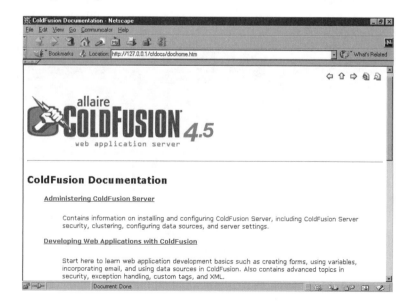

Note the tiny magnifying glass icon in the upper-right corner of your screen—that's the link that launches the Verity search, as pictured in Figure 17.2.

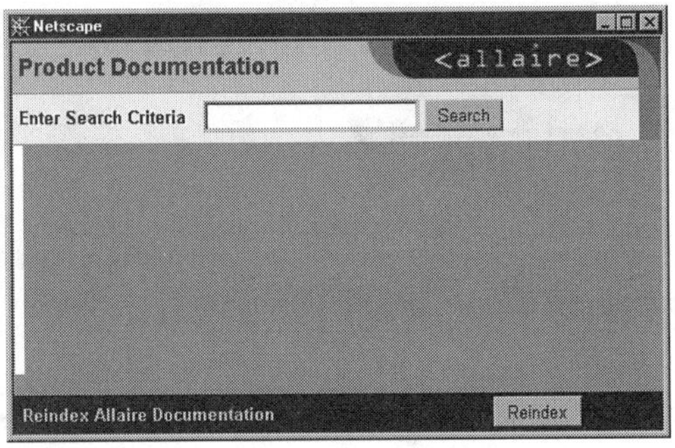

FIGURE 17.2

ColdFusion provides a Verity search of its extensive product documentation library.

Note that if you're running this Verity search for the first time, you'll see a notice asking you to index the collection. The process will take a few minutes to complete.

Note

This description assumes you're using ColdFusion Server 4.5. On older releases, look for a link or icon labeled "search." Note that ColdFusion versions released prior to the Allaire/Verity partnership in 1997 will not contain Verity technologies.

Type in a search term or two and hit the Search button. I searched for the words "Verity" and "search" and within a few seconds saw a page like Figure 17.3.

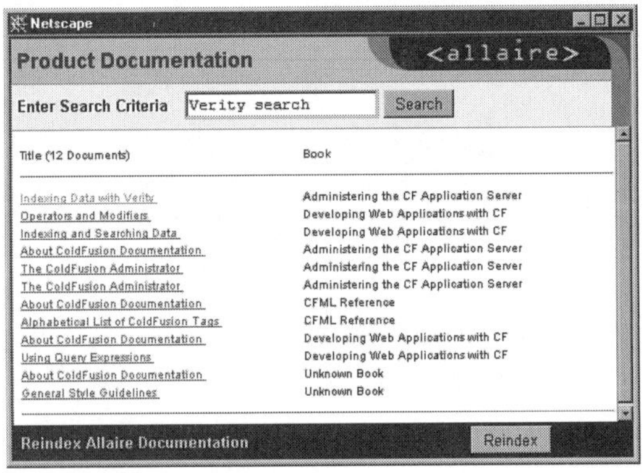

FIGURE 17.3

A sample Verity search results page.

Because all the documents found in my search are `.CFM` or `.HTM` files, Verity has provided direct links to the pages. In the column on the right, it also lists the "book" or category where the page was found.

Granted, ColdFusion's documentation is composed primarily of static files that all "live" in one master directory, but envision this type of a search on a large business intranet. In the results window, you'd see links and data describing possibly scores of documents. Are you beginning to understand just how valuable a tool Verity is?

Defining Verity Collections with ColdFusion Administrator

There are two ways to create a new Verity collection. The first and most straightforward method is to build a collection in ColdFusion Administrator. This method provides a graphic interface to find the files and folders you want to add to the collection, and it's pretty hard to go wrong.

The second method is a little trickier, but it has certain advantages over the graphic interface. In this method, you use a special tag called `<CFCOLLECTION>` in a ColdFusion template. This is ideal for situations in which a user or employee needs the ability to create or manage Verity collections, but doesn't have access to ColdFusion Administrator. You can use the tag to design a form page that will build, optimize, repair, or delete a collection automatically. This method will be described in the section "Integrating Databases into Verity Collections," later in the chapter.

First, take a look at the ColdFusion Administrator interface. Log in to the Administrator and choose the Verity link near the bottom of the navigation bar at the left of the screen. You will see something like Figure 17.4.

Notice that there is already one Verity collection listed there, the ColdFusion product documentation mentioned in the last section. To create a new collection, supply a name, a path, and a language in the input boxes at the bottom of the page. Name can be anything you'd like, and the default path will work fine. Note that Path is simply the location where Verity will store the index files—not the path of the files you want to add to the collection.

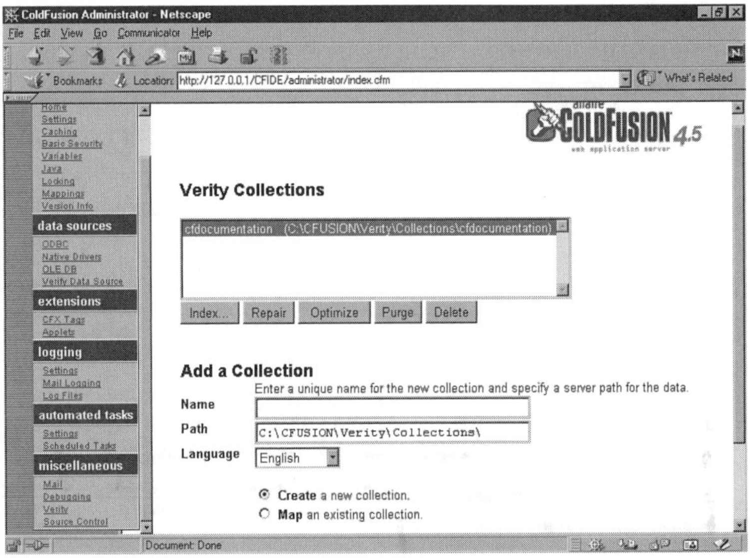

FIGURE 17.4

*ColdFusion Adminis-
trator's Verity
interface.*

Note If you choose a language other than English, ColdFusion requires the International Search Pack. The Search Pack is a separate option available from Allaire.

Leave the radio button set to Create a New Collection and press Apply. The page will reload, and you'll see your new collection added to the large list box at the top of the page.

Indexing a Collection with ColdFusion Administrator

Indexing a collection is the process of building a master index file that houses information about your documents. To do this, you start by defining the documents to be indexed. Select your new collection in the large list box and press the Index button beneath it. You'll see a form like Figure 17.5.

In this form, you supply a Directory Path that contains the files you want to index, either by typing in a path or via the Browse Server button. The check box below the Directory Path field is important—it controls whether the index should look for documents that reside in folders within the selected folder (checked) or not (unchecked).

FIGURE 17.5

Creating an index of files in ColdFusion Administrator.

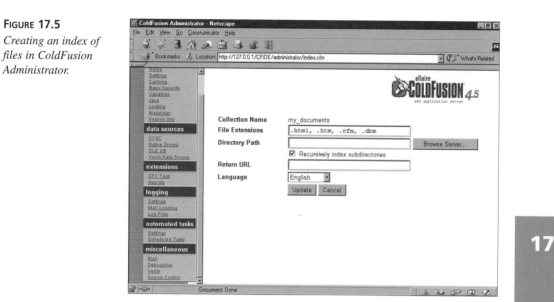

The File Extensions input box is also important because it contains a comma-delimited list of the file types you want Verity to index. By default, all the standard ColdFusion file types are included, but you might want to add other extensions, such as .doc for Microsoft Word files. A complete list of file types supported by Verity is shown in the table seen in Figure 17.6.

FIGURE 17.6

File Types Supported by Verity.

Supported Document Types	
Documents	**Versions**
Text files	
HTML, CFML, DBM, SGML, XML,	N/A
ANSI, ASCII, Plain Text	N/A
Word processors	
Adobe Acrobat (PDF) Adobe FrameMaker (MIF) Aplix Words Corel WordPerfect for Windows Corel WordPerfect for Macintosh Lotus AMI Pro Lotus AMI Pro Write Plus Lotus Word Pro Microsoft Office MS Rich Text Format (RTF) MS Word for Windows MS Word for DOS MS Word for Macintosh MS Notepad, WordPad MS Write, MS Works XYWrite	All All 4.2 5.x 6, 7, 8 2, 3 2, 3 all 96, 97 95, 97 1.x, 2.0 2, 6, 95, 97 4, 5, 6 4.0, 5.0, 6.0 all all 4.12
Spreadsheets	
Corel QuattroPro Lotus 1-2-3 for DOS/Windows Lotus 1-2-3 for OS/2 MS Excel MS Works	7, 8 2.0, 3.0, 4.0, 5.0, 96, 97 2 3, 4, 5, 95, 97 all
Presentation	
Corel Presentations Lotus Freelance MS PowerPoint	7.0, 8.0 96, 97 4.0, 95, 97

The final input box in Figure 17.5, Return URL, requires the name of the *Web path* to the location of your files. For example, if the files you want to index reside in the folder

```
c:\my_documents\web\my_site
```

and web is the root directory for your Web server, your Return URL would be

```
http://my_server/my_site/
```

Verity will use this Return URL entry to create links to your pages later, so it's important to get it right.

Finally, press the Update button in Figure 17.5. Your hard drive will begin churning away as Verity builds an index file of the documents you've specified. It might take a while, but remember that, for each churn you endure now, you're ensuring that you and your users won't have to wait long for search results.

When the indexing is complete, ColdFusion Administrator will return to the main Verity page.

Searching Verity Collections

Building search interfaces for Verity collections is surprisingly simple. Because the engine itself handles the tough stuff, all you need to do is supply it with a search term and create a page to display the results.

> **Note**
>
> ColdFusion Studio users can take advantage of the Verity Wizard, a tool for automatically generating search forms and displaying results. Even if you do choose to create your pages in the wizard, read through this section to see what's happening behind the scenes.

The Search Form

To illustrate the incredible powers of Verity, I've designed a bare-bones search form, as illustrated in Figure 17.7.

It collects one block of text and that will be passed on to the action page `verity_search_results.cfm`. The code for my form is shown in Listing 17.1.

FIGURE 17.7

*This extremely basic
search form collects all
that's needed to power
a Verity search.*

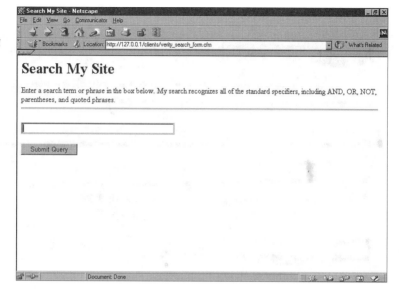

LISTING 17.1   verity_search_form.cfm

```
 1: <HTML>
 2: <HEAD>
 3:     <TITLE>Search My Site</TITLE>
 4: </HEAD>
 5:
 6: <BODY>
 7: <H1>Search My Site</H1>
 8:
 9: Enter a search term or phrase in the box below. My search recognizes all of
    ➥the standard specifiers, including AND, OR, NOT, parentheses, and quoted
    ➥phrases.
10: <HR>
11: <FORM ACTION="verity_search_results.cfm" METHOD="post">
12: <INPUT TYPE="text" NAME="criteria" size="40"><P>
13: <INPUT TYPE="submit">
14: </FORM>
15:
16:
17: </BODY>
18: </HTML>
```

It doesn't get any simpler than this—I've only used one text input box, which is defined
as the variable "criteria". Now on to the results page, which is a little more complex,
but not much.

The Results Page

Verity searches work much like a standard <CFQUERY>. To create a search, you use a special ColdFusion tag called <CFSEARCH> in your action pages. Like a query, <CFSEARCH> requires a NAME for the search, but instead of searching a datasource, it searches a COLLECTION, which must be set to the name of a valid collection appearing on the Verity page in ColdFusion Administrator.

Unlike a query, <CFSEARCH> doesn't require an SQL statement. Instead it uses a parameter called CRITERIA, which can be supplied dynamically from a form variable, as in my example. When a <CFSEARCH> executes, it returns values just like a query, except that, instead of returning a series of variables keyed to the field names of a database table, it returns a special set of variables unique to itself.

To display search results, you use a standard <CFOUTPUT> section and simply use these predefined variable names where you'd usually supply query variables, as I've done for my results page in Listing 17.2.

LISTING 17.2   verity_search_results.cfm

```
 1: <CFSEARCH NAME="search_diamonds" COLLECTION="diamonds" CRITERIA="#Form.
    ➥criteria#">
 2:
 3: <HTML>
 4: <HEAD>
 5:     <TITLE>The Results of Your Search</TITLE>
 6: </HEAD>
 7:
 8: <BODY>
 9: <H1>The Results of Your Search</H1>
10:
11: <HR>
12: <CFOUTPUT QUERY="search_diamonds">
13: <A HREF="#URL#">#Title#</A><BR>
14: Score: #Score#<P>
15: </CFOUTPUT>
16:
17:
18: </BODY>
19: </HTML>
```

My example searches a collection I titled "diamonds" when I created it on ColdFusion Administrator's Verity page. "diamonds" is short for "The Incredible Diamonds," a hypothetical rockabilly band for which I've designed a site.

Note the hash-marked variable in the <CFSEARCH> tag. This comes from the form, and will contain whatever text the user has typed into the text box. Note here one of the beauties of Verity—because I'm not using SQL, I don't have to be concerned whether the user has typed in quotation marks, parentheses, or any other non-alphanumeric characters. Verity handles it for me.

For the output section in Listing 17.2, I use the same type of <CFOUTPUT> section as I would if I were displaying the results of a query. The difference is that I use those special variables associated with <CFSEARCH>. They're listed in Table 17.1.

TABLE 17.1 Variable Names Returned by <CFSEARCH>

Variable Name	What It Holds
CurrentRow	The number of the item returned by the search. If a search returns five documents, the first would be 1, and so on, up to 5.
Custom1, Custom2	Optional, user-defined variables created with <CFINDEX TYPE="custom"> (described in the following sections of the chapter).
Key	The filename of the matched document.
Score	The document's *relevancy score*, which indicates how closely it matched the search term. By default, the documents with higher relevancy scores are displayed first in output.
Summary	A summary of the document, automatically generated by <CFSEARCH>.
Title	The title of the document, if Verity can find one. It draws the titles of HTML pages from the <TITLE> tags.
URL	The Web server path to the document.

Note in Listing 17.2 that my results page uses three of these variables. It creates an <A HREF> link to the path specified in #URL# and uses the #Title# variable to label that link. On a new line, it displays the item's relevancy score with #Score#.

When I load my form page in a browser and type in a search term, I see a results page like Figure 17.8.

In the search form, I typed in the quoted phrase "Matt Hogan"—Matt Hogan is the hypothetical lead singer and guitarist of the hypothetical rockabilly band The Incredible Diamonds. The results page shows five matches for that exact phrase, ranked by relevancy score.

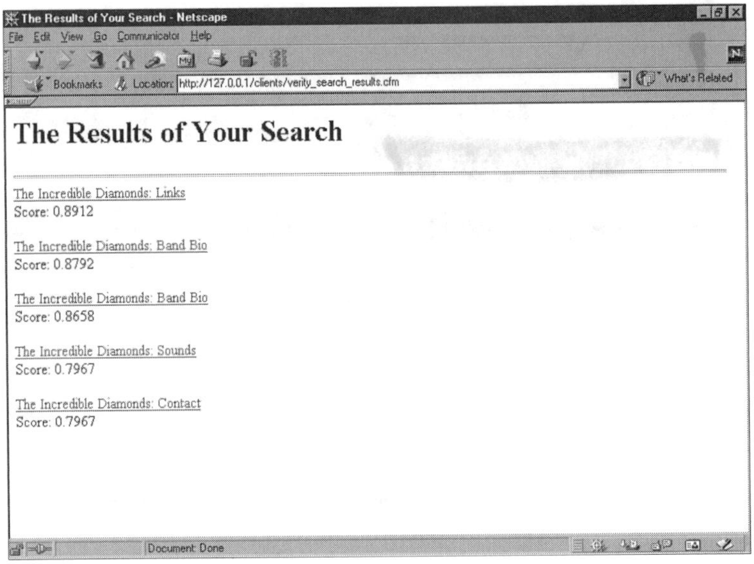

FIGURE 17.8

The results page for a Verity search on the collection `"diamonds"`.

The Results of Your Search - Netscape

File Edit View Go Communicator Help

Bookmarks Location: http://127.0.0.1/clients/verity_search_results.cfm

The Results of Your Search

The Incredible Diamonds: Links
Score: 0.8912

The Incredible Diamonds: Band Bio
Score: 0.8792

The Incredible Diamonds: Band Bio
Score: 0.8658

The Incredible Diamonds: Sounds
Score: 0.7967

The Incredible Diamonds: Contact
Score: 0.7967

Document: Done

Tip

<CFSEARCH> also returns two variables describing search results, RecordCount
and RecordsSearched. These enable you to perform actions such as returning
an error (rather than blank space) if no records are matched:

```
<CFIF search_diamonds.RecordCount IS 0>
    Your search did not produce any results
</CFIF>
```

Defining and Indexing Verity Collections with CFML Tags

The Verity interface in ColdFusion Administrator provides an easy way to define and
index collections, but there's another method that you might want to use if

- You want to allow users to define or index collections, and those users don't have
  access to ColdFusion Administrator.
- You want to create a one-click interface to reindex collections that change frequently.
- You host your ColdFusion site with a Web hosting service that supports Verity, but
  it does not give you access to ColdFusion Administrator.

To use this alternative method, you create template pages that use two tags, <CFCOLLECTION> and <CFINDEX>. When these pages are accessed or called as an ACTION from a form page, Verity will automatically perform the specified actions.

Using <CFCOLLECTION>

To work with a collection from a template page (rather than in ColdFusion Administrator), you'd include code like this:

```
<CFCOLLECTION ACTION="Create"
              COLLECTION="my_new_collection"
              PATH="C:\CFUSION\Verity\Collections\">
```

Recall that the creation of a collection in ColdFusion Administrator required you to specify three values. These same values are required by <CFCOLLECTION> as the parameters ACTION, COLLECTION, and PATH, described here:

- ACTION can be set to create, delete, repair, optimize, or map, the same options available in Administrator's Verity interface.

- COLLECTION is the name of a new collection to create, or the name of an existing collection on which to perform other ACTIONs.

- PATH specifies the location where Verity will store its index file. The default, C:\CFUSION\Verity\Collections\, will work fine for most. PATH is not used when you're performing ACTIONs on an existing collection.

Note

> Any of <CFCOLLECTION>'s parameters can be supplied dynamically. This gives you the ability to design a form to collect user input defining the name and storage location of the collection. The form's action page would use <CFCOLLECTION>, inserting user data for the COLLECTION and PATH parameters.

Using <CFINDEX>

<CFINDEX> works in much the same way as <CFCOLLECTION>, but it requires a different set of parameters to tell Verity things about the documents you want to add to your collection.

Just like the Index dialog in Administrator's Verity interface, the <CFINDEX> tag requires that you define a folder to index, specify whether you want subfolders to be searched, and accepts a comma-delimited list of the file types to index. The tag takes this format:

```
<CFINDEX COLLECTION="my_new_collection"
         ACTION="update"
         TYPE="path"
```

17

```
KEY="path_to_files"
URLPATH="http://my_server/some_folder/"
EXTENSIONS=".htm, .html"
RECURSE="Yes">
```

<CFINDEX> takes the following parameters:

- COLLECTION is the name of the collection to which you want to add documents.

- ACTION can be defined as update to simply add new documents, or refresh to clear out old indexed data before adding new documents.

- TYPE should be set to path if you want to index entire folders, or file if you want to specify certain files to index. A third option, custom, is described in the next section.

- KEY is the path containing the files you want to index. It is the same as Directory Path in Administrator's Verity interface.

- URLPATH is the same as Return Path in Administrator's Verity interface. It is the server path (such as http://my_server/my_files/) to the directories being indexed.

- EXTENSIONS accepts a comma-delimited list of file types to be indexed.

- RECURSE specifies whether you also want to index folders that live within the path specified in KEY. Valid entries are yes and no.

Note

Like <CFCOLLECTION>, the <CFINDEX> tag can also accept dynamic parameters supplied by a form. This enables you to create form and action pages to let users add documents to a Verity index without accessing ColdFusion Administrator.

Integrating Databases into Verity Collections

You've learned how to create a Verity search that examines document files on your server, but what about all that useful data that's tucked away in your ColdFusion datasources? No worry, because, with a little extra work, Verity can be configured to index database contents as well.

As a search engine, Verity could easily examine the data stored in your datasources—that's not the problem. The trouble is that it wouldn't know what text to return as results. Recall from Table 17.2 that Verity searches return five variables for matched documents: KEY, TITLE, SCORE, URL, and CURRENTROW. When dealing with database contents, two of these variables present a problem because how is Verity to know which of your field contents should be returned as the Key, and which should be returned as the Title?

To overcome this problem, Verity enables you to specify these things. It enables you to run queries on your datasources, and then add the results of the queries to your collection's index using the <CFINDEX> tag described in the previous section.

Adding Query Data to an Index

Adding data from queries is a two-step process. To see how it works, assume that I've created a Verity collection called "elvis." I also have a datasource called "elvis" that contains a table called "movies." To add this data to the collection's index, I create a page like Listing 17.3.

LISTING 17.3 Adding Query Results to a Verity Collection with <CFINDEX>

```
 1: <CFQUERY NAME="get_elvis_movies" DATASOURCE="elvis">
 2: SELECT * from movies
 3: </CFQUERY>
 4:
 5: <CFINDEX QUERY="get_elvis_movies"
 6:         COLLECTION="elvis"
 7:         ACTION="update"
 8:         TYPE="custom"
 9:         KEY="ID"
10:         TITLE="title"
11:         BODY="title, year, rating">
12:
13: <HTML>
14: <HEAD>
15:     <TITLE>Your Verity Collection Has Been Updated</TITLE>
16: </HEAD>
17:
18: <BODY>
19:
20: The following items have been added to your Verity collection:<P>
21:
22: <CFOUTPUT QUERY="get_elvis_movies">
23: #title#, #year#, #rating#<P>
24: </CFOUTPUT>
25:
26: </BODY>
27: </HTML>
```

When a page like Listing 17.3 is loaded in a browser, three things occur. First, the template runs a pretty standard <CFQUERY> on the "movies" table and retrieves all the data for each record it finds there.

Next, <CFINDEX> takes over. It takes the results of the specified QUERY, and because I've defined the ACTION as update, it will update the specified collection with data returned by <CFQUERY>.

The next line of the <CFINDEX> tag is TYPE="custom", which tells <CFINDEX> that I want to define which fields returned by my query should be treated like parts of a document. I can use any of the fields I'd like for Key and Title, but the field I define as BODY is particularly important because it is the one that will be examined by Verity when a user searches my site. To ensure that all my data gets searched, I add all my query fields to the BODY parameter, separating them with commas.

Finally, my page uses a simple <CFOUTPUT> section to show confirmation that the items have been added to my Verity index. If I add new data to my table later, I can simply reload this page to have the new data added to the index.

Tip

If the information in your datasources changes frequently, you might want to design a form-driven interface to add query data to your Verity indexes. Because <CFQUERY> and <CFINDEX> will both accept dynamic data, you can easily create a form that will allow you to specify what datasource contents to add to what Verity index.

Displaying Database Records as Search Results

When you create a Verity collection that indexes only files, it's easy to create a results page that will allow users to click through to the files matched by their searches. Each file has a related #URL# variable returned by <CFSEARCH> (refer to Location field in Figure 17.7).

But when you're working with collections populated by query data, it's not so easy. Your database records don't have a specific URL associated with them. Depending on the data you've supplied, this might not be a problem. For example, if you populate your collection with data from a datasource that holds only names and phone numbers, your results page might contain listings like this:

Buddy Bradley 555-1212

Jim Jones 555-1234

Skip Spence 555-2345

This page would, in itself, be useful to the user because it displays all the pertinent information she is looking for. But what if your datasource holds something like a product for sale? Simply displaying the product details on a results page won't do the trick, because you want the user to be able to see the product in its full glory, including related images and links to "Buy 100 of These Now," and other product pages.

In the example in the last section, you learned that when you use <CFQUERY> to populate a collection, <CFINDEX> allows you to specify one of your table fields to use as a KEY. You can recall this information later as the #Key# variable returned by <CFSEARCH>. Don't worry if this sounds confusing so far—look at Listing 17.4.

LISTING 17.4 Displaying Database Records as Search Results

```
 1: <CFSEARCH NAME="search" collection="elvis" criteria="#FORM.criteria#">
 2:
 3: <HTML>
 4: <HEAD>
 5:     <TITLE>The Results of Your Search</TITLE>
 6: </HEAD>
 7:
 8: <BODY>
 9: <H1>The Results of Your Search</H1>
10:
11: <HR>
12: <CFOUTPUT QUERY="search">
13: <A HREF="http://127.0.0.1/elvis/elvis_movie.cfm?code=#Key#">#Title#</A><BR>
14: Score: #Score#<P>
15: </CFOUTPUT>
16:
17:
18: </BODY>
19: </HTML>
```

This results page is similar to the one used to display file results, as in Figure 17.7. Instead of using the <CFSEARCH> variable #URL# to create links to the files returned by the search, this page points to a specific template file, elvis_movie.cfm. Immediately following the filename is the text ?code=#Key#, which will append the contents of #Key# and send it to the template as the variable code when a user clicks on the link.

The value returned by #Key# will be the primary key for the specified database record, assuming that you set things up this way when you used <CFINDEX> to populate your collection. Knowing that, it's pretty simple to build a page that will query your datasource for a particular record, and then display the contents of that record, along with other relevant data such as "Buy This Now," and so on. Take a look at Listing 17.5 for an example.

LISTING 17.5 elvis_movie.cfm

```
 1: <CFQUERY NAME="movies" DATASOURCE="elvis">
 2: SELECT title, released, rating FROM movies WHERE ID = '#code#'
 3: </CFQUERY>
 4:
 5: <HTML>
 6: <HEAD>
 7:     <TITLE>Elvis Movies</TITLE>
 8: </HEAD>
 9:
10: <BODY>
11: <CFOUTPUT QUERY="movies">
12: <B>Title:</B> #title#<BR>
13: <B>Year Released:</B> #released#<BR>
14: <B>My Rating:</B> #rating#<P>
15:
16: </CFOUTPUT>
17:
18: <A HREF="buy_it.cfm">Click here to buy this film now! Don't wait!</A>
19: </BODY>
20: </HTML>
```

This page would take the variable code, passed by the results page, and display the relevant record in all its HTML-ized glory (my example isn't very glorious, but you get the idea).

If your Verity collection contains *both* files and database information, you might use a <CFIF> statement in your results pages to create one display method for files, another for database records.

Code like the following would do the trick, because the #URL# variable returned by <CFSEARCH> is always empty if the matched item is a database record.

```
<CFIF URL IS "">

<A HREF="http://127.0.0.1/elvis/elvis_movie.cfm?code=#Key#">#Title#</A><BR>
Score: #Score#<P>

<CFELSE>

<A HREF="#URL#">#Title#</A><BR>
Score: #Score#<P>

</CFIF>
```

Summary

For sites that hold many types of documents or work with data from a variety of sources, ColdFusion's Verity search engine provides an excellent alternative to SQL queries. It works by building collections of data, which can include HTML and CFM files, along with various word-processor documents, spreadsheets, and even database records.

Verity builds an index of collected documents, and when it is used to perform a search, it examines this index rather than the files themselves. This is a very efficient search method, and it gives the developer the ability to create interfaces that can quickly search hundreds of documents on a site. Verity also supports search parameters such as parenthetical phrases, Boolean operators, and quoted phrases as input, just like the search engines you've used on the Web.

Using Verity is a two-step process. First, you define and index a collection of files, either through the Verity link in ColdFusion Administrator or from template pages, using a special tagset. Second, you use the special ColdFusion tag `<CFSEARCH>` to build a search interface and display results.

17

Q&A

Q **Is Verity an option I need to purchase separately?**

A No. Both the Professional and Enterprise versions of ColdFusion Server include Verity as part of the deal.

Q **My remote Web provider doesn't allow access to ColdFusion Administrator. Can I still use Verity?**

A If the provider supports Verity, you can still create and index collections from template pages using the `<CFCOLLECTION>` and `<CFINDEX>` tags. No Administrator access is required.

Q **How fast is Verity? Will it handle very large collections of files?**

A Compared to the time it would take a SQL query to perform a similar task, Verity is *blazing*. It will handle collections of hundreds of documents without batting a virtual eye, although, if you notice a decrease in performance you might want to subdivide large collections into smaller ones and search them individually.

Q **My client adds new documents to its site daily, and I'm getting tired of having to update the collection. What can I do?**

A You can build a form interface using `<CFINDEX>` that will allow your client's employees to reindex the collection each time they add a new document, or at the end of a work day.

Q Can I use Verity searches behind the scenes as I do with SQL queries?

A Yes, and the Verity engine includes special provisions designed for those sorts of tasks. Check your ColdFusion documentation for information on Verity operators.

Workshop

Just to see if you were dozing through today's lesson, here are a few quiz questions and exercises. Answers to quiz questions can be found in Appendix A at the back of the text.

Quiz

1. Name the two ways to create a new Verity collection.
2. Name the two ways to index a Verity collection.
3. When indexing a collection, why is the Return URL field so important?
4. What three parameters are required by <CFSEARCH> to perform a successful search?
5. What is contained in the #score# variable returned by <CFSEARCH>?
6. Describe the process used to add database records to a Verity collection.
7. What is different about the way files and database records are displayed as search results?

Exercises

1. Using ColdFusion Administrator, create a Verity collection that indexes all the .html and .cfm pages on your Web site. Design a two-page interface to search the collection and display results.
2. Using the <CFCOLLECTION> and <CFINDEX> tags, build an interface that enables you to create and populate a Verity collection.
3. Using <CFQUERY> and <CFINDEX>, create an interface that inserts data from one of your datasources into a Verity collection.

DAY 18

Working with Files and Directories

As a ColdFusion developer, you ought to do a little dance right here and now because you're about to learn how the development application you've chosen includes full support for uploading, managing, and even *creating* files from a Web browser. Using ColdFusion, you can design templates that enable you and your users to send images, word processor documents, database files, spreadsheets, programs, or any other type of file to a remote server. The best part is that any of these tasks can be done via a simple Web interface, using nothing but a browser. In today's lesson, you'll learn

- How ColdFusion works with files and directories
- Uploading files with <CFFILE>
- Managing and creating files with <CFFILE>
- Using <CFDIRECTORY> to work with remote directories

Understanding How ColdFusion Works with Files

Most of us think of our Web browsers primarily as viewing tools—applications designed to enable us to look at stuff on the Web and maybe download a file or two now and then. But as competition between the "big two" browser companies (Microsoft and Netscape) has increased, these once-lowly viewing applications have begun to support more interactive features.

One of the most useful features—and the least heralded—is the ability to upload files via a browser window. As a Web designer, it's likely you use some form of FTP (File Transfer Protocol) software to send your expertly crafted files to a remote server, but I'll bet you didn't know that you could perform the same action using nothing but Netscape's Navigator or Microsoft's Internet Explorer. If you did know that, keep that smug look and read on.

ColdFusion harnesses this hidden browser power with a tag called <CFFILE>. By using <CFFILE> in your templates, you can offer Web users (or clients running an intranet) the ability to send files to a Web server right from the browser on their home or office desktop. These files might be items you want to use on a Web site, such as images, HTML pages, or text. Or they might be non-Web files such as word processor documents, spreadsheets, or databases that you want to archive or make available for other users to download.

Note

Some Web hosting services don't allow use of <CFFILE> due to security concerns. If you host your ColdFusion files with an outside service, check with the systems administrator to see which <CFFILE> features are supported.

The beauty of <CFFILE> is that it makes the upload and file-management process as simple as using a Web form. For example, if one of your clients regularly updates a database file on a remote Web server, you can build a form page to walk that client's users through the upload. If you've ever spent an hour on the phone guiding an Internet newbie through the process of sending a file via FTP software, you can probably appreciate the convenience of a Web-based system that accomplishes the same tasks.

Caution

Not all browsers support file uploading, but most modern varieties do. If your users or clients access your site with older packages such as Lynx, Mosaic, or Cello (remember that one?), you might want either to heartily encourage an upgrade or to use alternative uploading methods.

To grasp how Web-based file management works, take a look at the sample form page in Figure 18.1.

FIGURE 18.1

A form enabling users to upload picture files from their browser.

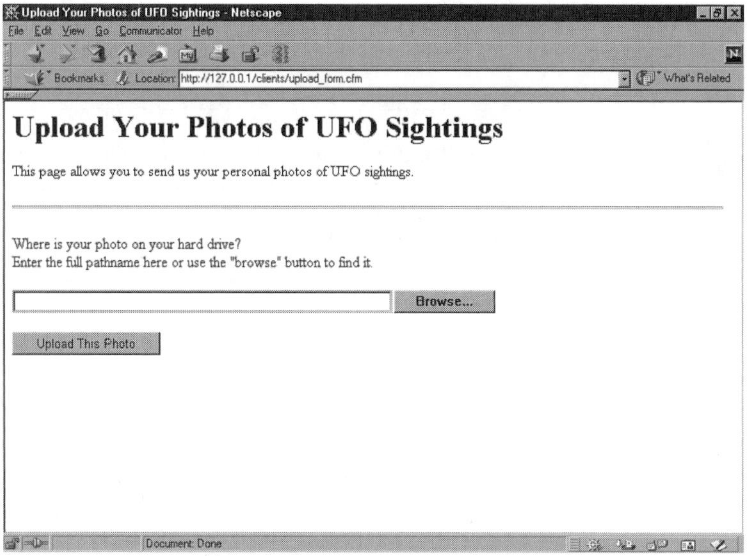

The page in Figure 18.1 is a quick-and-dirty form that prompts users either to specify a path where a picture resides on their hard drives or to use a special Browse button to find the picture. After clicking the Browse button, the user would see a standard dialog box like the one in Figure 18.2.

FIGURE 18.2

By clicking the Browse button, Windows users see a dialog box like this one.

18

All Windows users will be instantly familiar with the dialog box in Figure 18.2, and chances are they'll find it easy to navigate their hard drives to search for the photo they want to send. If a user is working with an operating system other than Windows, he'll see a different dialog box, but one that will still be familiar to him because it will have the same appearance as those used with other programs on his OS.

> **Note**
>
> Figure 18.2 shows a dialog box with the Files of Type list box expanded. This Windows 9x feature enables users to select the type of file (an image, a document, and so on) for which to browse. Depending on their operating system, your users might not see this feature.

A great thing about the form in Figures 18.1 and 18.2 is that it was created in about five minutes, and uses only about 15 lines of code. (The actual code is detailed in the next section.) The form was created in a ColdFusion template file (.CFM), although it could have also been built in a standard HTML page. So far there's no fancy ColdFusion trickery happening—the form is simply collecting data to pass on to an ACTION page where ColdFusion will come into play and <CFFILE> will be used to handle the passed data.

After a user locates a file on her hard drive and submits the form, she'll wait a bit depending on the size of the file and the speed of their connection. When the upload is complete, the user will see a confirmation message I designed to let her know the transfer succeeded. Because this particular form is designed to upload an image file, I might also design the confirmation page to display the actual uploaded image.

File uploading is only a third of the <CFFILE> arsenal. Similar Web forms can also be used to manage files on the server—to move, rename, or delete them—and even to create files by merging two or more text documents, for example. Another ColdFusion tag, <CFDIRECTORY>, can be used to further enhance file management, giving users the ability to create, move, and delete directories on the server via forms similar to the one in Figure 18.1.

> **Caution**
>
> As you begin to use tools such as <CFFILE> and <CFDIRECTORY>, it's important to keep security in mind. As with any tool that gives users direct access to your server, it's important to use failsafe measures to keep malicious users out of your important stuff. Specific security concerns are discussed in the notes and cautions that accompany each of the following sections. Familiarize yourself with them all before going live with a <CFFILE>-enabled application.

Using <CFFILE> to Accept Uploads

The <CFFILE> tag is most often used on an ACTION page, getting its necessary data from a form like the one illustrated in Figure 18.1. To get a feel for the sort of data the tag needs, take a look at Listing 18.1, which contains the code that created the form in Figure 18.1.

LISTING 18.1   The Code for upload_form.cfm, as Illustrated in Figure 18.1

```
 1: <HTML>
 2: <HEAD>
 3:    <TITLE>Upload Your Photos of UFO Sightings</TITLE>
 4: </HEAD>
 5: <BODY>
 6:        <H1>Upload Your Photos of UFO Sightings</H1>
 7:
 8: This page allows you to send us your personal photos of UFO sightings.<P>
 9: <HR>
10: <FORM ACTION="upload_action.cfm" ENCTYPE="multipart/form-data"
    ➥METHOD="post">
11: Where is your photo on your hard drive?<BR>
12: Enter the full pathname here or use the "browse" button to find it.<P>
13: <INPUT TYPE=FILE NAME="FileName" SIZE="50" ><P>
14: <INPUT TYPE=SUBMIT VALUE="Upload This Photo">
15: </FORM>
16: </BODY>
17: </HTML>
```

Much of Listing 18.1 will be familiar from previous lessons on forms. The <FORM> tag defines an ACTION page, there's an INPUT box to collect information, and there's a SUBMIT button to send the collected data along to the ACTION page for processing.

Note the differences, though. The <FORM> tag specifies a new ENCTYPE, multipart/form-data, which is absolutely required for <CFFILE> to work its magic later. Also, the INPUT box is a little different than those used to collect text. It uses TYPE=FILE to tell the user's browser that the form is looking for a pathname to the location of a file on the user's hard drive. Incidentally, TYPE=FILE is also the part of the form that automatically creates the nifty Browse button and accompanying dialog box pictured in Figure 18.2.

Another important feature of the INPUT box is NAME, which defines a variable, FileName, that is passed to <CFFILE> on the ACTION page. <CFFILE> uses this name, minus the path, to store the file on the Web server.

This form passes just one piece of information on to the <CFFILE> tag on the ACTION page: the filename the user has entered in the form. Listing 18.2 shows a sample ACTION page that might be used to handle the passed data.

18

LISTING 18.2 upload_action.cfm

```
 1: <HTML>
 2: <HEAD>
 3:    <TITLE>The Results of Your Photo Upload</TITLE>
 4: </HEAD>
 5:
 6: <BODY>
 7:
 8: <CFFILE ACTION="upload" FILEFIELD="FileName"
 9: DESTINATION="c:\in\" NAMECONFLICT="makeunique" >
10:
11: <H1>The Results of Your Photo Upload</H1>
12:
13: Your file has been uploaded to our server. Thanks, and keep watching the
    ➥skies.
14:
15: </BODY>
16: </HTML>
```

The ACTION page in Listing 18.2 serves two purposes. First, it uses <CFFILE> to process the uploaded file; second, it serves as a confirmation page to alert the user that the upload succeeded. You might recall using similar ACTION/confirmation pages with tags such as <CFUPDATE> and <CFINSERT> in Day 7, "Inserting and Changing the Contents of a Database with ColdFusion."

Caution

Templates that use <CFFILE> to accept uploads should be used with extreme caution because there are significant risks involved in allowing user uploads. In actual practice, form and ACTION pages such as those in Listings 18.1 and 18.2 should reside in a folder that is password-protected to keep out ne'er-do-wells and no-goodniks. Check your Web server's documentation to find out how to password-protect individual folders.

Just like a <FORM> tag, <CFFILE> requires a defined ACTION to know what it's supposed to do. In the previous example, the ACTION, not surprisingly, is upload, which tells <CFFILE> that a file is being uploaded.

When <CFFILE> sees ACTION="upload", it looks for other attributes that tell it more about the file being uploaded and what it should do with the file. In Listing 18.2, these attributes include FILEFIELD (which is set to the variable passed by the form, or FileName) and DESTINATION, which tells <CFFILE> where to store the uploaded file on the Web server.

Note Depending on your operating system and your version of ColdFusion Server, the DESTINATION attribute might require a trailing slash in the directory name, such as c:\in\ rather than c:\in.

Note When accepting an upload, the folder or directory name specified in DESTINATION must be write-accessible by ColdFusion Server. The process of setting write permissions is unique to your operating system and your security setup. Windows 9x users set write permissions by enabling file sharing in Network Neighborhood, whereas users of UNIX-based operating systems and Windows NT might need to set write permissions for the user who runs ColdFusion (usually the "admin" user).

The third attribute, NAMECONFLICT, tells <CFFILE> what to do if a file by that name already exists on the server. Listing 18.2 uses NAMECONFLICT="makeunique". This tells <CFFILE> that if the file being uploaded has the same name as a file already existing in the upload folder, <CFFILE> should automatically create a different name for the new file. The attributes used with NAMECONFLICT are detailed in Table 18.1.

TABLE 18.1 Attributes Used with NAMECONFLICT

Attribute	What It Does
makeunique	If the filename already exists in the upload directory, <CFFILE> automatically creates a unique name for the new file.
error	The new file isn't saved, and the user sees an error message.
skip	The file is simply skipped, without being saved. This attribute is often used when you want to perform some other action if the filename exists.
overwrite	The existing file is overwritten by the new file. Use this attribute with extreme caution.

Tip If you use virus software (and all Web server machines should), it's a good idea to run regular checks on the folder(s) you use to accept user uploads. Even if your upload pages are password protected, well-meaning users can unknowingly pass on virus-infected files. Be particularly careful to scan any executable files and data files that might contain macros or scripting.

Assigning <CFFILE> Attributes Dynamically

The ACTION page in Listing 18.2 uses static definitions for all <CFFILE> attributes except FILEFIELD. That is, FILEFIELD is set to the variable FileName, which was passed from the previous form, and all the other attributes are simply typed in on the ACTION page.

Realize that one of <CFFILE>'s great strengths is that any or all of its attributes may be dynamically assigned. To understand this concept, take a look at Figure 18.3.

FIGURE 18.3

An upload form prompting the user for an action if the uploaded file already exists.

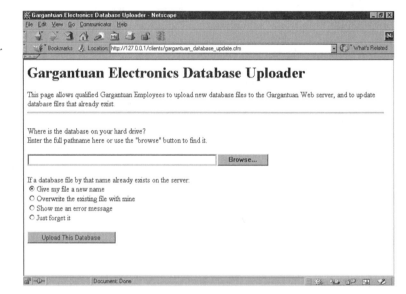

This form enables employees at Gargantuan Electronics to upload database files to the Web server. It serves two purposes for the company; first, it enables workers to update existing databases, and second, it enables them to send new databases to the server for storage.

The form gives employees four options if the file they want to upload already exists. It's no coincidence that there are four options; each of them is keyed to one of the four attributes accepted by <CFFILE>'s NAMECONFLICT parameter.

All four radio buttons in the form share the same NAME, FileAction, which is a variable that will be passed to the <CFFILE> tag on the form's associated ACTION page. The actual code for the form appears in Listing 18.3.

LISTING 18.3   gargantuan_database_update.cfm

```
 1: <HTML>
 2: <HEAD>
 3:     <TITLE>Gargantuan Electronics Database Uploader</TITLE>
 4: </HEAD>
 5:
 6: <BODY>
 7:
 8: <H1>Gargantuan Electronics Database Uploader</H1>
 9: This page allows qualified Gargantuan Employees to upload new database
10: ➥files to the Gargantuan Web server, and to update
11: ➥database files that already exist.
12: <HR>
13: <FORM ACTION="upload_database.cfm" ENCTYPE="multipart/form-data"
     ➥METHOD="post">
14: Where is the database on your hard drive?<BR>
15: Enter the full pathname here or use the "browse" button to find it.<P>
16: <INPUT NAME="FileName" SIZE="50" TYPE=FILE><P>
17: If a database file by that name already exists on the server:<BR>
18: <INPUT TYPE="radio" NAME="FileAction" VALUE="makeunique" CHECKED>
19:         ➥Give my file anew name<BR>
20: <INPUT TYPE="radio" NAME="FileAction" VALUE="overwrite">Overwrite
21:         ➥the existing file with mine<BR>
22: <INPUT TYPE="radio" NAME="FileAction" VALUE="error">
23:         ➥Show me an error message<BR>
24: <INPUT TYPE="radio" NAME="FileAction" VALUE="skip">Just forget it<P>
25:
26: <INPUT TYPE=SUBMIT VALUE="Upload This Database">
27: </FORM>
28:
29: </BODY>
30: </HTML>
```

The ACTION page that accompanies this form will then accept two dynamic parameters, FileName and FileAction. Both are used as attribute values in the ACTION page's <CFFILE> tag, as illustrated in Listing 18.4.

LISTING 18.4   upload_database.cfm

```
 1: <HTML>
 2: <HEAD>
 3:     <TITLE>Thanks for Uploading Your Database/TITLE>
 4: </HEAD>
 5:
 6: <BODY>
 7:
 8: <CFFILE DESTINATION="c:\database_files\" ACTION="upload"
 9:  NAMECONFLICT="#FileAction#" FILEFIELD="#FileName#">
```

continues

LISTING **18.4**   continued

```
10:
11: <H1>Thanks for Uploading Your Database</H1>
12:
13: Your database has been uploaded to the Web server. Please return to your
14:  duties.
15:
16: </BODY>
17: </HTML>
```

Overall, this ACTION page is very similar to the example in the previous section, but note the attributes accompanying <CFFILE>. Now both NAMECONFLICT and FILEFIELD get their values from data passed by the form. Also note that because the form's passed value for FileAction is plugged directly into NAMECONFLICT, it's important that the radio buttons on the form use the exact names and spellings of valid NAMECONFLICT attributes for their VALUEs.

Using <CFFILE> to Manage and Create Files

The examples so far have illustrated <CFFILE>'s ability to handle file uploads, but the tag can also be used to manage and create files by using similar methods.

The attribute that alerts <CFFILE> that a file is being uploaded is ACTION="upload". When an upload ACTION is called for, other associated attributes further define the terms of the action (FILEFIELD, DESTINATION, and so on). Other ACTIONs have their own associated attributes, as listed in Table 18.2.

TABLE 18.2   ACTIONs Supported by <CFFILE>

ACTION	*What It Does*	*Attributes Used with the* ACTION
upload	Uploads FILEFIELD to DESTINATION	FILEFIELD, DESTINATION, ACCEPT, NAMECONFLICT
move	Moves SOURCE file to DESTINATION	SOURCE, DESTINATION, ATTRIBUTES
rename	Renames SOURCE file to DESTINATION	SOURCE, DESTINATION, ATTRIBUTES
copy	Copies SOURCE file to DESTINATION	SOURCE, DESTINATION, ATTRIBUTES
delete	Deletes FILE	FILE
read	Sets a VARIABLE to the contents of FILE	VARIABLE, FILE

ACTION	*What It Does*	*Attributes Used with the* ACTION
readbinary	Creates a binary FILE object from the contents of VARIABLE	VARIABLE, FILE
write	Writes the contents of an OUTPUT variable to a FILE	OUTPUT, FILE, MODE, ADDNEWLINE, ATTRIBUTES
append	Writes the contents of an OUTPUT variable to the end of a FILE	OUTPUT, FILE, MODE, ADDNEWLINE, ATTRIBUTES

Note

As previously illustrated with the upload ACTION, any of the attributes associated with any of the ACTION types in Table 18.2 may be dynamically assigned.

18

As Table 18.2 shows, <CFFILE> is an extremely feature-rich tag. When used with dynamically assigned attributes, it has the ability to function as a full-featured remote management system. The following sections show some sample uses for <CFFILE>'s file management and creation ACTIONs.

Copying, Renaming, and Deleting Files with <CFFILE>

Gargantuan Electronics has requested a form that enables employees to perform some basic file-management tasks on the company Web server. Employees would like to be able to copy files from one location to another, rename files to match the company's file-naming scheme, and delete old files after they're no longer needed.

To accomplish this, I've designed a four-page application that consists of a form page that collects the necessary data and three unique ACTION pages that each use <CFFILE> to perform the desired task. For security, all the pages reside in a password-protected directory that is accessible only by Gargantuan employees.

Because there are three potential tasks, the form page actually contains three separate <FORM> sections, as illustrated in Figure 18.4.

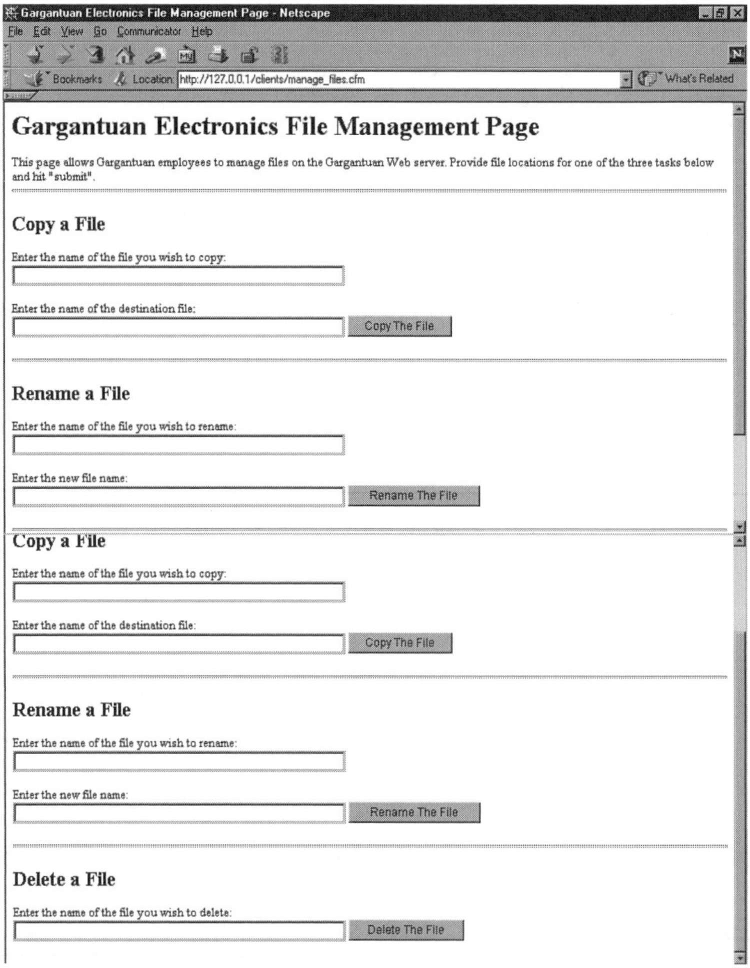

FIGURE 18.4

This form page uses three <FORM> sections to allow for three different file-management tasks.

Each of the three <FORM> sections is associated with its own ACTION page, as illustrated in Listing 18.5.

LISTING 18.5   manage_files.cfm

```
1: <HTML>
2: <HEAD>
3:    <TITLE>Gargantuan Electronics File Management Page</TITLE>
4: </HEAD>
5:
6: <BODY>
7: <H1>Gargantuan Electronics File Management Page</H1>
8: This page allows Gargantuan employees to manage files on the Gargantuan Web
```

```
 9:  server. Provide file locations for one of the three tasks below and
10:  hit "submit".
11:  <HR>
12:  <!--- THIS FORM SECTION COPIES A FILE --->
13:  <H2>Copy a File</H2>
14:  <FORM ACTION="copy.cfm" ENCTYPE="multipart/form-data" METHOD="post">
15:  Enter the name of the file you wish to copy:<BR>
16:  <INPUT TYPE="text" NAME="FileSource" SIZE="50"><P>
17:  Enter the name of the destination file:<BR>
18:  <INPUT TYPE="text" NAME="FileDest" SIZE="50">
19:  <INPUT TYPE=SUBMIT VALUE="Copy The File">
20:  </FORM>
21:
22:  <HR>
23:  <!--- THIS FORM SECTION RENAMES A FILE --->
24:  <H2>Rename a File</H2>
25:  <FORM ACTION="rename.cfm" ENCTYPE="multipart/form-data" METHOD="post">
26:  Enter the name of the file you wish to rename:<BR>
27:  <INPUT TYPE="text" NAME="FileSource" SIZE="50"><P>
28:  Enter the new file name:<BR>
29:  <INPUT TYPE="text" NAME="FileDest" SIZE="50">
30:  <INPUT TYPE=SUBMIT VALUE="Rename The File">
31:  </FORM>
32:
33:  <HR>
34:  <!--- THIS FORM SECTION DELETES A FILE --->
35:  <H2>Delete a File</H2>
36:  <FORM ACTION="delete.cfm" ENCTYPE="multipart/form-data" METHOD="post">
37:  Enter the name of the file you wish to delete:<BR>
38:  <INPUT TYPE="text" NAME="FileSource" SIZE="50">
39:  <INPUT TYPE=SUBMIT VALUE="Delete The File">
40:  </FORM>
41:
42:  </BODY>
43:  </HTML>
```

18

The following sections look at each <FORM> section and its associated ACTION page in detail.

The Copy ACTION

Take a look at the copy section of the form in Listing 18.5. The code looks like this:

```
<!--- THIS FORM SECTION COPIES A FILE --->
<H2>Copy a File</H2>
<FORM ACTION="copy.cfm" ENCTYPE="multipart/form-data" METHOD="post">
Enter the name of the file you wish to copy:<BR>
<INPUT TYPE="text" NAME="FileSource" SIZE="50"><P>
Enter the name of the destination file:<BR>
<INPUT TYPE="text" NAME="FileDest" SIZE="50">
<INPUT TYPE=SUBMIT VALUE="Copy The File">
</FORM>
```

This form sends two variables—FileSource and FileDest—to the ACTION page
copy.cfm. The ACTION page uses these variables to dynamically supply attributes for
<CFFILE>'s copy ACTION, as illustrated in Listing 18.6.

LISTING 18.6   copy.cfm

```
 1: <HTML>
 2: <HEAD>
 3:    <TITLE>Your File Has Been Copied</TITLE>
 4: </HEAD>
 5:
 6: <BODY>
 7:
 8: <CFFILE ACTION="copy" SOURCE="#FileSource#"  DESTINATION="#FileDest#"
 9:  ATTRIBUTES="ReadOnly">
10:
11: <H1>Your File Has Been Copied</H1>
12:
13: <CFOUTPUT>
14: The file #FORM.FileSource# has been copied to #FORM.FileDest#
15: </CFOUTPUT>
16: <P>
17: Return to Your Duties
18: </BODY>
19: </HTML>
```

The <CFFILE> tag uses the ACTION copy, and uses the variables passed by the form to
define SOURCE and DESTINATION. Note that the user must supply a full path and file name
for both SOURCE and DESTINATION for the copy to work. As a bonus, the tag also sets
read-only attributes to the new file to ensure that the new file can't be accidentally
overwritten or deleted.

Note

Several <CFFILE> ACTIONs use the ATTRIBUTES parameter. The attributes of a
file determine things such as whether it can be viewed, deleted, and
whether it is a hidden file that doesn't show up in directory listings.
<CFFILE> can set one or more of the following file attributes. (To set more
than one attribute, use a comma-delimited list in the ATTRIBUTES parameter.)

- ReadOnly
- Temporary
- Archive
- Hidden
- System
- Normal

Following the `<CFFILE>` tag, this `ACTION` page also uses a short `<CFOUTPUT>` section to dynamically display the source and destination names of the copied file.

The Rename `ACTION`

The `<FORM>` section that collects data for the `rename` `ACTION` is similar to the copy form because it also collects two items.

```
<!--- THIS FORM SECTION RENAMES A FILE --->
<H2>Rename a File</H2>
<FORM ACTION="rename.cfm" ENCTYPE="multipart/form-data" METHOD="post">
Enter the name of the file you wish to rename:<BR>
<INPUT TYPE="text" NAME="FileSource" SIZE="50"><P>
Enter the new file name:<BR>
<INPUT TYPE="text" NAME="FileDest" SIZE="50">
<INPUT TYPE="hidden" NAME="what_to_do" VALUE="rename">
<INPUT TYPE=SUBMIT VALUE="Rename The File">
</FORM>
```

The `ACTION` page associated with this `<FORM>` section is shown in Listing 18.7.

LISTING 18.7   `rename.cfm`

```
 1: <HTML>
 2: <HEAD>
 3:     <TITLE>Your File Has Been Renamed</TITLE>
 4: </HEAD>
 5:
 6: <BODY>
 7:
 8: <CFFILE ACTION="rename" SOURCE="#FileSource#"  DESTINATION="#FileDest#"
 9:  ATTRIBUTES="ReadOnly">
10:
11: <H1>Your File Has Been Renamed</H1>
12:
13: <CFOUTPUT>
14: The file #FORM.FileSource# has been renamed as #FORM.FileDest#
15: </CFOUTPUT>
16: <P>
17: Return to Your Duties
18: </BODY>
19: </HTML>
```

18

Listing 18.7 is very similar to 18.6, except for the `ACTION` performed. The `rename` `ACTION` also accepts `SOURCE` and `DESTINATION`, which are dynamically supplied by the form page. The `ATTRIBUTES` parameter (`ATTRIBUTES` "attribute"?) has also been set to read-only.

The Delete ACTION

The delete ACTION is the most succinct <CFFILE> task, but it's also the most dangerous. It takes just one attribute: the name of the file to delete. The <FORM> section from Listing 18.5 looks like this:

```
<!--- THIS FORM SECTION DELETES A FILE --->
<H2>Delete a File</H2>
<FORM ACTION="delete.cfm" ENCTYPE="multipart/form-data" METHOD="post">
Enter the name of the file you wish to delete:<BR>
<INPUT TYPE="text" NAME="FileSource" SIZE="50">
<INPUT TYPE=SUBMIT VALUE="Delete The File">
</FORM>
```

The single variable, FileSource, is passed to the ACTION page, where it is dynamically inserted into the <CFFILE> tag, as in Listing 18.8. <CFILE> performs the actual delete process, removing the file named in FileSource.

LISTING 18.8   delete.cfm

```
 1: <HTML>
 2: <HEAD>
 3:     <TITLE>Your File Has Been Deleted</TITLE>
 4: </HEAD>
 5:
 6: <BODY>
 7:
 8: <CFFILE ACTION="delete" FILE="#FileSource#">
 9:
10: <H1>Your File Has Been Deleted</H1>
11:
12: <CFOUTPUT>
13: The file #FORM.FileSource# has been deleted.
14: </CFOUTPUT>
15: <P>
16: Return to Your Duties
17: </BODY>
18: </HTML>
```

> **Tip**
>
> Because <CFFILE>'s delete ACTION is such a potentially dangerous tool, you might want to use a confirmation page in some <CFFILE> applications. For example, when a user submits a form that requests a deletion, you might create a template that asks, Are you really, really sure? before passing the delete data along to <CFFILE>.

Viewing File Object Attributes

When <CFFILE> performs any of its supported ACTIONs on a file, it temporarily stores data about the file and the ACTION in a special set of variables. All these special variables use the format #FILE.some_variable#, and they're ideal for tasks such as reporting successful uploads back to the user.

Figure 18.5 shows a modified confirmation page that tells users their UFO photo files have been uploaded successfully. It also uses file object variables to display a few details about the upload.

FIGURE 18.5

This modified confirmation page gives users more information about the files they've uploaded.

The code that created Figure 18.5 is displayed in Listing 18.9. In the <CFOUTPUT> section, note the special variables that begin with FILE.

LISTING 18.9 An Enhanced Version of upload_action.cfm

```
1: <HTML>
2: <HEAD>
3:    <TITLE>The Results of Your Photo Upload</TITLE>
4: </HEAD>
5:
6: <BODY>
7:
8: <CFFILE DESTINATION="c:\in" ACTION="upload" NAMECONFLICT="makeunique"
9: FILEFIELD="FileName">
```

continues

LISTING 18.9   continued

```
10:
11: <H1>The Results of Your Photo Upload</H1>
12:
13: <CFOUTPUT>
14: The image file you uploaded:<P>
15:
16: #FILE.ClientDirectory#\#FILE.ClientFile#<P>
17:
18: was saved on our server as:<P>
19:
20: #FILE.ServerFileName#<P>
21:
22: with a file size of:<P>
23:
24: #FILE.FileSize# bytes<P>
25:
26: </CFOUTPUT>
27:
28:
29: Thanks, and keep watching the skies.
30:
31: </BODY>
32: </HTML>
```

Four special variables are used in this page. #FILE.ClientDirectory# and #FILE.ClientFile# are used together, with a slash between them to show the full path of the file uploaded by the user. #FILE.ServerFileName# displays the name of the file as it appears on the remote server, and #FILE.FileSize# gives the size in bytes.

Table 18.3 displays a complete list of these special file object variables.

TABLE 18.3   File Object Variables

Variable	*What It Contains*
AttemptedServerFile	Returns a yes or no as to whether ColdFusion tried to save the file
ClientDirectory	The directory on the user's machine that holds the file
ClientFile	The name of the file as it appears on the user's machine
ClientFileExt	The extension of the file on the user's machine, without the period
ClientFileName	The same as ClientFile, but without the extension
ContentSubType	The MIME subtype of the file
ContentType	The MIME type of the file

Variable	What It Contains
DateLastAccessed	The date and time the file was last accessed
FileExisted	Tells whether a file by the same name existed on the server before the file was uploaded
FileSize	The size of the uploaded file
FileWasAppended	Used with the append ACTION, this returns a yes or no
FileWasOverwritten	Displays a yes or no as to whether the server file was overwritten by the user's file
FileWasRenamed	Displays a yes or no as to whether the user's file was renamed during the upload
FileWasSaved	Displays a yes or no as to whether ColdFusion saved the file
OldFileSize	The size of the server file that was overwritten by the user's file
ServerFile	The name of the file as it was saved on the server
ServerFileExt	The extension of the saved file, without the period
ServerFileName	The same as ServerFile, but without the extension
TimeCreated	The time the file was created on the server
TimeLastModified	The date and time the uploaded file was last modified

Tip

File object attributes are useful for more than just reporting statistics to users. For example, after an upload you might use a tag such as <CFINSERT> to add information on the uploaded file to a database table.

Reading and Writing with <CFFILE>

<CFFILE>'s read and write ACTIONs enable you to work with plain-text files on your server. They enable you to extract data from text files and to create new text files to hold data a template has obtained from a variable or a query.

Note

<CFFILE>'s read and write ACTIONs work only with plain-text, or ASCII files. They will not work with proprietary, binary formats such those in word-processing documents. A special ACTION, readbinary, *will* read binary files into a binary ColdFusion object—check your ColdFusion documentation if you need to use this advanced feature.

The Read ACTION

Say that a user has uploaded a plain-text file that details her most recent alien encounter. Using <CFFILE>, you could read this file into a variable that might be displayed on a Web page, inserted into a database, or both.

Listing 18.10 shows an example of <CFFILE>'s read ACTION. It uses a file object variable to get the name of the text file uploaded by the user, and then displays the actual contents of that text file on the Web page for confirmation.

LISTING 18.10   Using <CFFILE> to Read an Uploaded Text Document

```
 1: <HTML>
 2: <HEAD>
 3:    <TITLE>The Results of Your Text Upload</TITLE>
 4: </HEAD>
 5:
 6: <BODY>
 7:
 8: <CFFILE DESTINATION="c:\in\" ACTION="upload" NAMECONFLICT="makeunique"
 9:  FILEFIELD="FileName">
10:
11: <CFFILE ACTION="read" FILE="c:\in\#FILE.ServerFile#" VARIABLE="tale">
12:
13: <H1>The Results of Your Text Upload</H1>
14:
15: <CFOUTPUT>
16: The text file you uploaded reads as follows:<P>
17:
18: #tale#<P>
19:
20: </CFOUTPUT>
21:
22:
23: Thanks, and keep watching the skies.
24:
25: </BODY>
26: </HTML>
```

Listing 18.10 uses two <CFFILE> tags. The first saves the uploaded text file in the DESTI-NATION directory c:\in\. The second reads the text of the uploaded file into the variable tale, which is then used as output.

Figures 18.6 and 18.7 display, respectively, the user's story as it appears on her machine, and a browser view of the upload confirmation page in Listing 18.10.

FIGURE 18.6

The user's text file, as it appears in a text editor on her machine.

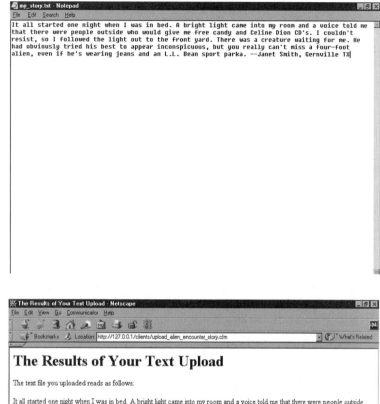

FIGURE 18.7

The upload confirmation page, including the contents of the text file uploaded by the user.

18

The `Write` and `Append` ACTIONs

Another `<CFFILE>` ACTION, `write` works much the same way as `read`, but in reverse. It takes information obtained from say, a variable or a query, and writes that data to a text file that can then either be viewed in a browser or made available for download.

The write ACTION assumes that you want to create a new text file in which to write data, although it has a companion ACTION, append, which adds designated text to an existing file.

To illustrate how this might work, assume that the UFO reporting site archives user's text files into a master file called encounters.txt. Using <CFFILE>'s append ACTION, an uploaded text file can be written to the end of the existing document. Listing 18.11 displays one method of doing so.

LISTING 18.11 Using <CFFILE>'s append ACTION to Write an Uploaded Text File to Another File on the Server

```
 1: <HTML>
 2: <HEAD>
 3:    <TITLE>The Results of Your Text Upload</TITLE>
 4: </HEAD>
 5:
 6: <BODY>
 7:
 8: <CFFILE DESTINATION="c:\in\" ACTION="upload" NAMECONFLICT="makeunique"
 9:  FILEFIELD="FileName">
10:
11: <CFFILE ACTION="append" FILE="c:\in\#FILE.ServerFile#"
12: OUTPUT="c:\in\encounters.txt">
13:
14: <CFFILE ACTION="read" FILE="c:\in\#FILE.ServerFile#"
15: VARIABLE="tale">
16:
17: <H1>The Results of Your Text Upload</H1>
18:
19: <CFOUTPUT>
20:  The text in your uploaded file has been added to the server file
21:  encounters.txt<P>
22:
23:  #tale#<P>
24:
25: </CFOUTPUT>
26:
27:
28: Thanks, and keep watching the skies.
29:
30: </BODY>
31: </HTML>
```

Using <CFDIRECTORY>

After you're familiar with <CFFILE>'s file-management ACTIONs, the companion tag <CFDIRECTORY> is a breeze to master. It supports only four ACTIONs, as listed in Table 18.4. All the ACTIONs use the associated attribute DIRECTORY to specify the directory or folder on which to act.

TABLE 18.4   ACTIONs Supported by <CFDIRECTORY>

ACTION	What It Does
create	Creates a new directory with the name specified in the attribute DIRECTORY.
delete	Deletes the directory named in DIRECTORY.
list	Lists the contents of specified DIRECTORY. This ACTION also accepts the optional attributes FILTER and SORT to determine file types to list, or sorting order, respectively.
rename	Renames DIRECTORY to the required attribute specified in NEWDIRECTORY.

 Note

> When you create a new directory with <CFDIRECTORY>, it automatically takes on the access privileges (read, write, execute) of the folder in which it has been created.

18

You reference <CFDIRECTORY> tags in pretty much the same way you use <CFFILE> for file-management tasks. For example, to rename a directory, you'd use code like this:

```
<CFDIRECTORY ACTION="rename" DIRECTORY="c:\my_old_directory"
NEWDIRECTORY="c:\my_new_directory">
```

To copy a directory, you'd use code like the following:

```
<CFDIRECTORY ACTION="copy" DIRECTORY="c:\my directory"
NEWDIRECTORY="c:\copy_of_my directory">
```

Remember that like <CFFILE>, <CFDIRECTORY> also accepts dynamically assigned parameters.

Summary

In previous days you've learned how ColdFusion is an excellent tool to promote interactivity, and you've learned how to work with text values input by your users. Today's lesson demonstrates that ColdFusion can handle much more than just snippets of text as input. With powerful tags such as <CFFILE> and <CFDIRECTORY>, you can give users the ability to create and update entire files on your server. You can also give your clients the ability to update their own Web content without having to master FTP software.

As with any application that gives users direct access to your server, <CFILE> and its associated tools involve a certain amount of risk. When you design applications that use the tag, it's extremely important to take security into consideration.

<CFFILE> supports a variety of ACTIONs that enable you to accept uploaded files, to manage files already on the server, and even to create new text files from information obtained by queries or other input methods. <CFDIRECTORY> does the same for directories on your server. Together, the two tags can be used to build a full-featured remote management system.

Q&A

Q What types of files can be uploaded and managed with <CFFILE>?

A <CFFILE> doesn't care much about the types of files users upload to your server. It simply accepts them and processes them based on the parameters you specify in the tag.

Q Why is it such a security risk to allow users upload access?

A It is a risk because crafty hackers can do a lot with directory access, even if they're not actually able to run files. Any form of direct access to a server's files or directories should be seen as a potential hole for intruders.

Q I built a page to enable users to upload files, but when I test it, ColdFusion tells me the DESTINATION directory doesn't exist. What gives?

A ColdFusion must have access to a directory before it can save files there. Check your operating system documentation for details on setting directory access privileges.

Workshop

Just to see whether you were dozing through today's lesson, here are a few quiz questions and exercises. Answers to the quiz questions can be found in Appendix A at the back of the text.

Quiz

1. True or false: When you create a form that enables users to upload a file, ColdFusion automatically creates a browse box to enable users to find files on their server.

2. Name three attributes used with <CFFILE>'s upload ACTION.

3. Where should your upload forms and ACTION pages reside on your server? (Hint: Think "security.")

4. Name the four attributes used with NAMECONFLICT.

5. What file types may be read and written with <CFFILE>?

Exercises

1. In a password-protected directory, create form and ACTION pages that enable users to upload a photo and a description of themselves to your server. Use <CFFILE>'s file object attributes to write information about the files to a database so that they may be displayed in a template.

2. In a password-protected directory, create a form that enables a client to upload a database file and thus update that client's ColdFusion datasource. Use file object attributes to log details about the upload to a database table.

3. In a password-protected directory, create a simple guestbook that accepts text files from a user and appends them to a master file.

18

DAY **19**

Using Advanced SQL Techniques

In Day 4, "Building a Database and Organizing Data," you learned how to create simple SQL statements that enable you to SELECT certain records from a
table in a datasource. In today's lesson, you'll learn more about SQL and its
advanced arsenal of selection techniques. You'll learn how to use SQL statements to work with databases that use unconventional table or field names, how
to create queries within queries, and how to use SQL's special aggregate functions to find out more about the data you've selected. Users of server-based
database applications such as Microsoft SQL Server, Oracle, and Sybase will
also learn how to save commonly used SQL statements as stored procedures.
Today's lesson covers:

- Column aliases
- Aggregate functions
- Table joins
- Subqueries

- SQL views
- Stored procedures

Understanding Column Aliases

In the introduction to SQL in Day 5, you learned that when you use `<CFQUERY>` to select records from a datasource, the selected records are returned as variable values corresponding to the field names in your table. Take a look at a sample Microsoft Access table in Figure 19.1.

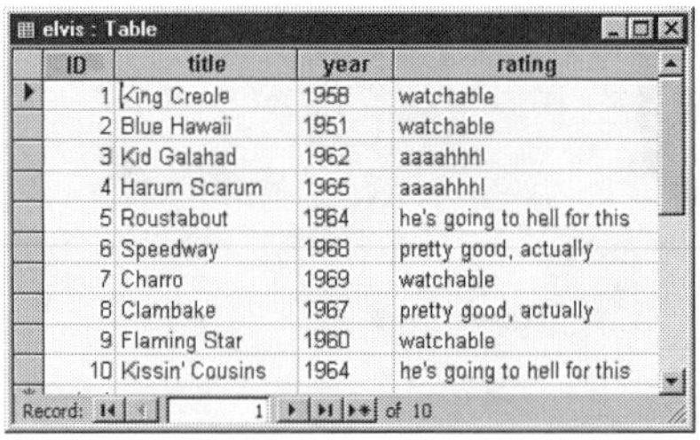

elvis : Table

ID	title	year	rating
1	King Creole	1958	watchable
2	Blue Hawaii	1951	watchable
3	Kid Galahad	1962	aaaahhh!
4	Harum Scarum	1965	aaaahhh!
5	Roustabout	1964	he's going to hell for this
6	Speedway	1968	pretty good, actually
7	Charro	1969	watchable
8	Clambake	1967	pretty good, actually
9	Flaming Star	1960	watchable
10	Kissin' Cousins	1964	he's going to hell for this

Record: 1 of 10

FIGURE 19.1
A sample database table in Microsoft Access, designed and named with ColdFusion in mind.

If you've already read Day 2, "Anatomy of a ColdFusion Application," you'll remember this same table from some of the examples there. To access records in this table, you might use a query like this:

```
<CFQUERY NAME="get_songs" DATASOURCE="elvis">
SELECT * FROM elvis
</CFQUERY>
```

This query would select all records in the table, and return the results as variable values using the names of the fields for variable names. To access these variables, you would use an output section that specifies field names as variables, like this:

```
<CFOUTPUT QUERY="get_songs">
Song Title: #title#<BR>
Year of Release: #year#<BR>
My Rating: #rating#<P>
</CFOUTPUT>
```

No problem—by now, this kind of query-and-output stuff should be old hat to you. In a perfect world, all database tables would look like Figure 19.1, with single-word field names and no weird spaces or nonalphanumeric characters that might spell trouble for ColdFusion. If you had created this table yourself, you would have used such naming conventions. But look at Figure 19.2, which shows a table more like one that a business client might supply.

FIGURE 19.2

A database table submitted by a client, using spaces and "troublesome" characters in field names.

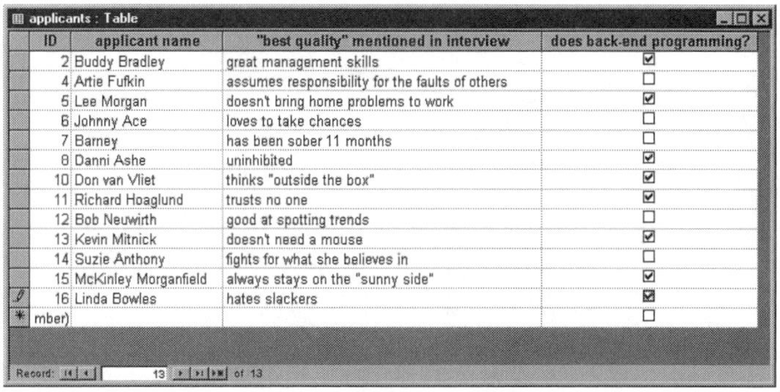

ID	applicant name	"best quality" mentioned in interview	does back-end programming?
2	Buddy Bradley	great management skills	☑
4	Artie Fufkin	assumes responsibility for the faults of others	☐
5	Lee Morgan	doesn't bring home problems to work	☑
6	Johnny Ace	loves to take chances	☐
7	Barney	has been sober 11 months	☐
8	Danni Ashe	uninhibited	☑
10	Don van Vliet	thinks "outside the box"	☑
11	Richard Hoaglund	trusts no one	☑
12	Bob Neuwirth	good at spotting trends	☐
13	Kevin Mitnick	doesn't need a mouse	☑
14	Suzie Anthony	fights for what she believes in	☐
15	McKinley Morganfield	always stays on the "sunny side"	☑
16	Linda Bowles	hates slackers	☑
mber)			☐

This sort of table presents some problems. ColdFusion doesn't like spaces, apostrophes, or dashes in field names because it interprets them as control characters.

NEW TERM *Control characters* are nonalphanumeric characters such as ", ', -, and # that programs such as ColdFusion interpret as something other than literal text. For example, when ColdFusion sees the # character, it assumes that you're specifying a variable name.

Normally, tables similar to Figure 19.2 would create havoc in ColdFusion applications, and would generate errors when you tried to use one of those field names as a ColdFusion variable. Your SQL statement might find the field names just fine, but when you try to present the results in a <CFOUTPUT> section, you would have to refer to an illegal variable such as #application name#, #"best quality" stated in job interview#. The spaces and quotation marks would confuse ColdFusion, and you would get all sorts of fancy error messages like the one shown in Figure 19.3.

One solution is to ask your client to change the field names in the database, but chances are the client has internal database forms and other applications that refer to those specific field names and making changes would be a big hassle. You probably wouldn't be in business long making these kind of haughty requests. Instead, you can use SQL's column alias feature to send ColdFusion variable names or column names that it will understand. Look at Listing 19.1, and pay special attention to the <CFQUERY> section.

19

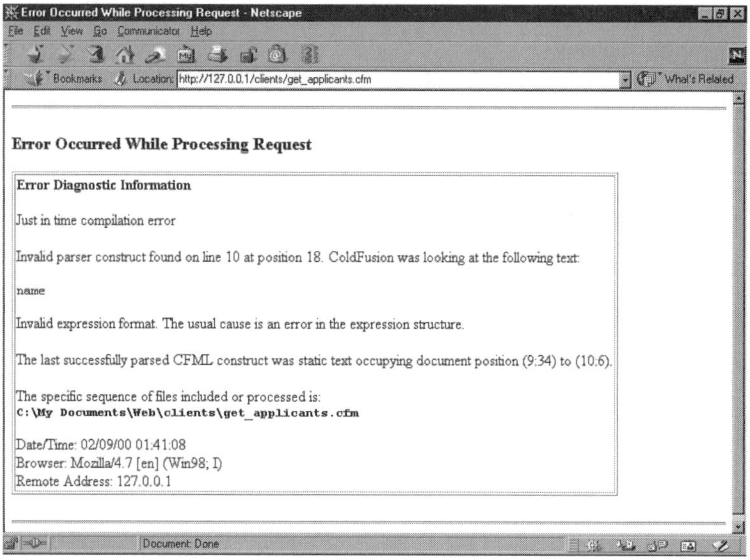

FIGURE 19.3

*An error message gen-
erated by ColdFusion
when a table's field
names use nonal-
phanumeric characters.*

LISTING 19.1   get_applicants.cfm

```
 1: <CFQUERY NAME="get_applicants" DATASOURCE="gargantuan">
 2: SELECT `applicant name` AS name, `"best quality" mentioned in interview`
➥AS quality, `does back-end programming?` AS back_end FROM applicants
 3: </CFQUERY>
 4: <HTML>
 5: <TITLE>Applicants for the Programming Position at
➥Gargantuan Electronics</TITLE>
 6: <BODY>
 7: <H1>Applicants for the Programming Position at Gargantuan Electronics</H1>
 8: <HR>
 9: <CFOUTPUT QUERY="get_applicants">
10: <B>Name:</B> #name#<BR>
11: <B>"Best Quality" as Stated in Interview:</B> #quality#<BR>
12: <B>Does Back-End Programming?</B> #YesNoFormat(back_end)#<P>
13: </CFOUTPUT>
14:
15: </BODY>
16: </HTML>
```

ANALYSIS   Listing 19.1 uses the SQL term AS on line 2 to create column aliases. AS requires
two things: the literal name of a column or field to select and a second, ColdFusion-
compatible name you want to use when referring to that column in later sections such as
<CFOUTPUT>. Note in Listing 19.1 that each literal name on line 2 is set off by backticks
(the ` character, usually found just below the Esc key) so that your SQL statement
doesn't try to interpret characters such as " as part of the statement.

When SQL sees a backtick used like those on line 2, it knows that everything between the first backtick and the next backtick should be interpreted literally—even control characters and spaces. This means that it will process the contents of backticked phrases as literal text, rather than trying to read characters like " as a reference to a text string.

For the purposes of the template file, each selected column (field name) is automatically renamed by SQL to the name specified after the AS term. For example, applicant name becomes name so that ColdFusion isn't confused by the space between the words; "best quality" mentioned in interview becomes quality so that ColdFusion doesn't choke on the quote marks, and so on. In the <CFOUTPUT> section, use the names or column aliases defined with the AS term rather than the actual field names.

The output from Listing 19.1 would resemble that resulting from any standard ColdFusion query, as illustrated in Figure 19.4.

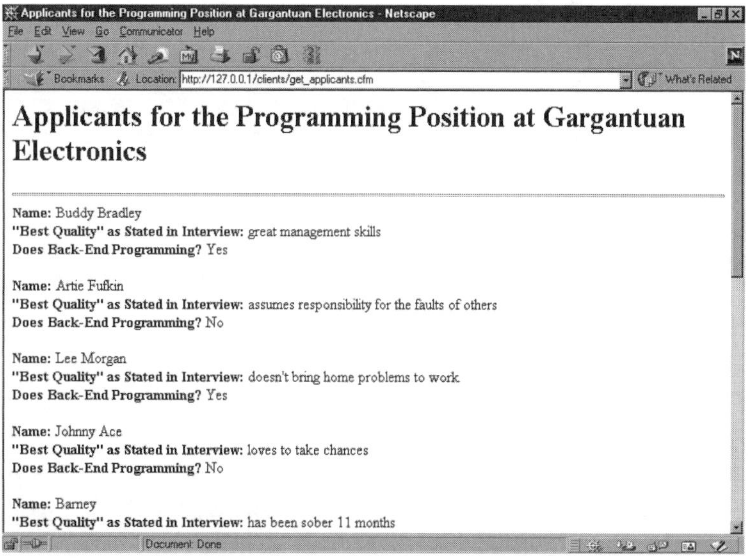

FIGURE 19.4

Using column aliases enables you to create conventional output from tables that include unconventional field names.

SQL column aliases are valuable for more than just getting around troublesome field names. For example, you can use a column alias to select a field that will be passed to a <CFINSERT> or <CFUPDATE> tag in which the datasource expects a field name other than the one selected.

Understanding Aggregate Functions

In Day 14, "Using ColdFusion Functions to Manipulate Data," you learned that ColdFusion has a special set of functions that can be used to modify variables or to display certain values, such as a time and date. SQL uses two types of functions: scalar and aggregate. You won't have to worry much about scalar functions because ColdFusion functions will perform the same tricks as SQL's scalar functions, but you'll find SQL's aggregate functions to be pretty useful tools.

NEW TERM *Aggregate functions* provide "data about the data" selected by SQL statements. That is, aggregate functions are used to report details about the records selected by a given SQL query.

To illustrate how SQL's aggregate functions are used, I added two fields, named years of experience and age, to Gargantuan's database table. Both use the data type number, and are set to the Microsoft Access default number type, "long integer." The table now looks like Figure 19.5.

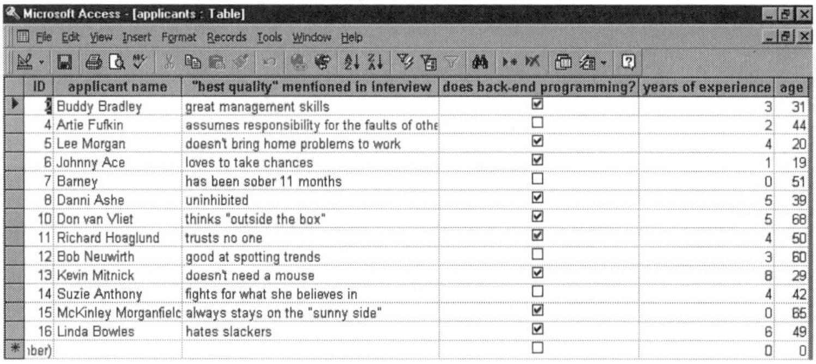

FIGURE 19.5

Gargantuan's table of job applicants, with two new fields that will record age and experience.

ID	applicant name	"best quality" mentioned in interview	does back-end programming?	years of experience	age
3	Buddy Bradley	great management skills	☑	3	31
4	Artie Fufkin	assumes responsibility for the faults of othe	☐	2	44
5	Lee Morgan	doesn't bring home problems to work	☑	4	20
6	Johnny Ace	loves to take chances	☑	1	19
7	Barney	has been sober 11 months	☐	0	51
8	Danni Ashe	uninhibited	☑	5	39
10	Don van Vliet	thinks "outside the box"	☑	5	68
11	Richard Hoaglund	trusts no one	☑	4	50
12	Bob Neuwirth	good at spotting trends	☐	3	60
13	Kevin Mitnick	doesn't need a mouse	☑	8	29
14	Suzie Anthony	fights for what she believes in	☐	4	42
15	McKinley Morganfield	always stays on the "sunny side"	☑	0	65
16	Linda Bowles	hates slackers	☑	6	49
(ber)			☐	0	0

Tip

You should never user a field name with spaces—like *years of experience*—unless you really like the extra work. I've done it here to simulate a troublesome name you might find in a client's database.

Listing 19.2 shows how to use aggregate functions to report on Gargantuan's new and improved table.

LISTING 19.2 Using Aggregate Functions in a ColdFusion Query

```
 1: <CFQUERY NAME="get_applicants" DATASOURCE="gargantuan">
 2: SELECT COUNT(`applicant name`) AS applicant_count,
 3:        MIN(age) AS minimum_age,
 4:        MAX(age) AS maximum_age,
 5:        AVG(age) AS average_age,
 6:        AVG(`years of experience`) AS average_experience
 7:        FROM applicants
 8: </CFQUERY>
 9:
10: <HTML>
11: <TITLE>Gargantuan Applicants</TITLE>
12: <BODY>
13: <H1>Gargantuan Applicant Report</H1>
14:
15: <CFOUTPUT QUERY="get_applicants">
16: So far, #applicant_count# applicants have applied for the back-end
➡programmer's position at Gargantuan.<P>
17: The applicants range in age from #minimum_age# to #maximum_age#.<P>
18: The average age of all applicants is #NumberFormat(average_age)#.<P>
19: The applicants have an average of #NumberFormat(average_experience,
➡ "9999.99")# years experience.<P>
20: </CFOUTPUT>
21:
22: </BODY>
23: </HTML>
```

ANALYSIS Several things are going on in Listing 19.2, so let's look at each one individually. First, it uses a <CFQUERY> on line 1 to examine the database of applicants. Because some of the field names on lines 2–7 contain spaces (applicant name and years of experience), those field names are surrounded by backticks. The SQL statement also uses AS to set up aliases, in which selected columns will become known as alternative variable names in the <CFOUTPUT> section that comes later, on line 15.

But notice that the column names I'm selecting are enclosed in special aggregate functions such as COUNT(), AVG(), MIN(), and so on. Remember the discussion of ColdFusion functions in Day 14? SQL functions work much the same way, performing some action on the variable that appears within the function's set of parentheses.

The aggregate functions used in this query do things such as count the number of records in the table, find the maximum and minimum number values for a specified field, and compute the averages of number values in other specified fields. Don't worry if you don't understand how exactly these functions accomplish these goals—you'll learn more about that in a moment.

19

After these functions have worked their magic, they temporarily store the results in internal SQL variables. To put these special variables into a format ColdFusion can understand, Listing 19.2 uses the AS command to create an alias for each of the variable/function sets: COUNT(`applicant name`) becomes applicant_count, MIN(age) becomes minimum_age, MAX(age) becomes maximum_age, and so on. Then, in the <CFOUTPUT> section in Listing 19.2, each variable is referred to simply by its alias. To see how this looks as output, check out Figure 19.6.

FIGURE 19.6

SQL's aggregate functions can be used to compute a field's maximium, minimum, and average values for display as output.

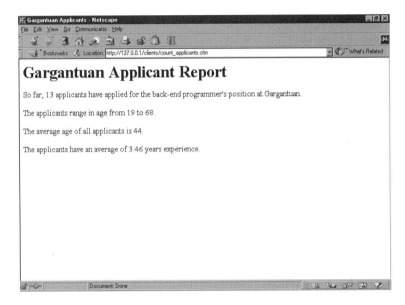

Notice in Figure 19.6 that the aggregate functions provide some pretty interesting "data about the data" selected from the applicants table.

- COUNT(`applicant name`) returns the number of records in the table.

- MIN(age) and MAX(age) return the minimum and maximum number values in the age field.

- AVG(age) computes the average value of all the numbers in the age field. The actual number AVG(age) returned was 43.6153846153846, but because that's not a very useful number for an age, I used ColdFusion's NumberFormat() function to round the value to a whole number automatically.

- AVG(`years of experience`) computes the average of values in years of experience. In this case, it might be useful to see at least a couple of decimal places with the number, so I used NumberFormat() with a mask of 9999.99 to display the number to two decimal places.

Tip

SQL's aggregate functions can also be used in queries that use a WHERE clause to limit data selection. In these cases, the functions will report only on the data selected by the WHERE clause. For example, the following query would return the minimum, maximum, and average values for only those applicants who do back-end programming:

```
<CFQUERY NAME="get_applicants" DATASOURCE="gargantuan">
SELECT COUNT(`applicant name`) AS applicant_count,
       MIN(age) AS minimum_age,
       MAX(age) AS maximum_age,
       AVG(age) AS average_age,
       AVG(`years of experience`) AS average_experience
       FROM applicants WHERE `does back-end programming?` = 1
</CFQUERY>
```

Look at Table 19.1, which lists SQL's aggregate functions. Depending on the data type of your table's fields, these functions report different values.

TABLE 19.1 SQL Aggregate Functions

Function	What It Reports on Text-Based Fields	What It Reports on Date Fields	What It Reports on Numeric Fields
AVG(*column*)	*Doesn't apply*	*Doesn't apply*	Finds the average of values in a column
COUNT(*)	Counts the number of rows in a table	Counts the number of rows in a table	Counts the number of rows in a table
COUNT(*column*)	Counts the values found in a column	Counts the values found in a column	Counts the values found in a column
MIN(*column*)	Finds the lowest alphabetic value in a column	Finds the earliest date in a column	Finds the lowest value in a column
MAX(*column*)	Finds the highest alphabetic value in a column	Finds the most recent date in a column	Finds the highest number in a column
SUM(*column*)	*Doesn't apply*	*Doesn't apply*	Adds the totals of all values in a column

19

> **Caution**
>
> Functions such as `AVG()` and `SUM()` are designed specifically to be used with columns that contain number values. If you try to use them with a field that contains text data, you'll get a sharply worded data mismatch error from your ODBC driver.

Understanding Table Joins

A *table join* is pretty much what it sounds like—using a single SQL statement to pull records from two different tables and presenting the results to ColdFusion as a single batch. Why would you want to do this? Check out the tables in Figures 19.7 and 19.8.

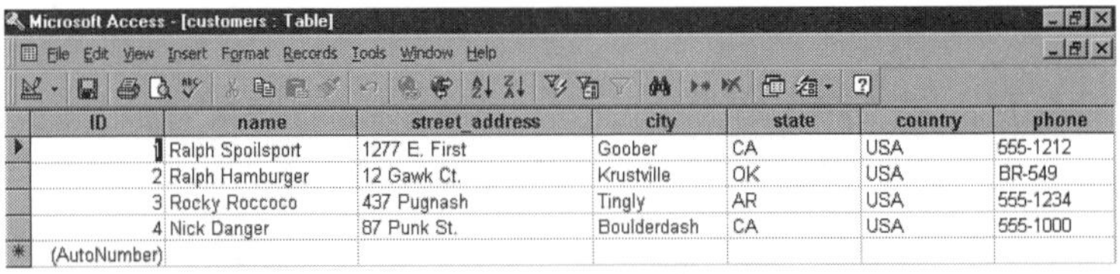

ID	name	street_address	city	state	country	phone
1	Ralph Spoilsport	1277 E. First	Goober	CA	USA	555-1212
2	Ralph Hamburger	12 Gawk Ct.	Krustville	OK	USA	BR-549
3	Rocky Roccoco	437 Pugnash	Tingly	AR	USA	555-1234
4	Nick Danger	87 Punk St.	Boulderdash	CA	USA	555-1000
(AutoNumber)						

FIGURE 19.7
The `customers` *table from TV Cop Pasta, Inc. displays shipping and contact information.*

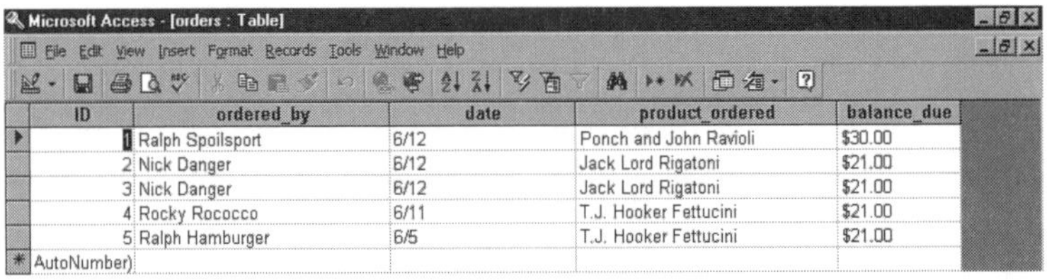

ID	ordered_by	date	product_ordered	balance_due
1	Ralph Spoilsport	6/12	Ponch and John Ravioli	$30.00
2	Nick Danger	6/12	Jack Lord Rigatoni	$21.00
3	Nick Danger	6/12	Jack Lord Rigatoni	$21.00
4	Rocky Rococco	6/11	T.J. Hooker Fettucini	$21.00
5	Ralph Hamburger	6/5	T.J. Hooker Fettucini	$21.00
AutoNumber)				

FIGURE 19.8
The `orders` *table from TV Cop Pasta, Inc. displays order details for each customer.*

Recall that when the TV Cop Pasta database was created in Day 4, the `customers` table and `orders` table were linked by the customer's name—as each record was entered in the `orders` table, it was assigned to one of the names in the `customers` table.

Each customer has only one entry in the `customers` table, but there may be several entries under that customer's name in the `products` table if the customer has placed more than one order.

> **Tip**
>
> Although it's certainly acceptable to use a text field such as `name` as the link between two tables, now that you know more about ColdFusion and SQL, you might want to start using numeric fields (such as `ID`) instead. SQL is much faster at processing numbers than text, which means that it has to do less work to find records related to a numeric field. Also, if you use a table's primary key (such as `ID`) as a means of linking, you ensure that every customer has a unique identifier.

Got that? Now assume that TV Cop Pasta needs a simple orders page that lists the dates and product names of each item ordered. No problem there because the details of each order are saved in the `orders` table.

But let's say that TV Cop Pasta also wants to display customer shipping information along with each order. That might be a problem because the customer info resides in a different table. It might be done with two separate queries, but there's an easier way.

Because the tables were linked, or related, by customer name when they were designed, you can exploit this fact by using a table join. Again, a table join uses a single query to pull data from two tables and assemble that data into one batch to be processed by <CFOUTPUT>. Look at an example in Listing 19.3. All the trickery happens in the query section.

LISTING 19.3   tv_cop_pasta_orders.cfm

```
 1: <CFQUERY NAME="get_orders" DATASOURCE="tv_cop_pasta">
 2: SELECT orders.ordered_by, orders.date, orders.product_ordered,
 3:        customers.name, customers.street_address, customers.city,
➥    customers.state
 4: FROM customers, orders
 5: WHERE customers.name = orders.ordered_by
 6: </CFQUERY>
 7:
 8: <HTML>
 9: <HEAD>
10:     <TITLE>TV Cop Pasta, Inc. Order Page</TITLE>
11: </HEAD>
12:
13: <BODY>
14: <H1>TV Cop Pasta, Inc. Order Page</H1>
15:
16: The following orders have been placed by customers of TV Cop Pasta, Inc.
17: <P>
18: <CFOUTPUT QUERY="get_orders">
19: <HR>
20: <B>Customer Information:</B><BR>
21: #name#<br>
22: #street_address#<BR>
23: #city#, #state#<P>
24:
25: <B>Product Ordered:</B><BR>
26: #product_ordered# on #date#
27:
28: </CFOUTPUT>
29:
30: </BODY>
31: </HTML>
```

19

ANALYSIS First, notice the FROM line in the query section. It lists two table names, separated by commas, from which you want to pull data. When you select data from two or more tables, every field name used in your query must be prefaced with one of the table names, such as `customers.state` or `orders.date`. This lets SQL know the table in which it will find the specified field.

So, the query in Listing 19.3 is simply selecting several fields from two different tables. But there's more. Note the WHERE clause:

```
WHERE customers.name = orders.ordered_by
```

This line tells SQL that you want to select customer fields only if a particular customer's name appears in the `orders` table. If the customer hasn't placed an order yet, his name, street address, and so on wouldn't be selected by the query.

> **Caution**
>
> When using table joins, the fields compared in the WHERE clause must have the same data type. Comparing a text field to a number field can lead to either errors or unpredictable results, depending on your database application.

This type of table join maintains the relationship you've already built into the two tables. Each order has a specific customer name associated with it.

After the data has been joined by the query, ColdFusion treats it just as it would any other query results. In your <CFOUTPUT> section, you just refer to the field name—no prefix is necessary.

The output from Listing 19.3 would look like this:

OUTPUT

```
- - - - - - - - - - - - - - - - - - - - - - - - - - - - - - - - - - - -
Customer Information:
Ralph Spoilsport
1277 E. First
Goober, CA

Product Ordered:
Ponch and John Ravioli on 6/12


- - - - - - - - - - - - - - - - - - - - - - - - - - - - - - - - - - - -

Customer Information:
Ralph Hamburger
12 Gawk Ct.
Krustville, OK
```

```
Product Ordered:
T.J. Hooker Fettucini on 6/5


- - - - - - - - - - - - - - - - - - - - - - - - - - - - - - - - - -


Customer Information:
Rocky Roccoco
437 Pugnash
Tingly, AR

Product Ordered:
T.J. Hooker Fettucini on 6/11


- - - - - - - - - - - - - - - - - - - - - - - - - - - - - - - - - -


Customer Information:
Nick Danger
87 Punk St.
Boulderdash, CA

Product Ordered:
Jack Lord Rigatoni on 6/12


- - - - - - - - - - - - - - - - - - - - - - - - - - - - - - - - - -


Customer Information:
Nick Danger
87 Punk St.
Boulderdash, CA

Product Ordered:
Jack Lord Rigatoni on 6/12
```

19

> **Tip**
>
> To avoid confusion, the <CFOUTPUT> section in Listing 19.3 displays query results in a linear fashion down the page. After you're familiar with the concept of table joins, you can experiment with using <TABLE> and <CFTABLE> tags to display this type of data.

Note in the output that each order is displayed along with related data from the customers table. If a customer has placed more than one order, you see that customer's information listed more than once.

Understanding SQL Subqueries

As you might expect, a SQL subquery is a `SELECT` within a `SELECT`. In a way, subqueries are similar to table joins, but certain situations may benefit from using one method rather than the other.

Take a look at a couple of TV Cop Pasta's tables in Figures 19.9 and 19.10.

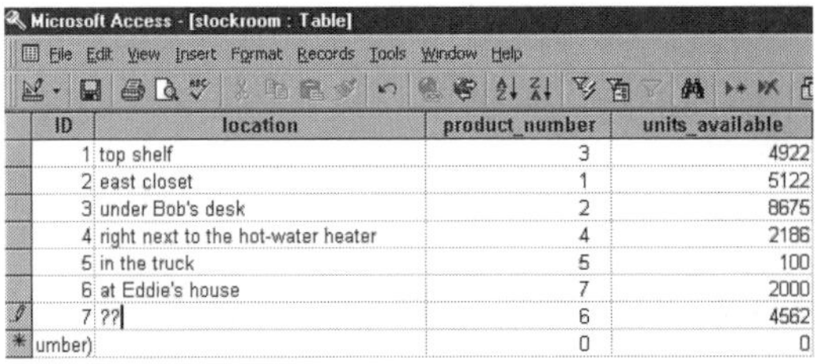

ID	location	product_number	units_available
1	top shelf	3	4922
2	east closet	1	5122
3	under Bob's desk	2	8675
4	right next to the hot-water heater	4	2186
5	in the truck	5	100
6	at Eddie's house	7	2000
7	??	6	4562
umber)		0	0

FIGURE 19.9
TV Cop Pasta's `stockroom` *table, showing product numbers, quantities, and locations of the products in the warehouse.*

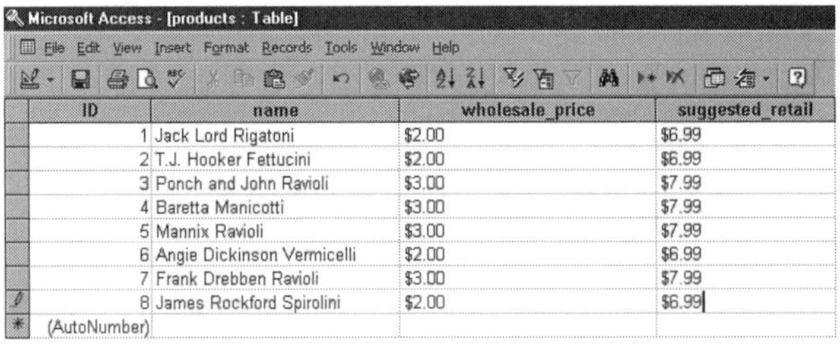

ID	name	wholesale_price	suggested_retail
1	Jack Lord Rigatoni	$2.00	$6.99
2	T.J. Hooker Fettucini	$2.00	$6.99
3	Ponch and John Ravioli	$3.00	$7.99
4	Baretta Manicotti	$3.00	$7.99
5	Mannix Ravioli	$3.00	$7.99
6	Angie Dickinson Vermicelli	$2.00	$6.99
7	Frank Drebben Ravioli	$3.00	$7.99
8	James Rockford Spirolini	$2.00	$6.99
(AutoNumber)			

FIGURE 19.10
TV Cop Pasta's `products` *table, showing the names and prices of each product.*

The design of these two tables reflects a very common way to set up a business database. The `products` table lists all items the company sells, and provides detailed information such as the product name and price. From there, all other tables that refer to an individual product use the item's `ID` number (as in the stockroom table in Figure 19.9) rather than the actual product name. Not only is this easier than typing long names into other tables, recall that it's also more efficient because ColdFusion and other database programs can search number fields much faster than text fields.

Assume that TV Cop Pasta needs a simple Web report of its product holdings. In itself that's a simple task—just query the `stockroom` table and display all results. But to add a twist that will help you understand subqueries, let's assume that TV Cop Pasta wants to display only ravioli products in the report. This is a little trickier because the `stockroom` table doesn't contain any product names—just ID numbers. Take a look at a solution in Listing 19.4.

LISTING 19.4   `ravioli_product_summary.cfm`

```
 1: <CFQUERY NAME="ravioli_products" DATASOURCE="tv_cop_pasta">
 2: SELECT ID, location, units_available FROM stockroom
 3: WHERE ID IN
 4: (SELECT ID FROM products WHERE name LIKE '%Ravioli%')
 5: </CFQUERY>
 6:
 7: <HTML>
 8: <HEAD>
 9: <TITLE>TV Cop Pasta Ravioli Product Summary</TITLE>
10: </HEAD>
11:
12: <H1>TV Cop Pasta Ravioli Product Summary</H1>
13: <HR>
14: <CFOUTPUT QUERY="ravioli_products">
15:
16: <B>Product ID:</B> #ID#<BR>
17: <B>Location:</B> #location#<BR>
18: <B>Units Available:</B> #units_available#<P>
19:
20: </CFOUTPUT>
21:
22: </HTML>
```

ANALYSIS This listing uses two tools to achieve the desired result: a subquery and the IN operator. Recall from the introduction to SQL in Day 4 that IN looks for a specified value in a series or in a list of values. In this case, the list supplied to IN is a subquery, as denoted by the parentheses surrounding it:

```
(SELECT ID FROM products WHERE name LIKE '%Ravioli%')
```

This subquery executes *before* the main SELECT statement. It looks for all product names that contain the text Ravioli and returns the product IDs to the parent query as a list of values.

The parent query, by way of IN, queries the stockroom table for each item on the list of IDs. The results look like Figure 19.11.

Note

Notice the differences between table joins and subqueries. Although they both enable you to work with data from multiple tables, a join maintains data relationships in your <CFOUTPUT> section, whereas a subquery simply uses a common field to find related data in two tables.

19

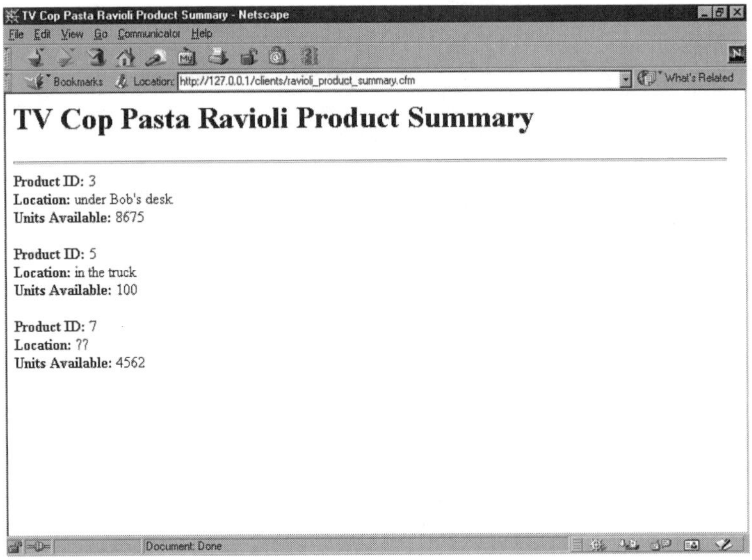

FIGURE 19.11

*The browser results
of Listing 19.4,*
`ravioli_product_
summary.cfm.`

Understanding SQL Views

Most modern database applications, including Microsoft Access, Microsoft SQL Server, Oracle, and so on support a valuable tool called the view.

NEW TERM A *view* is a saved SQL SELECT statement that lives in your database just as a table does. Just like tables, views can be named, queried, and updated.

To understand views, think of them as miniature tables created by queries—sort of like the structures discussed in Day 15, "Using Lists, Structures, and Arrays to Package Data," or like the results of a <CFQUERY>. When you create a view, you give it a name—usually like `view_someview` or `Vsomeview`—and it is permanently stored in your database along with tables, forms, reports, or any other type of information your brand of software supports.

Why would you want to use a view? Recall the earlier section on column aliases in which you used a query to select data on job applicants from Gargantuan's database, as follows:

```
<CFQUERY NAME="get_applicants" DATASOURCE="gargantuan">
SELECT `applicant name` AS name, `"best quality" mentioned in interview`
➥AS quality, `does back-end programming?` AS back_end FROM applicants
</CFQUERY>
```

This isn't a particularly long query, but there are plenty of punctuation marks and delimiters just begging for a typo. If you had to use this query in several pages on your site, you could save some time by using one of three methods:

- You could add the query to your application's `Application.cfm` file (see Day 16, "ColdFusion Client and Session Management"). This would enable you to display the query's results on any page in your site, without supplying the actual query on each page. The drawback is that the query will execute every time *any* page in your application is loaded, whether or not you need it to execute.

- You could save the query as a view named `view_get_applicants` or `Vget_applicants`, and then simply reference the view by name each time you need to access that data set.

- If you use a server-based database application such as SQL Server, Oracle, or Sybase (as opposed to file-based applications like Microsoft Access, dBASE, or FoxPro) you could save the SQL statement as a stored procedure within your database. Stored procedures are covered in the next section.

Views have advantages that go far beyond time-saving techniques. After a view is defined, you can query it just as you would a table. The results will be a subset of the data selected by the view. In the sample query mentioned earlier in the section, this is a pretty valuable feature because you can use the alias names `name`, `quality`, and `back_end` in your queries instead of the lengthier trouble names `applicant name`, `"best quality" mentioned in interview`, and `does back-end programming?`

To see how this works, you'll start by creating a view based on the sample query from this section.

Creating Views

There are two ways to create and store a view. The first way is to create a view in your database software. Different packages have different methods for creating views. In Microsoft Access, for example, you can simply create a query by using the automated Query Builder. Access considers a query the same thing as a view.

However, for a query that uses column aliases like the earlier example , it's actually a little easier to define the view by using the second method—using an SQL statement in a ColdFusion template page.

19

Note

This type of template page is not one that you would use as part of an application. It is designed to be loaded only once—to create a view—and then either deleted or stored somewhere out of your Web server path.

To add the column-alias query as a view in the gargantuan datasource, I used a page like Listing 19.5 to define the view Vget_applicants.

LISTING 19.5   Creating a View from a ColdFusion Template

```
 1: <CFQUERY NAME="get_applicants" DATASOURCE="gargantuan">
 2: CREATE VIEW Vget_applicants AS
 3: SELECT `applicant name` AS name,
 4:        `"best quality" mentioned in interview` AS quality,
 5:        `does back-end programming?` AS back_end
 6: FROM applicants
 7: </CFQUERY>
 8:
 9: <HTML>
10: Your view has been defined.
11: </HTML>
```

ANALYSIS   In the listing, the line that actually creates the view is

```
CREATE VIEW Vget_applicants AS
```

The SQL statement that follows will be saved in Gargantuan's database as the view Vget_applicants.

Tip

Although you can name views anything you like, it's a good idea to use a lowercase or uppercase v as a prefix. That makes it easy to distinguish view names from table names. This method is a general standard used by SQL programmers, so if someone else has to view your code later, she'll know what you were doing.

The text after the <CFQUERY> section is simply a confirmation message to let me know that things went the way I hoped they would.

After creating this page, I run it *once*, and only once, to permanently create the view in Gargantuan's database. Once the view exists, there's no reason to use this page again—if I accessed it more than once I'd usually get an error stating that the view already exists, depending on my database app. Because Microsoft Access treats views as queries, I can actually open the database file and see the results under the Query tab, as shown in Figure 19.12.

FIGURE 19.12

Microsoft Access saves views as queries.

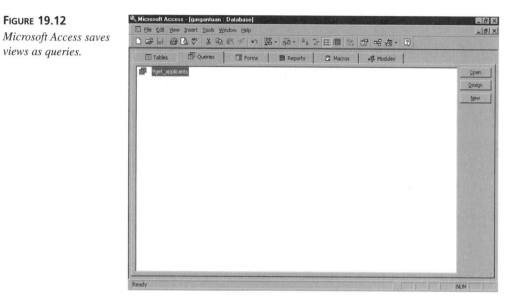

When I click the name of the query (view), I see something that looks a lot like the original applicants table, only the troublesome field names are now displayed as their aliases, as shown in Figure 19.13.

19

FIGURE 19.13

In many database applications, views can be browsed in the same way as tables.

name	quality	back_end
Buddy Bradley	great management skills	☑
Artie Fufkin	assumes responsibility for the faults of othe	☐
Lee Morgan	doesn't bring home problems to work	☑
Johnny Ace	loves to take chances	☑
Barney	has been sober 11 months	☐
Danni Ashe	uninhibited	☑
Don van Vliet	thinks "outside the box"	☑
Richard Hoaglund	trusts no one	☑
Bob Neuwirth	good at spotting trends	☐
Kevin Mitnick	doesn't need a mouse	☑
Suzie Anthony	fights for what she believes in	☐
McKinley Morganfielc	always stays on the "sunny side"	☑
Linda Bowles	hates slackers	☑
		☐

This is a key concept to understand because just as the view *looks* like a table, it can also be accessed just as a table would be accessed; for example, by a query.

> **Note**
>
> A view is generated dynamically—that is, when you reference a view, it automatically reflects any changes that have been made to the table queried by the view.

Accessing Views

After a view has been defined, it can be accessed in a standard query, like this

```
<CFQUERY NAME="get_applicants" DATASOURCE="gargantuan">
SELECT name, quality, back_end FROM Vget_applicants
</CFQUERY>
```

This has obvious advantages over the lengthier column-alias query, and it produces the same results. You can also use WHERE clauses or any other standard SQL tools to access a view, as follows:

```
<CFQUERY NAME="get_applicants" DATASOURCE="gargantuan">
SELECT * FROM Vget_applicants WHERE name LIKE 'B%'
</CFQUERY>
```

This query returns a subset of all records retrieved originally by the view, or more specifically, all names starting with B.

Introducing Stored Procedures

A *stored procedure* is a series of SQL statements that are saved within a database and can be recalled by ColdFusion (or other SQL-enabled applications) when the need arises.

> **Note**
>
> Currently, only server-based database programs support stored procedures. File-based applications such as Access, FoxPro, dBASE, and Paradox do not.

The actual mechanics of stored procedures get into some pretty heady stuff for a 21-day tutorial, but it's a good idea to understand the basic concept. If you someday find yourself working on a ColdFusion server that uses an Oracle or Sybase server as a datasource, you might want to do some further research into stored procedures.

In many ways, stored procedures are a lot like views, although they can accommodate much more sophisticated SQL functions. For example, the TV Cop Pasta application might use a stored procedure when a user purchases a product online. The procedure might perform a variety of functions (see the following examples), but all of them would be accessed by a single name.

- Check the `stockroom` table to see whether the specified product is on TV Cop Pasta's shelves. If the product isn't available, the procedure might automatically place an entry in the `back_orders` table to show that this product is in demand.

- If the product is available, the procedure might query the `customers` table to see whether the user is a return customer. If the user doesn't appear in the `customers` table, the procedure might add the user's form data to the `customers` table.

- After the customer's data has been established, the stored procedure might place it into the `orders` table along with data for the product ordered.

- When the order is successfully processed, the procedure might subtract 1 from the value in the `stockroom` table to reflect that one of the items has been sold.

Note

If you don't have the access or knowledge necessary to create stored procedures, be assured that all the automated tasks described in this section can also be implemented by using standard SQL statements and the `<CFIF>` tag.

After a stored procedure is defined in your database software, it is accessed with a special tag called `<CFSTOREDPROC>` or, alternatively, by a `<CFQUERY>`.

Stored procedures are extremely powerful and efficient tools, but they require a very extensive knowledge of your database software and of advanced SQL techniques.

19

Summary

Advanced SQL techniques are the key to getting the most from your datasources. By using tools such as aggregate functions and SQL views, you can create templates that do much more than blindly output records from a database.

For example, SQL's aggregate functions enable you to report "data about the data," such as automatically computing numeric averages, finding maximum and minimum values, and counting the number of records returned by a query. SQL's column alias feature enables you to work with databases that use field names that would otherwise be illegal in ColdFusion—possibly databases used by a client.

Table joins and subqueries enable you to process data from more than one table in a single query. With table joins, relationships between tables can be preserved in `<CFOUTPUT>` sections, such as relating a table of product orders to customer shipping data from another table. Subqueries function as `SELECT` statements within `SELECT` statements, giving you the ability to perform a query on a table and then perform a second query using results returned by the first.

Finally, SQL views and stored procedures offer two ways to store bits of SQL as part of your database file. These can be recalled later in ColdFusion templates, making them excellent timesaving devices that can greatly simplify your code.

Q&A

Q When I create a column alias, is it saved anywhere?

A No. Column aliases are relative to the template file in which they're created. To save a column alias so that it can be referenced throughout your applications, use a table view.

Q Why do I get SQL errors when I use aggregate functions?

A Some aggregate functions will work only with the number data type and will return errors if they encounter a text field. Check your data types carefully before using aggregate functions.

Q When I use a table join, why don't I have to use the table prefixes in my `<CFOUTPUT>` section?

A Because the join does this for you. `orders.name` becomes `name`, and so on. ColdFusion returns the results of a join exactly as it would the results from any standard SQL query.

Q How many tables can I join in a single query?

A In theory, some applications will let you join data from up to 23 tables. In practice, however, more than three or four joins on medium-to-large sized tables will start to tax your server's processor.

Q After I've created a view, can I use SQL's `UPDATE` and `INSERT` commands to change data that appears in the view?

A Yes, but remember that you are only changing the records selected by the view, not all the records in the original table.

Q Stored procedures sound pretty cool. Where can I learn more?

A Check your database software's docs for details on defining and testing stored procedures. In ColdFusion's documentation, look for the discussion of the `<CFSTOREDPROC>` tag.

Workshop

The workshop provides quiz and exercise questions to test your understanding of today's material. Answers to quiz questions can be found in Appendix A at the back of the text.

Quiz

1. Name at least three control characters that can give ColdFusion problems when used in variable names.

2. When defining column aliases, what character is used to delimit the original field name?

3. Name the two types of SQL functions. One of them isn't discussed in this book. Why?

4. Why is it preferable to relate two database tables by a numeric field such as ID instead of a text field?

5. Why does the subquery example in this chapter use the IN operator?

6. Name two ways to create a table view.

7. What type of database software do you need to use stored procedures?

Exercises

1. Create a database table that contains the names and ages of you, your family, and your friends. Design a template page that uses aggregate functions to report the average age, and the maximum and minimum ages.

2. Create a database table that simulates a table that might be presented to you by a client. Be sure to use lots of illegal characters in the field names. Create a view that uses column aliases to select all records in the table, and then design a simple template page that will query the view, rather than the table itself.

3. Create a second table that is related to the first by its ID field. Use both column aliases and a table join to present data from both tables in a single report page.

19

DAY 20

Using ColdFusion for E-Commerce Applications

Because ColdFusion can ably handle dynamic content, math computations, and relatively sophisticated program flow, it's ideal for building e-commerce sites. Many of the concepts you've learned in the last 19 days will come into play during today's discussion as you learn how to build store sites that are easy to navigate and transaction systems that transmit data securely. This lesson covers

- Considering prewritten commerce applications
- Planning an e-commerce site
- The four elements of online stores
- Online transaction methods

Considering Prewritten Commerce Applications

The goal of today's lesson is to acquaint you with the ColdFusion concepts behind e-commerce, but it's also important to know that you don't have to redesign the wheel when creating a commerce-ready site. As Web stores have become fairly common, many third-party developers have stepped in by providing complete applications that are written for ColdFusion.

To see some examples of prewritten applications available for free or for purchase, point your browser to Allaire's Web site and check out the application gallery:

```
http://www.allaire.com/developer/gallery/index.cfm
```

There you'll find several store applications ranging in sophistication and price. Most of the better applications feature an "example" link that will show you how the store looks in action.

If you're considering using one of these applications, rather than building your own, it's important to consider a few factors:

- What version of ColdFusion Server is required by the application?
- What are the server requirements? Does the Web server need HTTPS compatibility, for example?
- How is the store administered? For example, is it easy to add new products and product categories?
- Does the store layout suit you or your client's products?
- Does the store preserve user data by using cookies or client-state management techniques? (See Day 16, "Using ColdFusion Client and Session Management," for more on this subject.)
- Does the store's developer offer support?

Note

If you're considering using a prewritten app, rather than designing your own, don't let that keep you from finishing today's lesson. The concepts discussed here will help you understand what your chosen app is doing behind the scenes, and will be of particular value if you want to troubleshoot or customize the application on your own.

Planning an E-Commerce Site

As with any ColdFusion application, it's a good idea to start your e-commerce site by building a clear vision of what the site will and won't do, as well as how visitors will navigate your pages.

E-commerce sites typically have four basic elements:

- An administration section. The admin pages enable you or your client to enter, edit, or remove product data and to create categories by which products are organized.

- A catalog section. The catalog controls how users browse your products and what item information is presented.

- A shopping cart. The cart enables users to build a list of products they order as they browse your site. The cart must retain the list as the user moves from page to page. When the user is finished browsing and ordering, the contents of the cart are sent to the transaction section where they're totaled and processed.

- A transaction section. As described later in today's lesson, the transaction pages are where selected items are summarized and the customer enters billing and shipping data. If your site will use a secure transaction method, all transaction pages that send data to your server will need to use a secure protocol.

Because all these elements are interrelated, you can see why it's a good idea to know in advance what each will contain. For example, if your catalog will display a description of each product, you'll need to include a form element in the administration section to allow the store's administrator to input this information to the database.

The following three sections examine each of these elements in detail.

Tip	You might want to read through the next four sections in their entirety before planning your own store. It's important to understand all elements of an e-commerce site before mapping out one that suits you or your client's products.

Constructing an Administration Section

20

The administration section of your site is where you or the store's administrator will enter specific information on products (name, quantity in stock, shipping weight, stock number, and so on). From a developer's standpoint, a store's administration section is nothing more than a series of forms designed to input data into a database. By using form techniques discussed in Days 7, "Changing the Contents of a Database with ColdFusion," and 12, "Using Advanced Form Techniques to Manage Input," you can create an interface that's easy for you or other administrators to navigate.

Remember the database of Elvis movies that has popped up throughout this book? To keep things simple, assume that you're creating a store that will sell Elvis videos. You'll use my existing database as a starting point, and then create an administration section to enable you to enter new Elvis movies as they become available.

Because the existing database doesn't contain fields for things like prices, descriptions, and so on, you'll need to start by adding these. I made a copy of the original database, named it `elvis_store.mdb`, and opened it in Microsoft Access' Design view to enter information for the new fields. It looks like Figure 20.1.

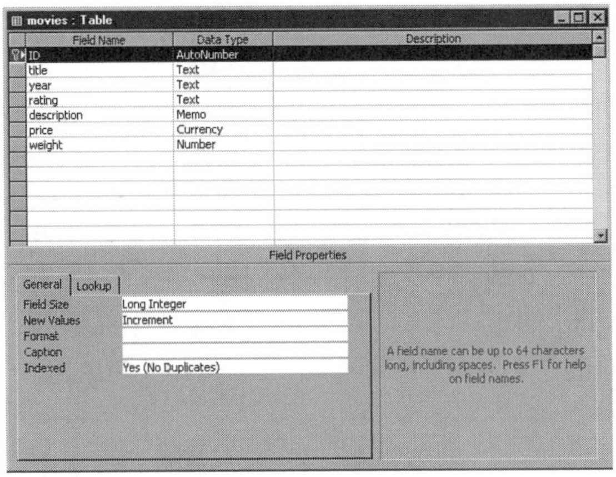

FIGURE 20.1

Adding product fields to the "movies" table in `elvis_store.mdb`.

Note the data types in Figure 20.1. Description is a memo field because it's likely to contain more than the 255 characters my software allows for a text type field. Price uses the currency data type, and Weight is set to contain a number. The example uses whole numbers, but if you want to include weights like 1.5, use the double type to specify a decimal.

Next, I'll define this database as a new datasource in ColdFusion Administrator and call it `elvis_store`. When that's complete, I have a working datasource and can start designing an administration page to put new data into it. If you've been reading this book in sequential order, then you've already done something like this in Day 12.

My page allows administrators to add and edit products in the database. In a Web browser, it looks like Figure 20.2.

FIGURE 20.2

The admin page for the Elvis store.

FIGURE 20.2

The admin page for the Elvis store.

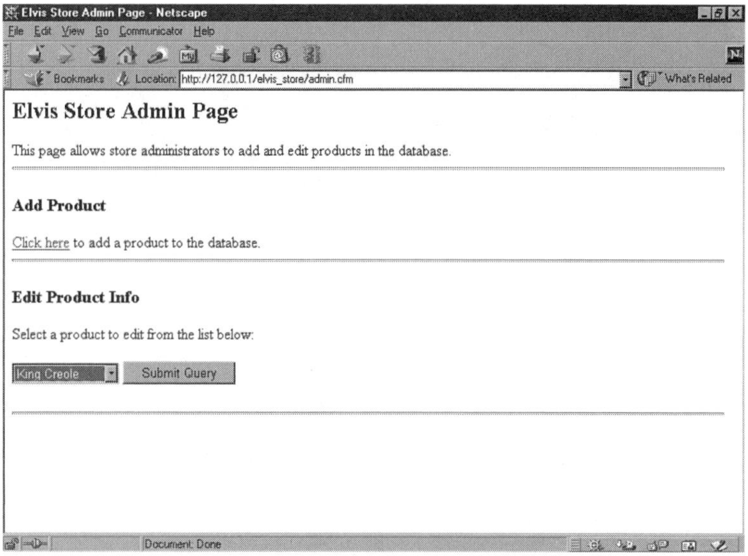

The code I used to produce the admin page is shown in Listing 20.1.

LISTING 20.1 admin.cfm

```
 1: <CFQUERY NAME="get_movies" DATASOURCE="elvis_store">
 2: SELECT * FROM movies
 3: </CFQUERY>
 4:
 5: <HTML>
 6:
 7: <TITLE>Elvis Store Admin Page</TITLE>
 8:
 9: <H2>Elvis Store Admin Page</H2>
10:
11: This page allows store administrators to add and edit products
    ➥in the database.
12:
13: <HR>
14:
15: <H3>Add Product</H3>
16: <A HREF="admin_edit.cfm">Click here</A> to add a product to the database.
17:
18: <HR>
19:
20: <H3>Edit Product Info</H3>
21: Select a product to edit from the list below:<BR>
22:
```

20

continues

LISTING 20.1   continued

```
23: <FORM ACTION="admin_edit.cfm" METHOD="post">
24:
25:     <SELECT NAME="ID">
26:
27:     <CFOUTPUT QUERY="get_movies">
28:         <OPTION VALUE="#ID#">#title#</OPTION>
29:     </CFOUTPUT>
30:
31:     </SELECT>
32:
33:     <INPUT TYPE="submit">
34:
35: </FORM>
36: <HR>
37:
38: </HTML>\
```

This page calls for an ACTION page titled admin_edit.cfm to process input. The page looks like Figure 20.3, and the code is illustrated in Listing 20.2.

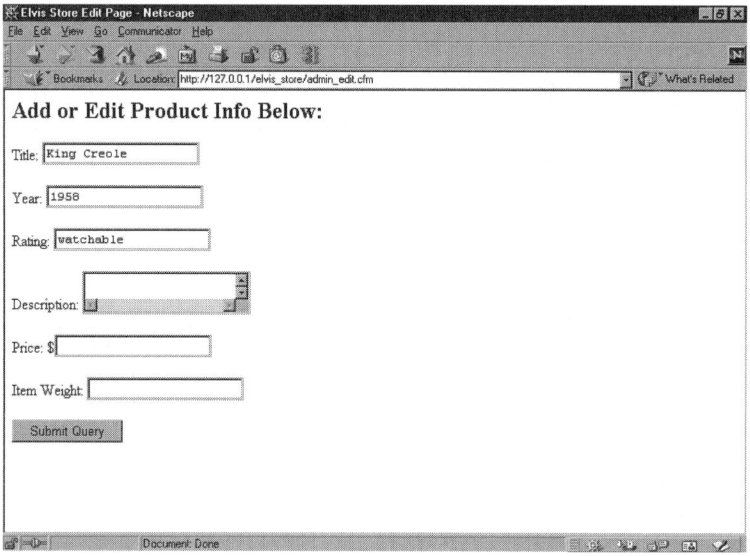

FIGURE 20.3

Editing product data in the Elvis store.

LISTING 20.2   admin_edit.cfm

```
1: <CFIF IsDefined("ID")>
2:
3:     <CFSET to_do = "edit">
```

```
 4:
 5: <CFELSE>
 6:
 7:     <CFSET to_do = "add">
 8:
 9: </CFIF>
10:
11: <CFIF to_do IS "edit">
12:
13:     <CFQUERY NAME="get_movies" DATASOURCE="elvis_store">
14:         SELECT * FROM movies WHERE ID=#form.ID#
15:     </CFQUERY>
16:
17: </CFIF>
18:
19: <HTML>
20:
21: <HEAD>
22:     <TITLE>Elvis Store Edit Page</TITLE>
23:
24: </HEAD>
25:
26: <H2>Add or Edit Product Info Below:</H2>
27:
28: <FORM ACTION="admin_update.cfm" METHOD="post">
29:
30: Title: <INPUT TYPE="text" NAME="title"
31:
32: <CFIF to_do IS "edit">
33:     VALUE="<CFOUTPUT>#get_movies.title#</CFOUTPUT>"
34: </CFIF>
35:
36: >
37:
38: <P>
39:
40: Year: <INPUT TYPE="text" NAME="year"
41:
42: <CFIF to_do IS "edit">
43:     VALUE="<CFOUTPUT>#get_movies.year#</CFOUTPUT>"
44: </CFIF>
45:
46: >
47:
48: <P>
49:
50: Rating: <INPUT TYPE="text" NAME="rating"
51:
52: <CFIF to_do IS "edit">
53:     VALUE="<CFOUTPUT>#get_movies.rating#</CFOUTPUT>"
54: </CFIF>
```

20

continues

LISTING 20.2 continued

```
55:
56: >
57:
58: <P>
59:
60:
61:
62: Description: <TEXTAREA NAME="description">
63: <CFIF to_do IS "edit">
64:     <CFOUTPUT>#get_movies.description#</CFOUTPUT>
65: </CFIF>
66: </TEXTAREA>
67:
68:
69: <P>
70:
71: <P>
72:
73: Price: $<INPUT TYPE="text" NAME="price"
74:
75: <CFIF to_do IS "edit">
76:     VALUE="<CFOUTPUT>#get_movies.price#</CFOUTPUT>"
77: </CFIF>
78:
79: >
80:
81: <P>
82:
83: Item Weight: <INPUT TYPE="text" NAME="weight"
84:
85: <CFIF to_do IS "edit">
86:     VALUE="<CFOUTPUT>#get_movies.weight#</CFOUTPUT>"
87: </CFIF>
88:
89: >
90:
91:
92: <CFIF to_do IS "edit">
93:     <INPUT TYPE="hidden" NAME="ID" VALUE="<CFOUTPUT>#get_movies.
        ➥ID#</CFOUTPUT>">
94: </CFIF>
95:
96: <P>
97:
98: <INPUT TYPE="submit">
99:
100: </FORM>
101:
102: </HTML>
```

Next you'll need an ACTION page for the form. It will need to either INSERT or UPDATE a record depending on the administrator's selection in the form. Mine looks like Listing 20.3.

LISTING 20.3   admin_update.cfm

```
<CFIF IsDefined("ID")>

    <CFSET to_do = "edit">

<CFELSE>

    <CFSET to_do = "add">

</CFIF>

<CFIF to_do IS "edit">

    <CFUPDATE DATASOURCE="elvis_store" TABLENAME="movies"
FORMFIELDS="title,year,rating,description,price,weight">

</CFIF>

<CFIF to_do IS "add">

    <CFINSERT DATASOURCE="elvis_store" TABLENAME="movies"
FORMFIELDS="title,year,rating,description,price,weight">

</CFIF>

<HTML>

<HEAD>
    <TITLE>Product Information Updated</TITLE>
</HEAD>

<BODY>
The information for product <CFOUTPUT>#form.title#</CFOUTPUT> has been
➥updated.<P>

<A HREF="admin.cfm">Return to Admin Page</A>
</BODY>
</HTML>
```

There isn't much to this ACTION page. It simply checks to see whether the variable to_do is set to "edit" or "add", performs the requested INSERT or UPDATE, and then alerts the user that the task is complete.

If you've been following along, you now have an administration section for your site.

20

> You don't want just any user to be able to edit your store's data, hence, administration pages should always be password protected on your server. This process varies depending on your Web server/operating system combination. You can also use ColdFusion to protect your admin pages by storing username and password combinations in a database and then checking user input against the contents before administration pages are displayed. See your ColdFusion documentation for details on the <CFAUTHENTICATE> tag.

Constructing a Catalog

Although the administration section was created using basic form techniques, the catalog section gets a little more complex. It needs to accomplish two tasks: It must display products to the user and save "ordered" items in a shopping cart so they can later be totaled when the user checks out.

Creating a Display Page for Your Products

Start by creating a page that will display all movies in the database. I used a pretty simple one, as shown in Figure 20.4.

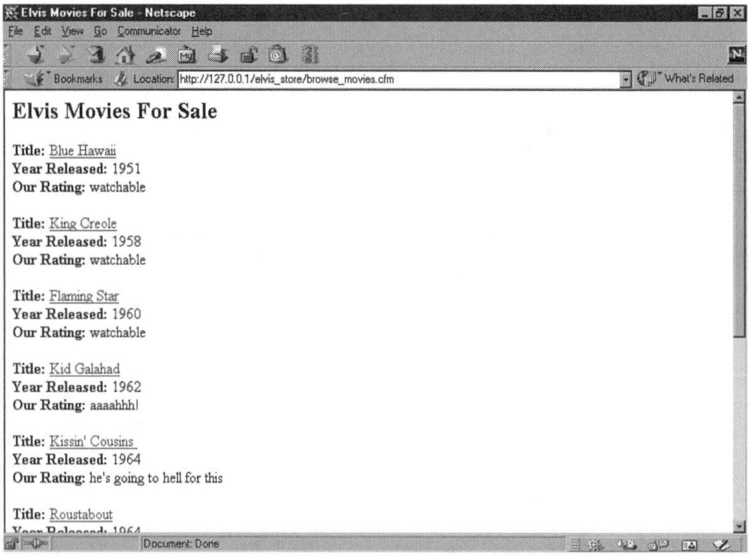

FIGURE 20.4

Displaying products in the catalog.

Elvis Movies For Sale

Title: Blue Hawaii
Year Released: 1951
Our Rating: watchable

Title: King Creole
Year Released: 1958
Our Rating: watchable

Title: Flaming Star
Year Released: 1960
Our Rating: watchable

Title: Kid Galahad
Year Released: 1962
Our Rating: aaaahhh!

Title: Kissin' Cousins
Year Released: 1964
Our Rating: he's going to hell for this

Title: Roustabout
Year Released: 1964

The code for Figure 20.4 is pretty straightforward by using the <CFOUTPUT> tag. It simply displays some of the data for each movie, and makes the title for each film a link to a secondary "details" page that you'll construct in a moment. First, take a look at the code that produced Figure 20.4, as shown in Listing 20.4.

LISTING 20.4   browse_movies.cfm

```
 1: <CFQUERY NAME="movies" DATASOURCE="elvis_store">
 2: SELECT ID, title, year, rating FROM movies ORDER BY year
 3: </CFQUERY>
 4:
 5:
 6:
 7: <HTML>
 8: <HEAD>
 9:    <TITLE>Elvis Movies For Sale</TITLE>
10: </HEAD>
11:
12: <BODY>
13:
14: <H2>Elvis Movies For Sale</H2>
15:
16: <CFOUTPUT QUERY="movies">
17:
18:    <B>Title:</B> <A HREF="details.cfm?ID=#ID#">#title#</A><BR>
19:    <B>Year Released:</B> #year#<BR>
20:    <B>Our Rating:</B> #rating#<P>
21:
22: </CFOUTPUT>
23:
24:
25: </BODY>
26: </HTML>
```

ANALYSIS The query on lines 1-3 simply searches the database for all movies and orders them by year. If you want to display your products alphabetically by name, numerically by ID, etc., you could instead use the corresponding field name in the ORDER BY clause on line 2.

The <CFOUTPUT> section on lines 16-22 displays the records returned by the query, but I've added a trick that should be familiar to you from previous lessons. The code on line 18 makes the title of an item a clickable link to a "details" page that will show just that item, with complete details including description, price, and so on. The page I created looks like Figure 20.5.

20

FIGURE 20.5

The detail page for the video "Blue Hawaii."

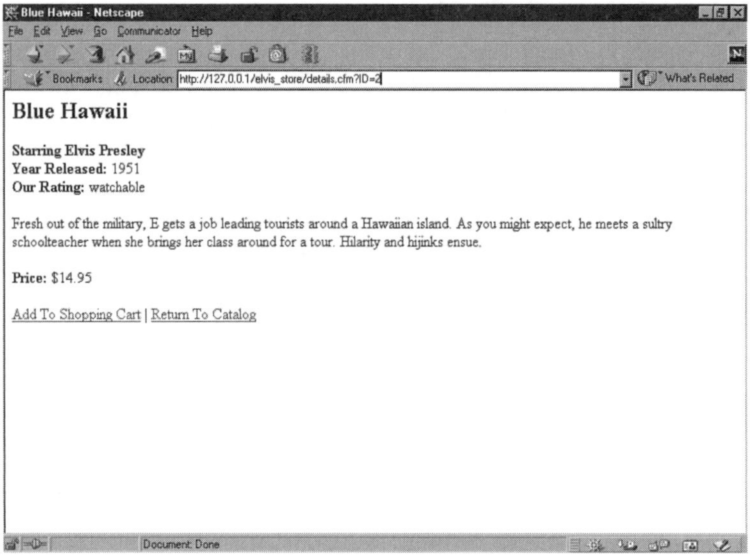

Blue Hawaii

Starring Elvis Presley
Year Released: 1951
Our Rating: watchable

Fresh out of the military, E gets a job leading tourists around a Hawaiian island. As you might expect, he meets a sultry schoolteacher when she brings her class around for a tour. Hilarity and hijinks ensue.

Price: $14.95

Add To Shopping Cart | Return To Catalog

> **Tip**
>
> When building a catalog, it's a good idea to have some data in your table of products so that you can ensure that it is displaying properly. For example, I used the admin pages created in the last section to fill in the price, description, and weight fields in my database.

The code that produced Figure 20.5 is still nothing out of the ordinary. It requires an ID (passed in the URL by the previous page) to retrieve and display data for a single record. The code is illustrated in Listing 20.5.

LISTING 20.5 details.cfm

```
1: <CFQUERY NAME="movie" DATASOURCE="elvis_store">
2:     SELECT * FROM movies WHERE ID=#ID#
3: </CFQUERY>
4:
5:
6:
7: <HTML>
8:
9: <CFOUTPUT QUERY="movie">
10:
11: <HEAD>
12:     <TITLE>#title#</TITLE>
```

```
13: </HEAD>
14:
15: <BODY>
16:
17: <H2>#title#</H2>
18:
19: <B>Starring Elvis Presley</B><BR>
20: <B>Year Released:</B> #year#<BR>
21: <B>Our Rating:</B> #rating#<P>
22:
23: #description#<P>
24:
25: <B>Price:</B> #DollarFormat(price)#<P>
26:
27: <A HREF="cart.cfm?ID=#ID#&action=add">Add To Shopping Cart</A> | <A
    ➥HREF="browse_movies.cfm">Return To Catalog</A>
28:
29: </CFOUTPUT>
30:
31:
32: </BODY>
33: </HTML>
```

ANALYSIS Listing 20.5 is pretty standard output-and-display, although I did use ColdFusion's `DollarFormat()` function on line 25 to control the way the price field is displayed.

On line 27 are two links, one of which will return the user to the main catalog page browse.cfm, and another that will direct the user to the shopping cart page you'll design in the next section. This latter link also appends a couple of variables to the URL, ID and ACTION, which will be required by cart.cfm.

Constructing a Shopping Cart

If your store is designed to sell only one quantity of just one product, you don't need a shopping cart at all. Such a site would only need to pass details on the selected item to the transaction page where the actual order would take place. In the real world of e-commerce, however, it's pretty likely that you'll want to give users the ability to select more than one product, and that's where the shopping cart comes in.

As a developer, you need to give your application the capability to "remember" products the user has selected so that they can be totaled at the end of the user's browsing session. One way to do this—not a particularly good one—would be to pass data for each selected item in the URL to each subsequent page. This would do the trick, but it would be a coding nightmare, and it would make certain features (such as deleting items from the cart) very difficult to achieve.

20

The solution is to use ColdFusion's client and session management, covered in Day 16's lesson. This enables you to create a session variable to hold the contents of the user's cart. Because the variable is temporarily stored on the ColdFusion server, you don't need to pass anything in the URL's of your pages—you simply read and write to the variable as necessary.

Recall that, to use session management, you first have to create a special file called Application.cfm to enable session variables throughout your application. The example in Listing 20.6 *must* be placed in the same directory as your store.

LISTING 20.6 Application.cfm

```
1: <CFAPPLICATION  NAME="elvis_store"
2:                 SESSIONMANAGEMENT="yes">
```

> **Tip**
>
> Listing 20.6 doesn't supply a TIMEOUT value for session management, so ColdFusion will default to 20 minutes. Any data your shopping cart saves in a session variable will be available for 20 minutes—plenty of time for our sample store. However, if your store contains lots of products or if you expect users to browse for long periods of time, you might want to add a higher value.

With session management enabled, you can now set a variable such as session.cart to contain details on a product the user adds to her shopping cart. This data will then be available to any page in your application, without having to send it in a URL or form field.

But, because the cart will hold more than one item, you need the ability to add and remove elements from the variable value. To do this, you can define session.cart as an array, that special type of variable we covered in Day 15, "Using Lists, Structures, and Arrays to Package Data." Recall that arrays can store complex data sets in much the same way that a database table stores data. For example, if you define session.cart as a two-dimensional array, you can store several details about each product:

```
session.cart[1][1] = item_1_title
session.cart[1][2] = item_1_price
session.cart[1][3] = item_1_weight
session.cart[1][4] = item_1_ID
```

A second item added to the cart would be defined as

```
session.cart[2][1] = item_2_title
session.cart[2][2] = item_2_price
session.cart[2][3] = item_2_weight
session.cart[2][4] = item_2_ID
```

By using an array, rather than a plain variable, you can add and remove items from the shopping cart with relative ease. You can also display the contents of the cart by using <CFLOOP> to run through the contents of your array. (You did this with ColdFusion lists in Day 15.)

The code for cart.cfm is shown in Listing 20.7.

LISTING 20.7   cart.cfm

```
 1: <!---set default action--->
 2:
 3: <CFPARAM NAME="action" DEFAULT="">
 4:
 5: <!---check to see if a cart array exists; define one if not--->
 6:
 7: <CFPARAM NAME="session.cart" DEFAULT="">
 8:
 9: <CFIF IsArray(session.cart) IS "false">
10:     <CFSET session.cart = ArrayNew(2)>
11: </CFIF>
12:
13: <!--if action is add, add selected item to cart array--->
14:
15: <CFIF action IS "add">
16:
17:     <CFQUERY NAME="movie" DATASOURCE="elvis_store" MAXROWS="1">
18:         SELECT ID, title, price, weight FROM movies WHERE ID = #ID#
19:     </CFQUERY>
20:
21:     <CFSET position=ArrayLen(session.cart)+1>
22:
23:
24:
25:     <CFSET session.cart[position][1]="#movie.title#">
26:     <CFSET session.cart[position][2]=#movie.price#>
27:     <CFSET session.cart[position][3]=#movie.weight#>
28:     <CFSET session.cart[position][4]=#movie.ID#>
29:
30: </CFIF>
31:
32: <!---if action is remove, remove item from cart array--->
33:
34: <CFIF action IS "remove_item">
35:
36:     <CFSET ArrayDeleteAt(session.cart, cart_ID)>
37:
38: </CFIF>
39:
40:
```

continues

20

LISTING 20.7   continued

```
41: <!---if action is clear, reset cart array--->
42:
43: <CFIF ACTION IS "clear">
44:
45:     <CFSET ArrayClear(session.cart)>
46:     <H2>Your Shopping Cart is Now Empty</H2>
47:     <A HREF="browse_movies.cfm">Return to Catalog</A>
48:
49: <!---for actions other than clear, display cart contents--->
50:
51: <CFELSE>
52:
53:     <CFPARAM NAME="total_cost" DEFAULT=0>
54:     <CFPARAM NAME="total_weight" DEFAULT=0>
55:
56:     <HTML>
57:
58:     <HEAD>
59:         <TITLE>Contents of Your Shopping Cart</TITLE>
60:
61:     </HEAD>
62:
63:     <H2>Contents of Your Shopping Cart</H2>
64:
65:     Please review all items and totals before proceeding to checkout.
66:
67:     <HR>
68:
69:     <!---loop through values in cart array, displaying each--->
70:
71:     <CFLOOP INDEX="loopcount" From="1" To="#ArrayLen(session.cart)#">
72:
73:         <CFOUTPUT>
74:         Title: #session.cart[loopcount][1]#<BR>
75:         Price: #DollarFormat(session.cart[loopcount][2])#<BR>
76:         Ship Weight: #session.cart[loopcount][3]#<BR>
77:         <A HREF="cart.cfm?action=remove_item&cart_ID=#loopcount#">Remove
           ➥This Item From Cart</A>
78:         <HR>
79:         </CFOUTPUT>
80:
81:         <CFSET total_cost=total_cost+session.cart[loopcount][2]>
82:         <CFSET total_weight=total_weight+(session.cart[loopcount][3])>
83:
84:
85:     </CFLOOP>
86:
87:
```

```
88:      <H3>Totals</H3>
89:
90:      <CFOUTPUT>
91:      Your Total Item Cost: #DollarFormat(total_cost)#<BR>
92:      Your Total Shipping Weight: #total_weight# pounds<BR>
93:      </CFOUTPUT>
94:
95:      <HR>
96:
97:      <CFOUTPUT>
98:
99:      <A HREF="cart.cfm?action=clear">Remove All Items From Your Cart</A> | <A
         ➥HREF="browse_movies.cfm">Return To Catalog</A> | <A
         ➥HREF="checkout.cfm?total_weight=#total_weight#&total_
         ➥cost=#URLEncodedFormat(total_cost)#">Check Out</A>
100:
101:     </CFOUTPUT>
102:
103: </HTML>
104: </CFIF>
```

ANALYSIS Listing 20.7 is a multifunction page that allows three defined actions.
The term `"action"` here doesn't mean a form action (such as
`<FORM ACTION="someactionpage.cfm">`) but rather a variable you create to
tell the cart page what to do.

For example, one of the actions defined in cart.cfm is add (lines 15-30), which is passed
when the user clicks Add To Shopping Cart on an item detail page. The other two actions
are defined on cart.cfm itself and are also passed in URLs—that is, cart.cfm contains
links back to itself to perform remove_item actions (lines 34-38) and clear actions
(lines 43-51). As with the multifunction pages covered in Day 12's forms discussion, this
is a code-saving technique that saves you from having to develop unique pages for each
action.

The following sections look at each action in cart.cfm and explain what the action does.

action IS add (lines 15-30)

Recall that the details page in the catalog uses a link like this to add an item to the cart:

```
<A HREF="cart.cfm?action=add&ID=2">Add To Shopping Cart</A>
```

When cart.cfm receives these parameters, it executes the code within the <CFIF> on line
15. It first runs a query on lines 17-19 to select the product associated with the passed
ID. Next, it finds out how many items currently exist in the cart array session.cart and
adds a value of 1 using <CFSET> to create a new variable, position (line 21). cart.cfm
then appends details on the ordered item to the cart array using <CFSET> tags (lines 25
through 28).

20

Finally, it executes the code between lines 51 and 104—the <CFELSE> section that displays cart contents to the user if the defined action is anything other than clear.

To do this, I've created a <CFLOOP> in lines 71 through 85 that uses an index, loopcount, to display the details of each item in the cart array. The loop tag uses a range like this:

```
FROM="1" TO="#ArrayLen(session.cart)#"
```

The ColdFusion function ArrayLen() returns the number of items in the array, so the loop will display each item until it reaches the last one.

Note that the <CFLOOP> displays each product along with a link to "Remove This Item From Cart" (line 77). This links back to cart.cfm (the current page), but it defines another action (remove) and passes a new variable called cart_ID (line 77), which will contain the specified product's index number in the array. Figure 20.6 shows how cart.cfm looks in a browser.

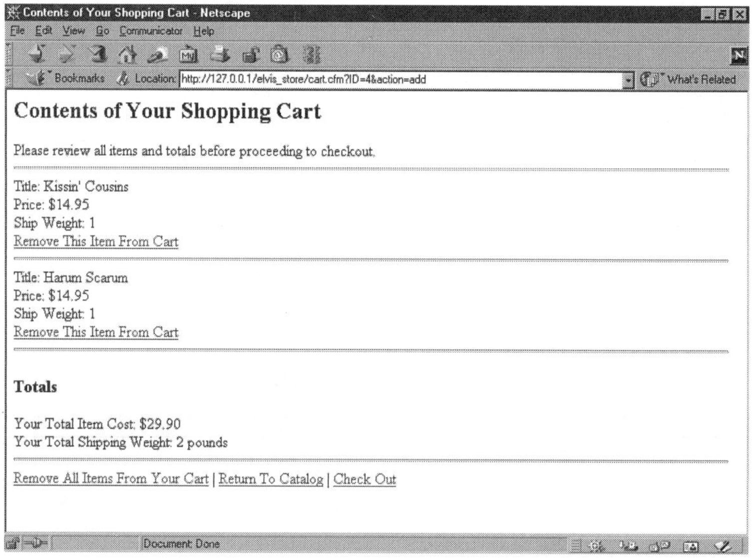

FIGURE 20.6

The cart page enables users to review items, remove them, or completely clear the cart.

The two <CFSET> tags (lines 81 and 82) in the loop section create "total" variables that have each item's price and weight added to them for each increment in the loop. Because these variables won't exist on the first increment of the loop, they have been defined with <CFPARAM> on lines 53 and 54.

Finally, after the loop completes, the variables total_cost and total_weight are displayed to the user (lines 91 and 92). I used the function DollarFormat() with total_price to add a dollar sign and display the value to two decimal places.

> **Tip**
>
> This sample shopping cart has been kept as simple as possible to aid in your understanding of common e-commerce practices. Some features you might consider adding to your own stores are
>
> - Product images
> - The capability to select multiple quantities
> - A search function to search for products by keyword or type
> - A category page to list products by type

action IS remove_item (lines 34-38)

When a user clicks one of the "Remove This Item" links on cart.cfm, the page will be reloaded with a new action (remove). These "Remove" links also pass the variable cart_ID, which specifies the product's position in the array.

The remove action is handled by the <CFIF> section on lines 34 through 38. There, a <CFSET> tag is used to delete the array item corresponding to the cart_ID (not the product field ID, because that would be different).

Finally, the revised cart is displayed to the user via the <CFELSE> statement on lines 51 through 104, just as described in the last section.

action IS clear (lines 43-51)

When the user clicks the link "Remove All Items From Your Cart" at the base of cart.cfm, the page is reloaded with the new action clear. The action is handled by yet another <CFIF> statement, this time on lines 43 through 51.

To clear the session variable that contains the user's cart, I've used the ColdFusion function ArrayClear() on line 45. This leaves the array session.cart defined, but it removes any items that have been placed there.

Finally, the page displays a simple notification to the user that the cart has been cleared, and offers a link back to the product catalog.

20

> **Tip**
>
> Because the sample cart uses session variables that time out, it will *not* retain a user's selected items if the user returns to a site hours or days after a browsing session. Most online stores use similar methods, but if yours requires that user selections be saved, you might add selections to a database using <CFINSERT>, rather than to less-permanent session variables.

Constructing Transaction Pages

When a user clicks the "Check Out" link on cart.cfm, he is taken to a new page called checkout.cfm, and the variables total_cost and total_weight are passed in the URL. To summarize this information, and to collect basic user data (not including credit card information, which will be discussed in the next section), I created a page called checkout.cfm, as illustrated in Figure 20.7.

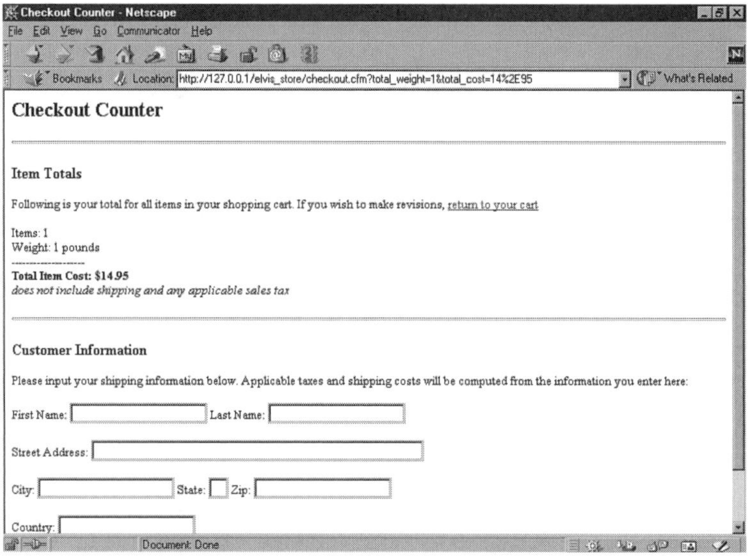

FIGURE 20.7

The checkout page summarizes purchases and collects basic user data that doesn't require heavy security.

The code for checkout.cfm is shown in Listing 20.8.

LISTING 20.8 checkout.cfm

```
 1: <HTML>
 2:
 3: <HEAD>
 4:
 5: <TITLE>Checkout Counter</TITLE>
 6:
 7: </HEAD>
 8:
 9: <H2>Checkout Counter</H2>
10: <HR>
11:
12: <H3>Item Totals</H3>
13:
```

```
14: Following is your total for all items in your shopping cart. If you wish
    ➥to make revisions, <A HREF="cart.cfm">return to your cart</A><P>
15:
16: <CFOUTPUT>
17:
18: Items: #ArrayLen(session.cart)#<BR>
19: Weight: #total_weight# pounds<BR>
20:
21: -------------------<BR>
22:
23: <B>Total Item Cost: #DollarFormat(total_cost)#</B><BR>
24: <I>does not include shipping and any applicable sales tax</I><P>
25:
26: </CFOUTPUT>
27:
28: <HR>
29:
30: <H3>Customer Information</H3>
31:
32: Please input your shipping information below. Applicable taxes and shipping
    ➥costs will be computed from the information you enter here:
33:
34: <FORM ACTION="checkout_process.cfm" METHOD="post">
35:
36: <CFOUTPUT>
37:
38: <INPUT TYPE="hidden" NAME="total_cost" VALUE="#total_cost#">
39: <INPUT TYPE="hidden" NAME="total_weight" VALUE="#total_weight#">
40:
41: </CFOUTPUT>
42:
43: First Name: <INPUT TYPE="text" NAME="first_name"> Last Name:
    ➥<INPUT TYPE="text" NAME="last_name"><P>
44: Street Address: <INPUT TYPE="text" NAME="street_address" SIZE="50"><P>
45: City: <INPUT TYPE="text" NAME="city"> State: <INPUT TYPE="text"
    ➥NAME="state" SIZE="2"> Zip: <INPUT TYPE="text" NAME="zip"><BR>
46: Country: <INPUT TYPE="text" NAME="country"><P>
47:
48: <INPUT TYPE="submit">
49: </FORM>
50:
51: </HTML>
```

20

Caution

The FORM ACTION specified in line 34 of Listing 20.8 links to an unsecured page. You'll want to leave it this way for testing purposes, but will need to change it to a secure link (such as https://some_server/some_processing _page) when your store goes live. You'll learn more about secure links in the following sections.

ANALYSIS Compared to the heavy coding you learned in the last section, transaction pages are a breeze. Listing 20.8 simply displays the totals passed by `cart.cfm` and uses a form to collect user data (lines 34-49). It's important to get this data before displaying a final total, because you'll need the user's state and/or ZIP Code to compute taxes and shipping costs later. The form also passes two hidden fields on lines 38 and 39 containing shipping and price totals.

The form uses an `ACTION` page called `checkout.cfm`, which will perform the actual machinations necessary to place an order. At this point in your application, you have collected several pieces of information to work with:

- An array variable, `session.cart`, which contains the title, price, weight, and product ID for each item selected by the user
- Two variables, `total_cost` and `total_weight`, containing data to be used in the transaction
- User data including a full name and address

It's time to take a pause from coding and consider what your store will do with the data you've collected. There are several options available, each depending on your budget, the capabilities of your server, and you or your merchant's methods of accepting payment.

Understanding E-Commerce Transaction Types

To decide how to complete your application, it's necessary to first consider the last element—the point at which the order is placed, or the *transaction*. Transaction methods range from secure Web forms that accept customer billing information and automatically set up product delivery, to less technical methods such as fax-back or call-back orders. Sites that employ the latter might lack flexibility and customer convenience, but they can still be sufficient to suit smaller budgets or sites that sell only a few, inexpensive products.

The following sections discuss the most common transaction types used with e-commerce sites.

Secure Web Transactions

If you've ordered products online from Web outlets such as Amazon.com or CDNow.com, you've participated in a secure Web transaction. Secure transactions employ special security measures to send the customer's information from the customer's computer to the merchant's (or bank's) computer. At the merchant's end, funds are automatically transferred from the customer's card to the merchant's billing account, and the order is automatically scheduled for delivery. Usually the method used to send data securely is some variation of the *SSL* or *HTTPS* protocols.

NEW TERM *SSL (Secure Socket Layer)* and *HTTPS (Secure Hypertext Protocol)* are protocols that enable a user's browser to communicate with a merchant's Web server. When the user submits a form that uses such protocols, the data is encrypted by the user's browser so that it can't be intercepted en route. Both the browser and the merchant's Web server must support the protocol for a secure transaction to take place.

> **Note**
>
> Most Web server packages offer secure links by enabling you to simply specify a link URL as `https://some_server/some_page`. The page that is returned will encrypt all user data sent to the server. Check your Web server documentation or with your Web hosting service for details on using SSL links.

After you have a user's credit-card data, you still need a way to credit a dollar amount to the merchant account. Most often this is done via third-party processing systems such as CyberCash, ICVerify, or ReadyCheck. These for-profit services enable you to send credit information and immediately get back a result code letting you know whether the user's card was successfully debited.

Sites that allow secure transactions are safe and convenient for both the customer and merchant, but they can also demand considerable time and expense to implement and maintain. For example, a store that doesn't already hold a credit-card merchant account with a bank will need to pay to initiate one; merchants who don't have an automated order fulfillment process will need to start one, and so on.

Email Ordering

In email ordering systems, the customer browses a merchant's site, selects some products, and then proceeds to an order form that sends an encrypted email to the merchant. In these systems, the merchant processes the order just as if the customer had visited a physical store by keying the credit card data into a credit-card processor or by completing a debit form.

20

> **Tip**
>
> The `<CFMAIL>` discussed in Day 13, "Using ColdFusion to Handle Email," is a great tool for enabling email orders, although you'll need to use a third-party tool (such as PGP) to encrypt the information sent to the merchant. You'll find several tools on Allaire's Web site that can be used to encrypt the contents of email messages.

As an alternative to sending credit-card data in email, some online stores prefer a simple call-back method, in which a Web form collects a customer's telephone number and sends email to the merchant. The merchant then phones the customer and takes the order. Not a very elegant method, but it might be all that you or your client requires.

> **Note**
>
> Sending credit card data in unencrypted mail is *not* recommended under any circumstances. Email is the Internet's least secure transmission method—unencrypted messages are fairly easy for snoopers to intercept, either in transmission or as they reside in the merchant's mail server.

Print-and-Fax Forms

In this method, the merchant's Web site hosts an order form designed to be printed out by the customer and then faxed to a specified phone number. By today's standards, this method is pretty archaic, but it's still common because it has several advantages: It's simple to implement, it requires no special security, and it's sometimes the only way to process Web orders when the merchant doesn't have a computer on-site. Print-and-fax systems are also offered by some sites as an alternative to online transactions for customers who are hesitant to send credit-card data over the Web.

> **Tip**
>
> ColdFusion applications can greatly enhance print-and-fax order systems. For example, you could use the data generated by `cart.cfm` and `checkout.cfm` to fill in a text form that could then be printed and faxed by the user.

Call-In Orders

Offering a phone number for purchases is by far the least advanced method of order-taking, but know that it's still the preferred method for lots of customers. It's also the easiest to implement, and usually doesn't require the merchant to do anything special to handle Web orders.

Unsecure Web Transactions

This method is mentioned here only so that you can be cautioned *not* to use it. In unsecured transactions, customer billing data is sent to the merchant's server using the standard, unsecure Web protocol—much the same way a form transmits data from user to server. Sending credit card information this way is particularly dangerous because it can allow others to "listen in" on the transaction and possibly extract the customer's data.

Secure transaction methods (such as SSL, introduced previously in today's lesson) are quickly becoming standard features on browsers and Web server software. It just doesn't make sense to take risks with unsecure transactions.

Completing Your Store Application

After you've decided how your store will accept payment and process orders, it's time to return to your sample store.

Space doesn't permit the illustration of all the transaction methods described in the last section, so we'll focus on one of the more common transaction types—the secure Web transaction.

To use this method, you'll need to build two more pages to complete the transaction section.

Your second transaction page, `checkout_process.cfm`, will perform three actions. It will first input the user's shipping data into a new database table, "customers," where it can be retrieved later by the folks who actually do the shipping. Then it will compute the user's shipping and tax from the state and ZIP Code they supplied on `checkout.cfm`. Finally, a form will collect the user's credit-card data and send it to a third and final `ACTION` page.

This final page, `checkout_complete.cfm`, will send information about the user and credit card to a payment processing service like CyberCash.

> **Note**
>
> All payment processing services require that you send special variables containing data on the customer and purchase. The names of these variables and the methods of transfer vary, depending on the service. The example here focuses on CyberCash, whose methods are typical of the industry. Check with your bank or processing service for details on what should be sent to them and how.

20

If the service reports that the transaction was successful, the page will add the user's items to an "orders" table and thank the user for the purchase.

checkout_process.cfm

The first step in completing the user's order is to place her customer data into a database table where it will be stored for shipping purposes. To do this, I created a new table in `elvis_store.mdb` called "customers" and within it created fields corresponding to the customer data passed by the form (`first_name`, `last_name`, `street_address`, `city`, and so on).

Tax and shipping details for your store will depend entirely on your product and how you plan to deliver it to customers. As a simple example of how this might work, assume that my physical store is in California, USA. California state tax only applies when products are shipped to California addresses, so my new page checkout_process.cfm can use pretty simple code to compute the tax to add to the user's total:

```
<CFIF form.state IS "CA">
    <CFSET tax = "total_cost * .0725">
<CFELSE>
    <CFSET tax = 0>
</CFIF>
```

Your mileage will vary depending on your location and local tax code.

Computing the shipping cost is a little more difficult. Depending on how I ship products (U.S. Postal Service, Federal Express, United Parcel Service, and so on), I can have several different shipping rates depending on the ZIP Code to which the product will be shipped. To handle this, I created a new table in my database called "shipping" and defined two fields within it, "zip" and "rate." In these I entered data corresponding to my shipping provider's per-pound rates to each ZIP or country code.

 Tip
> Your shipping service can usually provide you with rates for each ZIP or country code to which you ship. Often these are available in electronic form, making them easy to import into your database application.

Finally, your page needs to collect credit card data from the user. The full code looks like Listing 20.9.

LISTING 20.9 checkout_process.cfm

```
 1: <CFINSERT DATASOURCE="elvis_store" TABLENAME="customers"
    ➥FORMFIELDS="first_name,last_name,street_address,city,state,
    ➥zip,country">
 2:
 3: <CFIF form.state IS "CA">
 4:     <CFSET tax = form.total_cost * ".0725">
 5: <CFELSE>
 6:     <CFSET tax = 0>
 7: </CFIF>
 8:
 9: <CFQUERY NAME="get_shipping" DATASOURCE="elvis_store">
10:     SELECT rate FROM shipping WHERE state = '#form.state#'
11: </CFQUERY>
12:
13: <CFSET shipping = get_shipping.rate * form.total_weight>
```

```
14:
15: <CFSET total_billable = total_cost + tax + shipping>
16:
17: <HTML>
18:
19: <HEAD>
20:
21:     <TITLE>Credit Information</TITLE>
22:
23: </HEAD>
24:
25: <H2>Credit Information</H2>
26:
27: <CFOUTPUT>
28:
29: <H3>Totals</H3>
30:
31: Item Total: #DollarFormat(form.total_cost)#<BR>
32: Tax: #DollarFormat(tax)#<BR>
33: Shipping: #DollarFormat(shipping)#<BR>
34: --------------------<BR>
35: <B>Total Billable: #DollarFormat(total_billable)#</B>
36:
37:
38: <H3>Billing Information</H3>
39:
40: Please supply a credit-card number to which your purchase will be billed.
    ➡The cardholder must be identical to the name you supplied on the
    ➡previous page, #first_name# #last_name#.<P>
41:
42: <FORM ACTION="checkout_complete.cfm" METHOD="post">
43:
44: <INPUT TYPE="hidden" NAME="first_name" VALUE="#first_name#">
45: <INPUT TYPE="hidden" NAME="last_name" VALUE="#last_name#">
46: <INPUT TYPE="hidden" NAME="total_billable" VALUE="#total_billable#">
47:
48: Credit Card Number: <INPUT TYPE="text" NAME="cc"><P>
49:
50: Expires: Month <INPUT TYPE="text" NAME="cc_month" SIZE="2"> Year 20<INPUT
    ➡TYPE="text" NAME="cc_year" SIZE="2"><P>
51:
52: </CFOUTPUT>
53:
54: <INPUT TYPE="submit">
55:
56: </FORM>
57:
58: </HTML>
```

20

In the user's browser, the page looks like Figure 20.8.

FIGURE 20.8

The second transaction page computes tax and shipping charges, and then collects the customer's credit card data.

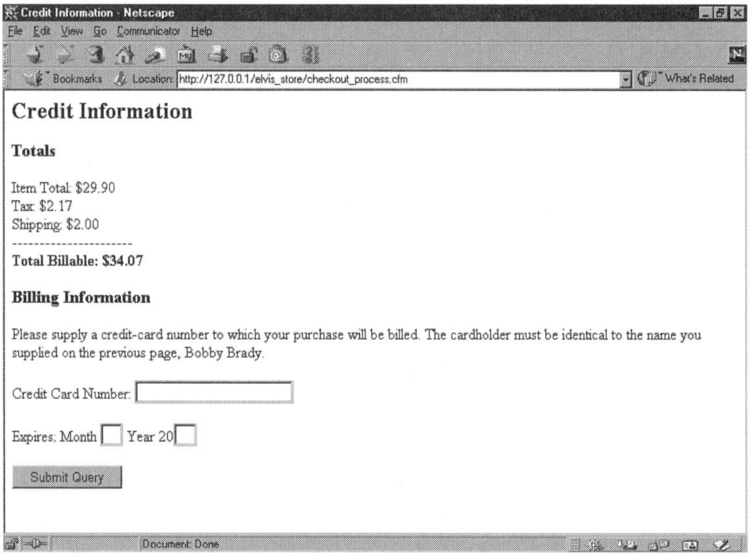

> **Caution**
>
> As with the previous form page, the example `checkout_process.cfm` does not specify a secure link (`https://`) in the form ACTION attribute. When your site goes live, you'll want to change this.

`checkout_process.cfm` first saves the user data you've collected so far by using `<CFINSERT>` to add it to the customers table. My fictitious business is based in California, so I used the code in the last section to compute tax on lines 3-7. If the user's state is "CA", the code multiplies the total item cost by a factor of .0725.

The query on lines 9-11 checks the shipping table for charges to the user's state. On line 13, I used `<CFSET>` to multiply the relevant shipping rate by the total product weight to produce a shipping cost. A third variable, `total_billable` is created by adding the total item cost, tax, and shipping (line 15). This is the sum that will be billed to the user's credit card later.

Lines 29-58 contain the output the customer will see. First, lines 31-35 show the various totals for product, tax, and shipping. Next, the form on lines 42-56 requests the customer's credit card data, which will be sent along to the ACTION page `checkout_complete.cfm`. For testing purposes, the form links to an unsecure ACTION page on line 42, but in your completed application you will probably want to point this to a secure link, such as `https://myserver.com/my_store/checkout_process.cfm`.

checkout_complete.cfm

The final transaction page has two jobs to perform. It must first send the user's billing data to a payment processing service and determine whether the purchase is successful. If so, it must also add the user's selected products to a new table called "orders" where it can be processed by shipping employees on the next business day.

Again, there are many banks and third-party services offering online credit card billing. Each has its own methods of communicating with its payment server, and each returns its own set of result codes to confirm or deny the payment.

The following example shows how you might use Cybercash to process payment. As with many payment systems, Allaire offers an add-on tag specially designed to work with CyberCash.

> **Tip**
>
> The CyberCash custom tag is part of Allaire's "Fuel Pack," a group of add-on utilities for ColdFusion Server. You'll find tags specific to other payment processing systems on Allaire's site in the tag gallery under the "Developers" link. Check your ColdFusion documentation for details on using custom tags.

When the CyberCash tag resides on your ColdFusion server, you use it by adding the following code to your page:

```
<CFX_CYBERCASH
    SERVER=""
    MERCHANTPASSWORD=""
    TRANSTYPE="  "
    ORDER_ID=""
    AMOUNT=""
    CCNUMBER=""
    CCEXP=""
    CCNAME=""
    CCADDRESS=""
    CCCITY=""
    CCSTATE=""
    CCZIP=""
    CCCOUNTRY="">
```

Each of the parameters corresponds to data you've already collected with your secure forms, and can be supplied dynamically, like this:

```
AMOUNT="#total_billable#"
```

When your page calls on the CyberCash tag, Cybercash will immediately return the results of the transaction in the form of special variables such as MStatus, MAuthNumber,

20

and MErrMsg. You can, in turn, use these variables in <CFIF> tags further down your page
to perform one action if the transaction succeeds, another if it does not.

If the transaction fails, your page will need to display an error message. If it succeeds,
you'll need to record the items ordered by the customer so they can be shipped. Assume
that your physical store has a shipping staff to deal with orders. Each morning, the shipping staff opens the company database and looks for new orders that need to be filled.

To simulate this environment in the sample Elvis store, I've created a new database table
called "orders". It contains just three fields: "item", "customer", and "filled" (a yes/no
datatype). The first two fields are related to other tables in the database. For example,
when a member of the shipping staff opens "orders", she sees a number in the customer
field that corresponds to an ID in the "customer" table. In the item field, she sees a number corresponding to a video in the "movies" table. When the staffer fills an order, she
places a check in the yes/no field "filled" to show that the item has been shipped.

The final transaction page runs a query to get the customer's ID from the customer table,
and uses each product's ID number from the session.cart variable to show the item
ordered. It inserts this data into "orders", as shown in Listing 20.10.

LISTING 20.10   checkout_complete.cfm

```
 1: <!---get customer ID--->
 2:
 3: <CFQUERY NAME="get_customer" DATASOURCE="elvis_store">
 4:     SELECT * FROM customers WHERE first_name = '#form.first_name#'
        ↪AND last_name = '#form.last_name#'
 5: </CFQUERY>
 6:
 7: <!---process payment--->
 8:
 9: <CFX_CYBERCASH
10:     SERVER="server_name"
11:     MERCHANTPASSWORD="password"
12:     TRANSTYPE="authonly"
13:     ORDER_ID="#session.cfid#"
14:     AMOUNT="#form.total_billable#"
15:     CCNUMBER="#form.cc#"
16:     CCEXP="#form.cc_month#/#form.cc_year#"
17:     CCNAME="#form.first_name# #form.last_name#"
18:     CCADDRESS="#get_customer.street_address#"
19:     CCCITY="#get_customer.city#"
20:     CCSTATE="#get_customer.state#"
21:     CCZIP="#get_customer.zip#"
22:     CCCOUNTRY="#get_customer.country#">
23:
```

```
24: <HTML>
25:
26: <HEAD>
27:
28:     <TITLE>Order Status</TITLE>
29:
30: </HEAD>
31:
32: <!---if payment fails, show error message--->
33:
34: <CFIF mstatus IS "fail">
35:
36:     Your order has not been processed. Our payment process returned the
        ➥following error:<P>
37:
38:     <CFOUTPUT>#MErrMsg#</CFOUTPUT>
39:
40: </CFIF>
41:
42: <!---if payment succeeds, add ordered items to orders table and show
    ➥confirmation--->
43:
44: <CFIF MStatus IS "succeed">
45:
46:     Your order has been processed. Your order ID is <CFOUTPUT>#session.
        ➥cfid#</CFOUTPUT>. Please print this page for your records<P>
47:
48: <CFLOOP INDEX="loopcount" From="1" To="#ArrayLen(session.cart)#">
49:
50:     <CFQUERY NAME="insert" DATASOURCE="elvis_store">
51:         INSERT INTO orders (item,customer)
52:         VALUES ('#session.cart[loopcount][4]#', '#get_customer.ID#')
53:     </CFQUERY>
54:
55:     <CFOUTPUT>
56:     Item Ordered: #session.cart[loopcount][1]#<BR>
57:     </CFOUTPUT>
58:
59: </CFLOOP>
60:     <P>Total Billed: <CFOUTPUT>#form.total_billable#</CFOUTPUT>
61: </CFIF>
62:
63: </HTML>
```

20

In analyzing Listing 20.10, be sure to remember that it is only an example of how a typical payment-processing page might work. The service you choose will determine how the process is handled, and what variables are available to you once the transaction is complete.

The query on lines 3-5 uses the customer's first and last name submitted by the form to get the rest of their information from the customers table. Next, the CFX_CYBERCASH tag is called on lines 9-22. The Cybercash system uses the variable mstatus to tell us whether the transaction has gone through, so the page uses that variable with <CFIF> to perform one of two actions. If the transaction fails (lines 34-40), the user sees the reason, which is contained in the Cybercash variable MerrMsg. If it succeeds (lines 44-61), the user sees a confirmation of their order.

For successful transactions, the listing displays an order confirmation number (session.cfid) to the user on line 46. It next uses a loop on lines 48-59 to insert the customer's ID and product selections into the order table (lines 50-53) and to display each product to the user (lines 55-57).

Summary

ColdFusion is an excellent back-end tool for e-commerce sites because it can automate so many of the processes necessary to display products and take customer orders. Several ColdFusion developers have recognized this fact and have created prewritten applications, some of which enable you to set up an entire store in just a few minutes.

If you're planning to build your own store application, begin by mapping out the four major elements of an e-commerce site: an administration section, a catalog, a shopping cart, and a transaction section. The first two of these use familiar tools like forms and queries to get data in and out of your products database.

The third element, the shopping cart, is a little more complex, but still a task for which ColdFusion is well suited. By using session management to store variables behind the scenes, you can give your customers the ability to store product information as they browse your site. When their visit is complete, you can direct them to a transaction section where their selected items are totaled and where they can place an online order in a secure environment.

Q&A

Q I already have an online store written in Perl or C. Can I integrate it with ColdFusion?

A In most cases, yes, although you'll probably need to know a little bit about your store's native language. The more integration you want, the more you'll need to know.

Q **Why is there such a huge price difference in prewritten store applications?**

A More expensive store apps usually offer more features, but the biggest difference is usually in support. Inexpensive sites typically offer no or little support, whereas the pricier models might even have an 800 number or direct email help.

Q **My client's database contains thousands of products. Is ColdFusion still the right e-commerce tool?**

A Yes. As you know, ColdFusion can handle pretty large databases with ease. For larger sites, you'll really need to plan out your catalog section and pay attention to how users will access products. By using subcategories and search boxes, you can make your large site easier to navigate.

Q **My client wants to use a fax-back or call-back ordering system. Should I talk him out of it?**

A If your client's business isn't online, or its employees aren't computer savvy, those older methods make great workarounds. After all, it wasn't too long ago that the majority of Web business used fax-back and call-back methods as their primary source of communication with customers.

Q **If I'm using a transaction type other than secure online ordering, how much of today's lesson applies?**

A Everything up to the final two sections. Even stores that use email or fax orders can benefit from having a well-designed product catalog and shopping cart system.

Q **If security is such an issue, why not use HTTPS links for all the pages on my site and be done with it?**

A Secure links have to encrypt and decrypt data each time a page is delivered. They can take up quite a bit of your server's processor time, so I advise using them only where necessary.

Workshop

20

Answers to quiz questions can be found in Appendix A at the back of this text.

Quiz

1. What are the four basic elements of e-commerce sites?
2. What are the functions of "browse" and "detail" pages in a catalog?
3. What must you do before using session variables (such as `session.cart`) in your shopping cart section?

4. Why is it necessary to store shopping cart selections in a session variable?

5. What does SSL stand for? How does it work, and why is it used?

6. Briefly describe how payment-processing services work.

Exercises

1. Set up the sample catalog described in this chapter and add a search function to the page browse_movies.cfm.

2. Customize the store's admin pages by adding a function to add and remove categories. You might also want to add a "categories" table to your database and a corresponding field in the "movies" table.

3. Enhance your transaction section by changing <FORM>s to <CFFORM>s and adding verification to form fields such as ZIP Code, and so on, You'll find details on <CFFORM> and verification in Day 11, "Enhancing Input Pages with Basic <CFFORM> Tags."

4. If you are the merchant of a physical store or service that accepts credit card payments, contact your bank and find out if it supports online processing for merchant accounts.

DAY **21**

Using ColdFusion's Debugging Tools to Troubleshoot Your Code

Although it might seem a little strange to find a debugging lesson at the end of your 21-day journey, there's a method behind the madness. Many components make up a complete ColdFusion application—the Web server, ColdFusion server, datasources, templates, SQL statements, CFML and HTML code, and so on. Each component has its own unique type of errors, so it's important that you first learn how each of the components works before you start to troubleshoot situations when it doesn't. Today's lesson covers

- Identifying the source of errors
- Troubleshooting Web server errors
- Troubleshooting ColdFusion and ODBC errors
- Using ColdFusion's advanced debugging tools

- Using ColdFusion Studio's Document Validator
- Introducing ColdFusion log files

Identifying the Source of Errors

First, realize that ColdFusion-related error messages can seem as cryptic as the Rosetta stone viewed through a soda bottle in a windstorm. In many cases in which errors occur, certain external factors might tell you more about what's wrong than the actual message itself. The most telling of these factors is *when* the error occurs—what you were doing when the error popped up.

For example, does the error occur when you try to load a template page, or does it rear its little head when you try to submit a form page? It's important to understand that the average ColdFusion application works with several components, including your Web server, the SQL language, your system's security setup, your database application and ODBC drivers, and yes, ColdFusion Server. One or more of these components can be confused by your code and report an error—this is where the *when* factor becomes important.

After you've identified which of these components is reporting an error, you've taken a giant step toward fixing the problem. The following sections examine each of the potential errors generated by each component in detail, starting at the lowest level.

Understanding Error Messages Generated by Your Web Server

Believe it or not, your Web server will probably be the component that complains least when you're building and testing ColdFusion applications. This is because the ColdFusion installer checks your Web server for compatibility, permissions, and other necessary parameters during the ColdFusion install process. After ColdFusion Server is up and running, only a few things can go wrong where your Web server is concerned.

Host Not Found

However astute and careful a developer you are, sooner or later you'll come across the common error pictured in Figure 21.1.

FIGURE 21.1

This browser error indicates that a Web server is not running, or could not be contacted at the specified address.

Mentioning this error might seem like the tech-support question, "Is the unit plugged in?" but be assured that Host Not Found errors do occur. Usually the solution is as simple as starting your Web server software. If you test your ColdFusion applications on a personal machine that doesn't serve files live on the Net, it's easy to forget to turn on Web service.

Note

If you get an error like the one shown in Figure 21.1 when accessing a remote Web server, there might be connection problems along your LAN or the Internet, or the remote server might be down for some reason. You can verify this with your operating system's command ping *X*, where *X* is the name or IP address of the server.

404 File Not Found

Another common Web server error is the dreaded File Not Found, as illustrated in Figure 21.2.

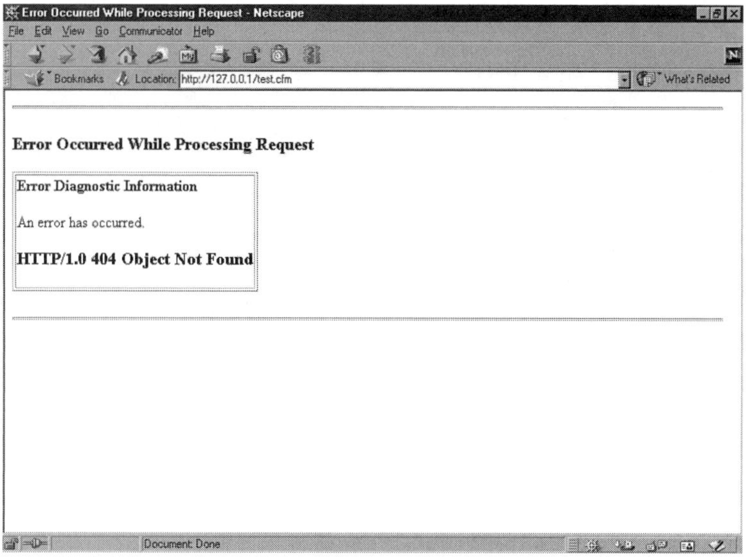

FIGURE 21.2

The dreaded File Not Found error is returned when a file doesn't exist.

21

Common reasons for a 404 error when working with ColdFusion are

- Your URL specifies an `.html` or `.htm` file extension instead of `.cfm`.

  Solution: Verify the file's extension.

- A dynamically generated link in a ColdFusion template isn't pointing to a valid file.

  Solution: In your browser, hold your mouse over the offending link and verify the URL as it appears in your browser's status bar. If you can't see the whole link, use your browser's View Source function.

- You've used one or more variables in a URL but have forgotten to include the question-mark symbol ? to set them off from the filename, such as

  ```
  http://www.myserver.com/products.cfmproduct_id=2&type=new
  ```

  This causes your Web server to look for a nonexistent file because it doesn't recognize the `.cfm` extension, and therefore it doesn't pass the file to ColdFusion for processing.

  Solution: Check your URLs (particularly those generated dynamically) to ensure they use the question mark to set off variables.

- The file or folder specified in your URL has security or permissions that cause it not to display.

  Solution: Check your Web server documentation for details on making files and folders available via the Web.

URL Syntax Errors

Another variation of the File Not Found error is shown in Figure 21.3.

Errors like the one shown in Figure 21.3 typically occur when your Web server tries to parse a URL that contains a space. This might have happened for one of a couple of reasons:

- You accidentally typed a space in a URL.

  Solution: Don't do it. It's best to avoid spaces in filenames that will be used on the Web, but if you absolutely have to, you can usually access the file by substituting the text %20 for each space in the filename.

- A variable value passed by a ColdFusion template contains a space. For example, you might need to dynamically pass a name to a template like this:

  ```
  <CFOUTPUT QUERY="applicants">

  <A HREF="applicant.cfm?name=#name#">#name#</A>

  </CFOUTPUT>
  ```

Because the variable #name# is likely to contain a space, your server will have trouble parsing the resulting URL.

Solution: Use the ColdFusion function URLFormat() to pass variables that might contain spaces:

```
applicant.cfm?name=#URLFormat(name)#
```

URLFormat() converts illegal URL characters to a format Web servers can understand (such as turning a space character to %20).

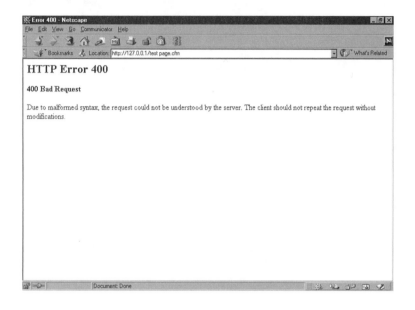

FIGURE 21.3

A syntax error reported by the Web server when it can't parse characters in a URL.

> **Note**
>
> When using URLFormat() to pass a variable, you don't need to worry about converting the variable values *back* to standard format on the template that receives them—ColdFusion does this automatically.

ColdFusion Not Running

If you request a .cfm file from your server and get an error like the one in Figure 21.4, you know that the ColdFusion service isn't running.

Possible causes for this error are

- The service has been stopped, shut down, or crashed. If you've had ColdFusion running successfully in the past, this usually isn't cause for alarm. It just means that the service isn't currently running, usually because it hasn't been started or it has been shut down.

21

Solution: Restart ColdFusion service and test that it's running by accessing the special Administrator URL:

`http://127.0.0.1/cfide/Administrator/index.cfm`

- The ColdFusion installation wasn't successful and now the program won't run.

   Solution: Reinstall ColdFusion Server and check out the installation troubleshooting tips listed at the end of Day 3, "Setting Up ColdFusion and Defining a Datasource."

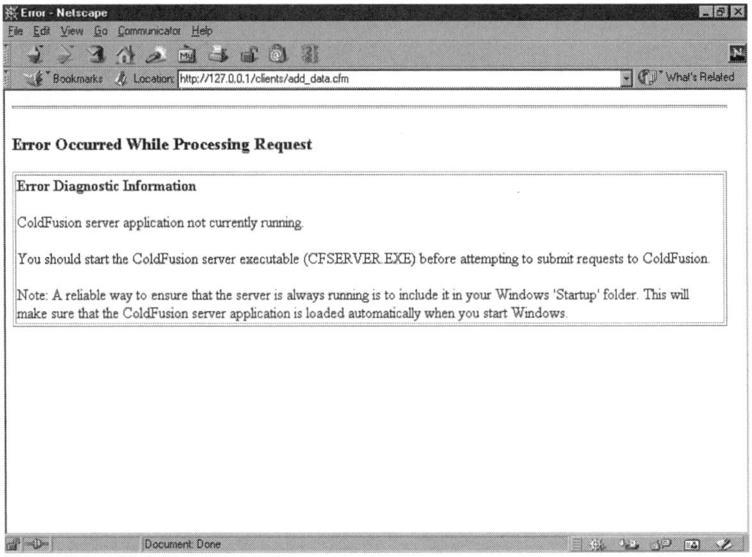

FIGURE 21.4

If ColdFusion services can't be found, the Web server returns this error message.

Tip

If you run ColdFusion on a live Web server, it's a good idea to make sure that it always runs on system startup to avoid errors like the one in Figure 21.4. Although the ColdFusion installer usually sets this feature for you, you can double-check your settings in the following ways:

- On Windows 9x systems, ColdFusion Server and ColdFusion RDS Service should have shortcuts in the default folder C:\Windows\Start Menu\Programs\StartUp.

- On Windows NT systems, ColdFusion runs as a service and should be set to run at startup in the NT Services Manager.

- On UNIX-based operating systems, ColdFusion should be listed in your system's startup script.

Understanding Error Messages Generated by ColdFusion

To avoid confusion, it's important to understand that ColdFusion errors come in two varieties. The first variety includes errors that come directly from ColdFusion Server and identify some problem with a template or process. The majority of these errors are the result of syntax problems, such as a misplaced `</CFIF>` or `</CFOUTPUT>` tag in your templates.

The second variety includes errors that are actually generated by components other than ColdFusion, but are passed on as ColdFusion errors to aid in development. The most common errors of this type are ODBC driver errors. These are displayed in ColdFusion's standard error format, but are labeled as ODBC errors so that you know it's your ODBC driver rather than ColdFusion that is complaining about your code.

Tip

> Most errors returned by ColdFusion include a reference to a line number and character position in your code. By turning on the line-numbering feature in ColdFusion Studio you can go right to the spot in your code that is creating the error. If you don't use Studio, you can use a text editor that displays line numbers (often called "programmers' editors") to find the offending line and position.

This section examines the errors that come directly from ColdFusion Server.

Mismatched Tags

If your template page contains a stray tag, such as an extra `</CFOUTPUT>` without a corresponding `<CFOUTPUT>`, you'll see an error like the one in Figure 21.5.

Fortunately, the error message will identify the offending tag, making it fairly easy to figure out what's wrong.

Tip

> Mismatched tag errors are common when working with lengthy `<CFIF>` statements. To avoid them, review your template's code as you would a flow chart—"if this...then that"—to verify a valid decision-making flow and to ensure closing `</CFIF>` tags are included.

21

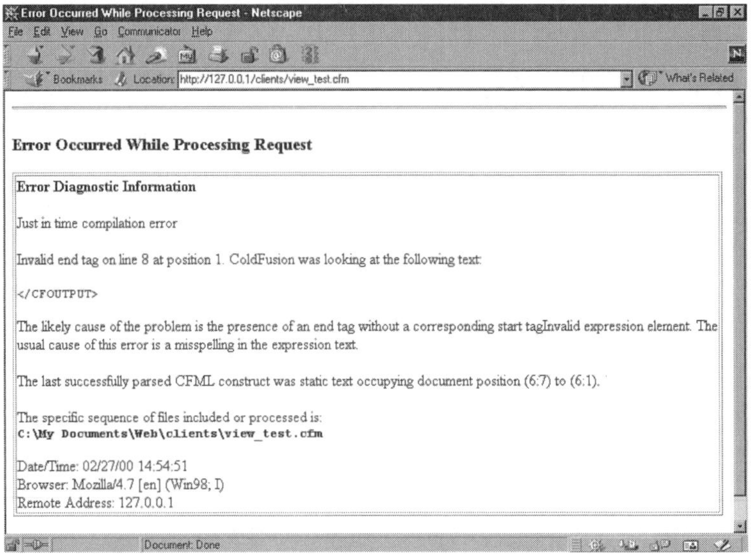

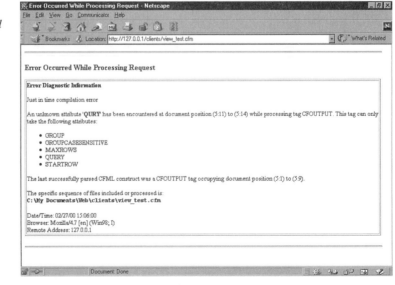

FIGURE 21.5

A stray </CFOUTPUT>
*tag results in an error
like this one.*

Solution: Carefully check your templates for valid tag pairs, or use ColdFusion Studio's Document Validator, as described later today.

Unrecognized Tag Attributes

If ColdFusion can't recognize an attribute in your tag (such as a misspelled "QURY" attribute in a <CFOUTPUT> tag), it reports an error like the one in Figure 21.6.

FIGURE 21.6

*A misspelled or invalid
tag attribute produces
an error like this.*

You'll see a similar error if you forget to use quotation marks around an attribute value, such as

```
DATASOURCE=my database
```

Solution: Fortunately, ColdFusion's error lists both the offending attribute or value as well as the valid attributes associated with a tag. Check your code to be sure that you're using a valid attribute and that the attribute is properly referenced.

Missing Pound Signs or Quotation Marks

If you forget to include an opening or closing pound sign when referencing a variable (such as name# or #name), or leave off a quotation mark when referencing a string, you'll get a somewhat cryptic error message that might resemble Figure 21.7.

FIGURE 21.7

A missing pound sign or quotation mark can really confuse ColdFusion and generate odd errors like this one.

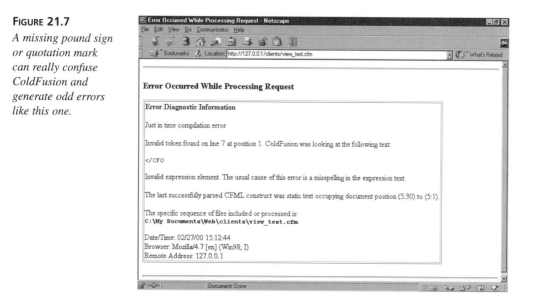

This type of error can be difficult to troubleshoot because it doesn't specifically tell you that a quotation mark or pound sign is missing. Instead, it tells you that ColdFusion had problems with the text or code that *comes before or after* the missing punctuation.

When items within quotation marks or hash marks aren't properly delimited, ColdFusion treats the preceding or following text as part of the string or variable and creates an error. When it gets confused this way, it simply stops processing your page and reports the last bit of code that was processed *successfully*.

21

The key to troubleshooting these types of errors lies in the following line of the error message: The last successfully parsed CFML construct was static text occupying document position (X) to (X).

Solution: Use ColdFusion's "last parsed" hints to track down the bad code in your file. More often than not, you'll find an error in your code at or around the line that was processed just before the error occurred.

> **Tip**
>
> In many error messages, ColdFusion tries to identify the code that has caused the error. Always use these hints in troubleshooting, particularly those that identify specific locations in your code.

Error Resolving Parameter

If a <CFOUTPUT> section encounters a variable that hasn't been defined (or that hasn't been returned by a query), you'll see something like the error in Figure 21.8.

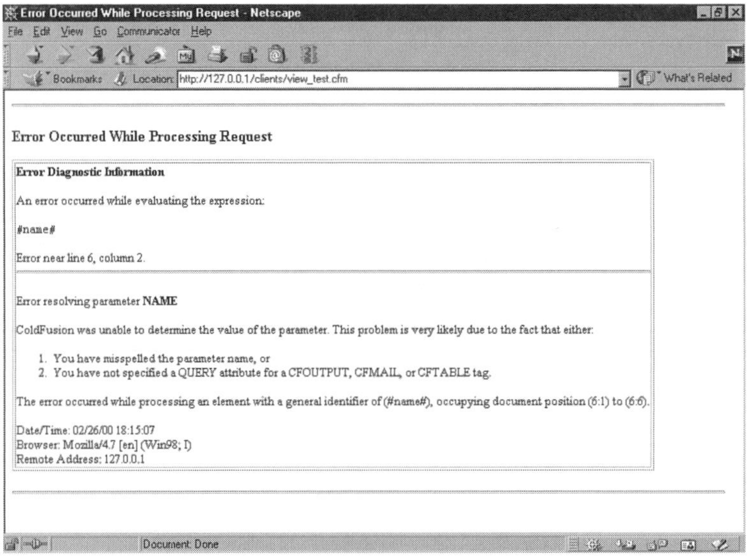

FIGURE 21.8

This error occurs when <CFOUTPUT> can't find a specified variable.

Possible reasons for this error include

* A misspelled variable name that doesn't match a variable returned by the query
* Referencing a nonquery variable that hasn't yet been defined

- A form variable for which the user provided no input
- The wrong query is specified in the <CFOUTPUT> tag

Solution: Trace the offending variable back to its source and make sure that it exists, is defined, and is spelled correctly. Also verify that the query name specified in <CFOUTPUT> refers to the correct <CFQUERY>. Both ColdFusion Studio and ColdFusion Administrator have debugging tools that help find these types of errors—both are covered later in today's lesson.

> **Tip**
>
> Use the <CFPARAM> tag when you're not sure whether a variable has been defined (such as with form input). It enables you to specify a default value if none exists. This helps eliminate "error resolving parameter" troubles.

Understanding Error Messages Generated by Your ODBC Driver

As mentioned in the last section, not all errors displayed by ColdFusion come directly from ColdFusion Server. The program also passes on a second variety of errors—those errors that come from other components, such as your ODBC driver.

Although these errors are displayed the same way as ColdFusion syntax errors, it's important to understand that they are generated by your ODBC components rather than ColdFusion itself. Read your error messages carefully—ColdFusion will tell you whether an error comes from an ODBC component, as illustrated in all the following examples.

Datasource Not Found

If your ODBC driver can't access a datasource, ColdFusion displays one of several errors that resemble the one in Figure 21.9.

There are several reasons for this type of error:

- You haven't yet defined the datasource referenced in your template.
- You misspelled the datasource name.
- You moved the database file after the datasource was defined in ColdFusion Administrator.
- The datasource has security or permission settings that don't allow it to be accessed.

21

FIGURE 21.9

A nonexistent or invalid datasource generates an error like this.

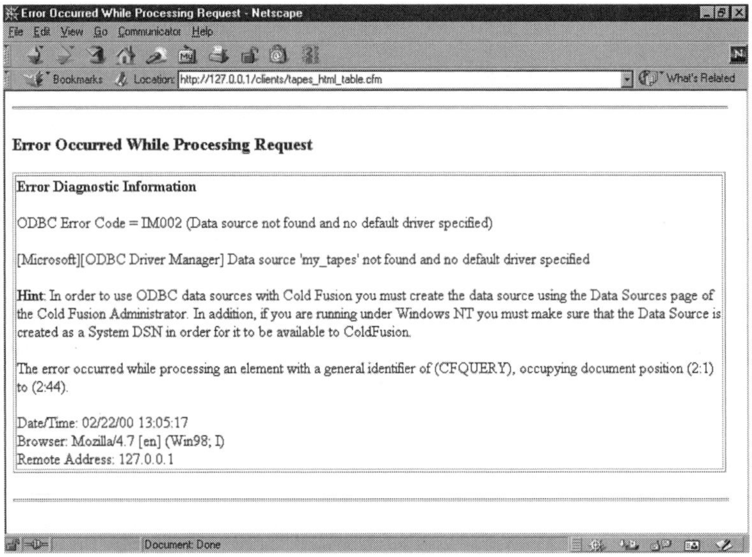

Solution: Under ColdFusion Administrator's OBDC link, use the Verify feature to identify problems with your datasource. You'll find an explanation of this feature in Day 3. This feature provides a more detailed explanation of potential datasource troubles than do standard error messages.

> **Caution**
>
> On Windows NT systems, datasources should always be defined in ColdFusion Administrator rather than from the ODBC Control Panel. This ensures that the user associated with the ColdFusion application has access to the datasource and avoids errors such as the one in Figure 21.9.

SQL Syntax or Logic Errors

Unless you're a veteran SQL programmer, you'll probably spend most of your ColdFusion debugging time working with faulty SQL statements. Although SQL is a relatively straightforward language, there's a lot of room for error and one misplaced quotation mark or misspelled word can halt your entire application.

SQL errors are always reported by your ODBC driver (via ColdFusion) and often resemble the error shown in Figure 21.10.

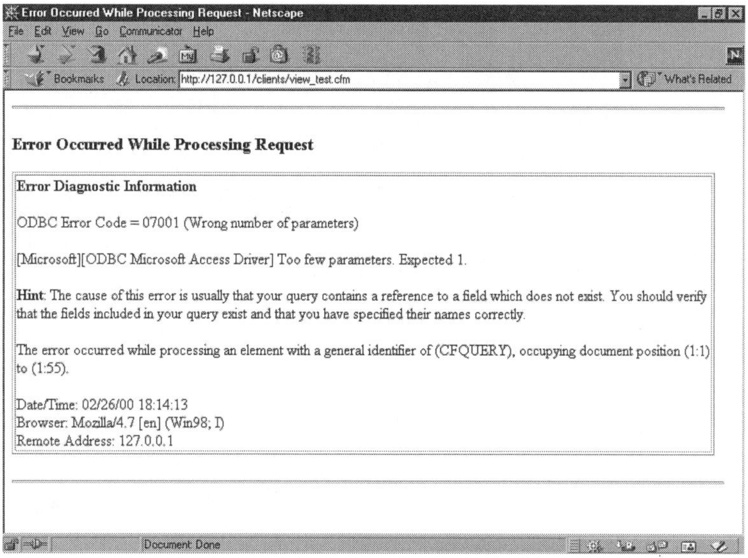

FIGURE 21.10

The common SQL error "too few parameters" is a catch-all error that may signify one of several problems with a query.

This section examines some common SQL errors, beginning with the one illustrated in Figure 21.10.

Too Few Parameters

This common error pops up when SQL can't find one or more of the items specified in your query. Causes include

- A misspelled field name, or a reference to a field that doesn't exist.
- Using a double quotation mark (") instead of a single quotation mark (') to denote a text string.
- A dynamic query is getting faulty or nonexistent information from a referring page, such as a form.

Solution: Use ColdFusion Administrator's enhanced debugging tools or the query DEBUG parameter (both described in the next section) to see the exact SQL statement passed to your ODBC driver. These tools will help you quickly identify the source of parameter problems.

Table Not Found

This is a pretty basic error, but it's also pretty common. It occurs when SQL can't find a table specified in your query. It looks like the error shown in Figure 21.11.

21

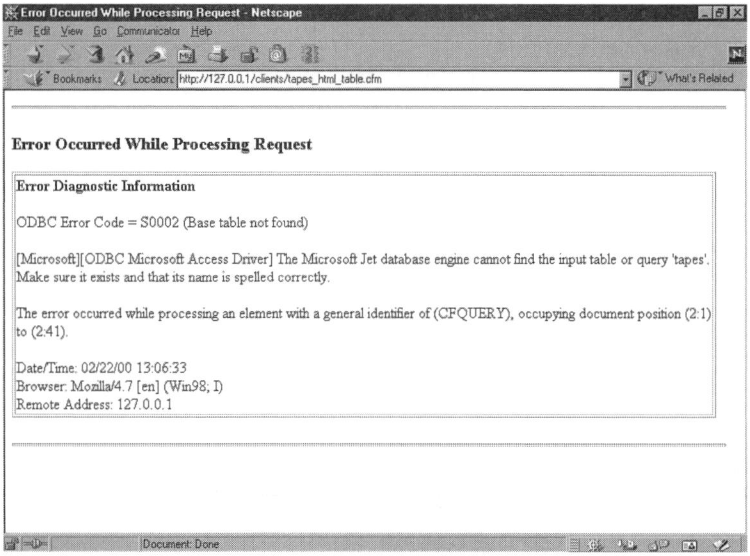

FIGURE 21.11

A misspelled or non-existent table name generates this type of error.

Solution: Check your query against the contents of your database to verify the spelling and existence of all table names.

Tip

> If you use ColdFusion Studio, you can eliminate lots of table- and field-related errors by using the drag-and-drop feature when building SQL queries. By dragging the table and field names from your datasource contents into your template's code, you ensure that all parameters are spelled correctly. Visual query builders such as Microsoft Query also help guard against spelling errors.

IS Instead of =

When building a query in a text editor, it's all too easy to substitute the required = parameter for IS, such as

```
SELECT * FROM applicants WHERE name IS 'Buddy Bradley'
```

This mistake produces an error like the one shown in Figure 21.12.

Solution: Your ODBC driver immediately reports this type of error, making it easy to correct in your template. Using the query builder in Studio, or an external app such as Microsoft Query can also help guard against such errors.

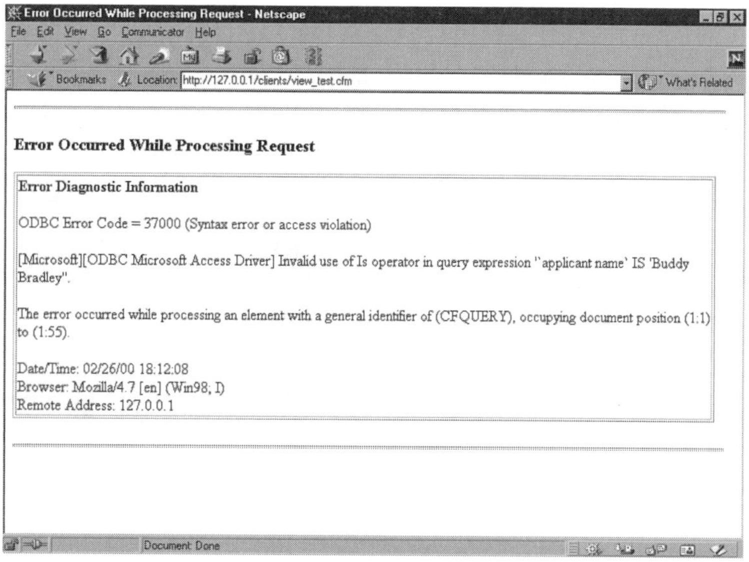

FIGURE 21.12

ColdFusion provides a very specific error message when IS is used instead of =.

Other SQL Errors

The complete range of possible SQL errors goes beyond the space available in today's lesson, but a few general rules of thumb will help you build and troubleshoot queries.

- For lengthy queries, use Studio's query builder or apps such as Microsoft Query. These ensure that all table names exist and are spelled correctly, and that your query uses the proper syntax.

- When an unspecific ODBC error occurs, narrow down the cause by removing all but the most basic elements of a query, then re-add the elements one by one until the trouble is identified.

- Remember to always use a single quotation mark to denote text strings, and no quotation marks at all with numeric fields. If your query is assigned parameters dynamically, make sure that referenced variables also use this convention.

- Look at your query as a group of components (such as an alias section, a select section, and so on), and troubleshoot each component individually by breaking it out into its own test query.

- Know the data types of each field in your tables, and use only operators that correspond to each type, such as numeric fields, text fields, date/time fields, and so on.

- Use ColdFusion Studio and ColdFusion Administrator to enhance your SQL debugging techniques, as described in the following sections.

21

Understanding ColdFusion's Debugging Tools

ColdFusion features several powerful reporting tools that can tell you much more about what's going on behind the scenes than its standard error messages can. When these tools are enabled, they cause your template pages to display some statistics at the bottom of the screen, as illustrated in Figure 21.13.

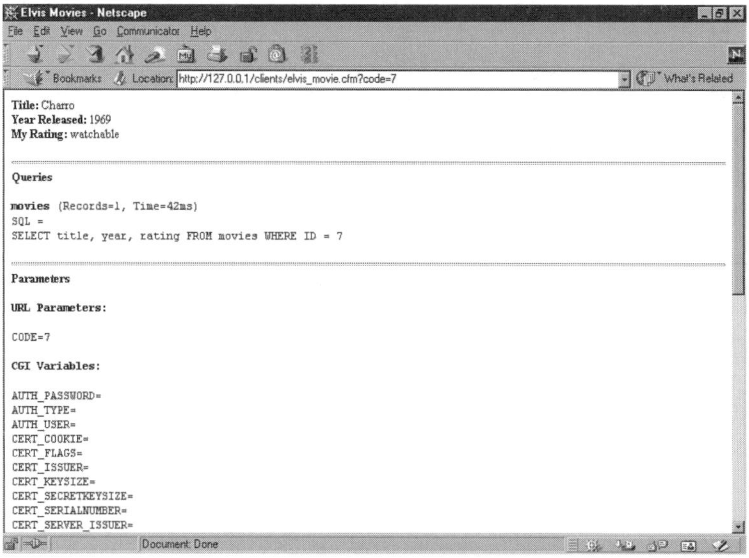

FIGURE 21.13

ColdFusion's debugging options may be set to display a detailed list of variable values and parameters at the end of a page's output.

In this example, you see a template page that worked just fine and returned some details about a database record. But note that following the first horizontal line there are several entries that tell more about the page, such as the actual text of the SQL query that was executed, the parameters sent by the page's URL, and so on. The template in Figure 21.13 worked successfully, but if it hadn't, you could find some valuable information about what went wrong in the details supplied.

These advanced debugging methods are enabled in one of two ways: You can enable them throughout your site by using the interface in ColdFusion Administrator, or you can enable them only for specific templates using the special DEBUG parameter as part of a URL.

ColdFusion Administrator's Debugging Features

To enable debugging features in Administrator, log in and choose the Debugging link in the lower-left column, as illustrated in Figure 21.14.

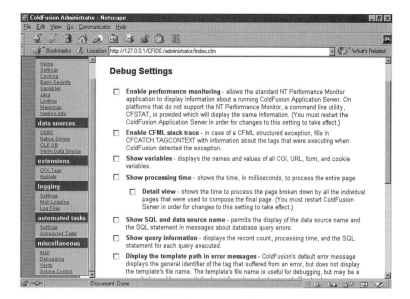

FIGURE 21.14

ColdFusion Administrator features a variety of powerful debugging tools.

Checking any box and then choosing Apply at the bottom of the page causes ColdFusion to display data along with the output of each of your template pages. The effects of each check box item are listed in Table 21.1. Some of these features go beyond simple template debugging, so don't worry if you don't understand all of them.

TABLE 21.1 Debug Settings in ColdFusion Administrator

Setting	What It Does
Enable performance monitoring	Allows Windows NT users to view information about ColdFusion performance in the NT Performance Monitor.
Enable CFML stack trace	Creates a special log when ColdFusion encounters a CFML structured exception.
Show variables	Displays the names and values of CGI, URL, form, and cookie variables. This feature also displays the time, in milliseconds, that ColdFusion took to process a template.
Show SQL and data source name	Displays the name of the datasource the actual contents of the SQL statement sent to the ODBC driver.
Show query information	Displays the number of records, processing time, and SQL statement for each query executed from a template.
Display the template path in error messages	Displays a template's file name and path.

21

> **Tip**
>
> The feature Show SQL and data source name is one of the most valuable tools in ColdFusion's debugging arsenal. By using it, you can find out exactly what text is being sent as an SQL query, and you'll often find that it wasn't what you'd expected. Similarly, Show query information will tell you what was queried, how long it took, and how many records were returned.

Enabling Debug Information for Specific Templates

If you're troubleshooting an entire application, it's not a bad idea to turn on the debugging options in Administrator so that you'll see them on every page. However, this approach might be overkill if you're having trouble with only one page. ColdFusion provides a second debugging option for cases like the latter.

Although single-page debugging doesn't give you all the options in Table 21.1, it does enable you to display some of the most commonly used debug displays.

- Debugging a single template page: Use the special variable `mode=debug` at the end of the page's URL:

  ```
  http://www.myserver.com/some_page.cfm?mode=debug
  ```

  This causes ColdFusion to display all parameters and CGI variables for the given page.

- Debugging a single query: Use the `DEBUG` parameter in your `<CFQUERY>` tag:

  ```
  <CFQUERY NAME="get_movies" DATASOURCE="elvis" DEBUG>
  ```

  This causes ColdFusion to display the SQL statement and query data for the given template.

Restricting Debug Output to Certain Viewers

Although the information presented by these debug tools is certainly valuable to *you*, it might not be so appealing to your site's users. By default, enabled debugging options are displayed to anyone who views your templates, but ColdFusion wisely enables you to restrict this output to specific IP addresses.

To enable an IP address, scroll down the debugging options page until you see a form like the one shown in Figure 21.15.

FIGURE 21.15

ColdFusion's debugging tools can be set to display only to users at specific IP addresses.

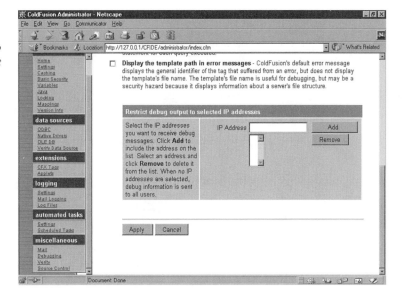

In the text box, supply the IP addresses of computers that you want to see debugging messages.

Tip

If you're developing applications on the same machine that runs ColdFusion Server, it's a good idea to enable debug displays for the special IP address 127.0.0.1. This allows you, and no one else, to view debug output.

Using ColdFusion Studio's Document Validator

ColdFusion Studio enables you to perform a quick check on a selected document by choosing Tools, Validate Document from the pull-down menus at the top of the screen (hotkey: Shift+F6). When you do this, the program will check for unknown variables, mismatched tags or pound signs, and other common coding errors. To display the results of the check, Studio opens a third window below the document, as illustrated in Figure 21.16.

21

FIGURE 21.16

ColdFusion Studio's Document Validator reports potential errors in a status window.

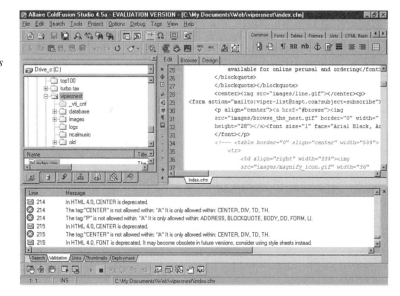

The validation window for the document in Figure 21.16 shows several potential errors, including bad HTML code, missing hash marks on variables, and so on. Clicking an individual error message causes the editor window to highlight the offending text, as shown in Figure 21.17.

FIGURE 21.17

Studio's Document Validator makes it easy to navigate to specific errors in your templates.

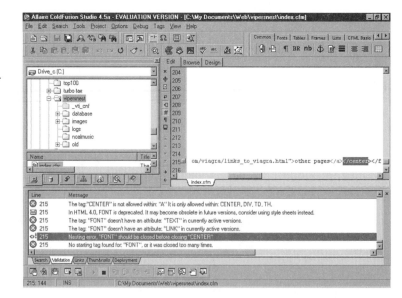

> **Tip**
>
> ColdFusion offers an even more sophisticated page-validation feature for experienced developers: Interactive Debugger. Although the use of this extremely powerful tool is a little too advanced for discussion here, know that it can identify code problems throughout an application. Interactive Debugger works both with files on your local server, and those hosted on RDS-compatible remote ColdFusion servers. Check Studio's documentation for details on using this tool.

Introducing ColdFusion Log Files

ColdFusion's standard troubleshooting tools will help you track the source of most coding errors you're likely to encounter, but you might eventually encounter problems not addressed by general debugging. Typically, these problems include unidentifiable server errors, Web server compatibility problems, or situations in which things just plain don't work, no matter what you try.

For these rare occasions, ColdFusion's expansive system of log files can help you find out what's going wrong. If you used the default installation paths, you'll find your log files in `cfusion\logs`. By default, ColdFusion Server maintains the following logs:

- `application.log` keeps track of all errors reported to users, logging each error with an associated IP address and browser information.
- `server.log` monitors system failure messages in cases when ColdFusion Server is unable to use a system resource or contact a specified remote server.
- `webserver.log` documents errors that occur between ColdFusion Server and your Web server.

> **Note**
>
> Several other types of advanced logs are available; these are enabled in ColdFusion Administrator under the link Logging, Settings.

> **Tip**
>
> If you encounter a ColdFusion problem that requires contacting Allaire technical support, be sure to have your log files accessible. Support persons will often refer to your log files to track down the source of problems.

21

Summary

As you've been building your own templates according to the lessons in this book, it's very likely that you've come across several of ColdFusion's unique error messages. Today's chapter assumed that you've now familiarized yourself with the various components of a ColdFusion application described in previous lessons, and showed you how to troubleshoot them.

One of the most important steps in fixing an error is identifying which component is reporting trouble. Web servers often report errors when pages aren't found or URLs are invalid; ColdFusion Server displays errors when it doesn't understand something in your template's code, and your ODBC driver will complain if it encounters an SQL statement it doesn't understand.

In addition to the default errors displayed by each of these components, ColdFusion offers a more detailed system of error reporting that can be enabled site-wide from ColdFusion Adminstrator, or can be used on a single template with the special variable mode=debug. ColdFusion Server also keeps extensive logs by default—these logs can be particularly valuable in tracking down problems not addressed by other methods. ColdFusion Studio users also have a powerful tool at their disposal in the Document Validator function. This feature can be used to check individual template pages for common coding mistakes that might produce errors when your pages are deployed.

Q&A

Q Are Web server errors reported by ColdFusion?

A Usually not, because they tend to occur before ColdFusion has had a chance to process a file. The Web server itself typically reports Web server errors.

Q When I load a template file, I don't see an error, but neither do I see the complete page. What's up?

A Certain types of errors can occur within a template page, meaning that only part of the page will display successfully. This is often true when using tables—a ColdFusion error might cause the closing </TABLE> tag not to load and your page would appear blank. To see what's really going on, use your browser's View Source command. You'll often find a ColdFusion error message embedded in the code.

Q **I've checked and double-checked my table names, and my ODBC driver is still reporting an Unknown Table error.**

A This problem can occur when using server-based database applications such as Oracle and Microsoft SQL Server. These apps typically require tables to be referenced with special three-part names that include the name of the desired database, the name of the database owner, and a table name.

Q **My template causes ColdFusion to return a vague message such as a `non-specific error has occurred`. What do I do?**

A It's rare that ColdFusion won't at least try to give you details about an error, but it does happen. Errors like this are often the result of severe syntax errors—check your code (particularly the `<CFIF>` structures) to make sure you have matching sets of tags, properly delimited variable names, and so on.

Q **I've enabled debugging options in ColdFusion Administrator, but I don't see them displayed. What's wrong?**

A Your system or Web administrator might have assigned one or more IP addresses to the debugging restrictions. You need to ask him or her to add your IP as well.

Q **Why does ColdFusion Studio's Document Validator report so many errors in my templates, even those that load successfully?**

A By default, the Document Validator tends to be a little overzealous and will report some formatting errors that don't necessarily affect on the way a page displays. You can customize the way Validator works by selecting Options, Settings and choosing the Validator tab.

Workshop

The workshop provides quiz and exercise questions to test your understanding of today's material. Answers to quiz questions can be found in Appendix A at the back of the text.

Quiz

1. Name the three main components that report errors in ColdFusion applications.
2. How are ODBC errors reported?
3. What CFML tag might be used to guard against ODBC errors that come from a dynamic query?
4. What special variable is used to debug an individual template page?
5. Name ColdFusion Studio's two primary debugging tools.
6. Which of ColdFusion's log files is of most use in troubleshooting application errors?

21

Exercises

1. This first exercise is a given: Use the principles outlined in today's lesson to trouble-shoot errors you might have encountered in previous applications.

2. Create a basic template page with <CFQUERY> and <CFOUTPUT> sections. Within it, add intentional typos that will duplicate each of the ODBC driver errors described in today's lesson.

3. Enable debugging options in ColdFusion Administrator and restrict their display to your own IP address. Load one of your applications and note the debugging messages as you navigate your pages.

WEEK 3

In Review

In your final week with ColdFusion, you tackled some pretty heady concepts. You learned how to use some of the application's advanced tools to maximize and customize your Web sites and how to build sophisticated applications that rival anything you've seen on the Web.

Day 15, "Using Lists, Structures, and Arrays to Package Data," focused on the complex variable types lists, structures, and arrays. You learned how these special tools are used when you need to store more than a single text string in a variable. You now know how to define, write to, and read from all three variable types.

Day 16, "ColdFusion Client and Session Management," urged you to look at your site's template pages as a whole entity, and introduced you to client and session management, the tool that allows your pages to share data without having to pass it via a form or URL. By now, you should know how to create sites that can store user data temporarily or permanently.

Day 17, "Finding Text with Verity," introduced you to Verity, the powerful search tool that comes bundled with ColdFusion Server. You learned how Verity is used to construct whole-site searches that can find text in documents including HTML pages, word-processor pages, and spreadsheets. You now know how to quickly create search engines that can help users find data in even the most complex sites.

Day 18, "Working with Files and Directories," gave you your first taste of using ColdFusion to work with files and directories on your Web server. You learned how tags such as <CFFILE> can enable you to add, remove, and edit files, and how <CFDIRECTORY> does the same for your directory structures.

With the tools you learned about in this lesson, you can now create an entire file-management system driven by a Web interface.

Day 19, "Using Advanced SQL Techniques," took you further into advanced development by introducing SQL techniques such as column aliases, multistatements, and views. After this lesson, you have a good working knowledge of SQL that will serve you well whether you use it with ColdFusion or any other SQL application.

Day 20, "Using ColdFusion for E-Commerce Applications," provided a step-by-step tutorial on building an online store. You learned about the four elements of e-commerce sites and learned about ColdFusion tools that help you create each of those elements. You also learned about transaction types and how to choose the one that's right for your or your client's store. At this point, you should be able to develop a complete store application from the ground up.

Day 21, "Using ColdFusion's Debugging Tools to Troubleshoot Your Code," completed your 21-day tutorial by teaching you about the various error messages that can crop up in ColdFusion development. You learned how to identify the source of errors, and gained some tips for troubleshooting common problems. By the end of this lesson (and this book), you should now have a firm knowledge of ColdFusion development and be ready to create advanced, feature-rich applications for you and your clients.

APPENDIX **A**

Answers to the Quiz and Exercise Questions

This appendix provides answers to the quiz and exercise sections at the end of each chapter.

Day 1

Quiz

1. What is ColdFusion's primary function? Name two good uses for the program.

    ColdFusion's primary function is serving dynamically generated pages from database information. Recent versions of the program have been added

2. How does ColdFusion work with CGI scripts?

    In some cases, ColdFusion can be used to replace existing CGI scripts and add functions that would have been difficult (or expensive) to build in

CGI. If you don't want to replace your existing scripts, ColdFusion will run just fine alongside CGI, and you can call CGI scripts from ColdFusion templates just as you can in standard HTML pages.

3. What is dynamic page generation?

Dynamic page generation is the process by which Web pages are built on-the-fly, at the moment a user's browser requests them. The opposite of a dynamic page is a static page, a standard HTML page that resides on a server.

4. How does a ColdFusion-driven Web page get from a server to a client?

When a user's browser (the client) requests a Web page named with the ColdFusion file extension (.CFM), it momentarily turns the request over to ColdFusion for processing. CF scans the template and does whatever actions are requested (queries a database and so on), then returns the resulting HTML code to the server for delivery to the user.

5. Who was Elizabeth Taylor's most recent husband?

Liz's seventh and latest stand at the altar was with Larry Fortensky, a decidedly unfamous construction worker and truck driver. They were divorced in 1996.

Exercises

1. Check out Allaire's Web site and browse the Frequently Asked Questions (FAQ) section on ColdFusion 4.

   No definite answer.

2. Also on Allaire's site, check out some of the links to other ColdFusion-driven pages. Note some of the ways others use ColdFusion in their design and compare them to your own design needs.

   No definite answer.

Day 2

Quiz

1. What are the three components of a ColdFusion application?

   The database, the datasource, and the template.

2. What does a user see at home when using his browser's view source function on a ColdFusion template?

   Standard HTML markup and text. ColdFusion tags and variables do not appear in output.

3. What are the three sections in a ColdFusion template?

The query, the HTML markup, and the output

4. What does SQL stand for, and what is it?

It stands for structured query language, and is a means of communication between an application and a database.

Exercises

1. Open a database file and identify the following elements: a table, a field, and a record.

No definite answer.

2. Open a database table and picture ways a record might be served up as a Web page.

No definite answer.

3. Open one of the sample template files included on the ColdFusion installation CD-ROM and identify the query and output sections.

You should have identified the query section as the part enclosed within the tags `<CFQUERY>` and `</CFQUERY>`, and the output section as that within `<CFOUTPUT>` and `</CFOUTPUT>`.

Day 3

Quiz

1. Name at least three questions you should ask a potential ColdFusion Web provider.

What version of ColdFusion does the provider use? How many datasources are supported? What is the process for updating a datasource? Where are databases stored?

2. What is ColdFusion Studio, and how is it different from ColdFusion Server?

ColdFusion Studio is a special program targeted at CF developers. It includes a semi-graphic interface for building template pages along with a single-user copy of ColdFusion Server. It sells for a fraction of the price of the server package, but can't be used to serve pages to others on the Web.

3. What are the two varieties of ColdFusion Server? How do they differ?

The two packages are ColdFusion Server Professional and ColdFusion Server Enterprise. They differ in the Web platforms they support. The Enterprise version also includes added features for secure e-commerce sites.

A

4. Which Web servers require special attention when installing ColdFusion Server?

On Windows platforms, some releases of the Apache server will need to be manually configured for ColdFusion. On Solaris platforms, Apache and Netscape users should check their docs as well.

5. Name two ways to start the ColdFusion Administrator.

The Administrator can be started from a Web page (all platforms), from the Windows "Start" menu (Windows NT and 9x), or from the system tray (Windows 9x only).

6. Describe the process of setting up a database as a ColdFusion datasource.

Open ColdFusion Administrator, choose the ODBC link under Datasources, browse for the database file, and name the datasource.

7. Name a reason you might need to stop ColdFusion service and describe how to do it.

You might need to stop the service if you're upgrading your Web server software or making other significant changes to your server. To start and stop service, use the utility in ColdFusion Administrator.

Exercise

1. If you don't already own a copy, download the demonstration edition of ColdFusion Server from Allaire's Web site and install it on your local computer.

No definite answer.

2. If you plan to host your site remotely, make a list of potential Web providers and contact them with the questions I discussed. Keep notes on their replies and compare them to hosting prices.

No definite answer.

3. Set up a sample datasource using a database existing on your system. Verify it using the verification utility in ColdFusion Administrator.

No definite answer.

Day 4

Quiz

1. What is an ODBC driver?

An ODBC driver is software that enables compatible programs to communicate with a database.

2. How is ColdFusion considered a "gateway" application?

It links a database to the Web by working in conjunction with the Web server software and ODBC.

3. What is a *schema*?

A schema is a visual map of a database showing tables, fields, and ways in which data is related

4. Why is it important to create a visual representation of a database before creating the actual file?

Creating a schema first allows you to determine whether data is being unnecessarily duplicated across tables, how each table will receive input, and how security should be set. It also helps work out bugs in database design.

5. On a 1973 Plymouth Fury, what color is the wire that switches between high and low headlight beams?

I still haven't figured this out, but I know it's not green—That's the dome light.

6. Why did I use lowercase letters and underscores in naming my database and tables?

To create a *filenaming convention*, or standard method that will keep things organized and portable from system to system.

7. What is a *primary key*?

A *primary key* is a value in a field that uniquely identifies a record.

8. Briefly describe the process of setting permissions on a table.

To set table permissions in most database applications, you first create a "user" or "users," then give the user read or write permissions to each table in your database.

9. Name three ways to get information into a database.

Using an input form, importing data, and retrieving it via a Web page form.

Exercises

A

1. Dream up a goofy, fictitious business and create a data map for it. If you have a real business, you can leave the goofy and fictitious parts out.

As you create your data map it should resemble the stages illustrated in Figures 4.2-4.5. Categories and input-output diagrams will vary depending on your business.

2. Design a small database for your "business" and enter some sample data.

No definite answer.

3. If you use a database application that supports list boxes (such as Microsoft Access), create a list box in one of your tables. It should draw information from another table in your database.

No definite answer.

4. Create a user in your database software. Set permissions on one of your tables to enable write permission from that user. Set another table to enable read-only access.

No definite answer.

5. Input some sample data into a database and explore input methods offered by your software.

No definite answer.

6. Check your word processing software's documentation to see whether it's ODBC compatible. If so, explore methods for reading and writing database information from word processing documents.

No definite answer.

Day 5

Quiz

1. What ColdFusion tags denote the beginning and end of a query section?

   <CFQUERY> and </CFQUERY>, respectively

2. In a basic SQL SELECT statement, what follows the word "FROM"?

   The name of the table we want to query

3. What are the two types of operators used in a WHERE clause?

   Relational operators and logical operators

4. Why are single quotes necessary when using a text string in a query?

   Single quotes identify the beginning and end of the text string and tell ColdFusion that the contents are to be evaluated as text. Occasionally, text strings contain characters that might otherwise be identified as special control characters, such as the equal sign or a comma.

5. What is the character that always appears in conjunction with the LIKE operator?

   The percent sign (%) always appears with the LIKE operator.

6. Which SQL command orders output alphabetically or numerically? How is it used?

   The ORDER BY command sorts output data by letter or number. It is placed at the end of a query, followed by a comma-delimited list of the fields by which to sort.

Exercises

1. Construct a sample database table with at least five fields. Set it up as a ColdFusion datasource and design a basic template that will query and output all records.

   Your query section should resemble Listing 5.2; your output section should look like Listing 5.3.

2. Using the same template file, refine the <CFQUERY> section to return only records where a field is equal to a value you specify. Use ORDER BY to sort the results alphabetically.

   Your query section should resemble Listing 5.18.

3. Refine your <CFQUERY> by using LIKE and the percent sign to search for a wild-card text string within a field, such as 'A%'

   Your query section should resemble Listing 5.16, with "A" instead of "D".

4. Construct a sample query that will search a hypothetical "orders" table for orders made between two calendar dates.

   Your query section should resemble Listing 5.14.

Day 6

Quiz

1. What is a *drill-down* application?

   A drill-down application consists of one page that shows a list of items and a second that shows detail on a selected item.

2. When you create a new folder to host ColdFusion template files, what two things do you need to do it?

   Folders that contain ColdFusion templates must be *shared* and allow for *execute* or *script* access, depending on your brand of Webserver.

3. What symbols open and close a ColdFusion comment?

   <! — · and — ·>, respectively.

4. In a URL passed to ColdFusion, what does the question mark (?) stand for?

   The question mark informs ColdFusion that the text following it will define a variable.

5. When should you use two hash marks (#) together?

   When you need to use a hash mark as literal text within <CFOUTPUT> tags. A common example is the hex code that identifies a background or font color.

A

Exercises

1. Return to the index and detail pages you built in this chapter and experiment with different ways of formatting the ColdFusion output. Try moving the fields around, making them bold, and so on.

   No definite answer.

2. Modify your template pages to produce some of the ColdFusion errors described in the section "Basic Troubleshooting." By understanding what creates these errors, you are better prepared to handle them when they occur in other projects.

   No definite answer.

3. Make your pages presentable by adding graphics and backgrounds. Use at least one graphic in the <CFOUTPUT> section.

   No definite answer.

Day 7

Quiz

1. What is the primary function of a form page?

   To collect data from the user and pass it on to an action page or program.

2. In the preceding examples, how does data input into a form page "get" to the action program or page?

   It is passed or "posted" in the form of a URL, behind the scenes.

3. What's the primary difference between the <CFINSERT> and <CFUPDATE> tags?

   The former is used to add new records to a table; the latter, to alter records already existing in a table.

4. Do input forms have to be coded as ColdFusion templates (.cfm files)?

   No. Form pages are a function of HTML and don't require ColdFusion. In the examples in this chapter, we created our forms as .cfm files only because we also used ColdFusion queries and output within the forms.

5. What is a "hidden" form field used for?

   To post data to an action page without having it appear in the page seen by the user.

6. Why does the <CFUPDATE> tag have to be supplied with a primary key, or ID field?

   Because the primary key field is the only one that uniquely identifies the record to be updated.

Exercises

1. Modify the confirmation page `insert.cfm` so that it also shows users the data they've just submitted to the database.

   No definite answer.

2. Design a Web form that will enable the Gargantuan administrator to add employee names to the Techs table.

   No definite answer.

3. Create a new file called `snippets.cfm`. Inside it, paste bits of queries or output you think might be useful on other projects. Describe each with "commented" text.

   No definite answer.

Day 8

Quiz

1. Where are Studio's resource tabs located by default?

   At the bottom of the resource area, or just below the two smaller windows at the left of the screen.

2. Before accessing remote files or datasources, what must you do first?

   You must first define a remote server in the Remote Files resource tab.

3. How do you access Studio's Tag Insight function?

   Begin typing a CFML or HTML tag and wait for the drop-down box to appear.

4. How do you launch the Table Wizard or Frame Wizard?

   Choose the appropriate edit tab just above the edit window and select the Table Wizard or Frame Wizard icon.

5. What does the SQL builder do?

   It provides a drag-and-drop interface to generate an SQL statement. After you craft a statement, it is inserted into your template page as text.

6. How do you toggle the resource area on and off?

   The F9 key toggles the resource area, giving more screen space to the edit window.

7. What must you first do to preview ColdFusion templates in the editor's Browse view?

   You must first define development mappings to tell Studio the URL of your Web server and related files.

A

Exercises

1. If you don't already have access to a copy of Studio, download the evaluation version from Allaire's Web site.

   No definite answer.

2. Define your local server in the resources area, or connect to a remote server and verify your connection by browsing the remote datasource and template files.

   No definite answer.

3. Create one of the sample template files from Day 7 using Studio. Use the SQL builder to create the necessary query.

   No definite answer.

4. Define a project using the Projects tab in the resource area. If you have more than one CF project on your system, define each of them.

   No definite answer.

5. Browse Studio's help references. Try a search for a keyword that interests you.

   No definite answer

Day 9

Quiz

1. Name three ways variables can be defined in ColdFusion applications.

   By the results of a query, by user input from a form, or by the `<CFSET>` tag. Other methods include server, session, and application variables, which are defined either within CF Administrator, or by your Web server.

2. Do `<CFIF>` statements have to be enclosed in `<CFOUTPUT>` tags?

   No.

3. Describe, in plain language, the flow of a `<CFIF>`-`<CFELSE>` statement.

   You should have answered something like the following: "If this is true, do this; if not, do that."

4. What is the distinguishing feature of the form input type `password`?

   When a user types text into a `password` form field, only asterisks are displayed.

5. Why are ColdFusion variables called "typeless"?

   Because their types don't have to be defined. Numbers will automatically be interpreted as numbers, text as text, and so on.

6. What is a variable scope?

Variable scopes are names appended to the names of variables to show the variable's source, such as from a query or from a form.

7. True or False: Hash marks are always used when defining a variable with <CFSET>.

False. You don't use the hash marks when defining the variable, but you do use them when you want the variable's value to be displayed later in the template.

Exercises

1. Using <CFIF>, create a two-template application that asks a question and returns a response depending on the user's answer.

No definite answer.

2. Use <CFIF> to create a simple form validation page in which a user must complete all fields before the form will be processed.

No definite answer.

3. Design a database table containing a list of people and their ages. Using this as a datasource, create a page using <CFSET> that will display the difference between two people's ages.

No definite answer.

Day 10

Quiz

1. What are the two modes of <CFTABLE>?

Text mode, which creates tables using the <PRE> tag, and HTMLTABLE mode, which creates tables in HTML 3.0.

2. If your table requires header fields, what parameter must you include in <CFTABLE>?

The COLHEADERS parameter, which alerts ColdFusion that the table will use column headers.

3. If your table requires rows that span multiple columns, which tool should you use to build it?

Plain old HTML tables, with <CFOUTPUT> used to populate the table rows that will contain data.

4. What is *nesting*?

Nesting occurs when you place one set of tags within another. Most ColdFusion tags support nesting.

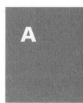

5. How many <CFOUTPUT> tags are necessary to build a grouped page?

   Two. The first defines the query and the field by which to group data. The second, or "child" output section shows how text will be displayed within a group.

6. What's the function of the HTML tag <A NAME>?

    <A NAME> sets up an invisible page anchor that can be referenced from within the document or from an outside link.

7. I have a database field that contains the following values: yes, yes, yes, no, maybe, yes, no, no. How many records would a query return if I used the DISTINCT tag on this field?

   Three: yes, no, and maybe.

Exercises

1. Create a page that uses <CFTABLE> to display the contents of a database. First, use the default <PRE> mode to display data, and then use HTMLTABLE.

   No definite answer.

2. Create a table using HTML <TABLE> tags and ColdFusion output. Use a title row that spans all columns, and end the table with a similar footer row. Use BGCOLOR to make one of your data columns display over a colored background.

   No definite answer.

3. Create a page that groups data into tables. Each group should have a header, followed by a table populated with data from that group.

   No definite answer.

4. Using SQL's DISTINCT, create index links to each of the grouped tables in the last exercise.

   No definite answer.

Day 11

Quiz

1. What happens when a user with a non-Java browser tries to view a ColdFusion-enhanced form page?

   They get either ColdFusion's standard "not supported" message, or error text you specify in the <CFFORM> tag.

2. Name the main feature supported by <CFINPUT> not supported by the standard HTML <INPUT> form tag.

<CFINPUT> supports text validation that can determine whether the user has input a valid phone number, ZIP code, and so on.

3. What's the difference between <CFINPUT> and <CFTEXTINPUT>?

<CFINPUT> also enables radio buttons and check boxes, whereas <CFTEXTINPUT> is designed specifically for text input. In addition, the latter creates boxes in JavaScript rather than HTML so you can customize box and font color.

4. What's the main benefit of using <CFSELECT> instead of a standard form <SELECT>?

<CFSELECT> simplifies the process of populating a select box with query output.

5. What is the parameter used with a query-driven <CFSELECT> to specify which option will be selected by default?

Not surprisingly, it's the SELECTED parameter, which must point to text from the field you specified as your VALUE. If you use the query field title as your VALUE, your SELECTED parameter will contain the text of a valid title in your table, such as "Some Book Title."

6. If you want to create a <CFSLIDER> that will show values 5, 10, 15, 20, and so on up to 100, what are the two parameters to use with the tag?

The RANGE parameter will be set to 5,100 and SCALE will be set to 5. This will enable the user to select values in increments of five, beginning with "5."

Exercises

1. Create a form that requires users to input a valid Social Security number. Customize the error message so that it reads "You Loser!" if they don't.

No definite answer.

2. Create a form that will collect user input in text boxes. Use <CFTEXTINPUT> to customize the color, font, and size of the boxes.

No definite answer.

3. Create a form that enables users to select more than one value from a SELECT box. Use <CFSELECT> and a query to create selections, and specify a selection to appear as the default.

No definite answer.

4. Create a slider that enables users to choose a decade between 1900 and the present using <CFSLIDER>.

No definite answer.

Day 12

Quiz

 1. Name the three situations in which you should use SQL updates instead of the ColdFusion equivalents.

When you need to insert data into more than one table, when your insert or update action is generally too complex to be handled with <CFINSERT> or <CFUPDATE>, or when you need to delete a record or records from a table.

2. How do you recover a record that has been accidentally removed with the DELETE command?

You don't.

3. What ColdFusion tag makes multifunction form pages possible?

<CFIF> enables you to perform more than one ACTION on a single page.

4. What are the primary differences between a form page designed to add a new record and one designed to edit an existing record?

Pages that enable users to input new records don't have VALUEs specified in their input fields. "Edit" pages do contain VALUEs, which are usually supplied by query results.

5. Name some uses for the <CFGRID> tag.

<CFGRID> provides an easy way to build input forms for tables that have lots of fields. It's also valuable for quickly displaying complex data that would get unwieldy in a standard HTML table.

Exercises

1. Create three sets of input forms and ACTION pages that use the SQL commands INSERT, UPDATE, and DELETE.

Your pages should resemble the examples in this chapter.

2. Create a multifunction form page that enables users to add, edit, or delete a database record. Use <CFIF> on your ACTION page(s) to determine which action should occur.

No definite answer.

3. Choose one of your database tables that contains five or more fields and design pages using <CFTREE> and <CFGRID> to display table contents. Create an ACTION page for your <CFGRID> to enable users to edit data in the grid.

No definite answer.

Day 13

Quiz

1. What is the primary function of the <CFMAIL> tag?

   It is used to send mail via a valid SMTP mail server.

2. What does <CFMAIL> display when it successfully sends a message?

   Nothing, which is why it's important to build your own confirmation messages into pages that use <CFMAIL>.

3. How do you use the results of a <CFQUERY> with a <CFMAIL> tag?

   You specify the QUERY parameter in your <CFMAIL> tag, and then supply query variables to any other parameters you want. For example, if your database table contained a field called user_email, you might supply the variable #user_email# with <CFMAIL>'s TO parameter to send mail to each user returned by the query.

4. What parameter must be set to use HTML code in message bodies?

   You use TYPE="HTML" in a <CFMAIL> tag to specify that you're sending HTML-enhanced content in your message body.

5. Name the three ACTION types used with <CFPOP>.

   They are GETHEADERONLY, GETALL, and DELETE.

6. How does <CFPOP> return the results of a mail check?

   It makes them available in the same way <CFQUERY> stores the results of a query. Each header element is assigned to a specific variable used with <CFPOP>. To display them, you'd use <CFOUTPUT query="x">, where x is the name you gave the <CFPOP> process.

Exercises

1. Create a database table containing names and email addresses of friends and family. Use <CFMAIL> to create a template that will send the same message to all of them. Tell them how you're destined for the high life as a ColdFusion developer.

   No definite answer.

2. Create a form page and an action page that will enable users to supply an email address, type in some text, and have that text returned to them as an email.

   No definite answer.

3. Create a template using <CFPOP> that will display the messages currently waiting on your mail server. Design a second page using <CFPOP>'s DELETE action that will enable you to remove unwanted messages.

   No definite answer.

A

Day 14

Quiz

1. When do ColdFusion functions require hash-mark delimiters?

   Just like variables, functions require hash marks when they appear between `<CFOUTPUT>` and `</CFOUTPUT>` tags. If they appear as part of a tag, such as `<CFIF SomeFunction(SomeVariable)>`, the marks aren't required.

2. Are function names case-sensitive?

   Function names are not case-sensitive, although it's a good idea to use ColdFusion's suggested case (such as `DollarFormat()`) to make them easy to identify in your template pages.

3. Name two functions that might be used to trim leading or trailing spaces from a text string.

   `LTrim()` strips leading spaces; `RTrim()` works on trailing spaces.

4. Briefly describe a date/time object.

   A date/time object is a special unit that may hold a month, date, and year, as well as an hour, minute, and second. It is created, manipulated, and displayed using date and time functions.

5. In the jargon of functions, what is a token?

   A token is the part of a string that appears between two delimiters. For example, if I specify that I want to use spaces as delimiters in this sentence, each word would be considered a token because it appears between spaces.

6. What is a mask?

   A mask is a bit of text that specifies how a function displays a variable. For example, using a mask such as `MM/DD/YY` with `DateFormat()` causes the date January 1, 2000 to display as `01/01/00`.

Exercises

1. Create a table in which at least one field contains dollar values. Add some values that contain commas for thousands, some that contain decimal points and trailing zeros, some that are whole numbers, and so on. Using ColdFusion functions, create a template that will query your table and display the results neatly aligned, each with dollar signs, commas, and two decimal places.

   Your output should use `DollarFormat()` and resemble Figure 14.3.

2. Create a table that contains the birth dates of friends and relatives. Using date and time functions, create a template that will show how many days separate two of the

dates. Also list the number of weeks, years, and months that separate the dates. (If you plan to display your handiwork to others, it's best not to use older people in your comparisons.)

Your template should use the function DateDiff().

3. Using <CFOUTPUT>'s GROUP parameter, create a template that displays records in groups, such as all employees in Production followed by all employees in Marketing. Use UCase() to create uppercase headers to identify each group.

No definite answer.

Day 15

Quiz

1. What is the default delimiter character for a list?

The comma. Other characters can be used when reading the list by specifying the DELIMITERS parameter in <CFLOOP>.

2. Name three ways to get data into a list.

By manually creating the list with <CFSET>; by dynamically generating list contents with a <CFQUERY>; or by assigning form input to a list.

3. What is a structure *key*?

It's a unique identifier for a bit of data stored in the structure.

4. Which of the three variable types covered in this chapter can be passed via a URL?

Only lists can be passed in URLs because they are made up of only plain text. Structures and arrays are more complex.

5. When assigning data to arrays, what do the two bracketed numbers after the array name stand for?

The first is the array row in which to insert data; the second refers to the array column.

6. What does the function ArrayLen do, and where would you use it?

It counts the length (in rows) of an existing array. It is often used with +1 to specify that data should be inserted after the last row counted.

Exercises

1. Create a Web form that lets users input a comma-delimited list of keywords. Use their input to search a database and return the results.

No definite answer.

A

2. Use the results of a query to populate a structure. On the same page, create a <CFOUTPUT> section that draws information from your structure.

No definite answer.

3. Use a query to create an array that mimics a two-dimensional table in your database.

No definite answer.

Day 16

Quiz

1. Describe the Web's statelessness.

You should have answered something like: Without using special tools, Web servers have no knowledge of things that have happened before.

2. Where should Application.cfm reside on your server?

In the root directory of the application it defines.

3. How long does an application variable persist?

For as long as the application continues to live on the server, or until the variable is "timed out" by a user setting.

4. In client-state management, when would you use the #CLIENT.URLToken# variable?

When you're concerned that your users' browsers might not support cookies. URLToken provides an alternative by passing the user's CFID and CFTOKEN to each page in your application.

5. In client-state management, what data is saved on the user's machine?

Using default settings, just the CFID and CFTOKEN values. The rest is stored on the server. ColdFusion can also be configured to save *all* client data to a local database or to a cookie on the user's machine.

6. How do you delete a cookie set with <CFCOOKIE>?

You reset the cookie using the special expiration parameter now.

Exercises

1. Create a two-page application consisting of a form and an ACTION page. Create an Application.cfm file to set default parameters for the page including background color, font face, and datasource name.

No definite answer.

2. Using the application from the previous exercise, enable client-state management and modify your ACTION page so that it adds the form input to client variables. Create a third page that reads these variables, using code such as #CLIENT.some_variable#. Use at least one of the reserved client variables in your display.

No definite answer.

3. Using the same application, use session variables to create a text display that appears for as long as the user browses in the current session. When the user leaves the session and returns later, she should see a new text message.

No definite answer.

Day 17

Quiz

1. Name the two ways to create a new Verity collection.

You can create Verity collections from ColdFusion Administrator, or by using the <CFCOLLECTION> tag in a template page.

2. Name the two ways to index a Verity collection.

You can index Verity collections from ColdFusion Administrator, or by using the <CFINDEX> tag in a template page.

3. When indexing a collection, why is the Return URL field so important?

It is used by Verity to provide the Web location of files returned by a search. If you enter the wrong Return URL, your search results will not link to the specified pages.

4. What three parameters are required by <CFSEARCH> to perform a successful search?

You need a NAME for the search, a COLLECTION to search, and some CRITERIA to search for.

5. What is contained in the #score# variable returned by <CFSEARCH>?

#score# holds a relevancy score showing how well the item matched the specified criteria.

6. Describe the process used to add database records to a Verity collection.

You first design a query to get the information from a datasource, and then you use <CFINDEX> to add the query data to the collection.

7. What is different about the way files and database records are displayed as search results?

Database records don't have an associated URL.

A

Exercises

1. Using ColdFusion Administrator, create a Verity collection that indexes all the .html and .cfm pages on your Web site. Design a two-page interface to search the collection and display results.

   No definite answer.

2. Using the <CFCOLLECTION> and <CFINDEX> tags, build an interface that enables you to create and populate a Verity collection.

   No definite answer.

3. Using <CFQUERY> and <CFINDEX>, create an interface that inserts data from one of your datasources into a Verity collection.

   No definite answer.

Day 18

Quiz

1. True or false: When you create a form that enables users to upload a file, ColdFusion automatically creates a browse box to enable users to find files on their server.

   False. This box is created by the <FORM> parameter TYPE=FILE. Your upload forms don't need to use ColdFusion at all, but your ACTION pages do.

2. Name three attributes used with <CFFILE>'s upload ACTION.

   DESTINATION, FILEFIELD, and NAMECONFLICT. You might also use the optional attribute ACCEPT, which takes a comma-list of file types that will be accepted as input.

3. Where should your upload forms and ACTION pages reside on your server? (Hint: Think "security.")

   In a directory that is password-protected at the server level. If you're dealing with extremely confidential data such as trade secrets, customer lists, and so on, you might want to add even more security measures. Some of these additional security measures will be discussed in Chapter 20, "Working with ColdFusion's Debugging Tools."

4. Name the four attributes used with NAMECONFLICT.

   They are error, skip, overwrite, and makeunique.

5. What file types may be read and written with <CFFILE>?

   <CFFILE>'s read, write, and append ACTIONs work only with text files. A special ACTION called readbinary will read binary content.

Exercises

1. In a password-protected directory, create form and ACTION pages that enable users to upload a photo and a description of themselves to your server. Use <CFFILE>'s file object attributes to write information about the files to a database so that they may be displayed in a template.

   No definite answer.

2. In a password-protected directory, create a form that enables a client to upload a database file and thus update that client's ColdFusion datasource. Use file object attributes to log details about the upload to a database table.

   No definite answer.

3. In a password-protected directory, create a simple guestbook that accepts text files from a user and appends them to a master file.

   No definite answer.

Day 19

Quiz

1. Name at least three control characters that can give ColdFusion problems when used in variable names.

   You could have listed any of these: a space, ", ', -, or #.

2. When defining column aliases, what character is used to delimit the original field name?

   The backtick, or "`" character.

3. Name the two types of SQL functions. One of them isn't discussed in this book. Why?

   The two types of SQL functions are aggregate and scalar. SQL's Scalar functions aren't discussed in this book because almost all of them can be duplicated with the standard ColdFusion functions .

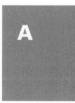

4. Why is it preferable to relate two database tables by a numeric field such as ID instead of a text field?

   Because SQL is more efficient at searching numeric fields. Also, if the ID field is one table's primary key, using it to relate the tables ensures that there is a unique identifier for every record in the table.

5. Why does the subquery example in this chapter use the IN operator?

   Because the subquery in the example will return more than one value. IN is necessary to tell SQL that it will be evaluating a list of values.

6. Name two ways to create a table view.

   Table views can be created natively in the database application, or by using an SQL statement in a ColdFusion template. The SQL statement is designed to be run only once.

7. What type of database software do you need to use stored procedures?

   A server-based program such as Oracle or Sybase.

Exercises

1. Create a database table that contains the names and ages of you, your family, and friends. Design a template page that uses aggregate functions to report on the average age, and the maximum and minimum ages.

   No definite answer.

2. Create a database table that simulates one that might be presented to you by a client. Be sure to use lots of illegal characters in the field names. Create a view that uses column aliases to select all records in the table, then design a simple template page that will query the view, rather than the table itself.

   No definite answer.

3. Create a second table that is related to the first by its ID field. Use both column aliases and a table join to present data from both tables in a single report page.

   No definite answer.

Day 20

Quiz

1. What are the four basic elements of e-commerce sites?

   An administration section, a catalog, a shopping cart, and a transaction section.

2. What are the functions of "browse" and "detail" pages in a catalog?

   A browse page provides a brief overview of several products, whereas a detail page presents all data for those who want to know more.

3. What must you do before using session variables (such as `session.cart`) in your shopping cart section?

   Enable session management by creating an `Application.cfm` file in your application's root directory.

4. Why is it necessary to store shopping cart selections in a session variable?

   So that the data can be read from, and written to, any page in the catalog. Without session variables, you'd have to pass the data from page to page in a URL.

5. What does SSL stand for? How does it work, and why is it used?

It stands for Secure Socket Layer. It is a security method by which data that passes between user and server is encrypted. It's particularly valuable for sending sensitive data such as credit card numbers.

6. Briefly describe how payment-processing services work.

Payment-processing services take customer and credit card data online. If a customer's card is successfully billed for the purchase amount, the service sends back data indicating that the purchase succeeded.

Exercises

1. Set up the sample catalog described in this chapter and add a search function to the page `browse_movies.cfm`.

   No definite answer.

2. Customize the store's admin pages by adding a function to add and remove categories. You might also want to add a "categories" table to your database and a corresponding field in the "movies" table.

   No definite answer.

3. Enhance your transaction section by changing `<FORM>`s to `<CFFORM>`s and adding verification to form fields such as ZIP Code, and so on, You'll find details on `<CFFORM>` and verification in Day 11.

   No definite answer.

4. If you are the merchant of a physical store or service that accepts credit-card payments, contact your bank and find out if it supports online processing for merchant accounts.

   No definite answer.

Day 21

A

Quiz

1. Name the three main components that report errors in ColdFusion applications.

   The Web server, ColdFusion Server, and the ODBC driver.

2. How are ODBC errors reported?

   They are passed to ColdFusion, which displays them as a Web page and identifies that the error has come from the ODBC driver.

3. What CFML tag might be used to guard against ODBC errors that come from a dynamic query?

The `<CFPARAM>` tag will check to see whether a parameter exists, and can be used to define a default value. This can help eliminate ODBC errors that occur when dynamic SQL parameters are empty or nonexistent.

4. What special variable is used to debug an individual template page?

   To debug a single page without enabling debugging features in Administrator, append the variable `mode=debug` to the template's URL.

5. Name ColdFusion Studio's two primary debugging tools.

   The Document Validator and the more sophisticated Interactive Debugger.

6. Which of ColdFusion's log files is of most use in troubleshooting application errors?

   The file `application.log` is the most useful because it maintains a record of every error ColdFusion has displayed to users.

Exercises

1. This first exercise is a given: Use the principles outlined in today's lesson to troubleshoot errors you may have encountered in previous applications.

   No definite answer.

2. Create a basic template page with `<CFQUERY>` and `<CFOUTPUT>` sections. Within it, add intentional typos that will duplicate each of the ODBC driver errors described in today's lesson.

   No definite answer.

3. Enable debugging options in ColdFusion Administrator and restrict their display to your own IP address. Load one of your applications and note the debugging messages as you navigate your pages.

   No definite answer.

ColdFusion Tags

This chapter describes each of the tags in the ColdFusion Markup Language (CFML). The introduction contains an alphabetical summary of ColdFusion tags, a list of new tags in ColdFusion 4.5, and a list of tags by category. The remainder of this chapter provides complete descriptions of each tag, listed alphabetically.

Alphabetical List of ColdFusion Tags

The ColdFusion Markup Language (CFML) consists of a set of tags you use in your ColdFusion pages to interact with data sources, manipulate data, and display output. Using CFML tags is very simple; tag syntax is much like HTML element syntax.

The following table provides brief descriptions of each CFML tag.

CFML Tag Summary	
CFML Tag	**Description**
CFABORT	Stops processing of a ColdFusion page at the tag location.
CFAPPLET	Embeds Java applets in a CFFORM.
CFAPPLICATION	Defines application name, activates client variables.
CFASSOCIATE	Enables sub-tag data to be saved with the base tag.
CFAUTHENTICATE	Authenticates a user and sets the security context for an application.
CFBREAK	Breaks out of a CFML looping construct.
CFCACHE	Caches ColdFusion pages.
CFCOL	Defines table column header, width, alignment, and text.
CFCOLLECTION	Creates and administers Verity collections.
CFCONTENT	Defines the content type and, optionally, the filename of a file to be downloaded by the current page.
CFCOOKIE	Defines and sets cookie variables.
CFDIRECTORY	Performs typical directory-handling tasks from within your ColdFusion application.
CFERROR	Displays customized HTML error pages when errors occur.
CFEXECUTE	Executes any developer-specified process on the server machine.
CFEXIT	Aborts processing of currently executing CFML custom tag.
CFFILE	Performs typical file-handling tasks from within your ColdFusion application.
CFFORM	Builds an input form and performs client-side input validation.

CFML Tag Summary (Continued)	
CFML Tag	**Description**
CFFTP	Permits FTP file operations.
CFGRID	Used in CFFORM to create a grid control for tabular data.
CFGRIDCOLUMN	Used in CFFORM to define the columns used in a CFGRID.
CFGRIDROW	Used with CFGRID to define a grid row.
CFGRIDUPDATE	Performs updates directly to ODBC data source from edited grid data.
CFHEADER	Generates HTTP headers.
CFHTMLHEAD	Writes text, including HTML, to the HEAD section of a specified page.
CFHTTP	Used to perform GET and POST to upload files or post a form, cookie, query, or CGI variable directly to a specified server.
CFHTTPPARAM	Used with CFHTTP to specify parameters necessary for a CFHTTP POST operation.
CFIF CFELSEIF CFELSE	Used to create IF-THEN-ELSE constructs.
CFIMPERSONATE	Allows you to impersonate a user defined in a security context defined in Advanced Security.
CFINCLUDE	Embeds references to ColdFusion pages.
CFINDEX	Used to create Verity search indexes.
CFINPUT	Used in CFFORM to create input elements such as radio buttons, checkboxes, and text entry boxes.
CFINSERT	Inserts records in an ODBC data source.
CFLDAP	Provides access to LDAP directory servers.
CFLOCATION	Opens a ColdFusion page or HTML file.
CFLOCK	Ensures data integrity and synchronizes the execution of CFML code.
CFLOOP	Repeats a set of instructions based on a set of conditions.
CFMAIL	Assembles and posts an email message.
CFMAILPARAM	Attaches a file or adds a header to an email message.

CFML Tag Summary (Continued)	
CFML Tag	**Description**
CFMODULE	Invokes a custom tag for use in your ColdFusion application pages.
CFOBJECT	Creates and uses COM, CORBA, or JAVA objects.
CFOUTPUT	Displays output of database query or other operation.
CFPARAM	Defines a parameter and its initial default value.
CFPOP	Retrieves messages from a POP mail server.
CFPROCESSINGDIRECTIVE	Suppresses extraneous white space, and other output.
CFPROCPARAM	Specifies parameter information for a stored procedure.
CFPROCRESULT	Specifies a result set name that other ColdFusion tags use to access the result set from a stored procedure.
CFQUERY	Passes SQL to a database.
CFQUERYPARAM	Reads, writes, and deletes keys and values in the system registry.
CFREGISTRY	Reads, writes, and deletes keys and values in the system registry.
CFREPORT	Embeds a Crystal Reports report.
CFRETHROW	Rethrows the currently active exception.
CFSCHEDULE	Schedules page execution with option to produce static pages.
CFSCRIPT	Encloses a set of CFScript statements.
CFSEARCH	Executes searches against data indexed in Verity collections using CFINDEX.
CFSELECT	Used in CFFORM to create a drop-down list box form element.
CFSERVLET	Executes a Java servlet on a JRun engine.
CFSERVLETPARAM	Used to pass data to the Java servlet. CFSERVLETPARAM is a child tag of CFSERVLET.
CFSET	Defines a variable.
CFSETTING	Define and control a variety ColdFusion settings.

CFML Tag Summary (Continued)	
CFML Tag	**Description**
CFSILENT	Suppresses all output that is produced by the CFML within the tag's scope.
CFSLIDER	Used in CFFORM to create a slider control element.
CFSTOREDPROC	Specifies database connection information and identifies the stored procedure to be executed.
CFSWITCH/CFCASE/CFDEFAULTCASE	Evaluates a passed expression and passes control to the CFCASE tag that matches the expression result.
CFTABLE	Builds a table.
CFTEXTINPUT	Places a single-line text entry box in a CFFORM.
CFTHROW	Raises a developer-specified exception.
CFTRANSACTION	Groups CFQUERYs into a single transaction; performs rollback processing.
CFTREE	Used in CFFORM to create a tree control element.
CFTREEITEM	Used with CFTREE to populate a tree control element in a CFFORM.
CFTRY/CFCATCH	Allows developers to catch and process exceptions in ColdFusion pages.
CFUPDATE	Updates rows in a database data source.
CFWDDX	Serializes and de-serializes CFML data structures to the XML-based WDDX format.

New Tags in ColdFusion 4.5

CFEXECUTE CFQUERYPARAM

CFHTTPPARAM CFRETHROW

CFIMPERSONATE CFSERVLET

CFMAILPARAM CFSERVLETPARAM

CFPROCESSINGDIRECTIVE CFSILENT

ColdFusion Forms Tags

CFAPPLET	CFINPUT
CFFORM	CFSELECT
CFGRID	CFSLIDER
CFGRIDCOLUMN	CFTEXTINPUT
CFGRIDROW	CFTREE
CFGRIDUPDATE	CFTREEITEM

Database Manipulation Tags

CFINSERT	CFQUERYPARAM
CFPROCPARAM	CFSTOREDPROC
CFPROCRESULT	CFTRANSACTION
CFQUERY	CFUPDATE

Data Output Tags

CFCOL	CFOUTPUT
CFCONTENT	CFTABLE
CFHEADER	

Exception Handling Tags

CFERROR

CFRETHROW

CFTHROW

CFTRY/CFCATCH

Extensibility Tags

CFCOLLECTION   CFSEARCH

CFEXECUTE   CFSERVLET

CFINDEX   CFSERVLETPARAM

CFOBJECT   CFWDDX

CFREPORT

File Management Tags

CFDIRECTORY

CFFILE

Flow-Control Tags

CFABORT   CFLOOP

CFBREAK   CFSWITCH/CFCASE/
                           CFDEFAULTCASE

CFEXECUTE   CFTHROW

CFIF/CFELSEIF/CFELSE   CFTRY/CFCATCH

CFLOCATION

Internet Protocol Tags

CFFTP   CFMAIL

CFHTTP   CFMAILPARAM

CFHTTPPARAM   CFPOP

CFLDAP

Java Servlet and Java Object Tags

CFOBJECT   CFSERVLETPARAM

CFSERVLET

Variable Manipulation Tags

CFCOOKIE   CFSCHEDULE

CFPARAM   CFSET

Web Application Framework Tags

CFAPPLICATION   CFERROR

CFASSOCIATE   CFLOCK

CFAUTHENTICATE

Other Tags

CFASSOCIATE   CFREPORT

CFCACHE   CFSCHEDULE

CFHTMLHEAD   CFSETTING

CFINCLUDE   CFSILENT

CFLOCK   CFWDDX

CFABORT

The CFABORT tag stops processing of a page at the tag location. ColdFusion simply returns everything that was processed before the CFABORT tag. CFABORT is often used with conditional logic to stop processing a page because of a particular condition.

Syntax   <CFABORT SHOWERROR="*error_message*">

SHOWERROR

Optional. Specify the error you want to display when CFABORT executes. This error message appears in the standard ColdFusion error page.

Usage   When combining CFABORT and CFERROR, remember that CFERROR is meant to redirect output to a specified page. CFABORT is intended to halt processing immediately.

If the CFABORT tag does not contain a SHOWERROR attribute value, processing stops immediately and the page contents are shown all the way up to the line containing the CFABORT tag.

When using CFABORT with SHOWERROR by itself (that is without defining an error page using CFERROR) page processing stops once the CFABORT tag is reached and the message defined in SHOWERROR is displayed to the client.

If you have a page in which you've defined both an error page using CFERROR and a CFABORT tag using the SHOWERROR attribute, ColdFusion redirects output to the error page specified in the CFERROR tag.

Example   cfabort

```
<!--- this example demonstrates the use of CFABORT
to stop the processing of a CFLOOP.  Note that in the second example, where CFABORT is used, the result
never appears --->

<HTML>
<HEAD>
<TITLE>CFABORT Example</TITLE>
</HEAD>
<BODY bgcolor=FFFFFF>

<H1>CFABORT Example</H1>

<P>
<H3>Example A: Let the instruction complete itself</H3>
<!--- first, set a variable --->
<CFSET myVariable = 3>
<!--- now, perform a loop that increments this value --->
<CFLOOP FROM="1" TO="4" INDEX="Counter">
    <CFSET myVariable = myVariable + 1>
</CFLOOP>
```

```
<CFOUTPUT>
<P>  The value of myVariable after incrementing through the loop
      #Counter# times is: #myVariable#
</CFOUTPUT>

<!--- reset the variable and show the use of CFABORT --->
<H3>Example B: Use CFABORT to halt the instruction</H3>

<CFSET myVariable = 3>
<!--- now, perform a loop that increments this value --->
<CFLOOP FROM="1" TO="4" INDEX="Counter">
      <!--- on the second time through the loop, CFABORT --->
      <CFIF Counter is 2>
          <CFABORT>
      <!--- the processing is stopped, and subsequent operations
      are not carried out by the CFAS --->
      <CFELSE>
      <CFSET myVariable = myVariable + 1>
      </CFIF>
</CFLOOP>

<CFOUTPUT>
<P>  The value of myVariable after incrementing through the loop
      #counter# times is: #myVariable#
</CFOUTPUT>

</BODY>
</HTML>
```

cfabort

CFAPPLET

Used in a CFFORM, CFAPPLET allows you to reference custom Java applets that have been previously registered using the ColdFusion Administrator.

To register a Java applet, open the ColdFusion Administrator and click the Applets button.

Syntax   <CFAPPLET APPLETSOURCE="*applet_name*"
             NAME="*form_variable_name*"
             HEIGHT="*height_in_pixels*"
             WIDTH="*width_in_pixels*"
             VSPACE="*space_above_and_below_in_pixels*"
             HSPACE="*space_on_each_side_in_pixels*"
             ALIGN="Left" or "Right" or "Bottom" or "Top" or "TextTop" or "Middle"
               or "AbsMiddle" or "Baseline" or "AbsBottom"
             NOTSUPPORTED="*message_to_display_for_nonJava_browser*"
             param_1="*applet_parameter_name*"
             param_2="*applet_parameter_name*"
             param_n="*applet_parameter_name*">

APPLETSOURCE
Required. The name of the registered applet.

NAME
Required. The form variable name for the applet.

HEIGHT
Optional. The height in pixels.

WIDTH
Optional. The width in pixels.

VSPACE
Optional. Space above and below applet in pixels.

HSPACE
Optional. Space on each side of the applet in pixels.

ALIGN
Optional. Alignment. Valid entries are:

- Left
- Right
- Bottom
- Top
- TextTop
- Middle

- AbsMiddle
- Baseline
- AbsBottom

NOTSUPPORTED

Optional. The text you want to display if the page containing a Java applet-based CFFORM control is opened by a browser that does not support Java or has Java support disabled. For example:

```
NOTSUPPORTED="<B>Browser must support Java to view
ColdFusion Java Applets</B>"
```
By default, if no message is specified, the following message appears:

```
<B>Browser must support Java to <BR>
view ColdFusion Java Applets!</B>
```

param*n*

Optional. The valid name of a registered parameter for the applet. Specify a parameter only if you want to override parameter values already defined for the applet using the ColdFusion Administrator.

Usage   Since Java applets must be pre-registered, the CFAPPLET tag can be very simple, taking the default parameter values as they were registered in the ColdFusion Administrator. You can also override parameters by invoking them directly in the CFAPPLET tag.

Example   cfapplet

```
<!--- This example shows the use of CFAPPLET --->
<HTML>
<HEAD>
<TITLE>CFAPPLET Example</TITLE>
</HEAD>

<BODY>
<H3>CFAPPLET Example</H3>

<P>Used in a CFFORM, CFAPPLET allows you to reference
custom Java applets that have been previously registered
using the ColdFusion Administrator.
<P>To register a Java applet, open the ColdFusion Administrator
and click the "Applets" link under the "extensions" section.
<P>This example applet copies text that you type into
a form.  Type some text, and then click "copy" to see
the copied text.

<CFFORM ACTION="copytext.cfm">
     <CFAPPLET appletsource="copytext" NAME="copytext">
</CFFORM>

</BODY>
</HTML>
```

cfapplet

CFAPPLICATION

Defines scoping for a ColdFusion application, enables or disables storing client variables, and specifies a client variable storage mechanism. By default, client variables are disabled. Also, used to enable session variables and to set timeouts for both session and application variables. Session and application variables are stored in memory.

Syntax   <CFAPPLICATION NAME="*application_name*"
   CLIENTMANAGEMENT="Yes" or "No"
   CLIENTSTORAGE="*datasource_name*" or "Registry" or "Cookie"
   SETCLIENTCOOKIES="Yes" or "No"
   SESSIONMANAGEMENT="Yes" or "No"
   SESSIONTIMEOUT=#CreateTimeSpan(*days, hours,*
    minutes, seconds)#
   APPLICATIONTIMEOUT=#CreateTimeSpan(*days, hours,*
    minutes, seconds)#
   SETDOMAINCOOKIES="Yes" or "No"
 >

NAME

The name you want to give your application. This name can be up to 64 characters long. Required for application and session variables to work. Optional for client variables.

CLIENTMANAGEMENT

Optional. Yes or No. Enables client variables. Default is No.

CLIENTSTORAGE

Optional. Specifies the mechanism for storing client variables:

- *datasourcename* — ColdFusion stores client variables in the specified ODBC or native data source. To use this option you must create a client variable storage repository using the Variables page of the ColdFusion Administrator.

- Registry — ColdFusion stores client variables in the system registry. This is the default.

- Cookie — ColdFusion stores client variables on the client machine in a cookie. Storing client data in a cookie is scalable to large numbers of clients, but this storage mechanism has some limitations. Chief among them is that if the client turns off cookies in the browser, client variables won't work.

SETCLIENTCOOKIES

Optional. Yes or No. Yes enables client cookies. Default is Yes.

If you set this attribute to "NO", ColdFusion does not automatically send the CFID and CFTOKEN cookies to the client browser; you must manually code CFID and CFTOKEN on the URL for every page that uses Session or Client variables.

SESSIONMANAGEMENT

Optional. Yes or No. Yes enables session variables. Default is No.

SESSIONTIMEOUT

Optional. Enter the CreateTimeSpan function and the values you want in days, hours, minutes, and seconds, separated by commas to specify the lifespan of any session variables that are set. The default value is specified in the Variables page of the ColdFusion Administrator.

APPLICATIONTIMEOUT

Optional. Enter the CreateTimeSpan function and the values you want in days, hours, minutes, and seconds, separated by commas to specify the lifespan of any application variables that are set. The default value is specified in the Variables page of the ColdFusion Administrator.

SETDOMAINCOOKIES

Optional. Yes or No. Sets the CFID and CFTOKEN cookies for an entire domain not just a single host. Applications that are running on clusters must set this value to Yes. The default is No.

Usage   CFAPPLICATION is typically used in the Application.cfm file to set defaults for a specific ColdFusion application.

CFAPPLICATION enables application variables unless they have been disabled in the ColdFusion Administrator. Using the SESSIONMANAGEMENT attribute to enable session variables is also overridden by the Administrator. See ../../ Administering_ColdFusion_Server/contents.htm*Administering ColdFusion Server*/a for information about the ColdFusion Administrator.

Server, Application, and Session Variables

Whenever you display, set, or update variables in the server, application, and session scopes, you should use the CFLOCK tag with the SCOPE attribute. For server variables, specify the "Server" scope. For application variables, specify the "Application" scope. For session variables, specify the "Session" scope. See CFLOCK for information about locking server, application, and session scopes.

If you are running ColdFusion on a cluster, you must specify either Cookie or a data source name for CLIENTSTORAGE; you cannot specify Registry.

Example   cfapplication1

```
<!--------------------------------------------------------------
   This example shows how CFLOCK can be used to guarantee the
   consistency of data updates to variables in the Application,
      Server, and Session scopes.
      You should copy the following code into an Application.cfm
   file in the snippets directory.
   -------------------------------------------------------------->
      <HTML>
      <HEAD>
          <title>Define Session and Application Variables</title>
```

```
</HEAD>

<BASEFONT FACE="Arial, Helvetica" SIZE=2>
<BODY bgcolor="#FFFFD5">

<H3>CFAPPLICATION Example</H3>

<P>CFAPPLICATION defines scoping for a ColdFusion application and
enables or disables the storing of application and/or session
variables. This tag is placed in a special file called
Application.cfm that is run before any other CF template in a
directory where the Application.cfm file appears.

<CFAPPLICATION NAME="ETurtle" SESSIONTIMEOUT=#CreateTimeSpan(0, 0,
 0, 60)# SESSIONMANAGEMENT="yes">
<!-------------------------------------------------------------
Initialize the session and application variables that will be
used by E-Turtleneck. Use the session scope for the session
variables.
------------------------------------------------------------->
<CFLOCK SCOPE="Session" TIMEOUT="30" TYPE="Exclusive">
    <CFIF NOT IsDefined("session.size")>
        <CFSET session.size = "">
    </CFIF>
    <CFIF NOT IsDefined("session.color")>
        <CFSET session.color = "">
    </CFIF>
</CFLOCK>

<!------------------------------------------------------------
Use the application scope for the application variable. This
variable keeps track of the total number of turtlenecks sold.
------------------------------------------------------------->
<CFLOCK SCOPE="Application" TIMEOUT="30" TYPE="Exclusive">
    <CFIF NOT IsDefined("application.number")>
        <CFSET application.number = 1>
    </CFIF>
</CFLOCK>
<CFLOCK SCOPE="Application" TIMEOUT="30" TYPE="ReadOnly">
    <CFOUTPUT>
    E-Turtleneck is proud to say that we have sold
    #application.number# turtlenecks to date.
    </CFOUTPUT>
</CFLOCK>
<!--- End of Application.cfm --->
```

cfapplication1

CFASSOCIATE

The CFASSOCIATE tag allows sub-tag data to be saved with the base tag. This applies to custom tags only.

Syntax

```
<CFASSOCIATE BASETAG="base_tag_name"
    DATACOLLECTION="collection_name">
```

BASETAG

Required. Specifies the name of the base tag.

DATACOLLECTION

Optional. Specifies the name of the structure in which the base tag stores sub-tag data. The default is AssocAttribs.

Usage

Call this tag within a sub-tag to save sub-tag data in the base tag.

ColdFusion saves sub-tag attributes in a structure whose default name is AssocAttribs. Use the DataCollection attribute to specify a non-default structure name. Specify a non-default structure name when the base tag can have multiple sub tags and you want to segregate sub-tag attributes.

If the custom tag uses an attribute collection, the attributes passed in the attribute collection are saved as independent attribute values, with no indication that they were grouped together in a structure within the custom tag.

Example

cfassociate

```
<!--- Find the context --->
<CFIF thisTag.executionMode is "start">
 <!--- Associate attributes
    This code occurs in a custom tag's
    sub tag. --->
 <CFASSOCIATE BASETAG="CF_TAGBASE">

 <!--- Define defaults for attributes --->
 <CFPARAM NAME="attributes.happy" DEFAULT="Yes">
 <CFPARAM NAME="attributes.sad" DEFAULT="No">
 ...
```

cfassociate

CFAUTHENTICATE

The CFAUTHENTICATE tag authenticates a user, setting a security context for the application. See the descriptions of the functions IsAuthenticated and AuthenticatedContext.

Syntax
```
<CFAUTHENTICATE SECURITYCONTEXT="security_context"
     USERNAME="user_ID"
     PASSWORD="password"
     SETCOOKIE="Yes" or "No"
     THROWONFAILURE="Yes" or "No">
```

SECURITYCONTEXT
Required. Security context with which the specified user is authenticated. This context must have been previously defined in the security system.

USERNAME
Required. User to be authenticated.

PASSWORD
Required. Password for the user.

SETCOOKIE
Optional. Default is Yes. Indicates whether ColdFusion sets a cookie to contain authentication information. This cookie is encrypted and its contents include user name, security context, browser remote address, and the HTTP user agent.

THROWONFAILURE
Optional. Default is Yes. Indicates whether ColdFusion throws an exception (of type SECURITY) if authentication fails.

Usage
Code this tag in the Application.cfm file to set a security context for your application.

Call the IsAuthenticated function to determine if the user has been authenticated. If you specify No for SETCOOKIE, you must call CFAUTHENTICATE for every page in the application (perhaps in an Application.cfm file).

If you specify THROWONFAILURE=Yes, you can enclose CFAUTHENTICATE in a CFTRY/CFCATCH block to handle possible exceptions programmatically.

Example cfauthenticate
```
<!--- This example shows the use of CFAUTHENTICATE
in an Application.cfm file --->
<CFIF NOT IsAuthenticated()>
 <CFTRY>
 <CFAUTHENTICATE SECURITYCONTEXT="Allaire" USERNAME=#user#
  PASSWORD=#pwd#>
 <CFCATCH TYPE="Security">
 <!--- the message to display --->
```

```
<H3>Authentication error</H3>
 <CFOUTPUT>
 <!--- Display the message. Alternatively, you might place
   code here to define the user to the security domain. --->
 <P>#CFCATCH.message#
 </CFOUTPUT>
 </CFCATCH>
 </CFTRY>
</CFIF>
<CFAPPLICATION NAME="Personnel">
 ...
```

cfauthenticate

CFBREAK

Used to break out of a CFLOOP. See Breaking out of a loop, later in this chapter, for more information.

Syntax <CFBREAK>

Example cfbreak

```
<!--- This example shows the use of CFBREAK to exit
a loop when a condition is met --->

<!--- select a list of courses and use CFLOOP to find a condition
and then break the loop --->
<CFQUERY NAME="GetCourses" DATASOURCE="cfsnippets">
SELECT *
FROM courses
ORDER by Number
</CFQUERY>
<HTML>
<HEAD>
<TITLE>
CFBREAK Example
</TITLE>
</HEAD>
<BODY bgcolor=silver>

<H1>CFBREAK Example</H1>
<P>This example uses CFLOOP to cycle through a query to find a desired
value. (In our example, a list of values corresponding to courses in the
cfsnippets datasource).
When the conditions of the query are met, CFBREAK stops the loop.
...
<!--- loop through the query until desired value is found,
    then use CFBREAK to exit the query --->
<CFLOOP QUERY="GetCourses">
    <CFIF GetCourses.Number is form.courseNum>
    <CFOUTPUT>
    <H4>Your Desired Course was found:</H4>
    <PRE>#Number##Descript#</PRE></CFOUTPUT>
    <CFBREAK>
    <CFELSE>
        <BR>Searching...
    </CFIF>
</CFLOOP>
</CFIF>

</BODY>
</HTML>
```

cfbreak

CFCACHE

CFCACHE allows you to speed up pages considerably in cases where the dynamic content doesn't need to be retrieved each time a user accesses the page. To accomplish this, it creates temporary files that contain the static HTML returned from a particular run of the ColdFusion page.

You can use CFCACHE for simple URLs and URLs that contain URL parameters.

Syntax
```
<CFCACHE
    ACTION="CACHE" or "FLUSH" or "CLIENTCACHE" or "OPTIMAL"
    PROTOCOL="protocol_name"
    TIMEOUT="#DateAdd(datepart, number, date)#"
    DIRECTORY="directory_name_for_map_file"
    CACHEDIRECTORY="directory_name_for_cached_pages"
    EXPIREURL="wildcarded_URL_reference"
    PORT= "port_number">
```

ACTION

Optional. Specifies one of the following:

- CACHE — Specifies server-side caching. The default is CACHE.

- FLUSH — Refresh the cached page. If you specify FLUSH, you can also specify the DIRECTORY and EXPIREURL attributes.

- CLIENTCACHE —Specifies browser caching.

- OPTIMAL—Specifies optimal caching through a combination of server-side and browser caching.

See the Usage section for more information.

PROTOCOL

Optional. Specifies the protocol used to create pages from cache. Specify either HTTP:// or HTTPS://. The default is HTTP://.

TIMEOUT

Optional. DateTime that specifies the oldest acceptable cached page. If the cached page is older than the specified datetime, ColdFusion refreshes the page. By default, ColdFusion uses all cached pages. For example, if you want a cached file to be no older than 4 hours, code the following:

```
<CFCACHE TIMEOUT="#DateAdd("h", "-4", Now() )#">
```

DIRECTORY

Optional. Used with ACTION=FLUSH. Specifies the fully qualified path of a directory containing the cfcache.map to be used when ACTION=FLUSH. The default is the directory of the current page.

CACHEDIRECTORY

Optional. Specifies the fully qualified path of the directory where the pages are to be cached. The default is the directory of the current page.

EXPIREURL

Optional. Used with ACTION=FLUSH. EXPIREURL takes a wildcarded URL reference that ColdFusion matches against all mappings in the cfcache.map file. The default is to flush all mappings. For example, "foo.cfm" matches "foo.cfm"; "foo.cfm?*" matches "foo.cfm?x=5" and "foo.cfm?x=9".

PORT

Optional. The port number of the web server from which the page is being requested. The port number defaults to 80. The port number is useful because the CFCACHE code calls CFHTTP. If the port number is specified correctly in the internal call to CFHTTP, the URL of each retrieved document is resolved to preserve links.

Usage   In its simplest form, all you need to do is code <CFCACHE> at the top of a page for it to be cached.

With the ACTION attribute, you can specify server-side caching, browser caching, or a combination of server-side and browser caching. The advantage of browser caching is that it takes no ColdFusion resources because the browser stores the pages in its own cache, thus, improving performance. The advantage of using a combination of the two forms of caching is that it optimizes performance; if the browser cache times out, the server can retrieve the cached data from its own cache.

In addition to the cached files themselves, CFCACHE uses a mapping file to control caching. It is named cfcache.map and uses a format similar to a Windows INI file. The mapping of a URL with parameters is stored as follows. Assume a directory "c:\InetPub\wwwroot\dir1" that has a CFM file called "foo.cfm", which can be invoked with or without URL parameters. The cfcache.map file entries for foo.cfm will look like this:

```
[foo.cfm]
Mapping=C:\InetPub\wwwroot\dir1\CFCBD.tmp
SourceTimeStamp=08/31/1999 08:59:04 AM

[foo.cfm?x=5]
Mapping=C:\InetPub\wwwroot\dir1\CFCBE.tmp
SourceTimeStamp=08/31/1999 08:59:04 AM

[foo.cfm?x=9]
Mapping=C:\InetPub\wwwroot\dir1\CFCBF.tmp
SourceTimeStamp=08/31/1999 08:59:04 AM
```

The cfcache.map file in a given directory stores mappings for that directory only. Any time the timestamp of the underlying page changes, ColdFusion updates the cache file for that URL only. ColdFusion uses the SourceTimeStamp field to determine if the currently cached file is up to date or needs to be rebuilt.

You can refresh the cache in the following ways:

- TIMEOUT attribute — ColdFusion tests the timestamp of the cached file against the TIMEOUT attribute. If the cached file's timestamp is older than TIMEOUT, the old file is deleted and a new one created. You can use fixed dates if necessary, but it's preferable to use relative dates. This is the preferred technique and it works for seconds, hours, days, weeks, years, etc.

- ACTION=FLUSH — You use ACTION=FLUSH to force the clean up of cached files. It can take two attributes, DIRECTORY and EXPIREURL.

- Manually — Manually or programmatically (using CFFILE) delete the .tmp files. This is not recommended.

Note the following regarding CFCACHE:

- CFCACHE requires that ColdFusion Server "simultaneous requests" be greater than 1. When a cache file is generated, the requested page requires two connections to satisfy the request. When a cached file is found, only one request is required.

- Debug settings have no effect on CFCACHE unless the template explicitly turns it on. When generating a cached file, CFCACHE uses <CFSETTING SHOWDEBUGOUTPUT="NO">.

- ColdFusion does not cache pages that are dependent on anything other than URL parameters.

- To use CFCACHE with the Secure Sockets Layer (SSL), specify PROTOCOL="http://". If you need to use SSL, you must run ColdFusion as a desktop application. Please note, however, Allaire strongly recommends that you run the ColdFusion Server as a service. For more details about using SSL, see Knowledge Base article #1096 at http://www.allaire.com/Support/KnowledgeBase/SearchForm.cfm.

- If a template returns an error for any reason, the error page gets cached.

Example   cfcache

```
<!--- This example will produce as many cached files as there
      are possible URL parameter permutations. --->
<CFCACHE TIMEOUT="#DateAdd("h", "-4", Now() )#">
<HTML>
<HEAD>
<TITLE>CFCACHE Example</TITLE>
</HEAD>
<BODY>
<H1>CFCACHE Example</H1>

<H3>This is a test of some simple output</H3>
<CFPARAM NAME="URL.x" DEFAULT="no URL parm passed" >
<CFOUTPUT>The value of URL.x = # URL.x #</CFOUTPUT>
</BODY>
</HTML>
```

cfcache

CFCOL

Defines table column header, width, alignment, and text. Only used inside a CFTABLE.

Syntax

```
<CFCOL HEADER="column_header_text"
    WIDTH="number_indicating_width_of_column"
    ALIGN="Left" or "Right" or "Center"
    TEXT="double_quote_delimited_text_indicating_type_of_text">
```

HEADER

Required. The text to use for the column's header.

WIDTH

Optional. The width of the column in characters (the default is 20). If the length of the data displayed exceeds the width value, the data is truncated to fit.

ALIGN

Optional. Column alignment, Left, Right, or Center.

TEXT

Optional. Double-quote delimited text that determines what displays in the column. The rules for the text attribute are identical to the rules for CFOUTPUT sections, meaning that it can consist of a combination of literal text, HTML tags, and query record set field references. This means you can embed hyperlinks, image references, and even input controls within table columns.

Example

```
cfcol
<!--- This example shows the use of CFCOL and CFTABLE
to align information returned from a query --->

<!--- this query selects employee information from the
cfsnippets data source --->
<CFQUERY NAME="GetEmployees" DATASOURCE="cfsnippets">
SELECT Emp_ID, FirstName, LastName, EMail, Phone, Department
FROM   Employees
</CFQUERY>

<HTML>
<HEAD>
<TITLE>
CFCOL Example
</TITLE>
</HEAD>

<BODY>
<H3>CFCOL Example</H3>

<!--- Note the use of the HTMLTABLE attribute to display the
CFTABLE as an HTML table, rather simply as PRE formatted information --->
```

```
<CFTABLE QUERY="GetEmployees" STARTROW="1" COLSPACING="3" HTMLTABLE>
<!--- each CFCOL tag sets the width of a column in the table,
as well as specifying the header information and the text/CFML
with which to fill the cell --->
    <CFCOL HEADER = "<B>ID</B>"
        ALIGN = "Left"
        WIDTH = 2
        TEXT = "#Emp_ID#">
    <CFCOL HEADER = "<B>Name/Email</B>"
        ALIGN = "Left"
        WIDTH = 15
        TEXT = "<a href='mailto:#Email#'>#FirstName# #LastName#</A>">
    <CFCOL HEADER = "<B>Phone Number</B>"
        ALIGN = "Center"
        WIDTH = 15
        TEXT = "#Phone#">
</CFTABLE>

</BODY>
</HTML>
```

cfcol

CFCOLLECTION

The CFCOLLECTION tag allows you to create and administer Verity collections.

Syntax

```
<CFCOLLECTION ACTION="CREATE" or "REPAIR" or "DELETE" or "OPTIMIZE" or
    "MAP"
    COLLECTION="collection_name"
    PATH="path_of_verity_directory"
    LANGUAGE="English" or "German" or "Finnish" or "French" or "Danish" or
    "Dutch" or "Italian" or "Norwegian" or "Portuguese" or "Spanish" or
    "Swedish">
```

ACTION

Required. Specifies the action to perform:

- CREATE — Creates a new collection using the specified path and optionally specified language.
- REPAIR — Fixes data corruption in the collection.
- DELETE — Destroys the collection.
- OPTIMIZE — Purges and reorganizes data for efficiency.
- MAP — Assigns an alias to an existing Verity collection.

COLLECTION

Required. Specifies a collection name or an alias if the ACTION is MAP.

PATH

Required for CREATE and MAP. Specifies a path to the Verity collection. The effect of the PATH attribute depends on the ACTION that you specify.

ACTION	What happens?
CREATE	CFCOLLECTION creates a directory for the use of Verity. The directory path is composed of the directory path specified in the PATH attribute with the name specified in the COLLECTION attribute appended to it. Thus, the full directory path is "path_name\collection_name\." For example, if the path name is "C:\Col\," and the collection name is "myCollection," the full directory path is "C:\Col\myCollection\."
MAP	The MAP action provides a name with which ColdFusion can reference an existing collection. This name is specified with the COLLECTION attribute. It is an alias for the collection, which can be used in CFINDEX, and to re-instate a collection after you have re-installed ColdFusion. The directory path specified with the PATH attribute is the full path name of the Verity directory. Therefore, to reference the directory created in the previous example, specify "C:\Col\myCollection\."

LANGUAGE

Optional for CREATE. To use the LANGUAGE attribute you must have the ColdFusion International Search Pack installed. Valid entries are:

- English (default)
- German
- Finnish
- French
- Danish
- Dutch
- Italian
- Norwegian
- Portuguese
- Spanish
- Swedish

Usage   CFCOLLECTION works at the collection level only. To add content to a collection, use CFINDEX.

Note the following regarding mapped collections:

- Mapping allows you to assign an alias to a Verity collection created by a tool other than ColdFusion.
- The ACTION, COLLECTION, and PATH attributes are required.
- The path must point to a valid Verity collection; mapping does not validate the path.
- Deleting a mapped collection unregisters the alias; the base collection is not deleted.

Example   cfcollection

```
<!--- This example shows the basic functionality
of the CFCOLLECTION tag (create, repair, optimize, delete) --->
<HTML>
<HEAD>
    <TITLE>CFCOLLECTION</TITLE>
</HEAD>
<BODY bgcolor=silver>
<H3>CFCOLLECTION</h3>

<!--- see if a collection name has been specificied ... --->
<CFIF IsDefined("form.CollectionName") AND
IsDefined("form.CollectionAction")>
    <CFIF form.CollectionName is not "">
        <CFOUTPUT>
        <CFSWITCH EXPRESSION=#FORM.CollectionAction#>
```

```
<CFCASE VALUE="Create">
 <CFCOLLECTION ACTION="CREATE"
 COLLECTION="#FORM.CollectionName#"
 PATH="C:\CFUSION\Verity\Collections\">
 <H3>Collection created.</H3>
</CFCASE>
<CFCASE VALUE="Repair">
 <CFCOLLECTION ACTION="REPAIR"
 COLLECTION="#FORM.CollectionName#">
 <H3>Collection repaired.</H3>
</CFCASE>
<CFCASE VALUE="Optimize">
 <CFCOLLECTION ACTION="OPTIMIZE"
 COLLECTION="#FORM.CollectionName#">
 <H3>Collection optimized.</H3>
</CFCASE>
<CFCASE VALUE="Delete">
 <CFCOLLECTION ACTION="DELETE"
 COLLECTION="#FORM.CollectionName#">
 <H3>Collection deleted.</H3>
</CFCASE>
</CFSWITCH>
```

...

cfcollection

CFCONTENT

Defines the MIME type returned by the current page. Optionally, allows you to specify the name of a file to be returned with the page.

Note The ColdFusion Server Basic security settings may prevent CFCONTENT from executing. These settings are managed using the ColdFusion Administrator Basic Security page. In order for CFCONTENT to execute, it needs to be enabled on the Basic Security page. Please refer to ../../ Administering_ColdFusion_Server/contents.htm*Administering ColdFusion Server*/a for more information about securing ColdFusion tags.

Syntax
```
<CFCONTENT TYPE="file_type"
    DELETEFILE="Yes" or "No"
    FILE="filename"
    RESET="Yes" or "No">
```

TYPE

Required. Defines the File/ MIME content type returned by the current page.

DELETEFILE

Optional. Yes or No. Yes deletes the file after the download operation. Defaults to No. This attribute only applies if you are specifying a file with the FILE attribute.

FILE

Optional. Denotes the name of the file being retrieved.

RESET

Optional. Yes or No. Yes discards any output that precedes the call to CFCONTENT. No preserves the output that precedes the call. Defaults to Yes. The RESET and FILE attributes are mutually exclusive. If you specify a file, the RESET attribute has no effect. See Note.

Note You should consider setting RESET to "No " if you are calling CFCONTENT from a custom tag and do not want the tag to have the side effect of discarding the current page whenever it is called from another application or custom tag.

Example cfcontent

```
<!--- This example shows the use of CFCONTENT to return the
contents of the CF Documentation page dynamically to the browser.
You may need to change the path and/or drive letter.
(graphics will not display) --->
<HTML>
<HEAD>
<TITLE>
CFCONTENT Example
```

```
</TITLE>
</HEAD>

<BODY>

<H3>CFCONTENT Example</H3>

<!--- Files may be set to delete after downloading,
allowing for the posting of changing content. --->
<CFCONTENT TYPE="text/html"
   FILE="c:\inetpub\wwwroot\cfdocs\main.htm" DELETEFILE="No">

</BODY>
</HTML>

<!--- This example shows how the RESET attribute changes textual
          output. --->
<HTML>
<HEAD>
<TITLE>
CFCONTENT Example 2
</TITLE>
</HEAD>

<BODY>
<H3>CFCONTENT Example 2</H3>


<P>This example shows how the RESET attribute changes the output for text.</P>
<P>RESET = "Yes ": 123<CFCONTENT type="text/html" reset= "Yes ">456</P>
<P>This example shows how the RESET attribute changes the output for text.</P>
<P>RESET = "No ": 123<CFCONTENT type="text/html" reset= "No ">456</P>
</BODY>
</HTML>
```

cfcontent

CFCOOKIE

Defines cookie variables, including expiration and security options. See the Usage section for important details.

Syntax   <CFCOOKIE NAME="cookie_name"
                  VALUE="text"
                  EXPIRES="period"
                  SECURE="Yes" or "No"
                  PATH="url"
                  DOMAIN=".domain">

NAME
Required. The name of the cookie variable.

VALUE
Optional. The value assigned to the cookie variable.

EXPIRES
Optional. Schedules the expiration of a cookie variable. Can be specified as a date (as in, 10/09/97), number of days (as in, 10, 100), NOW, or NEVER. Using NOW effectively deletes the cookie from the client's browser.

SECURE
Optional. Indicates the variable has to transmit securely. If the browser does not support Secure Socket Layer (SSL) security, the cookie is not sent.

PATH
Optional. Specifies the URL within the specified domain to which this cookie applies:

PATH="/services/login"

Note   If you specify a path, you must also specify a value for the DOMAIN attribute.

DOMAIN
Optional. Specifies the domain for which the cookie is valid and to which the cookie content can be sent. An explicitly specified domain must always start with a dot. This can be a subdomain, in which case the valid domains will be any domain names ending in this string.

For domain names ending in country codes (such as .jp, .us), the subdomain specification must contain at least three periods, for example, .mongo.stateu.us. In the case of special top level domains, only two periods are needed, as in .allaire.com.

When specifying a PATH value, you must include a valid DOMAIN.

Separate multiple entries with a semicolon (;).

Usage   Cookies written with CFCOOKIE do not get written to the cookies.txt file until the browser session ends. Until the browser is closed, the cookie resides in memory. If you do not have an EXPIRES attribute in a CFCOOKIE, the cookie set exists only as long as the client browser is open. When the browser is closed, the cookie expires. It is never written to the cookies.txt file.

Warning   Do not set a cookie variable on the same page that you use the CFLOCATION tag. If you do, the cookie is never saved on the browser; therefore, it is of no value.

Example   cfcookie

```
<!--- This example shows how to set a CFCOOKIE variable,
and also how to delete that variable --->

<!--- First select a group of users who have entered
comments into the sample database --->
<CFQUERY NAME="GetAolUser" DATASOURCE="cfsnippets">
SELECT EMail, FromUser, Subject, Posted
FROM   Comments
</CFQUERY>

<HTML>
<HEAD>
<TITLE>
CFCOOKIE Example
</TITLE>
</HEAD>

<BODY bgcolor=silver>
<H3>CFCOOKIE Example</H3>

<!--- if the URL variable delcookie exists,
set the cookie's expiration date to NOW --->
<CFIF IsDefined("url.delcookie") is True>
    <CFCOOKIE NAME="TimeVisited"
    VALUE="#Now()#"
    EXPIRES="NOW">
<CFELSE>
<!--- Otherwise, loop through the list of visitors,
and stop when you match the string aol.com in the
visitor's email address --->

<CFLOOP QUERY="GetAOLUser">
    <CFIF FindNoCase("aol.com", Email, 1) is not 0>
        <CFCOOKIE NAME="LastAOLVisitor"
        VALUE="#Email#"
        EXPIRES="NOW" >

    </CFIF>
</CFLOOP>

<!--- If the timeVisited cookie is not set,
set a value --->
```

```
        <CFIF IsDefined("Cookie.TimeVisited") is False>
            <CFCOOKIE NAME="TimeVisited"
            VALUE="#Now()#"
            EXPIRES="10">
        </CFIF>
</CFIF>
<!--- show the most recent cookie set --->
<CFIF IsDefined("Cookie.LastAOLVisitor") is "True">
        <P>The last AOL visitor to view this site was
        <CFOUTPUT>#Cookie.LastAOLVisitor#</CFOUTPUT>, on
        <CFOUTPUT>#DateFormat(COOKIE.TimeVisited)#</CFOUTPUT>
<!--- use this link to reset the cookies --->
<P><a href="cfcookie.cfm?delcookie=yes">Hide my tracks</A>

<CFELSE>
        <P>No AOL Visitors have viewed the site lately.
</CFIF>

</BODY>
</HTML>
```

cfcookie

CFDIRECTORY

Use the CFDIRECTORY tag to handle all interactions with directories.

Note   The ColdFusion Server Basic security settings may prevent CFDIRECTORY from executing. These settings are managed using the ColdFusion Administrator Basic Security page. In order for CFDIRECTORY to execute, it needs to be enabled on the Basic Security page.

If you write ColdFusion applications designed to run on a server that is used by multiple customers, you need to consider the security of the files and directories that could be uploaded or otherwise manipulated by CFDIRECTORY. Please refer to ../../ Administering_ColdFusion_Server/contents.htm*Administering ColdFusion Server/*a for more information about securing ColdFusion tags.

Syntax
```
<CFDIRECTORY ACTION="directory action"
        DIRECTORY="directory name"
        NAME="query name"
        FILTER="list filter"
        MODE="permission"
        SORT="sort specification"
        NEWDIRECTORY="new directory name">
```

ACTION

Optional. Defines the action to be taken with directory(ies) specified in DIRECTORY. Valid entries are:

- List (default)
- Create
- Delete
- Rename.

DIRECTORY

Required for all ACTIONs. The name of the directory you want the action to be performed against.

NAME

Required for ACTION="List". Ignored for all other actions. Name of output query for directory listing.

FILTER

Optional for ACTION="List". Ignored for all other actions. File extension filter to be applied to returned names, for example: *.cfm. Only one mask filter can be applied at a time.

MODE

Optional. Used with ACTION="Create" to define the permissions for a directory on Solaris or HP-UX. Ignored in Windows. Valid entries correspond to the octal values (not symbolic) of the UNIX chmod command. Permissions are assigned for owner, group, and other, respectively. For example:

MODE=644
Assigns all, owner read/write permission, group and other read/write permissions.

MODE=666
Assigns read/write permissions for owner, group, and other.

MODE=777
Assigns read, write, and execute permissions for all.

SORT

Optional for ACTION="List". Ignored for all other actions. List of query columns to sort directory listing by. Any combination of columns from query output can be specified in comma separated list. ASC or DESC can be specified as qualifiers for column names. ASC is the default. For example:

SORT="dirname ASC, filename2 DESC, size, datelastmodified"

NEWDIRECTORY

Required for ACTION="Rename". Ignored for all other actions. The new name of the directory specified in the DIRECTORY attribute.

ACTION=LIST

When using the ACTION=LIST, CFDIRECTORY returns five result columns you can reference in your CFOUTPUT:

- Name – Directory entry name.

- Size – Size of directory entry.

- Type – File type: File or Dir for File or Directory.

- DateLastModified – Date an entry was last modified.

- Attributes – File attributes, if applicable.

- Mode – (Solaris and HP-UX only) The octal value representing the permissions setting for the specified directory. For information about octal values, refer to the UNIX man pages for the chmod shell command.

You can use the following result columns in standard CFML expressions, preceding the result column name with the name of the query:

#mydirectory.Name#
#mydirectory.Size#
#mydirectory.Type#
#mydirectory.DateLastModified#
#mydirectory.Attributes#
#mydirectory.Mode#

Example   cfdirectory

```
<!----------------------------------------------------------------------
This example shows the use of CFDIRECTORY to display the contents of the snippets directory in CFDOCS.
---------------------------------------------------------------------->
<HTML>
<HEAD>
<TITLE>
CFDIRECTORY Example
</TITLE>
</HEAD>

<BODY>
<H3>CFDIRECTORY Example</H3>

<!--- use CFDIRECTORY to give the contents of the
snippets directory, order by name and size
(you may need to modify this path) --->
<CFDIRECTORY DIRECTORY="c:\inetpub\wwwroot\cfdocs\snippets"
     NAME="myDirectory"
     SORT="name ASC, size DESC">
<!--- Output the contents of the CFDIRECTORY as a CFTABLE --->
<CFTABLE QUERY="myDirectory">
     <CFCOL HEADER="NAME:"
             TEXT="#Name#">
     <CFCOL HEADER="SIZE:"
             TEXT="#Size#">
</CFTABLE>

</BODY>
</HTML>
```

cfdirectory

CFERROR

Provides the ability to display customized HTML pages when errors occur. This allows you to maintain a consistent look and feel within your application even when errors occur.

Syntax   <CFERROR
          TYPE="Request" or "Validation" or "Monitor" or "Exception"
          TEMPLATE="template_path"
          MAILTO="email_address"
          EXCEPTION="exception_type">

TYPE

Required. The type of error that this custom error page is designed to handle:

- Specify Exception to handle exceptions.

- Specify Validation to handle data input validation errors that occur when submitting a form. A validation error handler is only useful if placed inside the Application.cfm file.

- Specify Monitor to set up an exception monitor.

- Specify Request to handle errors that occur during the processing of a page. Request is the default.

See the table under CFERROR Error Variables for information about the variables and other constructs available from the templates used to handle each type of error.

TEMPLATE

Required. The relative path to the custom error handling page. The following table describes the template to use for each type of error.

Types and Their Corresponding Custom Error Pages	
Type	**Custom Error Page**
Exception	An exception-handling template that is dynamically invoked by the CFML language processor when it detects an unhandled exception condition. Exception-handling templates may be specified as part of an application, via the <CFERROR TYPE="Exception"> tag, or may be set via the ColdFusion Administrator. An exception-handling template can use the full range of CFML tags, making it significantly more powerful than <CFERROR TYPE="Request">. This template also has access to the error variables in the table under CFERROR Error Variables.

Types and Their Corresponding Custom Error Pages (Continued)	
Type	**Custom Error Page**
Request	This template can include only the error variables described in the table under CFERROR Error Variables and cannot include CFML tags. It is useful as a backup error handler for sites with high user interface requirements.
Validation	A validation error handler. It handles data input validation errors that occur when submitting a form. It is useful only if placed inside the Application.cfm file.
Monitor	An exception-monitoring template is dynamically invoked by the CFML language processor when it first detects an exception condition, before it searches for <CFTRY>/<CFCATCH> or <CFERROR> handlers for the exception.

Exception-monitoring templates are useful for monitoring and debugging exception handling within complex applications. |

MAILTO

Optional. The email address of the administrator who should be notified of the error. This value is available to your custom error page using the MailTo property of the error object, such as #Error.MailTo#.

EXCEPTION

Required if the type is specified as Exception or Monitor. The type of exception.

Usage The CFERROR tag is normally used to customize the error messages for all the pages in an application. As a result, you generally embed it in the Application.cfm file. For more information about the Application.cfm file, refer to ../../ Developing_Web_Applications_with_ColdFusion/contents.htm*Developing Web Applications with ColdFusion*/a.

To help ensure that error pages display successfully, pages you specify with CFERROR should not be encoded with the cfencode utility.

CFERROR Error Variables

The exception-handling template specified in the TEMPLATE attribute of the CFERROR tag may contain one or more error variables, which will be substituted by ColdFusion when an error is displayed.

Error Variables for Request, Exception, and Monitor Types

The following error variables are available when CFERROR specifies TYPE="Request",
TYPE="Exception" or TYPE="Monitor":

Variables for Request, Exception, and Monitor Types	
Error Variable	**Description**
Error.Diagnostics	Detailed error diagnostics from ColdFusion Server.
Error.MailTo	Email address of administrator who should be notified (corresponds to the value set in the MAILTO attribute of CFERROR).
Error.DateTime	Date and time when the error occurred.
Error.Browser	Browser that was running when the error occurred.
Error.GeneratedContent	The failed request's generated content .
Error.RemoteAddress	IP address of the remote client.
Error.HTTPReferer	Page from which the client accessed the link to the page where the error occurred.
Error.Template	Page being executed when the error occurred.
Error.QueryString	URL query string of the client's request.

Note   If you have specified `TYPE="Exception"` or `TYPE="Monitor"`, you
can substitute the prefix CFERROR for Error if you prefer this form; for
example, CFERROR.Diagnostics, CFERROR.Mailto or
CFERROR.DateTime.

Error pages where TYPE="Validation"

Error variables available when CFERROR uses TYPE="Validation" are as follows:

Custom Error Pages where TYPE="Validation"	
Error Variable	**Description**
Error.ValidationHeader	Text for header of validation message.
Error.InvalidFields	Unordered list of validation errors that occurred.
Error.ValidationFooter	Text for footer of validation message.

Example   cferror

```
<!--- This example shows the use of CFERROR. --->
<HTML>
<HEAD>
<TITLE>CFERROR Example</TITLE>
</HEAD>

<BODY>
<H3>CFERROR Example</H3>

<P>CFERROR provides the ability to display customized
HTML pages when errors occur. This allows you to
maintain a consistent look and feel within your
application even when errors occur. Note that no CFML
can be displayed in the resulting templates except
for the specialized error variables.
<P>CFTRY/CFCATCH provides a more interactive way to
handle your CF errors within a CF template than CFERROR,
but CFERROR is still a good safeguard against general
errors.
<P>You can also use CFERROR within the Application.cfm
to specify error handling responsibilities for an entire
application.

<!--- Example of CFERROR call within a template --->
<CFERROR TYPE="REQUEST"
     TEMPLATE="request_err.cfm"
     MAILTO="admin@mywebsite.com">

<!--- Example of the template to handle this error --->
<!---
<HTML>
<HEAD>
     <TITLE>We're sorry -- An Error Occurred</TITLE>
</HEAD>

<BODY>
<UL>
<CFOUTPUT>
     <LI><B>Your Location:</B> #Error.RemoteAddress#
     <LI><B>Your Browser:</B> #Error.Browser#
     <LI><B>Date and Time the Error Occurred:</B> #Error.DateTime#
     <LI><B>Page You Came From:</B> #Error.HTTPReferer#
     <LI><B>Message Content</B>: <BR><HR width=50%>
   <P>#Error.Diagnostics#<HR width=50%><P>
     <LI><B>Please send questions to:</B>
   <a href="mailto:#Error.MailTo#">#Error.MailTo#</A>
</CFOUTPUT>
</UL>
</BODY>
</HTML>     --->
```

cferror

CFEXECUTE

Enables ColdFusion developers to execute any process on the server machine.

Syntax   <CFEXECUTE
     NAME=" ApplicationName "
     ARGUMENTS="CommandLine Arguments"
     OUTPUTFILE="Output file name"
     TIMEOUT="Timeout interval in seconds">
     ...
</CFEXECUTE>

NAME

Required. The full path name of the application that is to be executed.

Note: On Windows systems, you must specify the extension, for example, .exe, as part of the application's name.

ARGUMENTS

Optional. Any command-line arguments that should be passed to the program.

If *ARGUMENTS* is specified as a string, it is processed as follows:

- On Windows systems, the entire string is passed to the Windows process control subsystem for parsing.

- On UNIX, the string is tokenized into an array of arguments. The default token separator is a space; arguments with embedded spaces may be delimited by double quotes.

If *ARGUMENTS* is passed as an array, it is processed as follows:

- On Windows systems, the array elements will be concatenated into a string of tokens, separated by spaces. This string is then passed to the Windows process control subsystem as above.

- On UNIX, the elements of the *ARGUMENTS* array is copied into a corresponding array of exec() arguments.

OUTPUTFILE

Optional. The file where the output of the program is to be directed. If this is not specified, the output appears on the page from which it was called.

TIMEOUT

Optional. Indicates how long in seconds the ColdFusion executing thread will wait for the spawned process. Indicating a timeout of 0 is equivalent to the non-blocking mode of executing. A very high timeout value is equivalent to a blocking mode of execution. The default is 0; therefore, the ColdFusion thread spawns a process and immediately returns without waiting for the process to terminate.

If no output file is specified, and the timeout value is zero, then the program's output will be directed to the bit bucket.

Usage   CFEXECUTE is available on Windows NT 4.0 and UNIX platforms. Do not put any other ColdFusion tags or functions between the start and the end tags of CFEXECUTE. Also, CFEXECUTE tags cannot be nested.

Exception   CFEXECUTE throws the following exceptions:

- If the application name is not found, an Application File Not Found exception will be thrown.

- If the output file cannot be opened, an Output File Cannot be opened will be thrown.

- If the effective user of the ColdFusion executing thread does not have permissions to execute the process, a security exception will be thrown.

- The time out values must be between 0 and some high number (to be determined).

Example   cfexecute

```
<!--------------------------------------------------------------------
This example illustrates use of the CFEXECUTE tag.
----------------------------------------------------------------------->
<HTML>
<HEAD>
<TITLE>CFEXECUTE</TITLE>
</HEAD>

<BODY>
<H3>CFEXECUTE</H3>
<P>
This example executes the Windows NT version of the netstat network monitoring program, and places its
output in a file.

<CFEXECUTE NAME="C:\WinNT\System32\netstat.exe"
     ARGUMENTS="-e"
     OUTPUTFILE="C:\Temp\output.txt"
     TIMEOUT="1">

</CFEXECUTE>
</BODY>
</HTML>
```

cfexecute

CFEXIT

CFEXIT can be used to:

- Abort the processing of the currently executing CFML custom tag.
- Exit the template within the currently executing CFML custom tag.
- Reexecute a section of code within the currently executing CFML custom tag.

Syntax   <CFEXIT METHOD="method">

METHOD
Optional. Specifies one of the following:

- ExitTag (default) — Aborts processing of the currently executing CFML custom tag.
- ExitTemplate — Exits the template of the currently executing CFML custom tag.
- Loop — Reexecutes the body of the currently executing CFML custom tag.

Usage   If a CFEXIT tag is encountered outside the context of a custom tag, for example in the base page or an included page, the tag acts exactly like CFABORT. CFEXIT can help simplify error checking and validation logic in custom tags.

CFEXIT behaves differently depending on location and execution mode:

METHOD attribute	Location of CFEXIT call	Behavior
ExitTag	Base template	Terminate processing
	Execution mode = Start	Continue after end tag
	Execution mode = End	Continue after end tag
ExitTemplate	Base template	Terminate processing
	Execution mode = Start	Continue from first child in body
	Execution mode = End	Continue after end tag
Loop	Base template	Error
	Execution mode = Start	Error
	Execution mode = End	

Example   cfexit

```
<!--- This example shows the use of CFEXIT, and
is a read-only example --->
<HTML>
<HEAD>
<TITLE>CFEXIT Example</TITLE>
</HEAD>

<BODY>
<H3>CFEXIT Example</H3>

<P>CFEXIT can be used to abort the processing of the
currently executing CFML custom tag.  Execution will resume
immediately following the invocation of the custom tag in the
page that called the tag.
<H3>Usage of CFEXIT</H3>
<P>CFEXIT is used primarily to perform a conditional stop
of processing inside of a custom tag.  CFEXIT returns control
to the page that called that custom tag, or in the case of
a tag called by another tag, to the calling tag.

<!--- CFEXIT can be used inside a CFML custom tag, as
follows: --->
<!--- Place this code (uncomment the appropriate
sections) inside the CFUSION/customtags directory --->

<!--- MyCustomTag.cfm --->
<!--- This simple custom tag checks for the existence
of myValue1 and myValue2.  If they are both defined,
the tag adds them and returns the result to the calling
page in the variable "result".  If either or both of the
expected attribute variables is not present, an error message
is generated, and CFEXIT returns control to the
calling page.  --->

<!--- <CFIF NOT IsDefined("attributes.myValue2")>
                <CFSET caller.result = "Value2 is not defined">
                <CFEXIT METHOD="ExitTag">
        <CFELSEIF NOT IsDefined("attributes.myValue1")>
                <CFSET caller.result = "Value1 is not defined">
                <CFEXIT METHOD="ExitTag">
        <CFELSE>
                <CFSET value1 = attributes.myValue1>
                <CFSET value2 = attributes.myValue2>
                <CFSET caller.result = value1 + value2>
        </CFIF> --->
<!--- End MyCustomTag.cfm --->

<!--- And place this code inside your page --->

<!--- <P>The call to the custom tag, and then the result:
<CF_myCustomTag
        myvalue2 = 4>
```

```
<CFOUTPUT>#result#</cFOUTPUT>  --->
<P>If CFEXIT is used outside of a custom tag, it functions
like a CFABORT.  For example, the text after this message
will not be processed:
<CFEXIT>
<P>This text will not be executed due to the existence of
the CFEXIT tag above it.

</BODY>
</HTML>
```

cfexit

CFFILE

Use the CFFILE tag to handle all interactions with files. The attributes you use with CFFILE depend on the value of the ACTION attribute. For example, if the ACTION is "Write, " ColdFusion expects the attributes associated with writing a text file. See the individual CFFILE topics below for details about which attributes apply to which ACTIONs.

Note The Basic Security settings may prevent CFFILE from executing. These settings are managed using the Basic Security page in the ColdFusion Administrator. In order for CFFILE to execute, it needs to be enabled on the Basic Security page.

If you write ColdFusion applications designed to run on a server that is used by multiple customers, you need to consider the security of the files that could be uploaded or otherwise manipulated by CFFILE. See ../../ Administering_ColdFusion_Server/contents.htm*Administering ColdFusion Server/*a for more information about securing ColdFusion tags.

CFFILE topics

- CFFILE ACTION="Upload"
- CFFILE ACTION="Move"
- CFFILE ACTION="Rename"
- CFFILE ACTION="Copy"
- CFFILE ACTION="Delete"
- CFFILE ACTION="Read"
- CFFILE ACTION="ReadBinary"
- CFFILE ACTION="Write"
- CFFILE ACTION="Append"

CFFILE ACTION attributes

Depending on the value you assign to the ACTION attribute of CFFILE, there are several additional attributes you can set. This table shows which attributes you can use with each CFFILE ACTION.

Attributes Used with CFFILE ACTIONs	
ACTION	**Attributes**
Upload	ACCEPT DESTINATION FILEFIELD NAMECONFLICT MODE ATTRIBUTES
Move	SOURCE DESTINATION ATTRIBUTES
Rename	SOURCE DESTINATION ATTRIBUTES
Copy	SOURCE DESTINATION ATTRIBUTES
Delete	FILE
Read	FILE VARIABLE
ReadBinary	FILE VARIABLE
Write	OUTPUT FILE MODE ADDNEWLINE ATTRIBUTES
Append	OUTPUT FILE MODE ADDNEWLINE ATTRIBUTES

Sections that follow describe these values and attributes in greater detail.

CFFILE ACTION="Upload"

Use CFFILE with the Upload action to upload a file specified in a form field to a directory on the Web server.

Note The MODE attribute applies to ColdFusion on Solaris and HP-UX, only.

Syntax
```
<CFFILE ACTION="Upload"
    FILEFIELD="formfield"
    DESTINATION="full_path_name"
    NAMECONFLICT="behavior"
    ACCEPT="mime_type/file_type"
    MODE="permission"
    ATTRIBUTES="file_attributes">
```

FILEFIELD

Required. The name of the form field that was used to select the file.

Note: Do not use pound signs (#) to specify the field name.

DESTINATION

Required. The full path name of the destination directory on the Web server where the file should be saved. A trailing slash must be included in the target directory when uploading a file. Use the backward slash (\) on Windows ; use the forward slash (/) on UNIX.

Note: The directory does not need to be beneath the root of the Web server document directory.

NAMECONFLICT

Optional. Default is error. Determines how the file should be handled if its name conflicts with the name of a file that already exists in the directory. Valid entries are:

* Error — Default. The file will not be saved, and ColdFusion will stop processing the page and return an error.

* Skip — Neither saves the file nor throws an error. This setting is intended to allow custom behavior based on inspection of FILE properties.

* Overwrite — Replaces an existing file if it shares the same name as the CFFILE destination.

* MakeUnique — Automatically generates a unique filename for the upload. This name will be stored in the FILE object variable "ServerFile. " You can use this variable to record what name was used when the file was saved.

ACCEPT

Optional. Use to limit what types of files will be accepted. Enter one or more MIME types, each separated by comma, of the file types you want to accept. For example, to allow uploads of GIF and Microsoft Word files, enter:

```
ACCEPT="image/gif, application/msword"
```

Note that the browser uses the file extension to determine file type.

MODE

Optional. Defines permissions for an uploaded file on Solaris or HP-UX. Ignored in Windows. Valid entries correspond to the octal values (not symbolic) of the UNIX chmod command. Permissions are assigned for owner, group, and other, respectively. For example:

MODE=644
Assigns the owner read/write permissions and group/other read permission.

MODE=666
Assigns read/write permissions for owner, group, and other.

MODE=777
Assigns read, write, and execute permissions for all.

ATTRIBUTES

Optional. A comma-delimited list of file attributes to be set on the file being uploaded. The following file attributes are supported:

- ReadOnly
- Temporary
- Archive
- Hidden
- System
- Normal

If ATTRIBUTES is not used, the file's attributes are maintained. If Normal is specified as well as any other attributes, Normal is overridden by whatever other attribute is specified.

Individual attributes must be specified explicitly. For example, if you specify just the ReadOnly attribute, all other existing attributes are overwritten.

Examples　The following example will create a unique filename if there is a name conflict when the file is uploaded on Windows:

```
<CFFILE ACTION="Upload"
    FILEFIELD="FileContents"
    DESTINATION="c:\web\uploads\"
    ACCEPT="text/html"
    NAMECONFLICT="MakeUnique">
```

Note　On Windows, you must include the backward slash (\) after the destination directory name. On UNIX, you must include the forward slash (/) after the destination directory. In this example, the specified destination directory is "uploads. "

Evaluating the results of a file upload

After a file upload is completed, you can retrieve status information using file upload parameters. This status information includes a wide range of data about the file, such as the file's name and the directory where it was saved. File upload status parameters use the "File " prefix, for example, `File.ClientDirectory`. The file status parameters can be used anywhere other ColdFusion parameters can be used.

The following file upload status parameters are available after an upload.

File Upload Parameters	
Parameter	**Description**
AttemptedServerFile	Initial name ColdFusion used attempting to save a file, for example, myfile.txt.
ClientDirectory	Directory location of the file uploaded from the client's system.
ClientFile	Name of the file uploaded from the client's system.
ClientFileExt	Extension of the uploaded file on the client's system without a period, for example, txt not .txt.
ClientFileName	Filename without an extension of the uploaded file on the client's system.
ContentSubType	MIME content subtype of the saved file.
ContentType	MIME content type of the saved file.
DateLastAccessed	Date and time the uploaded file was last accessed.
FileExisted	Indicates (Yes or No) whether or not the file already existed with the same path.
FileSize	Size of the uploaded file.
FileWasAppended	Indicates (Yes or No) whether or not ColdFusion appended the uploaded file to an existing file.
FileWasOverwritten	Indicates (Yes or No) whether or not ColdFusion overwrote a file.
FileWasRenamed	Indicates (Yes or No) whether or not the uploaded file was renamed to avoid a name conflict.

File Upload Parameters (Continued)	
Parameter	**Description**
FileWasSaved	Indicates (Yes or No) whether or not Cold Fusion saved a file.
OldFileSize	Size of a file that was overwritten in the file upload operation.
ServerDirectory	Directory of the file actually saved on the server.
ServerFile	Filename of the file actually saved on the server.
ServerFileExt	Extension of the uploaded file on the server, without a period, for example, txt not .txt.
ServerFileName	Filename, without an extension, of the uploaded file on the server.
TimeCreated	Time the uploaded file was created.
TimeLastModified	Date and time of the last modification to the uploaded file.

Tip   Use the File prefix to refer to these parameters, for example,
`#File.FileExisted#`.

Note   File status parameters are read-only. They are set to the results of the
most recent CFFILE operation. (If two CFFILE tags execute, the results of
the first are overwritten by the subsequent CFFILE operation.)

**UNIX
Examples**   The following three examples show the use of the MODE attribute for UNIX. The first
example creates the file /tmp/foo with permissions defined as rw-r-r-- (owner=read/
write, group/other=read).

```
<CFFILE ACTION="Write"
    FILE="/tmp/foo"
    MODE=644>
```

This example appends to the specified file and makes permissions read/write (rw) for
all.

```
<CFFILE ACTION="Append"
    DESTINATION="/home/tomj/testing.txt"
    MODE=666
    OUTPUT="Is this a test?">
```

The next example uploads a file and gives it rwx-rw-rw permissions (owner/group/
other=read/write).

```
CFFILE ACTION="Upload"
    FILEFIELD="fieldname"
    DESTINATION="/tmp/program.exe"
    MODE=755>
```

CFFILE ACTION="Move"

The CFFILE MOVE action can be used to move a file from one location on the server to another.

Syntax
```
<CFFILE ACTION="Move"
    SOURCE="full_path_name"
    DESTINATION="full_path_name"
    ATTRIBUTES="file_attributes">
```

SOURCE

Required. The full path name of the file to move.

DESTINATION

Required. The full path name of the directory to which the file will be moved. If you do not specify the file name, a trailing slash must be included in the target when moving a file. Use the backward slash (\) on Windows; use the forward slash (/) on UNIX.

ATTRIBUTES

Optional. A comma-delimited list of file attributes to be set on the file being moved. The following file attributes are supported:

- ReadOnly
- Temporary
- Archive
- Hidden
- System
- Normal

If ATTRIBUTES is not used, the file's attributes are maintained. If Normal is specified as well as any other attributes, Normal is overridden by whatever other attribute is specified.

Individual attributes must be specified explicitly. For example, if you specify just the ReadOnly attribute, all other existing attributes are overwritten.

Example   The following example moves the keymemo.doc file from the c:\files\upload\ directory to the c:\files\memo\ directory on Windows:

```
<CFFILE ACTION="Move"
    SOURCE="c:\files\upload\keymemo.doc"
    DESTINATION="c:\files\memo\">
```

Note   On Windows, you must include the backward slash (\) after the
destination directory name if you do not specify a file name. In this
example, the specified destination directory is "memo. "

CFFILE ACTION="Rename"

Use CFFILE with the Rename action to rename a file that already exists on the server.

Syntax   <CFFILE ACTION="Rename"
            SOURCE="full_path_name"
            DESTINATION="full_path_name"
            ATTRIBUTES="file_attributes">

SOURCE
Required. The full path name of the file to rename.

DESTINATION
Required. The full path name, including the new name, of the file.

ATTRIBUTES
Optional. A comma-delimited list of file attributes to be set on the file being
renamed. The following file attributes are supported:

- ReadOnly
- Temporary
- Archive
- Hidden
- System
- Normal

If ATTRIBUTES is not used, the file's attributes are maintained. If Normal is
specified as well as any other attributes, Normal is overridden by whatever other
attribute is specified.

Individual attributes must be specified explicitly. For example, if you specify just
the ReadOnly attribute, all other existing attributes are overwritten.

Example   The following example renames the file keymemo.doc to oldmemo.doc:

```
<CFFILE ACTION="Rename"
    SOURCE="c:\files\memo\keymemo.doc"
    DESTINATION="c:\files\memo\oldmemo.doc">
```

CFFILE ACTION="Copy"

The CFFILE tag can be used to copy a file from one directory to another on the server.

Syntax
```
<CFFILE ACTION="Copy"
    SOURCE="full_path_name"
    DESTINATION="full_path_name"
    ATTRIBUTES="file_attributes">
```

SOURCE

Required. The full path name of the file to copy.

DESTINATION

Required. The full path name of the directory where the copy of the file will be saved. If you do not specify a file name, you must include the trailing slash. On Windows, use the backward slash (\). On UNIX, use the forward slash (/).

ATTRIBUTES

Optional. A comma-delimited list of file attributes to be set on the file being copied. The following file attributes are supported:

- ReadOnly

- Temporary

- Archive

- Hidden

- System

- Normal

If ATTRIBUTES is not used, the file's attributes are maintained. If Normal is specified as well as any other attributes, Normal is overridden by whatever other attribute is specified.

Individual attributes must be specified explicitly. For example, if you specify just the ReadOnly attribute, all other existing attributes are overwritten.

Example   The following example saves a copy of the keymemo.doc file in the c:\files\backup\ directory:

```
<CFFILE ACTION="Copy"
    SOURCE="c:\files\upload\keymemo.doc"
    DESTINATION="c:\files\backup\">
```

Note   On Windows, you must include the backward slash (\) after the
destination directory name if you do not specify a file name. In this
example, the specified destination directory is "backup. "

CFFILE ACTION="Delete"

The CFFILE tag can be used to delete a file on the server.

Syntax   <CFFILE ACTION="Delete"
        FILE="full_path_name">

FILE
    Required. The full path name of the file to delete.

Example   The following example permanently deletes the specified file:

<CFFILE ACTION="Delete"
    FILE="c:\files\upload\#Variables.DeleteFileName#">

CFFILE ACTION="Read"

You can use the CFFILE tag to read an existing text file. The file is read into a dynamic
parameter you can use anywhere in the page like any other dynamic parameter. For
example, you could read a text file and then insert its contents into a database. Or you
could read a text file and then use one of the find and replace functions to modify its
contents.

Note   Using CFFILE ACTION="READ" reads the entire text file into memory.
Therefore, it is not intended for use with extremely large files, such as log
files, because they can bring down the server.

Syntax   <CFFILE ACTION="Read"
        FILE="full_path_name"
        VARIABLE="var_name">

FILE
    Required. The full path name of the text file to be read.

VARIABLE
    Required. The name of the variable that will contain the contents of the text file
    after it has been read.

Example   The following example creates a variable named "Message " that will contain the
contents of the file message.txt.

```
<CFFILE ACTION="Read"
    FILE="c:\web\message.txt"
    VARIABLE="Message">
```

The variable "Message" could then be used in the page. For example, you could display the contents of the message.txt file in the final Web page:

```
<CFOUTPUT>#Message#</CFOUTPUT>
```

ColdFusion supports a number of powerful functions for manipulating the contents of text files. You can also use the variable created by a CFFILE Read operation in ArrayToList and ListToArray functions.

See String Functions and Array Functions for more information about working with strings and arrays.

CFFILE ACTION="ReadBinary"

You can use the CFFILE tag to read an existing binary file, such as an executable or image file. The file is read into a binary object parameter you can use anywhere in the page like any other parameter. If you would like to send it through one of the Web protocols, such as HTTP or SMTP, or store it in a database, you should first convert it to Base64 (see ToBase64).

Syntax
```
<CFFILE ACTION="ReadBinary"
    FILE="full_path_name"
    VARIABLE="var_name">
```

FILE
> Required. The full path name of the file to be read.

VARIABLE
> Required. The name of the variable that will contain the contents of the binary file after it has been read.

Example   The following example creates a variable named "aBinaryObj " that will contain the ColdFusion Server executable.

```
<CFFILE ACTION="ReadBinary"
    FILE="c:\cfusion\bin\cfserver.exe"
    VARIABLE="aBinaryObj">
```

You can then convert the binary file to Base64 so that you could FTP it to another site for upload.

CFFILE ACTION="Write"

You can use the CFFILE tag to write a text file based on dynamic content. For example, you could create static HTML files from this content or log actions in a text file.

Syntax   <CFFILE ACTION="Write"
                  FILE="full_path_name"
                  OUTPUT="content"
                  MODE="permission"
                  ADDNEWLINE="Yes" or "No"
                  ATTRIBUTES="file_attributes">

FILE
Required. The full path name of the file to be created.

OUTPUT
Required. The content of the file to be created.

MODE
Optional. Defines permissions for a file on Solaris or HP-UX. Ignored in Windows. Valid entries correspond to the octal values (not symbolic) of the Unix chmod command. Permissions are assigned for owner, group, and other, respectively. For example:

MODE=644
Assigns the owner read/write permissions and group/other read permission.

MODE=666
Assigns read/write permissions for owner, group, and other.

MODE=777
Assigns read, write, and execute permissions for all.

ADDNEWLINE
Optional. Yes or No. If this attribute is set to Yes, a new line character is appended to the text that is written to the file. If this attribute is set to No, no new line character is appended to the text. The default value is Yes.

ATTRIBUTES
Optional. A comma-delimited list of file attributes to be set on the file being written. The following file attributes are supported:

- ReadOnly
- Temporary
- Archive
- Hidden
- System
- Normal

If ATTRIBUTES is not used, the file's attributes are maintained. If Normal is specified as well as any other attributes, Normal is overridden by whatever other attribute is specified.

Individual attributes must be specified explicitly. For example, if you specify just the ReadOnly attribute, all other existing attributes are overwritten.

Example   The following example creates a file with the information a user entered into an HTML insert form:

```
<CFFILE ACTION="Write"
    FILE="c:\files\updates\#Form.UpdateTitle#.txt"
    OUTPUT="Created By: #Form.FullName#
    Date: #Form.Date#
    #Form.Content#">
```

If the user submitted a form where:

```
UpdateTitle="FieldWork"
FullName="World B. Frueh"
Date="10/30/98"
Content="We had a wonderful time in Cambridgeport."
```

ColdFusion would create a file named FieldWork.txt in the c:\files\updates\ directory and the file would contain the text:

```
Created By: World B. Frueh
Date: 10/30/98
We had a wonderful time in Cambridgeport.
```

This following examples show the use of the MODE attribute for UNIX. The first, creates the file /tmp/foo with permissions defined as rw-r—r-- (owner=read/write, group/other=read).

```
<CFFILE ACTION="Write"
    FILE="/tmp/foo"
    MODE=644>
```

This example appends to the specified file and makes permissions read/write (rw) for all.

```
<CFFILE ACTION="Append"
    DESTINATION="/home/tomj/testing.txt"
    MODE=666
    OUTPUT="Is this a test?">
```

The next example uploads a file and gives it rwx-rw-rw permissions (owner/group/other=read/write).

```
CFFILE ACTION="Upload"
    FILEFIELD="fieldname"
    DESTINATION="/tmp/program.exe"
    MODE=755>
```

CFFILE ACTION="Append"

Use CFFILE with the Append action to append additional text to the end of an existing text file, for example, when creating log files.

Syntax

```
<CFFILE ACTION="Append"
       FILE="full_path_name"
       OUTPUT="string"
       ATTRIBUTES="file_attributes">
```

FILE

Required. The full path name of the file to which the content of the OUTPUT attribute is appended.

OUTPUT

Required. The string to be appended to the file designated in the DESTINATION attribute.

ADDNEWLINE

Optional. Yes or No. If this attribute is set to Yes, a new line character is appended to the text that is written to the file. If this attribute is set to No, no new line character is appended to the text. The default value is Yes.

ATTRIBUTES

Optional. A comma-delimited list of file attributes to be set on the file being appended. The following file attributes are supported:

- ReadOnly
- Temporary
- Archive
- Hidden
- System
- Normal

If ATTRIBUTES is not used, the file's attributes are maintained. If Normal is specified as well as any other attributes, Normal is overridden by whatever other attribute is specified.

Individual attributes must be specified explicitly. For example, if you specify just the ReadOnly attribute, all other existing attributes are overwritten.

Example

The following example appends the text string "But Davis Square is the place to be. " to the file fieldwork.txt which was created in the previous example:

```
<CFFILE ACTION="Append"
       FILE="c:\files\updates\fieldwork.txt"
       OUTPUT="<B>But Davis Square is the place to be.</B>">
```

CFFORM

CFFORM allows you to build a form with CFML custom control tags that provide much greater functionality than standard HTML form input elements.

Note   CFFORM requires the client to download a Java applet. Downloading an applet takes time, so using CFFORM may be slightly slower than using a simple HTML form. In addition, browsers must be Java-enabled for CFFORM to work properly.

Syntax
```
<CFFORM NAME="name"
        ACTION="form_action"
        ENABLECAB="Yes" or "No"
        ONSUBMIT="javascript"
        TARGET="window_name"
        ENCTYPE="type"
        PASSTHROUGH="HTML_attributes">

...
</CFFORM>
```

NAME
Optional. A name for the form you are creating.

ACTION
Required. The name of the ColdFusion page that will be executed when the form is submitted for processing.

ENABLECAB
Optional. Yes or No. Allows users to download the Microsoft cabinet (*.cab) file(s) containing the Java classes used for Java applet-based CFFORM controls. If Yes, on opening the page, users are asked if they want to download the CAB file.

ONSUBMIT
Optional. JavaScript function to execute after other input validation returns. Use this attribute to execute JavaScript for preprocessing data before the form is submitted. See ../../Developing_Web_Applications_with_ColdFusion/ contents.htm*Developing Web Applications with ColdFusion*/a for information on using JavaScript for form validation.

TARGET
Optional. The name of the window or window frame where the form output will be sent.

ENCTYPE
Optional. The MIME type used to encode data sent via the POST method. The default value is application/x-www-form-urlencoded. It is recommended that you

accept the default value. This attribute is included for compatibility with the
HTML FORM tag.

PASSTHROUGH

Optional. HTML attributes that are not explicitly supported by CFFORM. If you
specify an attribute and its value, the attribute and value are passed to the HTML
code that is generated for the CFINPUT tag. See the Usage section for more
information about specifying values.

Usage   The following custom control tags are available:

- CFINPUT — Creates a form input element (radio button, text box, or checkbox)
  and can validate form input.

- CFSELECT — Creates a drop down listbox.

- CFSLIDER — Creates a slider control.

- CFTEXTINPUT — Creates a text input box.

- CFTREE — Creates a tree control.

- CFGRID — Creates a grid control for displaying tabular data in a ColdFusion
  form.

- CFAPPLET — Embeds a registered Java applet in a ColdFusion form. Applets are
  registered in the ColdFusion Administrator.

You can add standard and dynamic HTML FORM tag attributes and their values to the
CFFORM tag by using the PASSTHROUGH attribute. These attributes and values are
passed directly through ColdFusion to the browser in creating a form.

If you specify a value in quotation marks, you must escape the quotation marks by
doubling them, for example,

PASSTHROUGH= "readonly= " "YES " " "

The ENABLECAB attribute is supported only for MS Internet Explorer clients that have
Authenticode 2.0 installed. Authenticode 2.0 can be downloaded from http://
www.microsoft.com/ie/security/authent2.htm.

Note   These CAB files are digitally signed using VeriSign digital IDs to ensure file
security.

Incorporating HTML form tags

CFFORM allows you to incorporate standard HTML in two ways:

- You can add standard FORM tag attributes and their values to the CFFORM tag.
  These attributes and values are passed directly through ColdFusion to the
  browser in creating a form. For example, you can use FORM tag attributes like
  TARGET to enhance your CFFORM features.

- HTML tags that can ordinarily be placed within an HTML FORM tag can also be
  placed between <CFFORM> and </CFFORM> tags.

For example, you use a standard HTML INPUT tag to create a submit button in a CFFORM:

```
<CFFORM
    <INPUT TYPE="Submit" VALUE=" Update... ">
</CFFORM>
```

Example   cfform

```
<!--- This example shows the use of CFINPUT controls in
a CFFORM --->
<HTML>
<HEAD>
<TITLE>
CFFORM Example
</TITLE>
</HEAD>

<BODY>
<H3>CFFORM Example</H3>

<CFIF IsDefined("form.oncethrough") is "Yes">
    <CFIF IsDefined("form.testVal1") is True>
    <H3>Results of Radio Button Test</H3>
    <CFIF form.testVal1 is "Yes">Your radio button answer was yes</CFIF>
    <CFIF form.testVal1 is "No">Your radio button answer was no</CFIF>
    </CFIF>
    <CFIF IsDefined("form.chkTest2") is True>
    <H3>Results of Checkbox Test</H3>
        Your checkbox answer was yes
    <CFELSE>
        <H3>Results of Checkbox Test</H3>
        Your checkbox answer was no
    </CFIF>
    <CFIF IsDefined("form.textSample") is True
     AND form.textSample is not "">
    <H3>Results of Credit Card Input</H3>
        Your credit card number, <CFOUTPUT>#form.textSample#</CFOUTPUT>,
        was valid under the MOD 10 algorithm.
    </CFIF>
    <CFIF IsDefined("form.sampleSlider") is "True">
    <H3>You gave this page a rating of <CFOUTPUT>#form.sampleSlider#
    </CFOUTPUT></H3>
    </CFIF>
    <hr noshade>
</CFIF>
<!--- begin by calling the cfform tag --->
<CFFORM ACTION="cfform.cfm" METHOD="POST" ENABLECAB="Yes">

<TABLE>
<TR>
    <TD>
    <H4>This example displays the radio button input type
    for CFINPUT.</H4>
```

```
      Yes <CFINPUT TYPE="Radio" NAME="TestVal1" VALUE="Yes" CHECKED="yes">
      No <CFINPUT TYPE="Radio" NAME="TestVal1" VALUE="No">
      </TD>
</TR>

<TR>
      <TD>
      <H4>This example displays the checkbox input type for CFINPUT.</H4>
      <CFINPUT TYPE="Checkbox" NAME="ChkTest2" VALUE="Yes">
      </TD>
</TR>

<TR>
      <TD>
      <H4>This example shows a client-side validation for
      CFINPUT text boxes.</H4>
      <BR>(<I>This item is optional</I>)<BR>
      Please enter a credit card number:
      <CFINPUT TYPE="Text" NAME="TextSample" MESSAGE="Please enter a Credit
      Card Number" VALIDATE="creditcard" REQUIRED="No">
      </TD>
</TR>

<TR>
      <TD>
      <H4>This example shows the use of the CFSLIDER tag.</H4>
      <P>Rate your approval of this example from 1 to 10 by sliding the
      control.
      <P>1 <CFSLIDER NAME="sampleSlider" LABEL="Sample Slider" RANGE="1,10"
        MESSAGE="Please enter a value from 1 to 10" SCALE="1" BOLD="No"
        ITALIC="No" REFRESHLABEL="No"> 10
      </TD>
</TR>
</TABLE>

<P><INPUT TYPE="SUBMIT" NAME="SUBMIT" VALUE="show me the result">
<INPUT TYPE="Hidden" NAME="oncethrough" VALUE="yes">
</CFFORM>

</BODY>
</HTML>
```

cfform

CFFTP

CFFTP allows users to implement File Transfer Protocol operations.

Note The CFFTP tag is for moving files between a ColdFusion server and an FTP server. CFFTP cannot move files between a ColdFusion server and a browser (client). Use CFFILE ACTION="UPLOAD" to transfer files from the client to a ColdFusion server; use CFCONTENT to transfer files from a ColdFusion server to the browser.

Note also that ColdFusion Server Basic security settings may prevent CFFTP from executing. These settings are managed using the ColdFusion Administrator Basic Security page. If you write ColdFusion applications designed to run on a server that is used by multiple customers, you need to consider the security of the files that the customer can move. Please refer to ../../Administering_ColdFusion_Server/ contents.htm*Administering ColdFusion Server*/a for more information about securing ColdFusion tags.

CFFTP topics:

- Establishing a Connection with CFFTP
- File and Directory Operations with CFFTP
- Accessing the Columns in a Query Object
- CFFTP.ReturnValue Variable
- Connection Caching

Establishing a Connection with CFFTP

Use the CONNECTION attribute of the CFFTP tag to establish a connection with an FTP server.

If you use connection caching to an already active FTP connection, you don't need to respecify the connection attributes:

- USERNAME
- PASSWORD
- SERVER

Note Changes to a cached connection, such as changing RETRYCOUNT or TIMEOUT values, may require reestablishing the connection.

Syntax
```
<CFFTP ACTION="action"
    USERNAME="name"
    PASSWORD="password"
```

```
SERVER="server"
TIMEOUT="timeout in seconds"
PORT="port"
CONNECTION="name"
PROXYSERVER="proxyserver"
RETRYCOUNT="number"
STOPONERROR="Yes" or "No"
PASSIVE="Yes" or "No">
```

ACTION

Required. Determines the FTP operation to perform. To create an FTP connection, use Open. To terminate an FTP connection, use Close. See Connection Caching for more information.

USERNAME

Required for Open. User name to pass in the FTP operation.

PASSWORD

Required for Open. Password to log in the user.

SERVER

Required for Open. The FTP server to connect to, as in ftp.myserver.com

TIMEOUT

Optional. Value in seconds for the timeout of all operations, including individual data request operations. Defaults to 30 seconds.

PORT

Optional. The remote port to connect to. Defaults to 21 for FTP.

CONNECTION

Optional. The name of the FTP connection. Used to cache a new FTP connection or to reuse an existing connection. If the *USERNAME, PASSWORD,* and *SERVER* attributes are specified, a new connection is created if no connection exists for the specified user. All calls to CFFTP with the same connection name will reuse the same FTP connection information.

PROXYSERVER

Optional. A string that contains the name of the proxy server (or servers) to use if proxy access was specified.

RETRYCOUNT

Optional. Number of retries until failure is reported. Default is one (1).

STOPONERROR

Optional. Yes or No. When Yes, halts all processing and displays an appropriate error. Default is Yes.

When No, three variables are populated:

- CFFTP.Succeeded – Yes or No.

- CFFTP.ErrorCode – Error number (See following Note for critical information.)

- CFFTP.ErrorText – Message text explaining error type

Note   Use CFFTP.ErrorCode for conditional operations. Do not use
CFFTP.ErrorText for this purpose.

PASSIVE

Optional. Yes or No. Defaults to No. Indicates whether to enable passive mode.

Example   cfftp<!--- This view-only example shows the use of CFFTP --->
```
<HTML>
<HEAD>
<TITLE>CFFTP Example</TITLE>
</HEAD>
<BODY>

<H3>CFFTP Example</H3>
<P>CFFTP allows users to implement File Transfer Protocol
operations.  By default, CFFTP caches an open connection to
an FTP server.

<P>CFFTP operations are usually of two types:
<UL>
      <LI>Establishing a connection
      <LI>Performing file and directory operations
</UL>
<P>This view-only example opens and verifies a connection,
lists the files in a directory, and closes the connection.
<!---
<P>Open a connection

<CFFTP ACTION="open"
USERNAME="anonymous"
CONNECTION="My_query"
PASSWORD="youremail@email.net"
SERVER="ftp.tucows.com"
STOPONERROR="Yes">

<P>Did it succeed? <CFOUTPUT>#CFFTP.Succeeded#</CFOUTPUT>
<P>List the files in a directory:
<CFFTP ACTION="LISTDIR"
    STOPONERROR="Yes"
    NAME="ListFiles"
    DIRECTORY="lib"
    CONNECTION="my_query">
<CFOUTPUT QUERY="ListFiles">
    #name#<BR>
</CFOUTPUT>

<P>Close the connection:
<CFFTP ACTION="close"
CONNECTION="My_query"
```

```
STOPONERROR="Yes">
<P>Did it succeed? <CFOUTPUT>#CFFTP.Succeeded#</CFOUTPUT>
--->

</BODY>
</HTML>
```

cfftp

File and Directory Operations with CFFTP

Use this form of the CFFTP tag to perform file and directory operations with CFFTP.

If you use connection caching to an already active FTP connection, you don't need to respecify the connection attributes:

- USERNAME

- PASSWORD

- SERVER

Syntax
```
<CFFTP
        ACTION="action"
        USERNAME="name"
        PASSWORD="password"
        NAME="query_name"
        SERVER="server"
        ASCIIEXTENSIONLIST="extensions"
        TRANSFERMODE="mode"
        FAILIFEXISTS="Yes" or "No"
        DIRECTORY="directory name"
        LOCALFILE="filename"
        REMOTEFILE="filename"
        ITEM="directory or file"
        EXISTING="file or directory name"
        NEW="file or directory name"
        PROXYSERVER="proxyserver"
        PASSIVE="Yes" or "No">
```

ACTION

Required if connection is not already cached. If connection caching is used, the ACTION attribute is not required. Determines the FTP operation to perform. Can be one of the following:

- ChangeDir

- CreateDir

- ListDir

- GetFile

- PutFile

- Rename

- Remove

- GetCurrentDir

- GetCurrentURL

- ExistsDir

- ExistsFile

- Exists

USERNAME

Required if the FTP connection is not already cached. If connection caching is used, the USERNAME attribute is not required. User name to pass in the FTP operation.

PASSWORD

Required if the FTP connection is not already cached. If connection caching is used, the PASSWORD attribute is not required. Password to log the user.

NAME

Required for ACTION="ListDir". Specifies the query name to hold the directory listing. See Usage for more information.

SERVER

Required if the FTP connection is not already cached. If connection caching is used, the SERVER attribute is not required. The FTP server to connect to.

TIMEOUT

Optional. Value in seconds for the timeout of all operations, including individual data request operations. Defaults to 30 seconds.

PORT

Optional. The remote port to connect to. Defaults to 21 for FTP.

CONNECTION

Optional. The name of the FTP connection. Used to cache a new FTP connection or to reuse an existing connection. If the *USERNAME*, *PASSWORD*, and *SERVER* attributes are specified, a new connection is created if no connection exists for the specified user. All calls to CFFTP with the same connection name will reuse the same FTP connection information.

ASCIIEXTENSIONLIST

Optional. A semicolon delimited list of file extensions that force ASCII transfer mode when TRANSFERMODE="AutoDetect". Default extension list is:

txt;htm;html;cfm;cfml;shtm;shtml;css;asp;asa

TRANSFERMODE

Optional. The FTP transfer mode you want to use. Valid entries are ASCII, Binary, or AutoDetect. Defaults to AutoDetect.

FAILIFEXISTS

Optional. Yes or No. Defaults to Yes. Specifies whether a GetFile operation will fail if a local file of the same name already exists.

DIRECTORY

Required for ACTION=ChangeDir, CreateDir, ListDir, and ExistsDir. Specifies the directory on which to perform an operation.

LOCALFILE

Required for ACTION=GetFile, and PutFile. Specifies the name of the file on the local file system.

REMOTEFILE

Required for ACTION=GetFile, PutFile, and ExistsFile. Specifies the name of the file on the FTP server's file system.

ITEM

Required for ACTION=Exists, and Remove. Specifies the object, file or directory, of these actions.

EXISTING

Required for ACTION=Rename. Specifies the current name of the file or directory on the remote server.

NEW

Required for ACTION=Rename. Specifies the new name of the file or directory on the remote server.

RETRYCOUNT

Optional. Number of retries until failure is reported. Default is one (1).

STOPONERROR

Optional. Yes or No. When Yes, halts all processing and displays an appropriate error. Default is No.

When No, three variables are populated:

- CFFTP.Succeeded – Yes or No.

- CFFTP.ErrorCode – Error number (See STOPONERROR variables, below)

- CFFTP.ErrorText – Message text explaining error condition

PROXYSERVER

Optional. A string that contains the name of the proxy server (or servers) to use if proxy access was specified.

PASSIVE

Optional. Yes or No. Defaults to No. Indicates whether to enable passive mode.

Usage   When `ACTION="ListDir"`, the Attributes column returns either "Directory" or "Normal." Other platform-specific values, such as "Hidden" and "System" are no longer supported.

When `ACTION="ListDir"`, a `"Mode"` column is returned. This column contains an octal string representation of UNIX permissions, for example, "777," when appropriate.

Note also that there is a CFFTP.ReturnValue variable that provides the return value for some of these actions. The actions for which this variable returns a value are as follows:

- GetCurrentDir
- GetCurrentURL
- ExistsDir
- ExistsFile
- Exists

The section CFFTP.ReturnValue Variable explains what is returned in this variable.

Note   Names of objects (files and directories) are case-sensitive; thus, using ListDir on "test.log " will not find a file named "test.LOG. "

CFFTP.ReturnValue Variable

The value of the CFFTP.ReturnValue variable is determined by the results of the ACTION attribute used in CFFTP.

CFFTP.ReturnValue Variable	
CFFTP Action	**Value of CFFTP.ReturnValue**
GetCurrentDir	String value containing the current directory
GetCurrentURL	String value containing the current URL
ExistsDir	Yes or No
ExistsFile	Yes or No
Exists	Yes or No

Accessing the Columns in a Query Object

When you use CFFTP with the ListDir action, you must also specify a value for the NAME attribute. The value of the NAME attribute is used to hold the results of the ListDir action in a query object. The query object consists of columns you can reference in the form:

queryname.columnname[row]

Where *queryname* is the name of the query as specified in the NAME attribute and *columnname* is one of the columns returned in the query object as shown in the following table. *Row* is the row number for each file/directory entry returned by the ListDir operation. A separate row is created for each entry.

CFFTP Query Object Columns	
Column	**Description**
Name	Filename of the current element
Path	File path (without drive designation) of the current element
URL	Complete URL for the current element (file or directory)
Length	Number indicating file size of the current element
LastModified	Unformatted date/time value of the current element
Attributes	String indicating attributes of the current element: Normal or Directory.
IsDirectory	Boolean value indicating whether object is a file or directory
Mode	An octal string representing UNIX permissions, when running on UNIX, for example, "rwxrwxrwx" in a directory listing is represented as "777".

Note   Previously supported query column values that pertain to system-specific information are no longer supported, for example, "Hidden" and "System."

Connection Caching

Once you've established a connection with CFFTP, you can reuse the connection to perform additional FTP operations. To do this, you use the CONNECTION attribute to define and name an FTP connection object that stores information about the connection. Any additional FTP operations that use the same CONNECTION name automatically make use of the information stored in the connection object. This facility helps save connection time and drastically improves file transfer operation performance.

If you need to keep the connection open throughout a session or longer, you can use a session or application variable as the connection name. However, if you do this, you must explicitly specify the full variable name with the Close action when you are finished. Note that keeping a connection open prevents others from using the FTP server; therefore, you should close the connection as soon as possible.

Note   Changes to a cached connection, such as changing RETRYCOUNT or TIMEOUT values, may require reestablishing the connection.

Example   The following example opens an FTP connection, retrieves a file listing, showing file or directory name, path, URL, length, and modification date. Connection caching is used to maintain the link to the server, and automatic error checking is enabled.

```
<CFFTP CONNECTION=FTP
    USERNAME="betauser"
    PASSWORD="monroe"
    SERVER="beta.company.com"
    ACTION="Open"
    STOPONERROR="Yes">

<CFFTP CONNECTION=FTP
    ACTION="GetCurrentDir"
    STOPONERROR="Yes">

<CFOUTPUT>
    FTP directory listing of #cfftp.returnvalue#.<P>
</CFOUTPUT>

    <CFOUTPUT>Return is #cfftp.returnvalue#</CFOUTPUT><BR>

<CFFTP CONNECTION="FTP"
    ACTION="listdir"
    DIRECTORY="/*."
    NAME="q"
    STOPONERROR="Yes">
<HR>FTP Directory Listing:<P>
<CFTABLE QUERY="q" HTMLTABLE>
    <CFCOL HEADER="<B>Name</B>" TEXT="#name#">
    <CFCOL HEADER="<B>Path</B>" TEXT="#path#">
    <CFCOL HEADER="<B>URL</B>" TEXT="#url#">
    <CFCOL HEADER="<B>Length</B>" TEXT="#length#">
    <CFCOL HEADER="<B>LastModified</B>"
     TEXT="Date(Format#lastmodified#)">
    <CFCOL HEADER="<B>IsDirectory</B>" TEXT="#isdirectory#">
</CFTABLE>
```

CFGRID

Used inside CFFORM, CFGRID allows you to place a grid control in a ColdFusion form. A grid control is a table of data divided into rows and columns. CFGRID column data is specified with individual CFGRIDCOLUMN tags.

See also CFGRIDROW and CFGRIDUPDATE tags.

Syntax
```
<CFGRID NAME="name"
       HEIGHT="integer"
       WIDTH="integer"
       VSPACE="integer"
       HSPACE="integer"
       ALIGN="value"
       QUERY="query_name"
       INSERT="Yes" or "No"
       DELETE="Yes" or "No"
       SORT="Yes" or "No"
       FONT="column_font"
       FONTSIZE="size"
       ITALIC="Yes" or "No"
       BOLD="Yes" or "No"
       HREF="URL"
       HREFKEY="column_name"
       TARGET="URL_target"
       APPENDKEY="Yes" or "No"
       HIGHLIGHTHREF="Yes" or "No"
       ONVALIDATE="javascript_function"
       ONERROR="text"
       GRIDDATAALIGN="position"
       GRIDLINES="Yes" or "No"
       ROWHEIGHT="pixels"
       ROWHEADERS="Yes" or "No"
       ROWHEADERALIGN="position"
       ROWHEADERFONT="font_name"
       ROWHEADERFONTSIZE="size"
       ROWHEADERITALIC="Yes" or "No"
       ROWHEADERBOLD="Yes" or "No"
       ROWHEADERWIDTH="col_width"
       COLHEADERS="Yes" or "No"
       COLHEADERALIGN="position"
       COLHEADERFONT="font_name"
       COLHEADERFONTSIZE="size"
       COLHEADERITALIC="Yes" or "No"
       COLHEADERBOLD="Yes" or "No"
       BGCOLOR="color"
       SELECTCOLOR="color"
       SELECTMODE="mode"
       MAXROWS="number"
       NOTSUPPORTED="text"
       PICTUREBAR="Yes" or "No"
       INSERTBUTTON="text"
```

```
DELETEBUTTON="text"
SORTASCENDINGBUTTON="text"
SORTDESCENDINGBUTTON="text">
```

</CFGRID>

NAME

Required. A name for the grid element.

HEIGHT

Optional. Height value of the grid control in pixels.

WIDTH

Optional. Width value of the grid control in pixels.

VSPACE

Optional. Vertical margin spacing above and below the grid control in pixels.

HSPACE

Optional. Horizontal margin spacing to the left and right of the grid control in pixels.

ALIGN

Optional. Alignment value. Valid entries are: Top, Left, Bottom, Baseline, Texttop, Absbottom, Middle, Absmiddle, Right.

QUERY

Optional. The name of the query associated with the grid control.

INSERT

Optional. Yes or No. Yes allows end users to insert new row data into the grid. Default is No.

DELETE

Optional. Yes or No. Yes allows end users to delete row data in the grid. Default is No.

SORT

Optional. Yes or No. When Yes sort buttons are added to the grid control. When clicked the sort buttons perform a simple text sort on the selected column. Default is No.

FONT

Optional. Font name to use for all column data in the grid control.

FONTSIZE

Optional. Font size for text in the grid control, measured in points.

ITALIC

Optional. Yes or No. Yes presents all grid control text in italic. Default is No.

BOLD

Optional. Yes or No. Yes presents all grid control text in boldface. Default is No.

HREF

Optional. URL to associate with the grid item or a query column for a grid that is populated from a query. If HREF is a query column, then the HREF value that is displayed is populated by the query. If HREF is not recognized as a query column, it is assumed that the HREF text is an actual HTML HREF.

HREFKEY

Optional. The name of a valid query column when the grid uses a query. The column specified becomes the Key no matter what the select mode is for the grid.

TARGET

Optional. Target attribute for HREF URL.

APPENDKEY

Optional. Yes or No. When used with HREF, Yes passes the CFGRIDKEY variable along with the value of the selected tree item in the URL to the application page specified in the CFFORM ACTION attribute. Default is Yes.

HIGHLIGHTHREF

Optional. Yes highlights links associated with a CFGRID with an HREF attribute value. No disables highlight. Default is Yes.

ONVALIDATE

Optional. The name of a valid JavaScript function used to validate user input. The form object, input object, and input object value are passed to the specified routine, which should return True if validation succeeds and False otherwise.

ONERROR

Optional. The name of a valid JavaScript function you want to execute in the event of a failed validation.

GRIDDATAALIGN

Optional. Enter Left, Right, or Center to position data in the grid within a column. Default is Left.

GRIDLINES

Optional. Yes or No. Yes enables rules (lines) in the grid control, No suppresses row and column rules. Default is Yes.

ROWHEIGHT

Optional. Enter a numeric value for the number of pixels to determine the minimum row height for the grid control. Used with CFGRIDCOLUMN

TYPE="Image", you can use ROWHEIGHT to define enough room for graphics you want to display in the row.

ROWHEADER

Optional. Yes or No. Yes displays row labels in the grid control. Defaults to Yes.

ROWHEADERALIGN

Optional. Enter Left, Right, or Center to position data within a row header. Default is Left.

ROWHEADERFONT

Optional. Font to use for the row label.

ROWHEADERFONTSIZE

Optional. Size font for row label text in the grid control, measured in points.

ROWHEADERITALIC

Optional. Yes or No. Yes presents row label text in italic. Default is No.

ROWHEADERBOLD

Optional. Yes or No. Yes presents row label text in boldface. Default is No.

ROWHEADERWIDTH

Optional. The width, in pixels, of the row header column.

COLHEADERS

Optional. Yes or No. Yes displays column headers in the grid control. Defaults to Yes.

COLHEADERALIGN

Optional. Enter Left, Right, or Center to position data within a column header. Default is Left.

COLHEADERFONT

Optional. Font to use for the column header in the grid control.

COLHEADERFONTSIZE

Optional. Size font for column header text in the grid control, measured in points.

COLHEADERITALIC

Optional. Yes or No. Yes presents column header text in italic. Default is No.

COLHEADERBOLD

Optional. Yes or No. Yes presents column header text in boldface. Default is No.

BGCOLOR

Optional. Background color value for the grid control. Valid entries are: black, magenta, cyan, orange, darkgray, pink, gray, white, lightgray, yellow.

A hex value can be entered in the form:

BGCOLOR="##*xxxxxx*"
where *x* is 0-9 or A-F. Use either two pound signs or no pound signs.

SELECTCOLOR
Optional. Background color for a selected item. See BGCOLOR for color options.

SELECTMODE
Optional. Selection mode for items in the grid control. Valid entries are:

- Edit — Users can edit grid data.
- Single — User selections are confined to the selected cell.
- Row — User selections automatically extend to the row containing selected cell.
- Column — User selections automatically extend to column containing selected cell.
- Browse — User can only browse grid data.

Default is Browse.

MAXROWS
Optional. Specifies the maximum number of rows you want to display in the grid.

NOTSUPPORTED
Optional. The text you want to display if the page containing a Java applet-based CFFORM control is opened by a browser that does not support Java or has Java support disabled. For example:

NOTSUPPORTED="<B> Browser must support Java
to view ColdFusion Java Applets</B>"
By default, if no message is specified, the following message appears:

<B>Browser must support Java to
view ColdFusion Java Applets!</B>

PICTUREBAR
Optional. Yes or No. When Yes, image buttons are used for the Insert, Delete, and Sort actions rather than text buttons. Default is No.

INSERTBUTTON
Optional. Text to use for the Insert action button. The default is Insert.

DELETEBUTTON
Optional. Text to use for the Delete action button. The default is Delete.

SORTASCENDINGBUTTON
Optional. The text to use for the Sort button. The default is "A -> Z".

SORTDESCENDINGBUTTON
Optional. The text to use for the Sort button. The default is "Z <- A".

Usage You can populate a CFGRID with data from a CFQUERY. If you do not specify any CFGRIDCOLUMN entries, a default set of columns is generated. Each column in the query is included in the default column list. In addition, a default header for each column is created by replacing any hyphen (-) or underscore (_) characters in the table column name with spaces. The first character and any character after a space is changed to uppercase; all other characters are lowercase.

Note CFGRID requires the client to download a Java applet. Downloading an applet takes time, so using CFGRID may be slightly slower than using a simple HTML table. In addition, browsers must be Java-enabled for CFGRID to work properly.

Select mode and form variables

Grid data is submitted in a CFFORM as form variables, depending on the value of the SELECTMODE attribute as follows:

- When SELECTMODE="Single", grid data is returned as *grid_name.selectedname* and the value of the selected cell.

- When SELECTMODE="Column", grid data is returned as a comma-separated list of all the values for the selected column.

- When SELECTMODE="Row", grid data is returned as *grid_name.colum1_name* and *grid_name.column2_name* and their respective values for the selected row.

- When SELECTMODE="Browse", no selection data is returned.

Using SELECTMODE="Edit"

When SELECTMODE="Edit ", one-dimensional arrays are used to store data about changes to the grid cells. For example, a one-dimensional array is used to store the type of edits made to grid cells:

gridname.RowStatus.Action [value]

Where *gridname* is the name of the CFGRID and *action* is U, I, or D for Update, Insert, and Delete, respectively.

ColdFusion also maintains both the value of the edited cell and the original value in one-dimensional arrays. You can reference this data in ColdFusion expressions as follows:

gridname.colname[value]
gridname.original.colname[value]

Where *gridname* is the name of the CFGRID, *colname* is the name of the column, and value is the index position containing the grid data.

Using the HREF attribute

When specifying a URL with grid items using the HREF attribute, the value of the SELECTMODE attribute determines whether the appended key value is limited to a single grid item or whether it extends to a grid column or row. When a user clicks on a linked grid item, a CFGRIDKEY variable is appended to the URL in the following form:

http://myserver.com?CFGRIDKEY=selection

If the APPENDKEY attribute is set to No, then no grid values are appended to the URL.

The value of *selection* is determined by the value of the SELECTMODE attribute:

- When SELECTMODE="Single", *selection* is the value of the column clicked.
- When SELECTMODE="Row", *selection* is a comma-separated list of column values in the clicked row, beginning with the value of the first cell in the selected row.

When SELECTMODE="Column", selection is a comma-separated list of row values in the clicked column, beginning with the value of the first cell in the selected column.

Example   cfgrid

```
<!--- This example shows the CFGRID, CFGRIDCOLUMN, CFGRIDROW,
and CFGRIDUPDATE tags in action --->

<!--- use a query to show the useful qualities of CFGRID --->

<!--- If the gridEntered form field has been tripped,
perform the gridupdate on the table specified in the database.
Using the default value keyonly=yes allows us to change only
the information that differs from the previous grid --->
<CFIF IsDefined("form.gridEntered") is True>
<CFGRIDUPDATE GRID="FirstGrid" DATASOURCE="cfsnippets" TABLENAME="CourseList"
KEYONLY="Yes">
</CFIF>

<!--- query the database to fill up the grid --->
<CFQUERY NAME="GetCourses" DATASOURCE="cfsnippets">
SELECT Course_ID, Dept_ID, CorNumber,
      CorName, CorLevel, CorDesc
FROM   CourseList
ORDER by Dept_ID ASC, CorNumber ASC
</CFQUERY>

<HTML>
<HEAD>
<TITLE>
CFGRID Example
</TITLE>
</HEAD>

<BODY>
<H3>CFGRID Example</H3>
```

```
<I>Try adding a course to the database, and then deleting it.</I>
<!--- call the CFFORM to allow us to use CFGRID controls --->
<CFFORM ACTION="cfgrid.cfm" METHOD="POST" ENABLECAB="Yes">

<!--- We include Course_ID in the CFGRID, but do not allow
for its selection or display --->
<!--- CFGRIDCOLUMN tags are used to change the parameters
involved in displaying each data field in the table--->

<CFGRID NAME="FirstGrid" WIDTH="450"
    QUERY="GetCourses" INSERT="Yes"
    DELETE="Yes" SORT="Yes"
    FONT="Tahoma" BOLD="No" ITALIC="No"
    APPENDKEY="No" HIGHLIGHTHREF="No"
    GRIDDATAALIGN="LEFT" GRIDLINES="Yes"
    ROWHEADERS="Yes" ROWHEADERALIGN="LEFT"
    ROWHEADERITALIC="No" ROWHEADERBOLD="No"
    COLHEADERS="Yes" COLHEADERALIGN="LEFT"
    COLHEADERITALIC="No" COLHEADERBOLD="No"
    SELECTCOLOR="Red" SELECTMODE="EDIT"
    PICTUREBAR="No" INSERTBUTTON="To insert"
    DELETEBUTTON="To delete" SORTASCENDINGBUTTON="Sort ASC"
    SORTDESCENDINGBUTTON="Sort DESC">
    <CFGRIDCOLUMN NAME="Course_ID" DATAALIGN="LEFT"
        BOLD="No" ITALIC="No"
        SELECT="No" DISPLAY="No"
        HEADERBOLD="No" HEADERITALIC="No">
    <CFGRIDCOLUMN NAME="Dept_ID" HEADER="Department"
        HEADERALIGN="LEFT" DATAALIGN="LEFT"
        BOLD="Yes" ITALIC="No"
SELECT="Yes" DISPLAY="Yes"
        HEADERBOLD="No" HEADERITALIC="Yes">
    <CFGRIDCOLUMN NAME="CorNumber" HEADER="Course ##"
        HEADERALIGN="LEFT" DATAALIGN="LEFT"
        BOLD="No" ITALIC="No"
SELECT="Yes" DISPLAY="Yes"
        HEADERBOLD="No" HEADERITALIC="No">
    <CFGRIDCOLUMN NAME="CorName" HEADER="Name"
        HEADERALIGN="LEFT" DATAALIGN="LEFT"
        FONT="Times" BOLD="No"
        ITALIC="No" SELECT="Yes"
DISPLAY="Yes" HEADERBOLD="No"
        HEADERITALIC="No">
    <CFGRIDCOLUMN NAME="CorLevel" HEADER="Level"
        HEADERALIGN="LEFT" DATAALIGN="LEFT"
        BOLD="No" ITALIC="No"
        SELECT="Yes" DISPLAY="Yes"
    HEADERBOLD="No" HEADERITALIC="No">
    <CFGRIDCOLUMN NAME="CorDesc" HEADER="Description"
        HEADERALIGN="LEFT" DATAALIGN="LEFT"
        BOLD="No" ITALIC="No"
SELECT="Yes" DISPLAY="Yes"
```

HEADERBOLD="No" HEADERITALIC="No">

</CFGRID>

...

cfgrid

CFGRIDCOLUMN

Used with CFGRID in a CFFORM, you use CFGRIDCOLUMN to specify individual column data in a CFGRID control. Font and alignment attributes used in CFGRIDCOLUMN override any global font or alignment settings defined in CFGRID.

Syntax

```
<CFGRIDCOLUMN NAME="column_name"
      HEADER="header"
      WIDTH="column_width"
      FONT="column_font"
      FONTSIZE="size"
      ITALIC="Yes" or "No"
      BOLD="Yes" or "No"
      HREF="URL"
      HREFKEY="column_name"
      TARGET="URL_target"
      SELECT="Yes" or "No"
      DISPLAY="Yes" or "No"
      TYPE="type"
      HEADERFONT"font_name"
      HEADERFONTSIZE="size"
      HEADERITALIC="Yes" or "No"
      HEADERBOLD="Yes" or "No"
      DATAALIGN="position"
      HEADERALIGN="position"
      NUMBERFORMAT="format">
```

NAME

Required. A name for the grid column element. If the grid uses a query, the column name must specify the name of a query column.

HEADER

Optional. Text for the column header. The value of HEADER is used only when the CFGRID COLHEADERS attribute is Yes (or omitted, since it defaults to Yes).

WIDTH

Optional. The width of the column in pixels. By default the column is sized based on the longest column value.

FONT

Optional. Font name to use for data in the column. Defaults to browser-specified font.

FONTSIZE

Optional. Font size for text in the column. Defaults to browser-specified font size.

ITALIC

Optional. Yes or No. Yes presents text in the column in italic. Default is No.

BOLD

Optional. Yes or No. Yes presents text in the column in boldface. Default is No.

HREF

Optional. URL to associate with the grid item. You can specify a URL that is relative to the current page:

../mypage.cfm

Or an absolute URL:

http://myserver.com/mydir/mypage.cfm.

HREFKEY

Optional. The name of a valid query column when the grid uses a query. The column specified becomes the Key no matter what the select mode is for the grid.

TARGET

Optional. The name of the frame in which to open the link specified in HREF.

SELECT

Optional. Yes or No. Yes allows end users to select a column in a grid control. When No, the column cannot be edited, even if the CFGRID INSERT or DELETE attributes are enabled. The value of the SELECT attribute is ignored if the CFGRID SELECTMODE attribute is set to Row or Browse.

DISPLAY

Optional. Yes or No. Use to hide columns. Default is Yes to display the column.

TYPE

Optional. Enter Image, Numeric, or String_NoCase. When TYPE="Image", the grid attempts to display an image corresponding to the value in the column, which can be a built in ColdFusion image name, or an image of your choice in the cfide\classes directory or a subdirectory, referenced with a relative URL. Built-in image names are as follows:

- cd
- computer
- document
- element
- folder
- floppy
- fixed
- remote

If an image is larger than the column cell where it is being placed, the images is clipped to fit the cell.

When TYPE="Numeric", data in the grid can be sorted by the end user as numeric data rather than as simple character text.

When TYPE="String_NoCase", data in the grid can be sorted by the end user as case insensitive text data like an Excel spreadsheet rather than as case sensitive character text.

HEADERFONT

Optional. Font to use for the column header. Defaults to browser-specified font.

HEADERFONTSIZE

Optional. Font size to use for the column header in pixels. Defaults to browser-specified font size.

HEADERITALIC

Optional. Yes or No. Yes presents column header text in italic. Default is No.

HEADERBOLD

Optional. Yes or No. Yes presents header text in boldface. Default is No.

DATAALIGN

Optional. Alignment for column data. Valid entries are: Left, Center, or Right. Default is Left.

HEADERALIGN

Optional. Alignment for the column header text. Valid entries are: Left, Center, or Right. Default is Left.

NUMBERFORMAT

Optional. The format for displaying numeric data in the grid.

NUMBERFORMAT mask characters

Mask characters you can use in the NUMBERFORMAT attribute correspond with those used in the NumberFormat CFML function. For more information about the NumberFormat function, see Chapter 2, "ColdFusion Functions," on page 253.

NumberFormat Mask Characters	
Character	**Meaning**
_ (underscore)	Optional digit placeholder.
9	Optional digit placeholder. Same as _, but shows decimal places more clearly.
.	Specifies the location of a mandatory decimal point.
0	Located to the left or right of a mandatory decimal point, to force padding with zeros.

NumberFormat Mask Characters (Continued)	
Character	**Meaning**
( )	Places parentheses around the mask if the number is less than 0.
+	Places + in front of positive numbers, - (minus sign) in front of negative numbers.
-	Place " " (space) in front of positive, - (minus sign) in front of negative numbers.
,	Separates thousands with commas.
L,C	Specifies left-justify or center-justify a number within the width of the mask column. L or C must appear as the first character of the mask. By default, numbers are right-justified.
$	Places a dollar sign in front of the formatted number. $ must appear as the first character of the mask.
^	Separates left from right formatting.

Example cfgridcolumn

```
<!--- This example shows the CFGRIDCOLUMN tag in action --->
...
<CFGRID NAME="FirstGrid" WIDTH="450"
    QUERY="GetCourses" INSERT="Yes"
    DELETE="Yes" SORT="Yes"
    FONT="Tahoma" BOLD="No" ITALIC="No"
    APPENDKEY="No" HIGHLIGHTHREF="No"
    GRIDDATAALIGN="LEFT"
    GRIDLINES="Yes" ROWHEADERS="Yes"
    ROWHEADERALIGN="LEFT" ROWHEADERITALIC="No"
    ROWHEADERBOLD="No" COLHEADERS="Yes"
    COLHEADERALIGN="LEFT" COLHEADERITALIC="No"
    COLHEADERBOLD="No" SELECTCOLOR="Red"
    SELECTMODE="EDIT" PICTUREBAR="No"
    INSERTBUTTON="To insert" DELETEBUTTON="To delete"
    SORTASCENDINGBUTTON="Sort ASC" SORTDESCENDINGBUTTON="Sort DESC">
    <CFGRIDCOLUMN NAME="Course_ID" DATAALIGN="LEFT"
        BOLD="No" ITALIC="No"
        SELECT="No" DISPLAY="No"
        HEADERBOLD="No" HEADERITALIC="No">
    <CFGRIDCOLUMN NAME="Dept_ID" HEADER="Department"
        HEADERALIGN="LEFT" DATAALIGN="LEFT" BOLD="Yes" ITALIC="No"
SELECT="Yes" DISPLAY="Yes" HEADERBOLD="No" HEADERITALIC="Yes">
    <CFGRIDCOLUMN NAME="CorNumber" HEADER="Course ##"
        HEADERALIGN="LEFT" DATAALIGN="LEFT"
```

```
            BOLD="No" ITALIC="No"
    SELECT="Yes" DISPLAY="Yes"
            HEADERBOLD="No" HEADERITALIC="No">
    <CFGRIDCOLUMN NAME="CorName" HEADER="Name"
            HEADERALIGN="LEFT" DATAALIGN="LEFT"
            FONT="Times" BOLD="No"
            ITALIC="No" SELECT="Yes"
    DISPLAY="Yes" HEADERBOLD="No"
            HEADERITALIC="No">
    <CFGRIDCOLUMN NAME="CorLevel" HEADER="Level"
            HEADERALIGN="LEFT" DATAALIGN="LEFT"
            BOLD="No" ITALIC="No" SELECT="Yes"
            DISPLAY="Yes" HEADERBOLD="No"
            HEADERITALIC="No">
                ...
```

CFGRIDROW

CFGRIDROW allows you to define a CFGRID that does not use a QUERY as source for row data. If a QUERY attribute is specified in CFGRID, the CFGRIDROW tags are ignored.

Syntax   <CFGRIDROW DATA="col1, col2, ...">

DATA
Required. A comma-separated list of column values. If a column value contains a comma character, it must be escaped with a second comma character.

Example   cfgridrow

...

```
<!--- use a CFLOOP to loop through the query and define CFGRIDROW
data each time through the loop --->
    <CFLOOP QUERY="GetCourses">
        <CFGRIDROW
    DATA="#Course_ID#,#Dept_ID#,#CorNumber#,#CorName#,
    #CorLevel#,#CorDesc#">
    </CFLOOP>
</CFGRID>
</CFFORM>

</BODY>
</HTML>
```

CFGRIDUPDATE

Used in a CFGRID, CFGRIDUPDATE allows you to perform updates to data sources directly from edited grid data. CFGRIDUPDATE provides a direct interface with your data source.

CFGRIDUPDATE first applies DELETE row actions followed by INSERT row actions and finally UPDATE row actions. Row processing stops if any errors are encountered.

Syntax
```
<CFGRIDUPDATE GRID="gridname"
        DATASOURCE="data source name"
        DBTYPE="type"
        DBSERVER="dbms"
        DBNAME="database name"
        TABLENAME="table name"
        USERNAME="data source username"
        PASSWORD="data source password"
        TABLEOWNER="table owner"
        TABLEQUALIFIER="qualifier"
        PROVIDER="COMProvider"
        PROVIDERDSN="datasource"
        KEYONLY="Yes" or "No">
```

GRID
Required. The name of the CFGRID form element that is the source for the update action.

DATASOURCE
Required. The name of the data source for the update action.

DBTYPE
Optional. The database driver type:

- ODBC (default) — ODBC driver.

- Oracle73 — Oracle 7.3 native database driver. Using this option, the ColdFusion Server computer must have Oracle 7.3.4.0.0 (or greater) client software installed.

- Oracle80 —Oracle 8.0 native database driver. Using this option, the ColdFusion Server computer must have Oracle 8.0 (or greater) client software installed.

- Sybase11 —Sybase System 11 native database driver. Using this option, the ColdFusion Server computer must have Sybase 11.1.1 (or greater) client software installed. Sybase patch ebf 7729 is recommended.

- OLEDB —OLE DB provider. If specified, this database provider overrides the driver type specified in the ColdFusion Administrator.

- DB2 —DB2 5.2 native database driver.

- Informix73—Informix73 native database driver.

DBSERVER
> Optional. For native database drivers and the SQLOLEDB provider, specifies the name of the database server machine. If specified, DBSERVER overrides the server specified in the data source.

DBNAME
> Optional. The database name (Sybase System 11 driver and SQLOLEDB provider only). If specified, DBNAME overrides the default database specified in the data source.

TABLENAME
> Required. The name of the table you want to update. Note the following:
>
> - ORACLE drivers — This specification must be in uppercase.
>
> - Sybase driver — This specification is case-sensitive and must be in the same case as that used when the table was created

USERNAME
> Optional. If specified, USERNAME overrides the username value specified in the ODBC setup.

PASSWORD
> Optional. If specified, PASSWORD overrides the password value specified in the ODBC setup.

TABLEOWNER
> Optional. For data sources that support table ownership (such as SQL Server, Oracle, and Sybase SQL Anywhere), use this field to specify the owner of the table.

TABLEQUALIFIER
> Optional. For data sources that support table qualifiers, use this field to specify the qualifier for the table. The purpose of table qualifiers varies across drivers. For SQL Server and Oracle, the qualifier refers to the name of the database that contains the table. For the Intersolv dBase driver, the qualifier refers to the directory where the DBF files are located.

PROVIDER
> Optional. COM provider (OLE-DB only).

PROVIDERDSN
> Optional. Data source name for the COM provider (OLE-DB only).

KEYONLY
> Optional. Yes or No. Yes specifies that in the update action, the WHERE criteria is confined to just the key values. No specifies that in addition to the key values, the original values of any changed fields are included in the WHERE criteria. Default is Yes.

Example cfgridupdate

```
<!--- This example shows the CFGRID, CFGRIDCOLUMN, CFGRIDROW,
and CFGRIDUPDATE tags in action --->
...
<!--- If the gridEntered form field has been tripped,
perform the gridupdate on the table specified in the database.
Using the default value keyonly=yes allows us to change only
the information that differs from the previous grid --->
<CFIF IsDefined("form.gridEntered") is True>
<CFGRIDUPDATE GRID="FirstGrid" DATASOURCE="cfsnippets"
 TABLENAME="CourseList"  KEYONLY="Yes">
</CFIF>
...
```

cfgridupdate

CFHEADER

CFHEADER generates custom HTTP response headers to return to the client.

Syntax   <CFHEADER
                 NAME="header_name"
                 VALUE="header_value">
           or
           <CFHEADER
                 STATUSCODE="status_code"
                 STATUSTEXT="status_text">

NAME
> Required if you do not specify the *STATUSCODE* attribute. A name for the header.

VALUE
> Optional. A value for the HTTP header. This attribute is used in conjunction with the *NAME* attribute.

STATUSCODE
> Required if you do not specify the *NAME* attribute. A number that sets the HTTP status code.

STATUSTEXT
> Optional. Text that explains the status code. This attribute is used in conjunction with the *STATUSCODE* attribute.

Example   cfheader

```
<!--- This example shows the use of CFHEADER --->
<HTML>
<HEAD>
<TITLE>CFHEADER Example</TITLE>
</HEAD>

<BODY>
<H3>CFHEADER Example</H3>

<P>CFHEADER generates custom HTTP response headers
to return to the client.
<P>The following example forces the browser client
to purge its cache of a requested file.
<CFHEADER NAME="Expires" VALUE="#Now()#">

</BODY>
</HTML>
```

cfheader

CFHTMLHEAD

CFHTMLHEAD writes the text specified in the TEXT attribute to the <HEAD> section of a generated HTML page. CFHTMLHEAD can be useful for embedding JavaScript code, or placing other HTML tags such as META, LINK, TITLE, or BASE in an HTML page header.

Syntax

```
<CFHTMLHEAD TEXT="text">
```

TEXT

The text you want to add to the <HEAD> area of an HTML page. Everything inside the quotation marks is placed in the <HEAD> section.

Example

cfhtmlhead

```
<!--- This example shows the use of CFHTMLHEAD --->
<CFHTMLHEAD TEXT="<TITLE>This is an example of a generated header</TITLE>
<BASE HREF='http://www.allaire.com/'>
">

<HTML>
<HEAD>
</HEAD>

<BODY>
<H3>CFHTMLHEAD Example</H3>

<P>CFHTMLHEAD writes the text specified in the TEXT attribute
to the &lt;HEAD&gt; section of a generated HTML page.  CFHTMLHEAD
can be useful for embedding JavaScript code, or placing other
HTML tags such as META, LINK, TITLE, or BASE in an HTML header.
<P>View the source of this frame to see that the title of the
page is generated by the CFHTMLHEAD tag.

</BODY>
</HTML>
```

cfhtmlhead

CFHTTP

The CFHTTP tag allows you to execute POST and GET operations on files. Using CFHTTP, you can execute standard GET operations as well as create a query object from a text file. POST operations allow you to upload MIME file types to a server, or post cookie, formfield, URL, file, or CGI variables directly to a specified server.

Syntax
```
<CFHTTP URL="hostname"
        PORT="port_number"
        METHOD="get_or_post"
        USERNAME="username"
        PASSWORD="password"
        NAME="queryname"
        COLUMNS="query_columns"
        PATH="path"
        FILE="filename"
        DELIMITER="character"
        TEXTQUALIFIER="character"
        RESOLVEURL="Yes" or "No"
        PROXYSERVER="hostname"
        PROXYPORT="port_number"
        USERAGENT="user_agent"
        THROWONERROR="Yes" or "No"
        REDIRECT="Yes" or "No"
        TIMEOUT="timeout_period">
</CFHTTP>
```

Note   Terminate CFHTTP POST operations with </CFHTTP>. Termination is not required with CFHTTP GET operations.

URL
Required. Full URL of the host name or IP address of the server on which the file resides.

PORT
Optional. The port number on the server from which the object is being requested. Default is 80. When used with RESOLVEURL, the URLs of retrieved documents that specify a port number are automatically resolved to preserve links in the retrieved document.

METHOD
Required. GET or POST. Use GET to download a text or binary file, or to create a query from the contents of a text file. Use POST to send information to a server page or a CGI program for processing. POST requires the use of a CFHTTPPARAM tag.

USERNAME
Optional. When required by a server, a valid username.

PASSWORD

Optional. When required by a server, a valid password.

NAME

Optional. The name to assign to a query when a query is to be constructed from a file.

COLUMNS

Optional. Specifies the column names for a query when creating a query as a result of a CFHTTP GET. If there are column headers in the text file from which the query is drawn, do not specify this attribute unless you need to overwrite the existing headers. If there are no column headers in the text file, you must specify the COLUMN attribute, or you will lose the data in the first row.

PATH

Optional. The path to the directory in which a file is to be stored. If a path is not specified in a POST or GET operation, a variable is created (CFHTTP.FileContent) that you can use to present the results of the POST operation in a CFOUTPUT.

FILE

Required in a POST operation if PATH is specified. The filename to be used for the file that is accessed. For GET operations, defaults to the name specified in URL. Enter path information in the PATH attribute.

DELIMITER

Required for creating a query. Valid characters are a tab or comma. Default is a comma (,).

TEXTQUALIFIER

Required for creating a query. Indicates the start and finish of a column. Should be appropriately escaped when embedded in a column. For example, if the qualifier is a quotation mark, it should be escaped as """". If there is no text qualifier in the file, specify a blank space as " ". Default is the quote mark (").

RESOLVEURL

Optional. Yes or No. Default is No. For GET and POST operations, when Yes, any page reference returned into the FileContent internal variable will have its internal URLs fully resolved, including port number, so that links remain intact. The following HTML tags, which can contain links, will be resolved:

- IMG SRC

- A HREF

- FORM ACTION

- APPLET CODE

- SCRIPT SRC

- EMBED SRC

- EMBED PLUGINSPACE

- BODY BACKGROUND
- FRAME SRC
- BGSOUND SRC
- OBJECT DATA
- OBJECT CLASSID
- OBJECT CODEBASE
- OBJECT USEMAP

PROXYSERVER

Optional. Host name or IP address of a proxy server.

PROXYPORT

Optional. The port number on the proxy server from which the object is being requested. Default is 80. When used with RESOLVEURL, the URLs of retrieved documents that specify a port number are automatically resolved to preserve links in the retrieved document.

USERAGENT

Optional. User agent request header.

THROWONERROR

Optional. Boolean indicating whether to throw an exception that can be caught by using the CFTRY and CFCATCH tags. The default is NO. See the Usage section for more information.

REDIRECT

Optional. Boolean indicating whether to redirect execution or stop execution. The default is YES. If set to NO and *THROWONERROR* is set to YES, execution stops if CFHTTP fails, and the status code and associated error message are returned in the variable CFHTTP.StatusCode. To see where execution would have been redirected, use the variable CFHTTP.ResponseHeader[LOCATION]. The key LOCATION identifies the path of redirection.

TIMEOUT

Optional. Timeout period in seconds. By default, the ColdFusion server processes requests asynchronously; that is, the ColdFusion server uses the timeout set on the URL in the browser, the timeout set in the ColdFusion Administrator, and the timeout set in the tag to determine the timeout period for the CFHTTP request.

When a URL timeout is specified in the browser, this timeout setting will take precedence over the ColdFusion Administrator timeout. The ColdFusion server then takes the lesser of the URL timeout and the timeout passed in the TIMEOUT attribute so that the request will always time out before or at the same time as the page times out. Likewise, if there is no URL timeout specified, ColdFusion takes the lesser of the ColdFusion Administrator timeout and the timeout passed in the TIMEOUT attribute.

If there is no timeout set on the URL in the browser, no timeout set in the ColdFusion Administrator, and no timeout set with the TIMEOUT attribute, ColdFusion processes requests synchronously; thus, ColdFusion waits indefinitely for the CFHTTP request to process.

Note that you must enable the timeout set in the ColdFusion Administrator in order for the ColdFusion Administrator timeout and the URL timeout to take effect. This setting is on the ColdFusion Administrator Server Settings page. Please refer to ../../Administering_ColdFusion_Server/contents.htm*Administering ColdFusion Server*/a for more information about ColdFusion settings.

Usage   Note the following:

- **HTTP GET** — A user can specify a URL that points to a text or binary file. The file will be downloaded and its contents stored in a CF variable or in a file so that the user can manipulate the data. The internal variable FileContent is available for text and MIME file types. The MimeType variable is available for all file manipulations. In addition, Header and ResponseHeader allow you to see the response headers. These variables can be accessed in the following manner:

  #CFHTTP.FileContent#

  #CFHTTP.MimeType#

  #CFHTTP.Header#

  #CFHTTP.ResponseHeader[*http_header_key*]#

  The ResponseHeader variable is a CFML structure; the other variables are strings. See the table at the end of this section for a summary of variables returned by CFHTTP.

- **GET file into a query** — To download a file in a ColdFusion page so that a query can be built using the file, the file must be either comma-separated or tab-delimited. Although risky, text qualification may be omitted. The file will be parsed and an appropriate query built from it. Columns may be specified in the attribute list so that the client can override the columns specified in the file. There is error checking within the tag that prevents a user from either entering an invalid column name or using an invalid column name that was specified in the original file. If such an illegal filename is encountered, the illegal characters are stripped. Such action could produce duplicate column names, so duplicate columns are renamed and inserted into the query header. The query has all of the functionality of a standard CFQUERY object.

- **HTTP POST** — CFHTTPPARAM tags can be nested inside a CFHTTP tag in a POST operation. The browser can be pointed to a URL specifying a CGI executable or a ColdFusion page. Since multiple CFHTTPPARAM tags can be nested in one CFHTTP tag, you can construct a multipart/form-data style post. A file content variable is created and this can be used in a CFOUTPUT. If PATH and FILE are specified, the data returned from the server is saved to the specified location.

- **Authentication** — CFHTTP supports Windows NT Basic Authentication for both GET and POST operations. However, Basic Authentication will not work if your Web server has enabled Windows NT Challenge/Response (Microsoft IIS).

- **Encryption** — CFHTTP is capable of using Secure Sockets Layer (SSL) for negotiating secured transactions over the wire.
- **CFHTTP.StatusCode**— CFHTTP provides the CFHTTP.StatusCode variable for access to the HTTP error string associated with the error if the *THROWONERROR* attribute is set to NO. See the following table for all the variables returned by CFHTTP.

CFHTTP Variables	
Variable Names	**Description**
#CFHTTP.FileContent#	Returns the contents of the file for text and MIME files.
#CFHTTP.MimeType#	Returns the MIME type.
#CFHTTP.ResponseHeader[*http_hd_key*]#	Returns the response headers. If there is only one instance of a header key, then the value may be accessed as a simple type. If there is more than one instance, then the values are placed in an array within the ResponseHeader structure.
#CFHTTP.Header#	Returns the raw response header.
#CFHTTP.StatusCode#	Returns the HTTP error code and associated error string if *THROWONERROR* is NO.

Example   cfhttp

```
<!-----------------------------------------------------------------
This example shows the use of CFHTTP to pull information from a web page.
----------------------------------------------------------------->
<HTML>
<HEAD>
<TITLE>
CFHTTP Example
</TITLE>
</HEAD>

<BODY>
<H3>CFHTTP Example</H3>

<P>This example shows the ability of CFHTTP to pull
the contents of a web page from the Internet, and shows how
you can get the following information by using CFHTTP variables:
</P>
<UL>
<LI>display the page (fileContent)
<LI>derive the MIME type of the page (mimeType)
<LI>find the header responses (responseHeader).
```

```
</UL>

<CFHTTP
    URL = "http://www.allaire.com"
    resolveurl = 1
    throwonerror = Yes
>
</CFHTTP>

<CFOUTPUT>
#cfhttp.filecontent#<BR>
<BR>
<H3><B>The mime-type:</B></H3><BR>
#cfhttp.mimetype#<BR>
<H3><B>The Status Code:</B></H3><BR>
#cfhttp.statuscode#<BR>
<H3><B>The Raw Header:</B></H3><BR>
#cfhttp.header#<BR>

</CFOUTPUT>

<H3><B>Output the Response Headers:</B></H3><BR>
<HR>

<CFLOOP collection=#CFHTTP.RESPONSEHEADER# item="httpHeader">
    <CFSET value = CFHTTP.RESPONSEHEADER[httpHeader]>
    <CFIF IsSimpleValue(value)>
        <CFOUTPUT>
            #httpHeader# : #value#<BR>
        </CFOUTPUT>
    <CFELSE>
        <CFLOOP index="counter" from=1 to=#ArrayLen(value)#>
            <CFOUTPUT>
                #httpHeader# : #value[counter]#<BR>
            </CFOUTPUT>
        </CFLOOP>
    </CFIF>
</CFLOOP>

</BODY>
</HTML>
```

cfhttp

CFHTTPPARAM

Required for CFHTTP POST operations, CFHTTPPARAM is used to specify the parameters necessary to build a CFHTTP POST.

Syntax
```
<CFHTTPPARAM NAME="name"
       TYPE="type"
       VALUE="transaction type"
       FILE="filename">
```

NAME
Required. A variable name for the data being passed.

TYPE
Required. The transaction type. Valid entries are:

- URL
- FormField
- Cookie
- CGI
- File

VALUE
Optional for TYPE="File". Specifies the value of the URL, FormField, Cookie, File, or CGI variable being passed.

FILE
Required for TYPE="File".

Example   cfhttpparam

```
<!--- This example shows the use of CFHTTPPARAM --->
<HTML>
<HEAD>
<TITLE>CFHTTPPARAM Example</TITLE>
</HEAD>

<BODY bgcolor=silver>
<H3>CFHTTPPARAM Example</H3>

<P>This view-only example shows the use of CFHTTPPARAM
to show the values of passed variables on another HTML
reference, accessed by CFHTTP.  The other file
could simply output the value of form.formtest,
url.url_test, cgi.cgi_test, and
cookie.cookie_test to prove that this page is working:

<H3>Sample Other File Listing</H3>
<CFOUTPUT>#HTMLCodeFormat("
```

```
<HTML>
<HEAD>
<TITLE>Sample Page</TITLE>
</HEAD>
<BODY>
<H3>Output the passed variables</H3>
<CFOUTPUT>
Form variable: ##form.form_test##
<br>URL variable: ##URL.url_test##
<br>Cookie variable: ##Cookie.cookie_test##
<br>CGI variable: ##CGI.cgi_test##
</CFOUTPUT>
</BODY>
</HTML>
")#</CFOUTPUT>

<H3>For CFHTTPPARAM code, see right frame</H3>
<!--- <P>
<CFHTTP METHOD="POST" URL="http://localhost/someotherfile.cfm">
<CFHTTPPARAM NAME="form_test" TYPE="FormField"
  VALUE="This is a form variable">
<CFHTTPPARAM NAME="url_test" TYPE="URL" VALUE="This is a URL variable">
<CFHTTPPARAM NAME="cgi_test" TYPE="CGI" VALUE="This is a CGI variable">
<CFHTTPPARAM NAME="cookie_test" TYPE="Cookie" VALUE="This is a cookie">
</CFHTTP>

<CFOUTPUT>
    #CFHTTP.FileContent#
</CFOUTPUT> --->

</BODY>
</HTML>
```

CFIF   CFELSEIF   CFELSE

Used with CFELSE and CFELSEIF, CFIF lets you create simple and compound conditional statements in CFML. The value in the CFIF tag can be any expression.

Syntax
```
<CFIF expression>
     HTML and CFML tags
<CFELSEIF>
     HTML and CFML tags
<CFELSE expression>
     HTML and CFML tags
</CFIF>
```

Usage
Note that when testing for the return value of any function that returns a Boolean, you do not need to explicitly define the TRUE condition. The following code uses IsArray as an example:

```
<CFIF IsArray(myarray)>
```

When successful, IsArray evaluates to YES, the string equivalent of the Boolean TRUE. This method is preferred over explicitly defining the TRUE condition:

```
<CFIF IsArray(myarray) IS TRUE>
```

Note
On UNIX, there is a switch that provides fast date-time parsing. If you have enabled this switch, you must refer to dates in expressions in the following order: month, day, and year. For example:

```
<CFIF "11/23/1998 " GT "11/15/1998 ">
```

This switch is set on the ColdFusion Administrator Server Settings page. Please refer to ../../Administering_ColdFusion_Server/contents.htm*Administering ColdFusion Server*/a for more information about ColdFusion settings.

Example
cfif

```
<!--- This example shows the interaction of CFIF, CFELSE,
and CFELSEIF --->
...
<H3>CFIF Example</H3>

<P>CFIF gives us the ability to perform conditional logic
based on a condition or set of conditions.
<P>For example, we can output the list of Centers from the
snippets datasource by group and only display them <B>IF</B>
the city = San Diego.
<hr>
<!--- use CFIF to test a condition when outputting a query --->
<P>The following are centers in San Diego:

<CFOUTPUT QUERY="getCenters" >
<CFIF city is "San Diego">
     <BR><B>Name/Address:</B>#Name#, #Address1#, #City#, #State#
```

```
    <BR><B>Contact:</B> #Contact#<BR>
</CFIF>
</CFOUTPUT>
```

<P>If we would like more than one condition to be the case,
we can ask for a list of the centers in San Diego <B>OR</B>
Santa Ana. If the center does not follow this condition, we
can use CFELSE to show only the names and cities of the
other centers.
<P>Notice how a nested CFIF is used to specify
the location of the featured site (Santa Ana or San Diego).
<!--- use CFIF to specify a conditional choice for multiple
options; also note the nested CFIF --->
<hr>
<P>Complete information is shown for centers in San Diego
or Santa Ana. All other centers are listed in italics:

```
<CFOUTPUT QUERY="getCenters">
<CFIF city is "San Diego" OR city is "Santa Ana">
    <H4>Featured Center in <CFIF city is "San Diego">San
    Diego<CFELSE>Santa Ana</CFIF></H4>
    <B>Name/Address:</B>#Name#, #Address1#, #City#, #State#
    <BR><B>Contact:</B> #Contact#<BR>
<CFELSE>
    <BR><I>#Name#, #City#</I>
</CFIF>
</CFOUTPUT>
```

<P>Finally, we can use CFELSEIF to cycle through a number
of conditions and produce varying output. Note that you
can use CFCASE and CFSWITCH for a more elegant representation
of this behavior.
<hr>
<P>
<!--- use CFIF in conjunction with CFELSEIF to specify
more than one branch in a conditional situation --->
<CFOUTPUT QUERY="getCenters">
<CFIF city is "San Diego" OR city is "Santa Ana">

<I>#Name#, #City#</I> (this one is in <CFIF city is "San
    Diego">San Diego<CFELSE>Santa Ana</CFIF>)
<CFELSEIF city is "San Francisco">

<I>#Name#, #City#</I> (this one is in San Francisco)
<CFELSEIF city is "Suisun">

<I>#Name#, #City#</I> (this one is in Suisun)
<CFELSE>

<I>#Name#</I> <B>Not in a city we track</B>
</CFIF>
</CFOUTPUT>

</BODY>
</HTML>
```
```

CFIMPERSONATE

Allows you to impersonate a user defined in a security context defined in Advanced Security. The ColdFusion Application Server enforces all the privileges and restrictions that have been set up for that user with the Advanced Security rules.

Syntax

```
<CFIMPERSONATE
    SECURITYCONTEXT="SecurityContext"
    USERNAME="Name"
    PASSWORD="Password"
    TYPE= "CF" or "OS">
    ...
    HTML or CFML code to execute
    ...
</CFIMPERSONATE>
```

SECURITYCONTEXT

Required. The security context in which the user should be authenticated. If the impersonation type is "CF ," then you should specify a security context that has already been defined using the ColdFusion Advanced Security Administrator. If the impersonation type is "OS," then you should specify an NT domain as the security context.

USERNAME

Required. The user name of the user you want to impersonate. You can create a rule within ColdFusion Advanced Security to restrict a user from being impersonated within a security context.

PASSWORD

Required. The password of the user that you want to impersonate.

TYPE

Required. The type of impersonation needed. This attribute can have the value – "CF " for impersonation at the application level or "OS" for impersonation at the operating system level. Operating System level impersonation means that the impersonation is of a user known to the operating system. Currently, this type of impersonation is available only for Windows NT and not for UNIX. When this type of impersonation is in effect, the operating system will automatically perform access control for access to any resources managed by the operating system such as files and directories. This is fast, since ColdFusion is not doing any extra checking, the OS is, but the OS is limited since only resources that are protected by the operating systemare protected. For example, the operating system cannot check for resource types such as Application, data sources etc.

Usage

CFIMPERSONATE is typically used to run a block of code in a secure mode. For impersonation of type "CF," there is automatic enforcement of access control of ColdFusion resources such as files, data sources, and collections between the start and end tags of CFIMPERSONATE. If CF type impersonation is turned on, the ColdFusion engine enforces the rules and policies specified for the user in the Advanced Security section of the ColdFusion Administrator. Therefore, there is no need to make multiple isAuthorized() calls in the code to protect each resource.

Refer to ../../Administering_ColdFusion_Server/contents.htm*Administering ColdFusion Server*/a for more information about Advanced Security.

Example

```
<!--- This example shows the use of CFIMPERSONATE to impersonate
a person with the user name Bill and the password BJ4YE.--->
<HTML>
<HEAD>
    <TITLE>CFIMPERSONATE Example</TITLE>
</HEAD>

<BODY>
<CFIMPERSONATE SECURITYCONTEXT="testContext"
    USERNAME="Bill"
    PASSWORD="BJ4YE"
    TYPE= "CF">

...
</CFIMPERSONATE>
</BODY>
</HTML>
```

CFINCLUDE

CFINCLUDE lets you embed references to ColdFusion pages in your CFML. If necessary, you can embed CFINCLUDE tags recursively.

For an additional method of encapsulating CFML, see the CFMODULE tag, used to create custom tags in CFML.

Syntax   <CFINCLUDE TEMPLATE="template_name">

TEMPLATE
A logical path to an existing page.

Usage   ColdFusion searches for included files as follows:

- Checks the directory in which the current page lives.
- Searches directories explicitly mapped in the ColdFusion Administrator for the included file.

Example   cfinclude

```
<!--- This example shows the use of CFINCLUDE to paste
pieces of CFML or HTML code into another page dynamically --->
<HTML>
<HEAD>
        <TITLE>CFINCLUDE Example</TITLE>
</HEAD>

<BODY>
<H3>CFINCLUDE Example</H3>

<H4>This example includes the main.htm page from the CFDOCS
directory.  The images do not show up correctly because
they are located in a separate directory.
However, the page appears fully rendered within the
contents of this page.</H4>
<CFINCLUDE TEMPLATE="/cfdocs/main.htm">

</BODY>
</HTML>
```

CFINDEX

Use the CFINDEX tag to populate collections with indexed data. CFINDEX and CFSEARCH encapsulate the Verity indexing and searching utilities. Verity collections can be populated from either text files in a directory you specify, or from a query generated by any ColdFusion query. Before you can populate a Verity collection, you need to create the collection using either the CFCOLLECTION tag or the ColdFusion Administrator. Use CFSEARCH to search collections you populate with CFINDEX.

Syntax

```
<CFINDEX COLLECTION="collection_name"
    ACTION="action"
    TYPE="type"
    TITLE="title"
    KEY="ID"
    BODY="body"
    CUSTOM1="custom_value"
    CUSTOM2="custom_value"
    URLPATH="URL"
    EXTENSIONS="file_extensions"
    QUERY="query_name"
    RECURSE="Yes" or "No"
    EXTERNAL="Yes" or "No"
    LANGUAGE="language">
```

COLLECTION

Required. Specifies a collection name. If you are indexing an external collection (EXTERNAL is "Yes"), specify the collection name, including fully qualified path:

COLLECTION="e:\collections\personnel"
You cannot combine internal and external collections in the same indexing operation.

ACTION

Optional. Specifies the index action. Valid entries are:

- Update — Updates the index and adds the key specified in KEY to the index if it is not already defined.

- Delete — Deletes the key specified in KEY in the specified collection.

- Purge — Deletes data in the specified collection leaving the collection intact for re-population.

- Refresh — Clears data in the specified collection prior to re-populating it with new data.

- Optimize — Optimizes the specified collection of files. This action is deprecated; use CFCOLLECTION instead.

TYPE

Optional. Specifies the type of entity being indexed. Default is CUSTOM. Valid entries are:

- File — Indexes files.
- Path — Indexes all files in specified path that pass EXTENSIONS filter.
- Custom — Indexes custom entities from a ColdFusion query.

TITLE

Required when TYPE="Custom". Specifies one of the following:

- A title for the collection
- A query column name for any TYPE and a valid query name

The TITLE attribute allows searching collections by title or displaying a separate title from the actual key.

KEY

Optional. A unique identifier reference that specifies one of the following:

- Document filename when TYPE="File"
- Fully qualified path when TYPE="Path"
- A unique identifier when TYPE="Custom", such as the table column holding the primary key
- A query column name for any other TYPE argument

BODY

Optional. ASCII text to index or a query column name. Required if TYPE="Custom". Ignored for TYPE="File" and TYPE="Path". Invalid if TYPE="Delete". Specifies one of the following:

- The ASCII text to be indexed
- A query column name when a valid query name is specified in QUERY

Multiple columns can be specified in a comma-separated list:

```
BODY="employee_name, dept_name, location"
```

CUSTOM1

Optional. A custom field you can use to store data during an indexing operation. Specify a query column name for any TYPE and a valid query name.

CUSTOM2

Optional. A second custom field you can use to store data during an indexing operation. Usage is the same as for CUSTOM1.

URLPATH

Optional. Specifies the URL path for files when TYPE="File" and TYPE="Path". When the collection is searched with CFSEARCH, this path name will automatically be prepended to all file names and returned as the URL attribute.

EXTENSIONS

Optional. Specifies the comma-separated list of file extensions that ColdFusion uses to index files when TYPE="Path". Default is HTM, HTML, CFM, CFML, DBM, DBML. An entry of "*." returns files with no extension:

EXTENSIONS=".htm, .html, .cfm, .cfml, *."
Returns files with the specified extensions as well as files with no extension.

QUERY

Optional. Specifies the name of the query against which the collection is being generated.

RECURSE

Optional. Yes or No. Yes specifies that directories below the path specified in KEY when TYPE="Path" will be included in the indexing operation.

EXTERNAL

Optional. Yes or No. Yes indicates that the collection specified in COLLECTION was created outside of ColdFusion using native Verity indexing tools.

LANGUAGE

Optional. To use the LANGUAGE attribute you must have the ColdFusion International Search Pack installed. Valid entries are:

- English (default)
- German
- Finnish
- French
- Danish
- Dutch
- Italian
- Norwegian
- Portuguese
- Spanish
- Swedish

Example   cfindex

```
<!--- This example shows how to utilize CFINDEX
to populate an existing collection with content --->
<HTML>
<HEAD>
<TITLE>
CFINDEX Example
</TITLE>
</HEAD>
<BODY bgcolor=silver>
```

CFINDEX Example

```
<!--- To index the collection, select the check box on the form --->
<CFIF IsDefined("form.IndexCollection")>
<CFINDEX ACTION="UPDATE" COLLECTION="Snippets"
  KEY="c:\inetpub\wwwroot\cfdocs\snippets" TYPE="PATH" TITLE="Test"
    URLPATH="http://127.0.0.1/cfdocs/snippets/" EXTENSIONS=".cfm"
      RECURSE="Yes">
  ...
```

CFINPUT

CFINPUT is used inside CFFORM to place radio buttons, checkboxes, or text boxes. Provides input validation for the specified control type.

CFINPUT supports the JavaScript onClick event in the same manner as the HTML INPUT tag:

```
<CFINPUT TYPE="radio"
    NAME="radio1"
    onClick="JavaScript_function">
```

Syntax
```
<CFINPUT TYPE="input_type"
    NAME="name"
    VALUE="initial_value"
    REQUIRED="Yes" or "No"
    RANGE="min_value, max_value"
    VALIDATE="data_type"
    ONVALIDATE="javascript_function"
    MESSAGE="validation_msg"
    ONERROR="text"
    SIZE="integer"
    MAXLENGTH="integer"
    CHECKED="Yes" or "No"
    PASSTHROUGH="HTML_attributes">
```

TYPE
Optional. Valid entries are:

- Text — Creates a text entry box control (default).

- Radio — Creates a radio button control.

- Checkbox — Creates a checkbox control.

- Password — Creates a password entry control.

NAME
Required. A name for the form input element.

VALUE
Optional. An initial value for the form input element.

REQUIRED
Optional. Enter Yes or No. Default is No.

RANGE
Optional. Enter a minimum value, maximum value range separated by a comma. Valid only for numeric data.

VALIDATE
Optional. Valid entries are:

- date — Verifies US date entry in the form mm/dd/yyyy.

- eurodate — Verifies valid European date entry in the form dd/mm/yyyy.

- time — Verifies a time entry in the form *hh:mm:ss*.

- float — Verifies a floating point entry.

- integer — Verifies an integer entry.

- telephone — Verifies a telephone entry. Telephone data must be entered as ###-###-####. The hyphen separator (-) can be replaced with a blank. The area code and exchange must begin with a digit between 1 and 9.

- zipcode — (U.S. formats only) Number can be a 5-digit or 9-digit zip in the form #####-####. The hyphen separator (-) can be replaced with a blank.

- creditcard — Blanks and dashes are stripped and the number is verified using the mod10 algorithm.

- social_security_number — Number must be entered as ###-##-####. The hyphen separator (-) can be replaced with a blank.

ONVALIDATE

Optional. The name of a valid JavaScript function used to validate user input. The form object, input object, and input object value are passed to the specified routine, which should return true if validation succeeds and false otherwise. When used, the VALIDATE attribute is ignored.

MESSAGE

Optional. Message text to appear if validation fails.

ONERROR

Optional. The name of a valid JavaScript function you want to execute in the event of a failed validation.

SIZE

Optional. The size of the input control. Ignored if TYPE is Radio or Checkbox.

MAXLENGTH

Optional. The maximum length of text entered when TYPE is Text.

PASSTHROUGH

Optional. HTML attributes that are not explicitly supported by CFINPUT. If you specify an attribute and its value, the attribute and value are passed to the HTML code that is generated for the CFINPUT tag. See the Usage section for more information about specifying values.

Usage   You can add standard and dynamic HTML FORM tag attributes and their values to the CFINPUT tag by using the PASSTHROUGH attribute. These attributes and values are passed directly through ColdFusion to the browser in creating a form.

If you specify a value in quotation marks, you must escape the quotation marks by doubling them, for example,

PASSTHROUGH= "readonly= " "YES " " "

Note CFINPUT requires the client to download a Java applet. Downloading an applet takes time, so using CFINPUT may be slightly slower than using a simple HTML form. In addition, browsers must be Java-enabled for CFINPUT to work properly.

Example cfinput

```
<!--- This example shows the use of CFINPUT to validate input --->
<HTML>
<HEAD>
<TITLE>
CFINPUT Example
</TITLE>
</HEAD>

<BODY bgcolor=silver>
<H3>CFINPUT Example</H3>

<!--- this example shows the use of CFINPUT within a CFFORM to
ensure simple validation of text items --->
<CFFORM ACTION="cfinput.cfm" METHOD="POST" ENABLECAB="Yes">

<!--- phone number validation --->
Phone Number Validation (enter a properly formatted phone number):
<BR><CFINPUT TYPE="Text" NAME="MyPhone" MESSAGE="Please enter telephone
number, formatted xxx-xxx-xxxx (e.g. 617-761-2000)" VALIDATE="telephone"
REQUIRED="Yes"><font size=-1 color=red>Required</FONT>
<!--- zip code validation --->
<P>Zip Code Validation (enter a properly formatted zip code):
<BR><CFINPUT TYPE="Text" NAME="MyZip" MESSAGE="Please enter zip code,
formatted xxxxx or xxxxx-xxxx" VALIDATE="zipcode" REQUIRED="Yes"><font
size=-1 color=red>Required</FONT>
<!--- range validation --->
<P>Range Validation (enter an integer from 1 to 5):
<BR><CFINPUT TYPE="Text" NAME="MyRange" RANGE="1,5" MESSAGE="You must
enter an integer from 1 to 5" VALIDATE="integer" REQUIRED="No">
<!--- date validation --->
<P>Date Validation (enter a properly formatted date):
<BR><CFINPUT TYPE="Text" NAME="MyDate" MESSAGE="Please enter a correctly
formatted date (dd/mm/yy)" VALIDATE="date" REQUIRED="No">

<INPUT TYPE="Submit" NAME="" VALUE="send my information">
</CFFORM>

</BODY>
</HTML>
```

CFINSERT

CFINSERT inserts new records in data sources.

Syntax
```
<CFINSERT DATASOURCE="ds_name"
          DBTYPE="type"
          DBSERVER="dbms"
          DBNAME="database name"
          TABLENAME="tbl_name"
          TABLEOWNER="owner"
          TABLEQUALIFIER="tbl_qualifier"
          USERNAME="username"
          PASSWORD="password"
          PROVIDER="COMProvider"
          PROVIDERDSN="datasource"
          FORMFIELDS="formfield1, formfield2, ...">
```

DATASOURCE
Required. Name of the data source that contains your table.

DBTYPE
Optional. The database driver type:

- ODBC (default) — ODBC driver.

- Oracle73 — Oracle 7.3 native database driver. Using this option, the ColdFusion Server computer must have Oracle 7.3.4.0.0 (or greater) client software installed.

- Oracle80 —Oracle 8.0 native database driver. Using this option, the ColdFusion Server computer must have Oracle 8.0 (or greater) client software installed.

- Sybase11 —Sybase System 11 native database driver. Using this option, the ColdFusion Server computer must have Sybase 11.1.1 (or greater) client software installed. Sybase patch ebf 7729 is recommended.

- OLEDB —OLE DB provider. If specified, this database provider overrides the driver type specified in the ColdFusion Administrator.

- DB2 —DB2 5.2 native database driver.

- Informix73 —Informix73 native database driver.

DBSERVER
Optional. For native database drivers and the SQLOLEDB provider, specifies the name of the database server machine. If specified, DBSERVER overrides the server specified in the data source.

DBNAME
Optional. The database name (Sybase System 11 driver and SQLOLEDB provider only). If specified, DBNAME overrides the default database specified in the data source.

TABLENAME

Required. Name of the table you want the form fields inserted in. Note the following:

- ORACLE drivers — This specification must be in uppercase.
- Sybase driver — This specification is case-sensitive and must be in the same case as that used when the table was created

TABLEOWNER

Optional. For data sources that support table ownership (such as SQL Server, Oracle, and Sybase SQL Anywhere), use this field to specify the owner of the table.

TABLEQUALIFIER

Optional. For data sources that support table qualifiers, use this field to specify the qualifier for the table. The purpose of table qualifiers varies across drivers. For SQL Server and Oracle, the qualifier refers to the name of the database that contains the table. For the Intersolv dBase driver, the qualifier refers to the directory where the DBF files are located.

USERNAME

Optional. If specified, USERNAME overrides the username value specified in the ODBC setup.

PASSWORD

Optional. If specified, PASSWORD overrides the password value specified in the ODBC setup.

PROVIDER

Optional. COM provider (OLE-DB only).

PROVIDERDSN

Optional. Data source name for the COM provider (OLE-DB only).

FORMFIELDS

Optional. A comma-separated list of form fields to insert. If this attribute is not specified, all fields in the form are included in the operation.

Example   cfinsert

```
<!--- This example shows how to use CFINSERT instead of CFQUERY
to place data into a datasource. --->
<!--- if form.POSTED exists, we are inserting a new record,
so begin the CFINSERT tag --->
<CFIF IsDefined ("form.posted")>
<CFINSERT DATASOURCE="cfsnippets"
    TABLENAME="Comments"
    FORMFIELDS="Email,FromUser,Subject,MessText,Posted">
<H3><I>Your record was added to the database.</I></H3>
</CFIF>
```

```
<!--- use a query to show the existing state of the database --->
<CFQUERY NAME="GetComments" DATASOURCE="cfsnippets">
SELECT  CommentID, EMail, FromUser, Subject, CommtType, MessText,
  Posted, Processed
FROM  Comments
</CFQUERY>
<HTML>
<HEAD>
<TITLE>
CFINSERT Example
</TITLE>
</HEAD>

<BODY bgcolor=silver>
<H3>CFINSERT Example</H3>

<P>First, we'll show a list of the available comments in the
cfsnippets datasource.

<!--- show all the comments in the db --->
<TABLE>
    <TR>
        <TD>From User</TD><TD>Subject</TD><TD>Comment Type</TD>
    <TD>Message</TD><TD>Date Posted</TD>
    </TR>
<CFOUTPUT QUERY="GetComments">
    <TR>
        <TD valign=top><a href="mailto:#Email#">#FromUser#</A></TD>
        <TD valign=top>#Subject#</TD>
        <TD valign=top>#CommtType#</TD>
        <TD valign=top><FONT SIZE="-2">#Left(MessText, 125)#
    </FONT></TD>
        <TD valign=top>#Posted#</TD>
    </TR>

</CFOUTPUT>
</TABLE>

<P>Next, we'll offer the opportunity to enter your own comment:
<!--- make a form for input --->
<FORM ACTION="cfinsert.cfm" METHOD="POST">
<PRE>
Email:<INPUT TYPE="Text" NAME="email">
From:<INPUT TYPE="Text" NAME="fromUser">
Subject:<INPUT TYPE="Text" NAME="subject">
Message:<TEXTAREA NAME="MessText" COLS="40" ROWS="6"></TEXTAREA>
Date Posted:<CFOUTPUT>#DateFormat(Now())#</CFOUTPUT>
<!--- dynamically determine today's date --->
<INPUT TYPE="Hidden" NAME="posted" VALUE="<CFOUTPUT>#Now()#</CFOUTPUT>">
```

```
</PRE>
<INPUT TYPE="Submit" NAME="" VALUE="insert my comment">
</FORM>

</BODY>
</HTML>
```

CFLDAP

CFLDAP provides an interface to LDAP (Lightweight Directory Access Protocol) directory servers like the Netscape Directory Server. For complete examples of CFLDAP usage, refer to ../../Developing_Web_Applications_with_ColdFusion/ contents.htm*Developing Web Applications with ColdFusion*/a.

Syntax

```
<CFLDAP SERVER="server_name"
        PORT="port_number"
        USERNAME="name"
        PASSWORD="password"
        ACTION="action"
        NAME="name"
        TIMEOUT="seconds"
        MAXROWS="number"
        START="distinguished_name"
        SCOPE="scope"
        ATTRIBUTES="attribute, attribute"
        FILTER="filter"
        FILTERFILE="<file_name>,<stanza_name>"
        SORT="attribute[, attribute]..."
        SORTCONTROL="nocase" and/or "desc" or "asc"
        DN="distinguished_name"
        STARTROW="row_number"
        MODIFYTYPE="REPLACE" or "ADD" or "DELETE"
        REBIND="Yes" or "No"
        REFERRAL="number_of_allowed_hops"
        SECURE="multi_field_security_string"
        SEPARATOR="separator_character"
        >
```

SERVER

Required. Host name ("biff.upperlip.com") or IP address ("192.1.2.225") of the LDAP server.

PORT

Optional. Port defaults to the standard LDAP port, 389.

USERNAME

Optional. If no user name is specified, the LDAP connection will be anonymous.

PASSWORD

Optional. Password corresponds to user name.

ACTION

Optional. Specifies the LDAP action. There are five possible values:

- Query — (Default) Returns LDAP entry information only. Requires NAME, START, ATTRIBUTES attributes. See Usage for more information.

- Add — Adds LDAP entries to the LDAP server. Requires ATTRIBUTES.

- Modify — Modifies LDAP entries on an LDAP server with the exception of the distinguished name ("DN") attribute. Requires DN, ATTRIBUTES. See the *MODIFYTYPE* attribute for additional controls.

- ModifyDN — Modifies the distinguished name attribute for LDAP entries on an LDAP server. Requires DN, ATTRIBUTES.

- Delete — Deletes LDAP entries on an LDAP server. Requires DN.

NAME

Required for ACTION="Query". The name you assign to the LDAP query.

TIMEOUT

Optional. Specifies the maximum amount of time in seconds to wait for LDAP processing. Defaults to 60 seconds.

MAXROWS

Optional. Specifies the maximum number of entries for LDAP queries.

START

Required for ACTION="Query". Specifies the distinguished name of the entry to be used to start the search.

SCOPE

Optional. Specifies the scope of the search from the entry specified in the Start attribute for ACTION="Query". There are three possible values:

- OneLevel — (Default) Searches all entries one level beneath the entry specified in the START attribute.

- Base — Searches only the entry specified in the START attribute.

- Subtree — Searches the entry specified in the START attribute as well all entries at all levels beneath it.

ATTRIBUTES

Required for ACTION="Query", Add, ModifyDN, and Modify. For queries, specifies the comma-separated list of attributes to be returned for queries. For queries, you can also specify the wild card "*" to get all the attributes associated with the entry. In addition, it can be used to specify the list of update columns for ACTION="Add" or "Modify". When used with ACTION="Add" and Action="Modify", separate multiple attributes with a semicolon. When used with ACTION="ModifyDN", ColdFusion passes attributes to the LDAP server without performing any syntax checking.

FILTER

Optional. Specifies the search criteria for ACTION="Query". Attributes are referenced in the form: "(attribute operator value)". Example: "(sn=Smith)". Default is "objectclass=*".

If you also specify the *FILTERFILE* attribute, the filter is considered to be a search string not a filter.

FILTERFILE

Optional. Specifies the name of a filter file and the name of the stanza tag within that file that contains the LDAP filter string specification. You can specify either an absolute path name or a simple file name to identify the file. If you use a simple file name, CFLDAP looks for it in ColdFusion's default LDAP directory. The default LDAP directory is C:\cfusion\ldap. The filter file must be in LDAP filter file format as defined in RCF-1558.

SORT

Optional. Indicates the attribute or attributes to sort query results by. Use a comma to separate attributes if more than one attribute is specified.

SORTCONTROL

Optional. Specifies how to sort query results. Enter "nocase" for a case-insensitive sort. By default, sorts are case-sensitive. You can also enter "asc" for an ascending sort and "desc" for a descending sort. You can enter a combination of these, for example, "nocase" and "asc". The default sort order is ascending.

DN

Required for ACTION="Add", Modify, ModifyDN, and Delete. Specifies the distinguished name for update actions. Example: "cn=Barbara Jensen, o=Ace Industry, c=US".

STARTROW

Optional. Used in conjunction with ACTION="Query". Specifies the first row of the LDAP query that is to be inserted into the ColdFusion query. The default is 1. See the Usage section for more information about the query object and query variables.

MODIFYTYPE

Optional. Indicates whether to Add, Delete, or Replace an attribute within a multi-value list of attributes, as follows:

- Add - appends the new attribute to any existing attributes.

- Delete - deletes the specified attribute from the set of existing attributes.

- Replace (default) - Replaces an existing attribute with the specified attribute or attributes.

Note that you cannot add attributes that already exist or that are NULL.

REBIND

Optional. Yes or No. If you set REBIND to Yes, CFLDAP attempts to rebind the referral callback and reissue the query via the referred address using the original credentials. The default is No, which means referred connections are anonymous.

REFERRAL

Optional. Specifies the number of hops allowed in a referral. Valid values for this are integers equal to or greater than zero. If you specify zero, you turn off CFLDAP's ability to use referred addresses; thus, no data is returned.

SECURE

Optional. Identifies the type of security to employ, CFSSL_BASIC or CFSSL_CLIENT_AUTH, and additional information that is required by the specified security type.

SECURE="CFSSL_BASIC,*certificate_db*"

or

SECURE="CFSSL_CLIENT_AUTH,*certificate_db,certificate_name,*
            key_db,key_password"

These fields have the following values:

certificate_db: The name of the certificate database file (in Netscape cert7.db format). You can specify either an absolute path or a simple file name.

certificate_name: The name of the client certificate to send the server.

key_db: Keyword database that holds the public/private key-pair (in Netscape key3.db format). You can specify either an absolute path or a simple file name.

keyword_db: The password to key database.

If you use a simple file name for *certificate_db* or *keyword_db*, CFLDAP looks for it in ColdFusion's default LDAP directory. The default LDAP directory is C:\cfusion\ldap.

Refer to the Usage section for information about the differences between the two types of security: CFSSL_BASIC and CFSSL_CLIENT_AUTH types.

SEPARATOR

Optional. Specifies the character that CFLDAP uses to separate attribute values in multi-value attributes. This character is used by the QUERY, ADD, and MODIFY action attributes, and is used by CFLDAP to output multi-value attributes. The default character is the comma (,).

Usage   If you use the Query ACTION, CFLDAP creates a query object, allowing you access to information in the three query variables as described in the following table.

CFLDAP Query Variables	
Variable Names	**Description**
queryname.RecordCount	The total number of records returned by the query.
queryname.CurrentRow	The current row of the query being processed by CFOUTPUT.
queryname.ColumnList	The list of the column names in the query.

The CFSSL_BASIC type of security provides V2 SSL, and the CFSSL_CLIENT_AUTH type of security provides V3 SSL. V2 SSL provides encryption and server authentication. V3 SSL adds to this certificate-based client authentication.

Both forms of security encrypt the conversation, and the server always sends a digital certificate to confirm that it is the right server.

For CFSSL_BASIC, you must also specify the CFLDAP attributes *USERNAME* and *PASSWORD* to authenticate yourself. V2 then encrypts the password prior to transmission.

For CFSSL_CLIENT_AUTH, you do not send a user name and password; instead, you perform authentication by a digital certificate that you send to the server. CFSSL_CLIENT_AUTH is much more secure; however, it is difficult to administer since all the clients must have certificates, which the server must be able to validate, and all the certificates must have keys associated with them and passwords to protect those keys.

Example   cfldap

```
<!--- This example shows the use of CFLDAP --->
<HTML>
<HEAD>
<TITLE>CFLDAP Example</TITLE>
</HEAD>

<BODY bgcolor=silver>
<H3>CFLDAP Example</H3>

<P>CFLDAP provides an interface to LDAP (Lightweight Directory Access
Protocol) directory servers like BigFoot
(<a href="http://www.bigfoot.com">http://www.bigfoot.com</A>).
<P>Enter a name (try your own name) and search a public LDAP resource.
...
<!--- If the server has been defined, run the query --->
<CFIF IsDefined("form.server")>
<!--- check to see that there is a name listed --->
<CFIF form.name is not "">
<!--- make the LDAP query --->
<CFLDAP
 SERVER="ldap.bigfoot.com"
 ACTION="QUERY"
 NAME="results"
 START="cn=#name#,c=US"
 FILTER="(cn=#name#)"
 ATTRIBUTES="cn,o,l,st,c,mail,telephonenumber"
 SORT="cn ASC">
<!--- Display results --->
    <CENTER>
    <TABLE BORDER=0 CELLSPACING=2 CELLPADDING=2>
    <TR>
        <TH COLSPAN=5><CFOUTPUT>#results.RecordCount# matches found
     </CFOUTPUT></TH>
    </TR>
```

```
        <TR>
            <TH><FONT SIZE="-2">Name</FONT></TH>
            <TH><FONT SIZE="-2">Organization</FONT></TH>
            <TH><FONT SIZE="-2">Location</FONT></TH>
            <TH><FONT SIZE="-2">E-Mail</FONT></TH>
            <TH><FONT SIZE="-2">Phone</FONT></TH>
        </TR>
        <CFOUTPUT QUERY="results">
        <TR>
          <TD><FONT SIZE="-2">#cn#</FONT></TD>
          <TD><FONT SIZE="-2">#o#</FONT></TD>
          <TD><FONT SIZE="-2">#l#, #st#, #c#</FONT></TD>
          <TD><FONT SIZE="-2"><A HREF="mailto:#mail#">#mail#</A></FONT></TD>
          <TD><FONT SIZE="-2">#telephonenumber#</FONT></TD>
        </TR>
        </CFOUTPUT>
        </TABLE>
        </CENTER>
</CFIF>
</CFIF>
</BODY>
</HTML>
```

cfldap

CFLOCATION

CFLOCATION opens a specified ColdFusion page or HTML file. For example, you might use CFLOCATION to specify a standard message or response that you use in several different ColdFusion applications. Use the ADDTOKEN attribute to verify client requests. See Warning for information about the interaction betweencookies and CFLOCATION.

Syntax   <CFLOCATION URL="url" ADDTOKEN="Yes" or "No">

URL
The URL of the HTML file or CFML page you want to open.

ADDTOKEN
Optional. Yes or No. CLIENTMANAGEMENT must be enabled (see CFAPPLICATION). A value of Yes appends client variable information to the URL you specify in the URL argument.

Warning   Do not set a cookie variable on the same page that you use the CFLOCATION tag. If you do, the cookie is never saved on the browser. Likewise, if you use a cookie to store a client variable, the client variable is never set.

Example   cflocation

```
<!--- This view only example shows the use of CFLOCATION --->
<HTML>
<HEAD>
<TITLE>CFLOCATION Example</TITLE>
</HEAD>

<BODY>
<H3>CFLOCATION Example</H3>
<P>CFLOCATION redirects the browser to a specified web resource;
normally, you would use this tag to go to another CF template or to
an HTML file on the same server.  The ADDTOKEN attribute allows you to
send client information to the target page.
<P>The following is example code to direct you back to
the CFDOCS home page (remove the comments and this information will
display within the frame):
<!--- <CFLOCATION URL="../../cfdocs/index.htm" ADDTOKEN="No"> --->

</BODY>
</HTML>
```

cflocation

CFLOCK

The CFLOCK tag provides two types of locks to ensure the integrity of shared data:

- exclusive lock
- read-only lock

An exclusive lock single-threads access to the CFML constructs in its body. Single-threaded access implies that the body of the tag can be executed by at most one request at a time. A request executing inside a CFLOCK tag has an "exclusive lock" on the tag. No other requests are allowed to start executing inside the tag while a request has an exclusive lock. ColdFusion issues exclusive locks on a first-come, first-served basis.

A read-only lock allows multiple requests to access the CFML constructs inside its body concurrently. Therefore, read-only locks should only be used when the shared data will only be read and not modified. If another request already has an exclusive lock on the shared data, the request will wait for the exclusive lock to be released before it can obtain it.

Syntax

```
<CFLOCK
     TIMEOUT="timeout in seconds "
     SCOPE="Application" or "Server" or "Session"
     NAME="lockname"
     THROWONTIMEOUT="Yes" or "No"
     TYPE= "ReadOnly/Exclusive ">
     <!--- CFML to be synchronized --->
</CFLOCK>
```

TIMEOUT

Required. Specifies the maximum amount of time in seconds to wait to obtain an lock. If a lock can be obtained within the specified period, execution will continue inside the body of the tag. Otherwise, the behavior depends on the value of the *THROWONTIMEOUT* attribute.

SCOPE

Optional. Specifies the scope as one of the following: Application, Server, or Session. This attribute is mutually exclusive with the *NAME* attribute. See the Scope section for valuable information.

NAME

Optional. Specifies the name of the lock. Only one request will be able to execute inside a CFLOCK tag with a given name. Therefore, providing the *NAME* attribute allows for synchronizing access to the same resources from different parts of an application. Lock names are global to a ColdFusion server. They are shared between applications and user sessions, but not across clustered servers. This attribute is mutually exclusive with the *SCOPE* attribute. Therefore, do not specify the *SCOPE* attribute and the *NAME* attribute in the same tag. Note that the value of *NAME* cannot be an empty string.

THROWONTIMEOUT

Optional. Yes or No. Specifies how timeout conditions should be handled. If the value is Yes an exception will be generated to provide notification of the timeout. If the value is No execution continues past the </CFLOCK> tag. Default is Yes.

TYPE

Optional. ReadOnly or Exclusive. Specifies the type of lock: read-only or exclusive. Default is Exclusive. A read-only lock allows more than one request to read shared data. An exclusive lock allows only one request to read or write to shared data. See the following Note.

Note   Limit the scope of code that updates shared data. Exclusive locks are required to ensure the integrity of these updates, but they have a significant impact on performance. Read-only locks are faster. If you have a performance-sensitive application, you should substitute read-only locks for exclusive locks wherever it is possible, for example, when reading shared data.

Usage   ColdFusion Server is a multi-threaded web application server that can process multiple page requests at any given time. Use CFLOCK to guarantee that multiple concurrently executing requests do not manipulate shared data structures, files, or CFXs in an inconsistent manner. Note the following:

- Using CFLOCK around CFML constructs that modify shared data ensures that the modifications occur one after the other and not all at the same time.

- Using CFLOCK around file manipulation constructs can guarantee that file updates do not fail due to files being open for writing by other applications or ColdFusion tags.

- Using CFLOCK around CFX invocations can guarantee that CFXs that are not implemented in a thread-safe manner can be safely invoked by ColdFusion. This usually only applies to CFXs developed in C++ using the CFAPI. Any C++ CFX that maintains and manipulates shared (global) data structures will have to be made thread-safe to safely work with ColdFusion. However, writing thread-safe C++ CFXs requires advanced knowledge. A CFML custom tag wrapper can be used around the CFX to make its invocation thread-safe.

Scope   Whenever you display, set, or update variables, in one of the shared scopes, use the *SCOPE* attribute to identify the scope as Server, Application or Session.

Within the ColdFusion Administrator, the Locking page, under the Server section, allows you to set different characteristics of the locking schema according to scope. The following table shows which features are available for Server, Application, and Session scope.

Features	Server	Application	Session
No automatic checking or locking	Yes	Yes	Yes
Full checking	Yes	Yes	Yes
Automatic read locking	Yes	Yes	Yes
Single Threaded Sessions			Yes

Each feature that you select has tradeoffs.

- No automatic checking or locking. If you select this button, no reads or writes are locked or checked for correct protection. You should select this only after you have run with full checking and know that there are no errors to handle and that all locking is handled programmatically. Selecting this button provides the fastest performance.

- Full checking. If you select this button, all unlocked accesses will be detected. You should select this when you are in debug mode. Selecting this button slows performance.

- Automatic read locking. If you select this button, all reads are locked and unlocked writes cause an error. Selecting this button also slows down performance considerably.

- Single-threaded sessions: If you select this button, the whole request has to finish before another request for the same session is processed. Selecting this button may have an effect on performance depending on the request pattern. For example, the total response time may increase if an application has multiple frames that can be refreshed at once, thus causing multiple requests to have to queue up and wait to be processed.

For an analysis of best practices with respect to locking, please refer to ../../ Administering_ColdFusion_Server/contents.htm*Administering ColdFusion Server.*

Deadlocks   CFLOCK uses kernel level synchronization objects that are released automatically upon timeout and/or abnormal termination of the thread that owns them. Therefore, ColdFusion will never deadlock for an infinite period of time while processing a CFLOCK tag. However, very large timeouts can block request threads for long periods of time and thus radically decrease throughput. Always use the minimum timeout value allowed.

Another cause of blocked request threads is inconsistent nesting of CFLOCK tags and inconsistent naming of locks. If you are nesting locks, you and everyone accessing the locked variables must consistently nest CFLOCK tags in the same order . If everyone accessing locked variables does not adhere to these conventions, a deadlock can occur. A deadlock is a state in which no request can execute the locked section of the page.

Thus, all requests to the protected section of the page are blocked until there is a timeout. The following tables show two scenarios that cause deadlocks.

Deadlock Scenario with Two Users	
User 1	**User 2**
Locks the session scope .	Locks the application scope.
Deadlock: Tries to lock application scope, but application scope already is locked by User 2.	**Deadlock:** Tries to lock the session scope, but session scope already is locked by User 1.

The following deadlock scenario could take place if you tried to nest a write lock after a

Deadlock Scenario With One User
User 1
Locks the session scope with a read lock.
Attempts to lock the session scope with an exclusive lock.
Deadlock: Attempts to lock the session scope with an exclusive lock, but cannot because the scope is already locked for reading.

read lock, as in the following code:

```
<CFLOCK TIMEOUT="60" SCOPE="SESSION" TYPE="ReadOnly">
        ...............
        <CFLOCK TIMEOUT="60" SCOPE="SESSION" TYPE="Exclusive">
        .........
        </CFLOCK>
</CFLOCK>
```

Once a deadlock occurs neither of the users can do anything to break the deadlock, because the execution of their requests is blocked until the deadlock can be resolved by a lock timeout.

In order to avoid a deadlock, you and all who need to nest locks should do so in a well-specified order and name the locks consistently. In particular, if you need to lock access to the server, application, and session scopes, you must do so in the following order.

1. Lock the session scope. In the CFLOCK tag, indicate the scope by specifying "SESSION" as the value of the SCOPE attribute.

2. Lock the application scope. In the CFLOCK tag, indicate scope by specifying "APPLICATION" as the value of the SCOPE attribute.

3. Lock the server scope. In the CFLOCK tag, indicate the scope by specifying "SERVER" as the value of the SCOPE attribute.

4. Unlock the server scope.

5. Unlock the application scope.

6. Unlock the session scope.

Note You can take out any pair of lock/unlock steps if you do not need to lock a particular scope. For example, you can take out Steps 3 and 4 if you do not need to lock the server scope. Similar rules apply for named locks.

For complete usage information on CFLOCK, see ../../ Developing_Web_Applications_with_ColdFusion/contents.htm*Developing Web Applications with ColdFusion*/ a.

Example   cflock

```
<!---------------------------------------------------------------
    This example shows how CFLOCK can be used to guarantee the
    consistency of data updates to variables in the Application,
        Server, and Session scopes.
        You should copy the following code into an Application.cfm
    file in the snippets directory.
    ------------------------------------------------------------->
        <HTML>
        <HEAD>
            <TITLE>Define Session and Application Variables</TITLE>
        </HEAD>

        <BASEFONT FACE="Arial, Helvetica" SIZE=2>
        <BODY  bgcolor="#FFFFD5">

        <H3>CFAPPLICATION Example</H3>

        <P>CFAPPLICATION defines scoping for a ColdFusion application and
        enables or disables the storing of application and/or session
        variables. This tag is placed in a special file called
        Application.cfm that is run before any other CF template in a
        directory where the Application.cfm file appears.</P>

        <CFAPPLICATION NAME="ETurtle" SESSIONTIMEOUT=#CreateTimeSpan(0, 0,
        0, 60)# SESSIONMANAGEMENT="yes">

<!----------------------------------------------------------------------
    Initialize the session and application variables that will be
    used by E-Turtleneck. Use the session scope for the session
    variables.
    ---------------------------------------------------------------------->
        <CFLOCK SCOPE="Session" TIMEOUT="30" TYPE="Exclusive">
            <CFIF NOT IsDefined("session.size")>
```

```
              <CFSET session.size = "">
          </CFIF>
          <CFIF NOT IsDefined("session.color")>
              <CFSET session.color = "">
          </CFIF>
      </CFLOCK>


<!---------------------------------------------------------------------
      Use the application lock for the application variable. This
      variable keeps track of the total number of turtlenecks sold. The
      application lock should have the same name as specified in the
      CFAPPLICATION tag.
--------------------------------------------------------------------->
      <CFLOCK SCOPE="Application" Timeout="30" Type="Exclusive">
          <CFIF NOT IsDefined("application.number")>
              <CFSET application.number = 1>
          </CFIF>
      </CFLOCK>
      <CFLOCK SCOPE="Application" TIMEOUT="30" TYPE="ReadOnly">
          <CFOUTPUT>
          E-Turtleneck is proud to say that we have sold
          #application.number# turtlenecks to date.
          </CFOUTPUT>
  </CFLOCK>
<!---------------------------------------------------------------------
      End of Application.cfm
--------------------------------------------------------------------->
<HEAD>
<TITLE>
CFLOCK Example
</TITLE>
</HEAD>

<BASEFONT FACE="Arial, Helvetica" SIZE=2>
<BODY  bgcolor="#FFFFD5">

<H3>CFLOCK Example</H3>

<CFIF IsDefined("form.submit")>
    <CFOUTPUT>
          Thank you for shopping E-Turtleneck. Today you have
          chosen a turtleneck in size <b>#form.size#</b> and in the color
          <b>#form.color#</b>.
    </CFOUTPUT>

      <!-------------------------------------------------------------
      Lock session variables to assign form values to them.
      ------------------------------------------------------------->
      <CFLOCK SCOPE="Session" TIMEOUT="30" TYPE="Exclusive">
          <CFPARAM NAME=session.size Default=#form.size#>
          <CFPARAM NAME=session.color Default=#form.color#>
      </CFLOCK>
      <!-------------------------------------------------------------
      Lock application variable application.number to find the total number
```

```
of turtlenecks sold.
--------------------------------------------------------------------->
<CFLOCK SCOPE="Application" TIMEOUT="30" TYPE="Exclusive">
    <CFSET application.number = application.number + 1>
</CFLOCK>

<CFELSE><!--- Show the form only if it has not been submitted. --->

<FORM ACTION="cflock.cfm" METHOD="POST">

<P>Congratulations! You have just selected the longest wearing, most comfortable turtleneck in the world.
Please indicate the color and size that you wish to buy.</P>
<table cellspacing="2" cellpadding="2" border="0">
<tr>
  <td>Select a color.</td>
  <td><SELECT TYPE="Text" NAME="color">
        <OPTION>red
        <OPTION>white
        <OPTION>blue
        <OPTION>turquoise
        <OPTION>black
        <OPTION>forest green
        </SELECT>
    </td>
</tr>
<tr>
  <td>Select a size.</td>
  <td><SELECT TYPE="Text" NAME="size" >
        <OPTION>XXsmall
        <OPTION>Xsmall
        <OPTION>small
        <OPTION>medium
        <OPTION>large
        <OPTION>Xlarge
        </SELECT>
    </td>
</tr>
<tr>
  <td>Press Submit when you are finished making your selection.</td>
  <td><INPUT TYPE="Submit" NAME="submit" VALUE="Submit">
    </td>
</tr>
</table>
</FORM>
</CFIF>
</HTML>
```

CFLOOP

Looping is a very powerful programming technique that lets you repeat a set of instructions or display output over and over until one or more conditions are met. CFLOOP supports five different types of loops:

- Index Loops
- Conditional Loops
- Looping over a Query
- Looping over a List
- Looping over a COM Collection or Structure

The type of loop is determined by the attributes of the CFLOOP tag.

cfloop

Index Loops

An index loop repeats for a number of times determined by a range of numeric values. Index loops are commonly known as FOR loops, as in "loop FOR this range of values. "

Syntax
```
<CFLOOP INDEX="parameter_name"
        FROM="beginning_value"
        TO="ending_value"
        STEP="increment">
    ...
    HTML or CFML code to execute
    ...
</CFLOOP>
```

INDEX
Required. Defines the parameter that is the index value. The index value will be set to the FROM value and then incremented by 1 (or the STEP value) until it equals the TO value.

FROM
Required. The beginning value of the index.

TO
Required. The ending value of the index.

STEP
Optional. Default is 1. Sets the value by which the loop INDEX value is incremented each time the loop is processed.

Examples
In this example, the INDEX variable is incremented for each iteration of the loop. The following code loops five times, displaying the INDEX value of the loop each time:

```
<CFLOOP INDEX="LoopCount"
    FROM="1" TO="5">
The loop index is <CFOUTPUT>#LoopCount#</CFOUTPUT>.<BR>

</CFLOOP>
```

The result of this loop in a browser looks like this:

The loop index is 1.
The loop index is 2.
The loop index is 3.
The loop index is 4.
The loop index is 5.

In this example, the STEP value has a default value of 1. But you can set the STEP value to change the way the INDEX value is incremented. The following code counts backwards from 5:

```
<CFLOOP INDEX="LoopCount"
    FROM="5"
    TO="1"
    STEP="-1">
The loop index is <CFOUTPUT>#LoopCount#</CFOUTPUT>.<BR>

</CFLOOP>
```

The result of this loop in a browser looks like this:

The loop index is 5.
The loop index is 4.
The loop index is 3.
The loop index is 2.
The loop index is 1.

Conditional Loops

A conditional loop iterates over a set of instructions while a given condition is TRUE. To use this type of loop correctly, the instructions must change the condition every time the loop iterates until the condition evaluates as FALSE. Conditional loops are commonly known as WHILE loops, as in "loop WHILE this condition is true."

Syntax `<CFLOOP CONDITION="expression">`

CONDITION
Required. Sets the condition that controls the loop. The loop will repeat as long as the condition evaluates as TRUE. When the condition is FALSE, the loop stops.

Example The following example increments the parameter "CountVar" from 1 to 5. The results look exactly like the Index loop example.

```
<!--- Set the variable CountVar to 0 --->
<CFSET CountVar=0>

<!--- Loop until CountVar = 5 --->
<CFLOOP CONDITION="CountVar LESS THAN OR EQUAL TO 5">

      <CFSET CountVar=CountVar + 1>
      The loop index is <CFOUTPUT>#CountVar#</CFOUTPUT>.<BR>

</CFLOOP>
```

The result of this loop in a browser would look something like:

The loop index is 1.
The loop index is 2.
The loop index is 3.
The loop index is 4.
The loop index is 5.

Looping over a Query

A loop over a query repeats for every record in the query record set. The CFLOOP results are just like a CFOUTPUT. During each iteration of the loop, the columns of the current row will be available for output. CFLOOP allows you to loop over tags that can not be used inside CFOUTPUT.

Syntax
```
<CFLOOP QUERY="query_name"
        STARTROW="row_num"
        ENDROW="row_num">
```

QUERY
Required. Specifies the query that will control the loop.

STARTROW
Optional. Specifies the first row of the query that will be included in the loop.

ENDROW
Optional. Specifies the last row of the query that will be included in the loop.

Example 1
The following example shows a CFLOOP looping over a query that works in the same way as a CFOUTPUT tag using the QUERY attribute:

```
<CFQUERY NAME="MessageRecords"
    DATASOURCE="cfsnippets">
    SELECT * FROM Messages
</CFQUERY>

<CFLOOP QUERY="MessageRecords">
    <CFOUTPUT>#Message_ID#</CFOUTPUT><BR>
</CFLOOP>
```

Example 2   CFLOOP also provides iteration over a recordset with dynamic starting and stopping points. Thus you can begin at the tenth row in a query and end at the twentieth. This mechanism provides a simple means to get the next n sets of records from a query.

The following example loops from the tenth through the twentieth record returned by "MyQuery ":

```
<CFSET Start=10>
<CFSET End=20>

<CFLOOP QUERY="MyQuery"
      STARTROW="#Start#"
      ENDROW="#End#">

      <CFOUTPUT>#MyQuery.MyColName#</CFOUTPUT><BR>

</CFLOOP>
```

The loop is done when there are no more records or when the current record is greater than the value of the ENDROW attribute.

Example 3   The advantage of looping over a query is that you can use CFML tags that are not allowed in a CFOUTPUT. The following example combines the pages returned by a query of a list of page names into a single document using the CFINCLUDE tag.

```
<CFQUERY NAME="GetTemplate"
      DATASOURCE="Library"
      MAXROWS="5">
      SELECT TemplateName FROM Templates
</CFQUERY>

<CFLOOP QUERY="TemplateName">
      <CFINCLUDE TEMPLATE="#TemplateName#">
</CFLOOP>
```

Looping over a List

Looping over a list offers the option of walking through elements contained within a variable or value returned from an expression. In a list loop, the INDEX attribute specifies the name of a variable to receive the next element of the list, and the LIST attribute holds a list or a variable containing a list.

Syntax
```
<CFLOOP INDEX="index_name"
      LIST="list_items"
      DELIMITERS="item_delimiter">
</CFLOOP>
```

INDEX
> Required. In a list loop, the INDEX attribute specifies the name of a variable to receive the next element of the list, and the LIST attribute holds a list or a variable containing a list.

LIST
> Required. The list items in the loop, provided directly or with a variable.

DELIMITERS

Optional. Specifies the delimiter characters used to separate items in the LIST.

Example   This loop will display the names of each of the Beatles:

```
<CFLOOP INDEX="ListElement"
    LIST="John,Paul,George,Ringo">
        <CFOUTPUT>#ListElement#</CFOUTPUT><BR>
</CFLOOP>
```

Although CFLOOP expects elements in the list to be separated by commas by default, you are free to specify your own element boundaries in the DELIMITER attribute. Here's the same loop as before, only this time CFLOOP will treat commas, colons, or slashes as list element delimiters:

```
<CFLOOP INDEX="ListElement"
    LIST="John/Paul,George::Ringo"
    DELIMITERS=",:/">
        <CFOUTPUT>#ListElement#</CFOUTPUT><BR>
</CFLOOP>
```

Delimiters need not be specified in any particular order. Note that consecutive delimiters are treated as a single delimiter; thus the two colons in the previous example are treated as a single delimiter between "George " and "Ringo. "

cfloop

Looping over a COM Collection or Structure

The CFLOOP COLLECTION attribute allows you to loop over a structure or a COM/DCOM collection object:

- A COM/DCOM collection object is a set of similar items referenced as a group rather than individually. For example, the group of open documents in an application is a type of collection.

- A structure can contain either a related set of items or be used as an associative array. Looping is particularly useful when using a structure as an associative array.

Each collection item is referenced in the CFLOOP by the variable name that you supply in the ITEM attribute. This type of an iteration is generally used to access every object within a COM/DCOM collection or every element in the structure. The loop is executed until all objects have been accessed.

The COLLECTION attribute is used with the ITEM attribute in a CFLOOP. In the example that follows, ITEM is assigned a variable called file2, so that with each cycle in the CFLOOP, each item in the collection is referenced. In the CFOUTPUT section, the name property of the file2 item is referenced for display.

Examples   This example employs a COM object to output a list of files. In this example, FFUNC is a collection of file2 objects.

```
<CFOBJECT CLASS=FileFunctions.files
      NAME=FFunc
      ACTION=Create>

<CFSET FFunc.Path = "c:\">
<CFSET FFunc.Mask = "*.*" >
<CFSET FFunc.attributes = 16 >
<CFSET x=FFunc.GetFileList()>

<CFLOOP COLLECTION=#FFUNC# ITEM=file2>
     <CFOUTPUT>
          #file2.name# <BR>
     </CFOUTPUT>
</CFLOOP>
```

This example loops through a structure (used as an associative array):

cfloop

```
...<!--- Create a structure and loop through its contents --->
<CFSET Departments=StructNew()>
<CFSET val=StructInsert(Departments, "John ", "Sales ")>
<CFSET val=StructInsert(Departments, "Tom ", "Finance ")>
<CFSET val=StructInsert(Departments, "Mike ", "Education ")>

<!--- Build a table to display the contents --->

<CFOUTPUT>
<TABLE cellpadding= "2 " cellspacing= "2 ">
     <TR>
     <TD><B>Employee</B></TD>
     <TD><B>Dept.</B></TD>
     </TR>

<!--- In CFLOOP, use ITEM to create a variable
      called person to hold value of key as loop runs --->
<CFLOOP COLLECTION=#Departments# ITEM= "person ">
     <TR>
     <TD>#person#</TD>
     <TD>#StructFind(Departments, person)#</TD>
     </TR>
</CFLOOP>
</TABLE>
</CFOUTPUT>

...
```

CFMAIL

CFMAIL allows you to send email messages via an SMTP server.

See also CFMAILPARAM.

Syntax

```
<CFMAIL TO="recipient"
        FROM="sender"
        CC="copy_to"
        BCC="blind_copy_to"
        SUBJECT="msg_subject"
        TYPE="msg_type"
        MAXROWS="max_msgs"
        MIMEATTACH="path"
        QUERY="query_name"
        GROUP="query_column"
        GROUPCASESENSITIVE="Yes" or "No"
        STARTROW="query_row"
        SERVER="servername"
        PORT="port_ID"
        MAILERID="headerid"
        TIMEOUT="seconds">
```

TO

Required. The name of the recipient(s) of the email message. This can be either a static address (as in, TO="support@allaire.com"), a variable that contains an address (such as, TO="#Form.Email#"), or the name of a query column that contains address information (such as, TO="#EMail#"). In the latter case, an individual email message is sent for every row returned by the query.

FROM

Required. The sender of the email message. This attribute may be either static (e.g., FROM="support@allaire.com") or dynamic (as in, FROM="#GetUser.EMailAddress#").

CC

Optional. Indicates additional addresses to copy the email message to; "CC" stands for "carbon copy."

BCC

Optional. Indicates additional addresses to copy the email message without listing them in the message header. "BCC" stands for "blind carbon copy."

SUBJECT

Required. The subject of the mail message. This field may be driven dynamically on a message-by-message basis. For example, if you want to do a mailing that updates customers on the status of their orders, you might use a subject attribute like SUBJECT="Status for Order Number #Order_ID#".

TYPE

Optional. Specifies extended type attributes for the message. Currently, the only valid value for this attribute is "HTML". Specifying TYPE= "HTML" informs the receiving email client that the message has embedded HTML tags that need to be processed. This is only useful when sending messages to mail clients that understand HTML (such as Netscape 2.0 and above email clients).

MAXROWS

Optional. Specifies the maximum number of email messages you want to send.

MIMEATTACH

Optional. Specifies the path of the file to be attached to the email message. Attached file is MIME-encoded.

QUERY

Optional. The name of the CFQUERY from which you want to draw data for message(s) you want to send. Specify this attribute to send more than one mail message, or to send the results of a query within a single message.

GROUP

Optional. Specifies the query column to use when you group sets of records together to send as a single email message. For example, if you send a set of billing statements out to your customers, you might group on "Customer_ID." The GROUP attribute, which is case sensitive, eliminates adjacent duplicates in the case where the data is sorted by the specified field. See the Usage section for exceptions.

GROUPCASESENSITIVE

Optional. Boolean indicating whether to group with regard to case or not. The default value is YES; case is considered while grouping. If the *QUERY* attribute specifies a query object that was generated by a case-insensitive SQL query, set the *GROUPCASESENSITIVE* attribute to NO to keep the recordset intact.

STARTROW

Optional. Specifies the row in the query to start from.

SERVER

Required. The address of the SMTP server to use for sending messages. The server name specified in the ColdFusion Administrator is used if no server is specified.

PORT

The TCP/IP port on which the SMTP server listens for requests. This is almost always 25.

MAILERID

Optional. Specifies a mailer ID to be passed in the X-Mailer SMTP header, which identifies the mailer application. The default is Allaire ColdFusion Application Server.

TIMEOUT

Optional. The number of seconds to wait before timing out the connection to the SMTP server.

Example   cfmail

```
<!--- This view-only example shows the use of CFMAIL --->
<HTML>
<HEAD>
<TITLE>CFMAIL Example</TITLE>
</HEAD>
<BODY bgcolor=silver>
<H3>CFMAIL Example</H3>
<P>This view-only example shows the use of CFMAIL.  If your CFAS mail
settings are configured successfully and the comments are removed,
you will be able to use this code to send simple email.
<!---
<CFIF IsDefined("form.mailto")>
    <CFIF form.mailto is not "" AND form.mailfrom is not "" AND
  form.Subject is not "">
    <CFMAIL TO="#form.mailto#"
        FROM="#form.mailFrom#"
        SUBJECT="#form.subject#">
            This message was sent by an
            automatic mailer built with CFMAIL:
            ===================================================
            #form.body#
  </CFMAIL>
        <H3>Thank you</H3>
        <P>Thank you, <CFOUTPUT>#mailfrom#: your message, #subject#, has
been sent to #mailto#</CFOUTPUT>.
        </CFIF>
</CFIF>
<P>
<FORM ACTION="cfmail.cfm" METHOD="POST">
<PRE>
TO:      <INPUT TYPE="Text" NAME="MailTo">
FROM:    <INPUT TYPE="Text" NAME="MailFrom">
SUBJECT:<INPUT TYPE="Text" NAME="Subject">
<hr>
MESSAGE BODY:
<TEXTAREA NAME="Body" COLS="40" ROWS="5" WRAP="VIRTUAL"></TEXTAREA>
</PRE>
<!--- establish required fields --->
<INPUT TYPE="Hidden" NAME="MailTo_required" VALUE="You must enter a
 recipient for this message">
<INPUT TYPE="Hidden" NAME="MailFrom_required" VALUE="You must enter a
 sender for this message">
<INPUT TYPE="Hidden" NAME="Subject_required" VALUE="You must enter a
 subject for this message">
```

```
<INPUT TYPE="Hidden" NAME="Body_required" VALUE="You must enter some text
 for this message">
<P><INPUT TYPE="Submit" NAME="">
</FORM> --->
...
```

CFMAILPARAM

CFMAILPARAM can either attach a file or add a header to a message. If you use CFMAILPARAM, it is nested within a CFMAIL tag. You can use more than one CFMAILPARAM tags within a CFMAIL tag in order to attach one or more files and headers.

See also CFMAIL.

Syntax

```
<CFMAIL
      TO="recipient"
      SUBJECT="msg_subject"
      FROM="sender"
      ...more attibutes...
>
      <CFMAILPARAM
            FILE="file-name"
      >
      or
      <CFMAILPARAM
            NAME="header-name"
            VALUE="header-value"
      >
      ...
</CFMAIL>
```

FILE

Required if you do not specify the NAME attribute. Attaches the specified file to the message. This attribute is mutually exclusive with the NAME attribute.

NAME

Required if you do not specify the FILE attribute. Specifies the name of the header. Header names are case insensitive. This attribute is mutually exclusive with the FILE attribute.

VALUE

Optional. Indicates the value of the header.

Example

cfmailparam

```
<!--- This example shows the use of CFMAILPARAM --->
<HTML>
<HEAD>
<TITLE>CFMAILPARAM Example</TITLE>
</HEAD>

<BODY>
<H3>CFMMAILPARAM Example</H3>

<P>
This example uses CFMAILPARAM to attach two files and add a header to a message.
```

```
</P>
<CFMAIL FROM="peter@domain.com" To="paul@domain.com" Subject="See Important Attachments and
Reply">
     <CFMAILPARAM NAME="Reply-To" VALUE="mary@domain.com">
     Please read the text file and view the new logo, and let us know what
     you think.
     <CFMAILPARAM FILE="c:\work\readme.txt">
     <CFMAILPARAM FILE="c:\work\logo.gif">
</CFMAIL>
</BODY>
</HTML>
```

CFMODULE

Use CFMODULE to invoke a custom tag for use in your ColdFusion application pages. CFMODULE can help deal with any custom tag name conflicts that might arise.

Use the TEMPLATE attribute to name a ColdFusion page containing the custom tag definition, including its path. Use the NAME attribute to refer to the custom tag using a dot notation scheme indicating the location of the custom tag in the ColdFusion installation directory.

Syntax
```
<CFMODULE TEMPLATE="template"
        NAME="tag_name"
        ATTRIBUTECOLLECTION="collection_structure"
        ATTRIBUTE_NAME1="value"
        ATTRIBUTE_NAME2="value"
        ...>
```

TEMPLATE

Used in place of NAME, defines a path to the application page (.cfm file) implementing the tag. Relative paths are expanded from the current page. Physical paths are not allowed. Absolute paths are expanded using the ColdFusion mappings.

NAME

Used in place of TEMPLATE, defines the name of the custom tag in the form "Name.Name.Name... " that uniquely identifies a subdirectory containing the custom tag page under the root directory for CF custom tags. For example:

```
<CFMODULE NAME="Allaire.Forums40.GetUserOptions">
```
Identifies the page GetUserOptions.cfm in the directory CustomTags\Allaire\Forums40 under the root directory of the ColdFusion installation.

ATTRIBUTECOLLECTION

Optional. A structure that contains a collection of key-value pairs that represent attribute names and their values. You can specify as many key-value pairs as needed. However, you can specify the ATTRIBUTECOLLECTION attribute only once. See Usage for more information.

ATTRIBUTE_NAME

Optional. Attributes you want your custom tag to use. You can use as many attributes as needed to specify the parameters of a custom tag. Each

Usage
You can use ATTRIBUTECOLLECTION and ATTRIBUTE in the same call.

Within the custom tag code, the attributes passed with ATTRIBUTECOLLECTION are saved as independent attribute values with no indication that the attributes were grouped into a structure by the custom tag's caller.

Likewise, if the custom tag uses a CFASSOCIATE tag to save its attributes, the attributes passed with ATTRIBUTECOLLECTION are saved as independent attribute values with no indication that the attributes are grouped into a structure by the custom tag's caller.

Example   cfmodule

```
<!--- This example shows the use of CFMODULE --->
<HTML>
<HEAD>
<TITLE>CFMODULE Example</TITLE>
</HEAD>

<BODY>
<H3>CFMODULE Example</H3>

<P>
This example shows the use of CFMODULE to call a sample custom
tag inline.
</P>
<P>
This example makes use of a sample custom tag that has been saved in the file myTag.cfm in the snippets
directory. You can also save ColdFusion custom tags in the Cfusion\CustomTags directory. For more
information about using Custom Tags, please refer to
<i>Developing Web Applications</i>.
</P>
<!--- show the code in the custom tag--->
<P>Here is the code in the custom tag.</P>
<CFOUTPUT>#HTMLCodeFormat("<CFSET X = attributes.x>
<CFSET Y = attributes.y>
<CFSET A = attributes.value1>
<CFSET B = attributes.value2>
<CFSET C = attributes.value3>
<CFSET caller.result = x + y + a + b + c>")#
</CFOUTPUT>
<!--- end sample tag --->

<CFSET attrCollection1 = StructNew()>
<CFSET attrCollection1.value1 = 22>
<CFSET attrCollection1.value2 = 45>
<CFSET attrCollection1.value3 = 88>

<!--- Call the tag with CFMODULE with Name--->
<CFMODULE
   Template="..\snippets\myTag.cfm"
      X="3"
      attributeCollection=#attrCollection1#
      Y="4">

<!--- show the code --->
<P>Here is one way in which to invoke the custom tag,
using the TEMPLATE attribute.</P>
<CFOUTPUT>#HTMLCodeFormat("<CFMODULE
      Template=""..\snippets\myTag.cfm""
```

```
        X=3
        attributeCollection=##attrCollection1##
        Y=4>")#
</CFOUTPUT>
<P>The result: <CFOUTPUT>#result#</CFOUTPUT> </P>


<!--- Call the tag with CFMODULE with Name--->
<CFMODULE
  NAME="myTag"
    X="3"
    attributeCollection=#attrCollection1#
    Y="4">


<!--- show the code --->
<P>Here is another way to invoke the custom tag,
using the NAME attribute.</P>
<CFOUTPUT>#HTMLCodeFormat("<CFMODULE
    NAME='myTag'
    X=3
    attributeCollection=##attrCollection1##
    Y=4>")#
</CFOUTPUT>
<P>The result: <CFOUTPUT>#result#</CFOUTPUT>


<!--- Call the tag using the short cut notation --->
<CF_myTag
    X="3"
    attributeCollection=#attrCollection1#
    Y="4">


<!--- show the code --->
<P>Here is the short cut to invoking the same tag.</P>
<CFOUTPUT>#HTMLCodeFormat("<CF_myTag
    X=3
    attributeCollection=##attrCollection1##
    Y=4>")#
</CFOUTPUT>
<P>The result: <CFOUTPUT>#result#</CFOUTPUT></P>


</BODY>
</HTML>
```

CFOBJECT

The CFOBJECT tag allows you to call methods in COM, CORBA, and JAVA objects.

Note   ColdFusion administrators can disable the CFOBJECT tag in the ColdFusion Administrator Basic Security page.

On UNIX, COM objects are not currently supported by CFOBJECT.

CFOBJECT topics

- CFOBJECT Type="COM"
- CFOBJECT Type="CORBA"
- CFOBJECT Type="JAVA"

CFOBJECT TYPE attributes

Depending on the value you assign to the TYPE attribute of CFOBJECT, there are several additional attributes you can set. This table shows which attributes you can use with each CFOBJECT TYPE.

Attributes Used with CFOBJECT TYPEs	
TYPE	**Attributes**
COM	ACTION CLASS NAME CONTEXT SERVER
CORBA	ACTION CONTEXT CLASS NAME LOCALE
JAVA	ACTION TYPE CLASS NAME

Sections that follow describe these values and attributes in greater detail.

CFOBJECT Type="COM"

CFOBJECT allows you to create and use COM (Component Object Model) objects. Any automation server object type that is currently registered on a machine can be invoked. You can use a utility like Microsoft's OLEView to browse COM objects. OLEView, as well as information about COM and DCOM, can be found at Microsoft's OLE Development web site http://www.microsoft.com/oledev/http://www.microsoft.com/oledev//a.

To use CFOBJECT, you need to know the program ID or filename of the object, the methods and properties available through the IDispatch interface, and the arguments and return types of the object's methods. The OLEView utility can give you this information for most COM objects.

Syntax
```
<CFOBJECT TYPE="COM"
    ACTION="action"
    CLASS="program_ID"
    NAME="text"
    CONTEXT="context"
    SERVER="server_name">
```

ACTION

Required. One of the following:

- Create — Use Create to instantiate a COM object (typically a DLL) prior to invoking methods or properties.

- Connect — Use Connect to connect to a COM object (typically an EXE) that is already running on the server specified in SERVER.

CLASS

Required. Enter the component ProgID for the object you want to invoke.

NAME

Required. Enter a name for the object.

CONTEXT

Optional. InProc, Local, or Remote. Uses Registry setting when not specified.

SERVER

Required when CONTEXT="Remote". Enter a valid server name using UNC (Universal Naming Convention) or DNS (Domain Name Server) conventions, in one of the following forms:

```
SERVER="\\lanserver"
SERVER="lanserver"
SERVER="http://www.servername.com"
SERVER="www.servername.com"
SERVER="127.0.0.1"
```

Example   cfobject

```
<HTML>
<HEAD>
<TITLE>CFOBJECT (COM) Example</TITLE>
</HEAD>

<BODY>
<H3>CFOBJECT (COM) Example</H3>
<!---
Create a COM object as an inproc server (DLL).
(CLASS= prog-id)
--->
<CFOBJECT ACTION="Create"
    TYPE="COM"
    CLASS=Allaire.DocEx1.1
    NAME="obj">

<!---
Call a method.
Note that methods that expect no arguments should
be called using empty parenthesis.
--->
<CFSET obj.Init()>

<!---
This object is a collection object, and should
support at a minimum:
Property : Count
Method : Item(inarg, outarg)
and a special property called _NewEnum
--->
<CFOUTPUT>
 This object has #obj.Count# items.
 <BR>
 <HR>
</CFOUTPUT>

<!---
Get the 3rd object in the collection.
--->
<CFSET emp = obj.Item(3)>
<CFOUTPUT>
 The last name in the third item is #emp.lastname#.
 <BR>
 <HR>
</CFOUTPUT>

<!---
Loop over all the objects in the collection.
--->
 <P>Looping through all items in the collection:
 <BR>
```

```
<CFLOOP COLLECTION=#obj# ITEM=file2>
 <CFOUTPUT>
   Last name: #file2.lastname# <BR>
 </CFOUTPUT>
</CFLOOP>
...
</BODY>
</HTML>
```

CFOBJECT Type="CORBA"

CFOBJECT allows you to call methods in CORBA objects. These CORBA objects must already have been defined and registered for use.

Syntax
```
<CFOBJECT TYPE="CORBA"
        CONTEXT="context"
        CLASS="file or naming service"
        NAME="text"
        LOCALE="type-value arguments">
```

CONTEXT

Required. Specifies one of the following:

- IOR — ColdFusion uses the Interoperable Object Reference (IOR) to access the CORBA server.

- NameService — ColdFusion uses the naming service to access server. "NameService" is only valid with the InitialContext of a VisiBroker Orb.

CLASS

Required. Specifies different information, depending on the CONTEXT specification:

- If CONTEXT is IOR — Specifies the name of a file that contains the stringified version of the IOR. ColdFusion must be able to read this file at all times; it should be local to ColdFusion server or on the network in an open, accessible location.

- If CONTEXT is NameService — Specifies a period-delimited naming context for the naming service, such as Allaire.Department.Doc.empobject.

NAME

Required. Enter a name for the object. Your application uses this to reference the CORBA object's methods and attributes.

LOCALE

Optional. Sets arguments for a call to init_orb(..). Use of this attribute is specific to VisiBroker orbs, and is currently available on C++, Version 3.2. The value should be of the form:

LOCALE=" -ORBagentAddr 199.99.129.33   -ORBagentPort 19000"

Note that each type-value pair has to start with a leading "-".

Usage   ColdFusion Enterprise version 4.0 and above supports CORBA through the Dynamic
Invocation Interface (DII). To use CFOBJECT with CORBA objects, you need to know
either the name of the file containing a stringified version of the IOR or the object's
naming context in the naming service. You also need to know the object's attributes,
method names and method signatures.

User-defined types (for example, structures) are not supported.

Example   cfobject

```
<CFOBJECT TYPE="CORBA"
 CONTEXT="IOR"
 CLASS="c:\\myobject.ior"
 NAME="GetName">
```

CFOBJECT Type="JAVA"

CFOBJECT allows you to create and use JAVA objects, and by extension EJB objects.

This support is currently only for NT, but will be extended to Solaris in the next release.

Syntax   ```
<CFOBJECT
      ACTION="Create"
      TYPE="Java"
      CLASS="Java class"
      NAME="object name"
>
```

**ACTION**
Required. Specifies "Create" in order to create the Java object or the WebLogic
Environment.

**TYPE**
Required. Specifies that the type of object, in this case, this is always "Java."

**CLASS**
Required. Specifies the Java class.

**NAME**
Required. The name used within CFML to access the object.

**Usage**   To be able to call Java CFXs or Java objects, ColdFusion uses a JVM embedded in the
process. The loading, location and the settings for the JVM are configurable using the
ColdFusion Administrator pages.
```

Any Java class available in the class path specified in the ColdFusion Administrator can be loaded and used from ColdFusion using the CFOBJECT tag.

Use the following steps to access Java methods and fields:

1. Call CFOBJECT to load the class. See Example.

2. Use the init method with appropriate arguments to call a constructor explicitly. For example:

    ```
    <CFSET ret = myObj.init(arg1, arg2)>
    ```

Calling a public method on the object without first calling the "init" method results in an implicit call to the default constructor. Arguments and return values can be any valid Java type (simple, arrays, objects). ColdFusion does the appropriate conversions when strings are passed as arguments, but not when they are received as return values.

Overloaded methods are supported as long as the number of arguments are different. Future enhancements will let you use cast functions that will allow method signatures to be built more accurately.

Calling EJBs

To create and call all the appropriate EJB objects, use CFOBJECT. The sequence in the second example assumes that the Weblogic JNDI is used to register and find EJBHome instances.

Example of Java Object

```
<!------------------------------------------------------------------------
This CFOBJECT call loads the class MyClass but does not create an instance object. Static methods and
fields are accessible after a call to CFOBJECT.
------------------------------------------------------------------------>
<CFOBJECT
    ACTION="CREATE"
    TYPE="Java"
    CLASS="myClass"
    NAME="myObj"
>
```

Example of EJB

```
<!------------------------------------------------------------------
The CFOBJECT tag creates the Weblogic Environment object, which is then used to get the InitialContext.
The context object is used to look up the EJBHome interface. The call to create() results in getting an instance
of stateless session EJB.
------------------------------------------------------------------------>

<CFOBJECT
    ACTION="CREATE"
    TYPE="JAVA"
    CLASS="weblogic/jndi/Environment"
    NAME="wlEnv">

<CFSET ctx = wlEnv.getInitialContext()>
<CFSET ejbHome = ctx.lookup("statelessSession.TraderHome")>
<CFSET trader = ejbHome.Create()>
<CFSET value = trader.shareValue(20, 55.45)>
```

```
<CFOUTPUT>
      Share value = #value#
</CFOUTPUT>
<CFSET value = trader.remove()>
```

CFOUTPUT

Displays the results of a database query or other operation. If you need to nest CFOUTPUT tags, please read the "Usage" section.

Syntax   <CFOUTPUT
             QUERY="query_name"
             GROUP="query_column"
             GROUPCASESENSITIVE="Yes" or "No"
             STARTROW="start_row"
             MAXROWS="max_rows_output">

             </CFOUTPUT>

QUERY

Optional. The name of the CFQUERY from which you want to draw data for the output section.

GROUP

Optional. Specifies the query column to use when you group sets of records together. Use this attribute if you have retrieved a record set ordered on a certain query column. For example, if you have a record set that is ordered according to "Customer_ID" in the CFQUERY tag, you can group the output on "Customer_ID." The *GROUP* attribute, which is case sensitive, eliminates adjacent duplicates in the case where the data is sorted by the specified field. See the *GROUPCASESENSITIVE* attribute for information about specifying a case insensitive grouping.

GROUPCASESENSITIVE

Optional. Boolean indicating whether to group with regard to case or not. The default value is YES; case is considered while grouping. If the *QUERY* attribute specifies a query object that was generated by a case-insensitive SQL query, set the *GROUPCASESENSITIVE* attribute to NO to keep the recordset intact.

STARTROW

Optional. Specifies the row from which to start output.

MAXROWS

Optional. Specifies the maximum number of rows you want displayed in the output section.

Usage   In order to nest CFOUTPUT blocks, you must specify the GROUP and QUERY attributes at the top-most level, and the GROUP attribute for all inner blocks except for the inner-most CFOUTPUT block.

Example   cfoutput

```
<!--- This example shows how CFOUTPUT operates --->

<!--- run a sample query --->
<CFQUERY NAME="GetCourses" DATASOURCE="cfsnippets">
SELECT Dept_ID, CorName, CorLevel
FROM courseList
ORDER by Dept_ID, CorLevel, CorName

</CFQUERY>
<HTML>
<HEAD>
<TITLE>CFOUTPUT</TITLE>
</HEAD>
<BODY>
<H3>CFOUTPUT Example</H3>

<P>CFOUTPUT simply tells ColdFusion Server
to begin processing, and then to hand back control
of page rendering to the web server.

<P>For example, to show today's date, you could write
#DateFormat("#Now()#").  If you enclosed that expression
in CFOUTPUT, the result would be <CFOUTPUT>#DateFormat(Now())#
 </CFOUTPUT>.

<P>In addition, CFOUTPUT may be used to show the results of
a query operation, or only a partial result, as shown:

<P>There are <CFOUTPUT>#getCourses.recordCount#</CFOUTPUT> total records
in our query.  Using the MAXROWS parameter, we are limiting our
display to 4 rows.
<P>
<CFOUTPUT QUERY="GetCourses" MAXROWS=4>
<PRE>#Dept_ID##CorName##CorLevel#</PRE>

</CFOUTPUT>

<P>CFOUTPUT can also show the results of a more complex expression,
such as getting the day of the week from today's date.  We first
extract the integer representing the Day of the Week from
the server function Now() and then apply the result to
the DayofWeekAsString function:

<BR>Today is #DayofWeekAsString(DayofWeek(Now()))#
<BR>Today is <CFOUTPUT>#DayofWeekAsString(DayofWeek(Now()))#</CFOUTPUT>

<P>
</BODY>
</HTML>
```

CFPARAM

CFPARAM is used to test for a parameter's existence, and optionally test its data type, and provide a default value if one is not assigned.

Syntax   <CFPARAM NAME="param_name"
                 TYPE="data_type">
                 DEFAULT="value">

NAME

The name of the parameter you are testing (such as "Client.Email " or "Cookie.BackgroundColor "). If you omit the DEFAULT attribute, an error occurs if the specified parameter does not exist.

TYPE

Optional. The type of parameter that is required. The default value is "any. "

Type Values	
Type Value	**Description**
any	any value.
array	any array value.
binary	a binary value.
boolean	a Boolean value.
date	a date-time value.
numeric	a numeric value.
query	a query object.
string	a string value or a single character.
struct	a structure.
UUID	a Universally Unique Identifier (UUID) formatted as 'XXXXXXXX-XXXX-XXXX-XXXXXXXXXXXXXXXX' where 'X' stands for a hexadecimal digit (0-9 or A-F). See CreateUUID.
variableName	a valid variable name.

DEFAULT

Optional. Default value to set the parameter to if it does not exist.

Usage   There are three ways to use CFPARAM:

- Test for a required variable — Use CFPARAM with only the NAME attribute to test that a required variable exists. If the variable does not exist, ColdFusion server stops processing the page and returns an error.

- Test for a required variable and for the type of variable — Use CFPARAM with the NAME attribute and the TYPE attribute to test that a required variable exists, and that it is of the specified type.

- Test for an optional variable — Use CFPARAM with both the NAME and DEFAULT attributes to test for the existence of an optional variable. If the variable exists, processing continues and the value is not changed. If the variable does not exist, it is created and set to the value of the DEFAULT attribute.

Example   cfparam

```
<!--- This example shows how CFPARAM operates --->
<CFPARAM NAME="storeTempVar" DEFAULT="my default value">
<CFPARAM NAME="tempVar" DEFAULT="my default value">

<!--- check if form.tempVar was passed --->
<CFIF IsDefined("form.tempVar") is "True">
<!--- check if form.tempVar is not blank --->
    <CFIF form.tempVar is not "">
<!--- if not, set tempVar to value of form.tempVar --->
        <CFSET tempVar = form.tempVar>
    </CFIF>
</CFIF>

<HTML>
<HEAD>
<TITLE>
CFPARAM Example
</TITLE>
</HEAD>

<BODY bgcolor=silver>

<H3>CFPARAM Example</H3>
<P>CFPARAM is used to set default values so that
the developer does not need to check for the existence
of a variable using a function like IsDefined.

<P>The default value of our tempVar is "<CFOUTPUT>#StoreTempVar#
  </CFOUTPUT>"

<!--- check if tempVar is still the same as StoreTempVar
and that tempVar is not blank --->
<CFIF tempVar is not #StoreTempVar# and tempVar is not "">
<H3>The value of tempVar has changed: the new value
is <CFOUTPUT>#tempVar#</CFOUTPUT></H3>
</CFIF>
```

```
<P>
<FORM ACTION="cfparam.cfm" METHOD="POST">
Type in a new value for tempVar, and hit submit:<BR>
<INPUT TYPE="Text" NAME="tempVar">

<INPUT TYPE="Submit" NAME="" VALUE="submit">

</FORM>

</BODY>
</HTML>
```

CFPOP

CFPOP retrieves and deletes email messages from a POP mail server. See also CFMAIL.

Syntax
```
<CFPOP SERVER="servername"
    PORT="port_number"
    USERNAME="username"
    PASSWORD="password"
    ACTION="action"
    NAME="queryname"
    MESSAGENUMBER="number"
    ATTACHMENTPATH="path"
    TIMEOUT="seconds"
    MAXROWS="number"
    STARTROW="number"
    GENERATEUNIQUEFILENAMES="boolean">
```

SERVER

Required. Host name (biff.upperlip.com) or IP address (192.1.2.225) of the POP server.

PORT

Optional. Defaults to the standard POP port, 110.

USERNAME

Optional. If no user name is specified, the POP connection is anonymous.

PASSWORD

Optional. Password corresponds to user name.

ACTION

Optional. Specifies the mail action. There are three possible values:

- GetHeaderOnly — (Default) Returns message header information only.

- GetAll — Returns message header information, message text, and attachments if ATTACHMENTPATH is specified.

- Delete — Deletes messages on the POP server.

Note   Two retrieve options are offered to maximize performance. Message header information is typically short and therefore quick to transfer. Message text and attachments can be very long and therefore take longer to process. See the Message Header and Body Columns table, which follows the CFPOP attribute descriptions, for information on retrieving header and body information form the query when you specify GetHeaderOnly or GetAll.

NAME

Optional. The name you assign to the index query. Required for ACTION="GetHeaderOnly" and ACTION="GetAll".

MESSAGENUMBER

Optional. Specifies the message number(s) for the given action. MESSAGENUMBER is required for ACTION="Delete". If it is provided for ACTION="GetHeaderOnly" or ACTION="GetAll", only referenced messages will be retrieved. If it is omitted for ACTION="GetHeaderOnly"or ACTION="GetAll", all messages available on the server are returned.

MESSAGENUMBER can contain individual message numbers or a comma-separated list of message numbers. Invalid message numbers will be ignored.

ATTACHMENTPATH

Optional. Allows attachments to be written to the specified directory when ACTION="GetAll". If an invalid ATTACHMENTPATH is specified, no attachment files are written to the server.

TIMEOUT

Optional. Specifies the maximum amount of time in seconds to wait for mail processing. Defaults to 60 seconds.

MAXROWS

Optional. Specifies the maximum number of entries for mail queries. This attribute is ignored if MESSAGENUMBER is specified.

STARTROW

Optional. Specifies the first row number to be retrieved. Default is 1. This attribute is ignored if MESSAGENUMBER is specified.

GENERATEUNIQUFILENAMES

Optional. Boolean indicating whether to generate unique file names for the files attached to an email message in order to avoid naming conflicts when the files are saved. The default is NO.

CFPOP Query Variables

The following table describes the query variables that are returned by CFPOP. The example illustrates their use.

CFPOP Query Variables	
Variable Names	**Description**
queryname.RecordCount	The total number of records returned by the query.

CFPOP Query Variables (Continued)	
Variable Names	**Description**
queryname.CurrentRow	The current row of the query being processed by CFOUTPUT.
queryname.ColumnList	The list of the column names in the query.

Message Header and Body Columns

The following table lists the message header and body columns that are returned by CFPOP when you specify the ACTION attribute to be either GetHeaderOnly or GetAll. All of the columns are returned if you specify GetAll, but only header information is returned when you specify GetHeaderOnly.

Message Header and Body Columns		
Column Name	**GetHeaderOnly returns**	**GetAll returns**
queryname.date	yes	yes
queryname.from	yes	yes
queryname.messagenumber	yes	yes
queryname.replyto	yes	yes
queryname.subject	yes	yes
queryname.cc	yes	yes
queryname.to	yes	yes
queryname.body	not available	yes
queryname.header	not available	yes
queryname.attachments	not available	yes
queryname.attachmentfiles	not available	yes

Usage To create a ColdFusion date/time object from the date-time string that is extracted from a mail message in the *queryname*.date column, use the following table to determine what to do.

Date-Time Parsing According to Locale	
Locale	**What to do?**
English (US) locale	Use the ParseDateTime function and specify the POP attribute, which converts the date-time value to Greenwich Meantime.
Other locales	Extract the date portion of the string and pass it to the LSParseDateTime function, then add or subtract the conversion time, depending on the locale.

See also the description of the SetLocale function.

For complete usage information on CFPOP, see ../../
Developing_Web_Applications_with_ColdFusion/contents.htm*Developing Web
Applications with ColdFusion*/a.

Example cfpop

```
<!--- This view-only example shows the use of CFPOP --->
<HTML>
<HEAD>
<TITLE>CFPOP Example</TITLE>
</HEAD>

<BODY>
<H3>CFPOP Example</H3>
<P>CFPOP allows you to retrieve and manipulate mail
in a POP3 mailbox.  This view-only example shows how to
create one feature of a mail client, allowing you to display
the mail headers in a POP3 mailbox.

<P>Simply uncomment this code and run with a mail-enabled CF Server to
see this feature in action.
<!---
<CFIF IsDefined("form.server ")>
<!--- make sure server, username are not empty --->
<CFIF form.server is not "" and form.username is not "">
    <CFPOP SERVER= "#server# " USERNAME=#UserName# PASSWORD=#pwd#
    ACTION= "GETHEADERONLY " NAME= "GetHeaders ">

    <H3>Message Headers in Your Inbox</H3>
        <P>Number of Records:
```

```
            <CFOUTPUT>#GetHeaders.RecordCount#</CFOUTPUT></P>
            <UL>
            <CFOUTPUT QUERY="GetHeaders">
                  <LI>Row: #CurrentRow#:  From: #From# -- Subject: #Subject#
         </CFOUTPUT>
            </UL>
      </CFIF>
      </CFIF>

      <FORM ACTION= "cfpop.cfm " METHOD= "POST ">
      <P>Enter your mail server:
      <P><INPUT TYPE= "Text " NAME= "server ">
      <P>Enter your username:
      <P><INPUT TYPE= "Text " NAME= "username ">
      <P>Enter your password:
      <P><INPUT TYPE= "password " NAME= "pwd ">
      <INPUT TYPE= "Submit " NAME= "get message headers ">
      </FORM>
      --->

      </BODY>
      </HTML>
```

CFPROCESSINGDIRECTIVE

Suppresses extraneous white space, and other output, produced by the CFML within the tag's scope.

Syntax

```
<CFPROCESSINGDIRECTIVE
    SUPPRESSWHITESPACE="Yes" or "No">
... any CFML tags here ...
</CFPROCESSINGDIRECTIVE>
```

SUPPRESSWHITESPACE

Required. Boolean indicating whether to suppress the white space and other output generated by the CFML tags within the CFPROCESSINGDIRECTIVE block.

Usage

If a CFPROCESSINGDIRECTIVE tag's scope includes another CFPROCESSINGDIRECTIVE tag, then the inner tag's settings override the enclosing tag's settings within the body of the inner tag, where they differ. If the enclosing tag specifies settings that the inner tag does not, those settings remain in effect within the inner tag's scope.

CFPROCESSINGDIRECTIVE settings do not apply to templates included via CFINCLUDE, CFMODULE, custom tag invocation, etc.

Example

This example shows the use of a nested <CFPROCESSINGDIRECTIVE> tag. The outer <CFPROCESSINGDIRECTIVE> tag suppresses unnecessary whitespace during computation of a large table while the inner <CFPROCESSINGDIRECTIVE> tag honors all whitespace to output the preformatted table.

```
<CFPROCESSINGDIRECTIVE SUPPRESSWHITESPACE="yes">
... any CFML tags here ...
<CFPROCESSINGDIRECTIVE SUPPRESSWHITESPACE="no">
<CFOUTPUT>#interesting_stuff#</CFOUTPUT>
</CFPROCESSINGDIRECTIVE>
```

CFPROCPARAM

The CFPROCPARAM tag is nested within a CFSTOREDPROC tag. You use it to specify parameter information, including type, name, value, and length.

Syntax

```
<CFPROCPARAM TYPE="IN/OUT/INOUT"
        VARIABLE="variable name"
        DBVARNAME="DB variable name"
        VALUE="parameter value"
        CFSQLTYPE="parameter datatype"
        MAXLENGTH="length"
        SCALE="decimal places"
        NULL="Yes" or "No">
```

TYPE

Optional. Indicates whether the passed variable is an input, output or input/output variable. Default is IN.

VARIABLE

Required for OUT and INOUT parameters. This is the ColdFusion variable name that you use to reference the value that the output parameter represents after the call is made to the stored procedure.

DBVARNAME

Required if named notation is desired. This is the parameter name. This corresponds to the name of the parameter in the stored procedure.

VALUE

Required for IN and INOUT parameters. This corresponds to the actual value that ColdFusion passes to the stored procedure.

CFSQLTYPE

Required. This is the SQL type that the parameter (any type) will be bound to. The CFSQLTypes are as follows:

CF_SQL_BIGINT	CF_SQL_IDSTAMP	CF_SQL_REFCURSOR
CF_SQL_BIT	CF_SQL_INTEGER	CF_SQL_SMALLINT
CF_SQL_CHAR	CF_SQL_LONGVARCHAR	CF_SQL_TIME
CF_SQL_DATE	CF_SQL_MONEY	CF_SQL_TIMESTAMP
CF_SQL_DECIMAL	CF_SQL_MONEY4	CF_SQL_TINYINT
CF_SQL_DOUBLE	CF_SQL_NUMERIC	CF_SQL_VARCHAR
CF_SQL_FLOAT	CF_SQL_REAL	

MAXLENGTH

Optional. Maximum length of the parameter.

SCALE

Optional. Number of decimal places of the parameter.

NULL

Optional. Specify Yes or No. Indicates whether the parameter is passed as a NULL. If you specify Yes, the tag ignores the VALUE attribute.

Usage   Use this tag to identify stored procedure parameters and their data types. Code one CFPROCPARAM tag for each parameter. The parameters you code vary, based on parameter type and DBMS. Additionally, the order in which you code CFPROCPARAM tags matters, depending on whether the stored procedure was coded using positional notation or named notation:

- Positional notation — Order is very important if the stored procedure was defined using positional notation. ColdFusion passes these parameters to the stored procedure in the order in which they are defined.

- Named notation — If named notation is used, the DBVarName for the parameter must correspond to the variable name in the stored procedure on the server.

Output variables will be scoped with the name of the VARIABLE attribute that was passed to the tag.

In 4.5 and above, CFML supports Oracle 8's REFERENCE CURSOR type. A REFERENCE CURSOR allows you to pass a parameter by reference. Therefore, parameters that are passed by reference can by allocated and deallocated memory within the course of one application. See the example for an illustration of the use of REFERENCE CURSORS.

Example   This example shows an Oracle 8 PL/SQL stored procedure, and the CFML code used to invoke it. In particular, it makes use of Oracle 8's support of the REFERENCE CURSOR type.

The following package *Foo_Data* houses a procedure *refcurproc* that declares two output parameters as REFERENCE CURSORS. The first parameter *pParam1* returns all of the rows in the EMP table, and the second parameter *pParam2* returns all of the rows in the DEPT table. In addition the procedure declares one input parameter as an integer, and one output parameter as a two byte char varying type. Before this procedure can be called by CFSTOREDPROC, it must be created, compiled and bound in the RDBMS environment.

cfprocparam

CREATE OR REPLACE PACKAGE Foo_Data AS

```
    TYPE EmpTyp IS REF CURSOR RETURN Emp%ROWTYPE;
    TYPE DeptTyp IS REF CURSOR RETURN Dept%ROWTYPE;
 PROCEDURE refcurproc(pParam1 in out EmpTyp, pParam2 in out DeptTyp, pParam3 in integer, pParam4
out varchar2);
 END foo_data;
```

```
CREATE OR REPLACE PACKAGE BODY Foo_Data AS
    PROCEDURE RefCurProc(pParam1 in out EmpTyp,
            pParam2 in out DeptTyp,
            pParam3 in integer,
            pParam4 out varchar2) IS
    BEGIN
        OPEN pParam1 FOR select * from emp;
        OPEN pParam2 FOR select * from dept;
        IF pParam3 = 1
        THEN
    pParam4 := 'hello';
        ELSE
    pParam4 := 'goodbye';
        END IF;
    END RefCurProc;
END Foo_Data;
```

The following CFML example shows how to invoke the RefCurProc procedure using CFSTOREDPROC, CFPROCPARAM, and CFPROCRESULT.

```
<CFSTOREDPROCPROCEDURE="foo_data.refcurproc"
                DATASOURCE="oracle8i"
                USERNAME = "scott"
                PASSWORD = "tiger"
                RETURNCODE="no"
>

    <CFPROCPARAM type="Out" CFSQLTYPE="CF_SQL_REFCURSOR"
        VARIABLE="param1">
    <CFPROCPARAM type="Out" CFSQLTYPE="CF_SQL_REFCURSOR"
        VARIABLE="param2">
    <CFPROCPARAM TYPE = "IN" CFSQLTYPE ="CF_SQL_INTEGER" VALUE = "1">

    <CFPROCPARAM TYPE="OUT" CFSQLTYPE="CF_SQL_VARCHAR" VARIABLE="FOO">

    <CFPROCRESULT NAME="rs1">
    <CFPROCRESULT NAME="rs2" RESULTSET="2">

</CFSTOREDPROC>

<b>The first result set:</b><br>
<hr>
<CFTABLE QUERY ="rs1" COLHEADERS HTMLTABLE BORDER ="1">
    <CFCOL HEADER = "EMPNO" TEXT = "#EMPNO#">
    <CFCOL HEADER = "EMPLOYEE NAME" TEXT = "#ENAME#">
    <CFCOL HEADER = "JOB" TEXT = "#JOB#">
    <CFCOL HEADER = "SALARY" TEXT = "#SAL#">
    <CFCOL HEADER = "DEPT NUMBER" TEXT = "#DEPTNO#">
</CFTABLE>

<hr>
<b>The second result set:</b><br>

<CFTABLE QUERY = "rs2" COLHEADERS HTMLTABLE BORDER = "1">
```

```
            <CFCOL HEADER = "DEPT NAME" TEXT = "#DNAME#">
            <CFCOL HEADER = "DEPT NUMBER" TEXT = "#DEPTNO#">
</CFTABLE>
<hr>
<CFOUTPUT>
<b>The output parameter is:</b>'#FOO#'
</CFOUTPUT>
```

cfprocparam

CFPROCRESULT

The CFPROCRESULT tag is nested within a CFSTOREDPROC tag. This tag's NAME parameter specifies a result set name that other ColdFusion tags, such as CFOUTPUT and CFTABLE, use to access the result set. It also allows you to optionally identify which of the stored procedure's result sets to return.

Syntax

```
<CFPROCRESULT NAME="query_name"
    RESULTSET="1-n"
    MAXROWS="maxrows">
```

NAME

Required. Name for the query result set.

RESULTSET

Optional. Specify this parameter to identify the desired result set if the stored procedure returns multiple result sets. Default is 1.

MAXROWS

Optional. Specifies the maximum number of rows returned in the result set. The default is to return all rows in the result set.

Usage

Specify one or more CFPROCRESULT tags to enable access to data returned by the stored procedure.

RESULTSET must be unique within the scope of the CFSTOREDPROC tag. If you specify the same result set twice, the second occurrence overwrites the first.

Example

cfprocresult

```
...
<!--- The following example executes a Sybase stored procedure
    that returns three result sets, two of which we want. The
    stored procedure returns the status code and one output
    parameter, which we display. We use named notation
    for the parameters. --->
<!--- CFSTOREDPROC tag --->
<CFSTOREDPROC PROCEDURE="foo_proc"
    DATASOURCE="MY_SYBASE_TEST"USERNAME="sa"
    PASSWORD=""DBSERVER="scup"DBNAME="pubs2"
    RETURNCODE="YES"DEBUG>
<!--- CFPROCRESULT tags --->
<CFPROCRESULT NAME = RS1>
<CFPROCRESULT NAME = RS3 RESULTSET = 3>
<!--- CFPROCPARAM tags --->
<CFPROCPARAM TYPE="IN"
    CFSQLTYPE=CF_SQL_INTEGER
        VALUE="1"DBVARNAME=@param1>

<CFPROCPARAM TYPE="OUT"CFSQLTYPE=CF_SQL_DATE
```

```
        VARIABLE=FOO DBVARNAME=@param2>
<!--- Close the CFSTOREDPROC tag --->
</CFSTOREDPROC>
<CFOUTPUT>
The output param value: '#foo#'
<br>
</CFOUTPUT>
<h3>The Results Information</h3>
<CFOUTPUT QUERY = RS1>#NAME#,#DATE_COL#
<br>
</CFOUTPUT>
<P>
<CFOUTPUT>
<hr>
<P>Record Count: #RS1.RecordCount# >p>Columns: #RS1.ColumnList#
<hr>
</CFOUTPUT>
<CFOUTPUT QUERY=RS3>#col1#,#col2#,#col3#
<br>
</CFOUTPUT>
<P>
<CFOUTPUT>
<hr>
<P>Record Count: #RS3.RecordCount# <P>Columns: #RS3.ColumnList#
<hr>
The return code for the stored procedure is:
 '#CFSTOREDPROC.STATUSCODE#'<br>
</CFOUTPUT>
...
```

cfprocresult

CFQUERY

CFQUERY passes SQL statements for any purpose to your data source. Not limited to queries.

Syntax

```
<CFQUERY NAME="query_name"
        DATASOURCE="ds_name"
        DBTYPE="type"
        DBSERVER="dbms"
        DBNAME="database name"
        USERNAME="username"
        PASSWORD="password"
        MAXROWS="number"
        BLOCKFACTOR="blocksize"
        TIMEOUT="milliseconds"
        CACHEDAFTER="date"
        CACHEDWITHIN="timespan"
        PROVIDER="COMProvider"
        PROVIDERDSN="datasource"
        DEBUG>

SQL statements

</CFQUERY>
```

NAME

Required. The name you assign to the query. Query names must begin with a letter and may consist of letters, numbers, and the underscore character (spaces are not allowed). The query name is used later in the page to reference the query's record set.

DATASOURCE

Required. The name of the data source from which this query should retrieve data.

DBTYPE

Optional. The database driver type:

- ODBC (default) — ODBC driver.

- Oracle73 — Oracle 7.3 native database driver. Using this option, the ColdFusion Server computer must have Oracle 7.3.4.0.0 (or greater) client software installed.

- Oracle80 —Oracle 8.0 native database driver. Using this option, the ColdFusion Server computer must have Oracle 8.0 (or greater) client software installed.

- Sybase11 —Sybase System 11 native database driver. Using this option, the ColdFusion Server computer must have Sybase 11.1.1 (or greater) client software installed. Sybase patch ebf 7729 is recommended.

- OLEDB —OLE DB provider. If specified, this database provider overrides the driver type specified in the ColdFusion Administrator.

- DB2 —DB2 5.2 native database driver.

- Informix73 —Informix73 native database driver.

DBSERVER

Optional. For native database drivers and the SQLOLEDB provider, specifies the name of the database server machine. If specified, DBSERVER overrides the server specified in the data source.

DBNAME

Optional. The database name (Sybase System 11 driver and SQLOLEDB provider only). If specified, DBNAME overrides the default database specified in the data source.

USERNAME

Optional. If specified, USERNAME overrides the username value specified in the data source setup.

PASSWORD

Optional. If specified, PASSWORD overrides the password value specified in the data source setup.

MAXROWS

Optional. Specifies the maximum number of rows you want returned in the record set.

BLOCKFACTOR

Optional. Specifies the maximum number of rows to fetch at a time from the server. The range is 1 (default) to 100. This parameter applies to ORACLE native database drivers and to ODBC drivers. Certain ODBC drivers may dynamically reduce the block factor at runtime.

TIMEOUT

Optional. Lets you specify a maximum number of milliseconds for the query to execute before returning an error indicating that the query has timed-out. This attribute is not supported by most ODBC drivers. TIMEOUT is supported by the SQL Server 6.x or above driver. The minimum and maximum allowable values vary, depending on the driver.

CACHEDAFTER

Optional. Specify a date value (for example, 4/16/98, April 16, 1999, 4-16-99). ColdFusion uses cached query data if the date of the original query is after the date specified. Effective only if query caching has been enabled in the ColdFusion Administrator. To use cached data, the current query must use the same SQL statement, data source, query name, user name, password, and DBTYPE. Additionally, for native drivers it must have the same DBSERVER and DBNAME (Sybase only).

Years from 0 to 29 are interpreted as 21st century values. Years 30 to 99 are interpreted as 20th century values.

When specifying a date value as a string, make sure it is enclosed in quotes.

CACHEDWITHIN

Optional. Enter a timespan using the ColdFusion CreateTimeSpan function. Cached query data will be used if the original query date falls within the time span you define. The CreateTimeSpan function is used to define a period of time from the present backwards. Effective only if query caching has been enabled in the ColdFusion Administrator. To use cached data, the current query must use the same SQL statement, data source, query name, user name, password, and DBTYPE. Additionally, for native drivers it must have the same DBSERVER and DBNAME (Sybase only).

PROVIDER

Optional. COM provider (OLE-DB only).

PROVIDERDSN

Optional. Data source name for the COM provider (OLE-DB only).

DEBUG

Optional. Used for debugging queries. Specifying this attribute causes the SQL statement submitted to the data source and the number of records returned from the query to be returned.

Usage   In addition to returning data from a ColdFusion data source, the CFQUERY tag also returns informations about the query. CFQUERY.ExecutionTime returns the time it took the query to execute in milliseconds.

CFQUERY creates a query object, providing you information in three query variables as described in the following table.

CFQUERY Variables	
Variable Name	**Description**
query_name.RecordCount	The total number of records returned by the query.
query_name.CurrentRow	The current row of the query being processed by CFOUTPUT.
query_name.ColumnList	Returns a comma-delimited list of the query columns.

You can cache query results and execute stored procedures. For information about caching CFQUERY results, executing stored procedures, and displaying CFQUERY output, see ../../Developing_Web_Applications_with_ColdFusion/ contents.htm*Developing Web Applications with ColdFusion*/a.

Example   cfquery

```
<!--- This example shows the use of CFQUERY --->

<HTML>
<HEAD>
    <TITLE>CFQUERY Example</TITLE>
</HEAD>

<BODY>
<H3>CFQUERY Example</H3>

<!--- define startrow and maxrows to facilitate
    'next N' style browsing --->
<CFPARAM NAME="MaxRows" DEFAULT="10">
<CFPARAM NAME="StartRow" DEFAULT="1">

<!--- query database for information --->
<CFQUERY NAME="GetParks" DATASOURCE="cfsnippets">
SELECT    PARKNAME, REGION, STATE
FROM      Parks
ORDER by ParkName, State
</CFQUERY>

<!--- build HTML table to display query --->
<TABLE cellpadding=1 cellspacing=1>
<TR>
    <TD colspan=2 bgcolor=f0f0f0>
    <B><I>Park Name</I></B>
    </TD>
    <TD bgcolor=f0f0f0>
    <B><I>Region</I></B>
    </TD>
    <TD bgcolor=f0f0f0>
    <B><I>State</I></B>
    </TD>
</TR>

<!--- Output the query and define the startrow and maxrows
    parameters. Use the query variable CurrentCount to
    keep track of the row you are displaying. --->
<CFOUTPUT QUERY="GetParks" StartRow="#StartRow#" MAXROWS="#MaxRows#">
<TR>
    <TD valign=top bgcolor=ffffed>
    <B>#GetParks.CurrentRow#</B>
    </TD>
    <TD valign=top>
    <FONT SIZE="-1">#ParkName#</FONT>
    </TD>
    <TD valign=top>
    <FONT SIZE="-1">#Region#</FONT>
    </TD>
    <TD valign=top>
    <FONT SIZE="-1">#State#</FONT>
```

```
        </TD>
    </TR>
</CFOUTPUT>

<!--- If the total number of records is less than or equal
to the total number of rows, then offer a link to
the same page, with the StartRow value incremented by
MaxRows (in the case of this example, incremented by 10) --->
<TR>
    <TD colspan=4>
    <CFIF (StartRow + MaxRows) LTE GetParks.RecordCount>
        <a href="cfquery.cfm?startrow=<CFOUTPUT>#Evaluate(StartRow +
        MaxRows)#</CFOUTPUT>">See next <CFOUTPUT>#MaxRows#</CFOUTPUT>
        rows</A>
    </CFIF>

        </TD>
    </TR>
</TABLE>
</BODY>
</HTML>
```

cfquery

CFQUERYPARAM

CFQUERYPARAM checks the data type of a query parameter. The CFQUERYPARAM tag is nested within a CFQUERY tag. More specifically, it is embedded within the query SQL statement. If you specify its optional parameters, CFQUERYPARAM also performs data validation.

Note For data, you must specify the MAXLENGTH attribute in order to ensure that maximum length validation is enforced.

See the Usage section for details.

Syntax

```
<CFQUERY NAME="query_name"
    DATASOURCE="ds_name"
    ...other attributes...
>
    SELECT STATEMENT WHERE column_name=
    <CFQUERYPARAM VALUE="parameter value"
        CFSQLType="parameter type"
        MAXLENGTH="maximum parameter length"
        SCALE="number of decimal places"
        DBNAME="database name"
        NULL="Yes" or "No"
        LIST="Yes" or "No"
        SEPARATOR="separator character"
    >
    AND/OR ...additional criteria of the WHERE clause...
</CFQUERY>
```

VALUE

Required. Specifies the actual value that ColdFusion passes to the right of the comparison operator in a where clause. See Usage section for details.

CFSQLTYPE

Optional. This is the SQL type that the parameter (any type) will be bound to. The default value is CF_SQL_CHAR. The CFSQLTypes are as follows:

CF_SQL_BIGINT	CF_SQL_IDSTAMP	CF_SQL_REFCURSOR
CF_SQL_BIT	CF_SQL_INTEGER	CF_SQL_SMALLINT
CF_SQL_CHAR	CF_SQL_LONGVARCHAR	CF_SQL_TIME
CF_SQL_DATE	CF_SQL_MONEY	CF_SQL_TIMESTAMP
CF_SQL_DECIMAL	CF_SQL_MONEY4	CF_SQL_TINYINT
CF_SQL_DOUBLE	CF_SQL_NUMERIC	CF_SQL_VARCHAR
CF_SQL_FLOAT	CF_SQL_REAL	

MAXLENGTH

Optional. Maximum length of the parameter. The default value is the length of the string specified in the VALUE attribute.

SCALE

Optional. Number of decimal places of the parameter. The default value is zero. Applicable for CF_SQL_NUMERIC and CF_SQL_DECIMAL.

NULL

Optional. Specify Yes or No. Indicates whether the parameter is passed as a NULL. If you specify Yes, the tag ignores the VALUE attribute. The default value is No.

LIST

Optional. Specify Yes or No. Indicates that the parameter value of the VALUE attribute is a list of values, separated by a separator character. The default value is No. See the SEPARATOR attribute for details.

SEPARATOR

Optional. Specifies the character that is to be used to separate the values in the list of parameter values specified by the VALUE attribute. The default separator is a comma. If you specify a list of values for the VALUE attribute, you must also specify the LIST attribute.

Usage   The CFQUERYPARAM is designed to do the following things:

- Allows the use of SQL bind parameters.
- Allows long text fields to be updated from an SQL statement.
- Improves performance.

The ColdFusion ODBC, DB2, Informix, Oracle 7 and Oracle 8 drivers support SQL bind parameters. However, at present, the ColdFusion Sybase 11 driver and Sybase native driver do not support SQL bind parameters.

If a database does not support bind parameters, ColdFusion still performs validation and substitutes the validated parameter value back into the string. If validation fails, an error message is returned. The validation rules follow:

- For types CF_SQL_SMALLINT, CF_SQL_INTEGER, CF_SQL_REAL, CF_SQL_FLOAT, CF_SQL_DOUBLE, CF_SQL_TINYINT, CF_SQL_MONEY, CF_SQL_MONEY4, CF_SQL_DECIMAL, CF_SQL_NUMERIC, and CF_SQL_BIGINT, data values can be converted to a numeric value.
- For types CF_SQL_DATE, CF_SQL_TIME and CF_SQL_TIMESTAMP, data values can be converted to a date supported by the target data source.
- For all other types, if the MAXLENGTH attribute is used, data value cannot exceed the maximum length specified.

The SQL syntax generated by the ColdFusion server is dependent on the target database.

For an ODBC, DB2, or Informix data source, the generated syntax of the SQL statement is as follows:

```
SELECT *
FROM courses
WHERE col1=?
```

For an Oracle 7 or Oracle 8 data source, the syntax of the SQL statement is as follows:

```
SELECT *
FROM courses
WHERE col1=:1
```

For a Sybase11 data source, the syntax of the SQL statement is as follows:

```
SELECT *
FROM courses
WHERE col1=10
```

Example   cfqueryparam

```
<!----------------------------------------------------------------------
This example shows the use of CFQUERYPARAM when valid input is given in
Course_ID.
---------------------------------------------------------------------->
<HTML>
<HEAD>
<TITLE>CFQUERYPARAM Example</TITLE>
</HEAD>

<BODY>
<h3>CFQUERYPARAM Example</h3>
<CFSET Course_ID=12>
<CFQUERY NAME="getFirst" DATASOURCE="cfsnippets">
    SELECT *
    FROM courses
    WHERE Course_ID=<CFQUERYPARAM VALUE="#Course_ID#"
    CFSQLType="CF_SQL_INTEGER">
</CFQUERY>
<CFOUTPUT QUERY="getFirst">
<P>Course Number: #number#<br>
 Description: #descript#
</P>
</CFOUTPUT>
</BODY>
</HTML>


<!----------------------------------------------------------------------
This example shows the use of CFQUERYPARAM when invalid numeric data is in Course_ID.
---------------------------------------------------------------------->
<HTML>
<HEAD>
<TITLE>CFQUERYPARAM Example</TITLE>
</HEAD>

<BODY>
```

```
<h3>CFQUERYPARAM Example With Bad Numeric Data</h3>
<CFSET Course_ID="12; DELETE courses WHERE Course_ID=20">
<CFQUERY NAME="getFirst" DATASOURCE="cfsnippets">
    SELECT *
    FROM courses
    WHERE Course_ID=<CFQUERYPARAM VALUE="#Course_ID#"
    CFSQLType="CF_SQL_INTEGER">
</CFQUERY>
<CFOUTPUT QUERY="getFirst">
<P>Course Number: #number#<br>
 Description: #descript#
</P>
</CFOUTPUT>
</BODY>
</HTML>
```

The CFQUERYPARAM tag returns the following error message when this example is executed.

VALUE
Invalid data '12; DELETE courses WHERE Course_ID=20' for
        CFSQLTYPE 'CF_SQL_INTEGER'.

```
<!---------------------------------------------------------------------
This example shows the use of CFQUERYPARAM when invalid string data is in Course_ID.
--------------------------------------------------------------------->
<HTML>
<HEAD>
<TITLE>CFQUERYPARAM Example</TITLE>
</HEAD>

<BODY>
<h3>CFQUERYPARAM Example with Bad String Input</h3>

<CFSET LastName="Peterson; DELETE employees WHERE LastName='Peterson'">
<---------------------------------------------------------------------
Note that for string input you must specify the MAXLENGTH attribute for validation.
--------------------------------------------------------------------->
<CFQUERY NAME="getFirst" DATASOURCE="cfsnippets">
    SELECT *
    FROM employees
    WHERE LastName=<CFQUERYPARAM VALUE="#LastName#"
    CFSQLType="CF_SQL_VARCHAR"
    MAXLENGTH="17">
</CFQUERY>
<CFOUTPUT QUERY="getFirst">
<P>Course Number: #FirstName# #LastName#
 Description: #Department#
</P>
</CFOUTPUT>
</BODY>
</HTML>
```

The CFQUERYPARAM tag returns the following error message when this example is executed.

VALUE
Invalid data 'Peterson; DELETE employees WHERE
LastName='Peterson'' value exceeds MAXLENGTH setting '17'.

cfqueryparam

CFREGISTRY

The CFREGISTRY tag reads, writes, and deletes keys and values in the system registry. CFREGISTRY is supported on all platforms, including Solaris and HP-UX.

Note   The ColdFusion Server Basic security settings may prevent CFRegistry from executing. These settings are managed using the ColdFusion Administrator Basic Security page. In order for CFRegistry to execute, it needs to be enabled on the Basic Security page. Please refer to ../../ Administering_ColdFusion_Server/contents.htm*Administering ColdFusion Server*/a for more information about securing ColdFusion tags.

CFREGISTRY topics

- CFREGISTRY ACTION="GetAll"
- CFREGISTRY ACTION="Get"
- CFREGISTRY ACTION="Set"
- CFREGISTRY ACTION="Delete"

CFREGISTRY ACTION attributes

Depending on the value you assign to the ACTION attribute of CFREGISTRY, there are several additional attributes you set. This table shows which attributes you can use with each CFREGISTRY ACTION.

Attributes Used with CFREGISTRY ACTIONs	
ACTION	**Attributes**
GetAll	BRANCH TYPE NAME SORT
Get	BRANCH ENTRY TYPE VARIABLE

Attributes Used with CFREGISTRY ACTIONs	
ACTION	**Attributes**
Set	BRANCH ENTRY TYPE VALUE
Delete	BRANCH ENTRY

Sections that follow describe these values and attributes in greater detail.

CFREGISTRY ACTION="GetAll"

Use CFREGISTRY with the GetAll action to return all registry keys and values defined in a branch. You can access these values as you would any record set.

Syntax

```
<CFREGISTRY ACTION="GetAll"
    BRANCH="branch"
    TYPE="data type"
    NAME="query name"
    SORT="criteria">
```

BRANCH

Required. The name of the registry branch containing the keys or values you want to access.

TYPE

Optional. The type of data you want to access:

- String — Return string values (default).

- DWord — Return DWord values.

- Key — Return keys.

- Any — Return keys and values.

NAME

Required. The name of the record set to contain returned keys and values.

SORT

Optional. Sorts query column data (case-insensitive). Sorts on Entry, Type, and Value columns as text. Specify any combination of columns from query output in a comma separated list. ASC (ascending) or DESC (descending) can be specified as qualifiers for column names. ASC is the default. For example:

```
Sort="value DESC, entry ASC"
```

Usage   CFREGISTRY returns #Entry#, #Type#, and #Value# in a record set that you can access through tags such as CFOUTPUT. To fully qualify these variables use the record set name, as specified in the NAME attribute.

If #Type# is a key, #Value# is an empty string.

If you specify Any for TYPE, GetAll also returns binary registry values. For binary values, the #Type# variable contains UNSUPPORTED and #Value# is blank.

Example   cfregistry

```
<!--- This example uses CFREGISTRY with the GetAll Action --->

<HTML>
<HEAD>
<TITLE>CFREGISTRY ACTION="GetAll"</TITLE>
</HEAD>
<BODY>
<CFREGISTRY ACTION="GetAll"
 BRANCH="HKEY_LOCAL_MACHINE\Software\Microsoft\Java VM"
 TYPE="Any" NAME="RegQuery">
<P>
<H1>CFREGISTRY ACTION="GetAll"</H1>
<CFTABLE QUERY="RegQuery" COLHEADERS HTMLTABLE BORDER="Yes">
<CFCOL HEADER="<B>Entry</b>" WIDTH="35" TEXT="#RegQuery.Entry#">
<CFCOL HEADER="<B>Type</b>" WIDTH="10" TEXT="#RegQuery.Type#">
<CFCOL HEADER="<B>Value</b>" WIDTH="35" TEXT="#RegQuery.Value#">
</CFTABLE>
</BODY>
</HTML>
```

cfregistry

CFREGISTRY ACTION="Get"

Use CFREGISTRY with the Get action to access a registry value and store it in a ColdFusion variable.

Syntax
```
<CFREGISTRY ACTION="Get"
        BRANCH="branch"
        ENTRY="key or value"
        TYPE="data type"
        VARIABLE="variable">
```

BRANCH
> Required. The name of the registry branch containing the value you want to access.

ENTRY
> Required. The registry value to be accessed.

TYPE
> Optional. The type of data you want to access:
>
> - String — Return a string value (default).
>
> - DWord — Return a DWord value.
>
> - Key — Return a key's default value.

VARIABLE

Required. Variable into which CFREGISTRY places the value.

Usage   CFREGISTRY does not create the variable if the value does not exist.

Example   cfregistry

```
<!--- This example uses CFREGISTRY with
    the Get Action --->

<HTML>
<HEAD>
<TITLE>CFREGISTRY ACTION="Get"</TITLE>
</HEAD>
<BODY>
<CFREGISTRY ACTION="Get"
  BRANCH="HKEY_LOCAL_MACHINE\Software\Microsoft\Java VM"
  ENTRY="ClassPath" TYPE="String" VARIABLE="RegValue">
<H1>CFREGISTRY ACTION="Get"</H1>
<CFOUTPUT>
<P>
Java ClassPath value is #RegValue#
</CFOUTPUT>
</BODY>
</HTML>
```

cfregistry

CFREGISTRY ACTION="Set"

Use CFREGISTRY with the Set action to add a registry key, add a new value, or update value data.

Syntax
```
<CFREGISTRY ACTION="Set"
     BRANCH="branch"
     ENTRY="key or value"
     TYPE="value type"
     VALUE="data">
```

BRANCH

Required. The name of the registry branch containing the key or value to be set.

ENTRY

Required. The key or value to be set.

TYPE

Optional. The type of data you want to set:

- String — Set a string value (default).

- DWord — Set a DWord value.

- Key — Create a key.

VALUE

Optional. The value data to be set. If you omit this attribute, CFREGISTRY creates default value data, as follows:

- String — Default value is an empty string: ""

- DWord — Default value is 0 (zero)

Usage   CFREGISTRY creates the key or value if it does not exist.

Example   cfregistry

```
<!--- This example uses CFREGISTRY with
    the Set Action to modify
        registry value data --->

<HTML>
<HEAD>
<TITLE>CFREGISTRY ACTION="Set"</TITLE>
</HEAD>
<BODY>
<!--- Normally you pass in a file name
    instead of setting one here. --->
<CFSET FileName="dummy.cfm">
<CFREGISTRY ACTION="Set"
 BRANCH="HKEY_LOCAL_MACHINE\Software\cflangref"
 ENTRY="LastCFM01" TYPE="String" VALUE="#FileName#">
<H1>CFREGISTRY ACTION="Set"</H1>
</BODY>
</HTML>
```

cfregistry

CFREGISTRY ACTION="Delete"

Use CFREGISTRY with the Delete action to delete a registry key or value.

Syntax   <CFREGISTRY ACTION="Delete"
        BRANCH="branch"
        ENTRY="keyorvalue">

BRANCH

Required. Specifies one of the following:

- For key deletion — The name of the registry key to be deleted. To delete a key, do not specify ENTRY.

- For value deletion — The name of the registry branch containing the value to be deleted. To delete a value, you must specify ENTRY.

ENTRY

Required for value deletion. The value to be deleted.

Usage   If you delete a key, CFREGISTRY also deletes values and subkeys defined beneath the key.

Example   cfregistry

```
<!--- This example uses CFREGISTRY with the Delete Action to remove
      a key from the registry  --->
<HTML>
<HEAD>
<TITLE>CFREGISTRY ACTION="Delete"</TITLE>
</HEAD>
<BODY>
<CFREGISTRY ACTION="Delete"
 BRANCH="HKEY_LOCAL_MACHINE\Software\cflangref\tempkey"
 ENTRY="LastCFM01">
<H1>CFREGISTRY ACTION="Delete"</H1>
</BODY>
</HTML>
```

cfregistry

CFREPORT

CFREPORT runs a predefined Crystal Reports report.

Syntax
```
<CFREPORT REPORT="report_path"
        ORDERBY="result_order"
        USERNAME="username"
        PASSWORD="password"
        FORMULA="formula">

</CFREPORT>
```

REPORT

Required. Specifies the path of the report. Store your Crystal Reports files in the same directories that you store your ColdFusion page files.

ORDERBY

Optional. Orders results according to your specifications.

USERNAME

Optional. The username required for entry into the database from which the report is created. Overrides the default settings for the data source in the ColdFusion Administrator.

PASSWORD

Optional. The password that corresponds to a username required for database access. Overrides the default settings for the data source in the ColdFusion Administrator.

FORMULA

Optional. Specifies one or more named formulas. Terminate each formula specification with a semicolon. Use the following format:

```
FORMULA="formulaname1='formula1';formulaname2='formula2';"
```

If you need to use a semi-colon as part of a formula, you must escape it by typing the semi-colon twice (;;), for example:

```
FORMULA="Name1='Val_1a;;Val_1b';Name2='Val2';"
```

Example   cfreport

```
<!--- This view-only example shows the use of CFREPORT --->
<HTML>
<HEAD>
<TITLE>CFREPORT Example</TITLE>
</HEAD>

<BODY>
<H3>CFREPORT Tag<H3>
<P>CFREPORT allows reports from the Crystal Reports Professional
```

report writer to be displayed through a ColdFusion interface.
The CFREPORT tag requires the name of the report to run;
CFREPORT can also pass information to the report
file being displayed to change the output conditions.

<P>This example would run a report called
"monthlysales.rpt " and pass it an optional filter condition to
show only the information for a certain subset of the report.

```
<CFREPORT REPORT='/reports/monthlysales.rpt'>
        {Departments.Department} = 'International'
</CFREPORT>
```

<P>Substitute your own report files and filters for this code
and CFREPORT can place your existing Crystal Reports into web pages.

```
</BODY>
</HTML>
```

cfreport

CFRETHROW

Rethrows the currently active exception. <CFRETHROW> preserves the exception's CFCATCH.TYPE and CFCATCH.TAGCONTEXT information.

See also CFTRY/CFCATCH.

Syntax   <CFRETHROW>

Usage   Use the <CFRETHROW> tag within a <CFCATCH> block. This tag is useful in error handling code when the error handler is not able to successfully handle the thrown error.

Example   cfrethrow

```
<!--- This example shows the use of CFRETHROW --->
<HTML>
<HEAD>
<TITLE>CFRETHROW Example</TITLE>
</HEAD>

<BASEFONT FACE="Arial, Helvetica" SIZE=2>
<BODY  bgcolor="#FFFFD5">

<H3>CFRETHROW Example</H3>

<!--- Rethrow a DATABASE exception. --->

<CFTRY>
    <CFTRY>
        <CFQUERY NAME="GetMessages" DATASOURCE="cfsnippets">
            SELECT  *
            FROM    Messages
        </CFQUERY>
    <CFCATCH TYPE="DATABASE">
        <!------------------------------------------------------------
        If the database signalled a 50555 error, we can ignore it,
        otherwise rethrow the exception.
        ------------------------------------------------------------>
        <CFIF CFCATCH.sqlstate neq 50555>
            <CFRETHROW>
        </CFIF>
    </CFCATCH>
    </CFTRY>

<CFCATCH>
    <h3>Sorry, this request can't be completed</h3>
    <h4>Catch variables</h4>
    <CFOUTPUT>
        <CFLOOP COLLECTION=#cfcatch# item="c">
            <br><CFIF IsSimpleValue(cfcatch[c])>#c# = #cfcatch[c]#</CFIF>
        </CFLOOP>
```

```
            </CFOUTPUT>
      </CFCATCH>
</CFTRY>

</BODY>
</HTML>
```

cfrethrow

CFSCHEDULE

CFSCHEDULE provides a programmatic interface to the ColdFusion scheduling engine. You can run a specified page at scheduled intervals with the option to write out static HTML pages. This allows you to offer users access to pages that publish data, such as reports, without forcing users to wait while a database transaction is performed in order to populate the data on the page.

ColdFusion scheduled events are registered using the ColdFusion Administrator. In addition, execution of CFSCHEDULE can be disabled in the Administrator. Information supplied by the user includes the scheduled ColdFusion page to execute, the time and frequency for executing the page, and if the output from the task should be published. If the output is to be published then a path and file is specified.

The event submission and its success or failure status is written to the \cfusion\log\schedule.log file.

Syntax

```
<CFSCHEDULE ACTION="Update"
        TASK="taskname"
        OPERATION="HTTPRequest"
        FILE="filename"
        PATH="path_to_file"
        STARTDATE="date"
        STARTTIME="time"
        URL="URL"
        PUBLISH="Yes" or "No"
        ENDDATE="date"
        ENDTIME="time"
        INTERVAL="seconds"
        REQUESTTIMEOUT="seconds"
        USERNAME="username"
        PASSWORD="password"
        RESOLVEURL="Yes" or "No"
        PROXYSERVER="hostname"
        PORT="port_number"
        PROXYPORT="port_number"
>

<CFSCHEDULE ACTION="Delete" TASK="TaskName">
<CFSCHEDULE ACTION="Run" TASK="TaskName">
```

ACTION

Required. Valid entries are:

- Delete – Deletes task specified by TASK.

- Update – Creates a new task if one does not exist.

- Run – Executes task specified by TASK.

TASK

Required. The name of the task to delete, update, or run.

OPERATION

Required when creating tasks with ACTION="Update". Specify the type of operation the scheduler should perform when executing this task. For now only OPERATION="HTTPRequest" is supported for static page generation.

FILE

Required with PUBLISH="Yes." A valid filename for the published file.

PATH

Required with PUBLISH="Yes." The path location for the published file.

STARTDATE

Required when ACTION="Update". The date when scheduling of the task should start.

STARTTIME

Required when creating tasks with ACTION="Update". Enter a value in seconds. The time when scheduling of the task should start.

URL

Required when ACTION="Update". The URL to be executed.

PUBLISH

Optional. Yes or No. Specifies whether the result should be saved to a file.

ENDDATE

Optional. The date when the scheduled task should end.

ENDTIME

Optional. The time when the scheduled task should end. Enter a value in seconds.

INTERVAL

Required when creating tasks with ACTION="Update". Interval at which task should be scheduled. Can be set in seconds or as Once, Daily, Weekly, Monthly, and Execute. The default interval is one hour and the minimum interval is one minute.

REQUESTTIMEOUT

Optional. Customizes the REQUESTTIMEOUT for the task operation. Can be used to extend the default timeout for operations that require more time to execute.

USERNAME

Optional. Username if URL is protected.

PASSWORD

Optional. Password if URL is protected.

PROXYSERVER

Optional. Host name or IP address of a proxy server.

RESOLVEURL

Optional. Yes or No. Specifies whether to resolve links in the result page to absolute references.

PORT

Optional. The port number on the server from which the task is being scheduled. Default is 80. When used with RESOLVEURL, the URLs of retrieved documents that specify a port number are automatically resolved to preserve links in the retrieved document.

PROXYPORT

Optional. The port number on the proxy server from which the task is being requested. Default is 80. When used with RESOLVEURL, the URLs of retrieved documents that specify a port number are automatically resolved to preserve links in the retrieved document.

Note You cannot use CFSCHEDULE and apply the Secure Sockets Layer (SSL) to your application.

Example cfschedule

```
<!--- This example shows an example of CFSCHEDULE --->
<HTML>
<HEAD>
<TITLE>CFSCHEDULE Example</TITLE>
</HEAD>

<BODY>
<H3>CFSCHEDULE Example</H3>
<P>CFSCHEDULE provides a programmatic interface to
the ColdFusion scheduling engine.  You can run a specified
page at scheduled intervals with the option to write out
static HTML pages.  This allows you to offer users access
to pages that publish data, such as reports, without
forcing users to wait while a database transaction is performed
to populate the data on the page.

<CFSCHEDULE ACTION="UPDATE"
    TASK="TaskName"
    OPERATION="HTTPRequest"
    URL="http://127.0.0.1/playpen/history.cfm"
    STARTDATE="8/7/98"
    STARTTIME="12:25 PM"
    INTERVAL="3600"
    RESOLVEURL="Yes"
    PUBLISH="Yes"
    FILE="sample.html"
    PATH="c:\inetpub\wwwroot\playpen"
    REQUESTTIMEOUT="600">
</BODY>
</HTML>
```

cfschedule

CFSCRIPT

The CFSCRIPT tag encloses a code segment containing CFScript.

Syntax
```
<CFSCRIPT>
 CFScript code goes here
</CFSCRIPT>
```

Usage   Use CFSCRIPT to perform processing in CFScript instead of CFML. Note the following regarding CFScript:

- CFScript uses ColdFusion functions, expressions, and operators
- You can read and write ColdFusion variables inside of CFScript

One use of CFSCRIPT is to wrap a series of assignment functions that would otherwise require CFSET statements.

For more information on CFScript, see ../../ Developing_Web_Applications_with_ColdFusion/contents.htm*Developing Web Applications with ColdFusion*/ a.

Example   cfscript

```
<!--- This example shows the use of CFSCRIPT --->
<HTML>
<HEAD>
<TITLE>CFSCRIPT Example</TITLE>
</HEAD>

<BODY bgcolor=silver>
<H3>CFSCRIPT Example</H3>

<P>CFSCRIPT adds a simple scripting language to ColdFusion
for those developers who are more comfortable with JavaScript
or VBScript syntax.

<P>This simple example shows variable declaration and
manipulation.
<CFIF IsDefined("form.myValue")>
<CFIF IsNumeric(form.myValue)>
<CFSET x= form.myValue>

<CFSCRIPT>
y = x;
z = 2 * y;
StringVar = form.myString;
</CFSCRIPT>
```

```
<CFOUTPUT>
<P>twice #x# is #z#.
<P>Your string value was: <B><I>#StringVar#</I></B>
</CFOUTPUT>
<CFELSE>
...
```

cfscript

CFSEARCH

Use the CFSEARCH tag to execute searches against data indexed in Verity collections. Collections can be created by calling the CFCOLLECTION tag, by using the ColdFusion Administrator, or through native Verity indexing tools. Collections are populated with data either with the CFINDEX tag, or externally, using native Verity indexing tools. Collections must be created and populated before any searches can be executed.

Syntax <CFSEARCH NAME="search_name"
        COLLECTION="collection_name"
        TYPE="criteria"
        CRITERIA="search_expression"
        MAXROWS="number"
        STARTROW="row_number"
        EXTERNAL="Yes" or "No"
        LANGUAGE="language">

NAME
Required. A name for the search query.

COLLECTION
Required. Specifies the logical collection name that is the target of the search operation or an external collection with fully qualified path. Collection names are defined either through the CFCOLLECTION tag or in the ColdFusion Administrator, Verity page.

Multiple ColdFusion collections can be specified in a comma-separated list:

COLLECTION="CFUSER, CFLANG"
If you are searching an external collection (EXTERNAL="Yes") specify the collection name, including fully qualified path:

COLLECTION="e:\collections\personnel"
If multiple collections are specified in COLLECTION and EXTERNAL is Yes, the specified collections must all be externally generated. You cannot combine internal and external collections in the same search operation.

TYPE
Optional. Specifies the criteria type for the search. Valid entries are:

- SIMPLE — By default the STEM and MANY operators are used.

- EXPLICIT — All operators must be invoked explicitly.

CRITERIA
Optional. Specifies the criteria for the search following the syntactic rules specified by TYPE.

MAXROWS
Optional. Specifies the maximum number of entries for index queries. If omitted, all rows are returned.

STARTROW

Optional. Specifies the first row number to be retrieved. Default is 1.

EXTERNAL

Optional. Yes or No. Yes indicates that the collection you are searching was created outside of ColdFusion using native Verity indexing tools. The default is No.

LANGUAGE

Optional. To use the LANGUAGE attribute you must have the ColdFusion International Search Pack installed. Valid entries are:

- English (default)
- German
- Finnish
- French
- Danish
- Dutch
- Italian
- Norwegian
- Portuguese
- Spanish
- Swedish

Usage   In the CRITERIA attribute, if you pass a mixed case entry (mixed upper and lower case), case sensitivity is applied to the search. If you pass all upper or all lower case, case insensitivity is assumed.

Every search conducted with the CFSEARCH tag returns, as part of the record set, a number of result columns you can reference in your CFOUTPUT:

- URL — Returns the value of the URLPATH attribute defined in the CFINDEX tag used to populate the collection. This value is always empty when you populate the collection with CFINDEX when TYPE="Custom".

- KEY — Returns the value of the KEY attribute defined in the CFINDEX tag used to populate the collection.

- TITLE — Returns whatever was placed in the TITLE attribute in the CFINDEX operation used to populate the collection, including the titles of PDF and Office documents. If no title was provided in the TITLE attribute, CFSEARCH returns CF_TITLE.

- SCORE — Returns the relevancy score of the document based on the search criteria.

- CUSTOM1 and CUSTOM2 — Returns whatever was placed in the custom fields in the CFINDEX operation used to populate the collection.

- SUMMARY — Returns the contents of the automatic summary generated by CFINDEX. The default summarization selects the best three matching sentences, up to a maximum of 500 characters.

- RECORDCOUNT — Returns the number of records returned in the record set.

- CURRENTROW — Returns the current row being processed by CFOUTPUT.

- COLUMNLIST — Returns the list of the column names within the record set.

- RECORDSSEARCHED— Returns the number of records searched.

You can use these result columns in standard CFML expressions, preceding the result column name with the name of the query:

```
#DocSearch.URL#
#DocSearch.KEY#
#DocSearch.TITLE#
#DocSearch.SCORE#
```

Example cfsearch

```
<!--- This example shows how to utilize CFSEARCH
to search an existing, populated collection --->
<HTML>
<HEAD>
<TITLE>
CFSEARCH Example
</TITLE>
</HEAD>

<BODY bgcolor=silver>
<H3>CFSEARCH Example</H3>

<!--- To index the collection, select the check box
on the form --->
<CFIF IsDefined("form.IndexCollection")>
<!--- Change KEY and URLPATH to reflect accurate key and URL
<CFINDEX ACTION="UPDATE" COLLECTION="Snippets"
  KEY="c:\inetpub\wwwroot\cfdocs\snippets" TYPE="PATH"
    TITLE="This is my test" URLPATH="http://127.0.0.1/cfdocs/snippets/"
      EXTENSIONS=".cfm" RECURSE="Yes">
<H3>Collection re-indexed</H3>
</CFIF>
<CFIF IsDefined("form.source") AND
IsDefined("form.type") AND IsDefined("form.searchstring")>

<!--- actually conduct the search --->
    <CFSEARCH NAME="SearchSnippets"
    COLLECTION="#form.source#"
    TYPE="#form.type#"
    CRITERIA="#form.searchstring#">

<!--- print out the search results --->
    <CFOUTPUT>
    <H2>#form.type# Search Results</H2>
```

```
        <P>#SearchSnippets.RecordCount# "hit
<CFIF SearchSnippets.recordcount is not 1>s</CFIF>" found
        out of #SearchSnippets.RecordsSearched# total record
        <CFIF SearchSnippets.recordcount is not 1>s</CFIF>
            searched.

        <P><I><B>#form.maxrows# records returned ...</B></I>

        <CFTABLE QUERY="SearchSnippets" MAXROWS="#maxrows#"
STARTROW="1" COLHEADERS HTMLTABLE>
            <CFCOL HEADER="SCORE" TEXT="#score#">
            <CFCOL HEADER="TITLE"
    TEXT="<a href='#url#' target='blank'>#title#</A>">
            <CFCOL HEADER="SUMMARY" TEXT="#summary#">
        </CFTABLE>
        </CFOUTPUT>

</CFIF>
...

cfsearch
```

CFSELECT

Used inside CFFORM, CFSELECT allows you to construct a drop-down list box form control. You can populate the drop-down list box from a query, or using the OPTION tag. Use OPTION elements to populate lists. Syntax for the OPTION tag is the same as for its HTML counterpart.

Note CFSELECT requires the client to download a Java applet. Downloading an applet takes time, so using CFSELECT may be slightly slower than using a SELECT element within an HTML FORM tag. In addition, browsers must be Java-enabled for CFSELECT to work properly.

Syntax <CFSELECT NAME="name"
   REQUIRED="Yes" or "No"
   MESSAGE="text"
   ONERROR="text"
   SIZE="integer"
   MULTIPLE="Yes" or "No"
   QUERY="queryname"
   SELECTED="column_value"
   VALUE="text"
   DISPLAY="text"
   PASSTHROUGH="HTML_attributes">

</CFSELECT>

NAME
Required. A name for the form you are creating.

SIZE
Optional. Size of the drop-down list box in number of entries.

REQUIRED
Optional. Yes or No. If Yes, a list element must be selected when the form is submitted, and the size of the drop-down list must be at least two. Default is No.

MESSAGE
Optional. Message that appears if REQUIRED="Yes" and no selection is made.

ONERROR
Optional. The name of a valid JavaScript function you want to execute in the event of a failed validation.

MULTIPLE
Optional. Yes or No. Yes permits selection of multiple elements in the drop-down list box. The default is No.

QUERY
Optional. Name of the query to be used to populate the drop-down list box.

SELECTED

> Optional. Enter a value matching at least one entry in VALUE to preselect the entry in the drop-down list box.

VALUE

> Optional. The query column value for the list element. Used with the QUERY attribute.

DISPLAY

> Optional. The query column displayed. Defaults to the value of VALUE. Used with the QUERY attribute.

PASSTHROUGH

> Optional. HTML attributes that are not explicitly supported by CFSELECT. If you specify an attribute and its value, the attribute and its value are passed to the HTML code that is generated for the CFSELECT tag. See the Usage section for more information about specifying values.

Usage   You can add standard and dynamic HTML FORM tag attributes and their values to the CFSELECT tag by using the PASSTHROUGH attribute. These attributes and values are passed directly through ColdFusion to the browser in creating a form.

If you specify a value in quotation marks, you must escape the quotation marks by doubling them, for example,

PASSTHROUGH= "readonly= " "YES " " "

CFSELECT supports the JavaScript *onClick* event in the same manner as the HTML INPUT tag:

```
<CFSELECT NAME="dept"
    MESSAGE="You must select a department name"
    QUERY="get_dept_list"
    VALUE="dept_name"
    onClick="JavaScript_function">
```

Example   cfselect

```
<!--- This example shows the use of CFTREE, CFSELECT and CFGRID in a
CFFORM. The query takes a list of employees, and uses CFTREE and CFSELECT
to display the results of the query.  In addition, CFGRID is used
to show an alternate means of displaying the same data --->

<!--- set a default for the employeeNames variable --->
<CFPARAM NAME="employeeNames" DEFAULT="">

<!--- if an employee name has been passed from the form,
set employeeNames variable to this value --->
<CFIF IsDefined("form.employeeNames") is not "False">
    <CFSET employeeNames = form.employeeNames>
</CFIF>

<!--- query the datasource to find the employee information--->
```

```
<CFQUERY NAME="GetEmployees" DATASOURCE="cfsnippets">
SELECT   Emp_ID, FirstName, LastName, EMail, Phone, Department
FROM     Employees where lastname
      <CFIF #employeeNames# is not "">= '#employeeNames#'</CFIF>
</CFQUERY>

<HTML>
<HEAD>
<TITLE>
CFSELECT Example
</TITLE>
</HEAD>

<BODY>

<H3>CFSELECT Example</H3>

<!--- Use CFFORM when using other CFINPUT tools --->
<CFFORM ACTION="cfselect.cfm" METHOD="POST" ENABLECAB="Yes">

<!--- Use CFSELECT to present the contents of the query by column --->
<H3>CFSELECT Presentation of Data</H3>
<H4>Click on an employee's last name and hit "see information for
this employee" to see expanded information.</H4>
<CFSELECT NAME="EmployeeNames" MESSAGE="Select an Employee Name"
  SIZE="#getEmployees.recordcount#" QUERY="GetEmployees"
   VALUE="LastName" REQUIRED="No">
<OPTION value="">Select All
</CFSELECT>
   ...
```

cfselect

CFSERVLET

Executes a Java servlet on a JRun engine. This tag is used in conjunction with the CFSERVLETPARAM tag, which passes data to the servlet.

Syntax

```
<CFSERVLET
    CODE="class name of servlet"
    JRUNPROXY="proxy server"
    TIMEOUT="timeout in seconds"
    WRITEOUTPUT="Yes" or "No"
    DEBUG="Yes" or "No">
    <CFSERVLETPARAM
    NAME="parameter name"
    VALUE="value"
    >
    ...
</CFSERVLET>
```

CODE

Required. The class name of the Java servlet to execute.

JRUNPROXY

Optional. Specifies a remote machine where the JRun engine is executing. By default, the JRun engine is assumed to be on the host running ColdFusion. To indicate the name of a remote host, specify the IP address of the remote host followed by a colon and the port number at which JRun is listening. By default, JRun listens at port 8081.

TIMEOUT

Optional. Specifies how many seconds JRun should wait for the servlet to complete before timing out.

WRITEOUTPUT

Optional. Boolean specifying if the text output of the tag should appear as inline text on the generated page or if it should be returned inside a ColdFusion variable for further processing . The default value, YES, means output is returned as text to appear inline on the generated page. Setting it to NO means no visible text is returned but, instead, the text is returned as the value of the CFSERVLET.OUTPUT variable. See the CFSERVLET Variables table under Usage for more information.

DEBUG

Optional. Boolean specifying whether additional information about the JRun connection status and activity is to be written to the JRun error log. The error log is in *JRunHome*/jsm-default/logs/stderr.log. Reading this log is helpful for debugging server-side problems. The default is No.

Usage   The syntax of the CFSERVLET tag is designed to be consistent with the HTML markup
            <SERVLET> and <PARAM> used by some web servers to invoke Java servlets from
            .shtml pages in what is known as SSI, Server-Side Includes.

CFSERVLET Variables	
Variable Name	**Description**
CFSERVLET.Output	Inline text output of the servlet is directed to this structure if the *WRITEOUTPUT* attribute is set to No.
CFSERVLET.*servletResponseHeaderName*	The CFSERVLET return structure also contains the values of any response headers returned by the servlet. To access a response header, specify its name in *servletResponseHeaderName*.

Note   The servlet must exist somewhere in the class path of the JRun engine
           executing the servlet. The JRun "servlet" subdirectory is a good location
           since it is already in JRun's class path and because classes in this directory
           are automatically reloaded by JRun if they change.

Example
```
<CFSERVLET  CODE="MyServletName"
     JRUNPROXY="236.3.3.4:8083"
     TIMEOUT="300"
     WRITEOUTPUT="YES">
     <CFSERVLETPARAM  NAME="Param1"  VALUE="Value1">
     <CFSERVLETPARAM  NAME="Param2"  VALUE="Value2">
     <CFSERVLETPARAM  NAME="Attribute1"  VARIABLE="CFVar1">
     <CFSERVLETPARAM  NAME="Attribute2"  VARIABLE="CFVar2">
</CFSERVLET>
```

CFSERVLETPARAM

The CFSERVLETPARAM is a child of CFSERVLET. It is used to pass data to the servlet. Each CFSERVLETPARAM tag within the CFSERVLET block passes a separate piece of data to the servlet.

See also CFSERVLET.

Syntax

```
<CFSERVLET
  ...>
  <CFSERVLETPARAM
  NAME="servlet parameter name"
  VALUE="servlet parameter value"
  >
  ...
  <CFSERVLETPARAM
  NAME="servlet attribute name"
  VARIABLE="ColdFusion variable name"
  TYPE="INT" or "DOUBLE" or "BOOL" or "DATE" or "STRING"
  >
  ...
</CFSERVLET>
```

NAME

Required. If used with the *VALUE* attribute, it is the name of the servlet parameter. If used with the *VARIABLE* attribute, it is the name of the servlet attribute. See the Usage section for details on passing parameters. See the Usage section for details on passing parameters.

VALUE

Optional. The value of a name-value pair to be passed to the servlet as a parameter.

VARIABLE

Optional. The name of a ColdFusion variable. See the Usage section for details on passing parameters. The value of which will appear in the servlet as an attribute. See the TYPE attribute for a way to pass data type information to the Java servlet.

TYPE

Optional. The data type of the ColdFusion variable being passed. By default, ColdFusion usually passes variables as strings; however, to ensure that the data is correctly type on the Java side, you can specify any of the following types: INT, DOUBLE, BOOL, DATE, or STRING. See the Data Types table under Usage for information about how these types map to Java object types.

Usage

There are two different ways that CFSERVLETPARAM can be used to pass information to the servlet: by value or by reference. Depending on the method used, this information appears in the servlet either as a parameter (by value) or attribute (by reference).

The first passes name-value pairs by value. This method uses the attributes *NAME* and *VALUE* to pass a simple name-value string pair to the servlet. The *NAME* attribute represents the name of the servlet parameter from which the string specified in the *VALUE* attribute can be retrieved. Although the servlet can use these parameters as input, it cannot change their values in the ColdFusion template.

The second passes a ColdFusion variable to the servlet by reference. This method uses the attribute *VARIABLE* to pass the specified ColdFusion variable by reference to the servlet. Within the servlet, the variable data is made available as servlet attributes in the form of Java objects. On the Java side, the data can be manipulated, even changed, and those changes will, in turn, change the value of the associated ColdFusion variable.

When used in this mode, the *NAME* attribute represents the name of the servlet attribute that will be created to hold the value of the ColdFusion variable. The *VARIABLE* attribute represents the name, not the #value#, of a ColdFusion variable. This ability to directly share ColdFusion variables with a servlet is a powerful extension to the servlet API because it allows even complex ColdFusion objects such as structures and result sets to be directly accessed from Java. The following table shows the mapping between ColdFusion data types (specified with the *TYPE* attribute) and the corresponding Java objects.

Data Types: CF versus Java	
Type	**in Java**
INT	java.lang.Integer
DOUBLE	java.lang.Double
BOOL	java.lang.Bool
DATE	java.util.Date
STRING	java.lang.String
Array	java.util.Vector
Structure	java.util.Hashtable
CF query result set	com.allaire.util.RecordSet (a WDDX-supplied utility class.)

Note   You need to have JRun 3.0 in order for the Name/Variable functionality to work. You can download the latest version of JRun at the following URL: http://www.allaire.com/products/Jrun/

In addition, in order to return a modified attribute to ColdFusion, thereby changing the value of the ColdFusion variable, you need to call the servlet API *setAttribute* method from the servlet to reset the value of the attribute.

Example

```
<CFSERVLET
      CODE="MyServletName"
      JRUNPROXY="236.3.3.4:8083"
      TIMEOUT="300"
      WRITEOUTPUT="Yes"
      DEBUG="Yes">
      <CFSERVLETPARAM NAME="Param1" VALUE="Value1">
      <CFSERVLETPARAM NAME="Param2" VALUE="Value2">
      <CFSERVLETPARAM NAME="Attribute1" VARIABLE="CFVar1" TYPE="BOOL">
      <CFSERVLETPARAM NAME="Attribute2" VARIABLE="CFVar2">
</CFSERVLET>
```

CFSET

Use the CFSET tag to define a ColdFusion variable. If the variable already exists, CFSET resets it to the specified value.

Syntax   `<CFSET variable_name=expression>`

Arrays

The following example assigns a new array to the variable "months".

`<CFSET months=ArrayNew(1)>`

This example creates a variable "Array_Length" that resolves to the length of the array "Scores".

`<CFSET Array_Length=ArrayLen(Scores)>`

This example assigns to index position two in the array "months" the value "February".

`<CFSET months[2]="February">`

Dynamic variable names

In this example, the variable name is itself a variable.

```
<CFSET myvariable="current_value">
<CFSET "#myvariable#"=5>
```

COM objects

In this example, a COM object is created. A CFSET defines a value for each method or property in the COM object interface. The last CFSET creates a variable to store the return value from the COM object's "SendMail" method.

```
<CFOBJECT ACTION="Create"
    NAME="Mailer"
    CLASS="SMTPsvg.Mailer">

<CFSET MAILER.FromName=form.fromname>
<CFSET MAILER.RemoteHost=RemoteHost>
<CFSET MAILER.FromAddress=form.fromemail>
<CFSET MAILER.AddRecipient("form.fromname", "form.fromemail")>
<CFSET MAILER.Subject="Testing CFOBJECT">
<CFSET MAILER.BodyText="form.msgbody">
<CFSET Mailer.SMTPLog="logfile">

<CFSET success=MAILER.SendMail()>

<CFOUTPUT> #success# </CFOUTPUT>
```

Example   cfset

```
<!--- This example shows how to use CFSET --->
<CFQUERY NAME="GetMessages" DATASOURCE="cfsnippets">
SELECT  *
FROM    Messages
</CFQUERY>
<HTML>
<HEAD>
<TITLE>
CFSET Example
</TITLE>
</HEAD>

<BODY bgcolor=silver>
<H3>CFSET Example</H3>

<P>CFSET allows you to set and reassign values to local or
global variables within a CF template.

<CFSET NumRecords = GetMessages.RecordCount>
<P>For example, the variable NumRecords has been declared on
this template to hold the amount of records returned from
our query (<CFOUTPUT>#NumRecords#</CFOUTPUT>).

<P>In addition, CFSET can be used to pass variables from other
pages, such as this example which takes the url parameter
Test from this link
(<a href="cfset.cfm?test=<CFOUTPUT>#URLEncodedFormat("
hey, you, get off of my cloud")#</CFOUTPUT>">click here</A>) to display
a message:
<P><CFIF IsDefined ("url.test") is "True">
    <CFOUTPUT><B><I>#url.test#</I></B></CFOUTPUT>
<CFELSE>
    <H3>The variable url.test has not been passed from
    another page.</H3>
</CFIF>

<P>Finally, CFSET can also be used to collect environmental
variables, such as the time, the IP address of the user, or any
other function or expression possible in ColdFusion.

<CFSET the_date =
 #DateFormat(Now())# & " " & #TimeFormat(Now())#>
<CFSET user_ip = CGI.REMOTE_ADDR>
<CFSET complex_expr = (23 MOD 12) * 3>
<CFSET str_example = Reverse(Left(GetMessages.body, 35))>
...
```

cfset

CFSETTING

CFSETTING is used to control various aspects of page processing, such as controlling the output of HTML code in your pages. One benefit of this option is managing whitespace that can occur in output pages that are served by ColdFusion.

Syntax <CFSETTING ENABLECFOUTPUTONLY="Yes" or "No"
     SHOWDEBUGOUTPUT="Yes" or "No"
     CATCHEXCEPTIONBYPATTERN="Yes" or "No"
>

ENABLECFOUTPUTONLY
Required. Yes or No. When set to Yes, CFSETTING blocks output of all HTML that resides outside CFOUTPUT tags.

SHOWDEBUGOUTPUT
Optional. Yes or No. When set to No, SHOWDEBUGOUTPUT suppresses debugging information that would otherwise display at the end of the generated page. Default is Yes.

CATCHEXCEPTIONSBYPATTERN
Optional. Yes or No. When set to Yes, it overrides the structured exception handling introduced in 4.5. Default is No.

Note Structured exception handling introduces a subtle upwards incompatibility. In 4.0.x, an exception was handled by the first CFCATCH block that could handle that type of exception. In 4.5, the structured exception manager searches for the best-fit CFCATCH handler.

Usage When nesting CFSETTING tags, you must match each ENABLECFOUTPUTONLY="Yes" setting with an ENABLECFOUTPUTONLY="No" setting for ordinary HTML text to be visible to a user. For example, if you have five ENABLECFOUTPUTONLY="Yes" statements, you must also have five corresponding ENABLECFOUTPUTONLY="No" statements for HTML text to be displayed again.

If at any point the output of plain HTML is enabled (no matter how many ENABLECFOUTPUTONLY="No" statements have been processed) the first ENABLECFOUTPUTONLY="YES" statement will block output.

Example cfsetting

```
...
<CFSETTING ENABLECFOUTPUTONLY="Yes">
This text is not shown
<CFSETTING ENABLECFOUTPUTONLY="No">
<P>This text is shown
<CFSETTING ENABLECFOUTPUTONLY="Yes">
<CFOUTPUT>
     <P>Text within CFOUTPUT is always shown
```

```
</CFOUTPUT>
<CFSETTING ENABLECFOUTPUTONLY="No">
<CFOUTPUT>
    <P>Text within CFOUTPUT is always shown
</CFOUTPUT>

</BODY>
</HTML>
```

cfsetting

CFSILENT

CFSILENT suppresses all output that is produced by the CFML within the tag's scope. See also CFSETTING.

Syntax <CFSILENT>

Example cfsilent

```
<HTML>
<HEAD>
<TITLE>CFSILENT</TITLE>
</HEAD>

<BASEFONT FACE="Arial, Helvetica" SIZE=2>
<BODY  bgcolor="#FFFFD5">

<H3>CFSILENT</H3>

<!--- This example shows the use of CFSILENT --->

<CFSILENT>
<CFSET a=100>
<CFSET b=99>
<CFSET c=b-a>
<CFOUTPUT>#c#</CFOUTPUT>

...
</CFSILENT>
<P>
Even information within CFOUTPUT tags does not appear within
the CFSILENT block.<BR>
b-c = <CFOUTPUT>#c#</CFOUTPUT>
</P>
</BODY>
</HTML>
```

cfsilent

CFSLIDER

Used inside CFFORM, CFSLIDER allows you to place a slider control in a ColdFusion form. A slider control is like a sliding volume control. The slider groove is the area over which the slider moves.

Note   CFSLIDER requires the client to download a Java applet. Downloading an applet takes time; therefore, using CFSLIDER may be slightly slower than using an HTML form element to retrieve or display the same information. In addition, browsers must be Java-enabled for CFSLIDER to work properly.

Syntax
```
<CFSLIDER NAME="name"
        LABEL="text"
        REFRESHLABEL="Yes" or "No"
        IMG="filename"
        IMGSTYLE="style"
        RANGE="min_value, max_value"
        SCALE="uinteger"
        VALUE="integer"
        ONVALIDATE="script_name"
        MESSAGE="text"
        ONERROR="text"
        HEIGHT="integer"
        WIDTH="integer"
        VSPACE="integer"
        HSPACE="integer"
        ALIGN="alignment"
        GROOVECOLOR="color"
        BGCOLOR="color"
        TEXTCOLOR="color"
        FONT="font_name"
        FONTSIZE="integer"
        ITALIC="Yes" or "No"
        BOLD="Yes" or "No"
        NOTSUPPORTED="text">
```

NAME
Required. A name for the CFSLIDER control.

LABEL
Optional. A label that appears with the slider control, for example:

LABEL="Volume %value%"
You can use %value% to reference the slider value. If % is omitted, the slider value appears immediately following the label.

REFRESHLABEL
Optional. Yes or No. If Yes, the label is not refreshed when the slider is moved. Default is Yes.

IMG

Optional. Filename of the image to be used in the slider groove.

IMGSTYLE

Optional. Style of the image to appear in the slider groove. Valid entries are:

- Centered
- Tiled
- Scaled

Default is Scaled.

RANGE

Optional. Determines the values of the left and right slider range. The slider value appears as the slider is moved.

Separate values by a comma, for example:

RANGE="1,100"
Default is "0,100". Valid only for numeric data.

SCALE

Optional. An unsigned integer. SCALE defines the slider scale within the value of RANGE. For example, if RANGE=0,1000 and SCALE=100, the incremental values for the slider would be 0, 100, 200, 300, and so on.

VALUE

Optional. Determines the default slider setting. Must be within the values specified in RANGE. Defaults to the minimum value specified in RANGE.

ONVALIDATE

Optional. The name of a valid JavaScript function used to validate user input, in this case, a change to the default slider value.

MESSAGE

Optional. Message text to appear if validation fails.

ONERROR

Optional. The name of a valid JavaScript function you want to execute in the event of a failed validation.

HEIGHT

Optional. Height value of the slider control, in pixels.

WIDTH

Optional. Width value of the slider control, in pixels.

VSPACE

Optional. Vertical margin spacing above and below slider control, in pixels.

HSPACE

Optional. Horizontal margin spacing to the left and right of slider control, in pixels.

ALIGN

Optional. Alignment value. Valid entries are:

- Top
- Left
- Bottom
- Baseline
- TextTop
- AbsBottom
- Middle
- AbsMiddle
- Right

GROOVECOLOR

Optional. Color value of the slider groove. The slider groove is the area in which the slider box moves. Valid entries are:

- black
- magenta
- cyan
- orange
- darkgray
- pink
- gray
- white
- lightgray
- yellow

A hex value can be entered in the form:

GROOVECOLOR="##xxxxxx"
Where x is 0–9 or A–F. Use either two pound signs or no pound signs.

BGCOLOR

Optional. Background color of slider label. See GROOVECOLOR for color options.

TEXTCOLOR

Optional. Slider label text color. See GROOVECOLOR for color options.

FONT

Optional. Font name for label text.

FONTSIZE

Optional. Font size for label text measured in points.

ITALIC

Optional. Enter Yes for italicized label text, No for normal text. Default is No.

BOLD

Optional. Enter Yes for bold label text, No for medium text. Default is No.

NOTSUPPORTED

Optional. The text you want to display if the page containing a Java applet-based CFFORM control is opened by a browser that does not support Java or has Java support disabled. For example:

```
NOTSUPPORTED="<B> Browser must support Java to
view ColdFusion Java Applets</B>"
```

By default, if no message is specified, the following message appears:

```
<B>Browser must support Java to <BR>
view ColdFusion Java Applets!</B>
```

Example   cfslider

```
<!--- This example shows how to use CFSLIDER
within CFFORM --->
<HTML>

<HEAD>
<TITLE>
    CFSLIDER Example
</TITLE>
</HEAD>

<BODY bgcolor=silver>

<H3>CFSLIDER Example</H3>
<P>CFSLIDER, used within a CFFORM, can provide
additional functionality to Java-enabled browsers.

<P>Try moving the slider back and forth to see the
real-time value change.  Then, submit the form to show
how CFSLIDER passes its value on to a new CF template.

<P>

<CFIF IsDefined("form.mySlider") is True>
<H3>You slid to a value of <CFOUTPUT>#mySlider#</CFOUTPUT></H3>

Try again!
</CFIF>
```

```
<CFFORM ACTION="cfslider.cfm" METHOD="POST" ENABLECAB="Yes">

1 <CFSLIDER NAME="mySlider" VALUE="12" LABEL="Actual Slider Value  "
   RANGE="1,100" ALIGN="BASELINE"
   MESSAGE="Slide the bar to get a value between 1 and 100" HEIGHT="20"
WIDTH="150" FONT="Verdana" BGCOLOR="Silver" GROOVECOLOR="Lime"
   BOLD="No" ITALIC="Yes" REFRESHLABEL="Yes"> 100

<P><INPUT TYPE="Submit" NAME="" VALUE="Show the Result">
</CFFORM>

</BODY>
</HTML>
```

cfslider

CFSTOREDPROC

The CFSTOREDPROC tag is the main tag used for executing stored procedures via an ODBC or native connection to a server database. It specifies database connection information and identifies the stored procedure.

Syntax   <CFSTOREDPROC PROCEDURE="procedure name"
          DATASOURCE="ds_name"
          USERNAME="username"
          PASSWORD="password"
          DBSERVER="dbms"
          DBNAME="database name"
          BLOCKFACTOR="blocksize"
          PROVIDER="COMProvider"
          PROVIDERDSN="datasource"
          DEBUG="Yes" or "No"
          RETURNCODE="Yes" or "No">

PROCEDURE
Required. Specifies the name of the stored procedure on the database server.

DATASOURCE
Required. The name of an ODBC or native data source that points to the database containing the stored procedure.

USERNAME
Optional. If specified, USERNAME overrides the username value specified in the data source setup.

PASSWORD
Optional. If specified, PASSWORD overrides the password value specified in the data source setup.

DBSERVER
Optional. For native database drivers, specifies the name of the database server machine. If specified, DBSERVER overrides the server specified in the data source.

DBNAME
Optional. The database name (Sybase System 11 driver only). If specified, DBNAME overrides the default database specified in the data source.

BLOCKFACTOR
Optional. Specifies the maximum number of rows to fetch at a time from the server. The range is 1 (default) to 100. The ODBC driver may dynamically reduce the block factor at runtime.

PROVIDER
Optional. COM provider (OLE-DB only).

PROVIDERDSN
> Optional. Data source name for the COM provider (OLE-DB only).

DEBUG
> Optional. Yes or No. Specifies whether debug info will be listed on each statement. Default is No.

RETURNCODE
> Optional. Yes or No. Specifies whether the tag populates CFSTOREDPROC.STATUSCODE with the status code returned by the stored procedure. Default is No.

Usage   Within a CFSTOREDPROC tag, you code CFPROCRESULT and CFPROCPARAM tags as necessary.

If you set the ReturnCode parameter to "YES", CFSTOREDPROC sets a variable called CFSTOREDPROC.STATUSCODE, which indicates the status code for the stored procedure. Stored procedure status code values vary by DBMS. Refer to your DBMS-specific documentation for the meaning of individual status code values.

In addition to returning a status code, CFSTOREDPROC sets a variable called CFSTOREDPROC.ExecutionTime. This variable contains the number of milliseconds that it took the stored procedure to execute.

Stored procedures represent an advanced feature, found in high-end database management systems, such as Oracle 8 and Sysbase. You should be familiar with stored procedures and their usage before implementing these tags. The following examples uses a Sybase stored procedure; for an example of an Oracle 8 stored procedure, see CFPROCPARAM.

Example   cfstoredproc

```
...
<!--- The following example executes a Sybase stored procedure
      that returns three result sets, two of which we want. The
      stored procedure returns the status code and one output
      parameter, which we display. We use named notation
      for the parameters. --->
<!--- CFSTOREDPROC tag --->
<CFSTOREDPROC PROCEDURE="foo_proc"
      DATASOURCE="MY_SYBASE_TEST"USERNAME="sa"
      PASSWORD=""DBSERVER="scup"DBNAME="pubs2"
      RETURNCODE="YES"DEBUG>
<!--- CFPROCRESULT tags --->
<CFPROCRESULT NAME = RS1>
<CFPROCRESULT NAME = RS3 RESULTSET = 3>
<!--- CFPROCPARAM tags --->
<CFPROCPARAM TYPE="IN"
      CFSQLTYPE=CF_SQL_INTEGER
            VALUE="1"DBVARNAME=@param1>

<CFPROCPARAM TYPE="OUT"CFSQLTYPE=CF_SQL_DATE
```

```
        VARIABLE=FOO DBVARNAME=@param2>
<!--- Close the CFSTOREDPROC tag --->
</CFSTOREDPROC>
<CFOUTPUT>
The output param value: '#foo#'
<br>
</CFOUTPUT>
<h3>The Results Information</h3>
<CFOUTPUT QUERY = RS1>#NAME#,#DATE_COL#
<br>
</CFOUTPUT>
<P>
<CFOUTPUT>
<hr>
<P>Record Count: #RS1.RecordCount# >p>Columns: #RS1.ColumnList#
<hr>
</CFOUTPUT>
<CFOUTPUT QUERY=RS3>#col1#,#col2#,#col3#
<br>
</CFOUTPUT>
<P>
<CFOUTPUT>
<hr>
<P>Record Count: #RS3.RecordCount# <P>Columns: #RS3.ColumnList#
<hr>
The return code for the stored procedure is:
 '#CFSTOREDPROC.STATUSCODE#'<br>
</CFOUTPUT>

...
```

cfstoredproc

CFSWITCH/CFCASE/CFDEFAULTCASE

Used with CFCASE and CFDEFAULTCASE, the CFSWITCH tag evaluates a passed expression and passes control to the CFCASE tag that matches the expression result. You can optionally code a CFDEFAULTCASE tag, which receives control if there is no matching CFCASE tag value.

Syntax

```
<CFSWITCH EXPRESSION="expression">
    <CFCASE VALUE="value" DELIMITERS="delimiters">
      HTML and CFML tags
    </CFCASE>
    additional <CFCASE></CFCASE> tags
    <CFDEFAULTCASE>
      HTML and CFML tags
    </CFDEFAULTCASE>
</CFSWITCH>
```

EXPRESSION

Required. Any ColdFusion expression that yields a scalar value. ColdFusion converts integers, real numbers, Booleans, and dates to numeric values. For example, TRUE, 1, and 1.0 are all equal.

VALUE

Required. One or more constant values that CFSWITCH compares to the specified expression (case-insensitive comparison). If a value matches the expression, CFSWITCH executes the code between the CFCASE start and end tags.

Separate multiple values with a comma or an alternative delimiter, as specified in the DELIMITERS parameter. Duplicate value attributes are not allowed and will cause a runtime error.

DELIMITERS

Optional. Specifies the character that separates multiple entries in a list of values. The default delimiter is the comma (,).

Usage

Use CFSWITCH followed by one or more CFCASE tags, optionally ending with a CFDEFAULTCASE tag. The CFSWITCH tag selects the matching alternative from the specified CFCASE and CFDEFAULTCASE tags and jumps to the matching tag, executing the code between the CFCASE start and end tags. There is no need to explicitly break out of the CFCASE tag, as there is in some other languages.

You can specify only one CFDEFAULTCASE tag within a CFSWITCH tag. CFCASE tags cannot appear after the CFDEFAULTCASE tag.

CFSWITCH provides better performance than a series of CFIF/CFELSEIF tags and the resulting code is easier to read.

Example cfswitch

```
<!--- This example illustrates the use of CFSWITCH and
CFCASE to exercise a case statement in CFML --->

<!--- query to get some information --->
<CFQUERY NAME="GetEmployees" DATASOURCE="cfsnippets">
SELECT   Emp_ID, FirstName, LastName, EMail,
      Phone, Department
FROM    Employees
</CFQUERY>

<HTML>
<HEAD>
<TITLE>
CFSWITCH Example
</TITLE>
</HEAD>

<BODY bgcolor=silver>
<H3>CFSWITCH Example</H3>

<!--- By outputting the query and using CFSWITCH,
we can classify the output without using a CFLOOP construct.
 --->
<CFOUTPUT QUERY="GetEmployees">
<CFSWITCH EXPRESSION=#Department#>
<!--- each time the case is fulfilled, the specific
information is printed; if the case is not fulfilled,
the default case is output --->
     <CFCASE VALUE="Sales">
     #FirstName# #LastName# is in <B>sales</B><BR><BR>
     </CFCASE>
     <CFCASE VALUE="Accounting">
     #FirstName# #LastName# is in <B>accounting</B><BR><BR>
     </CFCASE>
     <CFCASE VALUE="Administration">
     #FirstName# #LastName# is in <B>administration</B><BR><BR>
     </CFCASE>
     <CFDEFAULTCASE>#FirstName# #LastName# is not in Sales,
     Accounting, or Administration.<BR>
     </CFDEFAULTCASE>
</CFSWITCH>
</CFOUTPUT>

</BODY>
</HTML>
```

cfswitch

CFTABLE

Builds a table in your ColdFusion page. Use the CFCOL tag to define column and row characteristics for a table. CFTABLE renders data either as preformatted text, or, with the HTMLTABLE attribute, as an HTML table. Use CFTABLE to create tables if you don't want to write your own HTML TABLE tag code, or if your data can be well presented as preformatted text. See Usage for information about using the CFCOL tag with the CFTABLE tag.

Syntax

```
<CFTABLE QUERY="query_name"
        MAXROWS="maxrows_table"
        COLSPACING="number_of_spaces"
        HEADERLINES="number_of_lines"
        HTMLTABLE
        BORDER
        COLHEADERS
        STARTROW="row_number">

</CFTABLE>
```

QUERY

Required. The name of the CFQUERY from which you want to draw data.

MAXROWS

Optional. Specifies the maximum number of rows you want to display in the table.

COLSPACING

Optional. Indicates the number of spaces to insert between columns (default is 2).

HEADERLINES

Optional. Indicates the number of lines to use for the table header (the default is 2, which leaves one line between the headers and the first row of the table).

HTMLTABLE

Optional. Renders the table as an HTML 3.0 table.

BORDER

Optional. Adds a border to the table. Use only when you specify the HTMLTABLE attribute for the table.

COLHEADERS

Optional. Displays headers for each column, as specified in the CFCOL tag.

STARTROW

Optional. Specifies the query row from which to start processing.

Usage   You can use the CFCOL tag to align the data in the table , specify the width of each column, and provide column headers.

Note   CFCOL is the only tag that you can nest within CFTABLE.

Example   cftable

```
<!--- This example shows the use of CFCOL and CFTABLE
to align information returned from a query --->

<!--- This query selects employee information from the
cfsnippets datasource --->
<CFQUERY NAME="GetEmployees" DATASOURCE="cfsnippets">
SELECT Emp_ID, FirstName, LastName, EMail, Phone, Department
FROM Employees
</CFQUERY>

<HTML>
<HEAD>
<TITLE>CFTABLE Example</TITLE>
</HEAD>

<BODY>
<H3>CFTABLE Example</H3>

<!--- Note the use of the HTMLTABLE attribute to display the
CFTABLE as an HTML table, rather simply as PRE formatted information --->
<CFTABLE QUERY="GetEmployees" STARTROW="1" COLSPACING="3" HTMLTABLE>
<!--- each CFCOL tag sets the width of a column in the table,
as well as specifying the header information and the text/CFML
with which to fill the cell --->
    <CFCOL HEADER = "<B>ID</B>"
        ALIGN = "Left"
        WIDTH = 2
        TEXT  = "#Emp_ID#">

    <CFCOL HEADER = "<B>Name/Email</B>"
        ALIGN = "Left"
        WIDTH = 15
        TEXT  = "<a href='mailto:#Email#'>#FirstName# #LastName#</A>">

    <CFCOL HEADER = "<B>Phone Number</B>"
        ALIGN = "Center"
        WIDTH = 15
        TEXT  = "#Phone#">
</CFTABLE>

</BODY>
</HTML>
```

cftable

CFTEXTINPUT

The CFTEXTINPUT form custom control allows you to place a single-line text entry box in a CFFORM. In addition to input validation, the tag gives you control over all font characteristics.

Note   CFTEXTINPUT requires the client to download a Java applet. Downloading an applet takes time; therefore, using CFTEXTINPUT may be slightly slower than using an HTML form element to retrieve the same information. In addition, browsers must be Java-enabled for CFTEXTINPUT to work properly.

Syntax
```
<CFTEXTINPUT NAME="name"
        VALUE="text"
        REQUIRED="Yes" or "No"
        RANGE="min_value, max_value"
        VALIDATE="data_type"
        ONVALIDATE="script_name"
        MESSAGE="text"
        ONERROR="text"
        SIZE="integer"
        FONT="font_name"
        FONTSIZE="integer"
        ITALIC="Yes" or "No"
        BOLD="Yes" or "No"
        HEIGHT="integer"
        WIDTH="integer"
        VSPACE="integer"
        HSPACE="integer"
        ALIGN="alignment"
        BGCOLOR="color"
        TEXTCOLOR="color"
        MAXLENGTH="integer"
        NOTSUPPORTED="text">
```

NAME

Required. A name for the CFTEXTINPUT control.

VALUE

Optional. Initial value that appears in the text control.

REQUIRED

Optional. Yes or No. If Yes, the user must enter or change text. Default is No.

RANGE

Optional. Enter a minimum value, maximum value range separated by a comma. Valid only for numeric data.

VALIDATE

Optional. Valid entries are:

- date — Verifies US date entry in the form *mm/dd/yy.*

- eurodate — Verifies valid European date entry in the form *dd/mm/yyyy.*

- time — Verifies a time entry in the form *hh:mm:ss.*

- float — Verifies a floating point entry.

- integer — Verifies an integer entry.

- telephone — Verifies a telephone entry. Telephone data must be entered as ###-###-####. The hyphen separator (-) can be replaced with a blank. The area code and exchange must begin with a digit between 1 and 9.

- zipcode — (U.S. formats only) Number can be a 5-digit or 9-digit zip in the form #####-####. The hyphen separator (-) can be replaced with a blank.

- creditcard — Blanks and dashes are stripped and the number is verified using the mod10 algorithm.

- social_security_number — Number must be entered as ###-##-####. The hyphen separator (-) can be replaced with a blank.

ONVALIDATE

Optional. The name of a valid JavaScript function used to validate user input. The form object, input object, and input object value are passed to the specified routine, which should return TRUE if validation succeeds and FALSE otherwise. When used, the VALIDATE attribute is ignored.

MESSAGE

Optional. Message text to appear if validation fails.

ONERROR

Optional. The name of a valid JavaScript function you want to execute in the event of a failed validation.

SIZE

Optional. Number of characters displayed before horizontal scroll bar appears.

FONT

Optional. Font name for text.

FONTSIZE

Optional. Font size for text.

ITALIC

Optional. Enter Yes for italicized text, No for normal text. Default is No.

BOLD

Optional. Enter Yes for boldface text, No for medium text. Default is No.

HEIGHT

Optional. Height value of the control, in pixels.

WIDTH

Optional. Width value of the control, in pixels.

VSPACE

Optional. Vertical spacing of the control, in pixels.

HSPACE

Optional. Horizontal spacing of the control, in pixels.

ALIGN

Optional. Alignment value. Valid entries are:

- Top
- Left
- Bottom
- Baseline
- TextTop
- AbsBottom
- Middle
- AbsMiddle
- Right

BGCOLOR

Optional. Background color of the control. Valid entries are:

- black
- magenta
- cyan
- orange
- darkgray
- pink
- gray
- white
- lightgray
- yellow

A hex value can also be entered in the form:

BGCOLOR="##$xxxxxx$"
Where x is 0–9 or A–F. Use either two pound signs or no pound signs.

TEXTCOLOR

Optional. Text color for the control. See BGCOLOR for color options.

MAXLENGTH

Optional. The maximum length of text entered.

NOTSUPPORTED

Optional. The text you want to display if the page containing a Java applet-based CFFORM control is opened by a browser that does not support Java or has Java support disabled. For example:

NOTSUPPORTED="<B> Browser must support Java to
view ColdFusion Java Applets</B>"

By default, if no message is specified, the following message appears:

<B>Browser must support Java to
view ColdFusion Java Applets!</B>

Example   cftextinput

<!--- This example shows the use of CFTEXTINPUT --->

<HTML>
<HEAD>
<TITLE>
CFTEXTINPUT Example
</TITLE>
</HEAD>

<BODY bgcolor=silver>

<H3>CFTEXTINPUT Example</H3>

CFTEXTINPUT can be used to provide simple validation for text
fields in CFFORM and to have control over font information
displayed in CFFORM input boxes for text. For example, the field
provided below must not
be blank, and provides a client-side message upon erring.

<CFFORM ACTION="cftextinput.cfm" METHOD="POST" ENABLECAB="Yes">

<CFIF IsDefined("form.myInput")>
<H3>You entered <CFOUTPUT>#form.myInput#</CFOUTPUT> into the text box
  </H3>
</CFIF>

<CFTEXTINPUT NAME="myInput" FONT="Courier" FONTSIZE=12
 VALUE="Look, this text is red!" TEXTCOLOR="FF0000"
   MESSAGE="This field must not be blank" REQUIRED="Yes">

<INPUT TYPE="Submit" NAME="" VALUE="submit">
</CFFORM>

```
</BODY>
</HTML>
```

cftextinput

CFTHROW

The CFTHROW tag raises a developer-specified exception that can be caught with CFCATCH tag having any of the following type specifications:

- CFCATCH TYPE= "*custom_type*"
- CFCATCH TYPE= "APPLICATION "
- CFCATCH TYPE= "ANY "

Syntax   <CFTHROW
             TYPE= "exception_type "
             MESSAGE="message"
             DETAIL= "detail_description "
             ERRORCODE= "error_code "
             EXTENDEDINFO= "additional_information ">

TYPE

Optional. A custom type or the predefined type APPLICATION. None of the other predefined types should be specified because these types are not generated by ColdFusion applications. If you specify the exception type APPLICATION, you need not specify a type for CFCATCH, because the APPLICATION type is the default CFCATCH type.

MESSAGE

Optional. A message that describes the exceptional event.

DETAIL

Optional. A detailed description of the event. The ColdFusion server appends the position of the error to this description; the server uses this parameter if an error is not caught by your code.

ERRORCODE

Optional. A custom error code that you supply.

EXTENDEDINFO

Optional. A custom error code that you supply.

Usage   Use CFTHROW within a CFTRY block to raise an error condition.The CFCATCH block can access any accompanying information as follows:

- Message with CFCATCH.message
- Detail with CFCATCH.detail
- Error code with CFCATCH.errorcode.
- To get additional information, use CFCATCH.TagContext. TagContext captures the context of the exception; that is, the name and position of each tag in the tag stack, and the full path names of the files that contain the tags in the tag stack.

Note In order to see the information displayed by TagContext, use the ColdFusion Administrator to enable the CFML stack trace.Under Debugging in the ColdFusion Administrator, choose the checkbox next to "Enable CFML stack trace. "

Example cfthrow

```
<!--- This example shows the use of CFTHROW. --->

<HTML>

<HEAD>
<TITLE>
CFTHROW Example
</TITLE>
</HEAD>

<BASEFONT FACE="Arial, Helvetica" SIZE=2>

<BODY  bgcolor="#FFFFD5">

<H3>CFTHROW Example</H3>

<!--- open a CFTRY block --->
<CFTRY>
<!--- define a condition upon which to throw
    the error --->
     <CFIF NOT IsDefined("URL.myID")>
<!--- throw the error --->
          <CFTHROW MESSAGE="ID is not defined">
   </CFIF>

<!--- perform the error catch --->
<CFCATCH TYPE="application">
<!--- display your message --->
     <H3>You've Thrown an <B>Error</B></H3>
<CFOUTPUT>
<!--- and the diagnostic feedback from the
application server --->
  <P>#CFCATCH.message#</P>
     <P>The contents of the tag stack are:</P>
     <CFLOOP index=i from=1 to = #ArrayLen(CFCATCH.TAGCONTEXT)#>
          <CFSET sCurrent = #CFCATCH.TAGCONTEXT[i]#>
               <BR>#i# #sCurrent["ID"]# (#sCurrent["LINE"]#,#sCurrent["COLUMN"]#)
#sCurrent["TEMPLATE"]#
     </CFLOOP>
</CFOUTPUT>
</CFCATCH>
```

```
</CFTRY>

</BODY>

</HTML>
```

cfthrow

CFTRANSACTION

Use CFTRANSACTION to group multiple queries into a single unit. CFTRANSACTION also provides commit and rollback processing. See Usage for details.

Syntax
```
<CFTRANSACTION
    ACTION="BEGIN" or "COMMIT" or "ROLLBACK"
    ISOLATION="Read_Uncommitted" or
              "Read_Committed" or
              "Repeatable_Read" >
</CFTRANSACTION>
```

ACTION

Optional. The actions are as follows:

- BEGIN, which indicates the start of the block of code to be executed. It is the default value.

- COMMIT, which commits a pending transaction.

- ROLLBACK, which rolls back a pending transaction.

ISOLATION

Optional. ODBC lock type. Valid entries are:

- Read_Uncommitted

- Read_Committed

- Repeatable_Read

- Serializable

Usage   A transaction block is created within these tags:

```
<CFTRANSACTION>
    queries to be executed
</CFTRANSACTION>
```

Within the transaction block, you can commit a transaction by nesting the <CFTRANSACTION ACTION="COMMIT"/> tag or roll the transaction back by nesting the <CFTRANSACTION ACTION="ROLLBACK"/> tag within the block.

Within one transaction block, you can write queries to more than one database; however, you must commit or rollback the transaction to a particular database prior to writing a query to another database.

By using CFML error handling, you have control over whether each transaction is to be committed based on the success or failure of the database query.

Use the ISOLATION attribute for additional control over how the database engine performs locking during the transaction.

Example   cftransaction

```
<!--- This example shows the use of CFTRANSACTION --->

<HTML>
<HEAD>
<TITLE>CFTRANSACTION Example</TITLE>
</HEAD>

<BODY>
<H3>CFTRANSACTION Example</H3>

<P>CFTRANSACTION can be used to group multiple queries
using CFQUERY into a single business event.  Changes to data
requested by these queries can be committed on the basis of the success or failure of the query by using the
actions COMMIT and ROLLBACK, respectively.
<P>The following is a sample listing (see code in right pane):
<!------------------------------------------------------------------
        You can enclose the transaction in a CFTRY/CFCATCH block in order
        to catch database errors and make commitment or rollback or the
        transaction contingent on the errors received.
------------------------------------------------------------------->
<CFTRY>
<!------------------------------------------------------------------
Initialize commitIt to Yes.
------------------------------------------------------------------->
<CFSET commitIt = "Yes">
<CFTRANSACTION ACTION="BEGIN">
        <CFQUERY NAME='makeNewCourse' DATASOURCE='cfsnippets'>
        INSERT INTO Courses
                (Number, Descript)
        VALUES
                ('#myNumber#', '#myDescription#')
        </CFQUERY>

        <!------------------------------------------------------------------
        Rolls back the pending insertion if database exception is caught.
        ------------------------------------------------------------------->
        <CFCATCH TYPE="DATABASE">
                <CFTRANSACTION ACTION="ROLLBACK"/>
                <CFSET commitIt = "No">
        </CFCATCH>
        <CFIF commitIt>
                <CFTRANSACTION ACTION="COMMIT"/>
                <!------------------------------------------------------------
                Commits the pending insertion.
                ------------------------------------------------------------->
        <CFELSE>
                <CFSET commitIt="Yes">
        </CFIF>

        <CFQUERY NAME='insertNewCourseToList' DATASOURCE='cfsnippets'>
        INSERT INTO CourseList
                (CorNumber, CorDesc, Dept_ID,
```

```
        CorName, CorLevel, LastUpdate)
    VALUES
        ('#myNumber#', '#myDescription#', '#myDepartment#',
        '#myDescription#', '#myCorLevel#', #Now()#)
    </CFQUERY>
    <!----------------------------------------------------------------
    Rolls back the pending insertion if database exception is caught.
    ----------------------------------------------------------------->
    <CFCATCH TYPE="DATABASE">
        <CFTRANSACTION ACTION="ROLLBACK"/>
        <CFSET commitIt = "No">
    </CFCATCH>
    <CFIF commitIt>
        <CFTRANSACTION ACTION="COMMIT"/>
        <!--------------------------------------------------------------
        Commits the pending insertion.
        -------------------------------------------------------------->
    <CFELSE>
        <CFSET commitIt="Yes">
    </CFIF>
</CFTRANSACTION>
</CFTRY>

</BODY>
</HTML>
```

cftransaction

CFTREE

The CFTREE form custom control allows you to place a tree control in a CFFORM. User selections can be validated. Individual tree items are created with CFTREEITEM tags inside the CFTREE tag block.

Note   CFTREE requires the client to download a Java applet. Downloading an applet takes time; therefore, using CFTREE may be slightly slower than using an HTML form element to retrieve the same information. In addition, browsers must be Java-enabled for CFTREE to work properly.

Syntax
```
<CFTREE NAME="name"
       REQUIRED="Yes" or "No"
       DELIMITER="delimiter"
       COMPLETEPATH="Yes" or "No"
       APPENDKEY="Yes" or "No"
       HIGHLIGHTHREF="Yes" or "No"
       ONVALIDATE="script_name"
       MESSAGE="text"
       ONERROR="text"
       FONT="font"
       FONTSIZE="size"
       ITALIC="Yes" or "No"
       BOLD="Yes" or "No"
       HEIGHT="integer"
       WIDTH="integer"
       VSPACE="integer"
       HSPACE="integer"
       ALIGN="alignment"
       BORDER="Yes" or "No"
       HSCROLL="Yes" or "No"
       VSCROLL="Yes" or "No"
       NOTSUPPORTED="text">
```

```
</CFTREE>
```

NAME
Required. A name for the CFTREE control.

REQUIRED
Optional. Yes or No. User must select an item in the tree control. Default is No.

DELIMITER
Optional. The character used to separate elements in the form variable PATH. The default is "\".

COMPLETEPATH
Optional. Yes passes the root level of the treename.path form variable when the CFTREE is submitted. If omitted or No, the root level of this form variable is not included.

APPENDKEY

Optional. Yes or No. When used with HREF, Yes passes the CFTREEITEMKEY variable along with the value of the selected tree item in the URL to the application page specified in the CFFORM ACTION attribute. The default is Yes.

HIGHLIGHTHREF

Optional. Yes highlights links associated with a CFTREEITEM with a URL attribute value. No disables highlight. Default is Yes.

ONVALIDATE

Optional. The name of a valid JavaScript function used to validate user input. The form object, input object, and input object value are passed to the specified routine, which should return true if validation succeeds and false otherwise.

MESSAGE

Optional. Message text to appear if validation fails.

ONERROR

Optional. The name of a valid JavaScript function you want to execute in the event of a failed validation.

FONT

Optional. Font name to use for all data in the tree control.

FONTSIZE

Optional. Font size for text in the tree control, measured in points.

ITALIC

Optional. Yes or No. Yes presents all tree control text in italic. Default is No.

BOLD

Optional. Yes or No. Yes presents all tree control text in boldface. Default is No.

HEIGHT

Optional. Height value of the tree control, in pixels.

WIDTH

Optional. Width value of the tree control, in pixels.

VSPACE

Optional. Vertical margin spacing above and below the tree control in pixels.

HSPACE

Optional. Horizontal spacing to the left and right of the tree control, in pixels.

ALIGN

Optional. Alignment value. Valid entries are:

- Top

- Left

- Bottom

- Baseline

- TextTop

- AbsBottom

- Middle

- AbsMiddle

- Right

BORDER

Optional. Places a border around the tree. Default is Yes.

HSCROLL

Optional. Permits horizontal scrolling. Default is Yes.

VSCROLL

Optional. Permits vertical scrolling. Default is Yes.

NOTSUPPORTED

Optional. The text you want to display if the page containing a Java applet-based CFFORM control is opened by a browser that does not support Java or has Java support disabled. For example:

NOTSUPPORTED="<B> Browser must support Java to
view ColdFusion Java Applets</B>"

By default, if no message is specified, the following message appears:

<B>Browser must support Java to
view ColdFusion Java Applets!</B>

Example   cftree

```
<!--- This example shows the use of CFTREE in a CFFORM.
The query takes a list of employees, and uses CFTREE and CFSELECT
to display the results of the query.  In addition, CFGRID is used
to show an alternate means of displaying the same data --->
<!--- set a default for the employeeNames variable --->
<CFPARAM NAME="employeeNames" DEFAULT="">
<!--- if an employee name has been passed from the form,
set employeeNames variable to this value --->
<CFIF IsDefined("form.employeeNames")>
     <CFSET employeeNames = form.employeeNames>
</CFIF>
<!--- query the datasource to find the employee information--->
<CFQUERY NAME="GetEmployees" DATASOURCE="cfsnippets">
SELECT  Emp_ID, FirstName, LastName, EMail, Phone, Department
FROM    Employees where lastname
     <CFIF #employeeNames# is not "">= '#employeeNames#'</CFIF>
</CFQUERY>
```

```
<HTML>
<HEAD>
<TITLE>
CFTREE Example
</TITLE>
</HEAD>

<BODY>
<H3>CFTREE Example</H3>

<!--- Use CFFORM when using other CFINPUT tools --->
<CFFORM ACTION="cftree.cfm" METHOD="POST" ENABLECAB="Yes">
<!--- Use CFSELECT to present the contents of the query by column --->
<H3>CFSELECT Presentation of Data</H3>
<H4>Click on an employee's last name and hit "see information for
this employee" to see expanded information.</H4>

<CFSELECT NAME="EmployeeNames" MESSAGE="Select an Employee Name"
    SIZE="#getEmployees.recordcount#" QUERY="GetEmployees"
  VALUE="LastName" REQUIRED="No">
    <OPTION value="">Select All
</CFSELECT>

<INPUT TYPE="Submit" NAME="" VALUE="see information for this employee">

<!--- showing the use of CFTREE --->
<!--- Use CFTREE for an expanded presentation of the data --->
<!--- Loop through the query to create each branch of the CFTREE --->
<H3>CFTREE Presentation of Data</H3>
<H4>Click on the folders to "drill down" and reveal information.</H4>
<P>CFTREEITEM is used to create the "branches" of the tree.
<P>
<CFTREE NAME="SeeEmployees" HEIGHT="150" WIDTH="240"
    FONT="Arial Narrow" BOLD="No"
    ITALIC="No" BORDER="Yes"
    HSCROLL="Yes" VSCROLL="Yes"
    REQUIRED="No" COMPLETEPATH="No"
    APPENDKEY="Yes" HIGHLIGHTHREF="Yes">
<CFLOOP QUERY="GetEmployees">
    <CFTREEITEM VALUE="#Emp_ID#" PARENT="SeeEmployees" EXPAND="No">
    <CFTREEITEM VALUE="#LastName#" DISPLAY="Name"
        PARENT="#Emp_ID#" QUERYASROOT="No"
        EXPAND="No">
    <CFTREEITEM VALUE="#LastName#, #FirstName#"
        PARENT="#LastName#" EXPAND="No"
        QUERYASROOT="No">
    <CFTREEITEM VALUE="#Department#" DISPLAY="Department"
        PARENT="#Emp_ID#" QUERYASROOT="No"
        EXPAND="No">
    <CFTREEITEM VALUE="#Department#" PARENT="#Department#"
        EXPAND="No" QUERYASROOT="No">
    <CFTREEITEM VALUE="#Phone#" DISPLAY="Phone"
        PARENT="#Emp_ID#" QUERYASROOT="No"
        EXPAND="No">
```

```
            <CFTREEITEM VALUE="#Phone#" PARENT="#Phone#"
                EXPAND="No" QUERYASROOT="No">
            <CFTREEITEM VALUE="#Email#" DISPLAY="Email" PARENT="#Emp_ID#"
                QUERYASROOT="No" EXPAND="No">
            <CFTREEITEM VALUE="#Email#" PARENT="#Email#" EXPAND="No"
                QUERYASROOT="No">
        </CFLOOP>
        </CFTREE>
        ...
```

cftree

CFTREEITEM

Use CFTREEITEM to populate a tree control created with CFTREE with individual elements. You can use the IMG values supplied with ColdFusion or reference your own icons.

Note   CFTREEITEM incorporates a Java applet, so a browser must be Java-enabled for CFTREE to work properly.

Syntax
```
<CFTREEITEM VALUE="text"
       DISPLAY="text"
       PARENT="parent_name"
       IMG="filename"
       IMGOPEN="filename"
       HREF="URL"
       TARGET="URL_target"
       QUERY="queryname"
       QUERYASROOT="Yes" or "No"
       EXPAND="Yes" or "No">
```

VALUE

Required. Value passed when the CFFORM is submitted. When populating a CFTREE with data from a CFQUERY, columns are specified in a comma-separated list:

VALUE="dept_id,emp_id"

DISPLAY

Optional. The label for the tree item. Default is VALUE. When populating a CFTREE with data from a CFQUERY, display names are specified in a comma-separated list:

DISPLAY="dept_name,emp_name"

PARENT

Optional. Value for tree item parent.

IMG

Optional. Image name or filename for the tree item. When populating a CFTREE with data from a CFQUERY, images or filenames for each level of the tree are specified in a comma-separated list.

The default image name is "Folder. " A number of images are supplied and can be specified using only the image name (no file extension):

- cd
- computer
- document
- element

- folder
- floppy
- fixed
- remote

Use commas to separate image names corresponding to tree level, for example:

IMG="folder,document"
IMG=",document"

To specify your own custom image, specify the path and file extension:

IMG="../images/page1.gif"

IMGOPEN

Optional. Icon displayed with open tree item. You can specify the icon filename using a relative path. As with IMG, you can use an image supplied with ColdFusion.

HREF

Optional. URL to associate with the tree item or a query column for a tree that is populated from a query. If HREF is a query column, then the HREF value is the value populated by the query. If HREF is not recognized as a query column, it is assumed that the HREF text is an actual HTML HREF.

When populating a CFTREE with data from a CFQUERY, HREFs can be specified in a comma-separated list

HREF="http://dept_server,http://emp_server"

TARGET

Optional. Target attribute for HREF URL. When populating a CFTREE with data from a CFQUERY, targets are specified in a comma-separated list:

TARGET="FRAME_BODY,_blank"

QUERY

Optional. Query name used to generate data for the tree item.

QUERYASROOT

Optional. Yes or No. Defines specified query as the root level. As in Example 1, this option prevents having to create an additional parent CFTREEITEM.

EXPAND

Optional. Yes or No. Yes expands tree to show tree item children. No keeps tree item collapsed. Default is Yes.

Example   cftreeitem

<!--- This example shows the use of CFTREEITEM in a CFFORM.
The query takes a list of employees, and uses CFTREE and CFSELECT
to display the results of the query. In addition, CFGRID is used
to show an alternate means of displaying the same data --->

```
<!--- set a default for the employeeNames variable --->
<CFPARAM NAME="employeeNames" DEFAULT="">

<!--- if an employee name has been passed from the form,
set employeeNames variable to this value ---Auto>
<CFIF IsDefined("form.employeeNames")>
    <CFSET employeeNames = form.employeeNames>
</CFIF>

<!--- query the datasource to find the employee information--->
<CFQUERY NAME="GetEmployees" DATASOURCE="cfsnippets">
SELECT   Emp_ID, FirstName, LastName, EMail, Phone, Department
FROM     Employees where lastname
    <CFIF #employeeNames# is not "">= '#employeeNames#'</CFIF>
</CFQUERY>

<HTML>
<HEAD>
<TITLE>
CFTREE Example
</TITLE>
</HEAD>

<BODY>
<H3>CFTREEITEM Example</H3>

<!--- Use CFFORM when using other CFINPUT tools --->
<CFFORM ACTION="cftreeitem.cfm" METHOD="POST" ENABLECAB="Yes">

<!--- Use CFSELECT to present the contents of the query by column --->
<H3>CFSELECT Presentation of Data</H3>
<H4>Click on an employee's last name and hit "see information for
this employee" to see expanded information.</H4>
<CFSELECT NAME="EmployeeNames" MESSAGE="Select an Employee Name"
    SIZE="#getEmployees.recordcount#" QUERY="GetEmployees"
  VALUE="LastName" REQUIRED="No">
    <OPTION value="">Select All
</CFSELECT>

<INPUT TYPE="Submit" NAME="" VALUE="see information for this employee">

<!--- showing the use of CFTREE --->
<!--- Use CFTREE for an expanded presentation of the data --->
<!--- Loop through the query to create each branch of the CFTREE --->
<H3>CFTREE Presentation of Data</H3>
<H4>Click on the folders to "drill down" and reveal information.</H4>
<P>CFTREEITEM is used to create the "branches" of the tree.
<P>
<CFTREE NAME="SeeEmployees" HEIGHT="150" WIDTH="240"
    FONT="Arial Narrow" BOLD="No"
    ITALIC="No" BORDER="Yes"
    HSCROLL="Yes" VSCROLL="Yes"
    REQUIRED="No" COMPLETEPATH="No"
    APPENDKEY="Yes" HIGHLIGHTHREF="Yes">
```

```
<CFLOOP QUERY="GetEmployees">
    <CFTREEITEM VALUE="#Emp_ID#" PARENT="SeeEmployees" EXPAND="No">
    <CFTREEITEM VALUE="#LastName#" DISPLAY="Name"
        PARENT="#Emp_ID#" QUERYASROOT="No"
        EXPAND="No">
    <CFTREEITEM VALUE="#LastName#, #FirstName#"
        PARENT="#LastName#" EXPAND="No"
        QUERYASROOT="No">
    <CFTREEITEM VALUE="#Department#" DISPLAY="Department"
        PARENT="#Emp_ID#" QUERYASROOT="No"
        EXPAND="No">
    <CFTREEITEM VALUE="#Department#" PARENT="#Department#"
        EXPAND="No" QUERYASROOT="No">
    <CFTREEITEM VALUE="#Phone#" DISPLAY="Phone"
        PARENT="#Emp_ID#" QUERYASROOT="No"
        EXPAND="No">
    <CFTREEITEM VALUE="#Phone#" PARENT="#Phone#"
        EXPAND="No" QUERYASROOT="No">
    <CFTREEITEM VALUE="#Email#" DISPLAY="Email"
        PARENT="#Emp_ID#" QUERYASROOT="No"
        EXPAND="No">
    <CFTREEITEM VALUE="#Email#" PARENT="#Email#"
        EXPAND="No" QUERYASROOT="No">
</CFLOOP>
</CFTREE>
...
```

cftreeitem

CFTRY/CFCATCH

Used with one or more CFCATCH tags, the CFTRY tag allows developers to catch and process exceptions in ColdFusion pages. Exceptions include any event that disrupts the normal flow of instructions in a ColdFusion page such as failed database operations, missing include files, and developer-specified events.

Syntax
```
<CFTRY>
... Add code here
<CFCATCH TYPE="exceptiontype">
... Add exception processing code here
</CFCATCH>
... Additional CFCATCH blocks go here
</CFTRY>
```

TYPE

Optional. Specifies the type of exception to be handled by the CFCATCH block:

- APPLICATION (default)
- Database
- Template
- Security
- Object
- MissingInclude
- Expression
- Lock
- *Custom_type*
- Any (default)

Usage   You must code at least one CFCATCH tag within a CFTRY block. Code CFCATCH tags at the end of the CFTRY block. ColdFusion tests CFCATCH tags in the order in which they appear on the page.

If you specify the type to be ANY, do so in the last CFCATCH tag in the block so that all of the other tests are executed first.

Note   Specifying the type as ANY causes the ColdFusion Application Server to catch exceptions from any CFML tag, data source, or external object, which your application may not be prepared to handle.

Applications can optionally use the CFTHROW tag to raise custom exceptions. Such exceptions are caught with any of the following type specifications:

- TYPE="*custom_type*"
- TYPE="APPLICATION"

- TYPE="ANY".

The *custom_type* type designates the name of a user-defined type specified with a CFTHROW tag. CFCATCH has a catch handler that can catch a custom type by pattern, providing the custom type is defined as a series of strings concatenated together by periods, as in "MyApp.BusinessRuleException.InvalidAccount". CFCATCH searches for a custom type match starting with the most specific and ending with the least specific. For example, you could define a type as follows:

    <CFTHROW TYPE="MyApp.BusinessRuleException.InvalidAccount">

CFCATCH first searches for the entire type string defined in the CFTHROW tag, as follows:

    <CFCATCH TYPE="MyApp.BusinessRuleException.InvalidAccount">

Then it searches for the next most specific:

    <CFCATCH TYPE="MyApp.BusinessRuleException">

Finally, it searches for the least specific:

    <CFCATCH TYPE="MyApp">

The order in which you code CFCATCH tags designed to catch a custom exception type within an application does not matter. A CFCATCH tag searches for the custom exception types from most specific to least specific.

If you specify the type to be "APPLICATION, " the CFCATCH tag catches only those custom exceptions that have been specified as having the APPLICATION type in the CFTHROW tag that defines them.

The tags that throw an exception of TYPE="TEMPLATE" are CFINCLUDE, CFMODULE, and CFERROR.

An exception raised within a CFCATCH block cannot be handled by the CFTRY block that immediately encloses the CFCATCH tag. However, you can rethrow the currently active exception by using the CFRETHROW tag.

You can use the CFCATCH variable to access exception information:

- Type — Exception type, as specified in CFCATCH.

- Message — The exception's diagnostic message, if one was provided. If no diagnostic message is available, this is an empty string.

- Detail — A detailed message from the CFML interpreter. This message, which contains HTML formatting, can help determine which tag threw the exception.

- TagContext — The tag stack: the name and position of each tag in the tag stack, and the full path names of the files that contain the tags in the tag stack. See the note that follows this list for more information.

- NativeErrorCode — TYPE=Database only. The native error code associated with this exception. Database drivers typically provide error codes to assist diagnosis of failing database operations. If no error code was provided, the value of NativeErrorCode is -1.

- SQLSTATE — TYPE=Database only. The SQLState associated with this exception. Database drivers typically provide error codes to assist diagnosis of failing database operations. If no SQLState value was provided, the value of SQLSTATE is -1.

- ErrNumber — TYPE=Expression only. Internal expression error number.

- MissingFileName — TYPE=MissingInclude only. Name of the file that could not be included.

- LockName — TYPE=Lock only. The name of the affected lock (set to anonymous if the lock was unnamed).

- LockOperation — TYPE=Lock only. The operation that failed (set to Timeout, Create Mutex, or Unknown).

- ErrorCode — TYPE=Custom type only. A string error code.

- ExtendedInfo — TYPE=APPLICATION and custom only. A custom error message.

Note In order to see the tag stack displayed by TagContext, use the ColdFusion Administrator to enable the CFML stack trace.Under Debugging in the ColdFusion Administrator, choose the checkbox next to "Enable CFML stack trace. "

Example cftry

```
<!--- CFTRY example, using TagContext to display the tag stack. --->
<HTML>

<HEAD>
<TITLE>
CFTRY Example
</TITLE>
</HEAD>

<BASEFONT FACE="Arial, Helvetica" SIZE=2>

<BODY bgcolor="#FFFFD5">

<H3>CFTRY Example</H3>

<!--- open a CFTRY block --->
<CFTRY>

<!--- note that we have misspelled the tablename
"employees" as "employeeas" --->
<CFQUERY NAME="TestQuery" DATASOURCE="cfsnippets">
SELECT *
FROM EMPLOYEEAS
</CFQUERY>

<P>... other processing goes here

<!--- specify the type of error for which we are fishing --->
<CFCATCH TYPE="Database">
```

```
<!--- the message to display --->
    <H3>You've Thrown a Database <B>Error</B></H3>
<CFOUTPUT>
<!--- and the diagnostic message from the ColdFusion server --->
  <P>#CFCATCH.message#</P>
    <P>Caught an exception, type = #CFCATCH.TYPE# </P>
    <P>The contents of the tag stack are:</P>
    <CFLOOP index=i from=1 to = #ArrayLen(CFCATCH.TAGCONTEXT)#>
        <CFSET sCurrent = #CFCATCH.TAGCONTEXT[i]#>
            <BR>#i# #sCurrent["ID"]# (#sCurrent["LINE"]#,#sCurrent["COLUMN"]#)
#sCurrent["TEMPLATE"]#
    </CFLOOP>
</CFOUTPUT>
</CFCATCH>

</CFTRY>

</BODY>
</HTML>
```

cftry

CFUPDATE

The CFUPDATE tag updates existing records in data sources.

Syntax
```
<CFUPDATE DATASOURCE="ds_name"
        DBTYPE="type"
        DBSERVER="dbms"
        DBNAME="database name"
        TABLENAME="table_name"
        TABLEOWNER="name"
        TABLEQUALIFIER="qualifier"
        USERNAME="username"
        PASSWORD="password"
        PROVIDER="COMProvider"
        PROVIDERDSN="datasource"
        FORMFIELDS="field_names">
```

DATASOURCE
Required. Name of the data source that contains your table.

DBTYPE
Optional. The database driver type:

- ODBC (default) — ODBC driver.

- Oracle73 — Oracle 7.3 native database driver. Using this option, the ColdFusion Server computer must have Oracle 7.3.4.0.0 (or greater) client software installed.

- Oracle80 —Oracle 8.0 native database driver. Using this option, the ColdFusion Server computer must have Oracle 8.0 (or greater) client software installed.

- Sybase11 —Sybase System 11 native database driver. Using this option, the ColdFusion Server computer must have Sybase 11.1.1 (or greater) client software installed. Sybase patch ebf 7729 is recommended.

- OLEDB —OLE DB provider. If specified, this database provider overrides the driver type specified in the ColdFusion Administrator.

- DB2 —DB2 5.2 native database driver.

- Informix73—Informix73 native database driver.

DBSERVER
Optional. For native database drivers and the SQLOLEDB provider, specifies the name of the database server machine. If specified, DBSERVER overrides the server specified in the data source.

DBNAME
Optional. The database name (Sybase System 11 driver and SQLOLEDB provider only). If specified, DBNAME overrides the default database specified in the data source.

TABLENAME

Required. Name of the table you want to update. Note the following:

- ORACLE drivers — This specification must be in uppercase.

- Sybase driver — This specification is case-sensitive and must be in the same case as that used when the table was created

TABLEOWNER

Optional. For data sources that support table ownership (for example, SQL Server, Oracle, and Sybase SQL Anywhere), use this field to specify the owner of the table.

TABLEQUALIFIER

Optional. For data sources that support table qualifiers, use this field to specify the qualifier for the table. The purpose of table qualifiers varies across drivers. For SQL Server and Oracle, the qualifier refers to the name of the database that contains the table. For the Intersolv dBase driver, the qualifier refers to the directory where the DBF files are located.

USERNAME

Optional. If specified, USERNAME overrides the username value specified in the ODBC setup.

PASSWORD

Optional. If specified, PASSWORD overrides the password value specified in the ODBC setup.

PROVIDER

Optional. COM provider (OLE-DB only).

PROVIDERDSN

Optional. Data source name for the COM provider (OLE-DB only).

FORMFIELDS

Optional. A comma-separated list of form fields to update. If this attribute is not specified, all fields in the form are included in the operation.

Example   cfupdate

```
<!--- This example shows the use of CFUPDATE to change
records in a data source --->

<!--- if course_ID has been passed to this form, then
perform the update on that record in the data source --->
<CFIF IsDefined("form.course_ID") is "True">
<CFUPDATE DATASOURCE="cfsnippets"
TABLENAME="courses" FORMFIELDS="course_ID,number,Descript">
</CFIF>

<!--- perform a query to reflect any updated information
if course_ID is passed through a url, we are selecting a
```

```
record to update ... select only that record with the
WHERE clause
--->
<CFQUERY NAME="GetCourseInfo" DATASOURCE="cfsnippets">
SELECT    Number, Course_ID, Descript
FROM      Courses
<CFIF IsDefined("url.course_ID") is True>
WHERE    Course_ID = #url.course_ID#
</CFIF>
ORDER by Number
</CFQUERY>

<HTML>
<HEAD>
<TITLE>CFUPDATE Example</TITLE>
</HEAD>

<BODY bgcolor=silver>
<H3>CFUPDATE Example</H3>

<!--- if we are updating a record, don't show
the entire list --->
<CFIF NOT IsDefined("url.course_ID")>
<P><H3><a href="cfupdate.cfm">Show Entire List</A></H3>

<FORM METHOD="POST" ACTION="cfupdate.cfm">

<H3>You can alter the contents of this
record, and then click "submit" to use
CFUPDATE and alter the database</H3>

<P>Course Number <INPUT TYPE="Text" NAME="number"
 VALUE="<CFOUTPUT>#GetCourseInfo.number#</CFOUTPUT>">
<P>Course Description<BR>
<TEXTAREA NAME="Descript" COLS="40" ROWS="5">
<CFOUTPUT>#GetCourseInfo.Descript#</CFOUTPUT>
</TEXTAREA>
<INPUT TYPE="Hidden" NAME="course_id"
 VALUE="<CFOUTPUT>#GetCourseInfo.Course_ID#</CFOUTPUT>">
<P><INPUT TYPE="Submit" NAME="">
</FORM>

<CFELSE>
<!--- Show the entire record set in CFTABLE form --->
<CFTABLE QUERY="GetCourseInfo" HTMLTABLE>
<CFCOL  TEXT="<a href='cfupdate.cfm?course_ID=#course_ID#'>Edit Me</a>"
 WIDTH=10 HEADER="Edit<br>this Entry">
<CFCOL  TEXT="#Number#" WIDTH="4" HEADER="Course Number">
<CFCOL  TEXT="#Descript#" WIDTH=100 HEADER="Course Description">
</CFTABLE>
</CFIF>
```

```
</BODY>
</HTML>
```

cfupdate

CFWDDX

The CFWDDX tag serializes and de-serializes CFML data structures to the XML-based WDDX format. You can also use it to generate JavaScript statements instantiating JavaScript objects equivalent to the contents of a WDDX packet or some CFML data structures.

Syntax

```
<CFWDDX ACTION="action"
        INPUT="inputdata"
        OUTPUT="resultvariablename"
        TOPLEVELVARIABLE="toplevelvariablenameforjavascript"
        USETIMEZONEINFO="Yes" or "No">
```

ACTION

Specifies the action taken by the CFWDDX tag. Use one of the following:

- CFML2WDDX — Serialize CFML to WDDX format

- WDDX2CFML — Deserialize WDDX to CFML

- CFML2JS — Serialize CFML to JavaScript format

- WDDX2JS — Deserialize WDDX to JavaScript

INPUT

Required. The value to be processed.

OUTPUT

The name of the variable to hold the output of the operation. This attribute is required for ACTION=WDDX2CFML. For all other actions, if this attribute is not provided, the result of the WDDX processing is outputted in the HTML stream.

TOPLEVELVARIABLE

Required when ACTION=WDDX2JS or ACTION=CFML2JS. The name of the top-level JavaScript object created by the deserialization process. The object created by this process is an instance of the WddxRecordset object, explained in WddxRecordset Object .

This attribute applies only when the ACTION is WDDX2JS or CFML2JS.

USETIMEZONEINFO

Optional. Indicates whether to output time-zone information when serializing CFML to WDDX. If time-zone information is taken into account, the hour-minute offset, as represented in the ISO8601 format, is calculated in the date-time output. If time-zone information is not taken into account, the local time is output. The default is Yes.

Usage

Use this tag to serialize and deserialize packets of data used to communicate with the browser.

For complete information on WDDX, see the "Programming with XML " chapter in ../
../Developing_Web_Applications_with_ColdFusion/contents.htm*Developing Web Applications with ColdFusion*/a.

Example   cfwddx

```
<!--- This snippet shows basic use of the CFWDDX tag. --->
<HTML>
<HEAD>
        <TITLE>CFWDDX Tag</TITLE>
</HEAD>
<BODY>
<!--- Create a simple query  --->
<CFQUERY NAME='q' DATASOURCE='cfsnippets'>
        select Message_Id, Thread_id, Username from messages
</CFQUERY>

The recordset data is:...<P>
<CFOUTPUT QUERY=q>
        #Message_ID# #Thread_ID# #Username#<br>
</CFOUTPUT><P>

<!--- Serialize data to WDDX format --->
Serializing CFML data...<P>
<CFWDDX ACTION='cfml2wddx' input=#q# output='wddxText'>

<!--- Display WDDX XML packet --->
Resulting WDDX packet is:
<xmp><CFOUTPUT>#wddxText#</CFOUTPUT></xmp>

<!--- Deserialize to a variable named wddxResult --->
Deserializing WDDX packet...<P>
<CFWDDX ACTION='wddx2cfml' input=#wddxText# output='qnew'>

The recordset data is:...<P>
<CFOUTPUT QUERY=qnew>
        #Message_ID# #Thread_ID# #Username#<br>
</CFOUTPUT><P>
</BODY>
</HTML>
```

cfwddx

INDEX

G–H